PUBLICATION NO. 80: PATTERSON SMITH REPRINT SERIES IN
CRIMINOLOGY, LAW ENFORCEMENT, AND SOCIAL PROBLEMS

# OUR CONVICTS

BY

MARY CARPENTER

TWO VOLUMES IN ONE

*VOLUME ONE*

*Montclair, New Jersey*
PATTERSON SMITH
*1969*

*Originally published 1864*
*Reprinted 1969 by*
*Patterson Smith Publishing Corporation*
*Montclair, New Jersey*

SBN 87585-080-4

Library of Congress Catalog Card Number: 69-16229

TO

HENRY,

LORD BROUGHAM AND VAUX,

WHOSE HIGH AND VARIED POWERS

HAVE BEEN DIRECTED THROUGH A LONG LIFE TO PROMOTE THE WELFARE

OF HIS FELLOW MEN,

THESE VOLUMES

ARE MOST RESPECTFULLY INSCRIBED

BY

THE AUTHOR.

# CONTENTS OF VOLUME I.

# PREFACE.

THE Author of these volumes desires to offer to her readers some explanation of the circumstances and motives which have induced her to undertake a task little in accordance with her natural tastes and occupations; she hopes thereby to obtain for the work some of that candour and indulgence of which she is conscious that it stands in need.

From the commencement of the Reformatory Movement, now nearly fourteen years ago, she has had an active share in the proceedings. The preparation of two volumes on the subject*—the part she took in each of the three Conferences, assembled in Birmingham to promote the movement in 1851, 1853, and 1861,—together with the evidence she was called upon to give to the

---

* "Reformatory Schools for the Children of the Perishing and Dangerous Classes."—1850. "Juvenile Delinquents, their Condition and Treatment."—1853.

Committee of the House of Commons, which in
1852, 3, inquired into the condition of "criminal
and destitute children;"—all these brought her
into communication with persons connected not
only with the legislation, but also with the execution of our criminal law. The work in which
she has been since engaged, of developing some of
the institutions which were then the subject of
legislation, has brought her still more into communication with those who have the charge of
adult criminals; and has led her, while testing
the principles and system of management she had
adopted in reference to children, to perceive how
far these were applicable to men and women.  To
this subject her attention was especially drawn by
observation of the principles adopted in the Irish
Convict Prisons, with their results; and by a personal examination of these, during the Meeting of
the Social Science Association in Dublin in 1861,
with the advantage of full explanation of the
system from the Chairman of the Directors, Sir
WALTER CROFTON, whose mind had conceived it,
whose spirit had animated it, and whose devoted
and judicious labours, in conjunction with his

fellow Directors, had brought it to its present admirable condition.

Thus, while the Author made it the special object of her life to elevate the children of the perishing and dangerous classes, and to obtain for them that education and position, which, as the rising generation in a civilized and Christian community, they have a right to claim,—she has been led closely to consider the condition and treatment of adult criminals, of "Our Convicts," and has felt strongly impelled to endeavour to draw public attention to what she deems important information and principles respecting them.

But the very circumstances which led her to the preparation of the present work, have prevented her from giving to it that undivided attention which the subject required. The duties in which she had engaged herself bring with them frequent and unavoidable interruptions, and claims on time and thought; she trusts, however, that as she has, without neglecting those, given the best powers she could command to this engagement, she will receive the kind indulgence of her readers for the many defects they will discover.

The Author begs to present her thanks to all those who have kindly given her information, or whose works she has quoted; but especially she desires to offer her most respectful and grateful acknowledgements to M. D. HILL, Esq., Q. C., the Recorder of Birmingham, whose friendly counsels have ever been most kindly afforded to her, and have given her confidence, while she has warmly appreciated his elevated philosophical views, and his extensive experience on the subject of criminal legislation and reformatory treatment.


RED LODGE HOUSE, BRISTOL:
     *September 8th,* 1864.

# OUR CONVICTS

### AND

# THEIR TREATMENT.

## INTRODUCTION.

"OUR CONVICTS!" They are a part of our society! They belong to ourselves! They are not only subjects with us of the same great British Empire on which the sun never sets, but they belong to the same British Isles, the same small centre of civilization, the same heart of the world's life, the same Island, small in geographical extent, infinitely great in its influence on the nations,—whence must go forth laws, principles, examples, which will guide for better or for worse the whole world!

Fain would we say that these Convicts are not *ours*; that they have cut themselves off from us; that they have excommunicated themselves from civilized society by their own acts; that they no longer belong to us. The very name of "Convicts" excites in the mind an idea of moral corruption which would make one shrink from such beings with a natural repulsion, which would lead one to wish only that like the lepers of old they should dwell apart in caves and desert places, warning off the incautious passenger with the cry "unclean, unclean." We might desire to rid ourselves of them by sending them off to some remote region, where Nature herself should guard them with her impregnable walls of ice, scantily yielding them bare subsistence from a barren, grudging soil;—or to some spot where they should be cut off from the civilized world by the mighty ocean,—and where their fiend-like passions should be vented upon each other, not on peaceable and harmless members of society. Many would fain thus separate themselves from Convicts; would gladly thus rid themselves of the awful responsibility which lies in the words—"*Our Convicts.*"

*But they cannot!* These Convicts are men, are women, who were born among us, brought up among us, reared to manhood and to womanhood among us. We have mingled with them in the ordinary walks of life, we may even have eaten at the same board with them, and until the law put its fatal mark upon them, so that they were henceforth to be known as Convicts, we did not see anything in their outward appearance, whereby, in their various grades of society, we should have distinguished them from other men and women. But now this very legal sentence which makes us wish to separate them entirely from ourselves, only binds them closer to us. They were *free* agents while they were pursuing their mischievous calling, while they were transgressing the laws of God and of man, and we did not separate ourselves from them; had they been then branded by the indignation of society in England, they might have gone to other parts of the empire, and there retrieved their character or plunged into fresh crimes. We should not then have been responsible for them. But now all is changed The sentence of the law has placed them in our own keeping for many years. We cannot, now they are *legally proved* guilty of crimes against society, drive them from our country, or banish them from our shores, content that they shall still be responsible for their crimes to the Judge of all, before a higher tribunal. We have deprived them of the right to guide their own actions since that right has been abused; we subjugate their will, we confine them in our own country, and put them under such treatment as we consider best for them and for society. We therefore have doubly bound them to us, and ourselves to them. They are *ours*, and we *cannot*, if we would, shake off the responsibility arising from this relationship, however painful it is. It behoves us then to consider the "Treatment" which " Our Convicts" should receive.

Here, again, we shall be met by an unwillingness to regard such a subject as a part of our duty,—ours as private individuals,—as men who take no share in the management of public affairs,—as women. Why need *we* concern ourselves about the treatment of these persons whom the law has removed from troubling us, whom we shall not see again for years. Such matters, it may be argued, are beyond our sphere of knowledge; we have not studied these difficult questions; we cannot expect to understand this most perplexing and complicated subject; we do not comprehend the principles which guide our legislators. We are quite sure that they wish to do the best they possibly can; we see that they have built great prisons for these people, on the most new and approved plans; we know that Convicts must be very bad, and we had better leave the management of them in the hands of those who have undertaken the whole thing; —what have we to do with their treatment? We believe that every man and every woman in the kingdom has at the present time very much to do with the Treatment of Our Convicts. The events of the last two years have filled every one with consternation and fear for personal safety. But a short time since, gentlemen could not go about their lawful callings, or walk in the most public thoroughfares without danger to their property or even to their lives. Women have had to defend their houses from burglars, laying aside their natural timidity to protect their homes, and when found alone in unfrequented places have not only been murdered, but have suffered worse than loss of life from brutal monsters. And it has been discovered that most of these outrages, a disgrace to a civilized and a Christian country, have been committed by persons who had been subjected to the Convict Treatment adopted in our country, and many by those who, according to their sentence, were still under the responsibility of the Convict directors. It has been found that instead of becoming better in Convict Prisons they have become worse, more hardened, more reckless, more experienced in crime. Regard for personal safety, therefore, as well as duty to society, should imperatively call upon every one of mature judgment to study the whole subject, and thus to bring public opinion to bear upon the Government, so that a system may be altered, which, while so costly, is so much worse than useless,—so injurious to society.

We shall first consider who Convicts are.

The fact of their being classed together under the same brand of the law, by no means makes them of one nature or of the same degree of guilt. The commission of the same

legal crime by no means indicates the same moral depravity. Burglary may involve daring robbery and, murder,
and may be perpetrated by one long experienced in all the
arts of housebreaking, who wanders from county to county
like a wild beast seeking his prey, one who would be a
brigand or a bandit in a country under less controul than our
own;—while, perchance, an offence legally designated by the
same term is committed by a little girl of ten years old,
whose sole fault was, that having lost her Mother, and being
necessarily without proper care from her Father, who was
compelled to earn his daily bread, she had made her way into
a neighbour's house to supply her wants. Robbery from the
person may be perpetrated by a daring and experienced
Convict, ready to add violence or even murder to his theft;
or by a small child of nine years old, who is trying the
lessons which have been given to her diminutive fingers by a
wicked parent. We cannot classify Convicts by their nominal
crimes; we shall endeavour to form some correct idea of
them by other means.

It will be important, in the next place, to form some idea
of how persons arrive at the degree of hardened vice which
our investigation will disclose. We must try to learn the
cause of the disease as a guide in our treatment of it, and
as a means of checking its progress.

The principles which have been laid down by experienced
persons, and which have been proved to be true by actual
success, will next be considered; facts will be adduced in
demonstration of them.

After this preparation, we shall endeavour to form some
clear idea of the system of Convict discipline actually in
existence in our country, with its results. In doing this,

it must be clearly understood that no means of information are open to the writer but such as are perfectly accessible to every one who chooses to investigate the subject. The Prison Matron revealed secrets of the prison-house of which none but a resident in that abode of horrors could have been possessed. Persons officially connected with the Government Gaols have sources of information which none but those so circumstanced can obtain. They who enjoy personal intercourse with our rulers, may understand many things which are mysteries to those without the privileged circle. Access to the establishments obtained through persons in office, may reveal at a glance to an experienced eye what may be a lasting perplexity to the less privileged. But the writer of this work has enjoyed none of these advantages. Happily, however, there are open to all, sources of knowledge even more satisfactory, in the evidence which was laid before the Royal Commission last year, and from this, and from the witnesses before various Parliamentary Committees, we shall be able to obtain reliable information.

Of the *results* of the system adopted in Great Britain, we must form a judgment from less official sources, for unhappily in our country there has never yet been adopted such a system of identification and registration of criminals and their acts, as would give even the possibility of an approximation to truth from any criminal statistics that exist. We find even that in many cases the persons who may be supposed most cognisant of actual facts, and most in a position to obtain reliable statistics, arrive at conclusions most at variance with the reality which is patent to the public, and that they are most vague and theoretical in their statements We must, therefore, be satisfied with such amount of knowledge of results as we can obtain from ordinary facts and general opinions founded with reason upon them.

Having thus endeavoured, from such means of information as we possess, to obtain some distinct view of the Convict system adopted in Great Britain, and the results of it, we shall study the working of a system founded on different principles in the Sister Island; and here, an accurate identification and systematic registration of criminals throughout the country, will enable us to arrive at definite results, which may be considered reliable, as they are thoroughly supported by the independent testimony of public opinion. The writer has here had the advantage of both personal and official information respecting the working and the results of the Irish Convict System, which will be presented to the reader.

Whether removal to another country can take part in our Penal System will then be considered; and the evidence on the subject will be analysed, which was last year brought before the Royal Commission. Improvements in our present system will also be suggested, as they have been brought forward by many experienced persons.

In conclusion, we must remember that the Convicts are still *ours*, even after their punishment, and must return to our midst when they have been discharged from the Convict Prison. Society has a right to expect that during the period of a costly incarceration the best possible means shall be adopted by the Government for the reformation of those intrusted to them, for their preparation for re-absorbtion into the community; but, on the other hand, the Government must be supported in its efforts by society, and especially by that portion of it which is professedly

Christian. What has been done to promote this great object, and what may further be done, will be briefly stated.

May the earnest desire to promote in even the smallest degree the restoration of the erring, and to enlist the Christian public in the work, be kindly accepted as an excuse for the many defects and deficiencies which will be discoverable in these volumes! And may the Divine blessing rest on these humble efforts.

# CHAPTER I.

## WHO ARE OUR CONVICTS?

THE first sight of the inmates of a Convict Prison, to one un-accustomed to the criminal portion of our community, awakens emotions of mingled sorrow, pity and intense moral repugnance, never to be forgotten.

The Chaplain of an ordinary gaol, who has, in the course of his daily duty, been familiarised with vice, who has often striven to soften the obdurate criminal, and who knows but too well the meaning of the sullen hardened look,—who understands the significance of the audacious bearing, the significant gesture, —yet hopes that under his ministrations the culprit may become a penitent,—he shudders, when he is called on to lead the wor-ship of a thousand assembled together, more hardened, more audacious, compacted into one solid mass of crime, eventually to be separated and absorbed into the community. The criminals whom he had been used to exhort were solitary and powerless, abashed when face to face with one who strove to obey his master, Christ; these form one great community of vice,—no one feels abashed in presence of those who may be even worse than himself; the whole tone of the society is criminal. And each one is here powerful;—he is supported morally and physically by the sympathy of his fellows, and he knows that in concert they can, if so determined, terrify the surrounding country. Such were the Chaplain's first impressions of a Convict Prison.

The Magistrate of a crowded seaport town, who has been accustomed to see brought before him on the bench individuals who present every kind of degradation,—types of varied forms of vice,—would seem well prepared to see without surprise the interior of a Government Gaol. He is used to insolent daring, to the brazen effrontery of crime, to a crafty assumption of innocence. He has seen these exhibited in the excitement of the court; he has seen them subside in the solitude of the prison. He visits one of our penal establishments. He might expect that after a long period of solitude, in which the Convicts had received much spiritual instruction and help, when they were brought to a place constructed and arranged by our rulers to fit them for the world by training to labour, to good and regular habits, he should not recognise that low, cunning, daring, hardened expression, which he so well knew as marking the confirmed criminal; he might hope to see men who appeared likely to gain an honest livelihood in the world. He is disappointed. Far worse do these men look than those whom he has been accustomed to have before him in the discharge of his magisterial duty. The absence of any hopeful or good expression of countenance in the inmates of this Gaol, and their general air of settled wickedness, leave him at liberty to mark in one after another the low physical type indicating a settled and long formed habit of crime, varied only in degree, and in the peculiar expression which would lead him only to wonder whether he saw before him a coiner, a burglar, a garotter, or a murderer. Such was the aspect of the men whom he knew destined again to infest society with their dangerous presence.

What then must be the feelings of one, who unaccustomed like these to the contemplation of vice, is for the first time within a Convict Prison? Nothing external in the buildings and arrangements inspires terror, or indicates the corruption of the spirit within. All is well ordered. Scrupulous cleanness, a well constructed edifice, perfect finish in every detail, please the eye of the visitor. But the sight of the inmates as they file out from morning worship can never be forgotten! Why should each one look as if a good or holy feeling had never entered his soul? Why does the eye rest so seldom on any who have not a malignant scowl, an air of dogged endurance, a crafty smoothness of external aspect evidently concealing a depth of dangerous cunning? Are none of these reformed who have been long here? Can we hope that many of them will be changed before they enter the world? Their aspect absolutely forbids such an expectation.

These are our Convicts!

In the Government Prisons we see the Convicts in masses. There is an almost indescribable expression of countenance and peculiarity of demeanour pervading the whole body, which more or less infects each individual who has passed much time in these establishments. Those whose duty familiarizes them with this, recognise Convicts by a species of instinct or free-masonry when they meet them in the streets, see them loitering in thoroughfares, or detect them in the commission of theft. When discharged on a ticket-of-leave the destruction of their license paper does not prevent their recognition as Convicts by individuals not personally acquainted with them. The common observer will often shrink with a sort of mysterious dread from a group of men whose dress and physical condition do not indicate want, but yet who show no traces of honourable toil on their hands or clothes. They seem to have no sympathy with the interests of the world around, but to have a close understanding with each other, and a peculiar low expression unlike that of the labouring portion of society.

These are probably Convicts at large.

Whether, then, our Convicts are in confinement or at large in the world, the enormous amount of hardened crime, of almost fiend-like wickedness, of apparently hopeless apathy to all that is good, which is collected, condensed and coerced into external order within the walls of our enormous penal establishments, must strike with horror every thoughtful mind who seriously

contemplates it.  Still more appalling is it to realize the dreadful
fact that a torrent of vice from this sink of impurity annually
pours forth into the community, and irrigates the length and
breadth of the community, not with fertilizing, but with polluting
streams.  The hardened convicts who are discharged from their
confinement actually exist in society, whether they hide themselves in dens and haunts known only to the police, ready to
sally forth as burglars or murderers,—or whether, assuming an
externally respectable appearance, they mingle in the crowd,
saunter in the busy thoroughfare, and craftily select one victim
after another, until some inadvertence of theirs, or chance fortunate for the community, throws them into the hands of the
police and of justice.

We have hitherto spoken of Convicts as a class and as viewed
in masses, because as such they appear to the public, as such
they are dealt with in legislation.  But those who live with
them and work among them in their final separation from the
world see very great differences among them.  We shall endeavour in this chapter to gain some insight into the characters
and previous lives of convicts from the testimony of persons
whose position has enabled them to gain insight into them.

Among the inmates of Convict Prisons a large proportion will
necessarily be persons whose mode of life is criminal, for a
sentence of penal servitude is not usually passed on a first
offence ; some, however, will be casual offenders, not essentially
belonging to the criminal class.

The Rev. J. DAVIS, who has been Ordinary of Newgate for
20 years, gives in his evidence before the Royal Commission
much valuable information respecting the criminal class, derived
from his intercourse with them in their solitary confinement and
his frequent observation of them when at large.  Some of these,
he tells us, are men in the better classes of society, not habitual
criminals, "Men who commit one serious offence," he says (1928),
" such as forgery or embezzlement, are not always men of depraved minds, but a strong temptation has urged them to commit

crime, and public propriety requires a very heavy sentence to be passed; but they usually reform, and do not come under the power of the law again; a few do, but not many." Others, again, have been for a very long period living a life of crime without coming under the arm of the law. The convict GILL, who was last summer sentenced to a long term of penal servitude for housebreaking and the famous Will robbery at the Gaer, in Monmouthshire, stated, when somewhat subdued by solitude from his daring demeanour and persistent denial of his crime, that this was the nineteenth burglary he had committed! His Father was at the time awaiting his trial for another burglary. What a life must these men have been leading! "There are some men I have heard of," says Mr. DAVIS (1930-35), "who are now at liberty, and who have been the heads of gangs for many years, as many years as I have been at Newgate. One of the men that was caught in that last Bank robbery I have heard of for these 15 or 16 years. He was the man who sold the bank notes and bought the stolen bank paper. We have had the police again and again, but never could get information sufficient to convict him until this last trial. He has 25 years sentence, but I have heard of him for many years. He had not been previously convicted. That is an instance of a man living for many years by art in defiance of the law. There is one now at the west end of London who has been living for many years by dishonesty; but he is engaged in the more valuable kind of robberies, burglaries, and stealing of jewels and precious stones and articles of that kind; but he generally buys the articles, he does not go himself; but he has been so engaged for many years. All thieves have nicknames. That man has never been detected. I have heard this in conversation from the thieves who have been convicted, and who have been under sentence. They have talked over these matters. The same man who told me about the man I have spoken of was the one who gave the information upon which Jim the Penman was convicted, and the bankers of London have been saved £10,000 a-year since he was convicted, as far as we can judge; some of the friends of this man brought in notes, South American notes and others, on which they were to forge the names and get them out."*

We find here, then, at the commencement of our inquiry, two grand divisions of Convicts.

First, those who have not been habitually living a life of crime, but who may have been led by a sudden temptation or by peculiar circumstances to commit a crime which legally is followed by a sentence of penal servitude, and

Secondly, those who, whether or not they have been before convicted, have been for many years living in known defiance of the laws of God and of man.

It is important to keep in view these two classes. Experienced persons will usually be able to draw the distinction between them made by Mr. DAVIS, even without knowing the previous history of the criminal. In the Report of the Select Committee on Transportation, in 1856, Mr. JAS. SMART, the Superintendent of Police in Glasgow, makes a similar clear discrimination between those who may be called casual offenders and those who follow crime as a profession. He also states that the former are not necessarily debarred by their position as returned convicts from getting an honest livelihood. "I know a great many parties," he says (2143), "who have come back to Glasgow who have got into employment, and who are following a lawful employment. *But those were not of the class who have gone through the curriculum of the police courts, the sheriff's courts, and the justiciary courts, and who have committed every sort of offence.* I know a banker who was convicted and sentenced to transportation at

---

* Here and elsewhere when the Commission is mentioned reference is made to the "Report of the Commissioners appointed to inquire into the Operation of the Acts relating to Transportation and Penal Servitude," 1863. The numbers given are those appended to the questions. Where, as in this passage, the questions are not given, they are embodied in the answer, which otherwise is copied verbatim. Where an abstract of a witness's statements is given, the greatest care is taken to preserve his exact meaning.

Glasgow and was sent up here, and he got away in some four or five years' time, and is now in Glasgow doing well again. I know a forger also who got liberated, and who is following a lawful occupation ; and I know several other parties." He states, however, that these bear a very small proportion to the whole number of criminals who have come back. These belong to the first class, who are not deeply imbued with moral degradation, and of whom there is considerable ground for hope. These will not require further consideration at present. With respect to the second class, the habitual offenders, Mr. SMART says (2145), " The principal part of the criminals transported from Glasgow are almost hopeless, from the numerous convictions and from the short imprisonments which they have undergone in the police courts, and the lengthened imprisonments which they have received from the sheriff and jury ; and frequently the justiciary courts have sentenced them to long periods of imprisonment, even before resorting to transportation. The cases that come from those quarters are almost hopeless."

It should here be observed that the hopelessness expressed by Mr. SMART respecting the reformation of this last class does not arise from anything peculiarly bad in the individuals themselves, but from the fact of their having been suffered to continue their lawless course so long, receiving repeated short sentences which had no effect but to stimulate them to greater crimes and harden them by a sense of impunity. A person who has thus had frequent experience of all the proceedings of the law, acquires a degree of dangerous skill and acuteness in evading the pursuit of justice, a reckless daring, and a perfect callousness to all moral or religious influence, which renders him, when at last he he is sentenced to penal servitude, and becomes one of "our Convicts," a most difficult and perplexing case. Sir RICHARD MAYNE, Commissioner of the Metropolitan force since its foundation in 1829, speaks strongly of the evil arising from thus creating, as it were, by short imprisonments, a class of most daring convicts; in his evidence to the Commission (1766)

he mentions, in illustration, a remarkable case of a man named
ANDERSON,—

  "He was convicted on Oct. 28, 1850, and sentenced to 10 days; on Dec. 7,
1850, to 1 month; on Jan. 5, 1851, to 7 days; Dec. 8, 1851, to 1 month;
Nov. 11, 1852, to 6 days; on July 26, 1853, to 7 days; April 21, 1854, to
3 months; on Jan. 22, 1855, to 1 month; April 5, 1855, to 3 months. (1769.)
The offences committed were in some cases picking pockets.  On April 21,
1854, 3 months for picking pockets; January 22, 1855, 1 month for picking
pockets; April 5, 1855, 3 months; Sept, 7, 1855, 1 month for picking pockets;
April 24, 1856, 3 months for picking pockets; July 1, 1857, 6 months for picking pockets; March 19, 1859, 3 months for picking pockets; on Sept. 5, 1859,
3 years penal servitude. This sentence would not have expired till Sept. 1862;
he was released at the end of May, 1862, three months of his time having
been remitted.  On July 23, 1862, he was committed for three months, and in
November following he was sentenced to penal servitude for life.  All these
cases are, I think," says Sir RICHARD, "a great reproach to the state of the
law."

  The same witness tells us subsequently that the majority of
these cases are indictable offences, and that stealing from the
person is punishable with a long term of penal servitude, but
that "Magistrates very commonly deal with them, especially for
picking pockets, in that way."  It is the constant application of
the prosecutor to the Magistrate to deal summarily with the case,
when the sentence cannot be more than six months; and it is
the general practice of the criminal to plead guilty before the
Magistrate, in order to avoid information being obtained of
previous convictions.   Hence the numerous short imprisonments.
It was, probably, from this ignorance of his antecedents that the
Judge awarded him, when first he became a Convict, only three
years of penal servitude.  This being shortened, perhaps, from
a similar ignorance of his past career, he had time to commit a
fresh crime, and to receive another rest in gaol for three months,
while his sentence was still hanging over him, and while he
was probably supposed to be doing well, as his license was not
revoked.   He had scarcely regained his liberty from this incarceration, when some more daring offence brought upon him a
sentence of loss of liberty for life.   So now he is one of "Our
Convicts," whose future existence is regulated by our Govern-

ment; he may, indeed, be one of those very men who at Portland
are daringly demanding a return to their former luxurious
dietary, and who required armed soldiers to prevent them from
spreading terror through the country!

How skilful, as well as daring, these men become from their
long practice in crime, we may learn from the following case,
which is doubtless a sample of many others. The following is
from the report of the Gloucester Assize, Crown Court, in the
*Bristol Daily Post*, April 9, 1863 :—

*(Before Mr. Justice Crompton.)*

THE BURGLARIES AT CLIFTON AND BRISTOL.

" HENRY BLONDIN, *alias* CHARLES DOWD, musician, was indicted for a
burglay at the residence of —— —— Esq., at Clifton, and stealing twelve
knives, value £10, a silver cruet-stand, value £6, a silver waiter, value £4, and
other property, on the night of the 31st January. Mr. SAWYER prosecuted,
and having briefly stated the facts, called the following witnesses :—

" Mr. ——— : I am a banker at Bristol, and a magistrate. I live at
No. 11, Victoria-square, Clifton. The door of my house opens on the square,
and there is a walled garden at the back of the house. On the night of the
31st January, a little before eleven, I went round the house and saw that all
was safe. It was Saturday night. The shutters of the kitchen window were
closed; it looks to the back of the house into the garden. I noticed the back
door, which leads into the area; it was bolted and secure. Next morning
I received information that the house had been broken open. I went down-
stairs a little before seven, and found that drawers had been opened and
ransacked. This was chiefly in the kitchen. I missed some articles, including
a cruet-stand and a quantity of valuable plate. I gave information to the
police. I received from a man named WEBB, who then acted as my butler,
a large gimlet. [The gimlet was produced.] I gave it to Sergeant PEPPERELL.
I looked round the house; there was no appearance of violence having been
used in getting in.

" By Prisoner : I did not go into the garden till after the policeman came.
It appeared as if some one had got over the wall, but there was nothing
I could identify as a foot-track. I never saw the prisoner till I saw him
before the magistrates, that I know of.

" Sergeant PEPPERELL : On the 1st February I received information of the
burglary, and went to Mr. ——'s house. In the garden in which the kitchen
window opens I found marks, and also on the sill of the window; they were
dirty foot-marks. There are three compartments in the shutters, and the
centre one is fastened by an iron bar to the other two. I found that the
centre compartment could be opened from the outside. There were foot-marks
over walls adjoining the garden. I took the prisoner into custody on the

evening of the 2nd of February, and found on him a pocket-book, two small keys, a carpet-bag key, and a pawnbroker's ticket; also a large muffler handkerchief. After I apprehended him I went to the Swan public-house, and saw a carpet-bag and some other things there. I opened the carpet-bag with one of the keys which I found on the prisoner. In the carpet-bag was the cloth and brush which I have produced. The servant girl at the house gave me the carpet-bag. I had the gimlet I have produced from Mr. ———.

" By the Prisoner : I did not compare the foot-prints with prisoner's boots, because I did not then know he was the man.

" Witness (in reply to prisoner) said he took the prisoner's coat out of the carpet-bag without unlocking it, but when he took the cloth identified from the bag it was fastened quite close, and nothing could then be got out or put in without the bag being unlocked.

" The prisoner wished to ask the officer some questions about a book belonging to him which the officer had in his possession.

" His Lordship said he would not stop the question, but he warned the prisoner that it might have the effect of trying him on two charges at once."

It is unnecessary to enter into all the evidence, which was most complete in proving the crime, the prisoner questioning each witness with the skill of an experienced barrister.

" The prisoner addressed the jury in his defence. He remarked that the evidence had not shown that he had ever been seen near Mr. ———'s premises. He dwelt on one or two inconsistencies in the evidence as to where the carpet-bag was opened, whether in the club-room or a bed-room at the Swan ; and with regard to his arrest, said he had been ' led like a lamb to the slaughter.' Any one, he said, might have pushed the towel into the carpet-bag during his absence; the brush could not be identified, and as to the gimlet, he admitted purchasing it, but it was for his professional purposes as a repairer of harps. He begged the jury to consider the contradictions in the evidence, and if they entertained any doubt on the case to give him what was his right, the benefit of that doubt, by saying he was not guilty. Had his pecuniary circumstances permitted, he could have called witnesses who would have proved that he was at Bath on the night the burglary was committed.

" The Judge, in summing up, showed that the case for the prosecution had been entirely unanswered.

" The prisoner was found guilty.

" He was further charged with having been convicted at Newgate, under the name of Charles Taylor, in 1858.

" Prisoner said he was not so convicted.

" P.C. Clarke, of Bristol, put in a certificate, stating that Charles Taylor had been convicted of burglary in 1858, and was sentenced to four years' penal servitude. The witness said he was at the Old Bailey *and heard the prisoner plead guilty. He had known him 18 months in Bristol previous to* 1858.

some money; I asked him where he got it? He said he had picked a lady's pocket in St. Ann's Square. *I thought it very clever of him.* So we went and got something to eat, paid our lodgings, and went to bed; and I got into bad company from that time. Thus we went on for a long time, one thing led to another; at length *the police knew me quite well, from seeing me always among bad characters.* At last, I and another were apprehended in St. Ann's Square, on suspicion of pocket picking, and *sent to Salford prison for a month.*

"I was again taken up, and sentenced to two months' in Salford. When my time was up, and I was restored to liberty again, I soon forgot all my good resolutions I had formed during my imprisonment. I was soon taken again for the same offence, and got two months. When the time expired, my mother came to meet me at the gate, and tried to get me to go to work, *but I would not go.* I again took to my former wicked life, *and went on worse than before.* I went to Stockport fair, where I got £4. Then I took all the fairs and races within ten miles round Manchester, getting £3 or £4 at every place, sometimes more, till I came to Rochdale, then I was sent to Salford for fourteen days. I was not long out, when I was taken in Market Street, and sent back for three months. I was taken again, and got one month. When I came out I led just the same life for about six months; when I was taken again in Shude Hill, and sent back for three months more. When I came out the fever was very bad in Manchester, and I was confined to my bed. I was soon removed to the fever ward, and the fourth week I was sent home in a very weak state. A many of my companions *had gone off at this time with the fever.* They were not missed, *plenty rising up as fast as they died.* I was not long at my old game before I was taken up and sentenced to one month's imprisonment. When I came out, I went to Leeds fair, and stayed a week with some friends. I then went to Ripon hireings, and got £25. I then came to Manchester, and soon spent it all."

Mr. CLAY computes that at the age of 20, when this narrative was written, this young man had mulcted the public, during five years, of as much as £1800!

Now these persons, during all the years that they had been pursuing their iniquitous career, had not only been inflicting a great injury on society, which could be very inadequately represented by any pecuniary estimate of loss to the sufferers, but everyone connected with them must have more or less experienced an injurious influence.

"The extensive demoralization," says Mr. CLAY, in his 27th Report, "laid bare by the disclosures of the CLARKES, FLANAGAN, and others, cannot but shock the religious sense of every one who labours for, or desires, the real welfare of all classes. No doubt it is the moral aspect of the case which is beyond all measure of the greatest moment; at the same time it will not diminish solicitude in the matter if I present an economical view of it, and show how much the public has probably been plundered by the parties of this very small detachment from the pickpocket division of *la classe dangereuse.* FLANAGAN's fourteen years' course, and KELTY's twenty years—the latter worthy being still in practice—show, too plainly, that the land, or at least the police, is unequal to a successful contest with such characters, and it may, therefore, be of service to exhibit to the public the amount of depredation they are exposed to, in order that they may obviate, by their own watchfulness, those losses which, if once sustained, can seldom be recovered. The estimate offered is framed from a comparison of the separate statements made by each of the pickpockets, and after careful examinations of them." Of these, Mr. CLAY states further in a note, " T. M'GIVERIN and T. KELTY were then at liberty continuing their depredations. From information given by FLANAGAN to the Governor three more of the gang were apprehended, convicted, and sentenced to transportation,—LYNAM, BUCKLEY, and a woman named DICKENSON."

We shall not here present to the reader the painful details alluded to above, or those of the CLARKE family, as they will be sufficiently disclosed in a subsequent narrative of one of the gang, ELLEN CLARKE.

ESTIMATE OF THE LOSS INFLICTED ON THE PUBLIC BY THE UNDERMENTIONED PICKPOCKETS DURING THEIR SEVERAL CAREERS.

| | Name. | Age. | Career of Vice. | Estimate of Losses inflicted. |
|---|---|---|---|---|
| 1. | Richard Clarke ... | 18 | ... 6 ... | £2,820 |
| 2. | John Clarke ... | 20 | ... 5 ... | 500 |
| 3. | Edwd. Clarke ... | 15 | ... 3 ... | 1,650 |
| 4. | Ellen Clarke (O'Neill) | 17 | ... 2½ ... | 1,550 |
| 5. | John O'Neill ... | 21 | ... 9 ... | 1,450 |
| 6. | Thos. O'Gar ... | 18 | ... 6 ... | 300 |
| 7. | James O'Brien ... | 16 | ... 3¼ ... | 1,400 |
| 8. | Thos. M'Gwerin ... | — | ... 7 ... | 1,900 |
| 9. | Thos. Kelty ... | 30 | ... 20 ... | 11,570 |
| 10. | J. Flanagan ... | 28 | ... 14 ... | 5,800 |
| 11. | J. Thompson ... | 20 | ... 5 ... | 18,000 |
| 12. | J. Bohauna ... | — | ... 6 ... | 15,000 |
| 13. | J. Shawe ... | — | ... 3 ... | 600 |
| 14. | W. Buckley ... | — | ... 7 ... | 2,100 |
| 16. | S. Dickenson ... | — | ... 3 ... | 630 |

$$
\begin{array}{r}
32,000 \\
\end{array}
$$

Deduct for time past in prison ...     ...     7,000

25,000

Add for prison maintenance, cost of prosecution, &c.   ...    ...    ...    1,500

£26,500

Mr. CLAY adds,—

"In my Report for 1848, speaking of the Irish emigrants, I was led to remark,—'When these wretched people settled in a town, their children contributed largely to the hopeless class of young offenders. They are sent out, systematically, to beg; but the temptations of a town, the thronged streets, the places of low amusement, &c., soon convert the little beggar into an adroit thief.' The above list of thieves furnishes a remarkable commentary upon the observations just quoted, for only excepting the last two persons named, all the rest were either born in Ireland or of Irish parents."

It will be observed that these persons were sentenced to transportation. They were to be sent out of our own country, in the hope of our being henceforth freed from their depredations, and from their contaminating influence. They have ceased to be *our* Convicts. We transferred the difficult charge to others. We established their future home in our antipodal dominions; as far from us as the ocean would carry them. What kind of life they now are leading in the country they were forced to adopt,—what influence they spread there,— we know not;—we have thrown off all responsibility respecting them! Thus we trained men and women to become hardened in vice, expert in varied kinds of fraud, preying upon their fellow-citizens rather than earning their bread by the sweat of their brow. We allowed them so to grow up to maturity in the old country, and then to form a rising colony in the new ! We sent them unreformed,—we closed our ears to the horrors, the fiend-like wickedness, which men like these carried with them. The Coiners, the Housebreakers, the various classes of criminals whom Mr. CLAY describes in his Reports with such fearful truthfulness, were indeed all sent to our distant colonies, and we saw them no more;—but they left behind them a legacy of vice, and others take their place, as daring, as dangerous to society; these are now "our Convicts" whom we must deal with ourselves, for our colonies refuse to receive them !

One of these, now in Portland Convict Prison, lately made a remarkable disclosure of his own criminal acts. In the

Divorce Court on Saturday, June 4th, of the present year, in the case of "QUICK v. QUICK and QUICK," the plaintiff (who was the widow of HENRY BRANNON QUICK, a Solicitor, deceased in May, 1863,) sued for certain powers in the disposal of her late husband's property, in accordance with the intention in a will which was alleged to have been destroyed. It was stated, that

"On the 16th of October, 1862, the house in which Mr. and Mrs. QUICK lived at Haverstock Hill had been broken into, and a jewel-case and a dressing-case had been stolen. The plaintiff's case was that the will in question had been mislaid in the dressing-case by the deceased, and had been destroyed by the burglar.

"CHARLES KEMBELL was called to prove this part of the case. *He is now a convict at Portland*, and was brought up in the prison dress and in the custody of an officer. He stated that on the 16th of October, 1862, in the middle of the day, while the family were at dinner, he had climbed up to a balcony by a portico in the front of Mr. QUICK's house, and had made his way into a bedroom, and taken away a jewel-case and a dressing-case. He found some rings and some jewels, &c., in the jewel-case, and in the dressing-case a small parcel of papers, which he gave to a friend to see whether there was any paper-money among them. There was no paper-money, but there was a large paper in an envelope, with ' H. QUICK,' and ' This is my will,' written upon it. His friend read it and wished to keep it, but he took it from him and put it into the fire, for fear it might lead to his detection.

"Cross-examined: The police were after me at the time for *numerous robberies that I had committed in the same neighbourhood*, with the help of a gig and fleet horse. I was afterwards convicted and sentenced for one of the robberies. My friend had shown me the house before I committed the robbery. I decline to give the name of my friend, or to say where he is likely to be found. You will not know anything about him from me. I was questioned about the robbery last June by Captain CRAIG, the Governor of Pentonville prison. I did not tell him I had destroyed a policy of insurance as well as a will. At first I said that the will was not destroyed. That was not true; but I said it because I was then suffering a dreadful punishment for trying to make my escape, and I was not in a very good temper, and *I wanted other people to feel some of the sufferings I was enduring*. I did not wish to say anything that I thought would benefit Mr. QUICK, because he tried to arrest me while I was robbing a house next door but one to his, a day or two after I had robbed his house. He did not arrest me, *and I robbed the house and got away*. Last November a gentleman and lady brought me an affidavit in Pentonville prison, and read it over to me, and I swore to it and put my name to it. [In this affidavit the witness had given an account of the robbery, and had sworn that he and his friend had determined to destroy it, for fear it should lead to their detection.] He also deposed: I am quite certain that one of the documents I destroyed was a will, *as I am a scholar, and can read writing well*, and am familiar with wills, having observed that they were kept in similar places as dressing-cases by other persons whose houses I have robbed of such cases in a like manner, and I have invariably destroyed by fire such wills. *I can distinctly speak to the destruction of at least six of such wills by me, under the circumstances aforesaid.*"

What expense, annoyance, and lengthened legal proceedings were caused by the single wanton act committed by this man; what may have been the injury caused by the destruction of all these other legal documents, which were perfectly valueless to himself, but probably of unspeakable importance to others. The Convict GILL, after his nineteen burglaries, was not so lost to all consideration for others as to destroy the will which he had stolen. Observe again the desperate daring of his character in even attempting to escape from the secure Convict Prison at Pentonville, and his obdurate hardness and cruelty, which resisted all the softening religious influences of solitary confinement, and made him tell gratuitous falsehoods for the simple purpose of gratifying a vindictive feeling. However painful it may be to contemplate such heartless villany, it is necessary to realise its existence, in order to be able to form any opinion of the treatment needed for such Convicts.

Another division of the class of habitual plunderers on society must not be left unnoticed,—the Coiners. Though the frequency of convictions for passing base coin at particular times would lead to the supposition that there are individuals who make the manufacture of it their special calling, yet the public is probably not aware how completely this branch of fraud is organised, and how extensively it is practised. Mr. CLAY, in his twenty-eighth Report, especially directs his attention to the Coiners, a number of them being at that time in the gaol under sentence of transportation. He thus speaks in his Appendix to that Report,—

"The following narratives and statements relative to the making and passing of base coin, are given at some length (though all of them are compressed to less than half of their original bulk), under the impression that it is desirable to possess full particulars of a system chiefly carried on to the serious injury of the lower ranks of shopkeepers; and which, at the same time, holds out great temptations for the wilfully idle or casually unemployed operative to try a pursuit that, once entered upon, can scarcely, or by any possibility, be forsaken.

"The life of J. H., the writer of the first narrative, before he ventured on the career of a Coiner, is so full of warning of the miserable consequences that, in many shapes, beset the man who has surrendered himself into the power of drink, that I offer it as a fit introduction to these "*memoires pour servir,*" towards a due understanding of the extensive system which it illustrates. The entire narrative also supplies a characteristic commentary on the short but frequent records which appear in the assize and sessions calendars—relating to him and his family—to the following effect:—

| | | | | | |
|---|---|---|---|---|---|
| "J. H. (the father) | tried 1, | March, | 1846, | for uttering base coin, | acquitted. |
| | " 2, | Aug., | " | ditto, | 12 mos. imp. |
| | " 3, | Aug., | 1848, | ditto, | 18 mos. imp. |
| | " 4, | Feb., | 1851, | ditto, | 12 mos. imp. |
| Ellen H. (the mother) | " 1, | Dec., | 1847, | ditto, | 3 mos. imp. |
| | " 2, | Feb., | 1851, | ditto, | 12 mos. imp. |
| James H. (eldest son) | " 1, | April, | 1848, for felony, | | 6 mos. imp. |
| | " 2, | March, | 1849, for uttering base coin, | | acquitted· |
| | " 3, | Aug., | 1849, summarily convicted, | | 1 mo. imp. |
| | " 4, | Jan., | 1850, | ditto, | 3 mos. imp. |
| | " 5, | Feb., | 1851, for uttering base coin, | | 12 mos. imp. |
| Jane H. (daughter) | " 1, | April, | 1848, | ditto, | 9 mos. imp. |
| | " 2, | Nov. | 1849, | ditto, | 12 mos. imp. |
| John (son—a boy) | " 1, | Aug., | 1848, | ditto, | 9 mos. imp. |
| | " 2, | Sep., | 1849, summarily convicted | | 3 mos. imp." |

This table of convictions sufficiently shows how completely the family were engaged in this most nefarious occupation. Space will not permit the insertion of the narratives alluded to; one extract will suffice to show the extraordinary daring of those persons. Mr. CLAY derives it from the statement of a man, W. S.,—

"Few grown up people utter counterfeit money without being able to swallow it. I can give you a proof of this. A man, by name JOHN MURREL, was sentenced to three years' imprisonment to the Middlesex House of Correction. He was a seller of base coin. He was apprehended, with two others, and taken to Rosamond Street Station. Sometime during the night, a respectable man was placed in the same cell with them. He was speechless drunk, so they set about robbing him. They took from him two sovereigns and seven half-crowns; and as MURREL was the only one who could swallow them he was in possession of them in case of danger. The friends of the drunkard coming to bail him out in the morning, he asked for his money

The police, knowing the three men, and suspecting the truth, endeavoured to get the money, but without success, MURREL *had swallowed the seven half-crowns!* After his sentence he mentioned the fact to Dr. WAKEFIELD, the surgeon of Coldbath Fields."

Mr. CLAY says that he is indebted to the gentleman now named for a courteous letter, fully confirming W. S.'s otherwise incredible statement. Dr. WAKEFIELD writes :—

" The account given to you by the prisoner is perfectly true. The man swallowed seven *good* half-crowns upon entering the prison, as he said, under the apprehension of their being taken from him and forfeited. The half-crowns remained in his inside nearly eighteen months, when complaining of diarrhœa, he was taken to the Infirmary, and they all passed, perfectly black, but with very little loss of weight. They had, however, laid the foundation of disease in the intestinal canal, which produced ulceration, and, eventually, his death. This is by no means a solitary case, for we have had repeated instances of base *crown* pieces being swallowed, and passed away without detriment to the prisoner."

There is another division of the Convict class, whose offences are not against the property but against the persons of their fellow countrymen. Though crimes of violence may be sometimes the result of accidental irritation or passion, yet most commonly they indicate a life regardless of others, and habitually under the controul of the lower passions. This is especially the case with respect to those who commit outrages on the other sex, of whom so many must now be in the Government prisons, if they have not been already released on license again to infest society. We shall be excused for not investigating the histories of this class of Convicts.

We have hitherto been engaged in learning something respecting those Convicts who form the bulk of the inmates of our Government Gaols, the habitual criminals, those who are avowedly living by plunder. Most of these are persons belonging to the lower class of society, and if, for nefarious purposes, they assume for a time the external appearance and demeanour of a higher rank, they can be easily unveiled. But among the individuals composing the great masses of convicts already glanced at, are many who are not less dangerous to society, because they do not openly prey upon it. Such a case

is that of a man who had the extraordinary audacity to obtain
admission last year into the very Presence Chamber at a Royal
Reception. The following account of this man, whose conduct
at the time excited considerable sensation, is derived from the
*Daily Telegraph* of March, 1863 :—

" We cannot speak with precision as to the hulk, convict prison, or dockyard
in which Mr. SAMUEL TILLETT, late of Colchester, served his modicum of
seven years' transportation, to which he was condemned at the assize holden
at Chelmsford in the month of July, 1853, for the crime of forgery and fraud ;
but it is certain that he did receive such a sentence, that he underwent
a portion of it, and that, notwithstanding the indelible brand of convicted
felony, he was very recently presented at the Court of St. James's to his Royal
Highness the PRINCE of WALES, representing her Most Gracious Majesty on
that auspicious occasion. The Chief Baron POLLOCK was the judge who
tried TILLETT. It is quite within the range of probability for the learned
Chief Baron, in his full judicial robes, to have met with his quondam culprit,
complacent and confident, and arrayed in the orthodox snuff-coloured coat
and cut-steel buttons, in one of the corridors of St. James's. We can imagine
the amazement with which his Lordship might have regarded the impudent
varlet who had thrust himself into the society of English noblemen and
gentlemen. Let it be borne in mind that TILLETT's guilt was of no ordinary
degree. He was no mere perfunctory, or inadvertent perjurer. There is no
need to enter into a minute history of this person's malpractices, suffice it to
say that, as a conveyancer at Colchester, he became insolvent, *thereby bringing
many persons, who had reposed trust and confidence in him to actual beggary,*
and *that he was indicted for a gross act of perjury in his examination before the
County Court Judge, acting in assistance of the Insolvent Debtor's Court.* In
passing sentence, the Lord Chief Baron told him that the defence he put
forward amounted to 'the wicked fabrication of a falsehood ;' and that he had
as wickedly 'persevered to the last moment in endeavouring to fix imputations
of guilt upon persons who had brought him to justice. *I think,*' remarked his
Lordship, ' *that when a person of your station forgets what is due to his
profession, to his education, and to the claim society has upon him, he is justly
amenable to the severest punishment the law can afford. Nor has your conduct
since the transaction, nor up to the last moment you have addressed me, shown
anything like contrition or penitence that would give me reason to extend any
indulgence to you.*' And with this stinging admonition the Lord Chief Baron
sentenced SAMUEL TILLETT, the fraudulent and false-swearing conveyancer of
Colchester, to be transported for seven years."

Many cases of dishonesty and swindling, such as this, come
from time to time before the public, and each one is generally
attended with far greater suffering to society than the daring

burglaries and enormous thefts of jewels and large sums of money which shock and startle us. These last are usually committed on opulent persons who can retrive the loss; but the fraudulent swindlers frequently cause the ruin of persons in narrow circumstances, whose lives even sometimes sink beneath the blow. There must be many Convicts such as these in our Gaols, and in future pages allusion will again be made to them.

Willingly would we here conclude these narratives of crime, and most reluctantly are we compelled to give special notice to Female Convicts. It is well known to all persons who have the care of criminals, either old or young, that the treatment of females is far more perplexing than that of males. It demands, indeed, peculiar consideration and comprehension of the special difficulties to be grappled with.

The following may be regarded as a sample of the career of most of the Female Convicts who have completely plunged into crime. It is derived from *The Times*, February 16, 1864:— "Two women, named TREVES and CLOVES, were tried at the Middlesex Sessions last for shoplifting. They were sentenced, the former to 3, the latter to 4 years, penal servitude. TREVES, who is but 20 years of age, has already been convicted four times: for 3 months, in February, 1859; 10 months, in November, 1860; 3 months, January 4th, 1861; and 18 months January 4th, 1861. CLOVES has been in the same Gaol five times: for 3 months, October 23rd, 1854; 1 month, March 20th, 1855; 3 months, October 25th, 1858; 6 months, April 10th, 1859; and 3 months, April 26th, 1860." It is not known whether these women may not have been in other prisons; nor is it possible to obtain such information, as there is no general system established over the country whereby criminals may be identified and registered. But whether their previous convictions have been more or fewer, such a brief statement as this gives no idea of the individual women, nor of the peculiarities of their characters. The very susceptibility and tenderness of woman's nature render her more completely diseased in her whole nature

when this is perverted to evil; and when a woman has thrown
aside the virtuous restraints of society, and is enlisted on the
side of evil, she is far more dangerous to society than the other
sex. While we acknowledge this with deep sorrow, the conviction of it should only make us more anxiously desire to
comprehend the actual condition of those who have become so
deeply tainted with moral disease, in the hope of learning how
to effect a cure.

The Prison Matron's narrative has been so extensively read
that acquaintance with it may here be assumed. It presents
a true picture of what the unfortunate women who are the
subjects of it actually are when in a Convict Gaol. Peculiarities
of character, which are familiar to all who have had the care
of female Reformatories and Prisons, are there excited to a
frightful intensity, which is constantly increasing until they become a settled habit. Yet it does not appear that the women
there depicted, who seem like monsters when in that unnatural
condition, are different in their natures from other women who
may be met with at large in the world. An instance of this
will be adduced in illustration.

We have read in the narrative of the Prison Matron of the
extraordinary powers of deception existing in some of these
unfortunate female convicts. The woman whose case is about
to be given was not a convict, and the investigations made
into her history do not indicate that she had ever been in
prison. It seems strange that the law does not punish the
ruthless robbery of the good name of innocent persons which
this woman perpetrated, or such daring and extraordinary
frauds, and that a rest of three months in Gaol—for this only
it would be to a woman so hardened—should be the only termination of her career. The following is derived from the
*Birmingham Post* of Feb., 1863. It is headed,—

### "AN EXTRAORDINARY IMPOSTOR.

" On Tuesday the magistrates sitting in Petty Session in Wolverhampton,
the town whence the notorious ALICE GREY was committed, were engaged for

a considerable time in investigating the circumstances of a series of impostures committed by a young woman possessing all the personal attractions of the person first mentioned, and in no way inferior to her in artifice and cunning.

"Early in March, 1862, a respectably-dressed and prepossessing young woman was found in the street of Welshpool in a state of apparent insensibility. She was kept by the parish officers for about a week, when she left and proceeded by train to Newtown. On her arrival at the station in that town she was taken out of the carriage in a state of supposed unconsciousness. Three or four medical men were soon in attendance, and were completely at a loss to account for her symptoms. Mr. BAIRD, the Chief Constable of Montgomeryshire, happened, however, to be present, and the invalid's recovery was facilitated by his addressing her as ELIZABETH HODGES, the name by which she had gone in Welshpool, and by his asking her if she was not the same person who had been 'performing the dodge' in that town. Next she was found again insensible by the road side near Montgomery. Her position was first made known by three young men, against all of whom, when she had 'recovered,' she brought a most serious charge. So truthful appeared her statements that the three men were twice remanded upon the charge; but after the evidence of Chief-Constable BAIRD, and of another witness from Welshpool, a doubt was occasioned, and the men were discharged.

"Subsequently a woman, supposed to be the same person, was found on a railway-bridge near to Oswestry, with marks of violence in her throat. A man, who had been seen in her company a short time before, was arrested on suspicion of having attempted to strangle her. She was taken into the Workhouse the next morning, and it was assumed that she had dislocation of the jaw, but that she was injured the surgeon's assistant was satisfied. The woman was unconscious, and remained so during the following day, when, as the surgeon was talking near the bedside, the patient 'peeped out of one of her eyes,' and the surgeon's alleged suspicions were confirmed; but as she remained seemingly unconscious, he had her hair cut and her spine blistered. In a few days she was sent out. The surgeon had the charity to suppose the woman had been suffering from aggravated hysteria; but he writes, 'The marks on her throat were clearly caused by her own hands.'

"Nothing daunted, however, by this treatment, we find her in hospital again in January of this year. This time she is in London, and her name is given as HARRIET BELL. On the night of the 15th of January she was found by a porter on the arrival of a train at Paddington in a state of insensibility. It was conceived that she had taken poisons; and she was removed to St. Mary's Hospital, Paddington. The usual restoratives for poison were applied. On recovering, she pretended that she could not speak English, but only Welsh. A Welsh railway porter was sent for, to ascertain from her what she had taken. She said that she was on her way from Glasgow to Cheltenham to her brothers, who were soldiers, and that whilst in the train a man by sheer dint of superior strength overcame her, and committed an offence upon her person. He then gave her some wine or spirits, and whilst she was insensible robbed her of

£1 10s. Before she was discharged, however, she could speak English. Our readers may remember that three weeks ago it was recorded in the public journals that a woman was found in an unconscious state on the arrival of a train at Stroud from London-bridge. Restoratives were applied, but no motion of the heart was discovered, and Dr. BROWN *pronouncing the woman a corpse, recommended her removal to the dead-house.* Two surgeons (Mr. STEELE and Mr. LANGSTONE) were sent for, and when the latter had continued his efforts to restore animation for two hours, returning consciousness was perceived, and the woman was ultimately removed to the Stroud Workhouse, when she said that her name was BELL, that she had come from the United States to visit her father in Glasgow, and was proceeding thence to Chatham to visit her brother, who was a soldier. When in the Railway Station, she added, a respectably-dressed woman first drugged her, and then robbed her of 30s., her muff and shawl, and escaped in the confusion at Stroud. The report of this extraordinary recovery concluded by stating that ' every effort is being used by the police to trace the woman who perpetrated the robbery.' The Station-Master at Stroud gave her a free pass back to London and 5s. From London she made her way to Birmingham, where she feigned illness also at the Railway Station (New-street), was removed to Coventry, where she said she had friends, was driven round the city for an hour in the vain attempt to find those friends, and was returned to Birmingham. On the evening of the 10th instant she was found again insensible on the floor of a third-class carriage at Wolverhampton, and was removed to the South Staffordshire Hospital in that town. She was there recognised by Mr. KEOGH, the house-surgeon, who had removed from Shrewsbury Hospital to Wolverhampton, as the woman whom he had cupped and blistered in Shrewsbury. He accordingly regarded her as an impostor, had her arrested, and Captain SEGRAVE, the Chief-Constable, made inquiries, which resulted in the accumulated evidence given above.

" The Magistrates said that they believed she was the woman referred to in all the instances, and sentenced her to three month' imprisonment.

" The woman's statement is as follows:—' I left Chatham last Tuesday week, at 5.30 p.m., to proceed to Willenhall, to see my brother, a soldier, who was seriously injured on the railway. I arrived at London-bridge from Chatham, and took the train from Euston-square for Birmingham, where I arrived between eight and nine o'clock in the evening. I then booked for Wolverhampton, arriving late. Was asked in Birmingham by a lady if I was nurse in the Queen's Hospital, as she had seen some person there like me. She gave me some brandy to drink twice, which made me sick and senseless. She was in the same carriage with me. I had no further recollection. I was born in Russell Barracks, New York. My father is still lying there. He belongs to her Majesty's 36th Regiment. I have fourteen brothers, twelve in the army and two in the navy. My mother is at Chatham. She was to leave to join my father on the 18th of this month. My father has been 45 years a soldier. He was born in New Zealand in France. I am a widow. My husband's name was FORRESTER BELL. He was born in New Zealand in France, and has been dead about two and a half years. I was married in Glasgow. My husband enlisted there in the 36th Regiment, and died there. I have been in England seven years, and have worked in the Barracks at Chatham, having the care of dinners and books. I was apprenticed to Mrs. ROSSLEY, milliner, Longton-street, Chatham, and have been out of my time seven years. I have been a good deal in London, but never was in Montgomeryshire, Wales, or Salop.'"

This woman had not been in a Convict Prison, and was sentenced to only three months' imprisonment; but she exhibits all the bad features of some of the wretched females who are in them,—the same profound deception, the same remarkable power over her physical nature, enabling her to impose on the most experienced medical practitioners, the same intense love of notoriety and unscrupulous efforts to obtain it. We need not suppose that the women in Brixton Gaol were originally infinitely worse than others of their sex. The remarkable narrative of JANE CAMERON by the same author, gives a picture of the life of a female Convict, which must have almost an air of romance to those who are unacquainted with the characteristics of these unfortunate persons, yet it does not greatly surpass in variety of incident the unvarnished narrative of a young woman, ELLEN CLARKE, whose name appears in the list of pickpockets in page 24 ; her history given to Mr. CLAY, while lying under sentence of transportation in Preston Gaol, is verified by the independent histories of the other prisoners, her accomplices. We make no apology for introducing it here, though it has already appeared elsewhere.

"I was born at Stockport, my father was a pensioner, and had 1s. a day; my father and mother were both sober and industrious, *but my mother would have done anything to have got us meat.* My father was more shy,—he was a shoemaker. I went for nearly three years to a Roman Catholic School, at threepence a week. I went to the factory at ten years old and worked there till I was twelve. Then I went to service at Mosley, at a boarding school. I stayed there until I was fourteen. I then left on account of small wages. I came home and was sent by my father to learn to be a lad's cap maker. I was learning for three months, and then I came home again.

" When I came home I saw that my brother RICHARD was dressed very fine, besides having a gold ring and a watch. My brother was not then living at home regularly, *because he could not stand my father's reproaches.* I used to say to my father, ' How well RICHARD's dressed!' And my father would say, ' But who thinks anything of it? he's a prig.' *My mother was more unhappy about it than my father*, and often followed him about the town, begging him to come home. When I was just fifteen, my mother gave me threepence to go to Knoll Mill Fair, and I met my brother there. He told me what to do, and I stood before him so that nobody could see his hand while he picked a woman's pocket of 7s. 6d. and a purse. He gave me a shilling, and then told me to go home. I went into a show, and picked a young woman's pocket of 1s. 6d. *I trembled very much when I did it.* I met the young woman again in a short time and she was crying. I heard her say the money was her mother's. *I cried too, and would have given her the money back*, but was afraid of being took up. I dared not take the money home, so I took it to a stay shop, and paid it in advance towards a pair of stays. I remained at home three months *without doing anything more.* At the end of that time my little brother EDWARD was taken up for picking pockets and got three months. He had been taken up three times before, and had only been out three days. *During twelve months he had only been at liberty four days.*

" One of the witnesses against him was one of his own companions, and after he had been the means of convicting him, I leathered him just outside the court. I was taken up for the assault on this witness, and remanded in the New Bailey a week. I was then bailed out by two navvies. [These two men were perfect strangers; this kind of security is very common.] My mother met me in the street, and we were treated to some rum by a companion of my brother RICHARD's, JAMES O'B., who had £100 which he had stolen from a woman. My brother was then in Gloucestershire picking pockets. O'B. gave me money to complete the purchase of my stays. I had been at a fair with another young woman only for a day, and we got £3 between us. When I got home again, my mother had a letter from RICHARD, saying that he was put back for trial at Goucester for pocket-picking, and wanted money to pay for a counsellor. I went by the train to Oughton, and at the station picked a woman's pocket of 15s., which paid for my place to Kidderminster. I went in a waggon from Kidderminster to Worcester, with five or six other females, and got 15s. more from them. I stopped all night at Worcester. I went in an omnibus to the Gloucester station next morning, and picked a lady's pocket in the omnibus of £1 2s. I got into Gloucester on Friday night; saw my brother next morning; told him that I would try to get some money for a counsel, and went to the market, but it is a very poor market, and I only got 10s. 9d. I could not get enough money to fee my brother a counsel, and he received three months, having been recommended by the jury to mercy on account of his being so young. I then went to Derby, and then to Sheffield, where I saw O'NEILL, whom I had previously known in Manchester through my brother. I went to Rotherham Statute Fair and got about £4. I saw O'N. again, who said, ' I think you have done better than any of us !' for a great many pickpockets were there. I then went to Bam

Statute Fair, but got nothing, for it rained and no people came. I returned to Sheffield, and then went to Hull. I went to all those places by myself, having heard O'N. and his companions say they were going. It was the fair, and I got between £6 and £7. I seldom kept my money, for other travellers in the lodging-houses used to say they were hard up, and borrowed it from me. O'N. wanted me to live with him without being married, *but I would not.* My eldest brother JOHN was then in Hull, serving a month for picking pockets. I waited till he came out, and then he leathered me for coming away from home. I ran away from him and went to Leeds; there I met O'N. again, and the askings were put up for us to be married. I filled up the three weeks by going to Sheffield and York, and got about £10 or £11 at both places together. We were married at the Old Church. Up to this time I could only pick outside pockets, but O'N. taught me how to raise outside dresses and to pick inside pockets. I was married on the Thursday, and on the Saturday I got 10s. in the market. On Monday my brother EDWARD came to Leeds. We all went out, and EDWARD picked a pocket of 13s., but he had been watched, and we were all took up, *and we got three months.*

" After our liberation we went to Hull, and found PRINCE ALBERT was going to lay the foundation stone of Grimsby Docks. At Hull I got 17s. We went to Grimsby, and EDWARD and I got 30s. each. From Hull we went to Newark, where we got £7; then to Redford £4; then to Sheffield, where I was took up for 30s. I had just taken from a woman. *This brought me six weeks,* and O'N. (my husband) two months in Wakefield. I travelled after I came out until O'N. came out, and got in the fortnight about £15. Then we went to Selby, and got £4 in the market. Then to Hull, and got £5 at the station. Then to Manchester, when I and my husband went to live with my father. While I lived at Manchester I went out with O'N. almost every day by the trains six or seven miles out of Manchester, sometimes second, sometimes first class, having very good clothes. The largest sum I ever got was £22, going from Manchester to Stockport. *O'N. did nothing but 'shade me off.' He was a great drunkard, and I had to pay from 20s. to 35s. every week to the beer-shop for him. We carried on this way for about six months, making on the average about £10 a week.* We lived at my father's all this time. He used to fret and cry, and tell us we should get into disgrace, but we took no heed. He was too good-natured with us. We then heard that Preston Market was very throng on a Saturday, and for thirteen weeks we came over, O'N., RICHARD and I, every Saturday. O'N. and I went together, and RICHARD and O'G. At night we shared all equally. The largest sum I ever got at Preston was £17, and the smallest about £3. I used to call £4 and £5 nothing. It was owing to the wet day we went into the shop, few people being in the market, when the offence took place for which we are transported. *Although I was three years at school I never learnt to read.* Once when I was at Preston Station, I got some money in a purse (9s.) I took the purse, a red silk one, and put it in the water-closet on the Manchester side of the station. It was put behind the pipe over the seat. (This place was searched and the article found.) This was about two months ago. When I got a purse in a crowd, I used to take the money and put the purse into some man's pocket. I've done this 18 or 19 times. It was the best way of getting rid of the purse. J. O'N. lived with another young man in a furnished cellar. They dressed very well and each kept a woman. They used to have beefsteaks and beer regular to breakfast. I used to go out on Monday and get £2 and £3, which *would satisfy me for two days*, and then I would go again on Wednesday or Thursday, and again on Saturday, and generally got in the week about £20. I was never satisfied with less. O'G. did not do much ; he used to be clammed. My brother EDWARD was very daring. He could pick a woman's pocket as she was running along the street. If he had seen a thing that he fancied, he would say ' that's mine,' and watch his opportunity till he got it. JOHN had no heart (energy) for thieving. He lived on a woman who kept him. K. and M'G. were ' gins'; that is, they taught young theives and screened them when they were practising. K. kept a ' picking-up' woman ; that is, one who commits robberies in the street, K. coming up at the right moment to screen or rescue her."

Such is the narrative of this wretched young woman, at that time only about eighteen years of age. As she was living, she taxed the public for a luxurious maintenance for herself and her husband some £500 per annum, to finish her career in this country by transportation, a very costly procedure, and one not very certain in its results. The excellent Chaplain thus speaks of her :—

" ELLEN C. indeed possessed a natural disposition, which, had she been blessed with Christian parents, might have contributed to their and her own credit and happiness. Her narrative throughout betrays a wish to palliate their conduct, and at her interviews with them, since her conviction, she appeared quite forgetful of herself, and only solicitous to assuage their anxiety about her, and to warn her brother EDWARD from his dangerous course. This determined and skilful girl-thief of 17, who at the latter part of her short run of crime was not satisfied with less than a weekly booty of £10 or £20, ' trembled very much,' when she made her first successful essay upon the pocket of a young woman, from whom she purloined 18d. ' I met,' she says, ' the young woman again in a short time, and she was crying; I heard her say that the money was her mother's. *I cried too*, and would have given her the money back, but I was afraid of being took up.' What an affecting contrast between this girl's character and fate, as they are and as they might have been ! And how sad to think that our backward civilization *possesses, as yet, no means for saving from moral destruction thousands who, like this poor child, possess natural qualities which, by God's blessing, would amply repay the labour of cultivation !*"

This history affords a striking illustration of the evil arising from the existing state of the law; this allows a person to continue for years a course of depredations on society, unchecked except by an occasional short imprisonment, which produces no effect either in deterring or reforming the criminal. The evil to the individual of such a course is equally great; year after year adds fearfully to the weight of guilt, and burns in more deeply the criminal brand. Yet, while we lament the sinful course of this poor girl, we may also perceive in its details how much good, and what fine powers existed in her character, which under judicious and truly reformatory treatment, might have made her a valuable member of society. This is observable also in the life of JANE CAMERON, and is set forth so forcibly in a review of that work in the *Spectator* of November 28, 1863, that we here offer extracts from it.

"No one who reads this history will doubt for a moment that he has before him the actual life of a recently living woman, a life worth for all purposes of instruction whole columns of parliamentary talk. We, at least, never read such an answer to the theory now prevailing, which denies that criminals are human beings actuated by precisely the same impulses as the people who are not criminal, and considers them simply evil animals, to be lashed, and starved, and frightened into an endurable attitude towards the respectable classes. JENNIE CAMERON throughout her whole life was just an ordinary woman, governed by the emotions of all other women, and doing precisely the things they do under circumstances which made the doing an offence against society.

"Born in a Glasgow 'vennel,'—say one of the courts in Field Lane trans-ferred to a northern city—trained from childhood to beg, and bidden by her father to go on the streets before she was twelve years old, harlot, thief, and worse—for the final crime looks much more like being accessory to a murder than a mere violent robbery—JENNIE CAMERON was throughout simply an ordinary woman. There is not an impulse for good—except religious feeling, of which she had never heard—on which society relies for the good conduct of women which this girl did not display in a strong and permanent form. What impulse is it we trust to? Love! JENNIE CAMERON loved her associate BLACK BARNEY, the 'thieves' hero,' with all the power of her heart, remained absolutely faithful to him, and years after, when nearly reformed, could never speak of him without praise or evidence of strong feeling. But then her love was for the most expert thief in London, a man utterly bad, except that he never treated her unkindly, and instead of raising her it only plunged her deeper still. Is it the sense of honour? To the last day of her life she was

never without a sickening shame because she had once, in a fit of girl's wrath,
and drink, and jealousy, betrayed a 'pal' to the police; and for years she
attributed every calamity to the vengeance of fate for the one act which, when
recounting her life of crime, she described as her 'great wickedness.' But
then the honour she always strove to preserve was shown towards those
among whom she lived, and was, whether in itself virtue or vice, a weapon
*against* society. The conscience which pricked her was conscience, but it
bled because she had assisted justice, instead of impeding it. Do we rely on
maternal love? We know nothing more saddening in life than the history of
the love this girl bore to her single child, the efforts she made to support it,
how she begged for it, stole for it, realised Hugo's dream of Fantine for it, and
then, when it died, set herself by the body to drink down the grief which the
neighbours thought would kill her. Could the mother in Mayfair do more?
Only you perceive, where Mayfair lays down a carriage, the 'Vennel' sells
herself; where Mayfair only lacks luxury, the 'Vennel' starves; where
Mayfair strives by seclusion, and reading, and patience to obtain consolation,
the 'Vennel,' who cannot have seclusion, and knows not how to read, and
thinks of patience only as a needful help to successful crime, drinks away the
pangs. Or is it self-respect to which we are to look? JENNIE CAMERON was,
as we said, harlot, thief, and worse, yet once, when forced for some days to
join the professional beggars, she quitted them literally out of shame to find
herself fallen so low. Her pride of caste was as real and as sharply touched
as if she had been a lady forced to work publicly with her hands. Only you
perceive the moral superiority of thieves to professional beggars, which, by the
way, is a real one, is not so patent as is, for example, that of shopwomen to
servants; and so pride of caste was, instead of a defence, only a cause of
laughter. Is it a sense of housewifely duties? JENNIE, throughout her life,
avoided, when possible, all promiscuous living, kept her room to herself,
appreciated the cleanliness of the cells alone among the prison virtues, and
became, after her imprisonment an admirable domestic servant. One great
cause of her final reform, when after her first effort she had gone back to her
old associates, was a burning regret for the civilised home she had quitted, the
neatness, order, and, as she explicitly confessed, the regular and severe
industry. But then these qualities, born as she was, only helped to make her
an adroit thief, a careful housekeeper for a thief paramour, a successful trader
upon the streets. Or shall we appeal to the meaner qualities, which are so
little talked of, and so exceedingly potent in keeping society in its groove?
Fear! JENNIE CAMERON showed throughout conversations lasting for years
that she had never, through all her career, lost her terrible fear of gaol; that
she dreaded it as some minds dread death; that she feared every policeman
she met; that she was afraid of her paramour BLACK BARNEY, 'an awfu' mon
whan his blude was oop;' that the black hole gave her an actual though
temporary fit of insanity. It was to keep down fear that she drank till the
very thieves looked on her as one whose love for whiskey made her a dangerous
associate. But then, the fear of gaol, which makes you only lay plots the

deeper, has not the most moral effect. Shall we denounce love of idleness ?
This woman never had but one holiday in her life,—her paramour had stolen
a purse containing a hundred pounds, and they spent fifty in living like
respectable people at a quiet hotel, and the remainder was stolen from them
by a pickpocket,—and passed year after year in close hovels, pinched every
third week by hunger, and exposed to all manner of brutality, while the entire
remainder of her criminal career was expended in a prison which she detested
with all her heart. But then, the love of work which, in the respectable,
produces order and energy, in the unrespectable is very apt to produce
a feverish thirst for the excitement which is the substitute for regular labour.
Or, finally, was she deficient in that mental and physical weakness which is to
many respectables the most efficient of safeguards ? JENNIE CAMERON was all
her life, for her class, a weak woman. When her baby was born her
companions quizzed her for 'being as weak as a lady,' and in prison she was
given to violent fits of hysteria, ending in 'breakings-out.'

"In short, in all but training, religious and otherwise, guidance and means
of subsistence, JENNIE CAMERON was just woman, neither more nor less, and
those are the very things society can supply. Taken as a child out of the
'vennel'—by force if necessary—taught to work, and to think, and to pray,
she would have been just as decent a family mother as the millions around us,
with, perhaps, a crave for excitement, which would have been gratified by
a little too much reading of penny novels, and a capacity for loving which
would have expended itself on her husband and her children. Where is the
use of mere severity to such a woman as that? Its only effect was to harden,
and of all the purely restrictive force brought to bear upon JENNIE's life, the
sole effect was to make her adroit where she would have been careless, crafty
where she might have been audacious. That is a gain, it is true ; but how
trivial a one compared with that which would have been produced by education.
For this very woman's whole life is a proof of the doctrine which the first
glance at her life makes doubtful, that there is in man, once developed, something over which circumstances have no power. JENNIE CAMERON got her
education at last ; the education criminals want—the kindly contact of
a radically healthy mind. A prison matron took an interest in her, taught
her what kindness meant, and when her term had expired found her, with
another kindly mind, a place. She worked on for months as a housemaid, till
a bewildering crave possessed her for change, and she joined an old companion
worse in character than herself. She had no strong religious principle at any
time, and never professed any—the matron intimates that—she had no horror
of vice to get over, and not the faintest hope of retracing her steps to service.
Yet the education of kindness had done its work, had developed the resisting
strength, had let her know what was the decent life she was forfeiting, and
while living in the street-walker's room, she still fought her way back to
respectability. She refused to join her companion, lived on the savings of her
service, and, at last, when they were gone, forced herself to appeal once more
to the matron and her old employers. They, after delays, which, though

short, would have crushed anyone less resolved, decided to let her emigrate with them as a servant, and almost as the voyage ended she died, a Christian, the matron hopes; but, at all events, a finally civilised being. Suppose, instead of meeting the kindly matron, she had been crushed by a machine-like regularity of punishment, such as is now recommended, food insufficient for satisfaction, and therefore for maintaining decent temper; work a little too much for health; no communication with any but the chaplain, and just as much of physical torture as corresponds to the lash for men, what would society have gained?"

Fully do we subscribe to the views here expressed. Deep is our conviction that the female Convicts, appalling as their conduct may appear when thus presented to the public, and bad as it undoubtedly is, yet, every one, possess some traits of good feeling which the world knows little of, some aspirations after a better life which may have been stifled, but which Christian sympathy may re-awaken; some workings of God's spirit within which the loving heart of a fellow woman may rouse, to shake off from the soul the fetters of sin which have subdued it. May our rulers have wisdom to devise means to arrest these wretched ones in their career of vice, and to place them where they may have the possibility of true repentance. May the hearts of many Christian women be moved to help in their rescue!

# CHAPTER II.

## HOW ARE OUR CONVICTS MADE?

WE have now some idea of the individual Convicts who, after for years spoiling society, and living in luxury on their ill-gotten gains, are at length stopped in their guilty career by a long sentence of punishment. This idea, however strong and painful it may be to those who are unaccustomed to such narratives as have been here produced, is very faint in comparison with the reality, as those can testiy who have been brought by their duties into close contact with such persons, or who have perused the Prison Reports in which the excellent Chaplain of Preston Gaol presented annually his official experience. Such as it is, however, it must have impressed the mind with the necessity of stopping if possible such wholesale plunder of society; of protecting the public from such depredations, and, if possible, of bringing men and women, living in a manner so regardless of the laws of God and of man, to some degree of repentance,—to some conditon in which they may be able and willing to gain an honest livelihood.

But these persons have not suddenly become so lost to all good, so completely the slaves of sin. We should try to gain some insight into the nature of the temptations and circumstances which have plunged them to such a depth of wretchedness. Before attempting the cure we must learn the nature of the disease, and we must endeavour to ascertain whether there are not evils for the existence of which society is directly responsible, which must, unless removed, for ever perpetuate in our midst the mass of corruption from which we are suffering.

How do men and women arrive at a condition of so much depravity?

How far is society, directly or indirectly, to blame in the matter?

These are questions which we shall endeavour to answer in the present chapter.

Here is a brief history of a criminal career given by an old offender himself to the Chaplain of the Gaol, Rev. W. C. OSBORN, of Bath:—"I have been told a thousand times to go and get work, but it was never said to me during twenty years, while in or out of prison, 'I'll give you work.' Hence I have cost the country some two thousand pounds, and I expect to cost a great deal more yet. *I was sent to gaol for two months when a boy for stealing a loaf of bread, and no one cared for me.* I walked to the seaports, but in vain. I tramped, sore footed, thousands of miles when I was a lad, in order to get honest employment, but it did not answer. I was tempted to steal. I stole. I was imprisoned. I was sent to Bermuda. I have learnt the trade of a professional theif, and now I intend to follow it. I believe all philanthropy to be a mockery, and religion to be a delusion, and I care neither for God nor man. The gaol, penal servitude and the gallows, are all the same to me."

This is, probably, the history of thousands; and who is to be blamed? Are there no accessories to the life this man is leading? How was the boy who would "tramp sore footed thousands of miles to get honest employment" transformed into a man who disbelieved humanity,—who scoffed at religion and consequently defied the laws of God and man?

We will take other instances which have come under the personal knowledge of the writer. A woman in deep grief came to ask information from me how to learn any particulars respecting her son, who had lately committed suicide in a Convict Prison.

Suggestions how to obtain the sad information were given her, and inquiries put to her as to his history. She had made an unhappy marriage, and her husband, being much given to drink, treated her cruelly. Before the birth of this poor young man her husband had been particularly brutal to her. The child early showed signs of great irritability, and of a violent uncontrollable temper. The poor have not the means of correcting such a disposition, which are within reach of the rich. These can remove the child from irritating circumstances, change the scene for him, place him under proper control in a boarding-school, or engage the services of some one accustomed to the care of such cases to take care of him. What can a poor mother do with a wilful rebellious boy, when she has her own household work to attend to, her family to manage, and besides, a heartless drunken husband, who, far from controling his son, sets before him a bad example. The poor lad grew up under these auspices, until he openly defied the law and was sent to gaol for some months. He came out more hardened and daring; and was eventually sent to the Juvenile Prison at Parkhurst, where his conduct was so audacious, violent, and defiant of the officers, that he was sent to a Convict Prison; there, unable to endure the confinement and solitude, he terminated his imprisonment with his life. Who shall say that this poor fellow was a criminal in the sight of Him Who knoweth our frame and remembereth that we are but dust,—Who pitieth our weakness? How many may there be in our Lunatic Asylums who exceed this unfortunate young man in moral responsibility! Who can say what he might have become under different treatment?

The third case we will present is D——. We find him in one of the Convict Prisons under a sentence of four years' penal servitude. He does not pass through it without complaints of him. He professes an intention of emigrating, as the only chance of escaping from the thraldom of vicious associations; but having persisted in visiting his native city, and having £2 in his pocket, a greater sum than he had ever

before possessed, he fell in with his old companions, soon
squandered the greater part of it, and barely left himself
enough to proceed to Liverpool. There he again drank, behaved otherwise badly, and then disappeared with a large sum
of money from his lodgings. He was heard of next in gaol
in a distant town. Soon after his release he enlisted, and even
in the army he again got into prison. How was this wretched
young man brought up and trained to vice, and what had
society to do with his present condition? He was first seen,
about fourteen years ago, in a Ragged School, when about
twelve years of age. His wild appearance and close cropped
hair aroused suspicion that he had recently been discharged
from gaol. He acknowledged this, and said he had thence
made his way to this town. After a little while he was induced
to go to the Workhouse, instead of rambling about houseless;
but he did not stay there long, and was again in the streets.
Various efforts were made to induce him to accept a home
and work. For a time he would stay, and then leave. There
was no power of legal detention then over such boys. He
got into prison; there he had time for reflection, and would
have gladly sought the shelter of the Workhouse on his
discharge; but that was now refused him, and he was told to
get work. Of course that was impossible for such a youth;
so he resumed his Arab life. He stole a leg of mutton the
same evening, and was the cause of another boy's being sent
to prison; but he had become more cautious and escaped. He
came occasionally to the School, and showed, for the time,
a susceptibility of good influence; but it soon passed away.
He felt he was an outcast, and at war with society. In about
a year he was in prison for a longer time, for he was becoming
an adept in crime, and had learned to pick pockets. There
he again showed a tendency to good, and at his request, on his
discharge, was sent to a refuge at a distance. He did well for
about a year, but the roving spirit which had so long grown on
him was too powerful; he returned to the scene of his former

misdoings, was soon convicted of felony, and became a Government Convict! Can we wonder that this poor fellow was in the condition in which we found him?—that he seemed to all who attempted to controul or guide him an utterly hopeless case; that he himself should have felt himself the sport of circumstances over which, in his childhood, he had no controul? Yet he was not hopelessly bad, for he has been now for some years in the army, in a distant colony, doing well, and he has ever retained the most grateful remembrance of the kindness which was shown him, and of the instructions he received in the school, which, at the time, seemed like seed sown on stony ground, which would never bear fruit.

Now these three cases are probably representative ones of a large class of our Convicts, and they give us some idea of the way in which they became cut off from society. No individual person appears directly to blame for the condition of any one. And yet we can hardly hold any one of them morally responsible for his position in our Convict Prisons. What would any of the children of the upper classes become if so tossed about in the world? Is our society rightly constituted, or truly Christian, if young inexperienced persons, without proper parental guidance, are to be so left to the hard usage of the world?

We have frequently met, of late years, with Convicts of a very different stamp : men who could not in any way blame society for neglect or wrong treatment, who were not tempted by want of necessaries to commit fraud, who were not outcasts of society, or at war with it. It would be difficult, perhaps impossible, without intruding on domestic privacy, to trace out the steps by which that large class of Convicts has been raised, of whom the infamous WILLIAM ROUPELL is the glaring type. Men cannot arrive at such a degree of hardened wickedness suddenly, and without a long course of previous preparation. The training which society has given them is one received by many. There will always be temptations in the world to self-indulgence ; a desire for popularity; over estimation of external appearances; and recklessness as to the means by which these are to be gratified. We must always anticipate that there will be employers who are neglectful of proper precautions, and who, from reprehensible indolence, leave the management of their affairs too confidingly in the hands of others. Persons who make a fair show to the world will frequently be trusted more than they ought; we forget too often that when we pray "Lead us not into temptation," and hope to have our prayer answered, we are bound to try to avoid leading others into temptation. It is only when the world is far more Christianized than there is any likelihood of its being in our time, that these temptations and even incentives to crime, will not everywhere abound. It is Christian principle only, and the early training of such parents as desire above all to do their duty to God and to man, to which we must look to defend us against the evil which is in the world; we have never met with a single instance of crime in which there has not been some deficiency in the early influence, uncompensated for by later instruction. Such cases must, therefore, be left as exceptional ones in our inquiry. Yet it will be instructive to trace the career of such an one, for we may learn from it some valuable lessons. The following is extracted from the *Bristol Daily Post* of Feb. 9, 1864 :—

### "EXTRAORDINARY CAREER OF A SWINDLER.

"At the Middlesex Session, on Monday, EDWARD BATHURST, 40, who described himself as a 'gentleman,' and who was convicted last Session of fraudulently obtaining, by false pretences, the sum of £10, by means of a false check upon Messrs. ROBARTS, LUBBOCK and Co., bankers.

"Mr. RIBTON said this case was adjourned from the last Session to allow Mr. LEWIS, the attorney for the prosecution, to make some inquiries as to the character of the prisoner, and those inquiries having been made, he was then prepared to state the result of them in detail. He would state the facts, which would afterwards be proved by evidence. The history of the prisoner was curious and diversified, for it appeared that in 1844 *he was Her Majesty's Vice-Consul* at Copenhagen. In 1846 he became *Her Majesty's Vice-Consul* at Hayti, but soon after he left, and he did not know what then became of him until 1851. In that year he became a bankrupt, and appeared before Mr. Commissioner REYNOLDS for a large amount, Messrs. STULTZ, the eminent tailors, figuring among his creditors. Having got free of the Bankruptcy Court in England, he went to Australia, where *it appeared he carried on a system of swindling*. In 1855 he was Clerk to a Bench of Magistrates at Heidelburg, near Melbourne; and in that capacity he embezzled a large sum of money belonging to the Government, for which offence he was tried and convicted, and *sentenced to two years' imprisonment*. At the expiration of his sentence he left for Adelaide, where he was convicted of obtaining goods under false pretences, and sentenced to three years' imprisonment. The prisoner appealed against this conviction on some technical grounds, and this being successful the conviction was quashed. *Notwithstanding his character was well known in the colony,* a most extraordinary circumstance occurred; the Governor of South Australia, Sir RICHARD GRAVES MACDONALD, appointed him as a *Magistrate* at Gawler Town, about thirty miles from Adelaide. He did not hold his office long, and returned to Melbourne, *where he committed a fresh offence*. He there represented himself as a solicitor, and undertook to provide a counsel for a man who was to be tried for an offence. He took £10 from his wife, but on the trial coming on no counsel had been provided, he having appropriated the money to himself. For this offence he was again tried, and sentenced *to two years' imprisonment*, and at the expiration of this sentence he returned to England. He (Mr. RIBTON) held in his hand seven checks which the prisoner had drawn on Messrs. WILLIS, PERCIVAL and Co., of Lombard-street, six of them being for £10 each, and one of them for £25, and one promissory note on the London and Westminster Bank for £35. All these checks had been given without any funds whatever in hand to meet them.

"Mr. METCALFE said the prisoner had a wife and nine children in Australia.

"The Assistant-Judge said he had no doubt the prisoner had been defrauding the public, and thought to evade the law by obtaining money by means of false checks. He *had been guilty of a system of wholesale swindling, and, therefore, the smallest punishment the Court could think of giving him was, that he be kept in penal servitude for three years."*

Now here is a man who has twice held an honourable position under the Government between the years 1844 and 1851. We must infer, therefore, that he was possessed of some amount of talent, and that his character had stood well with the world. He then appears as a bankrupt; he does not seem to have been the victim of mercantile difficulties; among his creditors were fashionable tailors; we must presume, therefore, that he had been living beyond his means, incurring debts for his own personal gratification which he knew he could not pay,—certainly a species of swindling. This mode of life he more openly carried

on in a distant land, and obtained a position of respectability and
trust, when he availed himself of his office to "embezzle a large
sum of money belonging to the Government." It is hardly
credible that for so heinous an offence, involving serious breach
of trust, and aggravated by his antecedents, he should have
received only two years' imprisonment! Of course no change of
life could be expected from this; he is hardened by this short
punishment, again preys upon society, and is sentenced to only
three years, now that he has shown himself an unprincipled
hardened offender. Escaping from this punishment through his
skill in availing himself of technical objections, but with *his
character well known*, he is actually appointed as a magistrate!
Is not society now become an accomplice in iniquity? We may
hope that the Governor of the province was not aware of the
character of the man he was so elevating, though surely it was
his duty not to commit so grave a trust to one whom he did not
know to possess an unblemished reputation. But why did
society accept such a judge without protest? What confidence
can there be in a community the moral sense of which is so low?
This office did not last long; again he recommences his swindling career, and on this, the third conviction, he has again
only two years! Such was his career for nine years, and
now he again begins a similar one in England. Surely such
a man who had been in two hemispheres, engaged for so
long a period in "wholesale swindling," deserved the longest
instead of the "shortest punishment" that could be given him.
How on his fourth conviction could he be expected to be a safe
citizen in only three years? Without professing to understand
legal technical questions and difficulties, surely common sense
and common justice will concur in saying that such a succession
of crimes against society ought to be visited, to say the least,
with a very long separation from it. Surely the suspicion will
rise in the mind that a clever unscrupulous man, who calls
himself a gentleman, is punished with less severity than a
coarse ignorant poor man who has committed a crime. Such a

suspicion must act most injuriously on public morality, and the mere appearance which gives rise to it should be carefully avoided by the administrators of the law. Whether or not this man is now considered a " Convict," we must say that he ought to be one, and subjected to the most rigorous discipline. If the law as it now stands does not authorize longer punishments for such offences, surely it should be altered.

We have hitherto selected typical cases of various kinds of Convicts, and endeavoured briefly to trace their previous career, with a view to future consideration. Let us now observe the process by which boys and girls graduate in crime so as to become prepared to be Government Convicts.

If we enter the Female Convict Prison we may expect to find there a young girl, thirteen years of age! After the disclosures we have had of the hardened and almost hopeless condition of adult Female Convicts, such a spectacle must excite in the mind the greatest sorrow. Here a young child must have her future almost irrecoverably blighted. She is exposed to association with persons experienced in crime, but a small proportion of whom regain or take any honourable place in society, and who diffuse around them a pestilential moral atmosphere of their own. The Convict women themselves, hardened as they are, shudder (the Prison Matron tells us) at seeing a young girl come to be like them. What had that poor child done that her life should be thus blighted. The following paragraph is extracted from the *Bristol Daily Post*, Jan. 11, 1864,

## "A CHILD SENTENCED TO PENAL SERVITUDE.

"At the West Kent Quarter Session, held at Maidstone, on Thursday, before Mr. F. ESPINASSE, deputy-chairman, a girl, thirteen years of age, named EMMA G——, was indicted for robbing her mistress, ISABELLA COLLINGTON, residing at Greenwich. It appeared that the youthful prisoner had acted as servant to the prosecutrix about three weeks, but, owing to her untruthfulness and dilatoriness when sent on errands, she had been compelled to discharge her. Three days afterwards the father of the prisoner called upon the prosecutrix and handed to her a gold watch and chain, a portemonnaie, a pair of boots, two pairs of cuffs, and a pair of stockings which she identified as her property, and which had been found by the step-mother of the prisoner concealed under her bed. The jury upon this evidence before them returned a verdict of guilty. There had been no previous offence committed by the prisoner, who, to the surprise of every one in Court, was sentenced to four years' penal servitude!"

No wonder there was astonishment in every one in Court, that a young girl should be thus doomed on her first offence, and living with parents who would certainly have striven to correct her, for they returned, unasked, the stolen property, and thus became the unconscious agents of their daughter's ruin. No wonder there was astonishment that after the Reformatory Act has been made the law of the land for nearly ten years, after its steady progress in public opinion, any Magistrate should be found who, without one effort to reform her, should suddenly transform a young girl into a Convict.*

We have never heard of such extraordinary severity being exercised towards the other sex. Young boys have a longer career allowed them, and have usually several imprisonments before they are considered deserving of a sentence of penal servitude. We have already seen the career of poor D., after growing up to the age of 14 or 15, leading a wild Arab life. But then there were no Reformatories, and public opinion had not been awakened to the necessity of protecting the young vagrant, controlling and reforming the young thief, before he has acquired a *habit* of crime. What may we certainly expect to be the future of these young boys :—

"NEWPORT, MONMOUTHSHIRE, November, 1863.

"POLICE.—*Extraordinary Depravity of Three Lads.*—Yesterday, at the Town Hall, before the Mayor, WM. EVANS, and L. AUGUSTUS HOMFRAY, Esqrs., three ragged lads, named respectively THOMAS K——, aged 14; MOSES J——, aged 14; and RICHARD J——, aged 9, were charged with stealing five shillings and one pound package of sugar, the property of WM. THOMAS, grocer, Commercial Road. It appeared from the evidence of Mrs. SARAH

---

* Since this was written the Secretary of State kindly obtained a conditional pardon from the Crown for the poor girl, to enable her to be sent to a Reformatory instead of to a Convict Prison.

THOMAS, wife of the complainant, that the premises had been securely fastened about ten o'clock the previous evening, and the robbery must have been committed by some one who was concealed inside. The prisoners were then further charged with stealing a number of articles from the shop-window of MATTHEW ROE. In this case, which happened on the previous Monday, a clean sweep had been made of the contents of the shop-window, including twenty bundles of cigarettes, a number of fusee boxes, cigar tubes, pen-knives, &c., and the first defendant confessed that 'RICHARD J—— went under the counter, and stopped there all night,' and next morning they all divided five shillings, which he had 'found.' Sergeant WILLCOX, who, on Saturday, apprehended MOSES J—— and K—— sleeping on straw in an iron pig's cot, in the market, found upon them a number of articles, which Mrs. ROE identified as stolen from her shop. There was a third charge against the prisoners of stealing two fire-shovels, the property of Mr. ASTON, ironmonger. This robbery, the prisoner RICHARD J—— told the Police-sergeant had been committed by his brother and K——, and a witness, named SARAH JACKSON, deposed to having bought one of the shovels of the 'littlest of the prisoners,' RICHARD J——, for twopence and some cheese ! Mr. ASTON identified the shovels, which had been taken from his shop-door. The prisoners were severally sentenced to fourteen days' imprisonment for the robbery on Mr. ROE's premises, and a like term for that on Mr. ASTON's; K—— and MOSES J—— being ordered to be sent to the Reformatory for three years each, and RICHARD J—— for five years. It was stated that during the bark season J——'s parents earned from 20s. to 35s. per week. Their children *had been convicted twice before,* and K—— *no less than seven times.* It appeared that they had been pursuing their shop depredations on a *systematic scale,* and a man named STOCKWELL, who admitted having bought a pound of sugar of them for a penny, was severely reprimanded by the Bench, who stigmatised him as worse than the boys."—*Bristol Daily Post,* November 24, 1863.

Thus a boy of 14, and his accomplice of the same age, have been for some time pursuing their " shop depredations on a systematic scale ;" one having been convicted as many as seven times, without an attempt to reform him. A young boy of nine is being trained by these adepts, selling their stolen booty, and the prison brand is now put on him too, each of the three having a similar length of imprisonment. It will be well if three years' training in a Reformatory will make such experienced young thieves honest members of society. Why were they allowed to continue their depredations so long?

Here are two other cases which might pass unobserved among the police reports of a large city, did not a knowledge of their individual histories enable us to see in the following short paragraph the not distant approach to a Convict Prison. In the *Bristol Post* of February 24, 1864, we find the following:—

## "YOUNG PILFERERS.

" Two boys, named DONOGHUE and MAHONEY, who had been remanded on suspicion of stealing a coat, were again brought up, and it was proved that the coat had been taken from a shop kept by a person named W——, in the Horsefair. DONOGHUE was further charged with stealing another coat from the same complainant, and it appeared that the second coat had been pawned at the shop of Mr. JESSELL, St. Augustine's-back, by MAHONEY; but the pawn-ticket was found on DONOGHUE by P.C. HUGHES. The Magistrates sentenced the prisoners on the first charge to two months' hard labour."

The first named boy is one of a thoroughly bad family. Both father and mother have been frequently in prison for drunkenness and fighting. The oldest daughter has been several times in prison, and the younger ones were systematically sent out to steal, or beg, or sweep crossings, as the case might be. A miserable ragged boy, this was his only calling, and last summer he was brought before the Magistrates for seriously injuring a boy by throwing stones at him. He has been in Bridewell. What principle of duty, what possible means of gaining an honest livelihood can this wretched boy have when discharged from his two months' imprisonment? He has never had any good influence or instruction to incline him to right; he might have been sent to a Reformatory, and with a few years' training he might, as so many have done, have become a hard-working boy. But he has now no muscular power of working; his fingers are untrained to labour, his mind uncultured, his physical nature depressed by the vices of his parents. He must become one of the Convicts to be maintained by the country, and we can only hope for him that the system adopted in those establishments, when he arrives there, will be such as to correct the bad training of his youth.

The other boy, MAHONEY, might more easily have been saved. He had a poor widowed mother, who was not ill disposed, but was totally incapable either of maintaining or of controlling him. He was a regular street Arab. Any one who observed him would see a prophesy of an evil life written in his face, and would perceive that he was exactly one of those for whom the law has so wisely and mercifully provided in the Industrial Schools Act. If sentenced to such a school this poor lad would have had the discipline which every young child requires, and received the teaching and training which should be considered the right of every young human being. A Day Ragged School could do but little for him, for it could exercise little control, perhaps none, over him out of school. He came to the school in the companionship of a boy just discharged from Bridewell, and was thus the known companion of a thief. He begged for food. He had been at least three or four times previously before the Magistrates, and was therefore well known as a vagrant and a street Arab. These two facts being the legal indications of fitness for an Industrial School, the effort was made to get him sentenced to it, but unavailingly. Soon the police took him with five others before the Magistrates, one of whom was sentenced to a Reformatory for thieving; but this wretched boy, who might have been now sent to an Industrial School without the prison brand on him, was again thrown on the world. Now he has actually commenced his career of crime, and what is he to do when he comes forth into society from his solitary cell to starvation and misery. He *must* become a Convict.

These are not exceptional cases or unusual incidents; indeed, the frequency of their occurrence in our large towns prevents their attracting any public attention. Our gaols still contain multitudes of young boys who are thus training for our Convict Prisons. If a child in the higher walks of life were thus branded for life, universal attention would be excited, and public opinion would loudly exclaim against the cruelty of the proceeding. The notorious young girl, whose precocious wickedness in blasting the character of a Prison Chaplain, was afterwards proved by her conviction for perjury, was not

sentenced to penal servitude, though she had shown a moral
obliquity, that could not easily be exceeded, and which was
rendered more inexcusable by her position in society; she was
sentenced only to two years in a Reformatory, and being refused
admission into one, for fear of contamination to the other inmates,
she was placed under more private care.

During the last year, in the City of Bristol, "a boy of genteel
appearance," eleven years of age, the son of a Clergyman of the
Church of England, was brought before the Magistrates for
entering a shop, and, finding no one there, stretching over the
counter, opening the till, and abstracting money; the proceeding
had been seen by a passenger, and the money was found on the
boy. The act was certainly one indicating entire regardlessness
of the rights of others, and some experience in appropriation
of the property of others. Though the father urged to the
Court that "his son was a good boy, that he had never
been away from his mother, and that it might have been
the act of an infant," a Magistrate justly remarked, "he is
old enough to know right from wrong. If a poor ragged boy
were brought up here, he would have been punished, and we
cannot make distinctions." The case having been fully proved,
the Magistrates committed the culprit to prison for fourteen
days' hard labour, observing "that they could not pass over
such an offence." As *the law now stands*, it was impossible
justly to treat such an offence more leniently. To send a boy,
having a home where care and moral training might be
reasonably expected, to a Reformatory or Industrial School,
would have evidently been unnecessary, and even injurious.
Nothing else could have been done. Yet the case excited
considerable animadversion in the public press, and letters
appeared commenting on the severity of the sentence. No
voice is raised when such cases as these occur, as they do
most frequently,—

"HENRY H——— and THOMAS H———, *two ragged urchins*, were charged
with having three pieces of lead in their possession, supposed to have been

stolen. P.C. 33 saw the prisoners passing through a lane in Thomas-street with the lead on the previous evening. He suspected that they had not come by it honestly, and he followed the boys, taxed them with having stolen the lead, and from further inquiries he found that the property had been stolen from some void premises in Ring's-buildings, Pipe-lane, Temple-street. The three pieces of lead exactly corresponded with the end from which they had been broken off. The boys admitted having stolen the lead from Pipe-lane, and they were committed for trial."—*Bristol Post*, Feb. 25, 1864.

### "JUVENILE THIEVES.

" WILLIAM F—— and JOHN C———, two boys, 13 years of age, were charged with stealing three silver pencil-cases, value 3s., the property of Mr. ———, stationer, of Redcliff-hill. Complainant stated that *the urchins* came to his shop on the previous evening and asked for some trivial article, which he was about to reach from a shelf, when they made off, and on looking round he missed three pencil-cases. He rushed after them, and caught C—— a few yards off, and a constable caught the other. The boys said they threw the pencil-cases away. F——, *who had been before the Bench on a former occasion*, was sentenced to a month's imprisonment at the House of Correction, and it being C———'s first time, he received only a fortnight's imprisonment."—*Bristol Post*, Aug. 5, 1863.

Are these cases so much worse, morally, than that of the youthful robber of a till, who had been well brought up from infancy ? Yet the public does not consider these severe sentences, or reflect that while the Clergyman's son would be sheltered from the world's scorn, these boys were evidently on the way to a more daring criminal career. And are not such boys preparing for the next step, the commitment for trial, followed by a sentence of penal servitude,—which will probably be the fate of this poor boy :—

" WILLIAM D———, a lad, who had just come out of prison, after serving twelve months' imprisonment, was charged with stealing a piece of beef, value 1s. 6d., the property of JAMES TRULL. The offence was proved, and the prisoner was committed for trial."—*Bristol Post*, Feb., 1863.

Here we have in succession the various stages these boys go through when they have once received the prison brand, and are left, on discharge, in the same circumstances which led them to crime. After the first step they are compelled, as it were, to continue the course they have begun, for they are now necessarily excluded from all the respectable Day Schools, and association with decent boys who may be morally no better than they, but who have not received the stigma of a gaol.

This then is one of the most usual ways in which our Convicts are raised. They begin as wild neglected children; they have no true home influence; they learn in the streets all that ought to be far removed from the knowledge of the young; they are sent to prison; they come out more daring and qualified, by their having thus graduated in crime, to become the companions of more precocious thieves; one short imprisonment follows after another with the poor boy, until the character given of him at his trial obtains for him the final stamp of a Convict. Can we wonder at the hardened reckless bearing of a youth so trained? Could the early histories of the inmates of our Convict Prisons be ascertained, it would probably be found that a very large proportion had so begun their career in early youth. Of the consequences of these imprisonments of children, the Rev. T. CARTER, Chaplain of the Liverpool Gaol, thus speaks in a letter, addressed by him to the Mayor and Town Council, dated April 25, 1850 :—

"Suffer me to invite your attention to this fact: that of thirty boys and thirty girls, *not selected*, but taken in order from the respective registers of those in gaol in the month corresponding with the present one in 1847, eleven only do not appear to have been re-committed, *twelve have been transported since, twelve are now in gaol on re-commitments, and twenty-five have been re-committed (several frequently), and, with few exceptions, are known to be still living in criminal habits.* Now, leaving out of account the cost of apprehension, and that of carrying out the sentence of transportation, when awarded, the expense of prosecution and maintenance of these in gaol, on the nearest and fairest computation I can arrive at, may be stated to be £1,123 16s. 9d. But it will not escape remark, that the expense of juvenile crime is not to be estimated solely by that incurred while they remain in that category. There are, at the moment I write, *forty-three male and thirty-seven female adults in the gaol,* who commenced their career of crime as *juveniles,* and only four of whom have yet exceeded the age of twenty-one years. The aggregate number of times which these have been in the custody of the police is 678, of their commitments to gaol, 539; and the cost of their several prosecutions and maintenance, whilst herein, has been, on the lowest computation, £1,877 1s. 6d. Some are for trial, and possibly may be transported, thus entailing further heavy expense; but the rest, be it remembered, will, in the course of a few weeks, *be let loose upon society again*, to be maintained by the public, partly by plunder, and (if detected) partly out of the corporation purse. The amount of property *ascertained* to have been stolen by these is £255 17*s.* 2*d.*, inconsiderable perhaps in amount, but forming little or no criterion of the danger to which the public is exposed, or the extent of mischief such characters are capable of perpetrating."

Mr. CARTER states in the same letter that these facts are not unusual, and that if the same enquiry were made with respect to any other period, the same results would be found. Since that time a great change has been made in our legislation with respect to children, in consequence of the passing of the Reformatory Schools' Bill in 1854, and of the Industrial Schools' Bill in 1857. But though the former of those has been very extensively in operation throughout the kingdom, and the latter is highly valued wherever it is carried out—though H.M. Inspector of those Schools, Rev. SYDNEY TURNER, has given repeated reports of their success, wherever the principles on which they were originally founded are carried out ; and though the Royal Commission on Education spoke most strongly in favour of the system ; though it is now unnecessary for any young person under 14 to be now subjected to imprisonment, except as a preliminary to his being sent to a Reformatory, since he can be handed over to parental correction, or " cautioned and discharged," if his case does not appear a serious one ;—notwithstanding all this, we find the young delinquents still sent to prison ; we still find that when they have completed the " curriculum of crime" they have thus commenced, they help to fill our Convict Prisons.

Most truly did a Bristol Magistrate once declare, [*vide Bristol Post*, Oct. 16, 1862, when a "diminutive street urchin," who had been committing "Arab devastation at Clifton," was brought before him for stealing walnuts from a garden, "the prisoner deserved to go to gaol, ÓNLY HE THOUGHT THAT SUCH A STEP MIGHT RUIN HIM." He therefore handed the boy over to parental chastisement. But his example is not generally followed in our country; we will therefore add to his testimony the following important ones given before the Select Committee of the Lords in 1847, which are as true now as they were when delivered:

Mr. SMITH, the Governor of Edinburgh Gaol states,—"That he considers short commitments of young offenders *to have the most mischievous effect possible; it inures them to imprisonment by slow degrees, till it becomes no punishment at all.* * * * The fact that a boy has been imprisoned goes far to ruin him for life. * * * On comparing the sentences, we see that 62 out of every 100 are sentenced to not more than twenty days, 21 out of every 100 to no more than ten days, and nearly 2½ out of every 100 to no more than five days each. * * One person has been 110 times inprisoned in 15 years, the sentences ranging from five to sixty days. * * It is sad to think that 34 out of every 100 new criminals are such by the time they reach the age of twenty years; 19 out of every 100 at sixteen; and 4 out of every 100 at twelve years of age."

"I think as to children," says SERGEANT ADAMS (confining the term to children from seven to twelve), "prison discipline is *incompatible with their reform.* * * I have not the slightest doubt, that with children it would be better to apply ourselves to a Reformatory than to a deterring process· * * It is doubtless still necessary to hold out imprisonment as a terror to adults; but as far as a child is concerned, I do believe that prison discipline of any character operates *as a retarder rather than a promoter of reformation.* Confinement is needful; but it should be the confinement of a school, not of a prison. The mind of a child loses its elasticity and is injured by imprisonment."

"The discipline of prisons," says the Rev. WHITWORTH RUSSELL, "gives but little hope of the reformation of children, and I am confident that in the great majority of cases *the juvenile delinquent is rendered much worse, and much more dangerous to society by imprisonment.* I have visited prisons when children have been brought in for the first time, and I have seen them overwhelmed with fear and distress, clinging with instinctive dread even to the officer that brought them there; and I have seen those very children, three or four days afterwards, laughing and playing in the prison-yard with other convicts, and I felt then that the dread of a prison was gone from those children for ever."

Mr. Baron ALDERSON.—"As long as juvenile offenders are mixed up in our gaol with adults, no effectual improvement can take place. *I have known an instance in which a regular plan for robbery, which took place and was tried before me, was laid in one of what is called our best regulated gaols and on the treadmill.* The instrument there was a boy, and the principals were adult thieves."

Mr. Justice COLTMAN.—"It is to be borne constantly in mind that it is in a great degree from ignorance, and the immatured state of their reasoning powers, that children offend,—'Nequeunt curvo dignoscere rectum,'—and they are entitled to be treated with great indulgence, until they are able in some degree to understand the grounds on which the rules of right and wrong are founded; *and a gaol, however well conducted is, I fear, a bad school for them, and it fixes too dark a stain on their characters."*

"So far as I have experienced or have understood," says Lord COCKBURN,— "Imprisonment has very seldom, if ever, reclaimed juvenile offenders. It is chiefly for thefts that these boys were brought before us; and the case of a truly reformed thief, whether young or old, *who has already defied two or three convictions, is a phenomenon, I believe, of very rare occurrence indeed.* A thoroughly reformed thrice-convicted thief, I should like to know a well authenticated example of. And the reformation of the juvenile is what I despair of most. *The various and peculiar attractions of thieving, strong to the adult, seem nearly irrisistible to the young, to whose unformed minds,* moreover, *the habits of even the best conducted gaol are particularly hurtful."*

"The total number of juvenile offenders over Scotland," says the LORD JUSTICE CLERK, "has greatly increased since 1830, and they are now found in numbers in small quiet provincial towns, where formerly such were wholly unknown. The short imprisonments to which such offenders are subjected on summary convictions in Police Courts, or before the Sheriffs, generally produce no other effect than *to render them utterly indifferent to that* punishment, especially as the separate system in many places cannot be acted upon in regard to them. We have seen cases of lads of sixteen or seventeen, who from the age of ten or twelve and upwards, have been six, eight, or ten times convicted; sometimes tried before the Sheriff and a jury, and sentenced to long imprisonments, in which the separate system was acted upon, but returning *undeterred and unreformed.* But I ascribe the failure, as to boys, very much to the evils of association with bad companions during the short imprisonments to which they are at first subjected, and to the impossibility of making any impression on them during say forty or sixty days. *   * Certainly at present the *short* imprisonments seem only, in the ordinary case, to *harden* the offenders.

"I think," says Mr. TRACY, "that we produce but little improvement upon them in prison, according to the new system (separate confinement), with our best attention; their short sentences are, in my judgment, most objectional. *   * I have traced London thieves, step by step, from very tender years to manhood, who have been over and over again inmates of our prisons. It appears most distinctly that most of the juvenile offenders are set on by receivers of stolen goods, or by other thieves."

"A prison," says Mr. CARTER, in his Report to the Mayor and Magistrates of Liverpool, in 1847, "may have a deterring influence to a certain extent, so long as a boy is unacquainted with its interior; but on the present system, when a boy is committed for three or five days, it loses all its terror; *he leaves the prison more callous than when he entered it."*

"My decided opinion," says Mr. CHALMERS, the Governor of Aberdeen Prison, before the Lords' Committee (formed on an experience of 22 years), "is, that if a first imprisonment, however short, be not effectual in deterring persons from committing new offences, it is *in vain to expect that repeated short imprisonments will lead to different results.*"

Such are a few of the testimonies from high official sources to the great evil of committing young boys and girls to prison. The Parliamentary Committees, before which they were given, took place before there was any possibility of substituting a School for a Prison. The Industrial Schools' Act now does this, and the Juvenile Delinquent Act supplements a short imprisonment by legal detention in a Reformatory School. Yet Mr. J. WEATHERHEAD, the Governor of Holloway Prison, states to the Royal Commission, on the day of his giving evidence (March 30, 1863), that there were 51 juveniles in the prison, or young persons under 17 years of age. The numbers have been decidedly increasing during the last two years as much as 10 or 15 per cent. This prison is exclusively for the City of London, and this increase of number indicates an increase of juvenile crime in the metropolis. Out of the whole number two only were waiting to go to a Reformatory, which Mr. WEATHERHEAD stated was in the Isle of Wight; Parkhurst Juvenile Prison is therefore probably intended, as there is no Reformatory in that island. It is now more than a dozen years since the witnesses, assembled from all parts of Great Britain, at the first Reformatory Conference, in 1851, confirmed the evidence given by the Lords' Committee, and brought most incontrovertible testimony that prison discipline is not the right mode of dealing with juveniles; that it does not effect the end intended; that it is costly, because quite unsuccessful; and that it is unjust to a young boy or girl to inflict on one of immature years the punishment of an adult. Additional weighty evidence to the same effect was laid before the Committee of the House of Commons, appointed to inquire into the condition of "Criminal and Destitute Juveniles." Strange is it that so near the walls of our houses of legislature, which endorsed the principle, it should appear not to have been heard of or acted on, and that the same state

of things exists now which startled the public, and roused it
to action some dozen years ago.   It does not seem yet practically
understood in the metropolis of the kingdom, that prison training,
however good, can never prepare for an honest life of freedom
the unformed youths who are to become the next generation,
and that daily schooling in a gaol, with industrial teaching, do
not constitute alone the essence of reformation.   Here is the
evidence given in March, 1863, by Mr. WEATHERHEAD :—

"5275.—Can you give the Commission any opinion as to whether these
juveniles come frequently back to you ?—Some do frequently come back.

"5276.—Of the re-commitments to your prison, do the juveniles form
a larger or smaller proportion than the adults ?—They are greater in number.

"5277.—Are there many juvenile females ?—Not many.   There are a few.

"5278.—The larger proportion are males ?—Yes.

".5279.—What is the course of treatment pursued with respect to the
juveniles as contra-distinguished, if it is different, trom the treatment of the
adults ?—The juveniles are kept in a separate wing of the building ; they
attend school daily ; a good many of them are taught trades.   We teach trades
to those who *have received long sentences.*

"5280.—Upon the whole, the treatment of the juveniles is less penal than
that of the adults ?—Yes.

"5281.—*And yet you find a larger proportion of the juveniles return to
prison ?—I am sorry to say they do !*"

May these united and varied testimonies lead the magistracy
of our kingdom to pause before they place even one young child
in a position which is the first step to becoming one of "our
Convicts !"

Regarding it, then, as an acknowledged fact, that imprisonment
of children is the surest way to raise for our country a large
body of hardened Convicts, and to ensure a continually
recurring supply, what must we think of that system in our
country which, while professedly established to relieve destitution, does its part towards converting the pauper into the
criminal.   Without attempting to discover how many of our
Convicts were reared and prepared for a life of vice in a
Workhouse, we can state that the system often adopted for
juveniles in those establishments is such as must necessarily
lead to their becoming Convicts.   It does so indirectly by the

neglect of destitute children without their walls, and by the treatment of them very frequently when in the Workhouse. We have already traced the history of the wretched Convict D., and have seen him allowed to leave the Workhouse to which he had been taken, without any effort to detain or reclaim him. We saw him afterwards apply for admission, when discharged from gaol, without a home, and softened by his solitary confinement;—we saw him refused, and again driven to crime. It does so also directly. Workhouse authorities send boys to gaol again and again, only because unable to induce them to work. We find the following paragraph in a Bristol paper on May 29th of last year, which is headed,—

### "REFRACTORY JUVENILE PAUPERS.

" WILLIAM H,—— HENRY J—— and GEORGE Y——, three lads, were charged with refusing to work at the Bristol Union, Fishponds, of which they were inmates. HENRY D——, superintendent of labour there, stated that the prisoners were very refractory, had refused to sift some gravel, and one of them had threatened to dash his brains out. Mr. M——: Ah, but he didn't do it, you know (laughter). Now, you three gentlemen, what have you to say? Prisoners: We never refused to work, sir. The Magistrate said he believed them guilty of the charge; and Y—— and J——, who had been convicted for a similar offence only a short time ago, were sentenced to six weeks' hard labour, and H—— to 21 days' imprisonment.

Such a scene as this at Lawford's Gate hardly requires comment. The fact that the labour master of a Workhouse should be obliged to have recourse to magisterial authority and to the gaol to obtain a proper amount of work from boys entrusted to his care, of itself speaks volumes respecting the kind of influence and discipline used in such establishments. We never heard of the Master of a Reformatory or of an Industrial School being obliged to apply for such help. But passing by the reflections which such a fact would suggest, let us realize the treatment of these poor boys, condemned to imprisonment, protesting their innocence, on the sole evidence of the accuser, and with sarcastic expressions from their judge. What is to be their future, compelled by circumstances over which they had no controul, to become paupers and to be treated as such, and then, without breaking the laws of their country, or committing any offence beyond what would have been visited elsewhere with ordinary school correction, branded with the gaol mark, and probably taught that even such an abode is preferable to that provided for the destitute of their country. It is possible, indeed, that the gaol has nothing deterrent for these unhappy lads, and that they have intentionally made their way there to escape from the Workhouse; for the Chaplain of a gaol has told us of a lad who, "when advised to go to the Workhouse after his imprisonment here, replied that they should not keep him there, he would run away, *as he preferred the prison where he was better fed;*" and when on the point of leaving the gaol, when the same lad was asked what course he intended to take, he said, "*I will beg to get work in the brick craft during the summer, and come here in the winter !*"

The attention of the public has already been directed to the very great injury done to the destitute young of the country by subjecting them to the Workhouse treatment in connection with adult paupers. Surely many years will not elapse before destitute children may find in our country a true home, where they will not be trained even indirectly to be paupers or criminals.

Thus are young boys and girls prepared to become Convicts, by a certain, though it may be an indirect process. Their direct training to dishonesty has been vividly pourtrayed by DICKENS, and we have always believed that his picture was drawn after nature, as is usually his practice even in the delineations of life which appear the most extravagant; we have however supposed that these schools of vice belonged to a time when less attention than at present was paid to the true education of the young. We have heard indeed from the lady to whom the Mother of one of our reformatory scholars made the statement, that this worthless woman boasted to her of having trained at least fifty girls to pick pockets; that she lived at inns with these wretched gir's dressed as young ladies, and travelled with them in first-class carriages. This woman complained to another lady who had

obtained admission for her two daughters into an asylum, that
she should be deprived of their services, which was unjust, as she
had gone to great expense in having them trained by a first-rate
London pickpocket. The younger of these daughters, after
resuming her former course with her Mother, was five years in a
Reformatory, the Mother by her visits keeping up her powerful
and baneful influence over her mind. On her discharge she
again plunged her daughter into crime, and the wretched girl is
now in a Convict Prison. The elder daughter was more experienced, and, after a two years' imprisonment, she was sufficiently
skilful to live a career of crime, as she is now probably doing,
without detection. How successful she is in obtaining from the
public her ill-gotten wealth, is proved by her having boasted to
one of the ladies who had tried to save her, that she had six
times set up her Mother in a decent way of living by the proceeds
of her profession; as often had the woman shown an unwillingness to live any but a life of reckless wickedness. Such a case
might have been supposed to be a solitary one, but we learn
from Mr. DAVIS, the Ordinary of Newgate, that it is not so.
He says, in his evidence to the Commission,—"In speaking
of the penal class of London, it is such a comprehensive term.
These men get perhaps 10, or 15, or 20 boys. They get them
into a house and teach them how to pick pockets. There are a
great many men who commit the worst crimes in London, and
they are under that direction (of the ticket-of-leave men). The
others teach them, or instruct them, how to commit crimes of
different sorts," (1957—58.) Again, being asked (1987), "You
spoke just now of schools of crime for boys, which you say exist
now, regular Training Schools?" He replies, "Yes, and they
are watched now more by the police than they were, but there
are some still that you cannot find out; as soon as they are
found out they are blown upon, and there is no carrying
them on, they take a house in some remote district, and these
boys are well fed and well taught, and they plunder, and get a
good deal of money." Picking pockets, he says, is the most

lucrative part of the trade, "but it is more so with those who are able to watch men going into banking-houses, where there is a good deal of money passing," (1988.)

The metropolis is not the only school for such instruction. Mr. CLAY gives us the following statements respecting the training of young pickpockets, from one of the gang already mentioned as under sentence of transportation :—

"These girls," says one, "are natives of Dublin.  *  *  *  When they came to Manchester, they were quite plain in their dress, and no person on earth would suspect them. I believe there is nowhere their equal in being expert at ladies' dress pockets. When they first came to Manchester they got immense of money in shops and omnibuses.  *  *  *  When an omnibus leaves, they get into it, and being dressed like any gentlemen's girls, with one of these French baskets in their hands, they get close beside a lady, and contrive to place their shawl or mantle over the lady's dress pocket, which shades their hand.  *  *  *  When these two girls *and their mothers and myself* was getting a glass of liquor, they told me they was often sending £20 to their fathers and brothers in Dublin."

"The women now *travelling* look so maidenlified and comely in their person, that no human being would suspect their being pickpockets. Their attire is generally of the best, but it is not so with all. Some of the female *wires* are dressed in the first style. There are three of them attending the shops where the most ladies go; one woman acts as servant, while the *wire* acts mistress. When they go into one of these shops, as any other lady might do, they are on the watch to see when purses are pulled out, and the mistress gets close to the lady who has shown the purse, wires her of it, and then contrives to give it to the 'servant, who goes away, while the mistress remains in the shop, and if she is clever gets another purse before leaving it. There are now in Manchester three of the cleverest lady-wires travelling; one from Birmingham, one from Leeds, and one from Liverpool. The oldest of these three is about 24, and the youngest about 16. This youngest keeps a young man, who is dressed like any gentleman, with his gold watch and curb chain attached to it; and she dressed so that any magistrate that saw her would say she never could be anything of the sort, only her speech instantly condemns her. Last summer at Birkenhead and Chester Railway Stations one or two of these lady-like wires attended regularly. They frequent also private sales in town and country. To see them with books in their hands, like other ladies, and giving now and then a bid for an article,—but they never came away with anything *bought* at the sale. They look into the news-papers for intelligence about sales, and also about concerts, which they attend, never going inside, but watching as the people come out. I knew one woman and her man who got more money than any three women travelling. They had their own horse and gig, riding from fair to fair. Not long after coming out of Wakefield, where she had done twelve months, both she and her man got transported, about three years ago at Derby. She stood nearly five feet ten inches high, and her man the same. There is now in Manchester and Liverpool about fifty or sixty of these women wires, one day dressed up in their best, another day quite plain, to escape any information that may have been given."

The same informant gave Mr. CLAY a list of 103 males and 44 females whom he *had personally known* since 1838, and who have undergone transportation!

We might hope that these are isolated cases, and that the painful and vivid descriptions given of the den of thieves in Glasgow, by the author of JANE CAMERON, are either highly coloured or peculiar to that city; but we cannot. The following extracts from "Reports made of Notorious Harbours for Juveniles of both Sexes," made in 1856, in Liverpool, will reveal an amount of wickedness and direct training to crime most appalling. Forty-six cases are given; we take the first portion of them, and it will be observed that the prompters to crime often escape imprisonment while they lure on the young to destruction.

| Names of Parents | No. of Children | Means of getting living. | Parents convicted. | |
|---|---|---|---|---|
| C. B. | 4 | thieving | mother | This woman and her children have all been committed for thieving. She receives their plunder and harbours others. |
| P. B. and wife | 4 | " | ... | This man and woman keep two houses, one for young thieves to sleep in, the other for the receipt of their plunder. His children mix with the thieves. |
| B. S. | 2 | " | ... | This woman's two daughters are both harbourers of young thieves and receive their plunder. |
| J. C. and wife | 4 | " | both . | This man and woman, both committed for receiving, harbour young thieves, receive their plunder; their children mixing with them. |
| S. C. and wife | 4 | " | mother | A notoriously bad place. Both had frequent robberies committed in the house. Juveniles induced to come there and fetch their plunder. |

| Names of Parents. | No. of Children | Means of getting living. | Parents convicted. | |
|---|---|---|---|---|
| Mrs. C. | 2 | thieving | mother in gaol | This woman excels in villainy. Her house is a second hell. Her children are now going in her track. |
| S. J. and man | 3 | " | ... | This woman has no children of her own, but keeps her sister's children. She induces all the lads and girls she can to bring plunder to her house, and harbours them therein. |
| M. C. | 1 | " | ... | A receptacle for young thieves. Her own daughter and herself one too. Her house a harbour for young thieves and their plunder. |
| J. C. | 1 | " | mother | Mother and daughter thieves. Her daily work is trying to induce children to bring plunder to her house. |
| Mrs. L. | 3 | " | ... | Her three boys thieve; receives their plunder, and lives on it. Her house is a harbour for young thieves, who fetch their plunder there. |
| J. A. and M. A. | 3 | " | both | Father and mother in gaol for thieving. All their children thieves, and their house a harbour for young thieves and their plunder. |
| M. M. and wife | 6 | " | mother | This man has the name of being a tailor. His house is frequented by young shoplifters, who bring their plunder to his house, which is bought by his wife. She has been in custody for so buying. Their children mix with the thieves. |
| J. D. and wife | 4 | " | ... | The thieving propensities of this family have been handed down from father to son, on one side, and from the mother's brood on the other side. Their house is a diabolical school for crime, and Van Dieman's Land is their utmost expectation. |
| M. W. | 1 | " | mother | Mother and daughter thieves. The house is a harbour for young thieves. |
| S. B. and wife | 3 | receiving | father | This man and his wife keep a small shop in Preston-street, where young thieves bring their plunder for sale. Their children mix with the young thieves, and he has been in prison for felony. |

| Names of of Parents. | No. of Children | Means of getting living. | Parents convicted. | |
|---|---|---|---|---|
| M. J. | 4 | ... | mother | This woman has had several men living with her, who in their turn deserted her. Her house a harbour for thieves. She encourages her children to steal. One daughter transported, and she goes out stealing herself. |
| E. T. | 5 | " | ... | This woman keeps a notorious house for young thieves, who bring their plunder there. Several have been transported from her den. Her own children are thieves. |

With such constant and direct training to crime, it is no matter of surprise to learn that on the 4th of February, 1856, there were 91 boys in Liverpool Gaol. Of these, six only were there on their first conviction; ten had only once before been in custody. Excluding these, we find that the remainder had an average of three previous convictions each, many having had four, some only two. The ages usually range between 14 and 16, but one boy of 12 was there in prison on his fifth conviction. What a large body of Convicts are being thus trained for a future life of crime in our large towns. The following report of a house to house visit to the homes of these unhappy boys will give some faint idea of the influences under which our Convicts are reared. The first 20 on the list are a fair specimen of the whole:—

REPORTS OF A HOUSE TO HOUSE VISIT MADE TO THE PARENTS OF THE BOYS NAMED IN THIS LIST, WHO WERE IN WALTON GAOL FEB. 4, 1856.

| | Age. | No of times in custody. | |
|---|---|---|---|
| J. L. | 16 | 4 | Parents residing in 14, Berrington-hill. Honest, industrious people. This boy incorrigible. *His ruin traceable to the notorious* HANNAH CARR, *of Benjohnson-street, whose family and connections are all thieves.* |

| | Age. | No. of times in custody. | |
|---|---|---|---|
| T. J. | 16 | 4 | Father, a drunken debauched man, lived with the mother of this boy, by whom he had several children. *She being a profligate, the children turned out thieves.* He is now married to a decent woman, who will not allow the first children to remain in the house, lest they should contaminate her own. |
| J. C. | 15 | 2 | The father, a bricklayer, lives in Addison-street; married a second time. No care taken of children; allowed to go and mix with bad characters. |
| R. G. | 16 | 3 | Mother, a notoriously bad woman, encourages her son to steal. Harbours other lads and receives whatever plunder they bring. |
| M. L. | 15 | 4 | Father, bricklayer, out of work, in distress, large family. Mother seems anxious about her children. The boy's fall traceable to M. G. and M. F., houses in Wright-street. |
| W. R. | 14 | 4 | Cannot find the boy's parents at present, but no care has been taken. He was allowed to run wild. The Queen of Demons, viz., Old Granny HUNT, 55, Preston-street, was his home, where a number of other lads resort. This old woman's children and grand-children are all bad. |
| H. L. | 15 | 2 | Parents notoriously bad. Their children all bad, and their house an iniquitous harbour for juveniles of both sexes. Receives the proceeds of the plunder brought in. |
| H. B. | 16 | 3 | Parents (residing in a cellar) are bad, and bear bad characters. Children obliged to steal for their support. One son transported. |
| T. McJ. | 15 | 4 | Step-father bears a good character, but mother careless and took no interest until it became too late. The boy frequented a notorious house in St. Martin's-street. The woman in the cellar equally bad. |
| P. B. | 14 | 2 | Father in America. Step-mother in distress. The children obliged to get their living in the streets. |
| J. L. | 16 | 4 | His mother very poor. The notorious FITZPATRICK's and BURKE's houses his principal places of resort. |
| H. H. | 16 | 4 | A Manchester thief. The notorious HANNAH CARR's house his house when in Liverpool. |
| J. W. | 16 | 2 | The father and mother of this boy are to all appearance decent well-conducted people. Father worked as a moulder at Mr. P———'s, who gives him a good character. *A notorious house at the bottom of Preston-street the cause of the boy's fall.* |

|       | Age. | No. of times in custody. |                                                                                                                                                                                 |
| ----- | ---- | ------------------------ | ------------------------------------------------------------------------------------------------------------------------------------------------------------------------------- |
| J. T. | 11   | 2                        | ... ... ... ... ... ... ... ... ... ... ...                                                                                                                                      |
| T. W. | 16   | 4                        | The boy's parents are in America. He lives at 5, Dennison-street, and all that can truthfully be said is that nearly every house in that *street is filled with black-ballers and disorderly persons.* |
| J. B. | 16   | 4                        | Father, a dismissed cab-driver for drunkenness, *lives among a den of thieves*; he does nothing for a living. Mother and children obliged to pick up what they can for their support. |
| T. McC. | 14 | 4                        | Mother a very bad woman. Keeps a house inhabited by a number of low characters. *One son transported. She encourages her children to steal.*                                    |
| J. B. | 14   | ...                      | Step-father bears a good character. Mother unkind and severe, which is the only attributable cause for the boy leaving home.                                                     |
| M. B. | 15   | 2                        | The parents bear a good character, and appear to have taken as much care as they possibly can; but living in a bad neighbourhood is the only apparent cause.                      |
| M. O. | 12   | 1                        | Parents both drunken and dissipated; allow their children to go with any company they please, which is the cause of this boy's going bad.                                        |
| J. T. | 13   | 2                        | Father, a carter, in constant work, who cohabited with the boy's mother for several years—who was in her life time a most abandoned woman—by whom he had several children, all of whom turned out bad. |
| T. P. | 16   | 2                        | Father dead. Mother living with her daughter in a disorderly beerhouse, frequented by low characters. The boy allowed to associate with whom he pleases.                         |

Such statements as the foregoing inspire surprise, not that so
many young persons fall into crime in our large towns, but that
so many escape contamination. The repression of Training
Schools for vice falls rather under the magisterial province than
that of private individuals. There are however incentives to crime
which are within the reach of society to remove; among these
one of the most injurious is the corrupt literature of our time.
The late Rev. J. CLAY speaks strongly on this point in his
Twenty-third Report. "How far the inclination to crime is
encouraged or created by the reading of the 'The Newgate

Calendar Improved,' &c., may be inferred from the following statements. J. A., aged 18, convicted of housebreaking, says,— 'Now I will speak a few words about reading bad books. There is a book called '*The Newgate Calendar Improved*.' It contains the lives of the greatest vagabonds that ever was. I used to call it my catechism; and I read in that book until I began to think honesty and industry was a great shame. This book is a '*straight line*' for a young thief to work upon, and the first foundation and beginning of evil. I first began reading these bad books until I thought it was a sin to be honest, and from them to the beershops, where I got very well educated, and many fine lessons I heard, and from there to the concert room, where I began with bad women, and from there to the dancing school, which finally brought me within these walls. And now, in prison as I am, and taken from among my riotous companions, I am more content in my mind, along with the Bible, than if I was gaming for drink at the beershop. When I first came into prison I did not know the Lord's Prayer correctly, and now I know a great many prayers; and I am fully convinced that if I have lost my character, I have saved my soul from that place which I was fast running to."

Mr. CLAY adds,—"J. A.'s conduct since his liberation has been highly creditable, betokening in fact complete reformation."

J. N., aged 17, sentenced to transportation, writes thus:—

"  *   * At about 13 years of age, I began to read *The Newgate Calendar*, *and all such books as these, Jack Sheppard, Turpin, and different kinds of romances ;* this, with the *advice of wicked men, made me inclined to follow some of their examples, and to try if I could not imitate some of their evil deeds.* *   * In a short time I began to commit greater offences, one of which I got taken for, and got one month in prison at Salford House of Correction, which made me worse than ever, *through having so much liberty for talking by being three or four in a cell, and forty or fifty in a yard. The hearing them talk about the robberies they had committed, without being apprehended, I thought I would try myself.* So, when I got my liberty, I started with a fresh gang for a while," &c., &c.

"As a further proof," Mr. CLAY says in the same Report, "of the effects of the demoralising publications spoken of by J. A., I would refer to the case of H. J. K., aged 17, indicted for 'feloniously attempting to administer in a letter a quantity of deadly poison called oxalic acid to E. C., with intent to murder her,' reported in the *Times* of February 26th of the present year (1846). It is unnecessary to give all the details of the case here, as they may be easily referred to; it will suffice for my present purpose to say that the prisoner was convicted on his own confession, made in a letter to his brother, which contained the following passage:—' The fact was, I did for a long while read a great many of LLOYD'S Works, in which were some most wonderful characters; and I thought at the time that I would do as represented in the books, appear a most mysterious character, and then after that, write these letters, &c., &c.'

"I have conversed," Mr. CLAY says again, "during the last three years with 1234 males and 199 females who, though ignorant of almost everything good and useful, and of the meaning of the *words* 'virtue and vice,' have yet been made familiar with, if not enamoured of, the personification of the latter, as held up for their sympathies and imitations in the stories of TURPIN and SHEPPARD."

On Mr. CLAY's expressing his surprise to a young prisoner that he should be able to read the Testament, and yet have no idea of the meaning of the words he had read, he replied in a tone of indignation, "Why they never learned me the understanding of the words!" "But this same young man," he adds, "so uninstructed in the great and vital meanings of the Testament, could apply the mechanical faculty he had acquired, the instrument so dangerous when misapplied, to unlock the meanings of other books; he easily comprehended, assisted by coarse but intelligible engravings, the exciting stories of 'The Newgate Calendar *Improved*,' and of 'DICK TURPIN and his Black Mare!' And so, while the Book of Life has never been opened to his understanding and affections, other books, fraught with ruin and death, are made level to his capacity and enticing to his imagination."

It is to be feared that since this was written there has been no diminution in the taste for such exciting reading and for sensational novels, which fill the mind with the worst images and rouse the most lawless passions. A striking instance of this has recently occurred, an account of which is given in the *Reformatory and Refuge Journal* for January, 1864:—

## "YOUTHFUL ADEPTS IN CRIME.

" Our readers will have noticed a startling case of juvenile depravity, which attracted public attention about the beginning of December. Four lads, of whom the eldest appears to have been not more than seventeen, united for the perpetration of a series of evil deeds, to which, taking their youth into consideration, current history will scarcely afford a parallel. They broke into the premises of an ironmonger at Hull, and carried off some of his goods, entered the offices of the Electric Telegraph Company and possessed themselves of £10, besides planning and committing other violations of the law. All four agreed to fly together in a dog-cart into a country district to wait until the excitement occasioned by the robberies should have blown over. Two of them, however, being too late for the rendezvous, the other two set off without them. The laggards then engaged a cab, and agreed to murder the cabman and take possession of his horse and vehicle. One of them lost his courage and informed the driver of the project. His companion, who had suggested it, jumped out and ran away, but was speedily captured. The two lads that set off in the dog-cart broke it on the road, and offered the horse for sale to a dealer. The suspicions of the latter being aroused, he was the means of having them arrested and lodged in Hull Prison. The career of three out of four of these young miscreants was speedily cut short, one only remaining at large.

" *Upon their examination, the lads confessed that their imagination had been excited by the perusal of such works of fiction as the Life of Dick Turpin, Jack Sheppard, Paul Clifford and others.* We trust this avowal may be taken to heart by those who pander to the vitiated tastes of our depraved classes· Surely the bad influences to which youths are exposed in the wretched haunts among which our sin-bred populace first draw breath, need no aggravation from the pens of men of intellect and imagination. May our popular novelists learn a lesson from this occurrence, and, if they deal in criminal subjects at all, state facts as they are, with the veracious accompaniments of the criminal's habitual, trembling, apprehensive dread of discovery, his frequent subjection to poverty, hunger, cold and fatigue, ending in the privation of personal liberty and severe discipline, or still more severe monotony of prison life. No more suggestive lesson than this can be needed by the philanthropist. We most confidently appeal to such as have the well-being of society at heart, to unite with us in endeavouring to bring our various institutions and agencies within reach of the class to which these four boys belong. The energy, skill and audacity displayed by the lads, prove that from their earliest years they have been among such associates and associations as could but lead, as they have done, to their taking their place in the felon's dock. Could they have been removed, when they first showed signs of depravity, from their vicious haunts and companions, and placed in any of our numerous Reformatory Institutions, surrounded by pure industrial and religious influences, and guarded from outward immorality, how different might their course have been! Instead of being a curse to society they might, had they themselves been rescued, have been employing the natural talents conferred upon them by their Maker in endeavouring, by example and precept, to withdraw others from evil and lead them in the paths of rectitude. An occurrence of this description is well calculated to deepen our conviction of the necessity of the work in which we are engaged, and to quicken our energies in seeking to provide increased means for the prevention of crime and suppression of vice."

Closely connected with impure literature is the excitement and injurious tendency of low penny theatres, singing and dancing rooms, &c. All persons acquainted with the criminal class are aware that the intense longing for recreation of this kind often first induces the young boy or girl to steal, and that the associates there met with, and the immoral tendency of the performances, complete his ruin. The author of JANE CAMERON vividly pourtrays this in her narrative. The Rev. JOHN CLAY gives, in his Twenty-seventh Report, an account of a visit to the principal singing-room in Preston, by persons who were desirous of ascertaining the effect of such spectacles. The whole of the details are too revolting to be transcribed; the following extract will give some idea of the scene there witnessed:—

" There could not be less than 700 individuals present (young boys and girls, chiefly 14 years of age and upwards) and about one-seventh of them females. The pieces performed encourage resistance to parental control, and were full of gross innuendoes, 'double entendres,' heavy cursing, emphatic swearing, and incitement to illicit passion. Three-fourths of the songs were wanton and immoral, and were accompanied by immodest gestures. * * * This place is the manufactory and rendezvous of thieves and prostitutes. We saw several boys who had been recently discharged from prison. We did not see, during the evening, half-a-dozen respectable working-men. The audience consisted of that portion of society which demands our most especial care and attention—the rising generation. Many of them we could tell, by their conversation, were regular visitors. Some of the boys and girls were enabled to follow the singers in their songs, they could tell the names of the performers, their salaries, and converse on their relative merits. We did not see one female whose modesty seemed shocked or offended by anything said or done on the stage.

" We left the room about eleven o'clock, and there remained between 200 and 300 persons, one-fourth of whom would be juveniles. As we have said, the room contained at one period 700 spectators; but the entire number which visited it during the night must have reached 1000. We have visited many singing-rooms, both metropolitan and provincial, but for gross and open immorality, for pandering to the depraved tastes of an audience, for exciting the passions of the young, for sensual exhibitions, this place surpasses all. We left it with a firm conviction that we may build Mechanics' Institutes, erect and endow Churches, increase the number of Gospel ministers, and improve our prison discipline, *but while we tolerate this nuisance, we labour in vain.*"

Such are some of the influences which have formed the minds of our Convicts.

The limits of space forbid our giving more than this brief summary of the various ways in which the criminal class is constantly recruited in our country, and a faint sketch of the evil influences and training which persons now in our Government Prisons have probably received. We must not however conclude without alluding to one most fertile source of evil, which all persons concerned with the repression of crime, regard as a strong incentive to the commission of it, as well as a cause of the degradation of the criminal classes—the use of intoxicating liquors. The subject has been so often and so powerfully brought before the public that it is unnecessary here to do more than to refer to it. Yet, as Mr. CLAY's Reports are not now generally accessible, it may be instructive to copy from the concluding page of his Twenty-seventh Report, the following striking testimony of men actually suffering from the effects of drunkenness :—

" The Petition," Mr. CLAY says, " was drawn up after I had carefully read upwards of eighty written statements, by as many different prisoners, and was, as far as I could make it so, a digest of those statements. It was earnestly and clearly explained to the prisoners, that unless they *wished* to sign the petition, and also that the prayer of it might be granted, it would be improper to attach their names to it. They were also made to understand that their signing it, or otherwise, would not have the slightest influence on their position as prisoners. One man declined to sign it because the ' *wording* did not quite suit' him. As to the signatures themselves, I believe none were ever more heartily attached to a petition than these."

*"Petition presented to the House of Lords, in May last, by the Earl of Harrowby.*
            "To THE RIGHT HONOURABLE THE LORDS, &c., &c.
    " The Petition of the undersigned Prisoners in the County House of
            Correction, at Preston, in Lancaster,
" Humbly Sheweth,
    " That your Petitioners have had painful experience of the miseries, bodily
and spiritual, produced by beer-houses, and are fully assured that those places
constitute the greatest obstacles to the social, moral and religious progress of
the labouring classes.   They are alike injurious to old and young.   By frequenting them parents bring their families to disgrace and ruin, and children
are familiarised with vice and crime.   They combine whatever is demoralising
in the ale-house, pawn-shop, fence-shop, gaming-house and brothel.   Your
Petitioners have all been drawn, by frequenting beer-houses, into offences and
crimes of which they might otherwise have remained innocent.   We speak
from our own direct and bitter knowledge, when we declare that beer-houses
lead to Sabbath-breaking, blasphemy, fraud, robbery, stabbings, manslaughters
and murders !
    " Your Petitioners, therefore, desiring that others may be saved from the
fate which has overtaken them, humbly, but most earnestly, pray that your
Lordships would be pleased to take such measures as will, on the one hand,
lead to the entire suppression of the beer-house curse, and on the other,
promote whatever may hold out the prospect of wholesome and rational
amusement for the working population of the kingdom.
                    " And your petitioners will ever pray, &c.
                                        " *Signed by* 247 *Male Prisoners.*"

# CHAPTER III.

## PRINCIPLES OF CONVICT TREATMENT.

WE have now some idea of the persons forming the large body of men and women in our country who constitute "our Convicts."

Whatever may be the cause of their present condition, and however much or little they may morally be themselves to blame for it, the habitual offenders who constitute the largest proportion of the inmates of Convict prisons are in a state of absolute antagonism to society and disregard of ordinances, human and divine. They are usually hardened in vice, and they concern themselves with the law only to endeavour to evade it. They dislike labour of all kinds, and to supply their own wants exert themselves only by preying on the property of others. They are self-indulgent,—low in their desires,—ignorant of all knowledge that would profit them,—skilful only in accomplishing their own wicked purposes.

But they are still men and women, possessed of an immortal nature; still they are the children of the same Heavenly Father; still are they our fellow-citizens.

We have traced the course by which Convicts have arrived at their present very degraded and dangerous state. Though in some cases a succession of unfortunate circumstances, over which society had no direct control, may have carried on the unhappy victim from one step to another, in each plunging him deeper and deeper in an abyss of crime, from which he was unable to extricate himself, and for which society could not be held *directly* responsible,—yet even in these cases we must have perceived that the prevalence of a more Christian spirit in society, of a stronger moral repugnance to evil, of a greater readiness to help the weak, may have arrested the criminal in an earlier stage of his career.  But, in the great bulk of the instances adduced, young persons have become gradually hardened in guilt through causes over which they had no control, and for which society is *directly* responsible.  The practice still continues of sending children to prison, though for so long a time it has been declared by the highest authorities worse than useless, and though the existence of schools authorised by the Government renders this incarceration unnecessary.  The Workhouses do not yet provide a true home for destitute children, who find themselves better cared for in the hands of justice than in the keeping of those misnamed their guardians. Dens of infamy are still tolerated in our cities, to give to our young children that schooling to vice, which no one gives them to lead them in the right way.  The uncertainty of punishment, the glaring defects still existing in our criminal law, allure by impunity or slight punishment to repetition of crime.  Society *is* responsible for all this, and therefore is bound to remedy as far as possible the evils arising from these various abuses.  It is, then, our solemn duty, both as members of society and as professing Christians, to endeavour to bring these people to a sense of their responsibility to God and to man, and of their own immortal destiny,—to reform them.

To produce any permanent change in natures so perverted and hardened, it is evident that no merely external means can be of the slightest value.  While under compulsory detention they may be bribed or terrified into some degree of quietude and submission, but their *natures* are not touched by these means. They return from the monotony and forced propriety of their prison life, only with fresh zest for the exciting career from which they have been for a season snatched.  Their long abstinence from intoxicating stimulants is compensated for by increased excess. The hated forced labour of their servitude is at once abandoned for the wonted indolence of their old life. All who are acquainted with the histories of criminals, are well aware that this is the ordinary result of the present treatment of Convicts, and hence arises a profound and general disbelief in the possibility of reformation, among those whose duties lead them to a knowledge of the "dangerous class."

A different principle of management produces different results, and does effect real reformation, provided all external means are adopted in developing the principle which experience and sound judgment suggest.

We shall now endeavour to ascertain what are the true principles of the treatment of Convicts as individuals, and to show that these can be carried out in the legal punishment of criminals.

In the first place, the *will* of the individual should be brought into such a condition as to wish to reform, and to exert itself to that end, in co-operation with the persons who are set over him. The state of antagonism to society must be destroyed; the hostility to divine and human law must be subdued. This can never be done by mere force, or by any mechanical appliance. No fear of punishment, no hope of advantage, can produce a change of heart, or a true penitence towards God, and without this it is impossible that any reliable alteration in life can be effected. Severe suffering may subdue, and bring the individual into a state in which he may be more easily made sensible of his criminality towards God and towards man. But it is only when his heart is touched by the Christian sympathy of those around,—when he can be made to understand that his own personal efforts alone can raise him,—that all that he is now enduring only has in view his restoration to society as an honest member of it; it is only then that he truly repents of his sins, humbles himself before his Creator, earnestly seeks divine help, desires to atone for his past misdeeds, is united to his fellow-beings by the bonds of Christian love, willingly accepts the discipline appointed for him, and gratefully works with those set over him for his restoration to society.

That such a change as this, proved by the future life to be a genuine reformation, has ever been accomplished, may be discredited by many, but is nevertheless true. And wherever such reformation has been effected, of which many examples will occur in these volumes, it will be found that the moving spring has been some person of large and Christian heart, who worked on principles founded on human nature, and on God's moral and revealed law; who framed a system in accordance with these, and carried it out with earnest purpose, enlisting in his work the hearts of those with him, because it was evidently good and true.

Whatever system can be proved to be most truly reformatory will, of course, be the best for society as minimizing crime to the greatest extent; it should therefore be introduced into legal punishment, as it will most benefit the public at large, as well as the individual. Yet however firmly we may adhere to this reformatory principle, it is evident that we must not ignore or neglect another, viz., that it is the law both of God and of man that sin should be followed by suffering,—that what a man soweth that he must reap. These two principles are not opposed to each other, but are in perfect harmony, and if so worked will produce the best effects. How they may ·be harmonised has frequently been set forth most powerfully by Mr. Recorder HILL, who has so long devoted his special attention to this very subject, and has tested his views by extensive experience. The following extracts are from a paper of his, read at the general meeting of the Law Amendment Society, Jan. 12, 1863, and ordered to be printed :—

" The principles of secondary punishment may be reduced to three. First, the application of pain with the intention of proving to the sufferer, and to all who may learn his fate, that the profits of crime are overbalanced by its losses. This is the deterrent principle in action. The second principle is what BENTHAM calls that of *incapacitation.* So long as the criminal remains in gaol, society is protected from his misconduct, not by the deterrent operation of fear, but because he has for the time lost the power of offending. The third is the reformatory principle. Thus incapacitation deprives the malefactor of his power to do wrong,—deterrents overmaster by fear his desire for evil doing,—while by reformation that desire is extinguished, and is replaced by aspirations and habits which will furnish him with a safeguard against relapse.

"Now what is to prevent all these principles being combined in one and the same punishment. Reformation cannot be made the work of a day. It is a task which requires a tedious length of time for its assured performance. During this period the criminal will be subjected to incapacitation, while his long confinement will inspire the dread which necessarily attaches to the danger of again being deprived of liberty; a fear often undervalued by those who have never had the opportunity of estimating it by experience. It is true that by indulgences the pain and consequently the dread of incarceration may be to some uncertain extent diminished. But the vast majority of us are so constituted that imprisonment, always irksome, becomes by continuance all but intolerable.

"Of concessions to the prisoner, each of which, in the excitement of the hour is denounced as an indulgence, some are essential to prevent imprisonment from degenerating into an infliction far more revolting to contemplate than capital punishment itself; by permanently undermining the prisoner's health, and thus destroying his powers of self-maintenance— a consequence which, however lightly it may be viewed in the present temper of the public mind, would, when it was found to accrue, produce an excitement against harsh measures, exhibiting itself in bitter reproaches on the prison authorities for cruelty towards defenceless victims.

"Among these indispensable concessions I include food, clothing, ventilation, and exercise, upon a scale sufficient for the conservation of the bodily powers; nothing being added for enjoyment or even for comfort, except in so far as enjoyment and comfort unavoidably flow from arrangements which have the health of the prisoner for their sole object. Cleanliness of the person and of the habitation I do not class as indulgences, because, however salutary to the prisoner, they are not so appreciated by him; while the observances which they involve he finds annoying to a degree which difference of habits and manners utterly disqualifies us from duly estimating. Neither does any real objection lie against the indulgence (if it is to be so called) of education. On the contrary, by exciting the industry of the prisoner, and withdrawing his mind from debasing thoughts and reminiscences, it turns the malefactor's solitude to good account both for himself and for us. Nor indeed does the public mind in its normal condition visit these alleviations with censure. It reserves, and justly reserves, the weight of its indignation for those indulgences which pamper the sensual appetites of the criminal — an undue allowance of nutritious food made savoury to the palate,—intoxicating drinks, in any form and in any quantity, however small,—and indolence,—meaning thereby, any employment of the prisoner's time short of severe and long-continued labour. But let me ask who have opposed the introduction of these abuses into our prisons, with such earnest and ceaseless protests, as the advocates of reformatory treatment? Who, indeed, have so strong a motive for their opposition? The disbeliever in the practicability of reformation may, it is true, justly denounce these indulgences as diminishing the terror of imprisonment, and thereby weakening its exemplary effect; but the reformist, while he cordially joins in this condemnation, on the same ground goes further, and objects that to pamper the appetites is to defeat his object, by rendering reformation impossible. He knows well that it was the temptations of sensuality, together with other desires closely connected with the grosser appetites, which brought the malefactor to prison; and that if prison life is so ordered as to inflame instead of subdue these unruly appetites and desires, the prisoner will be discharged a far worse man than he entered. Therefore do I maintain that to hold reformatory treatment answerable for the course of false indulgence which has unhappily been pursued, or indeed for any toleration of it, is manifest error and injustice.

" Again, paradoxical as it may at first sight appear, reformatory treatment gives facilities for a freer use of the deterrent principle, and also for that of incapacitation, than can be otherwise obtained.

"Whatever threats may be held out by the law, public sentiment places limits to their execution which are found to be impassable. And for many years these limits have been constantly narrowing. The administration of even secondary punishments, on the scale of severity which universally prevailed when I began to practice in criminal courts forty years ago, would after the lapse of twenty years from that date have filled the audience with disgust and even consternation; while prosecutors, witnesses, and juries would, by their reluctance, and in many instances by their absolute refusal to act, have so impeded the course of justice as to compel a relaxation of rigour. And now, after a second interval of twenty years, punishments awarded at the commencement of that second interval, with the approbation of society, would shock the sensibilities of all classes, even while this *epidemic* of anger and alarm is still raging. Since it must always be borne in mind that to whatever height the thirst for vengeance may rise against malefactors in the aggregate, no sooner is an individual offender separated from the mass, brought under the public gaze, and presented as the object on which the severeties invoked are to fall, than a very different set of feelings comes into play, even among the loudest declaimers against the impunity to crime furnished by short sentences in Court, followed by lax discipline and preposterous indulgence in prison.

" But only let the public be convinced that imprisonment, with its attendant hardships, is the essential condition of reformation, and that if this object be not attained by short terms of confinement, it is to the benefit of the criminal as well as of society that they should be lengthened, and a check will be given to [that fatal disposition towards morbid leniency, which, with a constantly increasing force, is now paralyzing the hands of justice.

"Yet I am perfectly ready to admit that, while the introduction of the reformatory principle into the treatment of criminals offers no obstruction to the employment of deterrents, but on the contrary, as I have shown, removes a difficulty which stands in the way of the freer resort to such expedients, it nevertheless does impose a condition as to the manner in which they shall be used; which, however, it would be erroneous to assume impairs their efficiency—whatever that efficiency may be.

" In my observations I have only contemplated punishment by incarceration and hard labour—such visitations on the criminal being essential to his reformation. Now it must be noted that, in all but a small minority of cases, there is but little difficulty in guiding the aspirations of the prisoner into the right channel; since he soon becomes aware that the aims of those under whose control he is placed are benevolent, and, if successful, of the highest advantage to himself. Thus, the real difficulty of the arduous task undertaken by his instructors does not rest with the feelings and wishes of the prisoner, but with his habits. To the privations, then, which are necessarily incidental to the work of reformation, viz., confinement, labour, and abstemious living, he resigns himself with the patience which we all find it possible to command for evils out of which we expect to derive an ultimate benefit.

" With regard, however, to pain inflicted on the prisoner without such incidental necessity, but which has his suffering for its direct object, his feelings are very different. And these feelings lead to a settled hostility towards the inflictors and towards society itself whose ministers he knows them to be. I consider it, therefore, highly repugnant to the reformatory principle, and a serious impediment to reformatory action, that punishments like flogging should be administered as part of any system, devised with a view to the reformation of the criminal, because it is essential to that end that his mind should be brought into alliance with his governors and teachers, so that he should become an agent, and indeed the principal agent, in the great work. Nevertheless, should pain, intense even to agony, be deemed necessary for the protection of the public, the reformatory principle presents no bar to treatment founded on such necessity. For instance, suppose that for any crime which implied a love of cruelty in the malefactor, or indifference to the personal sufferings of his victims, it should be thought right to subject him to the lash: the only provision that would be requisite to prevent interference with his reformatory treatment, would be that the prisoner should undergo this infliction prior to the commencement of his training, and that it should be administered in another place, and by officers whom on his removal he will not see again.

" If I do not profess myself an advocate for inflictions like these, directed by what our President, Lord BROUGHAM, designates as ' simply penal legislation,' it is not that I am restrained by a morbid sympathy for criminals, or that I would shrink from awarding any amount of pain essential to the end and object of all criminal jurisprudence—the diminution of crime to the lowest attainable point. It is because I am not satisfied that what I may call pain for pain's sake is either necessary for the repression of crime or would be very efficient if so applied. With regard to its necessity, I must remark that the criminal classes in England (whose obduracy has been of late the subject of so much passionate comment) *are not in the state in which we should have found them, had not their treatment in prison been an outrage on all common sense and on all the lessons of experience.* They have had a training, to be sure, but if our object had been to confirm them in crime it would be very difficult indeed to imagine plans more exquisitely adapted to that purpose, or more successful in fulfilling it. Short terms of imprisonment—indulgences enervating or perverting the mind of the convict,—discharges not only without evidence of amendment, but against the strongest presumptions to the contrary—impunity when set at large, by keeping the police in the dark as to his character, whereby he lengthens his term of freedom between discharge and re-apprehension — deterrents diluted until they become innocuous to his feelings, and scarcely even unpalatable—and lastly, *incapacitation* absurdly abridged. If, then, such a process as this does not form the best *curriculum* for a liberal education in crime, all I can say is that I am unable to figure to myself a better, and I think I may safely defy even the commonwealth of felons to improve upon it.

"Having then to deal with a body of malefactors, who, by the united effect of self-education and perverted training in prison, have become hardened in crime to a frightful degree, there may be (although I shall be loth to yield the point) a necessity for resorting to the preliminary severities to which I have adverted—at least for a season.

"But, after all, I am persuaded we must not hope for much advantage from this class of inflictions. Although, by nine writers out of ten, the main efficacy of punishment is ascribed to deterrents, yet all experience goes to show that their value is so far below the popular estimate, that were it necessary (which assuredly it is not) to forego the advantages of the deterrent principle in order to avail ourselves of the other principles of punishment, such abandonment would be wisely made. In truth, however, such a sacrifice is not only unnecessary but impossible. *Reformatory treatment, to be sound and efficient, must be painful, and, therefore, however patiently borne, must be deterrent.* On this part of the subject, let me refer to the discourse to which I have already adverted. After citing instances not drawn from individual cases, but from the conduct, generation after generation, of large bodies of men, 'artizans who labour in unwholesome manufactures, selling themselves to certain death for a small increase of wages, which excess over the ordinary rate would in truth amount to only a trifling sum for their whole lives,' Lord BROUGHAM says,—'I surely have no occasion to go further in quest of evidence, if, indeed, any were needed, to demonstrate that the effect of punishment in deterring by example is exceedingly feeble upon the whole, and prodigiously over-rated in all systems of criminal jurisprudence, as well as by the philosophers who speculate upon the construction of codes, as by the lawgivers who trust to statutes for a protection against offences.' " *

The great object of *legal punishment* being then to minimize crime as much as possible, we have in the foregoing extract had the means clearly stated by which this may be effected.

First,—By deterring society and the individual from a further commission of crime.

Secondly,—By reformatory treatment, whereby the criminal will entirely alter his future life and become a useful member of society, instead of an injury to it.

Thirdly,—By "incapacitation," or preventing the criminal from ever injuring society again, either by death or by incarceration for life.

The last,—Incapacitation may be regarded as a primary punishment, and will not be considered in this work, in which is discussed the treatment of those who are to be restored to society.

Until within the last quarter of a century, the first of these, the deterrent principle, was the one generally acknowledged as the special object of the infliction of punishment by the law. The law is intended to be "a terror to evil doers." We are told that " the *fear* of the Lord is the *beginning* of wisdom," and the dread of punishment from human law is of course a great check on that large portion of the community, who are not restrained from evil by the fear of offending against the Heavenly Ruler. But, while punishment ought always to have a strongly deterrent element in it,—deterrent both to society and to the individual who has offended,—there should be nothing vindictive in it, for "vengeance is mine, I will repay saith the Lord;" the *old* law was "an eye for an eye, and a tooth for a tooth;" a Christian country should legislate in a very different spirit. Again, punishment inflicted by the law should have in view not only to deter from the commission of crime, but to exhibit

---

* Authorised Report of the Bristol Meeting of the National Reformatory Union, 1856, p. 54. See also Lord BROUGHAM'S Works, vol. 8.

to the community a detestation of crime for its own sake,—
a testimony against transgression of the laws both of God
and of man. This is forcibly expressed by the late Rev. F.
ROBERTSON, in his exposition of St. Paul's Epistles to the Corinthians,—"The general subject," he says, "has successively
brought before us the nature of human punishment, as not
being reformatory, nor exemplary, nor for safety's sake, but
*also as being declarative of the indignation of society*, and through
society, of the indignation of God against sin."

The deterrent principle will always be a prominent one in the
popular idea of the object of punishment. This is so on the
Continent. In the Report of the Select Committee on Transportation in 1856, we find in the Appendix a very valuable
abstract from Official Reports on Penal Discipline in most of
the countries of Europe ; the punishments, wherever mentioned,
have an entirely deterrent aspect. The punishments of chains,
of being fastened to a ring, of being kept in irons, are frequent;
the hardest and simplest fare is provided,—"one warm meal
and a pound of bread daily, and on Sundays a little meat," with
a straw mattress and pillow. Even the possibility of regaining
the lost position is in some cases precluded, the graver secondary
punishments involving a sort of civil death. The reformation
of the offender does not appear anywhere to form part of the
object of the punishments themselves. But though a sentence of
the law, when awarded by a judge, is intended to have especially
a deterrent effect, yet it has gradually been tacitly felt, and at
length openly acknowledged in our country, that the reformation
of the offender should form an essential part of all punishment
in which the offence is sufficiently grave to warrant a long
detention. The sentiment expressed last year by Sergeant
KINGLAKE, the Recorder of Bristol, in his charge to the Grand
Jury, will have, we doubt not, a general response from the
Bench,—"Whatever the particular punishment might be," he
said, "in reference to persons who had been previously convicted,
he trusted *that the system of reformatory conduct would always be*

*kept in view whilst the punishment was being carried out.*"   *   *
" While the punishment was made effective for all wholesome purposes, *it was possible that it might be accompanied with reformation on the part of the prisoner.*" The two objects, the deterring from crime and the reforming of the criminal, ought always to be associated together; no system is good in which both are not combined, and no theories of punishment are of any value unless they can be tested by results.

We shall now, then, proceed to bring forward some remarkable cases in which the principles we advocate have been carried out by individuals in different parts of the world, and quite unconnected with each other, but who have successfully combined deterrent punishment and reformation. Our first illustration is the system pursued by Colonel MONTESINOS in the prison of Valencia, in Spain. The following very instructive account of it is extracted from Mr. Recorder HILL's charge to the Grand Jury at Birmingham, as given in the "Repression of Crime," 532, 533 :—

" In the city of Valencia there has long been a penitentiary gaol, under the government of Colonel MONTESINOS, a gentleman who has made for himself a European reputation, by his skill in the treatment of his prisoners. He acted upon them by urging them to self-reformation. He excited them to industry, by allowing them a small portion of their earnings for their own immediate expenditure, under due regulations to prevent abuse. He enabled them to raise their position, stage after stage, by their perseverance in good conduct. When they had acquired his confidence, he entrusted them with commissions, which carried them beyond the walls of their prison; relying on his moral influence which he had acquired over them to prevent their desertion. And, finally, he discharged them before the expiration of their sentences, when he had satisfied himself that they deserved to do well, had acquired habits of patient labour, so much of skill in some useful occupation as would ensure employment, the inestimable faculty of self-denial, the power of saying ' No' to the tempter, and, in short, such a general control over the infirmities of their minds and hearts as should enable them to deserve and maintain the liberty which they had earned. His success was answerable to the wisdom and zeal of his administration. Instances of relapse but rarely occurred, and the Spanish Government, rightly judging that talent like this ought to have the widest scope, appointed him Inspector-General of all the prisons in Spain. It so happened, however, that the legislature of that country was minded to establish a new criminal code, and (for what reason I know not) held it advisable to convert sentences of imprisonment for long terms of years, which prevail on the Continent, into incarceration for life. This was done; but, unhappily, this was not the only, nor the most pernicious change. In the chapters of the new code, which relate to the management of prisons, governors are prohibited from offering those encouragements to the prisoners which had raised them step by step until they were fitted for the enjoyment of liberty; and they also make it imperative that every sentence of imprisonment shall be fulfilled to the last hour. The combined effects of these innovations teem with instruction. Prisons, which had been models of order and cleanliness, of cheerful industry, and of praiseworthy demeanour in general, now exhibit a painful contrast to that happy state of things; they have become the scenes of indolence, disorder and filth; and the prisoners are either reduced to despair, or urged upon plots for escape, which, in a multitude of instances, were followed by success."

The following additional information is derived from the same volume:—

"Colonel MONTESINOS, in his written memoirs, says, when explaining and advocating this measure, 'the commandant who knew how to choose his officers would have no untoward events to lament in his prison,' which is proved by the fact that during the twenty years of his governorship of the prison of Valencia he never needed an armed force for the guard within the walls, nor even for that which accompanied the gangs of prisoners who worked outside, amounting in number often to 400 men, for whom the convict officers were quite sufficient, and among whom there were never either plots nor desertions.

"For each hundred persons are required an overseer, chosen from among retired sergeants in the army, four 'cabos primeros' and four 'cabos segundos,' selected from the prisoners. It will cause surprise that the criminals themselves should be employed as cabos, and should be permitted to exercise authority, but the experience of many years has proved the utility and economy of the arrangement; its utility is shown in this, that selected with due discretion the men are thoroughly acquainted with their companions, with whom they live in constant intercourse; they understand their predilections and desires, are aware of their propensities, and foresee their actions, and thus are frequently able to avert the necessity of punishment. As they obtain consideration, besides a deserving benefit in other ways, from their office, they endeavour to retain it by performing its duties well. Moreover, this arrangement affords a stimulus to the rest to behave well, that they may in their turn be promoted. From among these latter are chosen the 'cabos segundos,' and from these, according to the proofs of reformation and of repentance they give, and provided they are under light sentences for only slight offences, are selected individuals to replace the vacancies which may occur among the 'cabos primeros.'"—p. 576.

"Colonel MONTESINOS is not now at the head of the prison of Valencia, having relinquished his office. By the system which he established, the prisoner was made aware that by behaving well, by applying himself to the acquisition of some art or trade, and by good moral conduct, he would ameliorate his present treatment and improve his future position; and *the desired result had been obtained of diminishing to two per cent. the annual re-commitments, which had formerly amounted to thirty-five per cent.* The publication of the new penal code, which converted sentences of imprisonment for a long period of years into imprisonment for life, and which deprived the governor of the prison of all power of alleviating the condition of the convict, however much he might deserve it, or however desirable it might be as a stimulus to the others, took from the unhappy prisoner all hope that his industry or good conduct would avail him anything. Unconsoled by the hope of improving their lot, Colonel M. observed that the convicts lost their energy, a feeling of despair spread among them, and their ardour in acquiring a trade abated; indeed, *that they continued to work at all was the result of discipline and consequent subordination, but they laboured without zeal, without any love of work*, and without the hearty goodwill they had exhibited before the introduction of the new penal code. Finding no means by which he could counteract this terrible evil, which utterly destroyed his system, Colonel M. resigned his appointment. He had, moreover, another reason, namely, that the promulgation of the said code was followed by the appointment of incompetent persons as officers, who, faulty in character, and having other unfavourable qualities, could not produce good results."—p. 571.

These facts are most important to our general argument, as proving, first, the power of right principles if carried out by persons who understand them, and with efficient instruments; and next, the hopelessness of the most enlightened efforts if counteracted by bad principles of management and inefficient officials. We shall next see the uselessness of the best organization without the animating spirit.

"The same material organization remains in the prison of Valencia, but the spirit of his internal arrangements has disappeared since the Colonel departed, to such a degree that in the workshops scarcely any work is done, and what is accomplished is badly performed; the remarkable cleanliness and order which was formerly observed has disappeared; desertions, then so exceedingly rare, were of those who worked outside the walls, now amount to a most disgraceful number, so that there have been as many as 43 convicts at once under heavy punishment for attempts to escape."

"There has been no imitators in Spain of the penal system of Colonel MONTESINOS, but as Inspector-General of all prisons in the kingdom, he established therein his system, which produced more or less favourable results, according to the character and disposition of their respective governors. Some improvement however was visible in all; workshops were introduced which were profitable to the treasury, and above all, the moral benefit to the convicts was very apparent. That the good results were not more universal was owing to an impediment, which, in spite of his utmost efforts, the Colonel was never wholly able to overcome. It arose thus:—When reorganising any establishment, he laid down a plan in accordance with his penal system, and himself put it in execution. During his stay there all went well, and every thing got into its proper place, but as soon as he went away, the imperfect regulations which the General Board of Prisons did not care to reform were brought back into force, and confusion again prevailed. Nevertheless, the doctrines of Colonel MONTESINOS remained, and gradually, with much labour on his part, regained their former ascendancy. The effects they produced were always good in a greater or less degree, and brought some revenue to the Treasury."—*Repression of Crime,* 571—573.

In this remarkable case it may be said by some, that the personal influence of one remarkable man produced these striking effects. But it was not so. He had discovered certain principles, which he believed would have the effect he desired. He had the personal qualities which would enable him to carry them out, and he devoted himself to the great and important work of developing them. He did this under peculiar disadvantages, for the simple deterrent principle appeared the prevalent one; he had no scientific organization or machinery to help him, and no well trained officials to execute his plans. But he fully succeeded, through the soundness of his principles and his own devoted efforts. Even when exercising the office of a general director, and shackled by government regulations, we find him succeeding, whenever there were in the gaols officials capable of understanding his system and putting them into execution; he thus proved that it was not any peculiarity of his own which was the secret of his success, but the soundness of his principles, administered by efficient and sympathizing officials.

We shall now present an account of a very striking instance of the reformatory power of a right principle, carried out by an individual man, as exhibited by Herr VON OBERMAIER in the Prisons of Munich. It is extracted from a letter of

GEORGE COMBE to the *Illustrated News*, and is inserted in Mr. HILL's "Repression of Crime," 578, &c.:—

"MUNICH, *July* 25, 1854.

"I have found here an unexpected illustration of the power of the moral sentiments and intellect to govern and reform criminals, without using the lash or any severe punishment, and also irrespective of all theory or system. Herr REGIERUNGSRATH OBERMAIER is the Governor of the Criminal Prison of this City, and has under his charge above 600 of the worst male convicts, collected from all the districts of Bavaria. Their sentences extend from eight to twelve years' imprisonment, and some of them for life. Their crimes have generally been attempts to murder, murder with extenuating circumstances, or highway robbery. A more unpromising set of convicts could hardly be imagined, and yet there are no separate cells, no severe discipline, no paid superintendents, except a turnkey to each ward, whose station is outside the door, and who does not see into the apartment. The prisoners are collected in workshops, to the number of ten, twenty, or thirty, according to the size of the room; for the prison is merely an old cloister, and they labour each in a trade under the superintendence of one of themselves. They sleep in similar groups, and have each a separate bed, a straw mattress, two very clean white sheets, a pillow, and a white blanket. In winter there is a large stove in each sleeping room, and also in each workshop. They eat in common, take exercise in the yard in common, and, in short, are under no perceptible restraint, except the prison bars and walls; and look much more like men working quietly in different kinds of production, in a great manufactory, than a collection of desperate criminals undergoing penal sentences. They card wool and flax, spin both, dye the wool, weave both, and dress both the linen and woollen cloth, so as to complete them for use. There are tailors', carpenters', shoemakers', and blacksmiths' workshops; and in none of them is any intelligence, except that of the convicts themselves, employed either to teach or superintend. The bars on the window are so slight, and so many tools are entrusted to the convicts, that escape could be easily accomplished, for outside there is only one soldier, and he cannot see a fourth of the windows; yet the culprits do not break the prison; they obey cheerfully, they work diligently; and there is an air of mental calmness about them that is truly extraordinary. Of course they differ in mental condition and moral expression, as their brains and training vary, but I mean to say that there is a moral calmness even in individuals with the worst brains, and a soft, moral, and intellectual expression in those who have the best brains, and been longest in prison, that speaks unequivocally of the success of their treatment.

"How has all been accomplished? By the genius of one man, Herr VON OBERMAIER! I say genius, because it appears to me that he and such men who are able, by the mere influence of their moral and intellectual faculties, to tame, guide, and instruct the rudest and most brutal of their countrymen, indicate a mental power, original, effective, and beneficient, which works independently of rules, and cannot be communicated, and which may, there-fore, be regarded as genius for the moral government of men. Be this as it may, I proceed to explain his method of treatment.

" 'How do you,' said I, ' deal with a rough, passionate, proud, determined character, who spurns your authority, and means to defy you if he can?' ' Every prisoner,' he replied, ' is brought before me on his entrance, and I converse with him. I ask him if his father or mother be alive; if he has a wife and children, brothers or sisters? and how they must feel degraded by his crime and sentence. I appeal to him through them; I tell him that I am his friend, not his enemy. That I regard him as sent to me to be reformed, and not merely to be punished. I explain to him the rules of the house, and tell him that they are all calculated for the improvement of the prisoners; that if he will be my friend, I shall be his; and that suffering and misery will overtake him here only in consequence of his own fault. The rudest natures,' continued he, ' can rarely resist such an appeal. The big tears often roll down cheeks that were never wet with weeping before, and I soon make them feel that my words are not speeches, but the expression of actual things. I give the new comer into the charge of the superintendent of the department for which he is most fitted, and recommend him to his care as his friend and adviser; and I appeal to the other men in his behalf. Should the new convict, as frequently happens, not believing in the reality of the law of kindness, begin to behave ill to his fellow convicts, they soon check him and set him right. The public spirit among them is in favour of obedience and steady conduct, and they say to him, " That conduct will not do here; Herr VON OBERMAIER is our friend, and we shall not allow you to act contrary to the rules of the house." '

" 'But,' said I, ' at night are not all abominations practised, or how do you restrain them ?' ' You see,' said he, ' that there is a space between each bed; an overseer, one of themselves, whom I can thoroughly trust, is on watch all night, with a bright light burning in every room, and every offence is observed and reported to me. I use persuasion with the offender—punish him by withholding part of his food, or depriving him of some other enjoy-ment—and he generally gives up his misconduct. When the general spirit of the men is directed towards virtue, an individual finds it extremely diffi-cult to persevere in vice in the face of their condemnation.'

" He maintained that criminals cannot be improved by severity, and that an enlightened spirit of humanity, emanating from the Governor, and through every individual of the prison, will supply the most perfect guarantee for obedience, diligence, and individual morality that can be procured. 'If once,' says he, ' the prison is pervaded by a sound public opinion, and the desire of improvement has gained the ascendancy, then the reformed penitents (büsser, for he avoids the word convicts) become such powerful instruments of further improvement that complete security in every department, and for every individual, is established; a security so great that one cannot expect always to find the like of it beyond the walls of the prison. When,' he adds, in large print, 'the whole system of a prison is founded on humanity, the most unbounded confidence in the overseers is the natural consequence; loyalty to the general good speedily becomes the object of all; and when this has once been established gross excesses, scandalous behaviour, and brutality are no longer to be apprehended; in general, they are no longer possible, and become exceptions very rarely occurring.'

" Here, then, we have a prison without classification of prisoners,—without a staff of moral superintendents,—without the prospect of abridged confinement, as a reward for good conduct,—without the lash, the solitary cell, the treadmill, the crank-wheel, pious visitors, or any of the other appliances, regarded as indispensable elements of prison discipline in England, and the place of them all is supplied by the enlightened humanity of one man.

" What conclusion then can be drawn from this example? In my opinion only one: that the spirit of enlightened humanity is the most effective instrument of prison discipline, the cheapest and the safest for the public, and the best adapted to reform offenders. But I do not say that in the hands of every man it is capable, without rules or assistance, of producing such results as I have described. But a man of an analytic and instructed intellect may observe the great principles which such geniuses are seen to follow, and the means by which they carry them into practice; and he may teach these to minds congenial to theirs, although not so highly gifted in self-originating power."

Mr. HILL adds to this narrative the following extract from "Revelations of Prison Life," by G. M. CHESTERTON, as showing the importance of giving encouragement to convicts :—

" Here, let me say, that the utmost care must be taken not to drive criminals, adjudged to undergo the longest sentences, into a state of desperation, by the withdrawal of all hope of alleviation. Perseverance in good conduct, unwearied industry, and perfection in mechanical arts, useful to the establishment, might be made to entitle convicts thus distinguished to an improved condition, to more generous fare, and to privileges of various kinds, graduated by a discreet consideration of what may befit so exceptional a society. My experience has revealed to me the *impossibility* of working exclusively by coercion. You must not, by extremities, reduce to despair; you must improve the disposition and elevate the mind by rational encouragement, assured that kindliness and discriminating mercy will beget suavity, and a grateful recognition evidenced by behaviour."

We shall now proceed to another even more remarkable instance of reformatory action, which was worked out by the late Captain MACHONOCHIE in the penal settlement of Norfolk

Island.   He thus states the principles on which he worked, in
a pamphlet published in Hobart Town, in 1839 :—

" The example of severe suffering, consequent on conviction of crime, has
not hitherto been found very effective in preventing its recurrence; and it
seems probable that the example of *necessary reform*, or, at least, *sustained
submission and self command through a fixed period of probation*, before obtaining release from the restrictions in consequence of such correction, would be
practically more so.   The idea that would be thus presented would be more
definite, more comprehensible, and more humbling to the false pride which
usually attends the early practice of crime, and derives gratification at once
from its successful perpetration, and from the bravado of thereby defying
menaced *vindictive* punishment.   And with reform, as the object of criminal
administration, the better feelings of even the most abandoned criminals
would from the beginning sympathize; whereas, when merely suffering and
degradation are threatened and imposed, it is precisely these better feelings
that both first and last are most revolted and injured by them.

" The sole direct object of secondary punishment should therefore, it is
conceived, be the *reform*, if possible, but, at all events, the adequate subjuga-
tion and training to self command of the individuals subjected to them; so
that, before they can regain their full privileges in society, after once forfeiting
them, they must give satisfactory proof that they again deserve and are not
likely to abuse them.   This principle does not proscribe *punishment, as such*,
which, on the contrary, will, it is believed, be always found indispensable, in
order to induce penitence and submission; nor, as may be already inferred,
does it lose sight of the object of setting a deterring example.   But it raises
the character of both these elements in treatment, placing the first in the
light of a *benevolent means*, whereas it is too often regarded as a *vindictive
end*, and obtaining the second by the exhibition of the law *constantly and
necessarily victorious over individual obstinacy*, instead of frequently defeated
by it.   It cannot be doubted that very much of the harshness and obduracy
of old offenders arises at present from the gratified pride of having braved
the worst that the law can inflict, and maintained an unconquerable will
amidst all its severities; and for this pride there would be no place, if
endurance alone could serve no useful end, and only submission could restore
to freedom.

" The end *reform*, or its substitutes, sustained submission and self command,
being thus made the first objects of secondary punishments, it is next contended that they can only be adequately pursued and tested,—first, by dividing
the processes employed into specific *punishment for the past*, and specific
*training for the future;* and next, by grouping prisoners together, in the latter
stage, in associations made to resemble ordinary life as closely as possible (in
particular, subdivided into smaller parties, or families, as may be agreed to
among the men themselves, with common interests, and receiving wages in
the form of marks of commendation, exchangeable at will for immediate

altogether, we were led at once to the necessity of having police supervision in the country.    We were in a very false position as to the public in general, from not being able to account for the ticket-of-leave convicts.    We felt that we must be able to say where these men were, or it would produce such a panic that the men would never get employment at all.    With regard to the supervision in Dublin, nothing can be more strict, for when anything bad is heard about a man his license is revoked immediately, and there is this fortnightly official list kept as a check.    This is merely a portion or extract from the list (*the same being handed in*); extracts from Mr. ORGAN's usual fortnightly reports; he has not confined himself simply to the prisoners discharged on ticket-of-leave, but he has habitually visited, also, other men who have been discharged under the Penal Servitude Act of 1853, whose sentences had expired, but who still resided in Dublin, over whom we have no legal check, but obtain this information.    He has visited them and placed them on our reports as well as the others; it is of course clear that any of these men unconditionally discharged could have closed their doors against him if they had wished, but this visitation has extended over some 400 or 500 people of this class in Dublin.    It is of importance because it brings a certain knowledge of these people to us that could not be attained in any other way, both as to the result of our system and the lives they were leading.    This report refers to what are called the old Act men—that means men who had been under sentence of transportation, and this document is with reference to men who were under sentence of transportation.    The first case that I come to is that of a man whose crime was burglary, there were former convictions, he had been bad in crime for eight years; there is his name, his residence, his employer's name, and his employment, and his wages.    The date of his conviction was in 1852, and he was discharged from the Convict Prisons the 9th September, 1857, he is still reported upon; he commenced to work at 8s. a week, but now his wages are much higher.    He had been sentenced to ten years' transportation; he was convicted in 1852 and his term expired in 1862, he is still on this list.    In the next case the crime was burglary, former convictions, and for years in crime; he was employed under a public body, his name is given, his residence, and wages; he has been out since the 5th July, 1857.    That was a case of ten years' transportation.    It also gives the general conduct of those men; there are observations to every one of them. I think that there are something like 140 men under the supervision of Mr. ORGAN, in Dublin, at this moment.

"I had, when in office, constant communication with the detective officers in the Dublin police, who were assisting Mr. ORGAN in the supervision of these men.    They were a very material assistance to me in carrying out the supervision.    They took a considerable amount of trouble when a case required it.

"Mr. ORGAN always went to the house of the employer and saw the man and the employer.    The man was sent for and Mr. ORGAN then spoke to him.

"I never heard that the circumstance of his going to visit these men so frequently was a means of discovering to their fellow workmen who they were.

The employers themselves, so far from objecting to his visits, encouraged them, and considered them to a very great extent a protection to themselves.

" The slightest infringement of the conditions of the license leads to a re-vocation of it. *I do not believe—and I have often put this forth when I was in the department—that any case could be proved of a man breaking the conditions of his license in Ireland, and remaining at large; he was sure to be put back to separation, and his license revoked.*

" If we found that a man was within a fortnight of the expiration of his sentence, and had infringed some of the conditions of the ticket-of-leave, we sent that man back to prison, for the sake of the principle. I do not know that it has ever occurred in a case so close as a fortnight, but it has done so close as a month or three weeks. The circumstance of his sentence being so nearly expired did not interfere with that in the slightest degree.

" They were generally easily caught. They were put in the 'Hue and Cry,' a warrant was issued, and there were very few cases in which they baffled us. At first there were a great many shifts and trials to evade, but ultimately and before long, when they found that many had their licenses revoked, and were brought back, they did not even try to baffle us as they did at first.

" In the county prisons, when prisoners are suspected or known to have been convicts, they send up a form containing particulars, with a description of the person suspected or known to be a discharged convict. That comes to the convict prison office, in order that the man may be identified; and very often when it is necessary, if a man at all demurs to his identification, a prison officer is sent down to identify him, and if found guilty of any crime, a letter is in all cases placed on the table of the judical officer, which has been written to the governor of the gaol, the letter being in these terms :—' Govern-ment Prisons' Office.—Sir,—The enclosed particulars of —— —— have been compared with the books of this office, and are correct. In the event of his being found guilty of the present charge the directors of convict prisons request that the notice of the judge may be particularly called to the circum-stance of his being an 'habitual offender,' with the view of his receiving a sentence proportionate to his perseverance in pursuing a course of crime. Please to notify the result of the trial to this office, and return the enclosure at the same time.' This is a case which actually occurred. A man was convicted for picking pockets. He was a convict, and this course was pursued with him. It entailed upon him a sentence of ten years' penal servi-tude. His character as an habitual criminal was taken into consideration by the judge. I am able to speak confidently on two most important points— information with regard to habitual offenders being sent in each case to the county prisons; and in the case of ticket-of-leave men that their licenses have been always revoked for an infringement of the conditions.

" It is not very difficult for an officer in Dublin to recognise a man of whom a description is sent from a provincial town. He has had this man perhaps within the last four or five years in his custody, and besides the general description, and the aid of photography, there is a margin left for observations; practically it is found that very few come into the Convict Prisons who have not been known in some way, and whose identification has not been made. The result is that the practice succeeds in a very great majority of cases, and operates very beneficially upon the minds of the convicts.

" The supervision of convicts in the country is thus carried on through the constabulary. There is a notification made to the inspector-general of the constabulary the moment a man is liberated, stating to what district he is going; the man then registers himself with the head of the police, states what he is going to do, where he is going to be employed, and reports himself to him once a month. If he removes from that district, his registration is transferred from the district he is in at that time, to the one to which he goes, so that he is traced from one place to another. If he does anything to infringe the terms of his license, the constabulary report him, and his license is revoked at once.

" He must come himself once a month, and report himself to the police, but it is evident that the police do not confine themselves to that, for, knowing where he is, they would look after him a little oftener, without interfering with him. I can state from my own experience that there is no undue espionage or oppression practised by the police.

" In the first instance I had a very large number of complaints from the convicts generally; they came almost in a body, stating that they would rather be kept to the end of their sentences than go out with such a stigma; but as it was quite evident that they would have had to remain to the end of their sentences, as they could not get out on any other terms, that feeling very shortly vanished, and they preferred being placed under police supervision. I have seen some hundreds of these people after being subjected to supervision, and with the exception of two cases, in which I recollect complaints being made of interference, nothing detrimental occurred. I state distinctly that in my opinion there has been no undue interference on the part of the police. It is quite probable that some man, when doing wrong, would state that he had been interfered with; but I know in general practice it is not true.

" I am quite sure that if police supervision were withdrawn to-morrow from the licensed convicts in Ireland, you would find but little employment for them, and you would have very serious trouble. I have no doubt that it is a very great protection to the public in Ireland."

Sir WALTER CROFTON's mature opinion respecting this system, is expressed in the following statement to the Commissioners. After speaking of the Intermediate Prisons, he says (3151) :—

"Another great point of difference between the English and the Irish Systems was the institution of supervision after liberation, and here I at once acknowledge what has been adduced against us, 'that there must have been very weak faith on the part of the directors in their own system, when they thought it necessary to supplement it by supervision after liberation.' I acknowledge, and I am sure that my colleagues would do the same, that I have a weak faith in any mere prison system, and I think it is far better, both for the public and the convict himself, to check his prison conduct and the prison system by the infallible test of observation when he is at liberty. During the process of classification I had taken the pains to go through somewhere between 2,000 and 3,000 convict cases, and I satisfied myself from their antecedents, and from other points brought to my notice during this examination, that a very great majority belonged to the criminal class, and would in ordinary course return to thieving. It therefore made it imperative, according to my mind, that we should not treat persons as casual offenders, who are in the convict prisons, but expressly as criminals living in crime by habit and repute. It was therefore necessary to surround, by every possible means, the commission of crime by obstructions. It was quite clear that if you could impress upon the minds of this class that if they pursued a course of crime after liberation, they would be brought back to prison again and have lengthened sentences entailed upon them; if you could tell them confidently that the conditions of the licenses would be enforced, it would serve in a great measure to indoctrinate them with the idea that crime would be unprofitable. I am quite sure that the success of the Irish System has been indebted mainly to a feeling on the part of the convicts from the commencement of their sentences, that they could not follow crime as a vocation with impunity. I believe firmly that the great evils which have occurred in England, and the very great expenditure consequent on crime, has arisen from our believing that the majority of the convicts in the government prisons were casual offenders. I am satisfied that there never was a greater delusion. If the police were taken into consultation, as I have always made a point of taking them into consultation in Ireland, the antecedents of these people would be reliably ascertained, and speaking of England I feel sure that the Commissioners would find that from 70 to 75 per cent. at least live by crime. It is with them a vocation—a business ; and I assert that we have no reason to assume that they are only waiting for employment in order to live honestly ; on the contrary, we are bound to assume, from their former lives, that they will not do so, and therefore should take such precautions as shall protect society against them ; and in the process of protecting society against them, we shall also protect them against themselves, and that I am, from practical experience, prepared to prove. These are the main features of the difference between the two systems, which start from different bases ; but it will observed that the Irish Convict System in its procedure makes cases against itself, and therefore its statistical results cannot be fairly compared with any other system."

These extracts from the evidence of the Chairman of the Board of Directors of the Irish Convict Prisons will have given some idea of the principles on which they are conducted,

and of their general management. The most minute details in
the system having been the subject of deep thought, and the
result of long experience, the evidence of Captain WHITTY,
at that time (March, 1863) sole Director, respecting the dietary,
gratuities, &c., will be valuable. It will be remembered that
Captain WHITTY had been formerly Governor of Portland
Convict Prison. Of his management of that prison the Rev. J.
W. MORAN, who was Chaplain there for five years from its commencement in 1848, speaks in high terms. He says, in his
evidence before the Commission (4745):—"The discipline at
Portland during the years I was there, was in every way
satisfactory. The discipline was such that it was most remarkable and pleasing. Captain WHITTY and I laboured together
there. He was the Governor, as also was Captain KNIGHT,
both of whom are very superior men, and everything was in
the most satisfactory state when I left the prison. There was
not the same number of prisoners then as there is now—viz.,
about 1,500—but between 900 and 1,000." Captain WHITTY
was therefore in a position to perceive and point out the
differences of discipline between the English and the Irish
Convict Prisons. Of this he says, generally,—"I think that
the earlier stages, up to the time that the men come to the
Intermediate Prisons, are certainly more rigid than in England.
That the whole period of confinement in Ireland, up to the
time when they go into the Intermediate Prisons, is a severer
system of punishment than in England."

The following are extracts from his evidence : —

"I think the points in which the Irish System is mainly distinguished
from the English System are, first, the greater stringency in the first period
of the sentence; that is, in the stage of separate confinement, in which the
prisoners in Ireland receive no meat diet for the first four months, and
have no occupation during the first three months but the distasteful labour of
oakum-picking; they receive no gratuity during the period of separate confinement, and that generally extends to eight or nine months. The second
distinction is, a more minute plan of classification on the public works as the
second stage. It consists in the use of a greater number of successive classes
through which the prisoners have to climb, and can thus be more effectually

sifted in their progress, for the purpose of dealing with them individually. Thirdly, there is a lower scale of gratuity in the earlier stages in the Irish Prisons, the higher rates being reserved for the later and superior classes, which makes this an important object of attainment to the prisoners, inducing in them the habit of looking forward, and of exerting and controlling themselves for a future benefit. Fourthly, the Intermediate Prisons, which are a special means of mental improvement, and of preparing the prisoner for the transition from confinement to liberty, and also of testing this preparation. Fifthly, there is a more rigid enforcement of the conditions on which the prisoners are set at large on license; there is a regular supervision, during the period of such licenses, either by the police or by an officer specially employed for the purpose. Sixthly and lastly, there is a process of tracing back, and placing before the judges, &c., the cases of habitual offenders. These appear to me to be the principal points on which the two systems differ." (3687.)

He thus states the system of gratuities in the Irish Prisons :—

" I am afraid I cannot correctly give you the English gratuities; as to the Irish gratuities, I have prepared a memorandum, but one distinction between the English and the Irish classification I should mention. In England, if a man's conduct is good in separate confinement, on being removed to the public works, he goes immediately into the first class; we require our men who go from separate confinement to commence in the third class, but we make this distinction, if they come with a good character they remain for only two months in that third class, whereas, if they come with a bad character they may be nine months in that class; but they all begin in the third class. I will now state what is the largest amount of gratuity which is attainable by a convict under a sentence of four years' penal servitude. I will take a man of the best character; he would be two months in the third class on public works; and eight weeks at a penny per week would amount to 8d. Then he would be for six months in the second class, or 26 weeks, and for those weeks he would get 2d. a week, making 4s. 4d. Then he would be in the first class twelve months, which are divided into two parts; for the first six months, or 26 weeks, he would receive 3d. a week, and during the second six months in the first class, or 26 weeks, he would receive 4d. a week; the first six months at 3d. yielding 6s. 6d., and the second six months at 4d. yielding 8s. 8d., and the two together for the year making 15s. 2d. Then this man would get into the advanced class, and a four years' man without any prison offences, his conduct being satisfactory, would be in that class 26 weeks; he would here receive 9d. a week, which in 26 weeks would amount to 19s. 6d. By that time he ought to have reached the Intermediate Prison. A four years' man is supposed to remain therein for five months before his discharge, these five months, or about 21 weeks at 2s. 6d. a week in the Intermediate Prison, giving £2 12s. 6d.; the total for a four years' man having a claim to a license would be £4 12s. 2d. (3695.)

" The total amount of gratuities that a man can receive in Ireland with a four years' sentence is about half the amount that he could receive under the same sentence in England, supposing that in both cases he earns the maximum." (3698.)

The dietary is a striking contrast to that in the English Convict Prisons :—

" I have an account here of the dietary for one convict at the Mountjoy Male Prison. On reception, for four months, he gets no meat; he gets in a week 3¼ lbs. of oatmeal, 10¼ lbs. of bread, 12¼ pints of milk, 2 ounces of rice, and 4 ounces of vegetables; they also get soup which is made of ox heads, but they get no actual meat given to them at all. They get no potatoes. The solid food in this case is only the oatmeal and the bread, and they would be together 14 lbs., 3½ lbs. of oatmeal and 10¼ lbs. of bread in a week. The oatmeal is made into porridge."

" In the next stage at Mountjoy the ordinary diet for the second four months in separation is oatmeal 3½ lbs., bread 10 lbs., milk 12½ pints, beef 1½ lbs. (weighed before cooking), rice 2 ounces, and vegetables 4 ounces, that is merely for the soup. The meat is boiled and made into soup; they get the meat only on two days in the week, Thursdays and Sundays, and that is at the rate of three-quarters of a pound each day, two days in the week. This dietary has been in force since 1860; it began experimentally; for some time it was tried for one month, and then the medical officer approved of its being tried for two months, and then for three months, and now it is the practice for four months. There were no ill effects produced by that diet. In the case of the small number of prisoners who are confined beyond eight months at Mountjoy, they get 12¼ ounces of oatmeal, 12½ ounces of rice, 11 pints of milk, and they also get coffee for breakfast, and some molasses for sweetening it, 11¼ lbs. of bread, 2 lbs. of beef (weighed before cooking), 4 ounces of vegetables, and 8 ounces of potatoes, that is after the eight months, but those men are put into association, and they work out of doors until they are removed; it is a small number only. There is no other diet given at Mounjoy, except to prisoners under prison discipline, who have bread and water."

" I will now give the dietary at Spike Island. The ordinary diet at Spike Island is 24¼ ounces of oatmeal, 24¼ ounces of rice, 12¼ pints of milk, 13 lbs. of bread, 2 lbs. of beef (weighed before cooking), and two ounces of vegetables. They get meat four times in the week, Tuesdays, Thursdays, Saturdays and Sundays, half-a-pound each day. On the other three days they only get stirabout, bread and milk, on Mondays, Wednesdays and Fridays. In the penal class at Spike Island they get no meat at all. We have two classes there, one called the penal class, and the probation labour class. These last are men who are exceedingly idle, and do nothing but pick oakum. They have a diet without any meat in it at all. They mind their deprivation so much that at present out of 700 men we have only four in that class. A reduction in the diet is very effectual in keeping up the discipline of the prison. I think that the diet at Spike Island is sufficient for the labour that the men perform, to keep them in health and strength. The medical officer never suggests any addition to be made to it. I believe that we have at this time eight in the penal class, four in the probation class, 96 in the third class, and 186 in the second class, 213 in the first class, 115 in advanced class, and 88 in a special class preparing for Intermediate Prisons.

"At Lusk and Smithfield the dietaries are quite different from the others· The Smithfield dietary is 12¼ lbs. of bread, ⅞ of an ounce of tea, 5¼ ounces of sugar, 3⁵⁄₁₆ pints of milk, 34 ounces of beef (weighed before cooking; they have 5 ounces of oatmeal, 5 ounces of vegetables, 10½ lbs. of potatoes, 1¹⁄₁₆ ounce of coffee, a proportion of chicory, and 8⅛ ounces of molasses. That is the Smithfield dietary, and these quantities have all been fixed by the medical officer. The dietary for Lusk is ⅛ of an ounce of tea, ⅔ of an ounce of sugar, 21½ ounces of oatmeal, 21½ ounces of rice, 11¼ lbs. of bread, 7⁴⁄₁₆ pints of milk, 2¼ lbs. of beef (weighed before cooking), they get that divided in in three days in the week), 14 lbs. of potatoes, five ounces of vegetables, 1⅛ ounce of coffee, a proportion of chicory, and 9⅓ ounces of molasses. I think a higher dietary is not given in any prison in England, but I cannot exactly compare the two. We tried to get it lowered, but the medical officer interfered and said that the men were out all day upon an exposed common, and got very wet, and therefore we had to raise it to that. The medical officer said that the health of the men was failing in consequence of their previous diet, and he said that the men required this to keep up their strength."

### With respect to the labour, Captain WHITTY says :—

"We have very little labour done that is capable of measurement; it is principally different kinds of quarrying work, filling up holes, and paring down the surface of the rock to the sea, to shape the fortification, and there is very little of that kind of work that is capable of being measured. We keep the men steadily at work, and we know what the cost of hired labour would be on the spot; we think that we are fairly justified in going near to that sum. Some of the work can be measured, and that is done by the Royal Engineers' department. We have no clerk of the works, as they have in English prisons, and we depend upon the Royal Engineers' department and their clerk of the works, under whom our men are employed, for the measurements. They report to us if the work is not satisfactory. I think that the men work very fairly there, quite as well as the free labourers. We keep a little under the amount given to the free labourers. We value the labour of each man about 1s. 6d. a day. A trifle under the wages of an ordinary labourer for that sort of work. We find out what labourers are employed for at Spike Island, when a contractor hires them. An able-bodied labourer would earn 1s. 8d. a day at Spike Island.

Captain WHITTY is able to state from his personal official knowledge the very important fact, that since he has been

Director of Convict Prisons in Ireland, there has never been anything in the shape of a mutiny or outbreak in them. He also says:—"I have not noticed any mutinous spirit general among them; we have had once or twice a little symptom of dissatisfaction; there have been violent acts done by individuals or by a few, but no combinations or outbreaks. There have been threats made by the men of one county against the men of another, of a sort of faction fight, but we have always managed to put those things down."

It is unnecessary to quote Captain WHITTY's description of the supervision of the licensed Convicts, as that is in every respect similar to what has been already stated by Sir WALTER CROFTON in his evidence. But our account of the working of the Irish Convict System would be incomplete without the personal testimony of Mr. ORGAN, to whom reference has been so often made in connection with the Intermediate Prisons. The cöoperation of a person of zeal, Christian spirit, and sympathising heart, was indispensable in the new and difficult work of supervision over Convicts on license; and at the same time it was essential that such a person should be an official who would strictly conform to the prison regulations, and who, in his labours, which might in a certain sense be termed voluntary, would be still guided by the superior wisdom and judgment of the Directors. Such an individual they were fortunate in finding in Mr. ORGAN, and they have always shown themselves ready to acknowledge his merits. But it would be very erroneous to suppose that he possesses unique qualifications, to which are due the success with which his efforts have been followed, and that it were in vain to hope for the same results if the system were adopted by any other person. Such objection was made, such difficulty started, when Reformatory Schools were first proposed. " Where," it was asked, " shall we find persons who will undertake so unpleasant and difficult a work, or who will have qualifications fitted for it? We know that there are individuals who possess special gifts, and who have had wonderful success in reforming young persons. But where will be found a DEMETZ, a WICHERN? How can we multiply the very few in our own country who have shown equal zeal, and who have had similar success? The Reformatory Schools will be a failure, for we know none who will be able and willing to give themselves to the work." It was answered then, that the work itself would raise up labourers, and prepare them, if faithful and zealous, to be equally successful with those who had first shown them the way. We had confidence in the existence in our country of a sufficient number of able and Christian men and women to afford such help, and our expectations have been realised. The work itself has trained the labourers in it, who humbly desire to be always learners as well as teachers, and who have applied themselves to it with loving hearts and devoted spirits. We cannot then doubt that whenever the Government of our country shall be ready to adopt the system which has been so successful in Ireland, persons will be found to work it with equal zeal and ability, who will encounter fewer difficulties than those which had to be surmounted at the commencement of the new work, because they have the advantage of the experience already acquired. Mr. ORGAN's exertions have obtained for him the esteem of all who are acquainted with them, and we trust that many will be found in our own country to emulate him. We will now, then, turn to his evidence before the Royal Commission. He tells them that he is known in his official position as lecturer to the Irish Intermediate Establishments, an appointment which he has held for more than seven years. His previous occupation was that of Superintendent of the adult evening schools in Dublin. "From early boyhood," he says, "I have been accustomed to appear as a teacher of adult labourers, who, after the close of their daily toil, repaired to the night schools over which I presided, and I have seen those men anxiously embracing the opportunity they had in an evening, but I have never seen greater anxiety or eagerness displayed to improve themselves by men of the non-criminal class than amongst the men from Smithfield and Lusk. Although they do hard work during the day, I have found no difficulty in inducing them to receive instruction for a certain limited time in the evening. They look forward to my going in amongst them with a kind of delight. My duties are to bring before the Convicts of Smithfield and Lusk subjects that are calculated to make them thinking beings. I speak to them upon social questions, such as taxes, strikes, combinations, illegal societies, industry, and honesty ; what they have to gain by the commission of crime, and what they have to lose, that is, in a temporal point of view, because I do not allow myself for a moment to infringe upon the duties of any of the respective chaplains. I have before me a copy of a little work of mine, containing the lectures which I deliver to the men, both at Smithfield and at Lusk. The subjects in this little book are— Air ; Water ; Plants ; Canada and her resources ; the Ocean ; Temperance and Self - control ; Australia, past and present ; Life, its battles, and how to fight them. My duties are not confined merely to giving lectures, but I exercise a supervision over the discharged Convicts. In addition to that I endeavour to procure employment for these men."

To understand the nature of Mr. ORGAN's work, and his mode of executing it, we must follow him in his details of it :—

" At the outset it was a labour of great difficulty to procure employment for those men on their discharge. I commenced my duties in February, 1856. I drew out a map of the county of Dublin, dividing it into baronies, laying down upon this map the different post towns, also the mills, and factories, and farms, showing the names of the proprietors, the nature of those works, and so on. Having done this, I set out to see such and such employer. Sometimes I was scoffed at, and on more than one occasion the hall door was closed in my face. Still I persevered, and I was very well satisfied, if, after going a distance of 40 or 50 miles, I should meet with one employer who would give one of my Smithfield men a chance to work out his character once more.

When I secured one, I visited both the employer and the employed, and I continue to do so down to the present time. The employer would ask me what control I had, or the government had, over the men. I, of course, explained, but I will give a case in point. Some five years ago I went to a gentleman who was a very large employer, and I saw him. I explained to him my mission. I was a long time in inducing him to give me a chance, but after many repeated visits I did succeed. He took one man. I visited that man once a fortnight, although he had removed from Dublin a distance of ten miles, and I visited the employer. That man succeeded in giving the employer satisfaction, and the employer afterwards applied for another, afterwards for another, and previous to my leaving Dublin this employer wrote the following letter, dated 21st February, 1863 :—' Dear Sir,—In reply to your letter, I beg leave to state that it was at your earnest solicitation that I was induced to take convicts into my employment, in the first instance. I have now had fully five years' experience of them, during which time they have given me universal satisfaction. I have one at present in my employment, in whose honesty I have such confidence that I have made him a sort of watchman, and he has for the last few days detected parties robbing me. Another saved enough to enable him to emigrate to Australia. A third, in shovelling up some manure, found a silver spoon, which he at once gave me. In conclusion I can only say that whenever you have an able-bodied man whom you can recommend, it will afford me much pleasure to give him employment.' This employer was one whom I secured, I assure you, after a great deal of trouble, through the character and conduct of the first man he had employed. I found great difficulty at first in procuring employment for them, but that difficulty has diminished since the employers have had experience of the men. Since such employers as these have been found, the difficulty, of course, does not exist now to so great an extent; but I think that, if I were to go over the same task again with other employers, I should have the same difficulty to encounter.

" My bi-monthly visits are valued very much by employers, who frequently say to me, ' I do not like to speak to the man for doing so and so. You had better do so; he will attend more to what you say than what I say.' I have frequently, in a country place, got 9 or 10 of these men behind a hayrick, and advise them what to do; in many cases they take a greater interest in their employment than ordinary workmen do, because they know that the employers have taken them out of prison, and thrown, as it were, a cloak of protection over them.

" I do not find that there is any sympathy with the criminals amongst the honest classes in Ireland, that would induce them the more readily to take these convicts into employment.

" In my supervision of the convicts who are placed under my charge, I communicate with the detective police on some occasions. I will explain the nature of my supervision, showing how the detective police and I work hand in hand. This letter which I am about to read explains the matter fully :—

'13, Richmond Fair View, Co. Dublin,
'January 10, 1863.

' Sir,—In reply to your inquiry as to my opinion of the working of the ticket-of-leave system in Ireland, I beg leave to submit the following statement of my practical experience day and night of the Smithfield men discharged on license and otherwise, and working and residing in the city and county of Dublin. It is perhaps necessary that I should state that I have been a detective police officer for eleven years, and therefore had an opportunity of making myself acquainted with the working of the new and old system of convict management in Ireland. My experience of the old system was of a most painful character, for the criminals came out of prison worse in fact than they entered, whereas on the other hand I have known very bad characters when discharged from your Intermediate Prisons to engage in steady labour, earning their bread, and absorbed amongst the honest members of the working community. It must have been only by perseverance that any Irish employer of respectable position could be induced to take into his work men who had been habitual thieves and burglars, for the aversion of all men of respectability in Ireland to employ convicts is very great. By this constant intercourse with the directors and yourself, I have on very many occasions been enabled to prevent the commission of additional crime, by visiting the abodes of the persons we had reason to believe intended doing wrong. I have never known a man discharged, and under your supervision, to be convicted of any act bordering upon violence on the person. I think the fact of a numerous and influential class of employers who have many of your discharged convicts in their establishments, is a proof of the great good which has resulted from the working of the Irish Convict System. I am prepared and willing at any time to give information in detail whenever circumstances may require me to do so.

'I remain, &c.,
' TIMOTHY MURPHY,
' Late Acting Inspector, Detective Depart-
ment, Dublin Metropolitan Police.

' To James P. Organ, Esq.,
5, Mespil, Co., Dublin.'

" I divide my visitation reports into three parts, one showing the number under the old Transportation Act; the next showing the number unconditionally discharged, over whom the Government have no control; and the next relates to the Penal Servitude Act of 1857, that gave those short sentences. I will now explain the nature of my supervision. In the visitation form of report there are columns showing, first, the date of a man's conviction, the length of his sentence, the date of his discharge from Smithfield or Lusk, the nature of his last crime, the number of former convictions recorded against him, his name, his residence, the name of his employer, the nature of his employment, the wages which he receives per week, the date if on ticket-of-leave, the date of his time being fully up, and in the margin is a remark upon each man which is made by me. Here is a case, for instance, of a man who was sentenced for ten years for receiving stolen goods, and having under his pillow a blunderbuss; his former character is this,—' A terror to the neighbourhood in which he resides'; his residence is about four miles from Dublin; his employer is Mr. So-and-so; he has remained with that employer since the 9th of April, 1856; he has been from that hour under my supervision; and my last remark was this,—' A man of sober and settled habits, with Mr. So-and-so for the last seven years, wife sober and industrious, has a pig and fowl.' With that kind of connection that exists between me and the discharged convicts, we are not ashamed to know one another, provided no one sees us. I provide employment for all who cannot secure it for themselves.

"Now I will refer to the men under the Act of 1857. The first man on my list was discharged on the 6th of February, 1861; felony was his last crime ; he had been 13 times convicted before, and had been known as a thief since 1845; his name and residence are here put down, and his employment, as before; he was last sentenced to four years; the observation is 'Keeping from crime, contrary to the opinion of many who knew him before.' He has been discharged two years and more now. He is in employment. I know his antecedents, that he was an habitual thief, but in the eleventh hour he gave it up.

"Referring to the connexion between the police and myself, when I find that a man is not going on according to my liking, and he has something suspicious about him, I go to the director, and I either bring the man up if within reach, or tell him about it. I say, ' I do not like the way in which this man is going on;' he may have too smooth an appearance for a hard-working man, or he may be lounging about, or I might find him in his home when he should be out working, or out when he should be in ; then the director takes a note of that; at the same time, if it happens that my suspicions are aroused at night, or when the director is not in the office, and the case is an urgent one, I do not wait for the director to come the following morning, but I go straight to the detective office at the castle-yard; I there tell the officiating inspector my doubts, and he, as a matter of course, has a close eye upon that man. Then in cases of suspicion I inform the detective authorities; they know that it is their interest and my interest to work hand-in-hand; and I point out to them sometimes, when I have my documents convenient, the last observation I have made upon the man."

It is very important to observe the manner in which voluntary benevolent effort may thus cöoperate with police agency. Mr. O. gives also a valuable testimony to the value of the control thus exercised over the Convicts to the men themselves, by enabling them more easily to get employment. He says :—

"The employers invariably prefer the ticket-of-leave men to convicts who are unconditionally discharged, because they are under more control. The question generally put by employers who have wealth and loose property lying about is, ' How long have the Government control over these men ?' They are always led in a very great degree by the number of years yet to run. Among the list of persons who have employed men who had been discharged from the Intermediate Prisons there are English employers in my district, and they are more generous, in fact, than the Irish. I have found no difficulty in getting English employers to give employment to these men, much less than with the Irish. With regard to any Englishman that I came across, I must say, although I may seem to speak against my own country, that he deals with me more generously. Among those men for whom I have obtained employment there were habitual criminals who had been committing crime for years. I have a case here in which there are 15 reconvictions against a man, and many cases in which there had been varying numbers of previous convictions. Now these men to whom I have referred are not all robbing; I see them every day at hard work. I keep up a regular visitation, and in point of fact I have never done. Those who are released on license are bound to report themselves to me in the same manner as those who are in the country are bound to report themselves to the constabulary. But I do not confine myself to the reports which are made to me by these men. I prefer visiting them at their own homes, and speaking to their employers. I always wish to obtain the opinion of the employer of a man from the employer himself. The police do not exercise any supervison over the convicts in Dublin, except what I have mentioned in the suspicious cases.

" I explain to the persons who employ these men, the control which the Government has over them whilst they are holders of a ticket-of-leave. I always lay the facts clearly before the employers, because if I were not straightforward with them, and I was once detected, I should never be able to show my face again. So that the employers are aware that these men whom they take into their service have been previously in the Convict Prisons. But the men with whom they work are not always aware of that fact. It is the interest of the employers to keep the other workmen in ignorance of the fact; and there is another thing, that if the honest workmen were to know this, I am sure they would take objection to it, and make the place too hot for a discharged prisoner. No difficulty has been found in keeping the matter concealed from the other workmen. The employer always does so. He communicates with me privately, and the other workmen are not acquainted with the characters of the men or their previous mode of life.

" I do not find any indisposition on their part to continue this intercourse with me, which they were obliged to keep up while under their tickets-of-leave; on the contrary, they appear to be grateful for what I have done for them. The success of the system very greatly depends upon its being possible to prevent the men who have been discharged from being recognised as former convicts, but in every case to let the employer know all about them. Also it proves that the Irish are not more tender in their feelings towards criminals than the English.

"The subject of industry very frequently engages our attention, and it is my duty, at least I think so, to explain the state of the home labour market and the foreign market. We never induce, compel, or urge any men to emigrate, and no man emigrates except through a matter of choice; but how does he emigrate? In Smithfield, across the rafters, I have the model of a ship and sails, and I get my young fellows more or less up in the practical working of a ship, and give them a knowledge of the technical terms of the rigging, and so on, and this cultivates in them a taste for the sea; and if they emigrate, they emigrate in this way, that some of them pay part of their passage, and work out the remainder. Some work their passage out. They do not emigrate except as a matter of choice. I do certainly point out to them, as far as I am able, the great advantages of breaking with their former companions, of concealing their shame, and of going where their antecedents are not known. I have a letter here in which one of them writes home for the purpose of bringing his brother and sister out; his brother is a convict at the present time; he himself worked out his passage to some part of America, and he has been writing home now for the purpose of bringing out his brother, and offering money to help the brother out.

"Those who go into the country and have their own friends or their own relations procure employment, I suppose, through them. We have the means of knowing what they are at because they write for their gratuities, and when they do that, or for the balance, they state with whom they are working, and they get no part of their gratuities unless the police authorities, or the head constable to whom each convict reports himself, certifies on the back of the letter that the man wants the money for a useful purpose, that his conduct is good, and that he is being employed by so-and-so. I have nothing to do with the payment of the gratuities except to recommend. For example, suppose I knew that a man wanted to purchase a pig, or to buy a bed or a suit of clothes, I write and say, 'I beg respectfully to recommend that this man may get so-and-so,' knowing that he intends to apply it to a useful purpose. This would apply to the men under my supervision; the police do that with regard to those men who are under their supervision. To those who go abroad the gratuities are paid at once, when it is fully understood that they are going.

"I have known cases in which the old associates of convicts have endeavoured to use their power over them, and from a fear of being betrayed to extort money from them. I have seen their former companions waiting in knots on the morning of their discharge, and endeavouring to induce them to go with them. I have known their former associates to come up 100 miles from different parts of Ireland in order to meet them on the morning of their discharge, and induce them to follow them. When men are of the principle of Reformatory Schools, apparently under the erroneous supposition that the same leading features exist in these as in the Government Prisons. The term "reformatory system" in reference to the Convict Prisons is inapplicable, because, as will be shown in this chapter, not only have they entirely failed in effecting reformation in their inmates, but because the principles on which they are conducted are totally at variance with those the soundness of which has been tested by the important experiments recorded in the last chapter, and which we, the Managers of Reformatories, have also proved to be true during the last ten years.

Whatever difference of opinion may be entertained respecting the true nature of reformatory treatment, we have a right to expect that a sentence of the law intended as the highest secondary punishment, shall be more severe than one pronounced on ordinary offenders; that the Convict Prisons shall be far more to be dreaded than county gaols. We know that in most of these a strict discipline is administered, as it should be; and we expect to find the treatment in the prisons for hardened offenders far more severe. What is our astonishment at learning from the evidence given to the Commission (824), that criminals prefer a sentence of three or four years' penal servitude to 18 months' or two years' imprisonment; and to find that the Chairman of the Directors of Convict Prisons attributes this circumstance "*to the fact that it is much milder discipline than exists in the county prisons*" (825). We are even more astonished to hear the following admission made respecting the treatment of those whom the public supposes to be undergoing the most severe secondary punishment the law awards in Convict Prisons; persons who have committed serious offences against society, or have persevered in a course of evil doing:—" *Convicts and the criminal population are aware that they are considerately treated*, and they must be. There are only two ways of dealing with men,— either to drive them or to lead them. If you drive them, *the public suffer from the effects of the demoralization, and if you lead them they gain by a large proportion being reformed*" (828). This statement, being made by the Chief Director, must be regarded as an authoritative declaration of the principles on which the Convicts are treated. It is made in reference to the dietary, but it underlies the whole system. A similar statement is made respecting labour :—"If you put a man to penal labour, it would interfere with the moral effect, and with the objects you had in view in training him for ultimate release" (834). "It (a deterring stage) would interfere in a great measure with the industrial and moral training of the larger proportion of the men" (833). We find (828) that "The object for which penal servitude as it now exists, and it has existed since it was introduced in 1848, was to train men for their release, either at home or abroad. Looking to the length of the sentences and the circumstances, the penal features were diminished, and the greater effort was thrown into the industrial training and the endeavour to reform." It is then here and elsewhere assumed that a man who has committed heinous crimes, will best be reformed by gratifying his wishes, instead of making him feel the consequences of his conduct; that he will be prepared for release into society, where he must expect difficulties and hardships, by shielding him from them in the place of his punishment !

The object of punishment will indeed be most completely answered if evil doers are prepared to be useful members of society " at home or abroad." Such is our object of course in the Reformatory Schools; though these are not regarded as penal establishments, we endeavour to maintain in them such *steady discipline* as may appear right and best to attain the end, without considering whether our scholars regard our restrictions or treatment irksome, and without endeavouring to lead them to obedience by indulgence of their appetites. We frame such regulations as appear to us best calculated to effect our end, and make strict justice and ready obedience the basis of them. Though we do not wish to make our dietary lower than is beneficial to the health and physical development of working boys and girls,—though we take care to have the food carefully prepared for them, so as to enable them to feel that relish for it which will promote digestion,—yet we should consider it very wrong to give to these children more palatable and abundant food than is procurable or found necessary by the labouring population in general, nor should we ever try to lead them by succumbing to their wishes. Finding such discipline necessary, even for young persons, when we learn that penal servitude is intended not only as a punishment, but as a preparation for a life of liberty, we are surprised to find it stated that men, *i.e., the Convicts, must either be driven or led !* Is that the order of society? Is it the principle of the government of our country to drive men, like the subjects of a despot, or to bribe and coax them into abstinence from rebellion? Will the Convicts when at large, either at home or abroad, find such the treatment they will receive from their fellow men? This system of "leading" Convicts is simply inducing them to submit to control, and to assume good prison conduct. The Director tells us, indeed, that the criminal population are *aware* that they are "treated considerately," and *they must be ;* for that if they are driven, when in penal servitude, "the public suffer from the effects of the demoralization," which we must interpret to mean, the Convict Prisons will be a constant scene of that rebellion and violence of which the public so often hears. If the first stage of their imprisonment is made penal, and if they have unattractive labour which they are obliged to perform, their minds, it is said, will be irritated, and they will not be in a fit state to receive the moral counsels and religious instruction which are intended to reform them. It is evident that a system founded on such indulgence and such avowed consideration of the wishes of the criminal classes, can neither be deterrent to them nor truly reformatory; the penal element of suffering as the consequence of sin is avowedly rejected, and nothing is substituted which will stimulate the culprit to that earnest effort to reform his life of which we spoke in the preceding chapter. However good the machinery adopted in these prisons, so erroneous a principle must be fatal to the success of its operations.

Before proceeding to consider the actual working of the English Convict Prisons, we must draw attention to another of the principles adopted in them which appears erroneous. The expression is often used by the chief Director and various officers in their evidence, that some kinds of work are more "reformatory" than others, and that under certain conditions the effect of the work is more reformatory than under others. It is difficult to understand what is really meant by work being in itself "reformatory." Reformation must spring from the inner spirit;— all judicious means which are likely to help in the work of reformation should of course be employed, and to be chosen rather than others which would not lead to that object. But how the selection of the most agreeable kind of work can help a Convict in his reformation we cannot conceive. If he has made the very first step towards a change of heart, as evinced in a better life,—if he is at all penitent for the evil he has inflicted on society, as well as the sin he has committed against God,—then the simplest evidence of this that he can give will be to perform willingly the very lowest drudgery,—to accept the least inviting food as more than he deserves,—to yield a cheerful obedience to the strictest regulations. If work is done in this spirit, reformation is going on, and the labour may be called reformatory. But we find no indication of any such meaning of the term so frequently used in this evidence. There is, on the contrary, everywhere traceable that spirit of consideration of the comfort and wishes of the criminal class which is in many passages distinctly avowed;—that labour is selected which they *like* the best on the ground that it is more "reformatory," but really because there is less difficulty in inducing the men to perform it, and it is therefore more profitable to the treasury. Work given under such conditions, and with such an evident object in view

as pecuniary interest, must be regarded as the very contrary
of "reformatory." These men are thus led quite to forget
their crime, and the debt they are under to society, which
would make the severest and least inviting labour their due;
—they find that though an honest man must take such labour
and means of maintenance as he can get, and be thankful for
it, yet they who are professedly suffering punishment for doing
their own will rather than their duty, are now to have their
wills considered in the selection of their occupation;—they
probably perceive too, very clearly, that other motives guide
in the arrangement of their occupations, than the sole object
of letting the law be a terror to evil doers beyond the prison
walls, and of bringing those within them to the condition of
obedient, self-denying, hard-working citizens. These remarks
are illustrated by the evidence of one of the Directors of the
Convict Prisons:—

"4208.—You stated in the early part of your evidence that you thought
the work done by the convicts at Portsmouth was less satisfactory than
that which was done at Portland and at Chatham?—Yes.

"4209.—Will you be so good as to give some further explanation of the
difference between the two?—The reason is because it is dockyard work;
there you see the men, or many of them, employed piling up timber, while
others of them are harnessed to carts like horses, dragging the carts about;
that is a kind of work in which you cannot engage the men's minds, nor get
them to take any *interest* in the work they are doing—they are more like
beasts of burden dragging carts about. It is well known that at Portland and
Chatham, and particularly at Portland, the men take the greatest possible
interest in their work, and they work like cart-horses. On the Verne works,
if, through any accident, there have been any wrong instructions given, the
*officers find the greatest possible difficulty in getting the men to pull their work
to pieces.* At Portsmouth, on the contrary, the men are mixing amongst all
the labourers and sailors while they are dragging cartloads of timber about
and doing other similar work; they are also employed in *cleaning chain cables
and picking junk and oakum, but, as I said before, that is not work which
engages the attention and the goodwill of the man.*"

We may doubt the expediency of making the Convicts drag
carts, if this is done so as to degrade them to the level of the
lower animals; we may also consider it injurious to sailors

and labourers to be exposed to contamination by working among
felons, and injurious to the Convicts to be tempted to communicate with free labourers; but what what must we think of really
useful labour being here objected to because it does not engage
the goodwill of the Convict!

"4210.—What effect do you infer from the fact of one class of work
being less *interesting* than another? Do you mean to convey this impression
to the Commission that you consider the labour is less reformatory?—It is
not only less reformatory, but it is less satisfactory in every point of view.
I mean *that it does not do the same good to the men themselves, nor to the
establishment.*

"4211.—*By good to the establishment you refer to productive labour?*—*Yes.*

"4212.—By good to the men you refer to the reformatory effect, and you
think that the more *interesting* the *work is the more likely that work is to
be reformatory in its effects?*—*Yes.* * * *

"4213.—With regard to the penal character of the work, which should
you say was the most irksome to the individual, the work at Portsmouth,
or the work at the other prisons?—I think the work at Portsmouth is the
most irksome.

"4214.—Is it the most penal?—I do not think the word penal is quite
the right word. I think it is the most irksome; but I do not think therefore
that it is the most penal."

We should have supposed that whatever useful work was
the most irksome in its nature ought to be given to those who
were in the lowest stage of penal discipline. In another part of
the same evidence "distasteful" diet and unattractive labour
are proposed for those who are deemed incorrigibles;—if that
which is "interesting" is the most "reformatory," surely such
would be desirable for those who most need reformation, and
who are here termed "incorrigibles."

"4263.—In some part of your evidence you stated that you thought it
was desirable that this class of persons so thrown into a prison for incorrigibles should be subjected to the most stringent penal discipline?—Yes,
I did.

"4264.—Will you give the Commission some idea of the sort of discipline
which you think would be applicable to such a class?—In the first place,
the diet should be, after being properly verified by the medical officer, one
that would be anything but tasteful to the prisoner, indeed, it should be
as *distasteful* as possible. Those prisoners should also have work to perform
which would not be the kind of work the prisoners labour at on the public

works, and I would not allow them to work together, but to work alone.
I would not let them exercise together, and they should have no remission
of sentence."

Thus all the treatment which is elsewhere called reformatory,
everything which was considered a stimulus to good conduct, is
withdrawn from these men, who most want reformation. There
is a latent distrust in the soundness of the principle in those
who profess it. Such inconsistencies necessarily arise when
the fundamental principles already stated are lost sight of;
when a system is not adopted which really enlists men in
their own reformation, while at the same time a firm, steady,
just discipline, removes temptation to evade the law.

The general arrangement of the time of penal servitude is
as follows :—The first 12 months are spent in the separate
prisons of Pentonville or Millbank, in solitude. This period
may be shortened to 10 months. During this time special
attention is paid to the prisoners' intellectual instruction and
religious teaching. They are then transferred to the Public
Works' Prisons; in which there are three stages. The prisoner
enters in the lowest,—in which there are three classes. In the
lowest class the man wears no stripe; in the second, one; in
the first, two. If a man sentenced to four years is in the
first class of the first stage at the end of a year, he is raised
to the second stage, in which he wears two blue stripes, in
addition to the two red. If, during the whole time he is in
the second stage he is perfectly well-conducted and gets V. G.
for labour for a year, he arrives at the third stage, in which
he wears a different dress and has some further little privileges.
When the specified time comes for the minimum period of
his sentence, he is recommended for remission of time ; all
forfeitures of time he has had recorded against him are
deducted from it. If a man has been very well-conducted
for a long time, and the Governor submits his case to the
Director, the latter judges whether any of the time he had
lost by misconduct should be given back to him. If he is

degraded to the third class, it takes a man three months to
get to the second class, and three months more to get to the
first class.    There are, then, three stages on the public works,
and a prisoner's full time there is divided into three stages,
dating from the end of the year of his sentence, which is
intended to be spent in solitude ; the time is shortened in
a certain proportion relatively to the length of his sentence,
if he does not forfeit the remission by idleness or misconduct;
and these are often punished by forfeiture of the remission
otherwise made.    The remission of a certain portion of his time
is therefore regarded by the prisoner as a *right*, unless he forfeits
it by gross misconduct.

The first stages of punishment in Pentonville and Millbank
being in separation, do not naturally vary from the system
which has been long before the public.    This period is considered as especially reformatory, on account of the religious
and secular instruction there given.    That this has not the effect
anticipated will appear as we proceed.    After the Convicts have
spent a longer or shorter time in these separate prisons, according to their conduct, they are transferred to the Public Works'
Prisons at Portland, Chatham, Woking, Dartmoor, Broadmoor.
Dartmoor is intended for those whose health is believed to be
unequal to the hard work required at Portland and Chatham;
Broadmoor is for those whose intellect is somewhat unsound.
The general system adopted in all is much the same; either
Chatham or Portland will therefore be selected, as either is
mentioned by the witnesses.

Chatham Prison is calculated for 1100 prisoners, each having
a separate cell.    The staff is as follows :—

| | |
|---|---|
| A GOVERNOR, | A CHIEF WARDER, |
| A DEPUTY-GOVERNOR, | SIX PRINCIPAL WARDERS, |
| A CHAPLAIN, | A HUNDRED WARDERS, |
| AN ASSISTANT CHAPLAIN, | A MEDICAL OFFICER, |
| A SCRIPTURE READER, | AN ASSISTANT MEDICAL OFFICER, |
| FOUR SCHOOLMASTERS, | A COOK, |

in all 119 officers, or, exclusive of the Governors, Chaplains and

Medical Officers, one to every ten prisoners. This does not appear to include the teachers of trades which are carried on in the prison, and for which there are doubtless skilled instructors. The prisoners are generally divided into 72 parties, including the prison parties, cooks, bakers, tailors, shoemakers and artizans. On the public works there are generally employed 55 or 60 parties. The number of men in each party varies, according to the nature of the work they are employed upon, from 10 to 25 ; a disciplined officer or warder is with each party; if the nature of the work renders it more desirable, and there is an officer to spare, he is attached to a large party. There is a principal officer to each district; the works are divided into so many districts. The Deputy-Governor visits the working parties every day.

The Governor states that it is the duty of the warders to see that the prisoners exert themselves. "After an experience of about six years," he says (998), "I believe that they work quite as well as free men paid by the day, as far as their strength admits and their capabilities." How far this is the opinion of others, we shall presently see. "We look upon the willingness for work—not the exact amount of work done." The officer in charge of each party puts V. G. against the name of each man if he is satisfied with his work, and this entry is checked by the principal warder. "If an officer considers that a man for any length of time is idle, he reports him to me," continues the Governor, "for being habitually idle. He will report him even if he is occasionally idle, and if he is idle to any extent he will make an entry to that effect in his book, and that man will be reported and he will be punished for it." "The punishment would depend on the previous character of the man, whether he was at the time in the first or second class. If he was a first-class man and it was his first report, he would, perhaps, be suspended from his classes for 28 days, to give him a trial, to see if he would improve. It would entail, perhaps, a forfeiture of about seven days of his remission, and he might recover, by subsequent good conduct, a portion of that, and that would depend again upon his after conduct."

The discipline and routine of Chatham Prison is derived from the evidence of the Governor, this being nearly the same as other Public Works Prisons.

The following is the *Time Table* as arranged for the summer:—

A.M.  5  0.—First bell rings.  Prisoners rise and muster, wash themselves, and clean the cells and the wards.  Breakfasts served out.

    5 45.—Breakfast.  Each man in his own cell.

    6 15.—Cells unlocked, and the prisoners taken to Chapel for prayers.  " The unlocking and marching to Chapel, the time they are at prayers, and the marching from Chapel again, occupies as as nearly as possible half an hour.  The service does not last above from ten minutes to a quarter of an hour."

    6 45.—Prisoners marched back to parade, and going to the working ground.  Marching back and serving dinners.  Work.

P.M. 12 15.—Dinner in cells.

    1 15.—Mustered, and marched to work.  Work.  March back.

    6  0.—Cells.  Take off working slops.  Go to Chapel.  At Chapel.  Return to cells.

    6 30.—Supper.

    7  0.—Cleaning shoes, shaving, changing any clothing that may be requisite, emptying slops, &c., and reading.

    7 45.—Take down hammocks, and go to bed.

    8  0.—Lights put out.  The third stage men are permitted to have a light an hour later.

In the dark months the prisoners rise half an hour later, going out to labour as soon as it is light, and returning earlier, so as to have a longer time for reading in the evening.

The following is the dietary of Portland Prison, as stated by the chief Director to have been approved by the Secretary of State (547).  "They proposed a diet table, which gave for breakfast one pint of tea, made with $\frac{1}{6}$ of an ounce of tea, on alternate days, sweetened with $\frac{3}{4}$ an ounce of raw sugar, with one pint of cocoa made from $\frac{3}{4}$ an ounce of cocoa, and $\frac{3}{4}$ an ounce of molasses and two ounces of milk daily; twelve ounces of bread for breakfast; for dinner, six ounces of cooked meat without bone, one pound of potatoes, six ounces of bread; for supper, one pint of oatmeal gruel, six ounces of bread;

on Mondays, Wednesdays and Fridays, for dinner, one pint of soup, one pound of potatoes, six ounces of bread."

Surely few labouring men either could afford, or would eat if they could, so large a dinner as is given to these Convicts four days in the week, one of these being Sunday, when the plea of hard work is not available. Nor, we presume, would labouring men allow themselves even on alternate days tea in *addition* to a pint of cocoa, made so substantial as this must be, a pound of cocoa and one of molasses being used for every twenty persons. We know that good and palatable cocoa can be prepared for Reformatory boys and girls, with a pound of cocoa and a quarter of a pound of sugar for every fifty. This is the ordinary dietary in Chatham Prison also, and the Convict Prisons for public works in general are on the same system. The Governor of Chatham Prison states in his evidence (1039 and 1040) that the prisoners in the second and third stages have "three ounces of bread and two ounces of cheese extra on Sunday, and half-a-pint of beer or porter in the third stage. They get a small suet pudding once a week on the Thursday; that is all as to their diet. There is one difference that I have not before mentioned; they get their meat roasted instead of boiled four times a week, and twice they have mutton instead of beef."

There is one cook in the establishment, and twelve prisoners are appointed to act as cooks under him, who are selected for their good conduct. The prisoners have their dinners served out to them by the other prisoners who are orderlies, and are every day told off in rotation to take that duty. Six are told off to each ward; 96 is the total number. A warder superintends each ward, and the dinners are placed at the doors of the cells, when each prisoner takes in his own. At times, in spite of the utmost vigilance of the officers, some of the orderlies abstract a portion of the meat before it is delivered to the prisoners; thus the dinner is not full weight. If the prisoner suspects that his dinner is deficient in quantity, when he takes out his meat,

which he does in the presence of the officer, before he takes it
into his cell, he says, "This is not my full weight, I must have
it weighed;" it is always weighed when a prisoner demands it.
The Governor says, "There are perhaps three or four cases
daily, but I do not suppose that we average six daily throughout
the year." When asked if he has reason to suppose that this
is done by ill-disposed prisoners for the purpose of vexation?
(1082) he replies, "I do not say that I have never known an
instance of that. I think that the men will sometimes incline
to be very annoying to the officers, and they may perhaps do it
more frequently out of viciousness, for there are prisoners who
will do anything that they dare to do to annoy the officers sometimes, but that is so exceptional that it is not worth taking
into account."

Great stress is laid by the chief Director on the prisoners
not being allowed to be in association. He appears quite
unaware how impossible it is to effect this. The men are of
course kept in their separate cells during the time when they
are not in Chapel or at work and prison duty. At Chapel they
would not be allowed to speak, but they are, however, in
sight of each other. Officers are present, who are raised
above them, to report any misconduct they observe. Still it
is impossible, when 1100 men are massed together, for any
ordinary staff of officers entirely to prevent conversation carried
on in an underhand manner, or secret communication between
ill-disposed prisoners. On the public works, however (1105),
the prisoners are allowed to converse quietly with each other;
any loose talking or laughing is forbidden. The warder is
supposed to be close to them and to hear what they say, but
it is evidently impossible for one warder to know what a whole
gang of from 10 to 25 men may be saying to each other. As it
is found that whispering cannot be prevented, that is not forbidden, and is not considered out of order.

Again, the warder is supposed to check all communication with
the outer world. How much there must have been before the

Chatham mutiny, the Governor himself testifies; how many things are secretly brought in to the prisoners is well known. There is no room for astonishment that this is the case, because whatever may be in theory the system of the Public Works Prisons the existing arrangements in these preclude the possibility of effecting any real separation of the Convicts from the outer world. We have already been told that at Portsmouth the Convicts work with free labourers. Mr. EVANS tells us (5990,1,2) on the Verne Batteries a portion of the casemated barracks is being done by free labourers, who work separately, but still within a few yards of the Convicts, and near enough to speak to them.

During the whole time that the prisoners are at work then, between eight and nine hours every day, they have the power of conversing with each other, though very quietly and without apparent breaches of decorum. The glaring profanity and open vice of the hulks, of which the Rev. J. DAVIS, the Ordinary of Newgate, says, "the conversation in those hulks was horrid," is indeed here suppressed. But the whispered communication of those criminal experiences and unholy thoughts which fill the minds of depraved Convicts must be even more dangerous, because less under the check of public opinion. Who can tell what lessons in crime, what subtle poison to the soul, is poured into no unwilling ears when the men are apparently engaged in work. Who knows what plots are formed when the men are crowded together under the sheds, if rain compels them to leave their work, and only a portion of them have occupation in stone-breaking. Thus doubtless have the prison mutinies been planned. What subjects of thought are suggested to those ignorant and impure minds during the long hours which they must afterwards pass alone in their solitary cells? Mr. DAVIS, the Chaplain of Newgate, truly says, "Where persons are brought up without anything like a well-regulated education, they fall into the habits or ways of those with whom they associate; and those wretched persons whom they meet with, and who are more depraved than they are, feel no shame in doing such kind of dreadful acts as they commit, and *the others are very much injured by their conversation*, their minds become more depraved, and they rapidly enter into their plans and devices, even of a nature hardly possible to speak of in terms too strong" (1926). "They are very free with their fellow thieves, and communicate to each other everything they have done, *and they take great pleasure and delight in it*"(1925). The Chaplain being asked (1926), "Have you formed any opinion as to the effect produced by the association of prisoners in a Convict Prison during the latter part of their imprisonment?" gives this important answer: "*It is very bad and very prejudicial.* The first part is good, and the way in which a Convict is treated is immensely better than it used to be, but in the latter part of their imprisonment they get together; the men from one part of England, from Newcastle and Birmingham, and other places, are told where to go in London,—they do not go to the same places where they have formerly been convicted; they are unknown to the police in London, and they carry on their depredations to a considerable extent. These men are often the leaders of others, and they either do the acts themselves or they teach other men to do them; they teach the less experienced how to carry on their wickedness. *Almost all the garotte robberies have been done in that way, and are under the leadership, either direct or indirect, of ticket-of-leave men who have been discharged.*" The police records of provincial towns would probably afford striking illustrations of the statements of the Chaplain of Newgate.

We now turn to the peculiar feature of these prisons—the labour of the Convicts at the Public Works. It is their conduct and diligence in these which chiefly decides the period of release from confinement, as indicated by certain marks.

It has often been perplexing to the public to hear that men of a very bad character are marked G. (good) or even V. G. (very good). We learn from the evidence before us that these letters are quite irrespective of the general conduct of the prisoners, and indicate only a good report of their work. "It is not always the worst of characters," the Governor says, "who work the worst." The V. G.s are given on the report of the warders, checked by the superintendent warder. The warders have gratuities given them in addition to their salaries, and these depend upon the general good conduct of their parties, both at work and in every other respect. The warder's gratuity is not of course regulated by his report, but by the opinion entertained of the conduct of the party and work of the men by his superiors, and especially by the Governor. Still, though the warder does not diminish his chance of getting his own gratuity by reporting the bad conduct of any of the men under him, if a favourable opinion is entertained of his zeal and judgment by his superior officers, yet there has not been a case in which a warder has reported favourably of his gang in which he has not had a gratuity. There must be, however, a strong temptation to the warder to avoid as much as possible unfavourable reports, irrespective of the fear of losing his gratuity from apparent incapacity to stimulate the men to labour, for the Governor says (1406), "When a man is idle, and an officer tells him to go on with his work, and tells him that such idleness as that will not do, and that he must report him, *that is very apt to elicit an insolent answer.*" Hence it is not a matter of surprise that the Chairman of the Commission, on examining one of the record books presented for inspection, should remark (1008), "It appears that is quite the exception when the letters V. G. are not set against them!" The gratuity which the Convict himself earns depends entirely upon the warder's report, checked, as we have already seen, by the superior officers. "He gets (1384, 1385), if he has V. G., 9d. a week credited to him, or 1½d. a day; if he gets G. for labour, he gets 1d. per day, or 6d. per week. If he does not get G. he gets nothing. He also gets something for his class; if he is in the first class he gets 6d. a week from that; if in the second class he gets 4d.

a week; and if in the third class he gets nothing." Bad conduct never diminishes the gratuities which they have earned: whatever they have earned is credited to them, unless there is a special order by a Director, who may forfeit the whole or half for serious offences. Hence, long sentenced men often have large gratuities coming to them; as those who receive such sentences will usually be very bad men, we are not surprised to be informed that at the Chatham mutiny some of the Convicts who were remarkably bad in their conduct had very large gratuities coming to them. Among the mutineers at Chatham, we are told, were "some whose 'licenses' were already issued, and actually in the possession of the Governor; and others recommended for discharge, *many of them with large gratuities*."—(Return of Convict Disturbances, Chatham, p. 14.)

But with all these inducements to diligence, with these short hours, and this ample fare, we have the opinion of competent witnesses that there is not half as much work done in a day by each Convict as would be effected by a single labourer in an ordinary day's work. It is evident that there must always be great difficulty in obtaining from Convicts the same amount of labour which will be performed by free labourers. The latter, in the natural and ordinary condition of existence, have strong motives for diligence and for such exercise of skill and intelligence as will make their labour most valuable. Free will, honest toil, if not too laborious, is itself pleasant and honourable. The man finds a satisfaction and comfort in the full exercise and development of his powers, and he returns from his day's work with cheerful look and active step. Where he is gaining a "fair day's wages for a fair day's work," he has a feeling of pride in the comforts, or even luxuries, which he can regard as his own, because obtained by his own exertions. If he has the blessing of a good wife and children, he has a greatly increased stimulus to exertion; he contentedly eats his hard fare, and submits unrepiningly to the inclemency of the weather, thankful if he can by the labour of his hands provide daily bread and needful comforts for those whom the Heavenly Father has entrusted to his care. There must under all circumstances be an immense difficulty, perhaps even an impossibility, in giving to persons in the artificial condition of Convicts any motives for labour at all equivalent to those which the Creator has given to free men. Persons who have been generally accustomed to live by crime, rather than by honest labour, will not naturally have pleasure in the exercise of their bodily powers in labour. But yet, on the other hand, the Convict has one great incentive to exertion which the free labourer has not; — his liberty and future position in life to a great extent depend upon it. Such a motive is of incalculable force, and instances have been given in a former chapter of its value in stimulating to exertion. But in these prisons it does not appear to have this effect. The Convicts not only do far less work than free labourers, but often sham sickness to avoid work altogether. Sir J. JEBB tells us (558-9, 561,) that at Portland Prison they "have thirty large separate cells for certain classes of offences, and that some Convicts used to be idle or *committed an offence* to go to one of the cells." He quotes the testimony of the medical man, Dr. HOUGHTON, who says, after recommending half diet for those in the cells, "I feel convinced that this arrangement will have more effect on the prisoners than many months of confinement on the present allowance; it will check all that shamming and scheming so common among prisoners *who are chiefly to be ruled through the stomach.* I also beg to observe that the separate cells are the most comfortable part of the prison, where they have books to read, and may *prefer to eat the bread of idleness to working*, and will otherwise be always a dead weight on the establishment." Sir J. JEBB adds that the recommendation of Dr. HOUGHTON to "reduce the diet of prisoners who were fond of going to the separate cells, had a most immediate and marked effect in stopping the practice." How little moral influence must exist in these prisons, if it is necessary to have recourse to so

low a motive in order to prevent men from shamming sickness
to escape work!

Respecting the work produced by the Convicts at the Public
Works' Prisons we may quote the evidence, given before the
Commissioners, of Mr. J. EVANS, who stated that he had been
employed as agent for several great railways, and who had
recently visited Portland Prison Works.

"5974.—What is your opinion as to the degree of industry shown by the
convicts in the performance of the work?—I must take into consideration
that it is forced labour, and that it is therefore not done willingly.

"5975.—Do the men exert themselves as much as you think can be
expected from them under the circumstances?—I think so; and I think
that great credit is due to the officials who get what they have got out of
the convicts. Perhaps it is desirable to get something more, *but I think
that there is a great deal of difficulty in getting it.*"

In making further deductions from the amount of work to
be expected, he says,—

"5977.—The prisoners have their prison discipline, and marching to and
from their work, in addition to their labour, and from what I saw, and
the inquiries I made, I consider that the officers are employed with them
as many hours as appear to me to be desirable, considering the arduous
nature of their duties. If I were employing free labour, my men, when
they went to their breakfasts or dinners, for instance, would sit down on
their work and get their meals, and be prepared to go to work immediately,
but, of course, in the case of these prisoners, they cannot do that, because
there are fissures in the rock, and all sorts of creeping holes, and, of course,
the prison officials look to the safety of their men in great measure; and,
in fact, that seems to be the first object, the safety of the prisoners; the next
point is the amount of work they can get out of them. They have to march
to the prison, and each man has to be searched, in order to see whether
he has any dangerous weapon concealed about him, and which they have
every opportunity of getting on their work. They are armed with picks,
crowbars, and chisels, which would be very desirable to them if they wanted
to break out of prison, and they have the knowledge how to make a mason's
chisel into a jemmy. I have watched all these proceedings just to see the
time that it took, and, of course, it reduces the amount of time they have for
labour.

"5978.—Are the convicts searched each time they go into the prison?—
Yes, and also out of it, every man is searched, at least every working party
has got a certain number to go to; a body of men walk up, and then the
officer having charge of them is responsible for them, and searches every

man; he passes his hand down to see whether there is any chisel or other
article concealed, and the party examined and checked by a superior officer
to see the warder has his number of men.

" 5979.—That is done to prevent their hiding a chisel, or any article of that
kind, which might be used in assisting them to break out of prison ?—Yes, or
to commit *an assault, because that sometimes happens.*  My memorandum is :
' I carefully watched the prisoners while at work, and I should say that *two
prisoners would do the work of one free quarryman*; but I am not surprised at
this state of things, because the work requires some degree of skill as well
as industry, *and we must bear in mind that it is forced labour, and not given
willingly.*  The above requires this qualification, that a great number of the
prisoners are entire strangers to work of any kind, and, in all cases, have
never been used to work of this nature, which requires a certain degree of
skill, as well as the will to work.' "

How completely a different system would produce a very
different effect is proved by the experiment of task work, tried
most successfully in Van Dieman's Land by Sir WILLIAM
DENNISON, who left this country for that colony in 1846.

" The instructions to him were (vide Commission, 697 and 698) that the
work was to be arranged in day work, so that a man of average power, by
working hard, could accomplish, *in the usual hours of labour, a day and
a quarter or a day and a half's work*, and thus reduce the period in the
probationary gang.  All the labourers in government custody were in probationary gangs, and they were to be allowed to have half the value of any
excess of labour in any days' work, if they liked, in tobacco, and so on.
The other half went towards completing their task before they could become
free.  Sir W. DENNISON, in his half-yearly report to the end of December,
1847, says that ' difficulties had been experienced in establishing a system
of task work, partly from want of officers, but it is now in operation in
many places, and will gradually be extended to all the convicts in the
employment of Government,'  Then in the next half-yearly report he says,
' The returns as to the working of the system of task work are very satisfactory, and every day tends to prove that it is producing a most beneficial
effect upon the conduct and discipline of the men.'  He also says that ' the
men working by task *have an interest in their work, and labour willingly,*
and their conduct is in every way improved.'  In the enclosed report,
the Comptroller-General says that ' *the introduction of task work has become
the stimulus to industry hitherto wanting*, and has in many cases produced
a remarkable revolution in the character of the coerced labour of the gangs.' "

The assaults upon officers in the Convict Prisons are a
peculiar feature of their condition.  " You have stated," said
a Commissioner to one of the Directors (4120) " that assaults

upon warders are somewhat common in these prisons?" He replies "Yes, in the *invalid prisons*, and sometimes it takes fits and starts in the Public Works' Prisons; but at Chatham Prison, ever since the outbreak which took place two years ago, I do not think there has been one single report of a prisoner, or not above one or two, of prisoners assaulting their officers. This will also go on at Portsmouth and at Portland for months and months together, and then there will be a sort of epidemic, and such cases will then occur, five or six or seven at once." Again (4094) he says,—"At Dartmoor, where many of these attacks occur, my last visit was made about a fortnight ago. I had to investigate *nine cases of assaults upon officers*, and I punished them all most severely, as they happened to be medically fit."

The Director of Millbank, Pentonville, and Brixton Prisons gives a similar report. On being asked by the Chairman—

"2298.—Have you many cases of assaults by prisoners on officers?" he replies: "Comparatively speaking, there are fewer assaults committed on officers in close prisons, as we term them, than have been committed on officers at the Public Works' Prisons; but I certainly have had some dreadful cases."

" 2299.—You do not think that the warders act under fear of violence from the prisoners?—Yes, I do. There are some of those prisoners now in Millbank whom it is very dangerous to approach, and the officers do not approach them without very great terror, and without taking very great precautions.

" 2300.—Are they influenced by fear of the prisoners in the reports they make respecting them?—It may be so, but I cannot say positively.

"2301.—Do you believe that they are not?—I think that they state generally what is the truth in making their reports.

" 2302.—You think that they are not afraid of reporting badly of a prisoner?—I cannot go so far as to say that, because I know that some of those prisoners are such desperate ruffians that the officers are probably more inclined to look over their offences than to report them."

When, in addition, cases of murder are far from being unknown—one very shocking case having occurred at Portland not long ago—we can easily imagine how little prison reports can give the real character of Convicts, and what a dreadful state of feeling must exist in these prisons. Dr. GUY,

the physician of Millbank Prison, gives a similar account:—
(3143), "Then again, their acts of violence and insubordination are almost incredible; it is wonderful what they will do,
and also what they will bear, with the *twofold object of deceiving
and annoying.*" He mentions the case of "one man who had
sewn his mouth and eyelids up with a needle. He had picked
it up about the prison, and contrived to secrete it. He seemed
to have no reason to assign for doing it, except that he thought
he would not eat any more!" Another man feigned madness
at times; his conduct had been brutal and disgusting in the
extreme. He persisted in not taking exercise, and would not
work. He was a very bad character, and had made several
assaults upon the warders, and had used most blasphemous
and wicked language (3135). Dr. GUY did not believe him
to be mad, and at his suggestion the man was threatened
with a flogging if he indulged in another outbreak, and on
his refusing to take exercise he lost his dinner.

" On the following day," Dr. GUY continues, " he said, ' If I cannot have
my dinner on my own terms, I will starve.' I said, ' I think you will bear
starvation very well,' and he took to starvation. But on the Sunday,
when his dinner was brought to him, he could not resist it, and he ate
his dinner, On the following day, Monday, he recommenced the system
of starvation, but he soon gave it up, and he went out to exercise; coir
was put into his cell, which he picked, and from that time, for more than
a month, he was as well-conducted a prisoner as we ever had in the prison."

Entries in the Chatham punishment-book, read by the Commissioners during the evidence of the Governor, are an illustration of the remarks of Dr. GUY, and show how dangerous
and unrestrained is the conduct of these Convicts. We read
in query 1412 : "The entry is—'Assistant - Warder WILMOTT
states, yesterday, about ten o'clock a.m., prisoner BROWN struck
another man, named HOLT, two heavy blows on the head with
a stone hammer; his head was severely cut; he was sent to
the infirmary and admitted. Prisoner admits it; he has nothing
to say. For some time the man's life was in danger.' " It
will be hardly credited that for such an offence the only

punishment was bread and water for three days, and half diet for four days! As the wounded man had said something impertinent to him which irritated him, and as the injury did not appear as serious as was first supposed, this brutal outrage was not thought a sufficient offence to report to the Director for further punishment! Another similar entry is observed the very next day in the same record (1422): "Throwing a piece of wood at another prisoner, and threatening to murder him. That man forfeited three days?—Yes." 1423. "There is another entry, 'For refusing to put on a pair of trousers when ordered, and using threatening language to the officer.' He was merely admonished?—Yes." 1424. "On the same day, for using highly insubordinate language and threatening, when visited by the chief warder, 'He was admonished.'" The prisoner states he was very sorry. "Then, on May 19th, for using threatening language towards the warder, and for resisting him in the execution of his duty, he forfeited seven days?— And he had two days' bread and water." If these men had not been Convicts they would surely have been visited with punishments much more severe. The immunity they receive shows how common must such offences be. In another case (1425), "striking another prisoner," entails only an admonition! How can warders dare to enforce a rigid discipline when their doing so may be followed by consequences so serious to them, and so trifling to the offender.

Such is the state of feeling and conduct among men who are supposed to be undergoing reformatory training! Prisoners, both old and young, soon learn how far misconduct will be tolerated, and act accordingly. The simple fact of the toleration of what would in society be very serious offences, of itself encourages to greater daring!

Though industrial occupation is the prominent feature of the Public Works' Prisons, yet, knowing the very degraded condition of most of the Convicts, we might have expected that considerable attention would be paid to their instruction, as a means of their moral and religious improvement, and as enabling them to obtain in their leisure hours such innocent and useful information as may occupy their minds well now, and be valuable to them in future life. But we learn from the evidence that the whole of the instruction given in these Convict Prisons is one half-day, or about three hours in the week. It is assumed, that a sufficient amount of schooling and religious instruction is given to the prisoners during the solitary twelve months at the commencement of their penal servitude. The religious instruction is confined to the daily prayers and the Sunday services, unless the Chaplains or Scripture Reader have occasionally a private interview with a prisoner. The deep ignorance and the hardened hearts of most of these Convicts renders it impossible that the period of instruction in Pentonville or Millbank, excellent as it doubtless is of its kind, can bring the prisoners' mind or heart to a condition in which they really profit by these brief intervals of cessation from their penal labours. Many, it is probable, come to the prison unable to read; such persons cannot have made such progress in the mere art of reading, the key as it were to all knowledge, as to render one lesson in a week of the least service to them. Of what use, then, can leisure hours be to such men in their solitary cells? What can they do there but pass away the time in as much physical comfort as possible? Surely Sunday, the day of rest from bodily toil, might have been profitably employed in some spiritual improvement or actual instruction;—this was suggested by one of the Commissioners, who asks (1325): "Might not that schooling take place on Sundays?—I do not think it possible," replies the Governor; "in fact, it would be quite impossible." (1326). "Might not the prisoners be so divided on Sundays that each of them could get a certain amount of schooling?—It is not possible."

A great objection is felt to the evening service at the Chapel, as being rather mischievous than otherwise, both by the Director and by the Governor. The former says: "I have always been of opinion that it would be better if there was no schooling whatever when the prisoners come to the public works; but they should have a great deal more of school instruction during the time they were undergoing separate confinement. I do not think the school instruction does much good; it is only half a day in a week, and not above four hours" (4373). He also expresses the decided opinion that any additional schooling would be of no advantage to the prisoner, if it took place in the evening. The Governor is of opinion that the evening service might be done away with, without any great disadvantage; because it would increase the time for labour, which he considers very desirable (1311, 1313). The Director is asked,—

"4383.—I understand you to be distinctly of opinion that any additional schooling would be of no advantage to the prisoner?—Decidedly not, if it took place in the evening.

"4230.—You would rather that the convicts should pass their time in labour than pass their time in going to evening service?—Yes.

"4231.—You do not think that in a religious point of view they gain any equivalent for that loss of time?—*I am certain that, in a religious point of view, it has a bad effect.*

"4232.—Do you think that they attend evening service without due feelings of reverence?—Not only that, *but the reverse.*

"4383.—You also think that the evening Chapel service is rather mischievous than otherwise?—Yes, I can also say that every Chaplain, save one, agreed with me, and that one I have never asked, because I knew it would be of no use."

Surely, if evening instruction and religious worship, after daily work, are not acceptable or beneficial to men who ought to be striving to improve and remedy past defects, there must be some radical defect in the system which should be removed.

The following is the scale of payments to Convicts authorised by the Secretary of State, as given by Captain O'Brien in his evidence to the Select Committee of 1856 :—

" £5 and under to be paid on discharge; above £5 and under £8, £4 to be paid on discharge, and balance at the end of two months. £8 and under £12, half to be paid on discharge, and half at the expiration of three months. £12 and under £20, £5 to be paid on discharge, and half the remainder in two months, and balance at the expiration of three months more." (560.)

The gratuities to prisoners after their discharge is at present paid through the police, who investigate the character of the applicant, and if it is unsatisfactory do not pay it. £240 were thus paid to 58 discharged prisoners through the police, the gratuities of the others being paid to the Prisoners' Aid Society. One man received in that year, in two payments, £15 17s. 9d.; another received £10, and another £7 10s. Sir RICHARD MAYNE expresses the belief that these gratuities diminish any deterring effect which sentences of penal servitude might otherwise have. They are even an inducement to crime. "There was a remarkable case which occurred," he says (1595) "within a day or two. I may state that the gratuities to Convicts released on tickets-of-leave are paid through the police, and a man, two days ago, when he received his gratuity, stated that he knew that several persons in the agricultural districts were very glad to get into prison, as they were so much better taken care of, and they had no fear whatever of it. I have the case here, and the name of the man who stated it."

Such, then, is our Convict system as described by those who are carrying it on. Let us hear the opinion of it given to the Commissioners by Sir R. MAYNE, who, as Commissioner of the Metropolitan Police, had peculiar opportunities of forming an opinion respecting its adaptation to the class intended. He thus speaks:—

"1607.—The whole system, I think, however humanely devised and intended, seems to me to be very inconsistent with the criminal condition of the parties, for instance, the permission to communicate by letter with their friends. I have had several letters sent to me by the Governor of Dartmoor Prison, requesting that inquiries should be made as to the characters of the parties who were corresponding with the convicts, *and in almost every case they have turned out to be very bad, of the worst sort, many of them keeping houses for the reception of thieves, and keeping up in the convict a knowledge of what was going on.* I think that very much diminishes the effects of the punishments.

"1669.—That sort of correspondence I think is calculated to keep up the spirits of the men, and make them feel that they are in communication with friends. I think that is mischievous, and with persons whose acquaintance they immediately renew on their release."

The effect of such correspondence on the prisoner's mind we can easily imagine. Shut out from the exterior world, which to his mind is entirely associated with scenes of vice, every letter he receives, couched though it may be in the most apparently inoffensive terms, awakens in him the remembrance of his past daring and places of vice;—every name mentioned is one which recalls his associates in evil doing, and rekindles the desire of rejoining them, if that has been in any way stifled by the instructions he is receiving. On these his imagination fixes itself, until, in another letter, he has a new reminder of his vicious career. It was only recently, within the last six months, that Sir RICHARD had received these inquiries, and the investigations they led to impressed his mind most strongly with the incompatibility of reformation with such correspondence.

"I think," he continues (1672) "that the condition of a convict felon is such that he should be excluded from all knowledge of what is going on elsewhere during the short sentences; it might form part of the remission if the sentences were longer. I may state also that the places of confinement appear to me to be very comfortable. * * * 1673. I have been to Chatham and to Portsmouth; I went over both of these lately, and at Chatham especially it struck me; there the walls or the partitions were of corrugated glass, which produces rather a cheerful effect inside. I went inside, and found that it was very light and agreeable; the temperature was pleasant, and the men had books, and were carrying on some trades. Another thing appeared to me to be inconsistent with their state and condition as felons. Their dietary is put up in their cells, and each man is told, for there it is printed, that he is entitled to have his food weighed and measured. One of the warders told me *that they sometimes required it to be done in order to spite them;* he said, 'We have sometimes had a great many who insisted on having their food weighed and measured.' Now these things seem to me to interfere with the condition of the criminal, and likewise the mode of employment at Portsmouth. I think that employing him in the dockyard generally is very bad, on account of the immediate personal communication that there is, and the comparison that arises between them and the free labourers, which is really very often to the disadvantage of the free man, with respect to his food, the state of his clothing, and his condition in every respect except that of being at liberty; likewise their employment in such a place as Southsea Common, where they have been employed for upwards of a year; it is a very agreeable place—one of the most cheerful places, I think, in England. They have been levelling and laying the turf, and it is now very much improved by them;—a place where the troops parade, and bands playing, and ladies and children walking about. In short, it is one of the pleasantest places in England, and it does not seem to me to be the place upon which to employ convicts. I think it is no punishment."

The police have been employed on duty in the dockyard for two or three years to prevent as far as possible any communication between the free labourers and the Convicts. But on the present system it seems impossible to prevent this, for Sir RICHARD says, in answer to the inquiry (1678) whether there is any communication carried on between the Convicts and the free labourers, "*I believe there is often,* because there have been things found which have been left in places which were a little secluded; and no doubt it was intended—in fact some have been convicted for it—that the free labourers should get the things away, and get them out of the yard if they could; but the police now make such a search that it is not easy to be done." Still there is the temptation held out, and it certainly is an anomaly that men receiving punishment should be allowed to be in such a position as to lure honest men into crime. They are even able to commit depredations themselves, for Sir RICHARD continues—

" When I was at Chatham the other day, on the repainting those gunboats laid up, which were built during the war, there were three or four pieces of copper, worth many shillings, found in a very out-of-the-way place, in one of those boats, and after the best examinations and inquiries that could be made, there seemed to be no doubt that some two years before that, when the boats were dismantled, the copper had been stolen by convicts, who had been employed in carrying it to the store, and had been left where it was found for the purpose of being taken away, but no opportunity had occurred for getting it away." 1679. " When so employed in the dockyards or on Southsea Common, it is very difficult to prevent them from having communication. The warders are few; the men are working about, and some of them are working in carpenters' shops by themselves, and it is impossible to prevent communication."

After reading such statements, as well as the admissions made by the various witnesses as to the amount of communication which can always take place between the Convicts, the very little possibility which exists of such communications coming under the notice of the warders,—the extremely small moral influence possessed by them, and the audacity and vindictiveness of the prisoners, pampered and indulged as they are,—no one can wonder at the various outbreaks which the public has been terrified and shocked, as occurring in the very places which were supposed to be intended for punishment and humiliation.  It would seem as if we have in our midst fortresses filled with savage enemies, ready to burst forth to kill and destroy.

The great Chatham mutiny occurred three years ago, in February, 1862, and it is said that that prison has been quiet since.  But as the public has heard of prison mutinies elsewhere, and the system remains in all these establishments without any radical alteration, it will be desirable to form some idea of its serious nature.  Full statements respecting it were given to the Commission by officials;—as these accord in general with an account which appeared in an article in " Meliora," which is briefer, we will present that to the reader.

" The Chatham mutiny commenced early in January, as Sir G. C. LEWIS stated in the House of Commons in answer to a question from Mr. Alderman SALOMONS, with the attempt of six Convicts to make their escape.*  They failed, but their endeavour became known to their comrades, who, testifying their sympathy by a general and continued uproar in both cells and chapel, proved the public feeling of the prison to be on the side of wrong.†  After the lapse of several days, order was restored, and no further outbreak occurred until Friday, Feb. 8.  Upon that day, when dinner was served to the men on St. Mary's Island, several—

" Began complaining that the food was not ' good enough' for them, and that the soup was ' poor.'  Mr. BURTON, the principal warder, ' promised that their complaint should be inquired into, when he was answered with an oath, and the contents of one of the soup tins dashed in his face.  This was the signal agreed upon for the commencement of the outbreak; and immediately afterwards the contents of innumerable tins of soup were thrown over Mr. BURTON, who was quickly drenched to the skin.  The greatest uproar

---

* *Times*, Feb. 16, 1861.        † *Western Daily Press*, Jan. 21, 1861.

now ensued, the convicts yelling, hooting, and swearing, hurling their dinner
utensils about, smashing the windows, throwing the remainder of their
dinner at the warders, and commencing to tear up the tables and other
articles of furniture.  *  *  *  The more desperate characters likewise
commenced pulling down the spouting round the building, with which they
armed themselves, while others endeavoured for this purpose to force away
the iron bars of the windows.' Subsequently most of the convicts returned
to their work, but on the arrival of a strong body of warders a large number
were marched, heavily ironed, to the punishment cells, where, throughout the
following Saturday and Sunday they 'created the greatest disturbances by
kicking the doors, hooting, and yelling.'* This proved, however, but the
precursor of an outbreak 'of a far more terrible character than any which has
yet taken place at this prison, spreading the utmost terror, not only among
the prison officials, but also throughout the whole town, when the fearful
excesses which were being enacted at the prison became known. When it
is stated that the whole 1,100 convicts succeeded in overpowering the keepers,
and obtaining complete possession of the establishment, which they held for
some time, actually setting fire to the prison, some idea of the alarming
nature of the outbreak yesterday may be imagined.  *  *  *  The keepers
on duty, about 150 in number, were all driven from the prison yard with
threats that they would all be murdered, if they did not make their escape.
*  *  *  The wildest uproar now ensued, and the scene which at this time
presented itself in the interior of the prison is described by the officials
as baffling description.  *  *  *  On hearing of the outbreak, Captain
GAMBIER and Captain POWELL (the Governor), together with the Deputy-
Governor, and the other principal officers of the establishment, were immediately in the prison yard with the hope of restoring order and inducing
the prisoners to return to their cells. With some hundreds of infuriated
ruffians to deal with, their efforts were of course useless; and there is no
doubt that had they remained among the convicts their lives would have
been sacrificed.' A large number of the convicts, rushing into the chief
warder's office, 'commenced destroying the books and papers, and every other
available article on which they could lay their hands—desks, tables, chairs,
and everything which could be broken up being quickly destroyed. They
then endeavoured to set the prison on fire, and the building was actually
fired in two or three places, from which the flames began to pour forth.'
A thousand troops were now summoned from the garrison, and 700, who
'were received by the convicts with the most dreadful yells,' charging the
prisoners, with the assistance of the warders 'using their truncheons with
the utmost freedom,' drove them back 'into their cells.' "†

"Involuntarily we contrast this and the similar employment
of military force to quell the outbreak at Portland Convict

---

* *Times*, Feb. 11, 1861.        † *Morning Star and Dial*, Feb. 13, 1861.

Prison some time ago, with the scene on Norfolk Island, when Captain MACHONOCHIE, six months after his arrival, employed the prisoners themselves to dismount the cannon which, until then, had always guarded the Superintendent's house, never afterwards to be used during his stay, but to fire a complimentary salvo. The amount of damage done in Chatham Prison has been estimated at £1,000.* Sir G. C. LEWIS, however, stated that "the Convicts broke some windows and upset some stores. That was, he believed, pretty nearly the extent of mischief which they did;" and he limited the number engaged in the revolt to "about 850."† It is certainly a striking circumstance that although the prison authorities were for a time completely at the mercy of the Convicts, none, as Sir G. C. LEWIS stated, suffered personal injury. Concerning the cause of the mutiny—

"He had investigated the matter with some care, but was unable to give any very clear explanation of the affair, nor could the officers of the prison satisfactorily account for it. The general cause, however, which certainly operated to a very large extent was, that the refuse of the hulks was transferred to Chatham prison on its first opening, and tainted the prison population, and some even of the inferior officers (!) Hence strict discipline could not be enforced without creating discontent, and the discipline at Chatham was strict compared with that which prevailed in the old hulks."†

"Nearly the whole day" (Wednesday, February 13th), we read in the *Times*, "was occupied in flogging those convicts who were examined yesterday by Sir JOSHUA JEBB and Captain GAMBIER, and who were proved to have been the ringleaders in the revolt on Monday afternoon. The convicts flogged were brought from the cells one at a time, and having been stripped, were fastened up to the halberds, when each man received three dozen lashes, laid on with terrible effect. Many of the convicts received their punishment with scarcely a cry; but as stroke after stroke fell on the backs of some of the most ruffianly characters, who particularly distinguished themselves in the recent outbreak, they set up piercing shrieks, mingled with frightful oaths and threats. Several of the men, on being released from the triangles, behaved with the greatest bravado, notwithstanding the intense pain they were enduring, and frequent threats were made that the 'business was not yet done,' and that on the first opportunity murder would be committed."‡

---

* *Morning Star and Dial,* Feb. 13, 1861.　　† *Times,* Feb. 16, 1861.
‡ *Times,* Feb. 14, 1861.

We need not give the account of the Portland mutiny, which required very strong measures to repress.  Paragraphs such as the following respecting Dartmoor not unfrequently meet our eye in the public prints :—

## "ATTEMPTED OUTBREAK OF CONVICTS AT DARTMOOR PRISON.

" For some weeks past the convicts at Dartmoor prison have been manifesting symptoms of renewing their attempts of outbreak and insubordination. On last Saturday evening, after the warders had served each convict with his supper, and clean linen for the ensuing day—being thus supplied with all their wants—they commenced to shout and hoot at their windows, and use threats of defiance towards the highest prison officials.  All the prisoners located in A and B Hall, No. 2 Prison, joined in one continued shout of defiance, and doggedly refused to close their cell doors.  Captain BEST (the deputy-governor), on being made acquainted with the disturbance, promptly appeared on the scene, accompanied by a strong body of warders, and a detachment of the Armed Civil Guard.  Captain BEST ordered the warders to close all the cell doors, on which the convicts commenced yelling, whistling, and knocking against the doors and partitions of their cells.  Quietness and good order were, however, ultimately restored.  But on Sunday afternoon, after having heard a most impressive lecture from the prison chaplain, all the convicts located in A Hall, No. 2 Prison, refused to enter their cells, and openly bade defiance to the warders, demanding their regular exercise, and that their cell doors should be left open, otherwise they would not return to their cells.  The governor had given orders that all the prisoners located in No. 2 Prison should be deprived of their Sunday's exercise, and not be allowed to assemble together on parade, also that their cell doors should be kept closed, as a punishment for their outrageous conduct on the previous evening.  The warders, with staves in their hands, courageously advanced on the infuriated convicts, and drove them towards their cells. The scene of tumult that ensued baffles description.  Shouting, yelling, imprecations, and threats of vengeance were uttered by the convicts if their demands were not complied with.  A detachment of the Civil Guard, with fixed bayonets and loaded arms, was then drawn up in front of A Hall, No. 2 Prison, and all the available officers that could be procured were despatched to aid the warders in charge of No. 2 Prison; the warders whose turn it was to be off duty for that day were also called into the prison at 11.30 a.m to act as a reserve.  The convicts, seeing such a formidable and determined force, after giving full vent to their lungs, succumbed to the warders, and returned to their cells.  Nine of the instigators, or rather ringleaders, were secured and removed to the refractory cells, to await the decision of Captain GAMBIER, the Visiting Director, who is expected to arrive at the prison in a day or two.  One of the ringleaders, named GRIFFITHS, has been sent back, on two different occasions, to the penal class at Pentonville Prison for murderous assaults on the warders at Dartmoor; so that, after completing his penance at Pentonville, he has been let loose at Dartmoor to carry out his murderous designs, and was allowed full scope to incite his companions in villany to acts of mutiny and insubordination. Only last month five of the convicts at Dartmoor underwent the punishment of the lash for violently assaulting the warders.

"At a future time our correspondent will inform the public as to the cause that leads to these different acts of violence and insubordination on the part of the convicts at the Dartmoor prison."—*Western Mercury*.

## "A TICKET-OF-LEAVE MAN.

"SAMUEL JOHNSON, a man who scarcely seemed to have recovered from the effects of his potations deep, was charged with being found drunk and incapable in Butter Lane, Temple. The prisoner, a ticket-of-leave man, it appeared had only been released from Dartmoor on the same day that he was found in a helpless state of drunkenness. He stated that he had lost his "papers" and the money which was given him upon his discharge, amounting to £2 10s. Mr. ROGERS (Magistrates' Clerk): This is a bad commencement of your new career. Prisoner: Ees."—*Post*, April 9, 1863.

## "ESCAPE FROM DARTMOOR PRISON.

"A man named JOHN KENNEDY was convicted for burglary at the Central Criminal Court on the 19th of September, 1859, and sentenced to a long term of imprisonment at Dartmoor. On the morning of Tuesday last he was seen in the chapel of the prison, but a few hours afterwards he could no longer be found. It was then ascertained that he had escaped over the wall by means of a rope. Later on the same day he was apprehended by a police-constable in a public-house at Ashburton, wearing an outer dress which he had obtained in some way not explained. The prisoner made an escape with three others about two years ago, and was brought back to the prison."—*Post*, June, 1863.

## "ATTEMPTED ESCAPE OF CONVICTS FROM DARTMOOR PRISON.

"An attempt was made by some of the convicts at Dartmoor on Friday, which served to show the excellent and very complete arrangements made for preserving order and preventing outbreaks and escapes amongst the wretched men who have been sent there for their crimes. A number of the convicts have latterly been employed in enclosing land between the prison and Two Bridges. On Friday evening last, when the signal was given for the men to cease work in order to return to the prison, seven men of one gang who had been working about a wall ran to the place where another gang was stationed, caught up their spades, and called upon the other men to join and make their escape. Four of the second gang joined, and the eleven made for a breach in the wall. There they were met by one of the Civil Guard, who said he would fire at the first man who attempted to pass.

The desperadoes then made for another officer, and by him they were as firmly resisted; and by this time the guard and officer had surrounded the rioters, and compelled them to submit. They were then marched off to their cells. Thus ended what, but for the efficiency of the guard, and the speed with which they were brought together, might have been a very serious affair. Captain GAMBIER, the Inspector of Prisons, had only just left Dart-moor when this daring attempt was made. A messenger found him in Plymouth, and he has gone to Dartmoor to inquire into the facts and award punishment to the offenders. But for his return to the prison the eleven offenders would have had to wait until the next official visitation for inquiry and judgment."—*Post*, Nov., 1863.

" There was a ' strike' at Dartmoor Prison on Monday morning, the convicts one and all refusing to work. They were accordingly marched back and confined in separate cells until their punishment has been decided on. A ringleader met every persuasion or order of the warders with the most dreadful imprecations and threats. The cause of the mutiny was the application of the new reduced scale of diet. For some months past the Governors of Convict Prisons have had orders to adopt the reduced scale of diet, which was approved by the Commission of Doctors, under the authority of the Secretary of State. Up to Sunday last these orders had not been adopted in Dartmoor Prison, and the old scale was adhered to. On that morning, however, it was announced to the convicts that the change was to be made. The dissatisfaction soon became apparent, and some well-disposed convicts gave the prison officials early information that a serious mutiny was contemplated. Prompt measures were therefore taken to prevent it."—*Bristol Post*, June 17, 1864.

Of the dangers to which warders are exposed in these Convict Prisons we have a specimen in the following, which appeared not long since in the public press :—

### "MURDEROUS ATTACK ON A CONVICT WARDER AT PORTSMOUTH.

" At the Borough Police Court, Portsmouth, on Friday afternoon, LOUIS FRANCIS, a convict, was charged with attempting to murder a convict warder named DEAN, doing duty at the prison at Portsmouth. By direction of the government authorities, Mr. SWAINSON, Admiralty Solicitor, appeared to prosecute. It was stated in evidence that on the 15th of December the prisoner formed one of a party of convicts under the charge of DEAN. There were fifteen in all, and they were employed in the junk store of Her Majesty's dockyard, cutting up old rope. About one-half the party had axes or choppers and knives, with which they were provided for the purpose of cutting up the old rope. The prisoner, on the morning in question, after some few words of conversation with DEAN, suddenly knocked him down with his fist, forced him on some of the old junk, and there knocked him

about in a frightful manner with his fist, kicked him in various parts of
the body with his hob-nailed boots, and after that obtained a heavy piece
of wood, twice the size of an ordinary policeman's truncheon, and struck
him over the head with it several times, causing the blood to flow profusely.
DEAN became insensible, and had been suffering ever since. *There were only
two men present desirous of interfering with the prisoner, but they were prevented from assisting the warder by the threats of the other armed convicts.
who intimated that they would serve them in the same way if they interfered.*
It also transpired that the prisoner had been previously convicted of offences
of this kind. The prisoner, who was a man of revolting appearance, was
committed for trial at Winchester."

This was shortly followed by the murder of another warder,
which occurred at Portland Prison, on September 8th, 1863.
The wretched young man who perpetrated it was under a sentence of three years' penal servitude, and was only 21 years of
age. Before he underwent the sentence of the law he appeared
very penitent, did not in any way extenuate his conduct, and
acknowledged to having feigned madness by giving way to fits
of violent passion, in order to escape punishment, and to having,
before his final act, committed other crimes nearly equal to
murder. What he might have been under different treatment
can only be surmised; from the deep penitence which he showed
before his execution, it is evident that he was susceptible of good
influences under judicious treatment. It is at any rate clear
that convict treatment which produces such scenes as the
following is not reformatory. The account is extracted from
the county papers :—

### "FEARFUL SCENE IN AN ASSIZE COURT.

" At Dorchester, on Wednesday, before Mr. Sergt. SHEE, ALFRED PREEDY,
a convict, was charged with the wilful murder of CHARLES EVANS, a warder in
the Portland Prison, on the 8th September last. On being called upon he
pleaded 'guilty of the act, but not of the intention,' which was received as a
plea of not guilty.

" Captain W. CLAY said: I am the Governor of the Portland Convict
Prison. The prisoner was brought to the gaol on the 14th of March. He
came from Millbank. He was in my custody up to the 8th September. He
was under sentence of three years' penal servitude. The murder was reported
to me on the 8th of Sept. I saw the body of EVANS, who was a shoemaker
warder of the prison.

"John Moore, a convict, was one of the cleaning gang of the ward on the 8th of September. The convicts take their dinners in their cells, and knives are pushed under the door, and after dinner they are collected in tins. I collected the tins and knives on the 8th of September, with Charles Evans, the warder, John Ashton and Jas. Scholfield. There were five other prisoners and a warder collecting the other side of the ward. I had collected at four or five cells before anything happened. I then came to the cell occupied by the prisoner Preedy. Evans unlocked the door and Scholfield put out his hand. The prisoner was standing with his knife and tin in his hand. He hesitated, then dropped his tin, pushed the knives out of the man's hand, rushed by him, and seized Mr. Evans. He struck him under the left ear with the knife. We dropped the trays and seized the prisoner. We had hold of him when the knife was in the wound, and he jerked the knife.

"At this moment a scene took place which, we believe, has never been witnessed in a court of justice. When the prisoner first came to the bar he looked a very harmless young man, but during the evidence he became restless, and sharply asked a question. Immediately after the answer the prisoner threw one leg and arm over the front of the dock, and very nearly succeeded in getting over. Two warders, who were in the dock, rushed at him and seized him, and other warders jumped into the dock, and an almost deadly struggle took place, the prisoner kicking, fighting, and roaring more like a wild beast than a human being, and it required ten strong men to hold him. Several had hold of his legs and arms, and some were holding him by the hair of his head. This continued for some minutes, and when it ceased it was only because he was held fast. The ferocity of the man was beyond anything that can well be imagined.

"The Surgeon of the gaol, who was in Court, went to him, and was then called by the Judge, to whom he stated that this was a repetition of what he had seen before in the gaol. His observation would not justify his saying that the prisoner was insane. His opinion was that he was perfectly sensible to all that was going on.

"The Judge then told the prisoner that the trial should proceed, because the Surgeon was of opinion that he knew what was going on.

"The Surgeon asked the prisoner if he knew him.

"Prisoner: Of course I do. Shake hands. You are a friend of mine.

"The prisoner then began struggling again, and was very violent.

"It was suggested to the Judge that, as well for the safety of the prisoner as for others, it would be better to put irons on him.

"The Judge said he did not like to do this; but the violence continuing, his Lordship gave way, and consented to the irons being put on.

"The prisoner was then heavily ironed and strapped, certainly as much as any maniac could be; but it was some time before this could be managed, on account of his extreme violence.

"After half an hour's delay, the Judge went out to consult Mr. Justice Byles, and their Lordships remained in consultation for a considerable length of time, and the prisoner appeared to be completely exhausted, and appeared as it were asleep.

"Another Surgeon was sent for, and

"Mr. Sergeant SHEE returned into Court, and ordered the prisoner to be taken into a private room and examined by the Surgeon. With some difficulty the prisoner was carried out of Court.

"After another half an hour's delay business was resumed, and the following witnesses were examined :—.

"ALFRED ANSON : I am a Surgeon of this town. Since the adjournment of the Court I have examined the prisoner, and in my judgment at this moment he is in perfect possession of his understanding, and is perfectly able to understand what is going on.

"JOHN GOOD, the Surgeon of the gaol, gave similar testimony.

"Dr. WILLIAM HOUGHTON, the Surgeon at the Convict Prison at Portland, confirmed the testimony of the other two medical men.

"The Judge then said the trial must proceed. It was extremely painful to him to be obliged to sanction the restraint under which the prisoner was placed, but from his conduct it was necessary that it should be continued, and so much force as was necessary, but not more, would be used to enable the trial to proceed.

"JOHN MOORE's evidence was then proceeded with :—I seized him first, and ASHTON seized his arm and wrenched it back. The prisoner cried out 'Murder!' and let the knife drop out of his hand. We had a struggle with the prisoner. He attempted to get down as if to the knife. I got on his back. He made a rush at ROBERTS, another warder, who came up. We then all secured him. EVANS ran round the hall, and I did not see him again.

"Several other witnesses corroborated this evidence.

"JAMES DOUGLAS, assistant warder, said he had charge of the refractory convicts. He received the prisoner in his custody, and asked him why he had murdered Mr. EVANS, and prisoner replied 'is he dead? I hope he is; I intended to murder him.' Witness said, 'You must have had some reason.' The prisoner put his hand up to his head and said, 'There, Mr. DOUGLAS, I must have done it, for I took my Bible down and swore that I would take his life as he opened the door, or on the first opportunity.' Witness said, 'Well, you would never have done that without some motive. What was your motive?' He replied, 'There was something between him and me that you don't know.'

"A good deal of additional evidence was taken ; and the learned Judge having summed up, the jury returned a verdict of guilty, and sentence of death was passed in the usual form."

———————

"After the murder PREEDY had been, on the 13th of September, received into custody, at the County Gaol, there to await his trial. His conduct for some time afterwards was very violent, and stringent measures were compelled to be resorted to to keep him in order. He said the reason for behaving so was to keep his thoughts from feeling his position. He destroyed his clothing, and was in a complete state of nudity for two days. He was put in irons by order of the magistrates, but after this he continued very quiet until his trial. After sentence had been passed upon him his conduct was of the most outrageous description. The irons with which he was bound at the trial remained on him up to the time of his execution, as it was considered unsafe to remove them, as he said that if he had his hands at liberty he would 'do' for the officials of the gaol who bound him. Notwithstanding that he was thus heavily bound, he 'butted' at the officials who attended him, swearing fearfully, and insulting those whose business brought them near him. Up to Friday, the 20th, he thought he should escape the hangman's hand, and stated that if he had known it was intended to prove he was insane he would have carried on much more. He knew what he was about whilst at the Assize Court, but thought it would make the judge and jury believe that he was not in possession of his faculties. He has been constantly guarded day and night, and when he retired to rest seemed quite exhausted by the extreme violence of his passions. The Rev. H. MOULE was most assiduous in his visits to the wretched culprit, but he refused to see him for some time after his condemnation. The day after PREEDY's trial his mother and aunt called at the Castle to seek an interview with him, but he obstinately refused to see them for a long time, but at last yielded to the entreaties of the Rev. H. MOULE. His conduct then was of a very violent nature, and he was much excited. None of his friends or relatives have called to see him since."

We have thus seen some of the indications of the evil existing within the Convict Prisons under the present system. We learn from the witnesses that the officers are afraid of the prisoners, and with good reason; — that the Convicts are fully aware of their power to do great injury to them, and have found by experience that offences against officers are punished with far greater leniency, when committed by Government Convicts, than they would be if perpetrated by ordinary persons without the walls. Hence a sort of tacit understanding grows up between the Convicts and the warders, — the former abstaining from prison irregularities sufficiently to obtain the necessary V. G., the latter not being unduly zealous to observe more than he is called upon to do. Though the dietary is very high, yet frequent thefts of food take place among the men whose duty gives them access to it, and insolent demands to have their rations weighed are made expressly to annoy the warders. The

worst possible communications go on among the prisoners, the
most daring plots can be concocted unknown to the warders,
intercourse can be carried on with free men not connected with
the prisons, and the Convicts even steal the prison property to
obtain in exchange for it illicit indulgences. All these evils are
mentioned incidentally by various official witnesses, and appear
to be the necessary result of the system adopted. Still more,
though industrial work is relied on as a great reformatory
means, and the diligent labour of the Convicts is spoken of with
great satisfaction by many of the official witnesses, yet other
competent judges acknowledge that it is not equal to half what
would be effected by ordinary labourers; indeed, the slow,
leisurely "government stroke" of Convicts is notorious to common observation.

Again, after the very great attention paid in the separate
prisons of Millbank and Pentonville to the religious instruction of the prisoners, it might have been expected that they
would at least have learned to value the means of spiritual
improvement. But we learn from the Director himself that it is
not so,—that the Convicts do not appear to appreciate it, and
that even the short portion of time dedicated every evening
to worship is worse than wasted. No traces are anywhere
discernible in these establishments of progress towards what
is better, of anxiety to retrieve the past. Simple abstinence
from glaring misconduct is sufficient to obtain a character of
"exemplary," and takes the place of positive effort to do
right.

With such an account of the Convict Prisons from officials,
who would naturally desire to present as favourable a report
of them as possible to the Commission, we do not wonder at
the popular belief that any one who enters these establishments must come from them worse than he was before. Those
who have not before been hardened offenders must become so,—
those who had belonged to a different class of society must be
degraded, and sink to the level of those around.

Mr. THWAITES, the Schoolmaster of the *Sterling Castle* Hulk, gives the following evidence on this subject to the Select Committee of 1856. Though it relates to the hulks, which are now discontinued, yet it is evident that there is no material change in the system or its effects; his remarks are, therefore, applicable now:—

"It is a great fallacy to suppose," says Mr. THWAITES (2951), "that all convicts are reputed thieves, because we have such a mixture of crimes and criminals that the great majority are not that class of men who live upon depredations. Those who live upon depredations, and have done so for a number of years, are not so large a class as the others." "I might say that I have known many instances where men have been sent to prison under transportation for a trivial offence, and, *after their schooling in the hulks, they have become the worst possible members of society*" (2939). And again, "Discipline is defied, and moral instruction is thrown away upon a great proportion of these men, for they are so mixed together that every villainous crime could be concocted by these men, and the officers have not an opportunity of detecting or knowing what is going on, from the way in which they are all classed together" (2674). "It has come to my own knowledge that men have absolutely been known to *plan deeds which they would do after they were liberated from the hulks*' (2944). " The hulks have had so debasing an influence that I have seen men who have lived in the highest stations before they came to the hulks as debased as the lowest men in them before they have left them; for instance, *I have witnessed a clergyman, and barristers, and officers from the army, who have been debased to a level with the lowest of the London thieves before they have left the hulks.*"

Not only do Convicts become greatly deteriorated under the system adopted in these prisons, but the extreme consideration adopted towards them removes any deterrent effect which they might reasonably be expected to have, makes culprits quite careless about returning to them, and has even in some cases been known to tempt persons to commit crime, in order to enjoy the comforts which they could not procure for themslves by honest labour. Mr. SMITH, who has been for twenty-two years Governor of the Edinburgh Prison, gives this evidence to the Commission respecting the results of the English convict system:—(4947). "I have had many Convicts who have undergone sentences of penal servitude, who have been re-committed

to the prison in Edinburgh during the last eight years; I have
frequently conversed with them, and I can only remember one
or two instances where the parties dreaded again being sent
to penal servitude.  The punishment itself did not appear to
have been formidable to them, and it was quite common for
them to speak with gusto of the light work and excellent rations
in the penal servitude prisons.  Repeatedly they have stated
to me that an English Convict Prison was not only more comfortable than a Scotch County Prison, but greatly more
comfortable than a Scotch Workhouse.  After a sentence, and
before removal, returned Convicts always grumble until they
can be removed to the superior comforts of the Convict Prison.''
What can be worse for the morality of the country than that
such an impression should be given to the classes from which
criminals spring, that a felon sentenced to the highest secondary
punishment in the kingdom is placed in a better position in what
most concerns him, his physical comfort, than an ordinary occasional offender; and in a very far better position than a pauper.
Such appears to be very decidedly Mr. SMITH's opinion, for,
when asked (4948), ''Do you think that the accounts given of
the punishment by the returned Convicts have or not the effect
of rendering it formidable in the eyes of the criminal classes
in Scotland?'' he answers,--''*I do not think that the accounts
given of penal servitude by the returned Convicts have the effect of
rendering it formidable in the eyes of the criminal classes; many of
them boast that the labour is light, and that the dietary is abundant
and good.*  The punishment, excepting perhaps the few months
of separate confinement at the commencement, was not formidable to themselves, and anything which they would say of
it would not I think be calculated to make it appear formidable
to others.  The dietary, I know, not only from the statements of
returned Convicts and the published dietary tables, but from
having personally examined it in three of the principal Convict
Prisons in England, is not only much superior to that of the
Scotch County Prisons and Poorhouses, but what is of much

greater and graver importance, it is far superior to that which the honest labouring man or mechanic, having a family to support, can possibly procure. The struggle for bread is the main struggle for life, and no punishment will ever appear very formidable to the poor where, for comparatively light labour, there is good and warm clothing, excellent lodging, and abundant food." Not only is there no deterrent effect produced on the criminal classes by the descriptions of English Convict Prisons given by returned Convicts, but there is a positive mischief done when these come back to their native counties after their association with the worst criminals in the Public Works' Prisons. "The effect produced," Mr. SMITH says (4949), "by the return to Scotland of habitual thieves and burglars, by far the most numerous class, is, I believe, of the most injurious kind. Many of these having in the Public Works at the Convict Prisons, unavoidably perhaps, come into contact with the worst class of prisoners from the large towns of Great Britain and Ireland, and from all parts of the world, *return to their native counties much worse than they were sent away. Very many instances of this have come under my observation. It cannot be doubted that such returned Convicts exercise a great and pernicious influence on the young.*" Respecting the effect of the system on the Convicts themselves, Mr. SMITH gives very important testimony. One would naturally have expected that, if no other benefit was gained by these men, they would have learned to work, and to feel the benefit arising from active exercise and the varied employment of their powers. It has been usual to account for the imagined difficulty they experience in getting work, which is adduced as an excuse for their relapse into crime, by saying that the stigma attached to them from having been in penal servitude prevents their being employed. Such men will of course experience more difficulty in getting work than men of unblemished reputation, and indeed this is a necessary consequence of their loss of character which we would not willingly remove. As we sow, we must reap. We shall find, however, hereafter that, when a right system of penal discipline is adopted, the Convict when at liberty wishes to work, and that if the employer is protected from danger by the Convict when at large being placed under police surveillance, there is no difficulty in his obtaining employment, and, on the contrary, many employers prefer on their own account having at their work men so situated. Let us hear Mr. SMITH's testimony on this subject also:—(4950). "Excepting those who have been sentenced for offences such as forgery, breach of trust, and assault" (whom he has before spoken of as not belonging to the regular criminal class), "and excepting also a class who may be termed occasional thieves, and who steal only under the influence of intoxicating liquor, *I have not observed that it is the wish of returned Convicts to maintain themselves by honest industry. Those who have been habitual thieves appear to go at once to their old haunts, and consort with such of their old associates as they can find.* The competition of the labour market of this country is so great that the Convict who wishes to do well is doubtless placed at a disadvantage. He has to contend against superior skill (which the well-doing man almost always possesses) and superior character, which enters as an element wherever the employer of labour can select his men. He has also against him the wholesome dislike which the honest labouring poor have to being associated in any way with persons who have been convicted of theft. The great want, however, is, I think, WANT OF WILL TO DO WELL. *Where there is great earnestness of purpose*, as I have seen in one or two instances of returned Convicts, THEY CONTRIVE TO GET ON, THOUGH THE STRUGGLE IS A HARD ONE."

Mr. SMITH considered the high dietary one of the great evils of the English Convict Prisons. He tells us that in all the prisons in Scotland they have for breakfast " oatmeal porridge, the Scotch national poor man's breakfast. The dietary for dinner in Scotland is bread and soup, the soup is made from barley and a certain quantity of bread, about two ounces of bullocks head to each individual boiled in the soup." They never have meat. There are three rates of diet, the first being equivalent to 24 ounces of wheaten bread per diem, the second 30, and the highest 36. Mr. SMITH never found the health of the prisoners break down under a diet equivalent to 24 ounces of bread daily.

The returns brought by Mr. SMITH respecting the relapses of Convicts are important. During the last ten years 604 prisoners have been sentenced at Edinburgh to penal servitude, giving a general average of 60 annually. But during the year ending Dec. 31, 1862, there were in the prison 54 male and female prisoners, who were returned Convicts. Of these 54, 23 have been liberated from penal servitude or transportation, and were recommitted to Edinburgh Prison before the expiry of their sentences; ten of them for theft. Of the 54, 15 were again sentenced to penal servitude. During the year, 56 were sentenced to penal servitude, therefore 15, or 27 per cent., were those on whom the costly process of imagined reformation had been bestowed only to make them more hardened than before, a greater pest to society, and again to be maintained at the expense of the nation, that they may again come forth her worst domestic foes.

How little the Government Convict Prisons are dreaded by those who have been subjected to their discipline, and how little good effect it appears to have had on them, is proved also by the Governor of Holloway Prison. There are about 380 prisoners. The dietary is much lower than in the Convict Prisons;—nine hours and 25 minutes is the time of daily labour;—the silent system is strictly enforced, and if a prisoner is detected speaking to another, while working in association, he is at once reported. The Governor has not the means of proving what prisoners have been under sentences of penal servitude except from themselves, but he is certain from what he has heard from other prisoners, and *from their general conduct and demeanour*, that from 20 to 24 have been Convicts. They have stated to him (5208) "that the diet is much better in the Government Prisons than at

Holloway, and some of them say *that they will commit themselves again for the purpose of getting back*, sooner than stop at Holloway for six months; they say they would sooner spend twelve months in a Convict Prison than six months at Holloway." Besides the dietary, he says (5209), "they speak of the silent system. They have a great horror of silence; secondly, they do not like the tread-wheel; thirdly, they are kept a great deal more strict, and the cell is a greater punishment to them."

Numerous cases might be cited in which criminals have not only shown an entire carelessness about what was intended to be a severe punishment, but have even *wished* to be maintained for a time at the public expense in Convict Prisons. As an illustration of this the following statements are valuable, being made by the Chief-Constable for Somerset, V. GOOLD, Esq., in a letter read before the Magistrates, at the Somerset Quarter Sessions, and dated Dec. 29, 1862. It is addressed to Sir W. MILES, M.P. :—

"SIR,—In compliance with the request expressed in your letter of the 24th inst., I beg to submit to you the result of my experience of the present system of granting 'tickets-of-leave,' and the mode in which, in my opinion, our convicts might be dealt with, so as to secure greater safety for the persons and property of the public.

"That the present system has failed appears to be generally admitted, and it is usually found that where any robbery, accompanied by unusual violence, or any skilful burglary is committed, the perpetrators are very frequently returned convicts. These men are let loose upon society before the expiration of their sentences, without the slightest notification to the police authorities, so that they cannot tell under what conditions they are at large, and many of this class have been re-convicted in this county before their previous sentences had expired.

"It is therefore clear that the present mode of treating convicts does not deter them from again committing crime. They are well-clothed, well-lodged, better fed than probably they had ever been before, lightly worked, and, after a certain term of imprisonment, are again allowed to go at large before the expiration of their sentences. They are under no surveillance, and return generally to their old habits and associates.

"In illustration of this statement it will not, I trust, be considered out of place to bring under your notice a few cases that have recently occurred in this county.

"In the first place, a ticket-of-leave man, who had actually committed a burglary on his way home from the convict establishment at Chatham, and was subsequently re-convicted, stated 'that he did not mind being sent back to the Convict Prison; that he lived much better there than he could at home; and had merely to ring his bell, and a servant in livery must attend on him.

"In another case, a notorious burglar from Birmingham, whom you sentenced to ten years' penal servitude at the last Quarter Session for housebreaking, and who had previously been convicted of robbery with violence, said he did not care being sent back, as the only thing he missed was his 'daily paper.'

"Again, at the last Assize, a prisoner who was charged with arson, after having been previously sentenced to penal servitude, expressed a hope 'that he might be again transported; that he lived better there than he did at home; and that he received fifteen pounds after the expiration of his former sentence.' "

The case alluded to is the following,—

## "ARSON.

"JOHN MOORE, a middle-aged labourer, was charged with setting fire to some turf, with a view to destroy a dwelling-house, the property of ANNE BELMONT. Mr. SPEKE appeared for the prosecution. The prosecutrix is a widow, and keeps the Sportsman's Inn at Exmoor. On the afternoon of the 26th of November the prisoner was there. About nine o'clock she repeatedly asked him to leave. Near to the house is a barn and stable, and in the barn there were two turf stacks. On the following morning a lodger named FRANCIS drew her attention to the barn, where the turf was on fire. On the previous evening, when he was told to leave, he did so, and FRANCIS afterwards saw him lying on the porch. He took him up and sat him on the porch, and afterwards heard him go towards the barn. On the following morning he saw smoke issuing from the barn, and found a quantity of turf on fire, which had been lit with sticks and straw, portions of which remained. On being charged with the offence by the policeman, he said that he had expected him all the day—that he hoped he should be transported, for he had served four years before, and lived better there than he did at home, and when he was transported he had plenty to eat, and brought home £15 with him.

" His Lordship : Did he say where he was transported to ?

" Policeman : Portsmouth, my lord.

" His Lordship : Portsmouth !

" This being the case for the prosecution his Lordship said there was no case to go to the jury. The prisoner had made just as much a mistake as had the policeman as to the place he was transported to. The prisoner had not done the right thing to be transported—he had not done enough, and the law must not be strained to transport the prisoner. (Laughter.) The prisoner must be discharged."

Captain MACHONOCHIE, in the last evidence which he gave before the Committee of 1856, states his strong conviction that the actual working of secondary punishment was one of the causes of the increase of crime. He thinks so, he says (3781), "Because all punishments upon minor criminals make them worse and worse from day to day, and progressively as the number of discharged criminals accumulates in the country, the public opinion of the lower classes becomes more and more brutal and ferocious, and by and by, when that number is still greater, your difficulties will be so much greater, because the influence of these demoralised prisoners extends very far and wide, and they lower the public opinion of the criminal."

Such effects of the existing system were predicted by Captain MACHONOCHIE in 1856. Sir RICHARD MAYNE tells us, in 1863, that a large increase in the crime of the metropólis took place in 1862; there was a great increase of crimes of violence, burglaries and highway robberies. (1599) "I certainly attribute this great increase of crime, he says, to the accumulation of criminals in the metropolis who have not the means of obtaining an honest livelihood, who have been released after undergoing very short sentences, and in some cases those sentences shortened mischieviously by tickets-of-leave, or letters of license. * * * (1580). I have watched it with great anxiety from the first, and it was the opinion of every police-officer, particularly those who were employed as detectives, that there was a large number of these men abroad who were living by the commission of crime, and that of those who were released from prison, although many of them did not commit crime themselves, yet they instigated others to the commission of crime, and gave them the benefit of their experience and skill." (1581). "Since the cessation of transportation there has been, of course, a large accumulation of old offenders every year." (1582). "That number must be gradually and steadily increasing every year. A number who are released have not the means, even of those who are disposed to do so, of living honestly, and I believe that the love of thieving and the love of criminal practices is like some other passions of human nature, and that you cannot eradicate them."

We have now formed as complete an idea as possible of the system adopted in our Convict Prisons in England, for it is derived from the very words of those who are officially engaged in their direction and management, as presented by them to the Royal Commission. There can be no misrepresentation. These prisons are built at enormous cost to the State, and contain accommodation, the comforts of which might be envied by a large proportion of our labouring population. No expense is spared which might conduce to the attainment of the end proposed. The establishments are under the general direction of gentlemen of distinguished position, who evidently believe that the system they are carrying out is as perfect as it can be made, and who give their utmost efforts to make it succeed. They are provided with an ample staff of officials in every gaol, and these are carefully selected men, who receive high encomiums from their superiors for their devotion to duty. Nothing is wanting to complete the whole system, as conceived and planned by those intrusted with this most important duty. The annual cost to the country of these Convict Prisons is above £220,000, after deducting the value of the Convicts' labour, as shewn in the Directors' Report for the year ending the 31st March, 1862. This sum, enormous as it is, would be well employed did the system succeed,— were our Convicts reformed,—*but they are not.* The prisons themselves do not attain to that state of steady discipline which is arrived at in well-ordered county gaols. We might point to various large gaols in different parts of the country, and bring as witnesses officials employed in them, who could declare that in their prisons such a state of discipline would never for a moment be tolerated, as is indicated by the facts that the officers are really afraid of the prisoners, whose personal violence is often most dangerous; that these feel their power so completely as to demand the weighing of their food, purposely to annoy their officers;—that they steal the rations of the other prisoners, and behave just so far in accordance with the regulations as to escape punishment. It may safely be asserted, without any fear of contradiction, that such a want of discipline and moral tone does not exist in any large gaol in the country. Mr. CLAY, of Preston, whose loving Christian character would not have brooked any undue severity, tells us of a man being brought to his gaol securely ironed, with the warning that unless under such restraint he would be intolerable. The man had been a year (half of his sentence) in other gaols, where he had been unmanageable, and the character of Preston Gaol for firm discipline had induced a removal of him there. The man was at once informed, Mr. CLAY tells us, that though he would be treated with kindness, yet that the discipline in the gaol would be more than a match for him, and that it would be useless to contend against it; his fetters were removed, and through the remainder of his time his conduct was perfectly satisfactory. Nor let it be said that these county gaols have not to deal with the hardened Convicts who are to be found in the Convict Prisons. Preston, Wakefield, Leicester, and others, receive a number of these very men from the Government to undergo a portion of their sentence, and we have already seen in the extracts from Mr. CLAY's reports the desperate character of many of the prisoners confined there. A wise firm discipline, too strong to tempt to infringement of its regulations, too benevolent in the spirit of its administration to provoke antagonism, is essential to any improvement, and to the simple establishment of a spirit of obedience. This, the witnesses prove to us, does not exist in our Convict Prisons.

Again, this under-current of a rebellious spirit, this bad public opinion, so to speak, which pervades the criminal thousands of well fed and tended desperadoes in our large Government establishments, is fostered by the constant quiet communication of thoughts and plots unfit for the ears of officers, which is even recognised by the authorities;—this produces an ever-smouldering flame of discontent, which is ready to burst forth into open rebellion. It has so burst forth, and proved the Convict Prisons to be a danger to the country. Warnings which have been given have been little heeded. Before the Chatham mutiny, Captain MEASOR, the Deputy-Governor of Chatham Prison, in an able pamphlet published in 1861 ("A Letter to Sir G. C. LEWIS, Bart., on the Administration, Results, and Expense of the present Convict System"), showed that the existing state of things must lead to a mutiny,—and it came. Dartmoor appears like a constantly active volcano, and even now, when we are assured that there is no longer danger of fresh outbreaks, we find that fire-arms are required to induce the convicts to accept without rebellion a dietary more accordant with their real wants. Even in this July, 1864, a year after the Directors hoped and believed, as intimated in their evidence before the Royal Commission, that a steady and settled discipline was established, the public are to be startled with such a paragraph as the following:—

"INSURRECTION OF CONVICTS AT PORTLAND.
"THE MUTINEERS FIRED UPON BY THE GUARDS.

"The officials belonging to the convict establishment at Portland were thrown into a state of great alarm and excitement on Tuesday by the insurrection of a gang of convicts. It appears that on that day the new dietary system had been introduced, and this caused much discontent amongst the convicts. After the men had been marched back from dinner, a gang employed in a stone quarry refused to work, and attacked one of the civil guards. The impression amongst the convicts appeared to be that the guards would not use the short Enfield Rifles with which they were armed, but in this they were mistaken. Several of the gang rushed upon the guard, attempting to knock him down with their pickaxes and shovels, when the officer discharged his weapon, the ball slightly wounding one of the ringleaders. By this time he had received assistance from his brother officers, who fired upon the mutineers, four or five of whom were shot, but not seriously injured. This measure had the effect of quelling the disturbance at once, and the party were marched back to prison, and confined in punishment cells."

Who would suppose that the "mutineers" here spoken of are criminals imagined by the authorities to be in the way of reformation, and that most of them are probably "exemplary" prisoners, with a daily mark of "Very Good!" Again, in a few days we read:—

### "THE CONVICT MUTINY AT PORTLAND PRISON.

"The feeling of insubordination among the convicts at the convict establishment here, in consequence of the introduction of the new dietary system, still continues to be exhibited, although no outbreak has taken place. Every day large numbers of the men refuse to work, alleging as an excuse that not sufficient food under the new dietary system is given them to keep their strength up. On Tuesday, a large body of men refused to leave their sheds after dinner and resume work, and it was not until the aid of the military was obtained that they would resume work. Almost every hour men are marched back handcuffed to the prison, and from inquiries we have made we are informed that about 230 have turned refractory, and are now confined in their cells. The ringleaders of the riot of Tuesday are recovering from the injuries which they received at the hands of the civil guards. It was expected that on Thursday, Friday, and Saturday the men would again turn mutinous, as a number of them were severely whipped on those days, but such was not the case. This is no doubt attributable to the fact that the guards have received orders to fire upon the convicts should another outbreak take place, and also to the excellent arrangements which have been made by Captain CLAY, the Governor of the Prison, and Captain DU CANE, Director of Convict Prisons, the latter of whom is now engaged in instituting inquiries respecting the outbreak, and in awarding punishment to the evil-doers. Every precaution has been taken to suppress a revolt should one unfortunately take place, *two detachments of the 64th Regiment being stationed in the vicinity of convict labour*, one overlooking the batteries on the east side of the island, and the other near the West Quarry, where the outbreak on Tuesday commenced. *In addition to this force there is a strong picket of the civil guard in the tower, should their assistance be needed.* The insubordinate convicts are confined to their cells and dieted on bread and water; but while thus treated some of them are very violent."

Any person experienced in the management of large institutions would need no further proof than the facts here alluded to, that the Convict Prisons are conducted in a manner which is most unsatisfactory. The possibility of "mutinies" and outbreaks on an organised plan, at once indicates that an entire change in the whole system is necessary. It proves that a bad tone pervades the establishments, and that among a set of men of whom a considerable proportion are desperadoes of the deepest dye, who are spreading their evil influence around, and are themselves deriving increased power from their excellent physical condition, and their sense of power to do evil. If these great receptacles of felons are not reforming them to a better life, they are preparing them to go forth far worse than before, and infinitely more injurious to society! That such is actually the case is testified by the two important witnesses who are selected from the metropolis of each great portion of the kingdom. They prove by actual demonstration that residence in the English Convict Prisons has actually added to the crime of the country, both in intensity and in quantity; and no favourable statement of results, such as we may find in criminal statistics given us by the Directors of such establishments, can shake the evidence such witnesses give of the dreadful facts, with the calmness of those who have been long habituated to them. Nor are their testimonies isolated. Few can have more extensive and general knowledge of the crime of London, the great receptacle of all that is good and all that is bad in the country, than Sir RICHARD MAYNE; few can have known more experimentally than Captain MACHONOCHIE the contagious nature of criminal influence; few can be better acquainted with the effect of such influences on the country than the experienced head of a county constabulary. These all give their own characteristic and independent testimonies to the same effect. The last even adds a new feature, which is borne out by other very striking evidence, that a Convict Prison on the system adopted in England, not only presents little terror to the habitual and experienced thief, but is considered a desirable resting place, where he will be treated with consideration, well fed, housed, and clothed, to come forth with money in his pocket to recommence an exciting career of crime on his discharge! What more do we need to prove the enormous evil of this system?

It will not be attempted yet to point out the errors in principle which appear to be the evident cause of these results. Any one who understands the cause of the success which was so remarkable in Munich, in Valencia, in Norfolk Island, and who admits the soundness of the principles set forth in the last chapter, will readily perceive why the English Convict Prisons are so great a failure,—why they are doing such enormous evil to the community.

Of the actual re-convictions from these prisons throughout the country there is no possibility of gaining a correct estimate, because there is no certain means of recognising in courts of justice which are discharged Convicts or license holders; we may, however, form some idea of these from the statistics of a single district, the West Riding of Yorkshire, which can be relied on, as accurate accounts have been there kept of the prisoners sent thence to the Convict Prisons, and their course subsequent to discharge has been carefully traced. These we learn from the volume which has had so extensive a circulation, "Observations on the Treatment of Convicts in Ireland, with some remarks on the same in England, by Four Visiting Justices of the West Riding Prison in Wakefield." In the Supplement to the Second Edition (February 1863) is the following statement:—

"The authorities of the English Convict system had officially declared it to be producing excellent results—that its 'success' was 'conspicuous'—and but few were disposed to question the statement. They kept their secrets so well, that only by a very round-about process were we able to estimate the proportion of ticket-of-leave men who returned to crime, as nearer to 50 per cent. than to 20 per cent., as stated in the official reports. We have since found that our estimate was too low, as regards the persons sentenced from the West Riding since 1854, whose sentences have expired, so that the result as to them could be ascertained from the police as well as from the prison records. Of all the *men* sentenced to terms of four years' penal servitude from the Riding during the years 1854, 1855, and 1856, 57 *per cent have either returned to prison or were known to be living by crime.* Only 22.4 per cent. were known to be living honestly. Taking all the persons sentenced from the Riding to terms of three or four years, from 1854 to 1858, 44 per cent. of the men, and 50 per cent of the women, had actually returned to prison before December, 1862, though those sentenced in the later years could have been discharged but a very short time. As to these last, returns from the police have not yet been obtained. We have no reason to think that such results are at all peculiar to the West Riding."

The authors make the following observations on the system itself :—

"The *semblance*, indeed, of the principle laid down by Lord GREY, that, 'upon the daily record of the conduct of the convict should depend his final release,' has been retained. A record *is* kept of the conduct of the convict. Upon his conduct during the period of separate confinement depends his classification on Public Works; and upon that classification depends his enjoyment of more or less of certain indulgences, such as gratuities, communication with his friends, beer, puddings, tea, &c. But so far is 'his daily conduct and industry' from being 'made to have a *certain and obvious effect* in determining the period of his release,' that, after the best inquiry we have been able to make, we cannot find that the daily conduct, and especially that *industry*, has any effect at all in determining that period· We cannot find that the release of the convict is ever deferred beyond the earliest day on which it can be granted, except in case of *positively bad* conduct, and then, except perhaps recently, only for short periods. This is a wholly different thing, acting upon the convict's mind in a wholly different way from that pointed out by Lord GREY. It is an entire abandonment of that which he pointed out as having 'contributed more than anything else to the gratifying reform which had (then) taken place, viz., the looking to *hope* as the principal means of exercising an influence on the minds of the convicts.' The remission of sentence ceases to be an object of *hope* as soon as it comes to be regarded as a matter of certainty and of right; and offers no motive for industry and *active exertion* to do well, when it is to be obtained by mere *passive* abstinence from gross breach of prison rules.

"If the forfeiture of any portion of the remission is the result only of positive misconduct,—and we cannot find that it is ever otherwise,—that is, *pro tanto*, 'trusting entirely to *fear*, as the instrument of government.' We are bound to say, however, that from all we can learn of the internal economy of the Public Works Prisons, it would seem that the application of this last principle has been somewhat inverted, and that 'fear' *of the convicts* has been the motive of many of the arrangements which have been adopted. The plan seems to be,—instead of affording to the convicts a motive to *active* good conduct, by making the *hope* of remission dependent on such conduct,—to propitiate and keep them from violent outbreaks, by allowing them the *possession* of certain indulgences, *e.g.*, by a diet so excessive, that we are assured by prisoners who have passed through the Public Works Prisons,—whose evidence on this point may be less exceptionable, as against their own interests,—that some of it cannot be eaten, but is destroyed lest it should be diminished. The usual effect of a policy which seeks to bribe off an enemy, is found in the repeated outbreaks which have occurred in those prisons so frequently, and of which the accounts which are allowed to ooze out are so imperfect that it is difficult to keep pace with them, or to ascertain the real facts relating to them.

"It is clear, however, that, though the convicts are but imperfectly governed by fear, and scarcely at all by hope, both these motives are strongly brought to bear upon the warders. Hope,—in that certain gratuities due to the warders are made to depend on the conduct of the convicts, *as reported by them;* which explains, in some degree, the 'Very Good prison characters' borne by most of the latter. Fear,—of the murderous assaults which these men have the will, and, as the results show, the power, to commit on any warder who renders himself obnoxious to them.

"Under such a system the inducements to the warders to be liberal with good reports and sparing with bad, are so strong, that we cannot wonder when we are informed, that the number of convicts who fail to obtain remission of their sentence on, or soon after, the earliest possible day, is very small. As little can we wonder that it has lost its power over them, as a motive to good conduct before discharge; and that,—with the abandonment of the principles to which Lord Grey pointed out we were 'indebted for the striking and happy contrast between the conduct that prevailed in the modern prisons and that which formerly existed in the hulks,'—the state of our modern Public Works' Prisons should be sinking back so rapidly, as we have strong reason to fear that it is, to the moral likeness of those dens of violence and abomination."

The enormous defects of the English Convict system attract the attention of other nations which are accustomed to expect from our country enlightened legislation on such subjects and faithful administration of the laws. A work has recently appeared in France, containing severe strictures on it, entitled "De L'Amélioration de la Loi Criminelle," par Bonneville de Marsangy, Conseiller de la Cour Impériale de Paris. The author says (Part ii., p. 91) :—

"L'imperfection du système de répression anglaise offre des aspects multiples, qu'il faut soigneusement distinguer. Elle tient notamment :

"1º A l'*organisation vicieuse* du système de servitude pénale substitué à la transportation, système qui, ainsi que le déclarait hautement le *speaker* de la Chambre des communes, président du grand jury de Nottingham, a pour résultat 'de rendre incertain l'effet des condamnations prononcées, et de diminuer la crainte des rigueurs de la loi chez les criminels.' * * *

"2º A l'*insuffisance des peines correctionnelles*, dont, suivant M. le Baron Bramwell, président de la Cour criminelle centrale, sont frappés les auteurs de graves méfaits contre les personnes et les propriétés. * * *

"3º A l'*impossibilité notoire où sont les tribunaux de connaître les anté-cédents judiciaires des inculpés*, et, par suite, de pouvoir leur appliquer une peine proportionnée à leur degré d'incorrigibilité. * * *

"7º Enfin *la déplorable exécution donnée à la mesure des tickets of leave.*

Ce sont là, pour tous ceux qui, sans engouement ni hostilité systématique, ont étudié la législation et l'état des faits en Angleterre, les vraies causes de la recrudescence criminelle qui a si fortement préoccupé l'opinion publique et le gouvernement. Je m'attache spécialement à cette dernière cause, parce qu'elle est l'objet principal que je me suis proposé dans les premiers chapitres de ce travail."*

M. MARSANGY thus speaks (p. 97) of the Convict Prisons :—

"Le rapport de la commission royale de 1863 prouve que le système pénitentiaire anglais a été énervé au delà de toute expression. La servitude pénale substituée à la transportation n'y a aucun caractère intimidant. La détention cellulaire qui constitue la première période du châtiment, y est très-rarement subie durant le temps prescrit (neuf mois). Loin de redouter la servitude pénale, les condamnés parlent avec satisfaction *des avantages* que leur assure cette peine ; du travail *doux et peu fatigant* auquel ils sont soumis ; de l'*excellente* nourriture qu'on leur distribue, et de la façon *confortable* dont ils sont traités."

The author here quotes the evidence of Mr. SMITH, which has been already cited. He continues :—

"Quant aux prisons de travaux publics (*public works prisons*), la com-mission royale reconnait que l'impression 'très-générale' est que leur système pénitentiaire n'a pas un caractère 'suffiisamment pénal.' Les convicts sont bien mieux pourvus dan ces prisons que les indigents des *workhouses* et les ouvrieres libres. 'Nous craignons, dit le chapelain de la prison de Newgate, que les convicts ne soient *trop bien traités;* car ils sont miex nourris que le pauvre qui gagne son pain par son travail.' Nous conclurons avec le lord *chief justice* 'qu'un tel régime pénitentiaire est peu fait pour disposer le condamné à l'amendement, et pour produire sur son esprit cette crainte salutaire du châtiment qui peut le détourner du crime et intimider par son exemple les autres malfaiteurs.'"

We must earnestly hope that such a condition of things will not much longer disgrace our country. The evil *can* be remedied, because it has been remedied in our Sister Isle. Let us no longer remain in apathy and silence. From time to time panics have taken possession of the public mind, and the daily papers have echoed the alarm ;—articles in our periodical literature have endeavoured to direct public opi-nion, and to point out the true cause of the gigantic evil. The powerful pen of "S. G. O." has shown in the columns

---

* The italics are those of the author.

of the *Times* how "Guilt Gardens" are cultured, and their fruit brought to an appalling size,—the fruit of the Upas tree which flourishes in them. But official reserve, and the confidence in the system evidently felt by our rulers, have hitherto prevented the public from so discerning the cause of the evil as to demand its cure for their own protection of life and property. It remained for the Royal Commission to enable these secrets to be thoroughly unveiled, and to let the public know from the directors and officers themselves, both the general principles and the details of the English Penal Servitude System, and to judge from them why "our Convicts" are the terror and disgrace of our Christian country! If any should imagine that the brief extracts from the evidence here given present too unfavourable an impression, let them study the evidence for themselves, and form their own opinion.

# CHAPTER V.

## DISPOSAL OF CRIMINALS, AND TICKETS-OF-LEAVE.

The disposal of discharged criminals is one of the most perplexing and difficult problems of our day. To establish and manage an institution — whether an Orphan Asylum, an Hospital, a Reformatory, or a Gaol—is a matter comparatively easy; but so to conduct it that the inmates, after having been the subjects of skilful management and under steady control, shall go forth as free agents, and without the help they have been receiving, to do their part in society under either favourable or adverse circumstances,—this is the trial,—this the difficulty. Yet it is thus only that we can test the success of our work,—the truth of the principles on which we have been carrying on our institutions. It would be of little advantage to society that we should be able to show them well-managed Reformatories, the premises neat and clean,—the boys obedient and diligent, strong and hardy, —the girls well-conducted, orderly and respectful—unless, on after trial, when our children are no longer under our care, it were found that the public money had been expended in producing hard-working youths of both sexes, able and willing to earn an honest living, and to do their part in society. Failures must always occur; there will always be many individuals unsusceptible of even the best efforts to improve them;—but these will not diminish confidence, if the public is satisfied with the principles carried out in the institutions. Society will always be ready to forgive criminals if it has reliable evidence of true repentance. Thus we have ourselves found that, while at the commencement of our reformatory work, we were sneeringly asked what we should do with our boys and girls when we had reformed them,—no question of the kind now arises, for employers of labour not only are willing to take our scholars when discharged, but even seek for them, preferring in their employment, for their own advantage, young persons who have undergone a steady, regular training in the Reformatory Schools.

Now it would be of course unreasonable to expect the results that can be attained with youths, in the case of adults, especially of persons who, as Government Convicts, are presumed to have committed very serious offences, or to have been frequently in commission of crime. The hardened and wilful offender cannot expect the same leniency from society as the young person who acts probably " sans discernement." There is a natural retribution which is part of the order of Providence; no human agency can remove it, though the Christian spirit may soften the consequences to the offender, and enable him to derive from it the precious fruits of repentance. We would not, if we could, obliterate in society a wholesome sense of repugnance to crime, nor show to the offender, however penitent he may seem, a kindness and consideration which we would not more cheerfully extend to the honest working man. This would truly be a premium on crime, and very injurious to the moral tone of society. But a readiness to admit really repentant sinners within the pale of society, and to give them a chance of retrieving character, certainly exists in our country;—and if the working classes do not come forward themselves to receive them, there are large employers of labour who readily do so, and who for many reasons are the proper persons to undertake the charge. The testimony of gentlemen connected with well-managed gaols in various parts of the country shows that persons who have been committed to them can get work after their discharge, *if they try*. In large communities direct efforts are frequently made to enable discharged prisoners to obtain work through the agency of institutions established for the purpose;—of these we shall speak in a future part of this work;—but even without such assistance there is not any general complaint made of great difficulty arising from the simple fact of a person having been in prison, irrespective of his subsequently proving himself indisposed to pursue an honest course of life. Mr. CLAY repeatedly shows in his reports, and in his evidence to Parliamentary Committees, that persons who were discharged from the Preston gaol did get into employment, and that inquiry as to their conduct through the police disclosed most satisfactory results. If, then, we find a general unwillingness on the part of the public to employ persons discharged from the Convict Prisons, where a sufficiently long time has been passed to give time for change of character, where special pains have been taken for their improvement, and where every advantage of training has been afforded them, such unwillingness must arise from the fact that the public do not believe in the efficacy of the system pursued, and have not confidence that it would be safe to employ any person who has been in a Convict Prison. Such disbelief in the reformation of Government Convicts exists universally throughout the kingdom.

The British public have long had reason to believe that there is "something very rotten" in this state of things. They have shown an extreme indisposition to employ persons who have been in Convict Prisons, not from a pharisaic feeling of standing aloof from so-called sinners,—not from hardness of heart, for no nation has ever shown a more Christian feeling towards erring brothers, or more overflowing benevolence towards those who want their need,—but simply because a profound and general disbelief exists in the probability of any persons being reformed in those prisons, or even coming out of them uncontaminated and not hardened in vice.

Now that this is the cause of the alleged difficulty is shown in the case of youths discharged from Parkhurst, a Juvenile Convict Prison, last year closed for that purpose.

The Director of that prison states, in his evidence before the Select Committee of 1856, not only the very great efforts he made to induce persons to take the boys discharged from Parkhurst into their employment, but the restless unsatisfactory conduct of the bulk of them, when efforts had been made to help them. He says (632): "I sent two boys to a gentleman, ————. He kindly took these two lads; their characters were good, and he treated them well; however, they soon left him; one, if not both, went on board ship at South Shields. I then taxed the philanthropy of a particular friend of mine, ————, an extensive coal-owner, and I sent him first and last a dozen in different drafts; they got very good wages, and were very well treated; they gave a great deal of trouble; they were very dissatisfied, and they gradually disappeared; but no dishonesty was even suspected among them. I then picked out a promising lad for a cabinet-maker at Liverpool; the cabinet-maker said that if this boy behaved himself properly and gave satisfaction, he hoped he would be the first of a succession of Parkhurst boys who might be sent to him; that he would take care that the other workmen knew nothing at all about him. I sent him down accordingly; he did well enough for three months, and then he left him, assigning some trifling reason; afterwards that boy got into a scrape, and his license was revoked. (633). He committed some offence; this was very unfortunate, as of course I could not ask the cabinet-maker to take any more; nor could I ask ———— to take any more, after the dozen whom I had sent him had left him. One lad I sent down to Bedford, and he has succeeded admirably, but he is the only one of those to whom I have had anything to say who has remained in his place; in fact, after their discharges with license, they will all roam; they will go upon what they term the tramp, and then it is a great fortune if they turn out well."

Such a statement as this, coming as it does from a Director of Convict Prisons, who has the special care of this department, sufficiently indicates that the system which produces such effects, however perfectly administered, is not founded on correct principles. It is not the simple fact of a person's having subjected himself to punishment and been in prison which prevents him from being able to obtain honest employment; the difficulty arises from a belief existing in the public mind that the individual has been contaminated by his residence in the gaol; also from a want of any certainty that the criminal has truly repented, and is prepared to do better if a fair opportunity is afforded him. These two causes naturally excite in the minds of employers of labour a fear of suffering injury from a discharged Convict, and in persons of the respectable working classes a dislike of being in any way associated with him; and in these originates the extreme repugnance which certainly exists in England to discharged Convicts. To remove this repugnance, and to give persons who have undergone a penal sentence that fair chance of retrieving their character and of gaining an honest livelihood, which they ought to have in a Christian country, the following conditions must exist:—

First,—The penal system must be such as to inspire general confidence that it is likely to produce a reformatory effect on the persons subjected to it.

Secondly,—Before release, the prisoner should be placed in such a condition of comparative liberty, and should have such degree of exercise of his own will, as may enable him to give some reliable proof of his determination henceforth to choose good and to eschew evil.

Thirdly,—He should be for some time after his discharge in a state of *conditional* liberty, so that if he proves by his conduct that he is not reformed, and is likely again to injure society, he may be sent back to a longer period of discipline.

Under these three conditions the fear of employing discharged Convicts will cease, and the extreme repugnance felt towards them in the public mind will be changed into the feeling which our Saviour inculcates towards our brethren who have offended "seventy times seven," but have repented, and have resolved to sin no more. Then there will be no difficulty in the disposal of our criminals, for society will receive them,—they will be absorbed into it, and they will no longer be marked out as "Convicts."

These conditions have not been fulfilled in England.

First,—There is no public confidence in the penal system which is adopted in England. If proof were wanting of this, we might fill volumes from the leaders and letters in many of the public journals of the end of 1862, and the commencement of 1863, and with extracts from the leading Quarterly Reviews and the periodical literature of that period. Without being able, perhaps, to understand what were the faults in the system of the Convict Prisons, the public knew that they must be bad, because the results were bad, and they feared to trust any one who had been in them. Let the system be entirely changed, and one adopted which has been proved by results to be successful, the results will be different, and the public will feel confidence.

Secondly,—There is at present in the English Convict Prisons no possibility of testing the sincerity of the prisoners' repentance. The Public Works' Prisons were probably intended to have this effect, and to prepare the Convicts for the world. But as long as we know that the prisoners in them cannot be trusted even to take their meals together;—that the trusted ones seize opportunities of stealing food from the others;—that tools have to be carefully abstracted from the prisoners to prevent violence; —that, notwithstanding constant precautions, terrible mutinies from time to time occur in those prisons, requiring for their suppression the aid of armed forces, and even the presence of a ship of war, the chief actors in these mutinies being prisoners who were designated "very good;"—and that even at the present time fire-arms are required to be at hand to suppress rebellions among prisoners who "are supposed to be reformed,"— when the public know all this, it is impossible that they can give any aid in the disposal of our Convicts. Society asks to see some reliable proofs of repentance, and asks it with reason, and no proofs are reliable which are not given by persons whose wills are released from strict prison bondage.

In future chapters it will be proved that these two conditions can be so carried out as to produce the results desired, and we may therefore feel assured that if they are so in England, the public will not be slow in comprehending the real value of the system, and co-operating, as elsewhere, with the Government, in the work of reforming the Convicts.

But for complete success in this, the third condition is indispensable, and has been acted on fully in the cases alluded to. The liberty of the criminal on his discharge must for some time be conditional on his good conduct;—if he still shows a disposition to injure society, he must be again subjected to reformatory discipline. Now this very important principle has been adopted by our Government in this country, since penal servitude was substituted for transportation, the trial of it having been first made in Australia. But unfortunately it has never been fully carried out in England, from causes which will presently be explained. Hence the great difficulty which now exists in our country in the disposal of our Convicts.

The apparent failure of a system of conditional freedom, from which excellent results were anticipated, is chiefly to be attributed to the want of a provision for the regular police supervision of all prisoners who are thus conditionally discharged. Now this question of police supervision involves much which is so little consonant with the tone of feeling in our country that it has excited considerable discussion. The subject received considerable attention by the Committee on Transportation in 1856, and Mr. ELLIOT presented in the appendix a *resumé* of replies to inquiries made by the Government to many Courts of Europe, respecting the system adopted in them about the disposal of criminals. The information conveyed in this paper is important, as proving the general acceptance in Europe of the principle that discharged prisoners should be placed under special surveillance;—since it would probably be obtained with much difficulty, if at all, through any other channel, copious extracts are here made from it:—

## BELGIUM.

"In BELGIUM, at the expiration of their sentences, persons convicted of crimes are placed, for a period of more or less length, under the surveillance of the police.

"The expense of each convict in prison in Belgium may be estimated at from 7½*d.* to 8*d.* a day."

## AUSTRIA.

"In AUSTRIA, as soon as a prisoner has finished his time of punishment, the administration makes a report of his private circumstances, and of his behaviour during the time of his detention, and delivers it to the head of the police, but the delinquent himself is to be sent to *the place where he resided before, and there he is subjected to more or less surveillance by the local authorities.*"

## PRUSSIA.

"The measures of precaution taken by the Government in regard to discharged prisoners consist of placing them under the surveillance of the police, and the exercise of this power has been regulated by a special law, dated the 12th of February, 1850.

"It is the custom in PRUSSIA, Baron DE KATTE tells us, in his evidence before the same Committee, to place a man under the surveillance of the police after the expiration of his sentence. This forms a part of his sentence, supposing a man has been condemned to two years' confinement, he is generally sentenced to three years of the surveillance of the police. It is not found practically that this surveillance is any hindrance to him in getting employment. The return of the prisoner is notified to the government of his district, and steps are taken to obtain monthly reports of him.

"In Prussia there is but a small number of persons who are continually coming back to prison. Though it is of course known that there are persons who habitually live by crime, yet care is taken that they should not transmit this to their offspring;—the children, for the last twenty years, have been removed from them, and educated in suitable establishments.

"Voluntary philanthropic societies are established near every large prison, the members of which frequently visit the prisoner while in confinement, and assist him on his discharge. These societies are regarded by the Government as very valuable."

## BAVARIA.

"As a measure of security the liberated penitentiary convicts are, after the completion of their sentences, subjected by law to a special surveillance of the police at their place of abode during five years.

" Prior to the discharge of the convicts who, in cases that require it, are provided with clothes and money for travelling at the expense of the establishment, the authorities of their place of abode are informed of the same, and at the same time of the trade or employment learnt by the liberated convict in the prison; in order that work be regularly provided for them, and that their favourable reception at their places of abode should promote that end, a union is established for the purpose of providing for discharged convicts."

## HANOVER.

" In HANOVER we are informed that the penal system cannot well extend its efficacy beyond the time of detention. Experience has, however, shown that the best penal institutions obtain their aim very imperfectly when *the confined, after being dismissed, are not put under sufficient control,* and do not receive the opportunity and means for earning their livelihood in an honest way.

" The local magistrates, to whose jurisdiction the dismissed individuals are directed, cannot therefore better execute their vocation than by assisting these individuals with their advice and help, to treat them with indulgence, though with firmness, and to stimulate them to order and activity.

" In order that the local magistrates may receive timely information, *so that precautionary police measures may be taken,* the authorities who conducted the inquiry have, at the time of sending the individuals into the penal institutions, immediately to furnish the local magistrates with the result of the inquiry, accompanied by a personal description, and remarks of the nature and duration of the punishment, and such other notices as may be serviceable; in particular cases even the communication of the documents of inquiry.

" As to the manner of the surveillance in respect to individuals dismissed from the penal institutions, general rules cannot well be given; the greater part must rather be left to the judicious consideration and circumspection of the local authorities. The precautionary arrangements for surveillance and care should be prepared beforehand, so that the individual at his arrival may be furnished with the proper directions. Such measures will be taken, according to the reasonable judgment of the magistrate, as may tend to lead the dismissed to a regular use of his personal liberty, and regular mode of life, keeping in view the more or less dangerous inclinations manifested by him. The extent of surveillance is not to be greater than circumstances require. *The public safety, however, must always be kept in view.* Afterwards it may be considered for what time the dismissed is to be ordered, perhaps, to report himself at certain times at the police of the circuit or place; for instance, in case of a pretended journey from the place or neighbourhood. Such control can usually cease at the end of a year, if urgent reasons do not require a prolongation. * *

In case a prisoner liberated from the penal institutions, and standing under surveillance, desires to change the district to which he is directed for another place, on account of any good reasons, information must be sent to the magistrate of the district to which the man intends to go. If any man under surveillance does not obey the regulations, or withdraws secretly from the district assigned to him, *police punishment is to be inflicted on him*, and, when requested, he may be treated in the same manner as suspicious and incorrigible vagabonds."

## SAXONY.

" The laws of SAXONY do not prescribe any fixed measures of precaution as to discharged prisoners: all of them, however, who can show evidence of reform are sent back to their native place; and unless some other district should voluntarily receive them, they cannot quit their domicile until they have earned in it *a certificate of good conduct for one whole year*. After they have gained such a certificate no district is at liberty to refuse them admission. The *police of their native place are warned beforehand of their approaching liberation, with orders to exercise a surveillance over them*."

## NASSAU.

" In NASSAU dangerous convicts are placed *after their liberation under the surveillance of the police for not less than one, or more than five years*. This surveillance consists of:—

" 1. The superior police authorities are empowered to direct—

" That the individual under their surveillance do not quit his domicile, or the limits assigned to him after nightfall, without permission from the police.

" That such individual do not remain in any place if his presence there seems dangerous.

" 2. The judicial and police authorities may at any time visit the domicile of such individual.

" The breach of such orders is punished with imprisonment.

" In Nassau there is a society also for the care and superintendence of individuals discharged from the Houses of Correction and Discipline, and also from the Lunatic Asylums."

## BADEN.

" The native who is condemned to imprisonment in a house of correction is at the same time, as far as public safety seems to be endangered by him, sentenced to be placed under the superintendence of the police; this superintendence cannot be awarded for less than one year, and not longer than for five years.

" The effects of being placed under the superintendence of the police are the following :—

" 1. The person placed under such superintendence may not leave his native place, or any other domicile, which, with the permission of the police he may have chosen, during the night, without being allowed to do so by the Mayor,—and not for eight days without leave of the police authorities.

" 2. The judicial and police authorities have the power to search his home at any time.

" If the person placed under the superintendence of the police leaves his domicile or place of residence without permission, he is, at the request of the police authorities, punished with three months' close confinement.

" The person placed under the superintendence of the police is freed from it for the time to which he has been sentenced, by giving bail for a sum to be fixed by the judge.

" The bail is forfeited when the person placed under superintendence of the police commits a new crime, which is punishable with imprisonment in a house of correction, and such crime has been committed within the time for which bail has been accepted.

" If the new crime punishable with imprisonment in a house of correction is less than the first, the bail can be declared in part forfeited in proportion to the crime.

" The bail forfeited to be paid to the Treasury, deducting the indemnification to be made to the party offended against, if the author of the offence is not able to furnish that sum."

## THE HANSE TOWNS.

" In HAMBURGH a private society is established in order to facilitate the liberation of prisoners, and to provide against their relapsing into error; dangerous criminals are, moreover, placed under the surveillance of the police."

" In LUBECK care is taken to facilitate the re-entry of criminals into society by delivering them the money *they have earned by extra work in their leisure hours*, sometimes by taking steps to render their means of subsistence secure. A private society has been formed for co-operating with the authorities in this particular."

" In BREMEN no regulations have been made with regard to placing criminals under restraint after their liberation, nor are they necessary, as such restriction may at any time be decreed by the sentence of a court of justice. There is, nevertheless, a private society for the superintendence and care of liberated convicts."

## WURTEMBERG.

" In WURTEMBERG the following regulations are made for the superintendence of criminals after their liberation from prison.

" When the authorities of the district in which the prisoner's domicile is situate receive notice as to his approaching release and capabilities for work, they are bound to provide for at least his temporary employment, and to make every arrangement consistent with that object; and for this purpose the extra

wages (if any) which the prisoner has earned while in prison, or any other
property that he may possess, is to be sent by the executive of the prison
to the said authorities.

"If the prisoner departs from the route laid down in his certificate of
liberation,'he renders himself liable to be treated as a vagabond.

"The authorities of the district in which the prisoner's domicile is situate
must advise the executive of the prison on his arrival, and not till then is his
name removed from the prison roll; but when he does arrive the police
regulations are put in force for his surveillance.

"The liberated convict need not be sent home, if he can mention some
other place, to the satisfaction of the prison authorities, where he will be able
to obtain a livelihood, and in that case they must be informed of his arrival
in that place. Nevertheless the authorities of the district in which the
released convict's domicile is situated must be informed of it, and the prison
executive must satisfy itself of his arrival in the place of his settlement.

"Those released convicts for whom employment is found by the society
for providing for such persons, must be particularly informed as to who
the district manager of their new place of destination is, and this last-
mentioned person is charged with the duty of bringing them before the
master and the district clergyman, before whom his certificate of discharge
is laid, in order to take proper measures for his superintendence and moral
and religious care. Notice is then to be given to the district assistant
society of his entrance, and of the amount of the savings which have been
delivered to the district authorities to his account by the executive of the
prison, in order that they may be laid out to the best advantage by the
assistant society, with the advice of the authorities of the district.

"Prisoners who have committed an offence punishable by confinement,
or have been guilty of repeated vagrancy, if the sentence does not order them
to be placed after their liberation under the especial surveillance of the police
of the district in which the prison is situated, must be conveyed on their
release from prison to their respective houses, *in order to put in force the
further police regulations against them.* In like manner, foreign pauper
prisoners, after their liberation, must be conveyed to the frontier, and
not till then is their property, viz., the savings they have made in prison,
delivered to them."

The regulations for "Confinement to the Domicile," as it
is termed, are extremely minute, and too long for insertion
here. The tenor of them may be gathered from the following
extracts:—

"One of the principal means adopted for the moral and social reformation
of liberated Convicts is the confining them to certain prescribed limits.

"This is accomplished by the local police with the assistance of any trustworthy person, and particularly of the district clergy, and members of the
society for the care of liberated convicts.

" The persons so placed under restraint are summoned once a week before the Inspector of the district, on some day not previously fixed, and he interrogates them as to their circumstances, employment, &c., and reports accordingly to the Court of the district. Sometimes an inhabitant of the district takes upon himself the duty of superintending one of the persons so restricted, and he reports his conduct to the Inspector once a fortnight, and the latter to the Court of the province every quarter of a year.

" Every person under such restraint, if he is in receipt of assistance from the public purse, must use his best endeavours to find employment, and if he cannot succeed, he may be compelled to accept such as the Inspector finds for him.

" *Particular care is taken that their children attend the public schools,* and if they are absent from them without sufficient reason, the Schoolmaster has to inform the Inspector, lest the cause of their absence should be the departure of the parents from the limits prescribed, or any other infringement of the police regulations.

" If a person under restraint quits the locality to which he is restricted, the proper authorities are informed of it by the Inspector, and the necessary steps are taken to bring him back.

" *A list and description of all the persons under restraint in the district is kept at each police office,* together with an account of the duration of the sentence, the limits prescribed, and the nature of their employment, copies of which are sent to the chief and all the neighbouring officers, &c., &c."

The object of the voluntary society alluded to above, is to co-operate with the police authorities in the restoration of a criminal to society.

" Since employment suited to this purpose, and religious and secular instruction, are provided in the penal settlements in Wurtemberg, and the moral reformation of the prisoners is attempted in them, the society bases its efforts upon the results produced in the penal establishments ; and the operation of the society commences where that of the State ends, namely, at the return of the liberated convict into social life. The society makes it its duty to bring to the knowledge of the Government the results of its experience, and to act, when requested, upon the suggestions made by the executive authorities of the penal establishments.

" All are invited to co-operate with the society who have a sincere desire to promote its objects, regardless of the differences of station, sex, or religion."

The details of the operation of this society are very valuable. Connected with it are numerous " assistant societies." The whole working of them appears very complete, and the results amply reward the labour bestowed.

## SWEDEN.

"In SWEDEN discharged prisoners are placed under the surveillance of the police, until they can succeed in either getting themselves hired in service, or finding some other means of subsistence. If in a given time they neither procure one nor the other, they are liable to be again sent to the public works for a definite period."

## NORWAY.

"In general no steps are taken with regard to criminals who have served their time of confinement. The only measure in connexion therewith is, that when a more serious offender is freed from prison before his time is out, by the King's free pardon, the rule is to discharge him only on condition that, for a certain period thereafter, he shall not be found in any of the towns where penal establishments are situated, or in any of the districts belonging thereto, unless such should be his place of residence. Any one offending against this regulation is re-imprisoned, but is soon again discharged, usually after about six months. The object of this arrangement is, as far as possible, to prevent masses of discharged criminals collecting in particular places, especially such as are the seats of the penal establishments. In the meantime this object can be very imperfectly obtained, no legal enactment enabling the authorities to apply this rule to the far more numerous class of offenders who undergo the whole period of punishment to which they have been condemned."

## TUSCANY.

"In TUSCANY numerous societies are in active operation, at Florence, Volterra, and San Gunizano, to provide occupation for liberated convicts.

"The average annual cost of prisoners during the last six years in the penitentiaries, after allowing for the profit derived from their labour per head, has been £6 14s.; to this add £2 16s. for the cost of guards, &c., making a total annual cost of £9 10s. per head.

"The number of guards found necessary are five per cent. to the number of prisoners."

By none of these Governments is transportation adopted for criminals. In many of the countries here mentioned there would be a natural impossibility of employing any such means of thus relieving themselves of the difficulty of dealing with crime. Norway, it is stated, has never had any penal colony, and, as far as is known, has never felt the want of one. In Sweden, public opinion has always been against transportation, viewing it as an unsatisfactory punishment, and also one which would be very costly for a country which possesses no colonies of its own. Even supposing it possible that a foreign power would consent to open some of its penal settlements for the reception of Swedish criminals, there would be serious considerations of national law and of private justice for hesitating to make use of the opportunity. Whenever the subject is alluded to in the other official answers, similar opinions are given. No application was made to France, so many valuable works being accessible on the criminal law of that country. The only information given by Portugal is respecting transportation, for which the size of her colonies give great facilities. About 260 being transported annually, no want is probably experienced of special arrangement for the comparatively small number of those who remain at home. In Russia no mention is made of surveillance of discharged criminals, the report being chiefly occupied with the system of punishment, and of transportation to Siberia and the Caucasus.

Leaving, then, out of consideration the two last-named countries, the peculiar circumstances of which render them essentially different from all the others mentioned, we may make the following statement of the system which has been acted on, more or less, by them all :—

Persons suffering imprisonment are considered to owe their labour to society, and if any gratuities are allowed they are for *extra work* done in leisure hours. These are generally reserved for their use after discharge.

In almost all cases criminals when set at liberty are liable to be under police supervision. In some cases there is a conditional discharge under surveillance; in others there is a direct sentence of supervision after imprisonment of from one to five years. In many States the superintendence of the police is very strict, the object being to make each State *absorb its own criminals* without annoying other districts, and to protect society in it.

In order to secure this, information is sent to the authorities of the place to which a criminal is returned; in some cases special notices are sent respecting his conduct in prison, and the way in which he may be most advantageously employed; he is thus at once under surveillance when he reaches his destination.

Private societies are very generally instituted, to co-operate with the Government in the restoration of the offender, and in some cases the supervision is intrusted to them.

Such, then, are the principles generally recognised in these States.  Offenders after receiving punishment are to have every opportunity of regaining their character, and a benevolent public helps them to do so, and is ready to receive them on condition of good conduct;—but at the same time society must be protected, and this can be done in the case of one who has broken the laws of the country, only by a special watchfulness being exercised over him, to arrest him in his career, if he shows a disposition to continue the same evil courses.  In the States of Europe from which these returns are sent, there appears to be no doubt as to the justice or the expediency of this course.

In our own country, however, the necessity of the adoption of such measures has not 'been generally acknowledged, nor has there been a recognition of the principles on which they are founded.  Private benevolence has done much to relieve discharged prisoners; but this voluntary benevolence has not been so organised as to effect the object throughout the country.  Until, indeed, the disposal of our criminals by transportation was nearly stopped, the attention of the Government does not appear to have been directed to any systematic method of giving gradual and conditional liberty to prisoners in England.  This course appears to be most safe as regards the culprit himself, and most just to society which has a right to protection.  The person who has seriously offended against the laws of his country has no right to expect confidence to be reposed in him until he has proved satisfactorily that he is deserving of it, and yet he may justly ask to have a fair opportunity of trial; on the other hand, society has a right to protection, and to some guarantee that persons who have proved themselves dangerous members of it shall not be permitted again to be at liberty among their fellow citizens, without some check. Both these objects can be accomplished by a combination of police surveillance and voluntary benevolence, and have actually been so where these have been wisely directed. If there has been a failure we shall find that the conditions have not been complied with.

We now proceed to examine the system of conditional freedom in our own country,—the principle and practice of the "ticket-of-leave" system. In order to arrive at a correct judgment respecting it we must divest ourselves of the prejudice against the class of men designated in England "ticket-of-leave men." We know well that the very name has of late years been one of terror, presenting to the mental view those habitual criminals whose vocation is to prey upon society, to defy all law human and divine, and from whose violent attacks there can be no safety until they are again incarcerated. This impression is so strongly impressed on the public mind that whenever any great crime is committed we expect to find that its author is a "ticket-of-leave man." When we learn from numerous attempts at house-breaking in a neighbourhood, that a band of burglars is visiting our vicinity, we conclude that they are "ticket-of-leave men." No discrimination is generally made between those who have been in the Convict Prisons, and have completed their sentence, and those who are nominally under conditional freedom;—and as there is a strong popular conviction that criminals come worse out of the Convict Prisons than they enter them, we cannot wonder at the prejudice existing against persons in any way connected with English Convict Prisons. But the prejudice is not against the system in itself considered;—if we cross the Channel we shall find that in our Sister Isle no such dread exists of the very name of "ticket-of-leave men." On the

contrary, employers of labour gladly give them work, and even
go to the prison doors to engage them; the respectable portion
of society does not keep aloof from them, and they regain their
lost place in society, or make one if they never before had one
to lose. We go further across the ocean to our antipodes, the
great island Continent in which we are striving to plant our
principles and our institutions. We find that there, in Western
Australia, land-holders are glad to employ men under "tickets-
of-leave," and that though persons who have formerly been
Convicts form a large proportion of the community in country
districts, the tone of morals is not deteriorated. It cannot be
then the "ticket-of-leave" system which is wrong, but some
defects in its administration which prevent its beneficial operation. These we shall learn from the evidence given before the
Royal Commission.

The principle of a conditional discharge was originated first in
the Colonies, where men who had been transported were, after
a time, set at liberty under certain conditions. But a large
number of men remained in confinement in England who had
received sentences of transportation, about 9000 at the end of
1852, when transportation was discontinued; the sentences were
always long, as it was intended that they should be abridged
nearly one-half by good conduct under confinement. The system
of conditional freedom was therefore extended to them also. It
appeared to possess great advantages, and to be founded on
a true principle.

Since it is quite impossible that the reformation of any one
can be relied on as real, as long as he is in an unnatural
condition and under coercion, which he must be while in
prison, to give a Convict his freedom, under condition that it
shall be forfeited at once if he proves by his conduct that he
is not reformed, is evidently a most satisfactory way of ascertaining the safety to the public of his return to society.
Besides, the slight control and surveillance which are implied
in the license itself, and essential to the development of the

system, are an excellent preparation to one whose voluntary action has been cramped for many years, to enable him to use his liberty without abusing it.

The following conditions are indorsed on the license of every Convict so liberated in the United Kingdom:—

"NOTICE.

"1. The power of revoking or altering the License of a Convict will most certainly be exercised in case of his misconduct.

"2. If, therefore, he wishes to retain the privilege, which by his good behaviour under Penal Discipline he has obtained, he must prove by his subsequent conduct that he is really worthy of Her Majesty's clemency.

"3. To produce a forfeiture of the License *it is by no means necessary that the holder should be convicted of any new offence. If he associates with notoriously bad characters, leads an idle and dissolute life, or has no visible means of obtaining an honest livelihood, &c., it will be assumed that he is about to relapse into crime, and he will be at once apprehended, and recommitted to prison under his original sentence.*"

This notice is so explicit, and so distinctly asserts that a new offence is not necessary for the forfeiture of the license, that the public at first reposed confidence in the Government that its provisions would be carried into effect. But it soon became evident that in England no means were being taken to enforce the conditions of the license, that the whole of the warning to the Convict was a mere delusion, that this ticket-of-leave was quite unnecessary to protect the Convict from the danger of being apprehended as a runaway from prison, and did not defend the public from the risk of being at the mercy of unreformed criminals. This official document was, then, a mere useless form, which the Convict, for his own safety, would generally hasten to destroy, as being a silent witness against him in any new crime he may commit.

This state of things appeared to be not accidental but intentional, for Mr. WADDINGTON stated in his evidence before the Select Committee of 1856, that no effort had been made by the Home Office to follow these ticket-of-leave men, and to

find out their course of life generally. "It was thought far
better," he says (243), "to give no directions whatever to the
police upon the subject, *but to leave them precisely in the situation of men who had served out the whole period of their license*."

The public certainly laboured under a great misapprehension
on the subject, being little aware that it was the avowed intention of the Home Office not to enforce the conditions, but to
place a Convict still under sentence in the position of one whose
punishment had been fully carried out! The same witness
states (247): "It is necessary to exercise the power (of revoking licenses) *very strictly indeed, for the protection of the public.
If it were not so the whole advantage of the license would be at an
end*." It certainly does seem extraordinary that, with such an
acknowledged necessity, so few licenses have been revoked,
especially as the same gentleman says (244): "We have
received a great deal of voluntary information upon the subject, of course from the heads of the police of different places,
not only of men who have misconducted themselves, but of
men who were likely to do so."

Much important evidence was brought before that Committee
of the injurious effect arising from disregard of the terms of the
license. The result of the discharge into society of a number of
Convicts on license, without any provision having been made
for enforcing the conditions of the license, is thus described by
Mr. SMART, the Superintendent of the Police in Glasgow, in
his evidence to the Committee of 1856 :—

"2102—2109.—Ticket-of-leave men find their way into Glasgow, no inti-
mation having been made either to the Sheriff of the county or to the Lord
Provost of the city, or to the magistrates of Glasgow, or to the police.
Dozens of them turn up in a night. They are found in certain houses of
Glasgow known to be bad; but no intimation is sent before them; we have no
notice of their arrival at all. Very frequently strangers come amongst us;
parties we do not know; parties who have not been transported from Glasgow.
We know that they are ticket-of-leave men, because many of them admit that
they are so, and we have taken other means of ascertaining it from their
associates, and the parties with whom they are lodging, and so on, and we
have found beside tickets-of-leave in their possession frequently. We have

had sometimes, of male and female parties in Glasgow, probably from 70 to 80, that is as many as that who were known to us; but I have no doubt that there are a good many of them that we do not even know of. *Now, to have given the ticket-of-leave system fair play, there should have been first organised a proper police over the whole country.* There would have been a police to have counteracted their operations, which has not been the case. Communications would have been easy among the police; and if these parties were found in Glasgow returning to their old practices, we should have had police at various other towns to communicate with, and should have been able to put them on their guard against their operations."

Mr. SMART states that no interference would ever be exercised if a man were conducting himself properly; on the contrary, he is always ready to encourage and help such. He suggests, however (2140), "that when a man is liberated, word should be sent to the Sheriff of the county in which he is liberated that he is at large, and that he is going to reside at Glasgow. Then if he follows his lawful occupation, neither the police nor anybody else should interfere with him; but that if, on the contrary, he does not get into lawful employment, they are to be put on their guard." On being asked (2170),—"Whether he does not believe that if the police had information respecting a license-holder he would be so dodged by them that he would find it impossible to get employment," Mr. SMART replies, "I think there is more danger from the system at present, *from nobody knowing who they are. I think the greatest danger exists under the present circumstances, and that would be obviated to a great extent were proper instructions given to the heads of police; and they would take care that the officers did not interfere improperly or unnecessarily.*" Mr. SMART states that there have been 61 re-transported; of these about 12 were persons who had received a conditional pardon previously to the Act of 1853. Only three or four have had their license withdrawn.

Mr. JAMES M'LEVY, a detective officer at Edinburgh, gave similar evidence to the Committee. He cannot tell how many license-holders have returned, but his experience leads him to the conviction that the system is not a good one, because the men who have been on the public works are not reformed,

"The men are as bad when they come back to Edinburgh, *or much worse*, than before they went away."—2286.   He mentions six who have been sentenced to 21 years since their return, two to 15 years, and one for life; also four or five others who are leading a very bad life, associating with thieves, and living in bad houses, but who have not been convicted since they came home.   Besides these, two were convicted in a Police-court sentence to 60 days each, and then returned to the same place where they came from.   " I will explain," he says (2326), " one case of a ticket-of-leave man, the first that I saw at Edinburgh.   His name was G. B. ; he was just seven weeks home, and within these seven weeks there were seven different acts of theft against him, *and not an officer in Edinburgh knew that he was home.*   I recovered the articles which had been stolen in the seven different acts in a broker's shop, and the broker told me that generally the thief came and sold the goods to him ; the same night I watched at eight o'clock, and found him coming with some more stolen goods to the same shop."

Society might have been saved much of the injury arising from these crimes, and the enormous expense of punishing it, if there had been proper provision for carrying out the conditions of the license;—still more, if the Convict system had been such as to produce a reformatory effect on the criminals.

In London a similar experience is given to the Committee by Police Sergeant LOOME.   He states that the police never received any instructions respecting the conditions of the license, or any duty to be performed to the holders of it, and it was the general practice of the police not to interfere with them in any way, if they were trying to maintain themselves honestly by work.   He knows of some who have been doing so, and succeeding, but he says (2620): "I think the majority have conducted themselves very badly since they have been home ; where one is reformed after coming back, I think I may say ten or twelve return to their old habits.   (2618). Some have been sent away to very heavy penal servitude for house-breaking and for highway robbery. They may commit twenty very serious offences before they are detected after coming back; and I have seen them the same day that they have come back with their old companions again. (2619). I do not think they ever tried to get into work; I have seen them when they have come back, in a day or two, and they are continually, day and night, with those parties with whom they associated before they were transported, a great many of whom have been in prison continually." When the Convicts return with their licenses, he says that they usually commit daring offences, burglary, highway robbery, &c. " They frequently, after they come home," he says (2692), " turn to uttering counterfeit coin, because, if they are once committed for uttering counterfeit coin, it is only a misdemeanour, and they can perhaps only have twelve or eighteen months. They cannot transport for a misdemeanour, and these fellows are aware of that, I have no doubt, and that is why they do it."

Though the actual results had been so unsatisfactory in London, Sir RICHARD MAYNE expressed to the Committee of 1856 an opinion respecting the soundness of the principle of discharging prisoners on license, which is important as coming from one who, from his position, would be well qualified to judge. He says (3388), " My opinion is that the system of a ticket-of-leave, as far as it releases persons, *keeping them under the power of subsequent punishment by a revocation of the license, is a good one.*" To effect this, which is indeed the very essence of the system, and the condition under which the license is granted, it is evident that some degree of supervision of the Convict is necessary. " *Unquestionably,*" as Sir RICHARD states in the same evidence, " *information ought always to be sent to his office respecting all ticket-of-leave men sent to London.*" No notification of the kind, he says, has ever been made, and as it is the usual practice of the license-holders to destroy the document which might be a witness against them in case of fresh transgression, it is entirely accidental whether the police recognise a ticket-of-leave man or not. Convicts were sent forth, then, into society without any arrangement being made to secure the due fulfilment of the conditions to the criminal, and safety from his outrages to the public. On the contrary, while it is the ordinary practice of the police to keep convicted thieves under special supervision, these license-holders were privileged with immunity, for an order was issued by Sir RICHARD, in accordance with what he understood to be the intention of the Government, to restrain them from what would have been their practice otherwise in reference to ticket-of-leave men. It is as follows :—

"The superintendents are to instruct the constables and sergeants of their divisions, with reference to the experiment that is to be tried of releasing convicts on ticket-of-leave,— that the police are to be careful not to interfere with them, so as to prevent their following any honest course for earning their living; with this view, should any of these parties have obtained employment, notice is not to be given to the employers that they have been convicted, *nor when seen in public houses are they to be pointed out to the landlord, and required to leave, as in other cases of convicted thieves and suspected characters.*"—3377.

A special immunity for irregular conduct is thus to be given to these licensed Convicts!

The result of these restrictions on the police, Sir RICHARD further says, is "that they are *not* to trace out the ticket-of-leave men." "I am fully persuaded that the instructions have been generally carried out, not only from the general confidence I have that a police order is obeyed, but I have not had complaints of a departure from those instructions. I have seen statements in the newspapers, but I have not had any cases verified before me, in which the police have acted contrary to, or differently from, the spirit of those instructions."—3412.

Such being the position of the question in 1856, as regards the central police authorities in the metropolis, we shall not be surprised to learn from the same source that 174 licenses had already been revoked from the known commission of fresh crime, while a great number had committed crime without their licenses being revoked, because the sentence for the subsequent crime extended far beyond the original sentence. (3365, 3372.)

"But again," says Sir RICHARD (3372), "I think that the number of licenses revoked, or the number out on license who have been convicted, does not show the extent of the evil arising from such numbers of experienced and skilful criminals being set at large in our state of society. In last January I called for a return from each superintendent, as far as his knowledge went, without making special inquiries, but from that which was under the eye of the police, as to the occupations of those who were known to be out on tickets-of-leave. I have got that return here. I do not know whether the Committee would wish me to read it; it shews that there was a considerable number of those who, I think, it is not unreasonable to suppose, were living, at least partly, by criminal pursuits, by the commission of crime, and yet against whom no specific crime could be proved so as to make it a justifiable case for the Secretary of State to revoke the license. Most of these cases are of persons associating with thieves day and night, and not known to have any honest means of earning a living;—under these circumstances the police conclude that they are living by criminal courses."

The following table presents an abstract of the paper here alluded to, which was given in to the Committee, and inserted in the Appendix of their Report:—

| No. of Division. | No. of Ticket-of-leave Convicts known to be living in this Division. | Since reconvicted. | Doubtful,— Living dishonestly or associate of thieves. | | Does not work. No honest means of living. | Occasional work. | Living honestly. |
|---|---|---|---|---|---|---|---|
| A | 0 | ... | ... | ... | ... | ... | ... |
| B | 10 | ... | ... | ... | 5 | 5 | ... |
| C | 0 | ... | ... | ... | ... | ... | ... |
| D | 12 | 1 | left & unknown 2 | | 6 | 2 | 1 |
| E | 4 | 1 | 2 | unknown 1 | ... | ... | ... |
| F | 8 | 2 | 4 | ... | 1 | ... | 1 |
| G | 10 | ... | 9 | ... | ... | ... | 1 |
| H | 16 | ... | ... | ... | 13 | ... | 3 |
| K | 13 | ... | 7 | ... | ... | ... | 6 |
| L | 3 | ... | 1 | ... | ... | ... | 2 |
| M | 9 { 3 recently returned | ... | 7 | ... | ... | ... | 2 |
| N | 5 | ... | 2 | ... | 1 | ... | 2 |
| P | 20 | ... | ... | ... | 15 | ... | 5 |
| R | 3 | 2 | ... | ... | ... | ... | 1 |
| S | 7 | ... | 6 | ... | ... | ... | 1 |
| T | 3 | ... | ... | ... | ... | ... | 3 |
| V | 4 | 1 | 1 | ... | .. | ... | 2 |
| | 127 | 7 | 39 | unknown 3 | 41 | 7 | 30 |

Among these is one very bad case of murder and of burglary;
only one case is mentioned in which a license has been revoked,
and in that instance the man, having absconded, was still at
large. Of the remainder, only one-fourth are believed to be
living honestly. The rest, after their costly punishment, are
more or less a burden and an injury to society. These 127
whom the police have discovered in their districts are but a
very small fraction of those who have been sent out, for we
learn from the same source that more than 5000 were released
under license, during the two years in which the Act has been
in operation (3368).

Of the difficulty, or even impossibility, of ascertaining which
are ticket-of-leave men, Mr. Recorder HILL speaks in his
evidence before the same Committee, quoted by himself, in
his "Repression of Crime." From a want of any information
being sent to the authorities, he states that numbers of persons
out on license never are identified; that they are not recognised
when they again commit crimes, and, consequently, that the
statistics which have been given, indicating that a very small
per centage of license-holders have been reconvicted, are founded
on very insufficient data. He thus speaks (1790) :—

"It is said that the number of reconvictions does not amount to more
than 8 per cent. of the number of convicts discharged on tickets-of-leave.
Now, no doubt it is quite true that 8 per cent. of the convicts discharged
on tickets-of-leave have been reconvicted, but I am by no means convinced
that *only* 8 per cent. have been reconvicted ; and it is quite clear that
before that inference can be safely drawn it must be known that ticket-of-
leave men can always be identified. But from the observations which I
have made, and the inquiries which I have made, I have come to a very
strong opinion that, not only are they not always identified, but that a vast
number of them escape identification; and the probability is that a very
considerable number of ticket-of-leave men have been reconvicted who are
not known to have been previously convicted, and who therefore stand in
our tables as convicted for the first time. I will offer to the Committee, if
they will permit me, some facts in proof of that conclusion. I have carefully questioned the heads of the police at Birmingham as to whether they
have any means of identifying all the ticket-of-leave men in Birmingham;
they assure me that they have not, and they have given me very strong
proof that they have not. In the month of November of last year I asked

them to make out a list of all the ticket-of-leave men in Birmingham, and to watch carefully their conduct for a certain time, and then to make to me a report. They did so. They thought it fair and reasonable to tell each person that his conduct would be watched; that he would not be interfered with if he were doing well, but that his conduct would be observed and noted down. At the end of six weeks they sent me a schedule, which I have before me, and by that schedule I found that there were 19 men whom they considered as ticket-of-leave men. Within the last few days I have received another report, in which they tell me they have discovered that five of those men were not ticket-of-leave men. Well, but 19 men for the town of Birmingham seems to be a very small number of licensees. I observe that Colonel JEBB says that 198 ticket-of-leave men belong to Warwickshire; they have been sent to Warwickshire. I do not know how the assignment is made, but they are in his evidence assigned to Warwickshire. Birmingham has very nearly half the population of the whole county, and I have not only observed that fact, but I have ascertained the proportion of prisoners convicted at the sessions in Birmingham on the one hand, and in all the other parts of the county on the other; and without taking the Committee through the details of the calculation, which I can do if they wish, I find that there ought to be 80 ticket-of-leave men in Birmingham, whereas only 19 could be found, and of those, five turned out eventually to be not ticket-of-leave men. I then questioned the police upon that difference, and they tell me that they have reason to believe that there are at least 40 in Birmingham, but they cannot venture, with respect to more than those of whom they have given me the names, to state that they are ticket-of-leave men; but 40 would be only half the number, according to the basis given by Colonel JEBB. Therefore, as far as the experience of Birmingham goes, I think I am justified in saying that there is sufficient difficulty in detecting a ticket-of-leave man to make me pause before I accept the 8 per cent. as an accurate statement."

What security, then, could the public feel that they were protected from injury from these license-holders, when the police were actually unaware which they were!

After such evidence as the foregoing, and more of a similar character, the Select Committee of 1856 passed the following resolutions:—

"11. That the system of *licenses to be at large*, as *tickets-of-leave*, authorised by section 9 of this Act, has been too short a time in operation in this country to enable the Committee to form a clear and decided opinion, either as to the effects which it has already produced, or as to its probable ultimate working.

"12. That this system appears to be founded upon a principle wise and just in itself, viz., that of enabling a convict to obtain, by continued good conduct while undergoing his punishment, the remission of a portion of his sentence, upon the express condition, however, *that in case of subsequent misconduct, his liability to punishment shall revive for the residue of the term specified in the original sentence."*

The Committee do not, however, appear satisfied that this condition had hitherto been observed, for they thus express their views in subsequent resolutions :—

"15. That to render this system of tickets-of-leave adapted both for the reformation of offenders and the interests of the public, the conditions endorsed on the tickets-of-leave *ought to be enforced more strictly than appears to have been hitherto the case.*

"16. That every convict, on his release with *a ticket-of-leave, ought to be reported to the police of the town or district to which he is sent."*

The hopes excited by the Report of the Select Committee of 1856 that a more efficient administration of the ticket-of-leave system would be adopted, were doomed to be disappointed. No change appeared intended. As the number of Convicts increased who were discharged from our Government prisons, the consequences foretold by Captain MACHONOCHIE and others were realised. Crime of a peculiarly audacious and organised kind increased fearfully. The panic of 1862 and the succeeding spring will not soon be forgotten. The following petition, presented to the House of Commons early in 1863, shows the facts of the case, and the anxious desire of many, who saw with alarm the consequences that must arise from the number of unreformed Convicts, who would be set at conditional liberty without control :—

"THE HUMBLE PETITION OF THE UNDERSIGNED,
"SHEWETH,

" That the outrages recently committed by convicts discharged on tickets-of-leave have occasioned much public alarm, and show the urgent necessity there is that those men should be placed under the supervision of the police.

" That a considerable number of ticket-of-leave holders are now at large—2,069 having been discharged in 1861, and 2,297 in 1862—and that tickets-of leave have been now extended to those who were sentenced for five years and upwards, under the Act of 1853, and, therefore, to all convicts to be discharged subsequently to 1862.

" That, whatever may be the result of the Commission at present sitting, tickets-of-leave having been promised to those convicts, cannot now be withheld from them.

" That, even if transportation should by any means be resumed, a large number of those whose time for release has nearly arrived could not be sent out of the country, but must be discharged in England.

" That the number of convicts who must be so discharged within the present year appears from the judicial statistics to be considerably more than two thousand.

" That your petitioners having understood that partial measures have been taken to make the convicts about to be discharged on tickets-of-leave known to the police of the metropolis, but no measures having been taken to extend that knowledge to other parts of England, are apprehensive that the effect must be to drive discharged convicts, who may be criminally disposed, from London to the large provincial towns and country districts, where they will be wholly unknown and therefore more dangerous.

" Your petitioners therefore pray that your honourable House will be pleased to present a humble address to Her Majesty, that Her Majesty will command that each holder of a ticket-of-leave shall, on being liberated, be reported to the police of the district to which he may be sent throughout England, and that such other measures be taken as shall secure the enforcement of the conditions endorsed on the license."

The appointment of a Royal Commission early in 1863 revealed more clearly the danger which threatens the country, from the system now adopted in discharging Convicts, and from the non-observance of the terms of the license.

We are again informed (*vide* evidence of Mr. EVEREST, 126) that there is no mode of finding out *that a person is the holder of a ticket-of-leave if he is disposed to conceal the fact.* Numbers of persons, therefore, have been convicted of offences, being holders of tickets-of-leave, who were not known to be such at the time of their conviction. The knowledge that a criminal was actually a license-holder would of course make the sentence more severe, and there would be every effort on the part of the prisoner to conceal it. The recognition of the licensed Convicts depends, then, only on the *chance* of their being recognised by officials who had known them, and who think fit to give information of the fact. It is evident, therefore, that official statistics of the number of relapses of persons who have undergone penal servitude in England are not of the slightest value, because there are no reliable facts on which they can be founded. We shall, consequently, not quote them in this volume.

Yet even with this fundamental difficulty in the way of their recognition, since these persons are of disorderly habits, and have often contracted peculiarities of manners and appearance which point them out to the experienced eye, we should expect to find that a large number of these license-holders have been discovered in the breach of the conditions, and the license revoked. As many as 8653 licenses had been issued under the old transportation system, and up to the end of 1859, and of these 875 were revoked, about one-tenth ;* but in the two following years 2490 licenses were issued, with the conditions above quoted annexed, and only 11 were revoked ;† the revocations were generally after some fresh offence, not involving another sentence of penal servitude, and in the very small number of cases where there was no reconviction, very strong representationshad been made as to the mode of life that was being led by the licensee (136). The public have been perplexed by such facts, and have wondered why there was this evident unwillingness to protect society by the removal of those who had no right to their freedom, the conditions on which they held it being broken.

We learn next from the same evidence (200-205) that though there has been no formal decision at the Home Office that the resolutions of the Committee of the House of Commons should not be acted on, yet, in fact, the recommendations have *not* been attended to, neither as to the more strict enforcement of the conditions,—this is of course shown by the small number of reconvictions, — nor as to the superintendence of the police. This last of course could not be exercised unless there were official means afforded them of recognising the licensees, but these do not exist.

Mr. WADDINGTON, in his evidence, gives the following reasons for the course which has thus been pursued to the extreme detriment of the public :—

"424.—The law which enables licenses to be granted did not provide for any investigations before a Magistrate, or for any way in which a prisoner

---

* *Vide* Commission Report (117).     † *Vide* Appendix to Commission, D.

could be heard upon an allegation as to his subsequent bad character, and the absence of any such provision has, I think, been the cause of the Secretaries of State declining to enforce that condition upon a mere or *ex parte* report of the police, excepting in the few cases of which you have heard, in which the evidence has been so strong of repeated misconduct, corroborated by Magistrates generally, as well as by repeated police reports, that it has been thought it might be acted upon even without any formal hearing at which the prisoner could defend himself.

"430.—Have you never compelled them to report themselves periodically to the police?—Never; it has always been thought, and that is my opinion, that if a system of surveillance by the police is to be introduced into this country, it ought to be done by Act of Parliament. I confess that I should be very sorry to be a party to introducing it without such an Act; it has never been heard of in this country before."

We find, then, that though the criminal enjoys his liberty on condition of submitting to such restrictions, his feelings of dislike of surveillance are to be considered, rather than the safety of the public whose laws he has violated, and the duty of obedience to the regulations annexed to his license. Still more,—we are astonished to learn from Sir RICHARD MAYNE, on whom, as Commissioner of the City Police, the duty devolved of seeing that the police carried out instructions respecting the Convicts:—(1824). "It may appear strange for me to say so, but until a few months ago I never saw a ticket-of-leave, *and did not know what was endorsed upon it;*—it was no business of mine."

It thus appears that though the Convict, on receiving his license to be at large conditionally on his good conduct, is distinctly warned that *he will be at once apprehended* if he is found associating with notoriously bad characters, leading an idle and dissolute life, or even without visible means of obtaining an honest livelihood, there are no means adopted to carry out these provisions;—the head of the police is not even aware of them, and the witnesses from the Home Office inform the Commissioners, not only that these conditions have not been carried out, but that a legal impediment exists as to the apprehension of the licensee and the revocation of his license, which they have never attempted to remove; they even

feel an objection to carrying out the resolution, which was the
basis of the Act of 1857,—the supervision by the police,—on
which condition alone the release of the Convict is safe to the
public.

Are we now astonished at all the crimes which have been
committed in our country by these persons? They come forth
from the Convict Prisons with their sentences unexpired, without
having given any reliable proof of reformation; they defy the
law, for they know by experience that, either through inability
or negligence, it will not or does not touch them; they are
in good physical condition, and recruited in strength for fresh
outrages; they know from the correspondence they have carried
on with their "friends" where to find them; they have better
clothes and more money in their pockets than they have ever
obtained by honest labour; and thus they go forth, undeterred
by the way in which they have passed the last few years, to
throw a fresh infusion of crime into the country, and to tempt
others, by their apparent impunity, to commit similar outrages
on society.  We shall find in Sir R. MAYNE's evidence that their
position as license-holders even gives them facilities to commit crime, and shields them from too troublesome inquiries
from the police, who have actual orders not to meddle with
them, because they are supposed to be reformed.

Sir R. MAYNE informs the Commissioners, as he had done the
Committee of 1856, that, not by an "express order, but an order
consistent," he says (1819), "as I conceived, with the desire of
the authorities; it was, I believe, by the Secretary of State's
desire; the order was issued in March, 1856, in consequence of
several complaints made that the police were preventing persons
from getting employment who might otherwise obtain it and
become reformed." The order was the same as that given in his
former evidence, p. 192. He continues: (1822). "I do not think
that I was aware that the ticket-of-leave was given as a matter
of course. I looked upon it then that the ticket-of-leave was
rather a certificate of a reformed man." (1624). "With regard

to those who were released on tickets-of-leave, the police were directed not to notice them, as they were looked upon as persons who must be considered reformed, and therefore the police were directed not to notice them, lest it might make them known, and interfere with their getting employment." These Convicts, then, are absolutely a class privileged to offend the law without interference.   The Public Houses Act makes it penal to harbour known thieves, and the police constantly visit the houses these persons are known to frequent; (1626) they point them out to the publicans or the refreshment-house keeper, and say, " You are committing an offence;" "that person is a thief," and so on, (1628) but the ticket-of-leave man they do not point out.   They know that he has been a thief, they may have seen him actually resuming his old career, and the familiar associate of notorious thieves;—but as he is supposed to be reformed, nothing is to be said to him—he is not to be interfered with.   Besides, as it is understood by the police authorities that it would not be legal to apprehend license-holders for violating the conditions of the license, they have not even the same power of apprehending these, which they have in case of other suspicious characters. It is evident, then, that the natural effect of such a system on men who are holders of tickets-of-leave is what Sir RICHARD states in his evidence it actually is: (1792) " *The natural effect*," he says, " *is to give them opportunities to commit crime which they might not otherwise have !*"   Can more be said than this against the system, as carried out in England?

Statistic returns have often been brought before the public, showing the very small number of relapses which have occurred. But we have already seen that, under the existing system, no reliance can be placed on them.   Sir R. MAYNE says :—

"1557. I should state that these returns are very imperfect, *because the police have no certain means of knowing whether the parties are on ticket-of-leave or not.*" (1558). "I suppose," he is asked, "although you have no particular information as to ticket-of-leave men, or as to penal servitude men, a great many of them are perfectly well-known to the police ?—Numbers." (1559.) "And a great number also unknown ?—Yes; after three years or more of penal servitude *a man generally comes out looking fatter*, and it is then difficult to recognise him; the police have, in fact, a great deal of difficulty in recognising them, *and they are strictly cautioned not to speak to a man unless they can certainly identify him.*"

Notwithstanding this difficulty of identification, however, we find the following results in the Report of the Directors of Convict Prisons for 1863 :—

Total number of convicts received in 1863: Males   ...   ... 2848

STATEMENT OF MALE CONVICTS AND LICENSES REVOKED
DURING THE YEAR 1863.

Reconvicted, not during the currency of former sentence...   ... 538
Reconvicted during the currency of former sentence...  ...  ... 106
                                           644
Revocations of license  ...  ...  ...  ...  ...  ...  ...  ...  ... 83

Such has hitherto been the state of the administration of the ticket-of-leave system in our country. That it has failed, as so administered, no one can deny. Many glaring examples have been already adduced of persons who have committed most serious crimes, while at large on the conditions of their license. Mr. Recorder HILL mentions, in his "Repression of Crime," a most striking instance of the evil of allowing licensees who were known to the police to be living a disorderly life, to retain their liberty until they had actually committed a crime. Among the 19 ticket-of-leave men whom Mr. HILL mentions, in his evidence before the Committee of 1856, as having been recognised by the Birmingham police, was one of the name of THOMAS WOTTON. Of this man he thus speaks in his charge to the Grand Jury, March, 1857 :—

"WOTTON had been adjudged to transportation for fifteen years. He obtained his ticket-of-leave and came to reside at Birmingham. Having myself requested the Superintendent of Police to watch, for six weeks, the conduct of all ticket-holders known to be in the town, and then to report to me their course of life, I received, as regards THOMAS WOTTON, the following information :—'Went to work at Nottingham. He states that he came to Birmingham at the suggestion of the Nottingham police. He has always borne (since known to the Birmingham police) a bad character, and keeps company of thieves, and has again taken to thieving.'* The report from

* Second Report Transportation Committee, House of Commons, 1856, p. 159.

which I cite this passage is made upon testimony of Inspector GLOSSOP, Sub-Inspector TANDY, and Police-Sergeant MANTON. I transmitted the document to the Home Secretary; but he informed me he was of opinion that it did not show 'sufficient reason to revoke the licenses of any of these convicts.' He stated, however, that he had 'desired the Inspector of Police, at Birmingham, to warn those among them who were suspected of having returned to dishonest practices, that their conduct would be carefully watched, and that on the first occasion of any offence, however slight, being legally brought home to them, their licenses would be cancelled.' In the same letter I was also informed that Sir GEORGE GREY had 'recently adopted the practice, in certain cases, of restricting the licenses, so as to prevent the return of convicts to their former associates.'* And believing that if ticket-holders were not permitted to seek harbour in the larger towns, they could not persist in a dishonest course of life without quickly falling into the hands of justice, I was well satisfied to have obtained so much by my interposition. But, gentlemen, we cannot reflect upon the consequences which followed this lenient decision, and still less upon the consequences which might have followed it, without most painful feelings being excited in our breasts. I will not parade the narrative of WOTTON's outrage before you. I would have refrained from adverting to it, if it did not appear to me to raise an unanswerable objection to the course of dealing with ticket-holders, advocated by Sir GEORGE GREY in the passage from his letter just read to you. Here we have a convicted felon—his sentence yet hanging over him. He is well known to be pursuing his nefarious career. The station-master at the railway observes him and his companions quit Birmingham for the north, and is satisfied they are on their way to the perpetration of some crime. Yet all this time the hands of justice are paralyzed!"

The journals of the day will give us the subsequent history of this man allowed to be at liberty while thus violating the conditions of his license. (*Vide* "Repression of Crime," 678-9.)

### "A BURGLAR SHOT BY A CLERGYMAN.

"The most daring case of burglary which ever took place in Derbyshire occurred between one and two o'clock on Saturday morning last, at the residence of the Rev. J. NODDER, of Marsh Green, Ashover, about eight miles from Chesterfield. The house in which the reverend gentleman resides stands by itself in a secluded place, about half-a-mile from the village. Mrs. NODDER slept in a room in front of the hall, and Mr. NODDER in an apartment at the back of the building, adjoining the servants' bedrooms. An infant, about seven weeks old, slept in a cot in Mrs. NODDER's room, but it awoke between one and two o'clock; while Mrs. NODDER was attending to it she heard a noise, which she first thought was occasioned by her husband stirring the fire in his room, and she took no further notice of it. In a

---

* Second Report Transportation Committee, House of Commons, 1856, p. 11.

minute afterwards she heard the noise again, and went to the window of her bedroom and drew the blind a little on one side, when she saw the figure of a man outside the window, and close to the glass. She was in her night-dress, and immediately drew back, put on her slippers, lifted the baby out of the cot with one hand, and rushed out of the room, shutting the door after her, and holding it in her hand. While she was doing this, six of the lower panes of glass in the window and the centre framework were smashed, and two men entered the room through the window, by means of a ladder, which they had procured from the stackyard adjoining the house. Mrs. NODDER held the door until she was overpowered, when she rushed into a passage on the stairs and locked the door, leaving the burglars fastened in the room. They were provided, however, with a 'jemmy,' or small crow-bar, and with this instrument they broke the panels of the door, and unlocked it, and so got into the passage communicating with the bedrooms. The first room they entered was that occupied by a lady named Miss HEELEY, a niece of the reverend gentleman, who was so alarmed that she lifted up the lower sash of the window and jumped into the yard, a height of fourteen feet, with nothing on her but a night-gown, and in this state ran for three-quarters of a mile into the village to the rectory-house. After escaping from her room, Mrs. NODDER went into that occupied by her husband, and called out, 'Papa, papa, here are thieves, and they'll murder us.' She had locked the bedroom door after her, and Mr. NODDER jumped out of bed and armed himself with a pair of large horse pistols, which were loaded, on the top of a cupboard, which contained the reverend gentleman's plate. The burglars outside called out, 'Now lads; now lads, come on, they're here !' Mr. NODDER, who was in the room, called out, 'If you enter here I'll shoot you.' The burglars took no heed, but prized the door open, and one of them entered the room with a black mask over his face, and a black gown on his body, which covered his clothes. He had a candle in his left hand which he held down towards the lower part of his body. Mrs. NODDER, who was greatly alarmed, said to her husband, 'Oh, my dear, give them what they want, or they'll murder us.' Mr. NODDER stepped about three yards back, said to the man, 'I'll give you what you want,' and fired one of the pistols at the man, and the shot entered his abdomen. The burglars now made a precipitate retreat, and as the man ran the shot fell from his clothes. They fled into a bedroom and jumped through a window, taking the glass and framework with them. They had to alight in the yard, which was about fourteen feet from the ground, and adjoining the window through which Miss HEELEY had jumped a short time before. Mr. NODDER rang the alarm-bell immediately, which brought about a dozen persons to the place, and a search was immediately instituted for the wounded man, as it was believed that he was so crippled with the shot and the leap through the window that he could not escape from the neighbourhood. Information was also given to Mr. HOLMES, Superintendent Constable of the district, and also to Mr. RADFORD, Superintendent of the Chesterfield Borough Police,

both of whom made a minute investigation of the premises.  The burglar
who had been shot left traces of blood in the direction in which he had run,
and the marks of blood and pieces of flesh on the window through which they
had leaped left no doubt that either one or both of them were severely cut.
A large yard-dog, which was turned loose at night, made no alarm, it having
been drugged.  Footmarks were traced from the hall across the flower garden,
and in the direction in which they had run, by Mr. RADFORD, Mr. MILNES,
a county magistrate, who resides near, and Mr. NODDER himself; and in
a field, about 200 yards distant, Mr. RADFORD found a mask and a dress,
which had been used as a disguise, and three others were found during the
morning, clearly showing that at least four persons were engaged in the
burglary.  Miss HEELEY, the lady alluded to above, lies in a precarious state.
She is suffering severely from an injury to the spine, and great nervous
excitement.  The police have obtained a clue to the burglars, which, we hope,
will lead to their detection.  A butcher who was travelling from Wirksworth
to Chesterfield market overtook a man at Kelstedge, near Ashover, whose leg
was bandaged up and much swollen, and who lay by the roadside, just within
a gate.  The man, whose hands were cut, asked for a ride to Chesterfield,
and he gave the driver one shilling to take him.  He was assisted into the
cart, and gave two different stories of how he had become lame.  First, he
said, he had been robbed; and, secondly, he said he had been engaged in
a prize-fight for £50.  On their arrival at Chesterfield the man was put
down at the White Horse, where he had his boots and clothes cleaned, and he
was conveyed to the Chesterfield station in the omnibus, and took a ticket for
Derby.  From what information has been gleaned, there is reason to believe
that the burglars belong to a Nottingham gang." — From the *Times* of
February 23, 1857.

-------

" It was said that this man was traced to Derby, where he took a ticket
for Birmingham.

" The suspicion that the wounded burglar had come to this town was
strengthened by the discovery of part of a Birmingham newspaper in a
plantation near the reverend gentleman's house; and on Monday morning
Mr. HOLMES, the Ashover Superintendent of Police, came to Birmingham
to consult the police as to the steps necessary to be taken.  Inspector
GLOSSOP at once determined to search the houses where dwell the A 1
burglars.  The most likely of these he thought was a house in Duddeston-
row, kept by Mrs. HADEN, the wife of a notorious receiver of stolen property,
whom the Recorder transported for life a few years back.  Mr. GLOSSOP knew
that here, when ' at home,' lived a man known to the police, and his associates, by the name of 'SHOG,' who some time back 'left his country for
his country's good,' for fourteen years; but who found his country so inconsolable on account of his loss, that in 1855 he accepted a ticket-of-leave, and
once more made Birmingham detectives happy by the knowledge that he was
in their midst, carrying on his ' little game' more successfully than ever.

There being no doubt that by associating with his old friends 'SHOG' had
made the recall of his ticket-of-leave possible, Mr. GLOSSOP had communicated
with the Recorder, and the Recorder had communicated with the Home
Secretary, and the Home Secretary had communicated with somebody or
nobody, as the case may be; but 'SHOG' remained at large. In spite of the
snubbing thus administered to the police, Mr. GLOSSOP thought he might as
well inquire after the health of 'SHOG,' or anybody else who might be
Mrs. HADEN's lodger that morning. Down to Duddeston-row he and HOLMES
went. No one found, though evidence most satisfactory that all Mrs. HADEN's
beds had been occupied during the night, one of these probably by the owner
of a fur cap, very wet, which Mr. GLOSSOP put in his pocket, not oblivious of
the fact that on the night of the robbery rain came down in torrents. He
also noted the presence of a bottle of hartshorn and oil, a medicament
useful in case of a sprain, whether caused by the leap from a clergyman's
window or otherwise. The hospitals were then searched, and all the doctors
and leech-women in the neighbourhood of Duddeston-row visited, but yet no
trace of gun-shot patient discovered. Towards dusk the officers again visited
Mrs. HADEN and found her preparing for tea. Though only herself and son
were in the house, Mr. GLOSSOP observed that three cups were on the tray.
The only explanation she gave of this was, 'I always do put three cups;' and
once more was she relieved of her prying visitors. Fresh inquiries were made
in the neighbourhood, and at last, in Allison-street, Mr. GLOSSOP found a
woman who acknowledged that at ten o'clock that morning she had applied
six leeches to the sprained ankle of a man who was at Mrs. HADEN's.
Back to Duddeston-row the officers went; neighbours positively affirmed
that no man had left Mrs. HADEN's house during the day; but, ultimately,
Mr. GLOSSOP visited an adjoining back yard, where lived a woman who
occasionally did a bit of 'charing' for Mrs. HADEN. She denied that any
one was in her house; she was indignant at the proposal to let a strange
gentleman inspect her bedroom; so Mr. GLOSSOP seized a candle, and proposed to do so without her company. He had his foot on the first step, when
a voice from the room above, in a resigned though tremulous tone, called out,
'It's all right, Mr. GLOSSOP; come up.' 'Oh, SHOG,' said the officer, recognising the voice, 'is that you?' 'Yes; come up,' was the reply made, as
Mr. GLOSSOP entered the room. There, in bed, lay the 'wanted' ticket-of-
leaver, a well-made, desperate-looking, thick-set fellow, with huge drops of
perspiration trickling down his face—this distilling process being probably
the result of the minute's confab. held with the lady of the house, as at
'SHOG's' side lay the woman's husband, who had doubtless rushed upstairs,
on hearing the approach of the officers, and whispered into his ear, 'They're
coming.' 'SHOG' was carefully conveyed to Moor-street prison in a cab, as
he was unable to walk. On Mr. GLOSSOP hinting that he wished to see
whether he was wounded, the captured burglar at once stripped, saying he
might as well do it first as last, and then it became obvious that the police
had at last got the 'right man in the right place.' Immediately under his

stomach, extending over a considerable space, were shot marks, inflammation, and lacerations. Mr. Solomon, surgeon, was at once sent for, in order that the shots might be extracted (both for 'Shog's' own relief, and to be used in evidence against him), but it was discovered that none had been left in the wounds, all of which were no more than skin-deep. A bystanding detective having remarked that there couldn't have been much powder in the pistol, 'Shog' said, very indignantly, 'If you had it in you, you'd have known whether there was much powder in it or not.' He'd as soon have been shot dead as taken, he said; 'but anyhow he'd only be lagged for life, and he'd work as little as he did before.' His name is Thomas Wotton. Both before and since his transportation he was known to the police as the leader of a most desperate gang of burglars, who make Birmingham their head-quarters. And yet such a scoundrel was granted a ticket-of-leave, and allowed to retain it, in spite of the representations of Recorder and police.

"Wotton was brought before the Magistrates yesterday, and an order made for his being taken to Derby."—From the *Birmingham Journal* of February 25, 1857.

---

"At the assizes at Derby, on Thursday, Thomas Wotton, *alias* 'Shog,' the Ashover burglar, was arraigned before Mr. Justice Wightman for breaking into the house of the Rev. J. Nodder, at Ashover, on the 20th February. The prisoner, to the surprise of most persons in Court, pleaded 'guilty.' The learned judge, after commenting with severity on the offence, and lamenting the mistaken leniency which had liberated such a criminal on a ticket-of-leave, sentenced the prisoner to be transported for twenty-five years."—From *Aris's Birmingham Gazette* of March 23, 1857.

Similar instances are not uncommon, though the result may not always be so disastrous, and though a warning may not always have been given. We rarely turn to the newspaper reports of criminal courts without finding an account of some crime committed by a person who is discovered to be on a ticket-of-leave. The following, which occurred in the present month of August, 1864, is only remarkable as being an example of a license being again granted after its revocation, while the culprit was undergoing the same sentence:—

"A TICKET-OF-LEAVE MAN's CAREER.

"At Lambeth, on Friday, Richard Kiley, a ticket-of-leave man, in custody on various charges of swindling, was finally examined. A police-officer gave a history of the prisoner's career as follows:—His father had been a leading merchant in the City, and lived in first-rate style at the west end of London.

*In January*, 1853, *the prisoner was sentenced to* 15 *years' transportation for forging* a bill for £150, and attempting to fix an innocent man with the offence. *In* 1856 *he was at large on a ticket-of-leave, which, owing to a further offence, was revoked in* 1859. *In* 1861 *he was again at large*, and he took Albert-lodge, a handsome villa at Sutton, at £100 a year rental, for two years certain. This enabled him to carry on extensive swindling for three months, giving reference to two swindlers, named ROBERTSON and STEVENS, who kept offices in the city. At the end of three months he absconded from Albert-lodge without paying his quarter's rent. He was next found living in Hanler's-buildings, on the 20th ultimo, with a young woman who had been his servant. In that place several articles, her property, were found, and also duplicates of property taken from Albert-lodge. When apprehended, other charges were brought against him, one for obtaining a carriage and harness from Mr. ADELBERT, of Long-acre; another for obtaining a carriage from Mr. KING, of Long-acre, and several others, including one for obtaining £700 worth of gin from a distiller, who declined to prosecute. The evidence in two cases (that of Mrs. BUTLER and Mrs. ADELBERT) rendered them quite clear against the prisoner, the former as an act of felony, and the latter one of conspiracy to defraud, and he was committed on both to take his trial."

Here is another case where a man receives a ticket-of-leave while undergoing a second sentence of penal servitude, and remains at liberty, though he is sent for a month to prison while under this conditional freedom, and is "one of the most notorious characters in the locality." The account is extracted from the *Bristol Post* of June 2, 1864:—

### "LAWFORD's GATE PETTY SESSIONS.

#### "THE HOUSEBREAKING CASE AT HENBURY.—ESCAPE AND RECAPTURE OF ONE OF THE PRISONERS.

"JAMES LEE, *a ticket-of-leave man*, and GEORGE SMITH, two of the most notorious characters in this locality, were brought before the Bench on a charge of breaking and entering the dwelling-house of WILLIAM LOADER, at Henbury, on Sunday evening last. Mr. ALMAN defended the prisoners. It appears that on the evening in question Mr. LOADER and his family attended divine service, and during their absence the prisoners gained access to the premises by getting in at the bedroom window, having previously tried to force the back-door with a "jemmy." On returning home from church Mr. LOADER heard a noise, and on getting to the premises he saw the two prisoners coming from the back kitchen. SMITH was apprehended on the spot, but LEE succeeded in making his escape. He was, however, apprehended the same evening, on Henbury-hill, by Sergeant WOOD. On the premises being examined, it was found that every drawer in the house had been broken open, and a number of articles of different kinds had been packed up and brought down stairs, ready to be taken away. A silver spoon was missed, together with the contents of two missionary boxes (chiefly coppers), as well as a small sum from the complainant's cash-box. A crow-bar was left behind. An application was now made by Sergeant Wood for a remand, for the production of two or three witnesses, and the magistrates remanded the accused till Saturday. *The prisoner Lee, we learn, is now out on a ticket-of-leave.* He was tried at the January Quarter Session, in 1851, for stealing 10s. 6d. from the person of Mrs. Arnold, Temple-street, and was sentenced to *four years' penal servitude.* He was also tried at the June Session, 1859, for breaking and entering the shop of Mr. Ashley, Dean-street, St. Paul's, and stealing one gold and six silver watches, together with other articles, value £40. *For this offence he was sentenced to six years' penal servitude.* He only came *out of prison on the 12th May,* having been com-mitted for a month for an assault. P.C.'s White and Bowden conveyed the prisoners to Lawford's Gate on Monday; but just before coming to the place a crowd followed them, and the prisoner Lee managed to escape. The con-stable, however, pursued him and re-captured him near St. Jude's Church, and, having conveyed him to the House of Correction, returned to the assistance of his brother constable, who got roughly handled by the mob, lost his hat and walking-stick, and after a tremendous struggle succeeded in taking the prisoner to the cell. Both the constables had their heads broken, and were otherwise injured by the mob, who afterwards surrounded the House of Correction, threw stones at the door, and behaved, we are told, in the most outrageous manner."

A peculiar ferocity and daring in resisting the administration of justice is observable in these persons. It is not often that prisoners are brought up handcuffed before the magistrates assembled in Petty Sessions, except in such cases as the follow-ing, which are extracted from the same paper in May of the present year. In this case the culprit is twice sent to prison while under conditional freedom, without his license being revoked :—

### "A DANGEROUS FELLOW.

"James Cocum, who appeared in court handcuffed, was charged with attempting to steal a watch, the property of William Tillett, Park-street. P.C. 239 deposed that whilst he was coming down Park-street on the previous day, he saw the accused seize the complainant's watch, which was in his waistcoat pocket. Being attached to a guard, however, he did not succeed in making off with it. Witness at once took him into custody, and conveyed him to the Central Station. On being asked what he had to say in his defence, he said that it was his own fault. Sergeant Woollacott then explained why the prisoner was handcuffed. He stated that at a quarter to eleven o'clock that morning he was about to let the accused out of his cell, when the latter, who had a quart jug and a cup in his hands, said he would not come out. He then struck witness on the head with a jug, and inflicted a severe cut. On the previous night he came down to the station, and said some one was going to kill him. Witness remonstrated with him, and advised him to go home, but he remained outside the station some two or three hours afterwards. He then had a piece of a poker in his possession. He believed the defendant was not in his right senses. Mr. WILLIAMS stated that at half-past four on the previous day, as he was walking down John-street with Mr. Superintendent HANDCOCK, they were met by COCUM, who told them that he was beset by six ruffians who were after him, and he could not walk the streets for them. He said he had a poker and a knife with him to take vengeance upon them. They handed him over to his mother. Mr. WILLIAMS, the Clerk of the Magistrates, *stated that the accused was a ticket-of-leave man, and had only come out of Bridewell that day week.* He had been drinking for a long time, and that had apparently affected his intellect. He was remanded to the Bridewell for the purpose of being examined by the medical officer."

### "A DARING THIEF.

"JAMES COCUM, a young man, was brought up on remand, on a charge of attempting to steal a watch from the person of WILLIAM TILLET, in Park-street. The case was heard before the Magistrates on Tuesday, when P.C. 239 proved that the prisoner seized Mr. TILLET's watch and chain, and was in the act of wrenching it from the button-hole of his waistcoat, when the constable, who was coming down Park-street at the time, apprehended him and prevented the theft. When before the Magistrates on Tuesday, and while at the station, his conduct was so strange and violent that he was remanded for the medical officer to see him, but it appeared that *his furious conduct was entirely owing to drink.* The Magistrates committed him to *three months' hard labour,* as a rogue and vagabond found attempting to pick pockets."

Even near the Metropolis, where it might have been imagined that facilities existed for recognising ticket-holders and obtaining a revocation of their licenses, we find daring burglars committed for three months only, while perpetrating depredations under their original sentence. In the *Times* of June 3rd, 1864, we find the following:—

### "WANDSWORTH.

"WILLIAM ENZOR, CHARLES MORTIMER and THOMAS BARKER, were finally examined on a charge of being concerned in stealing wearing apparel of the value of £20, the property of Miss G——, residing at Eaton-lodge, Upper Richmond-road, Putney.

"Mr. WILSON defended the prisoners.

"It appeared that Eaton-lodge is situated at the corner of a turning called 'The Avenue,' from which a man could climb to a wall, and then to a verandah, and thence into Miss G——'s bedroom window at the back. About four o'clock in the afternoon of the 2nd of February last, Miss G——'s servant went up to the room, and found the door fastened on the inside, and, believing that her mistress was there, she went down stairs again. She went up at ten minutes to five o'clock, and she then found the door open, and the room in great confusion. From the wardrobe a black silk dress was missed, and from the room two cloaks, an alpaca dress, and a shawl. The evidence affecting the prisoners was that three men were seen with a pony and cart loitering about the place at the time in question, and the witnesses spoke more particularly to the identity of ENZOR and MORTIMER. On the 12th of the same month the three prisoners were seen with the same pony and cart at Holloway, loitering about for the purpose of committing a felony. PINDER, a constable of the S division, detained the pony and cart, but the prisoners escaped. They were, however, captured soon afterwards, and committed from the Clerkenwell Police Court for *three months' imprisonment*, which expired on the 21st of May, and they were apprehended by LEVI, of the V division, on the present charge, as they left Coldbath-fields Prison. It also appeared that ENZOR was convicted at the Surrey Sessions of May, 1820, in the name of WILLIAM JONES, for stealing a basket of plate from a house, *and he was sentenced to four years' imprisonment.*—The prisoners were committed for trial."

The police are not safe in the discharge of their duty, when apprehending such ferocious desperadoes, as come forth with an assumed good character from our Convict Prisons. Such men as the subject of the following police report, rather remind us of the brigands of some notoriously ill-governed country, than the inhabitants of civilised and law-loving England. It is extracted from the *Western Daily Press* of April 16, 1864 :—

"MURDEROUS ATTACK BY A BURGLAR UPON POLICE CONSTABLES.

"At the Police Court, yesterday, JOHN SMITH, *alias* GOODENOUGH, a middle-aged, swarthy-complexioned man, of medium stature, but possessing a most villanous cast of countenance, was charged with resisting his lawful apprehension, under a warrant charging him with having committed a burglary at the parish of Alverstoke, in the county of Southampton, and stolen therefrom a variety of articles, the property of SAMUEL WHEELER, and also with violently assaulting P.C.'s 51, 199, and 200, with intent to do them grievous bodily harm.

"DAVID HARVEY deposed that he was Superintendent of Police for the county of Southampton, and brought a warrant (produced) to Bristol to apprehend the prisoner. He came to Bristol with others, and communicated with the force of this city. Had been seeking for the prisoner for more than two months past, and his application to the Court was to remove him to Gosport, in the county of Southampton.

"The prisoner said he was willing to go with the Superintendent.

"Superintendent HARVEY said they *had five very clear cases of burglary against him at present.*

"Mr. WILLIAMS, addressing the Bench, said the only question was whether they would deliver him up. If the Superintendent would give them the assurance that the prisoner should not go from the jurisdiction of the Court before the grievous offence with which he was now charged had been adjudicated upon, the Magistrates would probably consent.

"The Superintendent gave the required promise. He stated that he had the prisoner's companion, a man named STEWART, now in custody, and he wished to take the prisoner to Gosport.

"Mr. WILLIAMS : In the event of his discharge he would be brought back to this city.

"Mr. HOLLINGTON, Superintendent of the Chertsey (Surrey) Constabulary, said he would take the responsibility upon himself.

"P.C. PERROTT, No. 199, then deposed as follows :—He stated that last night, about ten o'clock, he was in the neighbourhood of Back-lane, Bedminster. From information he received from Mr. YATES he found that P.C.'s HUGHES (200) and CLARK (51) were seeking after a man. Mr. YATES said the prisoner was the person. He accosted him, and just then he (prisoner) bolted. He followed him down the lane, and said, 'I beg your pardon, sir, is your name Smith ?' He said, 'For why ?' He then informed him that he was a police-officer, and there was a gentleman in the street who wanted to speak to him. That brought him 100 yards up the lane. He then saw him put his hand into his pocket. CLARK was coming down. The prisoner then drew a pistol, *which was loaded and capped.* CLARK and himself closed upon him and threw him down. He got up, and they threw him down again. With that HUGHES came up, and they all three struggled with him a long time. *The pistol was a six-barrelled revolver. The prisoner tried to shoot them,* and he (PERROTT) made sure one of them would be shot. *He bit his* (PERROTT'S) *hand.* He called CLARK and HUGHES to assist him, but they could not, as they were trying to wrest the pistol from him. He then got the prisoner by the throat until he let his hand go. He had been badly kicked, and he also received a tremendous blow upon the arm.

"P.C. HUGHES (200) said he was called to the assistance of PERROTT. The prisoner made a most desperate resistance, and struck him (HUGHES) in the face, and cut his cheek open with the revolver. He kicked him about the body, and, in consequence of the friends of the man and a female who were there and attempted to rescue him, they were beaten very badly. His (witness's) legs and body were in such pain that he could scarcely move. They had a most desperate struggle there. The prisoner was a very powerful man, though he was small in stature. In searching the prisoner's house they found a great deal of property and a *quantity of bullets and caps.*

" Mr. BIDDLECOMBE, late Chief Superintendent of the Surrey Constabulary, said that *eight years ago he had twenty-five cases of burglary against the prisoner.* He was tried at Hertford and sentenced to ten years' transportation. *He had been out eight or nine months, and he believed he had since committed about twenty-five burglaries in his neighbourhood. He had broke out of more gaols than any other man in England.* He had three governors of three different gaols, Hertford, Reading and Winchester, who would prove as many escapes. [The revolver was here produced.]

" The prisoner was then handed over to the police authorities to be conveyed to Gosport."

## "FINDING A TREASURE.

" STEWART, the accomplice of the notorious burglar SMITH, who has been committed for trial at Gosport, is at present a prisoner in Bristol, having been brought here by Mr. Superintendent DREW. He has confessed to having pledged here a large quantity of stolen property, and on Monday he made known to the police authorities that he had hidden fifty watches in a field at Long Ashton, which were the proceeds of a burglary. Search was made, and the watches were found. The detectives are endeavouring to trace other valuables."

Such men as SMITH carry contamination with them wherever they go. Two respectable men, not knowing his character, had assisted in his rescue, and were brought up for the offence, which was clearly proved.

" Mr. —— said the Magistrates had formed their opinion about the case. The prisoners had acted exceedingly wrong and wickedly, and they deserved severe punishment. They assisted a vile thief to escape, if possible, and they would be committed each for two months, with hard labour.

" Mr. WILLIAMS told JONES he could not expect to get into Mr. ——'s employ again.

" JONES said the evidence that had been given was ' lies from beginning to end.'

" The prisoners were then removed in custody."

Thus a man who had been in respectable employment had his character blighted by association with such men.

Multitudes of cases as striking might be gathered without difficulty from the public journals; one more only will be here cited from the volume of the "Four Justices," mentioned by them in the Introduction, p. 13. The individual was at that time (1862) a prisoner in the convict department of Wakefield Prison :--

"J. H., having been several times previously convicted, was sentenced to seven years' transportation on August 5, 1852. Being then only sixteen, he was sent to Parkhurst, where his behaviour was such that, on Feb. 22, 1856, he was removed to the penal class at Pentonville for eight months, on the ground of *three years' continual bad conduct*. His conduct in the cell at Pentonville, and we may observe, generally when he was in separate confinement, was 'good.' From Pentonville he was sent to Portsmouth, and on September 4, 1857, he received the 'privilege which by his good behaviour under penal discipline he had obtained,' and was discharged on ticket-of-leave, having two years, all but a month, of his sentence unexpired. We understood that it was then the practice, before discharging a man on license, to require him to name some person likely to employ him, and to ascertain the character and fitness of such person. J. H. was thus consigned to his own father, who had been described in the form originally sent with J. H. as having been himself eight times in prison, and as being the father of 'a family of passers of bad coin.' If we are surprised at this, we are less surprised at what followed—viz., that on October 16, 1857, J. H., having been at large for six weeks, was again committed for fresh crime ; that on October 21, 1857, he was convicted and sentenced to four years' penal servitude; that after ten months' 'good conduct' in cell, being sent to Portland, he, there, for 'idleness, insubordinate conduct, and trying to incite other prisoners to follow his example'—in fact, for being a ringleader in the mutiny, the alleged ground of which was non-remission of sentence, under the Act of 1853, though his was not of that kind—for this he received twenty-four lashes, was reduced to third class, adjudged to forfeit past service as regards stages and all gratuity, and was again sent to the cell at Pentonville for five months ; again forwarded to Portsmouth, and again, *mirabile dictu*, 'obtained for his good behaviour under penal discipline' another ticket-of-leave on February 21, 1861. He had then eight months of his sentence unexpired, which is one month less than the maximum period which, by the regulations, may be remitted in case of 'continued good conduct.' This time the Discharged Prisoners' Aid Society received J. H., but did not long retain their hopeful *protégé*. After again being at large for six weeks, he was again committed on April 8, 1861, and, on August 7, sentenced to ten years' penal servitude, under which he is now at Wakefield, the credentials brought with him being 'character bad, conduct in gaol very good.' Should this system of convict management continue to maintain that 'stability' which we are told it has acquired (Report of Directors for 1860, Memorandum, p. xxxvi.), we cannot but feel an unusual degree of confidence in a calculation of the orbit which J. H. is still likely to describe, founded on the preceding *data*. We cannot but see, 'looming in the future,' Her Majesty's clemency again invoked, to reward, by a remission of two years and some months of sentence, another course of 'good conduct' in separate confinement, and of 'continual bad conduct' for years in association, with a few more mutinies on public works, and to enable J. H. to take another short walk abroad, in order to qualify himself (should nothing more serious occur) for a fourth progress through the deterrent discipline of the Convict Prisons.*

" It is barely necessary to observe that the above remarks were published several months before the revived panic of 1862 had brought the public mind to conclusions yet more adverse to the convict system existing in England, than those to which we have been led."

An analysis of the cases of prisoners sentenced to penal servitude in our large towns would doubtless present very instructive information respecting the causes of vice, the effects of imprisonment, and the working of the ticket-of-leave system, as at present administered. These it would not often be easy to obtain. The Chaplain of the Bristol Gaol, however, the Rev. CHARLES BRITTAN, has kindly furnished the following table from his private notes :—

"BRISTOL QUARTER SESSIONS, OCTOBER 27, 1863.

7 years' Penal Serv., E. M., on Ticket-of-leave, expiring June 18, 1864.

| | | | | |
|---|---|---|---|---|
| 6 ditto | ditto, | E. S.,ᵃ | ditto, | ditto. |
| 5 ditto | ditto, | M. A. B. | ditto, | ditto. |
| 4 ditto | ditto, | E. F. | | |
| 4 ditto | ditto, | J. Y. | | |
| 3 ditto | ditto, | E. S. | | |
| 3 ditto | ditto, | L. P. | | |
| Imprisonment for } 3 months } | | G. S. | ditto, | expiring Dec. 30, 1863. |

*a* E. S. had also previously undergone a sentence of 4 years' penal servitude.

"QUARTER SESSIONS, DECEMBER 30, 1863.

4 years' Penal Serv., J. B., on Ticket-of-leave, expiring April 12, 1864.

| | | |
|---|---|---|
| 3 ditto | ditto, | W. T. |
| 3 ditto | ditto, | S. A. J. |
| 3 ditto | ditto, | L. R. |

---

* " We learn that 'to persons sentenced to penal servitude for a second or any subsequent time, after January 1, 1863, the regulations as to remission of sentence issued in 1857 are not to apply;' but whether such persons are to receive remission under some other regulations, or none at all, does not yet appear."

"QUARTER SESSIONS, April 7, 1864.

4 years' Penal Serv.,   J. B.
4 ditto     ditto,     T. D.
4 ditto     ditto,     W. G.
4 ditto     ditto,     I. S.[a]

     [a] I. S. had had 7 years' transportation in 1851.

" QUARTER SESSIONS, July 5, 1864.

8 years' Penal Serv., H. P. on Ticket-of-leave, expiring April 13, 1865.
4 ditto     ditto,     C. C.
4 ditto     ditto,     W. C.
4 ditto     ditto,     M. T.
4 ditto     ditto,     E. B.

Imprisonment for 12 months }   J. E.[b]

Imprisonment for 2 months }   E. D.     ditto,     expiring Oct. 24, 1864.

     [b] J. E. had 3 years' penal servitude in 1856.

"It appears, therefore, that in the years ending Midsummer, 1864, *twenty* persons were sentenced to penal servitude in Bristol; of these twenty, *five* were on ticket-of-leave at the time of reconviction.

"Three others who had previously undergone sentences of penal servitude were now sentenced to imprisonment. *Two* of them being on ticket-of-leave.

"Making a total of *seven persons* recommitted whilst on ticket-of-leave,— four of them being women."

Of these persons sentenced to penal servitude, nine were women — a large proportion. Of the whole number four women and one man were holders of licenses when they committed the present crime, the man being at liberty after *two* sentences of penal servitude. Others may of course have been also license-holders, without the fact having been discovered, but these the Chaplain knew to be so. Of the remaining Convicts, two were brothers, now sentenced to penal servitude, after several previous convictions;—the youngest of the two had commenced his criminal career at the age of *nine*, being now twenty-three years of age; he had been imprisoned severally for one, two, six, and ten months! One of the women, now convicted for the first time, was the accomplice of a ticket-of-leave woman, lately arrived in Bristol, who herself was acquitted from want of evidence, and her license was not revoked, though the fact of her committal proved her to be the companion of a thief. Of the other license-holders, one woman had only a short imprisonment, on medical grounds; three were acquitted from want of evidence; one of these, however, had been before in prison while under license, and consequently was liable to revocation of license, as was another who had a short imprisonment. Such are the results of the present system in one place and in one year.

The principle of conditional freedom which is here strongly advocated is, however, in no way shaken by these results, because they are clearly traceable to defects in the existing system.

They are as follows:—

First,—The want of a really reformatory character in the English Convict Prisons; — hence the inmates are not prepared for freedom, and all subsequent efforts to benefit them are comparatively useless. A large proportion of those who received a ticket-of-leave have given no reliable proof that they are fit for freedom.

Secondly,—No arrangements are made for carrying into effect the conditions of the license;—the authorities of the district to which the licensee is going are not informed of his arrival;—no surveillance of his conduct is arranged for;—difficulties are even thrown in the way of the exercise of the same watchfulness over him by the police, as over other suspicious characters. Hence the Convict is aware, that the conditions under which he is at large are habitually violated, that the hands of the authorities are restrained; thus the law is set at nought.

Thirdly,—There is no system adopted in England, as there is elsewhere, by which habitual offenders and reconvicted felons and license-holders can be recognised, and their offences registered, so that their sentence on a fresh conviction may be proportioned to their moral depravity.

Fourthly,—The arrangements for revoking licenses are so

incomplete and ineffective that license-holders, even if known
to be such, frequently receive a few months' imprisonment in
a common gaol, instead of a revocation of their license.

How widely the defects in the working of the license system
in England have attracted attention, is shown by the following
extract from the work of M. de MARSANGY, which has been
already quoted. He thus speaks of the ticket-of-leave system
(p. 95) :—

" Aucun homme sérieux ne conteste, en Angleterre, que la libération
préparatoire ne soit par elle-même une précieuse et féconde institution.
En effet, elle ne repose pas, comme la grâce, sur une pensée de pure
miséricorde ; elle est motivée par un triple intérêt de justice, de sécurité
publique et d'économie. Que veut la justice? Qu'on frappe le malfaiteur
d'une peine suffisante pour le réformer. Que veut la sécuritié publique ?
Que l'expiation sévère de cette peine provoque les condamnés à s'amender,
afin de faciliter leur reclassement dans la société ; afin qu'étant ainsi réformés
et reclassés, ils puissent ne plus troubler l'ordre par de nouveaux crimes.
Que veut l'économie? Que tout en tenant compte des nécessités de la répression, on s'efforce diminuer le plus possible les frais énormes qu'impose
l'expiation,* afin de degrever d'autant le budget de l'Etat. Rien donc à la
fois de plus sensé, de plus généreux et de plus utile que le but auquel tendent
les *tickets-of-leave*. Aussi ce système, si favorablement accueilli en 1853 par le
Parlement et par l'opinion, n'a-t-il rien perdu de la légitime confiance qu'il
inspirait. La Commission Parlementaire de 1857 et la Commission Royale
de 1862 persistent à considérer les *tickets-of-leave* comme une mesure
'sage et excellente en soi.'† Maintenant, que cette mesure n'ait pas pro-
duit en Angleterre les fruits qu'on en espérait; que même elle ait pu,
contrairement à l'assertion de Lord GREY,‡ contribuer à l'accroissement du
nombre des crimes; faul-il logiquement en conclure qu'elle soit dangereuse
ou inefficace? Non évidemment; car les plus parfaites institutions peuvent
ne produire que de funestes résultas si elles sont mal ou inhabilement
pratiquées, et à plus forte raison, si elles le sont à contresens de leur principe
et de leur but, et au mépris des plus formelles prescriptions de la loi !
Toute la question se réduit donc à savoir si le Bill de 1853, que a établi
les *tickets of leave*, stipule des garanties *suffisantes* et si ce Bill a été
*ponctuellement exécuté* notamment en ce qui touche les quatre conditions
radicales de ce système ; l'*amendement* des condamnés ; leur *patronage*, leur
*surveillance ;* enfin, la *révocation des licenses* en cas d'inconduite."

_____

* "Il résulte d'un rapport fait au Parlement, en juillet 1860, que 5465 convicts déportés
ont coûté chacun 180 livres sterl., soit 4500 fr. l'un, au total 24,592,500 livres.

† "Rapp. de la Comm. Royale de 1862.

‡ " 'Je conteste très-fortement que les désordres dont on se plaint avec raison soient,
en général, l'œuvre des condamnés bénéficiaires des *tickets-of-leave*.' V. la *Belgique*
judiciaire, article déjá cité de M. Casier."

After having fully discussed each of these points, and shown great failure in all of them, M. MARSANGY thus expresses his opinion (p. 123):—

"Pour moi, ce que je ne puis comprendre, c'est qu'en présence des énergiques réclamations de l'opinion et de la presse, le Parlement anglais qui, en 1853, avait, sur la motion de LORD GREY, appuyée par Lord BROUGHAM, édicté le bill généreux des *tickets of leave,* ait pendant dix années toléré, de la part de l'administration, *une exécution de ce bill qui était la plus manifeste violation du principe et du but; de la lettre et de l'esprit de la loi!"*

The evils which now exist can be remedied, for they do not attend the working of the system elsewhere. A new Act has just passed through the Legislature regulating some of these points; others do not require fresh legislation, but can be remedied by those who have the direction of this department of Government. Much will depend on the public opinion of society whether such changes are made as will check the enormous evil, which, if allowed to continue much longer, will be deeply rooted in our country, and render insecure both property and life.

The whole subject of the ticket-of-leave system has been so forcibly set forth by the Four Justices, whose extensive experience has given them ample means of forming a judgment, that we will conclude this chapter with an extract from their work (pp. 52, 54, &c.):—

"There can be no question that such a system as this [the ticket-of-leave system as carried out in Ireland] is a most powerful deterrent from crime, because it produces so much greater certainty of detection. What really deters the criminally disposed is not so much the *amount* of punishment as the certainty that *some* punishment will follow upon crime. What encourages them is not so much mildness of punishment as the hope of impunity.

"But the discharged convict who is criminally disposed knows that under this system he is likely, if reconvicted of felony, to receive a much *longer* sentence,—which is what he really dreads,—than he would otherwise. His identification being thus secured, all his antecedents are readily ascertained, and systematically brought before the court which tries him, and he receives a sentence proportionate to his *former* offences, as well as the last.

"A secondary advantage derived from it is that criminal statistics are made

more trustworthy.  While it swells the amount of crime which is apparent,
it lessens proportionately, what is more dangerous, the amount which is
unknown.  While it shows worse results as against the whole penal system
of which it is a part, it gives us confidence that we know, more nearly, the
worst.  The opposite system—that of putting the discharged convict as much
as possible out of sight—gives better 'returns' by lessening the number of
*known* reconvictions, but leaves us with painful doubts as to the *unknown*
number. * * *

" The avowed objections to police supervision in England are various.

" One is that it would be a hard case, even an encroachment on the liberty
of the subject, that the man who is still under sentence of penal servitude
for crime, though conditionally permitted to be at large, should not enjoy
his liberty without being hampered by such restrictions.  It is admitted
that there are a few bad ones for whom such restrictions would be, in itself,
desirable, but that it would be hard, for their sakes, to inflict it on the large
well-disposed majority.  We, who have the misfortune to learn, that in our
Riding, nearly half the men who are known to be discharged convicts are
living dishonestly, and many are 'captains among thieves,'* can hardly
sympathise with this sentiment.  How many of these men are license-
holders, how many absolutely discharged, we have, through official reserve,
no means of knowing; but we, certainly, should not feel our liberties as
Englishmen encroached upon, if the former were obliged, from time to
time, to let the police know whereabouts they are to be found.  For we
know that,—owing to the uncontrolled liberty allowed to a few men (who,
as Sir J. JEBB says, 'have by their crimes rendered themselves liable to
the most rigorous imprisonment for the whole of their sentences') before
the expiration of those sentences,—the property and personal security of
millions of honest men are every day in danger.† * * *

" It is said that this supervision would be to place their fate in the hands of
the police, who might *trump up* charges against them, and get their licenses
unjustly revoked.  But, in the same sense is the fate of every Englishman in
the hands of the police, who may *trump up* a charge against him, as 'learned
counsel for the defence' often contend, and sometimes successfully, that they
have done against many a 'prisoner at the bar.'

" Another objection is that the reporting to the police would ' *brand* the
man as a *criminal*.'  One would have thought, that the 'brand' was rather
stamped by the perpetration of crime, and by the verdict of the jury which
pronounced him guilty, than by telling the police that he is at large, and
where he is to be found.

" But the main objection is one which comes from the ticket-of-leave men
themselves; and we must do credit to their discernment and skill when we

---

* " In the *towns*, 72 out of 104 whose character is ascertained, are reported as dishonest,
being 68 per cent."

† " These anticipations were published in June, 1863.  How far they have been verified,
let the reports of the Criminal Courts during the latter part of that year bear witness."

say that they have seized upon the position with great judgment, and maintained it with remarkable success. Having won the authorities wholly to their side, they have made it well-nigh impregnable. They say, 'We desire to live honestly, but we cannot get work. The police are our especial enemies. They dog us, tell people what we are, and then everybody turns his back upon us. To require us to report ourselves to them will make matters much worse. Some of us steal as it is, but then we shall all steal, or starve, for no one will employ us.'

"This is a plausible argument. The major premiss is true to a great degree. There *is* an objection to employ ticket-of-leave men. We have already seen how much that difficulty has been increased by the recklessly indiscriminate mode in which tickets-of-leave have been granted in England. *We believe it to be still further aggravated by the absence of any of that control over the ticket-of-leave man, and of those means of enforcing the conditions on which he is, professedly, at large, which police supervision would supply.* It arises, we have seen reason to believe, far less from any mere sentiment as to the 'brand,' than from a reasonable apprehension that he may prove a dangerous person to have anything to do with; and, so far, is likely to be diminished, rather than increased, by the knowledge that a strong control is exercised over him.

"But it is said that police supervision will make the man known as a discharged convict. The question is, can it, in the majority of cases, be concealed? And are not the exceptions, for the most part, those of men over whom it is most desirable that some control should be kept, viz., the 'first-class thieves,' as they call themselves, who travel from place to place, as 'organising masters,' so to speak, of crime; and in large towns, where the worst men congregate?

"No doubt, if the fact that any given man has been a convict could be wholly obliterated from everybody's memory, and never more mentioned, he might get employment where it is now denied him. But, in the majority of cases, it will creep out somehow or other. The authorities tell us that the men, when discharged, generally go back to the place from whence they came, where of course somebody knows who they are, and can guess where they have been. This being so, some zealous policeman now and then catches the scent, and thinks he has found a mare's nest. He, like the 'general,' thinks a discharged convict must be a dangerous animal, and that it is his duty as a man, still more as a policeman, to warn any unconscious employer of his danger in harbouring such a reptile. No doubt, in that way, a well-disposed license-holder may sometimes be driven from honest employment.

"But such cases are, we believe, exceptional, and when they do occur, arise precisely from the *want* of that very thing which it is alleged would aggravate the evil: viz., the giving to the police systematic and official information, instead of leaving them to ferret it out through irregular channels. It is their duty to look after suspicious characters. That a man has been a convict, no doubt, raises a certain degree of presumption that he may be such a character. If a man arrives in their neighbourhood, whom they know or suspect to be a returned convict, they are obliged, in the discharge of their duty, to endeavour to ascertain whether he is living honestly or not; and if they have any reason to suspect the latter, to keep a sharp look-out after him.

" From our knowledge of the police (which is not inconsiderable, having been constantly in contact with them as magistrates, acting in very populous districts), we have no doubt that *when they are once satisfied* that a discharged convict is endeavouring to live honestly, they have not the slightest disposition to interfere with him, but, on the contrary, are ready to help him. In the returns to the enquiries we recently made, we were much struck by the evident satisfaction and pleasure which the police had in recording the number of discharged convicts in their several districts who were living honestly, where such was the case. But *before* this is ascertained, and in order to ascertain the man's honest or dishonest purposes, they are obliged—especially if he do not settle down in one locality—to practise a certain amount of that watching and *dogging* which really constitutes *espionage*.

" If they knew that every man discharged on license was bound to report to them his arrival in their district, and his movement to any other, all necessity for such watching and dogging would cease, because they would always know where to find him, if necessary ; and, instead of the irregular and real *espionage* over him which now exists, we should have authorised *supervision*, to be exercised as a matter of regular routine, according to prescribed rules, and involving far less danger of a man's chance of employment being injured by some over-officious under-policeman, who would thus have neither the merit of a discovery, nor the pleasure of communicating a secret, to stimulate his zeal, besides having his proper course of duty more clearly pointed out."

Let wise measures be speedily taken, and let the public co-operate with them ; then there will be little difficulty in the disposal of our Convicts. Society will receive into her midst the repentant sinners.

# CHAPTER VI.

## TRANSPORTATION.

WE shall not attempt in this work to enter fully into the history of Transportation, because our object is rather to ascertain what are sound principles on this subject, and how they can be brought into operation at the present time. It is absolutely impossible that we should ever resume the system of Transportation as it has been carried on, because the Colonies declare that they will not have their new territories peopled with the refuse of the old country, and because our legislative have been made so fully aware of the enormous wickedness which has been perpetrated under the former system, that we may be certain that no government will attempt to re-establish it. Still it will be useful briefly to consider, in the first place, the history of the system; then we shall learn what has been the cause of the great evils which have arisen; and we may afterwards consider under what conditions any kind of deportation or emigration of Convicts may still be continued.

The following brief sketch of the recent position of the question was given to the Select Committee on Transportation, in 1856, by Mr. WADDINGTON, the Permanent Under Secretary of State for the Home Department :—

"The first deadly blow," he says (5, &c.), "which was struck at the system of Transportation to the Australian Colonies, was given by a Committee of the House of Commons in 1838, generally known as Sir WILLIAM MOLESWORTH's Committee. The Report of that Committee of 1838 was extremely adverse to Transportation, and recommended its discontinuance, both as a great injustice to and a serious infliction upon the Colonies, and also as a bad punishment in itself, failing to *deter criminals at home or reform them abroad;* in fact, it is impossible to have a report more decidedly adverse to it. There was at that time a very strong party in the Colony opposed to Transportation; not, however, at that time so strong, I believe, as those who were in favour of it. That Report of course gave great strength to the opponents of Transportation; and though the system continued, yet the opposition increased in strength, I believe, every year. Unfortunately, in a few years preceding the year 1845, from 1840 to 1845 inclusive, the Government thought it right to send out an enormous quantity of convicts to the Colony of Van Dieman's Land; there were no less than the enormous number of 17,000 convicts sent out in those six years. The consequences of that were most diastrous; the supply was infinitely greater than the demand; they could not be employed by the settlers; they were congregated in immense numbers on public works. A frightful degree of crime was produced, and a proportionate degree of alarm; and the result was that though Transportation to Van Dieman's Land was suspended for two or three years, still, the feeling against it gaining additional strength, leagues were formed; the local legislatures passed resolutions against it; an Australian league was formed two or three years afterwards to put an end to it, and the consequence was that at the end of the year 1850 Transportation to New South Wales and South Australia was discontinued. It continued for two years longer to Van Dieman's Land, with a still increasing opposition, and at the end of 1852 it was abandoned to Van Dieman's Land also, leaving as our only outlet the little Colony of Western Australia."

The League alluded to in the foregoing extract was a very important one. Our own Colonies, attached as they were to the mother country, felt themselves compelled to unite together to defend themselves against the enormous evil which they were suffering from her. Of the amount of crime with which we were inundating the new country, some conception may be formed from the following extract from the speech of the Attorney-General, in the Legislative Assembly, September 27, 1850 :—

"According to the Quarter Sessions returns it would be found that the transported class had a greater share of the crime among them than he had stated. But it was from the calendar of the Sydney Gaol during the last year that he had drawn the proportion which he had estimated. Sixteen hundred and odd prisoners had passed through that gaol, upwards of one thousand of those were of the transported class. If the amount of crime in these two classes had been equal, and had not exceeded the proportion of crime among the free classes to the numerical strength of that class, there would have been eleven hundred prisoners less in that gaol during the year, and there would of course have been a corresponding diminution of expense. But if there had not been a transported class mingled up among the free population, *and necessarily exercising a contaminating influence*, it was not probable that they would have had more than five or six hundred prisoners in the gaol during the entire year. The Assizes during the past year, as well as the state of the Metropolitan Gaol, had proved that the same proportion in crime was still maintained. At Goulburn September Assizes there were nine of the transported class out of thirteen prisoners. At Bathurst, in February last, out of nineteen, fifteen were free by servitude; and at the last assizes of that place, out of twenty-two there were thirteen of the transported class. There were nine of the most heinous crimes—murder, manslaughter, robbery with arms or violence, and stabbing—two only of those were of the free class. At the Assizes at Maitland, September, 1850, out of twenty-six there were twenty-one of the transported class; nine tried for murder, rape, robbery, and stabbing—two only of these were of the free class. At Brisbane Assizes, in May last—and he would call the special attention of those in that district to the fact—out of eighteen on the calendar, there was only one of the free class—a native of the colony. Three soldiers were tried who were not on the calendar; one found guilty of assault, the other two acquitted. The only capital case was for murder, and both the prisoners were found guilty, and executed; one was a ticket-of-leave holder, who arrived by the *Havering* in November or December last; the other was emancipated; and they murdered an unfortunate free shepherd, who was on the same station, under cruel and atrocious circumstances. It was deserving of particular remark also, as had been noticed by the hon. member for Roxburgh, that nearly all the heinous offences were committed by persons of the transported class. Out of every nine cases of this description, there were not more than two committed by persons of the free class. The state of the Bathurst gaol, at the time of the last Assizes, had been particularly inquired into, and it was found that out of nineteen persons confined there under the Master and Servants' Act, and as rogues and vagabonds and incorrigible drunkards, there were but two of the free class, a fact worthy of particular attention on the part of those gentlemen who contended for the superiority of the description of labour now asked for."

But these figures inadequately represent the injury done to the Colonies. The Committee of the League truly state that—

" The calculation of the evils of Transportation should not be limited to the Criminal Courts,—they should be traced to the remoter consequences—the expenses should be estimated of apprehending, prosecuting, and punishing all these transported persons; the pecuniary losses should be considered, the social evils, the domestic misery, which these crimes occasion, and of which the effects will remain for generations—families rendered destitute—children brought up in wickedness—associates made evil, or confirmed in vicious principles and habits, by the contagion of such numerous and constantly recurring examples."

Feeling strongly the consequence, not only to the great island continent, but to the whole of Australasia, of a continuance of the practice of inundating the new world with the refuse of the old, a large public meeting was held at Sydney on the 16th of September, 1850, when the New South Wales Association was formed, after which the following petition was drawn up and extensively signed. It forcibly sets forth the position of the question:—

"TO THE QUEEN's MOST EXCELLENT MAJESTY.

"The humble Petition of the Inhabitants of the Australasian Colonies of New South Wales, Victoria, Van Dieman's Land, South Australia, and New Zealand,

" SHEWETH,—

" That it is the glory and happiness of your Majesty's Petitioners to form a part of your Majesty's empire, united to Great Britain by mutual ties of interest, affection and duty; possessing the domestic and moral habits, the literature, the laws, and the religious faith of the illustrious nation which gave them birth.

" That the past belongs to the Parent State, the future alone to your Petitioners; and among the bright visions of the future, there is not one more cheering than that which exhibits these Colonies as the grateful refuge, and the pleasant home, of millions of honest and industrious men, the redundant population of Great Britain and Ireland.

" That the magnificent capabilities of these Colonies as fields for emigration are greatly impaired, and your Petitioners, as Colonists, grievously injured, by the wrongs inflicted, directly on Van Dieman's Land, and indirectly on all the other Colonies of Australasia, through Transportation; the appalling results of which have been disclosed by Parliamentary inquiries, and have been repeatedly attested and depicted with expressions of horror by your Majesty's Ministers.

" That although your Majesty's Government has been pledged to the discontinuance of Transportation to Van Dieman's Land, it nevertheless continues unabated.

" That the actual result, if not the avowed object, of the present system is, through Van Dieman's Land, to inundate all the Australasian Colonies with the worst convicts of the Mother Country; and that such a policy is not only an outrage upon your Petitioners, but a breach of your Majesty's most gracious promise, that no criminals should be transported by Great Britain to her Colonies, without their consent, expressed through their several Legislatures; which promise was conveyed by the circular dispatch of the Right Honourable the Earl GREY to the Colonial Governors, dated 7th August, 1848.

"That, although the social and moral mischiefs of the system render its merely economical results comparatively insignificant, your Majesty's Petitioners cannot but advert to the fact, that the criminals so cast upon them are, too commonly, improvident and intemperate, and are many of them diseased in body and mind; thus becoming a burthen on the industry and resources of these infant communities.

"That by persisting in their present penal policy, your Majesty's Government will make the Australasian dependencies, against their repeated protest, the great receptacle for the crime of the empire, and will subject them to all the moral and pecuniary evils of direct Transportation;—evils, which are not only the occasion of an exhausting drain upon their charity and benevolent institutions, and of enormously increased taxation for police and gaols, but the cause of social depravity, degradation, and wretchedness.

"That your Majesty's Petitioners desire to transmit to their posterity an inheritance, unencumbered by the pauperism, and unpolluted by the crime of the empire.

"*That the inundating of feeble and dependent Colonies with the criminals of the Parent State is opposed to that arrangement of Providence, by which the virtue of each community is destined to combat its own vice.*

"That although the stupendous power of Great Britain may enable her to continue these aggressions with impunity, injustice so revolting has aroused your Petitioners to unite in solemn appeal to those Eternal Principles which should preserve the weak from the oppression of the strong, and which should, more especially, restrain a Parent State from thus injuring her offspring. And your Petitioners submit that their relation to the Mother Country, as Colonists, so far from repealing, renders of stronger obligation, that Rule of Justice which Commonwealths, as well as private persons, are bound to reverence and practice; and which commands them, to do unto others, as they would that others should do unto them.

"Your Majesty's Petitioners, therefore, humbly beseech your Majesty to procure the immediate cessation of Transportation to Van Dieman's Land; and, further, that your Majesty will be graciously pleased to abandon altogether a penal policy, which your Majesty's Petitioners feel to be so injurious, so unjust, and so oppressive.

"And your Majesty's Petitioners, as in duty bound, will ever pray, &c."

That the British Government had virtually granted the the prayer of the petition is proved by the fact that in House of Lords, in a debate on Transportation, Earl GREY said, on the 5th of March, 1847 (as quoted in the Report of the Association, p. 6):—

"The Government had resolved to make a change, which amounted to nothing less than the total abolition of the system of Transportation. When a system of that nature was carried on at the Antipodes, it was utterly impossible that any other result should follow, than that which had been actually witnessed. He thought the papers which had been recently laid upon the table, proved that the anticipations of failure had been but too well founded. *He would not disgust their Lordships by going into the horrible, the monstrous details.* The system was frightful, and it was a disgrace to the British nation that such a system should have existed under the British flag. There was all the evidence which it was possible to have, that the system worked badly. It must also be remembered that the expenditure connected with the carrying out of the system in Van Dieman's Land, on the part of the mother country, had been extremely large; he had no hesitation in saying that had the same been expended in a well-considered system of employing convicts at home, the same number of convicts might have been effectually punished in this country. But while to the mother country the system had been expensive, *to the colony it had been absolute ruin.* The charge thus thrown upon the colony had made it bankrupt. By this system many of the most valuable settlers in Van Dieman's Land had been forced to quit the island, and thus a most serious blow had been inflicted on the prosperity of the colony. Until this large influx of convicts, the career of the colony had been one of almost unexampled prosperity; but from that time the state of things was greatly altered."

The corruption here spoken of in Van Dieman's Land was not confined to that Island. Though direct Transportation to New Zealand had been resisted, the report tells us (p. 5):—

"Her proximity to this Colony, and to Tasmania, and the easy and frequent intercourse which already existed, and which the certain establishment of steam communication must increase, exposed her also to the introduction of convicts—the refuse of Van Dieman's Land; thereby causing her to suffer, in general estimation, as a field for emigration, although her climate and soil, and her position with reference to the Islands of the Pacific, and to the western coast of North America, now in course of such rapid settlement and colonization, proclaim her great importance as an entrepôt for British commercial enterprise in the Southern Hemisphere.

"Van Dieman's Land," the Report continues, "not only claims their sympathy, but excites their deepest solicitude. *There,* the social disorganization is not less portentious, than the moral evils are appalling. *There,* the emancipists are in great numerical excess of the emigrants, and the introduction of representative institutions will, it is much to be feared, place that Island in the political possession of the convict party. An Association has been formed there, called 'The Tasmanian Union,' which threatens complete ascendancy. *This 'Union' is an alliance of the emancipists, against the emigrants—the former class being arrayed in the bitterest hostility against the latter."*

It would be unnecessary here to dwell on the dangers to civilised society in general of such a state of things, were it not, that, now the immediate danger is past, which was threatened by the position in which our Antipodal Colonies were placed,—many persons, who probably were not aware of the circumstances attending that crisis, have again recurred to the idea of Transportation as the most feasible way of disposing of our Convicts. The subject was fully investigated by the Royal Commission, and we derive the following information both from the questions of Mr. WADDINGTON and the answers of Mr. EVEREST, who had been for fifteen years principal clerk in the Criminal Department of the Home Office; we shall render it more succinct and clear by leaving the form of question and answer, and interweaving both into a narrative.

In the year 1842 there were no sentences to penal servitude, all being sentenced to Transportation; these received a free pardon after a certain time, except in cases of misconduct, which very seldom occurred. The bulk of these Convicts were sent to Australia; the others were kept in confinement in the hulks, as there were no Public Works' Prisons then on shore. The free pardon was usually granted at the end of about four years in the case of a seven years' sentence; of six years in the case of a fourteen years' sentence; and in cases of Transportation for life, after about eight years. The time of discharge depended entirely, however, on the conduct of the Convict; it was the practice to recommend a certain number out of the whole who were confined, on the ground of good behaviour during the previous three months, but the rules on that subject were not very fixed and defined.

The following is a table showing the number of Convicts who were sentenced to Transportation during eleven years, commencing with 1842, from a paper delivered in by Mr.

EVEREST, and inserted in the Appendix of the Report of the Commission:—

| Year. | Sentenced to Transportation. | In the Hulks. | Transported to Australia. |
|---|---|---|---|
| 1842 | 4,481 | 315 | 4,166 |
| 1843 | 4,448 | 1,455 | 2,993 |
| 1844 | 3,651 | 372 | 3,279 |
| 1845 | 3,247 | 705 | 2,542 |
| 1846 | 3,157 | 1,449 | 1,708 |
| 1847 | 3,262 | 2,040 | 1,222 |
| 1848 | 3,600 | 1,703 | 1,897 |
| 1849 | 3,202 | 1,593 | 1,609 |
| 1850 | 3,173 | 708 | 2,465 |
| 1851 | 3,338 | 898 | 2,440 |
| 1852 | 2,896 | 355 | 2,541 |
| Total | 38,455 | 11,593 | 26,862 |

At the end of this period about 9000 remained in the hulks, under sentence of Transportation. The Colonies, except Western Australia, then refused to receive more Convicts;—the last batch of Convicts was sent out to Tasmania in 1852. In pursuance of an Act passed in 1853, a new sentence of penal servitude was introduced, and all sentences under fourteen years were abolished, but these continued to be passed to a limited extent until the year 1857. By the Act of 1853 the system of ticket-of-leave was made legal, as applicable to persons under sentence of Transportation, of whom we have seen that there were 9000 remaining beside all those sentenced to fourteen years' Transportation. Those who had a sentence of seven years had their ticket-of-leave granted to them after three years; those under a ten years' sentence, in four years; a fourteen years' sentence, in six years; a twenty years' sentence, after eight years; and a life sentence might be brought under consideration in ten years, but the release was not to follow unless the merits of the case justified it, and after a consideration of the enormity of the case. Several persons still remain in the Convict Prisons whose claims have been refused on account of the enormity of their crimes. A case recently occurred of the release on license of a man who had been fifteen years in confinement for murder, though his conduct had been good through the whole time. The sentences to penal servitude that were substituted for Transportation were much shorter, and these were carried out in full—there was no remission by ticket-of-leave, and there was considerable doubt whether any penal servitude men could be transported. The Committee of the House of Commons in 1856 specially inquired into the working of the system, which led to a new Act in 1857, by which Transportation was abolished altogether, the sentences of penal servitude were extended to the old periods of Transportation, a new sentence of three years was added, and the system of granting licenses was extended to all these sentences.

The following table is a continuation of the former one, and gives the disposal of the Convicts under the new system:—

| Year. | Sentenced to Transportation. | Sentenced to Penal Servitude. | Total Sentenced. | In Convict Prisons. | Transported to Western Australia. |
|-------|------|------|------|------|------|
| 1853 | 2,086 | 623 | 2,709 | 2,109 | 600 |
| 1854 | 360 | 2,382 | 2,742 | 2,462 | 280 |
| 1855 | 375 | 2,215 | 2,590 | 2,105 | 485 |
| 1856 | 345 | 2,370 | 2,715 | 2,217 | 498 |
| 1857 | 138 | 2,703 | 2,841 | 2,309 | 532 |
| 1858 | ... | 2,419 | 2,419 | 1,869 | 550 |
| 1859 | ... | 2,383 | 2,383 | 2,159 | 224 |
| 1860 | ... | 2,436 | 2,436 | 2,140 | 296 |
| 1861 | ... | 2,678 | 2,678 | 2,372 | 306 |
| 1862 | ... | 3,369 | 3,369 | 2,587 | 782 |
| Total | 3,304 | 23,578 | 26,882 | 22,329 | 4,553 |

This enormous mass of Convicts annually enlisted in our criminal ranks awakens in the public mind a desire that we should in some way rid ourselves of them, and the wish naturally arises that we could in some way rid ourselves of them by Transportation. And, though we know that it cannot possibly be resumed in our Colonies, because they absolutely refused to receive them, except, indeed Western Australia, of which more will shortly be stated, yet arguments are often brought forward in favour of an attempt to` resume it in some other parts of the globe. We have heard Transportation defended, in the first place, because it is said that "great empires have been founded by Convicts." Specific instances have not usually been adduced in support of this assertion, and, indeed, if any were mentioned, it would probably be found that these were far from being parallel cases. In early days we used to read of the Roman Empire being originated by a few bandits. These were certainly a very different set of men, from those that go forth from our Convict Prisons. Rough and rude as they probably were, they did not destroy but establish law and order, and step by step created the marvellous empire which, even after its decay, will ever be the wonder of the world. Those were not men, pampered by a corrupt system, hardened by a long course of immorality, such as we have already seen our Convicts to be. Or again (we again quote the report),—

"Should it be objected that, out of similar materials, a great empire has been created in the United States, it may be replied that, though England adopted, in the seventeenth century, the system of Transportation to her North American plantations, the number of convicts was too small—and that of free labourers too large, in the old provinces of North America—to have allowed this infusion of a convict population to produce much effect on the development of these communities. 'Our own times (says Mr. HERMAN MERIVALE, in his twelfth lecture on Colonization, vol. 2, p. 4) are the first which have witnessed the phenomena of communities in which the bulk of the working people consists of felons serving out the period of their punishment. In the middle of the last century,' he adds, 'Maryland was estimated to contain 107,208 inhabitants, of whom 1,981 only were convicts. Yet Maryland was *one of the principal receptacles for criminals.*' [See SADLER on Population, vol. 1, p. 447.] Thus, while in Maryland, the principal receptacle for convicts in the United States, the convict class was never so much as two to fifty in proportion to the emigrant and native classes; in New South Wales, the former class, even now, constitutes one-fifth of the population (and in which calculation infants and young children are included); and in Van Dieman's Land their numbers are far more than double those of the emigrants and natives,"—p. 41.

But even supposing that empires have been commenced by any such agency, we certainly at the present day have no right to use it, and to entail on a new community the certain moral injury which any numbers of such a population must cause. We know well from the history of our own Colonies, that not only was direct crime immensely increased by Transportation, but also that a tone of society was created which was even more injurious. An illustration of this we will present from the article in "Meliora" before quoted, "Our Convict System," April, 1861 :—

"In the thickly-populated districts especially, public opinion in some degree shielded the convict from the extremity of oppression; but that great tyranny was exercised even at the seat of government (though sinking to a trifle when compared with the cruelty perpetrated up the country), the following conversation in 182—, will serve to show. The speakers are the author of 'Settlers and Convicts,' and an old resident in the Colony, who narrates a few instances of such horrors as afterwards came to the knowledge of Capt. MACONOCHIE by hundreds.

"You may wonder, my lad," he said, "at what you read about the treatment of prisoners; most people do when they first come. But you'll see things yet up the country, that these Sydney doings are only child's play by the side of.

"You don't mean to say," I replied, "that I shall meet with anything worse than this case I have just read. Here is an offence called by three different names; three several charges are made upon it; three several trials, three several sentences, and three several punishments following. A man gets drunk, has his clothes stolen, and is afraid to go home to his master. He his tried first for drunkenness, a second time for making away with his clothing, and a third time for absconding. His sentence is in sum total one hundred lashes, which, with the cat-o'-nine-tails, is really nine hundred lashes.

"Why, I have known the same act to be called by five different names and five sentences passed upon the prisoner for it. It was in the case of a government servant belonging to a magistrate near me. The man, as in the case you read, had got a drop of liquor from a travelling dealer. His master's son, a very pert young fellow, began to curse at and threaten him. The man retorted; a constable was sent for, whom he knocked down and escaped from. He then ran off into the bush, taking with him, as he passed his own hut, about three parts of a cake he had by him ready baked. The young fellow prosecuted him for drunkenness, insolence, theft (the piece of bread, for rations are considered the master's till used), and bushranging; and then the magistrate made the constable swear the assault against him. He got twenty-five lashes for drunkenness, twenty-five for insolence, fifty for bushranging, six months to an iron gang for stealing the cake, and three months for assaulting a peace-officer in the execution of his duty. The flogging he got before going to the iron gang frightened him; and on receiving sentence for some trivial offence at the iron gang, he escaped before the punishment was inflicted, took to the bush, joined a gang of bushrangers, who had arms, committed several robberies with them, was taken with arms in his hands, and hanged. The man was a quiet, hard-working, honest fellow, but he could not stand flogging, and he was fond of liquor. The crime he was sent here for he committed when drunk, and it was perhaps the only one he had to answer for. That man was murdered; and so hundreds upon hundreds have been, and are being, every year in this cursed country.

\*          \*          \*          \*          \*

"The fact is, flogging in this country is such a common thing, that nobody thinks anything of it. I have seen young children practising on a tree, as children in England play at horses. I have now got a man under me who received 2,600 lashes with the cat in about five years, and his worst crime was insolence to his overseer. The fact is, that the man is a red-hot Tipperary man, and when his blood gets up, you could not make him hold his tongue if you were to threaten to hang him. Since I have had him he has never had a lash, just because I take no notice of what he says. The consequence is, there is nothing in the world that man would not do for me if he could.

\*          \*          \*          \*          \*

"What I tell you now, I tell you on the authority of my own eyes. I was sent for to Bathurst Court House, to identify a man supposed to have taken the bush, from the farm I have charge of. I had to go past the triangles, where they had been flogging incessantly for hours. I saw a man walk across the yard with the blood that had run from his lacerated flesh squashing out of his shoes at every step he took. A dog was licking the blood off the triangles, and the ants were carrying away great pieces of human flesh that the lash had scattered about the ground. The scourger's foot had worn a deep hole in the ground by the violence with which he whirled himself round on it to strike the quivering and wealed back, out of which stuck the sinews, white, ragged and swollen. The infliction was one hundred lashes, at about half-minute time, so as to extend the punishment through nearly an hour. The day was hot enough to overcome a man merely standing that length of time in the sun; and this was going on in the full blaze of it. However, they had a pair of scourgers who gave one another spell and spell about, and they were bespattered with blood like a couple of butchers."

However exceptional such scenes as these may be, yet the fact that they have taken place, and were even not uncommon, warns us of the danger to which we are exposing, by Transportation, countries dependent on us. The danger of such a proceeding is well stated by Mr. HASTINGS, in an address made by him at a Special Meeting of the Social Science Association, February 17, 1863:—

"The first of the general objections is the great injury and annoyance which any system of Transportation entails on our free Colonies. By the Transportation of criminals you bring discredit on emigation. You hold that out as a punishment which you ought to give as a reward. You corrupt the blood of young communities. You lower the estimation of all Colonies in every part of the world. You create feelings of suspicion and jealousy between the mother country and her dependencies, where nothing but good will and amity ought to prevail. Now I have sometimes heard it urged—I have read lately a distinct statement—that we may do what we like with the waste territories of our distant dependencies, and that we may use them, if we choose, for the disposal of our criminals. I deny that proposition. I deny that we possess any such absolute right. *We hold our vast Colonial dominions not for our own exclusive benefits, but as trustees for the interests of their future inhabitants, of the empire and the whole world.* I say, too, that in this case the old legal maxim, *Sic utere tuo ut alienum non lædas*, is strictly applicable. The owner of flowing water may use it, but not to another's injury; and so are we entitled to use the great stream of emigration for all lawful purposes, but we have no right to poison it to our neighbour's wrong. Moreover, I contend that the argument which has been used very freely during the last few months, that convict establishments are necessary for the foundation of all Colonies, is an extraordinary argument to produce at the present day. If it could ever have been legitimately employed, which I doubt, looking to the history of ancient colonization, looking to such Colonies as that at the Cape, founded by the Dutch, and of the Canadas, founded by the French and by ourselves, which, as far as I know, never had a convict among them,— it at least is most extraordinary that, in face of the events of the last twenty years, such an argument should be advanced to grown people. Look at the Colony of Queensland; look at South Australia; look at New Zealand. The inhabitants of all these settlements have refused convict labour, and their prosperity has been far more rapid than that of the Colonies which have attempted to bolster themselves up by the importation of felons. This is one of the *post hoc propter hoc* arguments which are so commonly used. I deny that the success of the original Australian settlements was due to convict labour. I say that it was in spite of convict labour, and notwith- standing its blighting influence, by the energy of their inhabitants and the enterprise of Englishmen, that those Colonies attained to their present splendid position."

But though all reason, justice, and morality distinctly declare that the system of Transportation can never be resumed, yet a strong belief even now exists among some that the dread of Transportation is great in the criminal class, and has a wholesome deterrent effect. Hence, again, a desire exists in the public mind of devising some means of renewing it. Many judges tell us of the horror and despair they have witnessed when a sentence of transportation has been passed.

Sir MICHAEL BARRINGTON mentions in his evidence before the
Select Committee of 1856, striking instances of the effect of
sentences of Transportation, during some very serious agrarian
disturbances in 1831, in Ireland. There was then a special
commission appointed, when 50 or 60 persons had to be tried
for offences, which, under the existing laws, might have been
punished with death. Instead of trying them for the capital
offence, executing some and discharging the least culpable,
as was probably expected, the whole number were sentenced
to Transportation; they were removed straight from the dock,
and escorted by a body of dragoons to Cork, whence they
were sent off, without being permitted to bid farewell to their
friends. The effect was most striking. "From that period
(Sir M. BARRINGTON says, 2329), for nearly 20 years, there was
not a more peaceful part of Ireland than the county of Clare,
which I attribute to the immediate effect of Transportation."

We must, however, perceive that the effect here spoken of
is referable to certain circumstances which do not form part of
the more recent mode of carrying out the punishment.

In the first place, there was a certainty that *all* would be
punished who were found guilty of thus disturbing the peace
of the country. This *certainty of consequences* has, of itself,
a very deterrent effect. While death was the penalty awarded
by the law, there was a natural tendency to calculate on the
chances of escape, and the unwillingness on the part of judges
and juries to offend humanity and public feeling by wholesale
executions. Sir M. BARRINGTON tells us that in these agrarian
offences such calculations are actually made. "I have known
it," he says (2405), "from approvers who have told us that
they have so calculated; they have said, 'There will be so
many of us transported, and the rest will get off;' and there
has been that kind of calculation. * * * In that very
case which I mentioned, of houghing the cattle and killing
them, in that way, the approvers told me, that they calculated
that some of them might be transported, but they had no

idea that the whole of them would be; two of them became approvers, and the remaining 14 were all transported, and that had a most admirable effect." On the other hand, the same witness says (2337), "There is no instance of a number of men, convicted of anything but murder, in which there would not be a selection made for the execution of some. For instance, in a Whiteboy case, eight or ten are convicted of a capital offence, punishable with death; some would be selected for execution, and some let off, and then the letting off of some neutralizes the effect of the execution of the others."

In the second place, the suddenness of the punishment, and the *immediate* removal of the prisoners from any hope of seeing their friends, formed a considerable part of its impressiveness. "I know that at that special commission at Clare," says Sir M. BARRINGTON (2332), "they were taken out of the country so rapidly and so suddenly, that the scene was awful; the Convicts threw their shoes and handkerchiefs to their families as tokens and remembrances; I am sure it had a much stronger effect than if some of them had been executed three or four weeks afterwards, having the consolation of friends and party to support them."

And, thirdly, under no circumstances can the punishment of Transportation now have the terrors with which it was invested thirty years ago, the period to which Sir M. BARRINGTON refers. "Transportation to Botany Bay" was then a most awful sentence;—Australia was a *terra incognita* to the mass of the people,—the end of the world,—the bourne from which scarcely any traveller returned; postal communication was difficult and almost impossible, and the transported felon was regarded as having undergone a sort of civil death. But the last quarter of a century has entirely changed the whole aspect of the subject. Australia has been regarded as an El Dorado by the ignorant; reports of enormous fortunes acquired, have made emigration to the antipodes an object of desire instead of terror, to the restless and daring;—instead of immediate removal from the land of their fathers, it is well known that the Convicts remain for a considerable time before their departure, in prisons, where they are provided with every necessary, and even with comforts which they could never have procured for themselves by honest means, and whence they may at stated intervals communicate with their friends.  Transportation can never again be regarded by the criminal population with the dread which it inspired thirty years ago ; the deterrent influence it may once have had is for ever gone.  Where it still is regarded with some degree of fear, it is because an erroneous idea exists of what is meant by it.  Mr. LOOME, Police-Sergeant, states to the Select Committee of 1856, that the criminal class express a "great horror of Transportation, but on asking them what they mean by the horrors of Transportation, they have said," he says (2592), " 'We are confined, perhaps, two, three, or four years on board some ship before we go out, and after we go out we are worked in gangs; and then, when we get our liberty out there, we cannot get back.  If we get imprisonment here, on our discharge, we are at home again.' "  But even in that very Committee, while some speak of the "great horror of Transportation" entertained by the criminal class, one of the Judges of the High Court of Queen's Bench, the Hon. Sir W. ERLE, informs the Select Committee of 1856, in his answer (3344)— "By all that part of the community who have any place in English society, I think Transportation is as much dreaded as ever it was.  There are isolated criminals who have given themselves up to the practice of dishonesty, and have no confirmed place; to them *Transportation is often a matter of hope. Such men as these I frequently have before me, and their wish is to be transported.  They say, 'My position in society is such that it would be better for me to be transported;' that is as to the isolated individual.*"

Sir J. JEBB gives, in the Appendix to his evidence before the Commission (p. 145), the following opinion of the effect of Transportation on the criminal class :—

"I say it with all due respect for the opinions of others, but I say it because my own experience rests upon an extended experience and upon facts, that the deterring effect of Transportation has been gradually diminishing in the eyes of the criminal classes, concurrently with an increasing necessity of providing some more sentences to replace the loss of capital punishment. *It is little dreaded by the majority of the men, and is even less so by the women. Few of them have anything to lose ; any change must be for the better.*

"Lord CAMPBELL observes in his evidence :

"'I think that if the country is to send people abroad as emigrants, and to take care of them, if you call that Transportation, that, instead of being a *punishment*, it may be a *reward*.'

"If it be said it can surely be made a punishment! a consideration of the details for throwing convicts on a desert island, and ruling them when landed, will make any one shrink from so fearful a responsibility. In whatever form it might be attempted, it would be surrounded with insuperable difficulties, keeping in mind that a watchful public would not long tolerate the dark atrocities of Norfolk Island. It would be next to impossible to avoid them, unless the convicts were introduced in a small proportion to the thriving community among whom they might be set free, and there the object would be to make them happy.

"A satisfactory solution of this question may not be hoped for, where the interests of the mother country and the colony are diametrically opposed ; the former seeking to be relieved of her worst criminals, and to obtain a formidable punishment; the latter deserving to receive only the best, and such as are likely to prosper."

Transportation no longer exists, then, as the awful punishment which it used to be regarded as some thirty or even twenty years since, nor can it ever be so again. We will again quote Mr. HASTINGS, in the same address :—

"I can quite understand that, in former times, when convicts were first sent to Australia, seeing that it was at that period almost a *terra incognita;* that there was no free population and no wealth in the settlement; that the voyage of many months to a distant and inhospitable shore was clothed with all the terrors of imagination—in those days, I can imagine it possible that a sentence of Transportation may have deterred, in some measure, from crime. But in the present day, when the continent of Australia contains more than a million of English inhabitants, in the enjoyment of one of the most fertile soils and finest climates in the world—when it is known to be teeming with metallic riches—when, in fact, it is the very El Dorado of the working population of this country—do you suppose you can prevent men from committing crime by telling them you are going to send them, free of expense, to such a country as that? It seems to me to be one of the most extravagant delusions which ever entered the mind of man. Let me refer you to an example. There was a man of the name of REDPATH, who some years ago committed a crime which, considering his position and knowledge, was one of the worst he could be guilty of — that of swindling people out of their money when he was in a position of trust, and swindling them in order to gratify his mean and miserable ambition of living in greater luxury and display than he could do with his honest salary. That man was transported for life, and every one conceived that a very severe punishment had been pronounced upon him. Now what is the fact? REDPATH is spending his days in Western Australia, living free and at his own pleasure on an annuity provided him by his friends — I have no doubt enjoying every comfort and many luxuries. Take the case of ROUPELL. He will go out, most probably, as REDPATH did, and in a few years will be living in the same comfortable manner. And this, we are told, is the highly deterrent punishment! But if this be so with regard to such men as REDPATH and ROUPELL, how much more is the punishment non-deterrent in its nature when applied to men who, if they remained in this country, never could have hoped to earn more than a few shillings a week, but, if transported to a colony, may look forward to good wages as secure, and even to rising into the position of owners of property in a few years! I repeat that it is a delusion on the part of the public to imagine that this can be a deterrent punishment."

But while the public have been compelled to abandon all idea of sending our criminal population in general to the Colonies, the notion has still been strongly advocated by many, of establishing penal Colonies where the very worst criminals might be securely placed, and prevented from doing further injury to society.

The Lord Chief Justice of England, Lord CAMPBELL, expresses, in his evidence before the Select Committee of 1856, the unsuitable nature of such places as the Falkland Islands, or the Hebrides, which have been mentioned as adapted for penal settlements. He says (4008):—

" The object of Transportation, in my view of it, cannot be accomplished, unless the prisoner is sent to some country where there is a *demand for his labour*, where he can become a useful citizen, and where he may re-establish himself in society. There has been a talk of having a penal settlement in one of the Hebrides, or in one of the Falkland Islands, without really colonizing. *I do not believe that that would at all produce the effect, because it would be little better than merely keeping the imprisonment with hard labour at home.* The persons so dealt with would acquire no new status; they could not acquire property, they could not maintain their families respectably. It is stated on good authority, that in the colonies there are now (or there were a year or two ago) 40,000 convicts who had been transported, who were reputably maintaining themselves by their industry. In such a settlement as the honorable member represents, not one of the individuals could gain the status which is now enjoyed by those 40,000 parties."

Mr. ELLIOT, the Assistant Under-Secretary of State in the Colonial Department, expresses himself forcibly in his evidence before the Select Committee of 1856, respecting the evil of sending our Convicts to any place where they would form the whole population, and would have no opportunity, therefore, of being received again into society. Thus, he truly remarks, there would be no influence of public opinion, and the horrors of Norfolk Island may be again anticipated. It is extraordinary, after the evidence on the subject which has been so long before the public, that the question should have been recently revived of sending our Convicts to some exclusively penal settlement. The public prints continually presented the suggestions of some individuals to send them to the Falkland Islands, to Labrador, to the most uninviting region that could be discovered, whether in the tropics or near the frozen zone. Mr. ELLIOT thus speaks of similar proposals which were made eight years ago :—

" We have had the Falkland Islands suggested, and the Auckland Islands suggested, and the Chatham Islands proposed. I think that all those proposals mistake the difficulty with which we have to grapple. Those places would all do very well for retaining men while in bondage, but I really think that the nearest common in Surrey would be a better place still. *I think that so long as a man is locked up in prison you can keep him as well at home*, and you can more easily get good officers, who are also under the influence of public opinion, if anything is done amiss. The difficulty is to *provide for the convicts when they become free men in a large community*; for that purpose the Falkland Islands are wholly unsuited (415). I think that the territory of the Hudson's Bay Company is just as objectionable, from being too cold, as are several other places that have been thought of, from being too hot; you can hardly create an English Siberia; and there is the further objection that this would be very dear (418). I have heard the suggestion of converting some of the Scotch Islands—some of the Hebrides—into receptacles for convicts, and I think it comes under the same class as those of the Falkland Islands and others I have mentioned;

they would be very well for a Penitentiary, but, really, Wandsworth Common
is quite as good, and quite as unobjectionable (421). In the Hebrides the
convicts might have greater liberty, but I do not see that they would be better
able to provide for their own subsistence. The reason why I think this, is
that we all know ;the immense distress which has been experienced by the
free inhabitants of the Hebrides;—if they could not live there, I do not
believe that prisoners could by their own exertions" (510).

Such a settlement must necessarily lose all the value to the
Convict of giving him an opportunity of regaining a social
status, and, as a purely penal institution, it would not have
the advantages of one in our own country, while it would be
far more expensive and difficult of management. Sir WALTER
CROFTON's opinion on this subject has great authority, coming
from one of such high experience. The following passage is
extracted from his speech at the Meeting before alluded to, of
the Social Science Association :—

"It is known to every one connected with criminal matters that the
convicts are anxious to go to Western Australia. Many of the advocates
of Transportation say — ' Perhaps Western Australia would not deter
these men; but we will have some new penal settlement, some rugged,
bleak place, the very sight of which shall deter them.' And what are they
to be made to do do? Work—erect their own prisons, and be made to do
all that is needed. Now, I will invite consideration to those persons who
are committing offences of the most desperate character; and I ask, how
are they to be so easily made to do everything—to become such handy
men, the moment they arrive at this bleak and barren spot? I think it
will be obvious that we shall have to maintain a large force to accompany
them; and what will be the position of the troops who do accompany these
men? We shall be punishing our soldiers equally with our convicts. Much
has been said that we are not to return to the system of Norfolk Island or
Port Arthur; but I say, if we send these men out to a new penal settlement, they are the very class of men who were sent to Norfolk Island and
Port Arthur. It is the same course over again. It is no use to talk
about better administration. Sir GEORGE ARTHUR gave in evidence before
Sir WILLIAM MOLESWORTH's Committee in the House of Commons, that
at Port Arthur he knew men there constantly committing murder, for the
purpose of being sent to Hobart Town—for what? To be hung in the
course of a fortnight for their offence. And what is also of consequence,
is the fact, that the commanding officer of the troops gave in evidence that
his regiment was perfectly demoralised by coming in contact with these
people. Now, I want to know how we can for one moment expect a

repetition of this state of things? Is it likely we should repeat a condition of things which frightened us so much in 1840? A penal settlement
must be enormously expensive. Is it possible we should pay a large bill,
year after year, for these men who never could be finally disposed of?"

A purely penal settlement such has been thus suggested may
be regarded as morally and physically impossible; an experiment so costly and so certain of failure, will surely never again
be tried by our Government.

It was remarked in the last chapter, that of all the States of
Europe from whom answers to inquiries were received by the
British Government, only Portugal and Russia employ Transportation under any form as a secondary punishment. The
following is the statement from those countries:—

### PORTUGAL.

"In the year 1847, 329 convicts were transported, 34 in 1848, 300 in
1849; and in the present year (1850) upwards of 400 are ready for Transportation, which gives as a medium about 260 convicts annually.

"When these convicts from Portugal arrive at the different provinces
they are enlisted in one of the military corps, if their age and health
permit; and if not enlisted for any of these reasons, or on account of
other considerations, such as the social position of the individuals, they
are sent by the governor to reside at the places which may be considered
most convenient, keeping in view the affording them the facility of procuring the means of subsistence, subject, however, *to the constant vigilance
of the local authorities.*

"Except with such as are enlisted, no further expense is incurred with
the convicts beyond that of their conveyance; and when their term of
Transportation is up, the provincial authorities furnish them, on requesting
it, with passports for returning to the kingdom, otherwise they continue to
reside in the province as free subjects. That system of Transportation to
the transmarine provinces may be considered beneficial, from the improvement which in general is observed in the behaviour of the convicts, and
no reasons have yet been brought forward to warrant its discontinuance."

In Russia, Transportation to remote parts of the empire forms
a leading feature in the penal code, and this punishment is of
a peculiarly severe character. No mention is made, in the
abstract given of a very elaborate treatise received from
Russia, of any attempt at reformation, or any provision for
criminals on discharge.

RUSSIA.

"The punishments denominated 'capital' consist of—
1. Death.
2. Hard labour in the mines, in a fortress, or in the public factories and workshops.
3. Transportation to Siberia.
4. Transportation beyond the Caucasus.

"The characteristic of the whole of these so-called 'capital' punishments is that they carry with them a complete political and civil death. The individual loses his rank and all his rights, personal, social, and political; his marriage may be annulled on the demand of his wife; he ceases to be a member of his family, and is as utterly deprived of all his privileges as if he were naturally dead.

"The number of persons who received sentence in the year 1847 to these punishments, except death, amounted to the following:—

| | | |
|---|---|---:|
| Hard labour | ... ... ... ... ... | 1095 |
| Transportation to Siberia | ... ... ... | 1860 |
| Ditto | beyond the Caucasus ... ... | 175 |
| Ditto | (simple) to Siberia ... ... | 644 |
| Ditto | to other remote governments ... | 259" |

The position of these two States is very different from our own. In the case of Portugal, what is termed Transportation is really nothing more than a forced emigration to a country where the culprit is enabled to begin anew to gain an honest living, under a certain degree of surveillance. The possibility of thus disposing advantageously of the criminal population of the country, evidently removes the necessity of devising measures for absorbing them into the home population. In Russia, on the contrary, Transportation is of a more absolutely penal character than it has ever been in our own country. There is no hope of retrieving the past, of regaining a place in society, or of establishing a new home in a distant colony;—the Convict is doomed to a political and civil death, and society is separated from him for ever. Our Nation desires to reclaim her erring children.

It is, then, evidently impossible in our country that we should ever be able to dispose of our criminals under the conditions with which Portugal can transfer them to her vast dependencies. It is, we believe, equally impossible that the British Govern-

ment should ever abandon the idea of reformation in the
treatment of Convicts, and adopt the system pursued by Russia.
Those countries cannot, therefore, be regarded in any way as
examples to us, nor can any advantages which they may
derive from the system which they pursue, afford any argument
for our adopting a similar course. There is a great and
universal truth in the declaration of the Colonies in their
address to the Sovereign:—" The inundating of feeble and
dependent Colonies with the criminals of the Parent State
is opposed to that arrangement of Providence by which the
virtue of each community is destined to combat its own vice."
Every district should grapple with the evils for which it alone
is responsible; no country has a right to pollute the shores
of another with its crime; no society ought, in justice to itself,
to receive into its midst, for any pecuniary or commercial
advantages which may be offered, a mass of crime which may
take root in the country, lower its moral tone, and undermine
the very springs of its social constitution. May our Colonies,—
inheriting from the Parent State a love of moral purity,—ever
resist any attempt to pollute their shores with the presence
of vice, as did of old our New England brethren. At the
Anti-Transportation meeting, before alluded to, Lord LYTTELTON
said :—

" I remember the settlers of New Plymouth holding a public meeting when
that colony was, as it always has been, suffering from want of labour. A
resolution was proposed to the effect that, on certain conditions and with certain regulations, convicts should be received from this country. The report
of that meeting, which appeared in the public newspapers, stated that the
gentleman who brought forward the resolution, stood in a minority of one."

May a similar feeling ever pervade our Colonies, and may
our rulers ever feel the solemn responsibility expressed in the
declaration of Earl GREY to the House of Lords, in March, 1847,
that if Transportation is continued, "Van Dieman's Land will
become what Norfolk Island was, *a vast horde of criminals, with
nothing but their keepers!*" May posterity never have to reproach
our country with having thus established a "reign of terror"

instead of a kingdom of peace! May the principle set forth by Lord JOHN RUSSELL to the House of Commons on June 10th, 1847, be ever the guide of our policy,—"It has been too much the custom to consult the convenience of Great Britain by getting rid of persons of evil habits, and to take that view of the question alone. In planting provinces which might become Empires, they should endeavour to make them, not seats of malefactors and Convicts, but communities which may set examples of virtue and happiness."

That the reader may have some faint idea of the class of persons alluded to as the inhabitants of Norfolk Island, where there were 1400 colonial Convicts when Captain MACONOCHIE was sent to the Island, of whom one hundred were *murderers*, under commutation of sentence, we copy the following narrative of one of them from the article in "Meliora" above alluded to:

"CHARLES ANDERSON was born at Newcastle-on-Tyne. His father, a sailor, was drowned, leaving a widow and two little sons. She soon died, and her children, helpless and friendless, were sent to the workhouse. There, untaught and uncared for, they remained until old enough to go to sea. At nine years of age, CHARLES was apprenticed to a collier, where he was knocked and buffeted about, and weathered many a storm. His apprenticeship over, he joined a man-of-war, and was in the battle of Navarino, where he was severely wounded in the head. He recovered, but ever afterwards irritation or drink would bring on violent fits of excitement. In a seaport in Devonshire a street row arose among a party of drunken sailors, in which ANDERSON was engaged. Some shops were broken into, and he, no doubt violent enough, was arrested, tried, and sentenced to seven years' Transportation for burglary. With no one to interpose in his behalf, the sentence was fulfilled, and at the age of eighteen he was sent to New South Wales. Doomed to a punishment involving the deepest degradation, for a crime of the committal of which he was not conscious, the bitterest hostility against his kind took possession of his breast. Utterly ignorant, both mentally and morally, he had little idea of patient submission, which, indeed, physical disease rendered impossible. No wonder, then, that violence created violence. His floggings were almost innumerable; but, sturdy and staunch for good or evil, punishment had no effect upon him. His was no spirit to give in to harshness, and kindness was never dreamt of.

"Upon his arrival in the colony he was sent to Goat Island (an insulated rock in Sydney harbour, famous in the records of convict discipline) as an

English or first-convicted prisoner. He remained there about two months under treatment so severe that, to escape it, he absconded. Apprehended and taken to Sydney Barracks, he there received 100 lashes for this offence; and upon being returned to Goat Island he received 100 more lashes, and was to wear irons for twelve months, in addition to his original sentence. Before completing it he had received 1,200 lashes for trivial offences, such as looking round from his work, or at a steamer in the river, &c. He again absconded, was re-apprehended, taken back to the island, and received 200 lashes; afterwards he was tried for the same offence, and was sentenced to 100 lashes more, and to be chained to a rock for two years, with barely a rag to cover him. He was fastened by his waist to the rock with a chain twenty-six feet long, and with trumpet irons on his legs. A hollow scooped out in the rock, large enough to admit his body, served for his bed, and his only shelter was a wooden lid perforated with holes, which was placed over him and locked in that position at night, being removed in the morning. He was fed by means of a pole, with which the vessel containing his food was pushed towards him. None of his fellow-prisoners were permitted to approach or speak to him, under penalty of 100 lashes, which his former messmate underwent in consequence of giving him a piece of tobacco. Regarded as a wild beast, people passing in boats would throw him bits of bread or biscuit. Exposed to all weathers, and without clothing on his back and shoulders, which were covered with sores from repeated floggings, the maggots rapidly engendered in a hot climate feeding upon his flesh, he was denied even water to bathe his wounds, such denial being not an unusual portion of the punishment to which he had been condemned; and when rain fell, or by any other means he could obtain liquid, he would lie and roll in it in agony.

" Several weeks had thus been passed in torture, when Sir RICHARD BOURKE hearing of him repaired at once to the spot. He asked ANDERSON if he would work, but he answered he would not; adding, that if he worked, he would be punished, and if he did not work, he would be punished the same. His Excellency then sent him to Macquarie for life. There he was set to labour in irons, his occupation being to carry lime in baskets on his back, from the kilns to barges in the Government service lying off the settlement. His overseer, ANTHONY, a Frenchman, used to threaten that the lime and salt water should burn the flesh off his back, and in effect it did burn off the skin, causing excruciating agony. Again the unhappy man absconded, and travelling several hundred miles, joined the aborigines. His native associates having attacked and killed some settlers, were pursued by the police, who, falling in with ANDERSON, seized and carried him back to Macquarie, where he received 200 lashes, and was returned to his gang. Three months afterwards a fellow convict and he agreed to kill ANTHONY, and ANDERSON declaring himself tired of life, said he would do the deed, and be hanged for it. According, next morning, he felled ANTHONY to the ground with his spade, and death ensued. The soldiers on guard stabbed ANDERSON in five places, and when seized, he had to be conveyed to the hospital. His wounds being cured, he was tried at Sydney and sentenced to death, but was respited and sent to Norfolk Island to work in chains for life. When Captain MACONOCHIE subsequently arrived there, the offences on the island recorded against ANDERSON were—ten times violent assault, and three times scheming to avoid labour, besides charges of insolence and insubordination. Though then only twenty-four, he looked forty years old. The captain was told he was 'cranky,' and he found that his fellow-prisoners amused themselves with teasing and making him vicious. This was at once forbidden. ANDERSON being one of the colonial convicts, the prohibition from Government to place that class under the mark system, precluded him from its influence. Casting about, therefore, for any means of reclaiming the unhappy creature now sunk deep in wickedness, Captain MACONOCHIE thought some unruly bullocks which had to be kept in bounds, would usefully exercise his superfluous energies, and would, besides, separate him for a time from his fellows. Many thought 'BONY,' as he was nicknamed, and his bullocks would come to grief. But strict orders were given that none should interfere with him, and very soon a marked change was apparent in the man. He became less wild, felt himself of some value, and won praise for his good conduct and successful management of his bullocks. He and they grew tractable together. He knew instinctively that high and strong tempers will not bend to the lash; and often were the anxious watchers of the experiment amused by the just insight into criminal discipline which ANDERSON displayed in the treatment of his charge. The cattle-training served its purpose well for a time, but as his mind improved, sailor-like, he hankered for his own old ‘work. His physical liability to excitement continuing, Captain MACONOCHIE feared collisions if he associated with other men: moreover, his constitution was so shattered as to unfit him for hard work; and it occurring to the captain that a signal station on Mount Pitt (the highest point on the island) would be an advantage, he resolved to erect one, and place ANDERSON in charge. His delight was extreme, for he now felt himself a man again; and dressed in sailor costume, he soon regained the bearing of a man-of-war's man. The top of Mount Pitt was cleared, a hut built, and a flag-staff, provided with a code of signals, was raised. The smallest boat could there be seen, and the settlement at once knew if anything were in sight. ANDERSON's patch of garden was his great delight; the gift of a new flower was highly prized, and the best potatoes on the island grew there. Of these it was his special pride to bring a freshly-dug basketful, to be served at the captain's dinner table.

" Sir GEORGE GIPPS visited the island three years after Capt. MACONOCHIE's arrival, and while driving through its beautiful scenery, ANDERSON was seen tripping along in his trim sailor dress, full of importance, with his telescope under his arm. ' What little smart fellow may that be?' asked Sir GEORGE. ' Who do you suppose? That is the man who was chained to the rock in Sydney Harbour.' ' Bless my soul, you do not mean to say so!' was the astonished rejoinder.

" As he regained his self-respect, ANDERSON revealed a noble generous heart, and a gay and sociable disposition; but his excitability eventually became madness, and not long after, the benefactor who had restored him, and hundreds like him, to the feelings and duties of humanity, was peremptorily recalled from the scene of his philanthropic labours, ANDERSON was seen in a lunatic asylum by one whom he had known as a friend of the captain in Norfolk Island. The poor fellow recognised his visitor, and spoke of nothing but Captain MACHONOCHIE and his family.

"The early portion of this narrative," the writer continues, "was taken chiefly from ANDERSON'S own lips at Norfolk Island, and cannot, therefore, be wholly relied upon for accuracy; but the terrible incident of his being chained to the rock was well known in the colony, and Captain MACONOCHIE had heard it spoken of long before he saw the man; while the other events in his career were but too common to need corroboration."

From the Captain's records we have also the following extract, which shows, as does also the foregoing one, how great was the moral influence he exercised over even these wretched persons, who seemed to have lost their human nature, but who were still our fellow men :—

" An unhappy prisoner, one of a most unhappy family, of whom *the mother, two brothers, and a sister had all been executed for different acts of violence, and who was himself little better than a wild beast,* was tried for his life on the island for stabbing the gaoler; and the line of defence that he took was to plead insanity and act accordingly. Being an ignorant, coarse-minded man, his only idea of this was to address volleys of obscenity to the Court and all concerned with it on trial, and this he maintained for a considerable time. At length he ceased, and was found guilty and sentenced to death; and when led away, being asked how he came to falter in his purpose, he replied, ' Didn't you see Master A—— come in ? I couldn't go on that way before him.' This was one of my sons, then a boy of fifteen, who, even at that age, had taken much to the object of reforming the prisoners, and used frequently to attend the gaol, and read the Bible with them; and this wretched man so much respected his youth and innocence that he compromised what he must have considered his only chance of life, rather than pollute his ears with his previous abominations."

Though enough has probably been here stated to satisfy our readers of the impossibility of again resuming Transportation as a secondary punishment, yet, as the Report of Sir WILLIAM MOLESWORTH's Committee has not been here quoted, we may give the following extracts from it, contained in a valuable letter of Mr. FREDERICK HILL's, in the *Daily Telegraph* of January 23rd, 1863 :—

"I now proceed to treat of Transportation. That my opinions on this subject have not been formed suddenly, is shown by the fact that they were expressed, more than twenty years ago, in my Fourth Annual Report as an Inspector of Prisons; and again, and more fully, ten years since, in my book entitled 'Crime: its Causes and Remedies.' These opinions, which I can see no reason whatever to change, are in accordance with the dictum of the great and far-seeing BACON, who declared that 'it is a shameful and unblessed thing to take the scum of people, and wicked condemned men, to be the people with whom you plant.'

"Those who have joined in the clamour for returning to Transportation, whilst strangely over-looking existing, known and well-tried remedies close at hand, and requiring only their more general adoption, seem utterly to forget the monstrous evils to which this lazy remedy, this transfer of a burden —transfer with aggravation—from one quarter of the world to another, gives rise; but to refresh their memory, and to guard the public generally on the subject, I will give a few extracts from the able and luminous Report made in 1838 by a Select Committee of the House of Commons, presided over by the lamented Sir WILLIAM MOLESWORTH. Indeed, it is greatly to be desired that the whole of this Report, which, if the minutes of evidence be omitted, is within a very moderate compass, should be republished, and in a cheap form.

"After speaking of the lottery character of the punishment of Transportation, and stating that they found that it was most dreaded by accidental offenders, and least by habitual criminals, and after giving much other important matter, the Report proceeds as follows:—

"'The catalogue of convictions in New South Wales by no means exhausts the catalogue of crimes committed; for Judge BURTON, in his charge to the grand jury of Sydney (to which document your Committee have already referred), after giving a vivid description of the "crimes of violence, the murders, the manslaughters and drunken revels, the perjuries, the false witnesses from motives of revenge or reward, which in the proceedings before him had been brought to light"—after mentioning several cases of atrocious crimes as characteristic of the general want of principle in the colony—after referring to the "mass of offences which were summarily disposed of by the magistrates, and at the several police offices throughout the colony"—spoke of the "numerous undiscovered crimes, which every man who heard him, or to whom the report of his words should come, would at once admit to have occurred within his own circle of knowledge;" and then he said, "the picture presented to men's minds would be of the most painful reflection. It would appear to one who would look down upon that community, as if the main business of them all were the commission of crimes, and the punishment of it; as if the whole colony were in motion towards the several courts of justice; and the most painful reflection of all must be, that so many capital sentences, and the execution of them, had not had the effect of preventing crimes by the way of example"'—(page 27).

"Two or three pages further on in the Report is the following:—

" 'Of the state of society in the towns of these colonies a general idea may be formed from a description of Sydney, according to the accounts given of it by its chief police magistrate, and by Mr. Justice BURTON. In 1836 Sydney covered an area of about 2000 acres, and contained about 20,000 inhabitants ; of this number 3500 were convicts, most of them in assigned service, and almost 7000 had probably been prisoners of the Crown. These, together with their associates among the free population, were persons of violent and uncontrollable passions, which most of them possessed no lawful means of gratifying ; incorrigibly bad characters, preferring a life of idleness and debauchery, by means of plunder, to one of honest industry. Burglaries and robberies were frequently perpetrated by convict servants in the town and its vicinity, sometimes even in the middle of the day. * * * The drunkenness, idleness, and carelessness of a great proportion of the inhabitants afforded innumerable opportunities and temptations, both by day and by night, for those who chose to live by plunder. * * * Those of the emancipists who possessed property had generally acquired it by dishonest means—by keeping grog-shops, gambling-houses, by receiving stolen goods, and by other nefarious practices ; they led a life of gross licentiousness, but their influence was such that one-fourth of the jurors who served in the civil and criminal courts in the years 1834, 1835, and 1836, belonged to that number. More immorality prevailed in Sydney, than in any other town of the same size in the British dominions ; there the vice of drunkenness attained its highest pitch ; the quantity of spirits consumed in Sydney was enormous. * * * With a free population little exceeding 16,000, Sydney contained 219 public-houses, and so many unlicensed spirit-shops that the chief magistrate felt himself incompetent to guess at the number. The greater portion of these public-houses were kept by persons who had been transported convicts, and who were notorious drunkards, obscene persons, fighters, gamblers, receivers and harbourers of thieves, and of the most depraved of both sexes, and who existed upon the depravity of the lower orders. Such, according to the authorities we have quoted, are the towns to which Transportation has given birth ; and such are the inmates furnished to them by the criminal tribunals of this country.

" 'In the country districts of New South Wales and Van Dieman's Land the proportion of convict men to women is as 17 to 1. As the greater proportion of the agricultural labourers belong to the criminal population, they constitute a peasantry unlike any other in the world ; a peasantry without domestic feelings or affections, without parents or relations, without wives, children, or houses ; one more strange and less attached to the soil they till, than the negro slaves of a planter. They dwell crowded together in miserable huts ; the hours of recreation which they can steal from the night are usually spent in the unlicensed spirit shops found in the vicinity of every estate. In these places, kept by some ticket-of-leave man or emancipated convict, the assigned servants of settlers generally purchase the means of gratifying their appetites for liquor, gambling, and every species of debauchery, by the proceeds of their depredations on the flocks and herds and other property of their masters. The vicious habits of the lower orders, the manner in which they are allowed to live and associate with the convicts, the inefficiency of the police, and the general want of principle in the colony of New South Wales, are vividly depicted in the charge, already so frequently mentioned, of Judge BURTON to the grand jury at Sydney' (p. 30).

"In another part of the Report, the Committee describe a fearful state of things among the convicts in Norfolk Island, a place where Transpor- tation was exhibited in the darkest hue, since to that island were sent, as to a second and yet worse place of Transportation, some of the convicts who in New South Wales were convicted of fresh offences. But, as the condition of that island was afterwards greatly ameliorated under the wise and zealous government of Captain MACONOCHIE, I shall not quote that part of the report, but content myself with observing that, had the scene of such monstrous evils been nearer home, no such delay could have taken place in applying a remedy; and that, after all, the cure was not permanent, seeing that on the removal of Captain MACONOCHIE the former state of things again in part returned.

"After speaking of Norfolk Island, the Report continues:—

"'Your Committee will not lengthen this Report by describing the penal settlements of Van Dieman's Island, where the severity of the system is as great, if not greater, than that at Norfolk Island, and where culprits are as reckless, if not more reckless; committing murder, to use the words of Sir GEORGE ARTHUR, "in order to enjoy the excitement of being sent up to Hobart Town for trial, though aware that, in the ordinary course, they must be executed within a fortnight after arrival." Your Committee, however, cannot help referring to a remarkable document with respect to a penal settlement in Van Dieman's Land, called Macquarie Harbour (which is now abandoned). It contains an account of the number and of the fate of the convicts who attempted to escape from Macquarie Harbour from the 3rd of January, 1822, to the 16th of May, 1827. From that return it appears that out of 116 who absconded, 75 are supposed to have perished in the woods, one was hanged for murdering and eating his companion; two were shot by the military; eight are known to have been murdered and six eaten by their companions; 24 escaped to the settled districts, 13 of whom were hanged for bush-ranging, and two for murder; making a total of 101 out 116 who came to an untimely end' (p. 16).

"Surely nothing but an overwhelming necessity ought to induce us to contemplate for a moment a return to a system fraught with such evils as these, even allowing for all the improvements which could possibly be introduced into it."

We now proceed to consider the present position of the subject.

In consequence of the violent opposition of the Colonies to the reception of any more Convicts, it became apparent to the Government that, without a most formidable conflict with all the Australian Colonies, Transportation must cease.

"The result was," Mr. ELLIOT informs us (Committee of 1856, 295-299), "that the Government of that day, by which time Lord DERBY was Prime Minister, and Sir JOHN PAKINGTON was Secretary of State for the Colonies, must, I presume, have felt satisfied that it was impossible to carry on this system in the face of an almost unanimous opposition in the colonies; and there was also this other fact, which could hardly have failed to weigh with the Government, that as soon as the colonists were opposed to it, all the benefits of Transportation ceased. One great advantage of the system was, that so long as the colonists would employ the convicts, so that they had a good chance of occupation, they cost the public no more money; but when once the colonists were resolved to have nothing to do with them, the Government would have had on its hands an indefinite number of able-bodied criminals in a pauper condition, to be supported by British money. It was announced at the end of 1852, by a dispatch from the Secretary of State, that Transportation to Van Dieman's Land would cease henceforth. There was an Order of Council to carry that out. The Order in Council was passed in January, 1854. The Secretary of State's dispatch, announcing the intention of putting an end to Transportation, was written and sent in December, 1852."

The system thus virtually ceased, as regarded the Colonies generally. One Colony only remained which did not join in the general opposition—Western Australia,—and there such Convicts were sent, as it was thought necessary to send abroad, in 1853.

"About the year 1850," Mr. ELLIOT informs us in the same evidence (308, 316), "the population of Western Australia, impressed probably with the stagnant condition in which they found themselves, compared with other Australian colonies, had applied to the Government to send them convicts; this colony alone of all the British colonies was desirous to have convicts. The climate of Western Australia is exceedingly good. The soil is not so good, especially in situations near the sea, and there is, unfortunately, a great want of good harbours. These facts, combined with an exceedingly injudicious plan on which the colony was originally settled, had caused it very much to languish, and hence, doubtless, the readiness of the inhabitants to receive a supply of convict labour and perhaps, also, to enjoy the indirect advantages of a very large government expenditure. Western Australia in 1850 contained less than 6,000 European inhabitants, including men, women and children. That was about twenty years after the formation of the original settlement.

It was in 1849 and 1850 that Western Australia applied to the Government of this country to send convicts to that colony. There were no dissentients who made their sentiments known; it was the unanimous desire of those who took an interest in public affairs, resident colonists and persons connected with them in this country. The wish was assented to; a small party of convicts was dispatched immediately.

"When the inhabitants applied for convicts to be sent to Western Australia (350), it might not unreasonably have been hoped that, by an abundant supply of cheap labour, and also the advantage of a great demand for produce, the colony would have become attractive, and that settlers of capital would have entered; in short, it might have been hoped that something would have happened resembling more or less what did take place in former years in New South Wales and Van Dieman's Land; but scarcely had the Government given its consent to send convicts to Western Australia, when gold was discovered in New South Wales. The moment that this took place, no man of enterprise or capital who was going to Australia would think of proceeding to a languishing settlement on the Western Coast; he rather went to Eastern Australia, and consequently Western Australia has made but little progress.

"At first sight it appears remarkable (362, 363) that, when we have all been so anxious to find an outlet for convicts, we have the inhabitants of Western Australia lamenting that they do not receive more convicts, and yet that the departments in this country are unable to find more to send. The explanation is, first, that the number sentenced is so much reduced, and next, that you can only send one description of convicts so great a distance. You ought to send a man who has a certain period of his term still to serve; otherwise it is not worth while to go to so great an expense; and he ought to be in good health, and capable of some special employment. Now, when all these conditions are put together, it has turned out to be difficult to find a sufficient supply for the wants of the colony of such men as would be acceptable to them, or as it would be any advantage to this country to send; because, if you send a convict who is sickly, or if you send a convict who turns out a lunatic, which often happens, the colony justly says that Great Britain is bound to take care of him, and to pay for his maintenance."

Such was the evidence presented to the Committee of 1856. The following extract from the evidence to the Royal Commission, by the Director appointed to make the selection of Convicts for Transportation to Western Australia, gives important information on several points. It shows that Transportation is decidedly regarded, both by the Convicts and by the officials, as a boon; and that to receive this boon the men selected are, not those whose character may be fairly regarded to be best, and who are not deeply sunk in crime; but those who, being reconvicted, were probably the worst men, though, from their familiarity with penal discipline, they had learnt not to be the worst prison characters;—besides these the life cases, who had served the time laid down in the printed notices,—men, who, by the nature of their sentences, must have committed very serious offences;—these were the men who received this privilege, and helped to colonize a new world!

"4246.—What is it that guides you in making that selection (viz., of convicts to go to Australia)?—In the case of the last ship that went out to Western Australia it was determined that a certain proportion of the men going out in that ship should be composed of reconvicted men, men who were license-holders, and who had eighteen months and upwards of their sentences to serve, dating from the first of July next, the supposed period when the ship shall have arrived at the colony. Another portion of the men was to consist of reconvicted men, not license-holders, who had eighteen months and upwards of their sentences to serve, dating from next July, and then the remainder was to be made up of long-sentenced men, commencing from life downwards. After those selections were made, we received instructions from the Home Office that the life cases were not to go, unless they had served the time laid down in the printed notices to convicts in this country. They had not gone through that time, and, therefore, they had to be taken out.

"4247.—There were, I believe, some few who had?—*Yes, thirteen, and they were men who had been to Bermuda.*

"4248.—You select from all the prisoners, but you are bound to take a certain number from each?—No, I am not. I might take them all from one, but we do not do that; we always give each prison its fair share, *because the convicts look forward to it very much indeed.*

"4249.—You give each prison its fair share, so making it still a question of number in every case?—Yes.

"4250.—You do that, because the convicts look forward to it as a boon?—Yes.

"4251.—*Have you not just stated that you select for this purpose the reconvicted men, and, therefore, the men of the worst character?*—It does not always follow that reconvicted men are of the worst character. *I mean the worst prison characters; many of these reconvicted men are not so.*

"4252.—Looking not to the prison character, but rather to the previous life of the prisoner, is it not a reasonable conclusion that a reconvicted man is a man of bad character?—It might be so supposed, but I have no instructions to select men of good character."

Of these reconvicted men, he is afterwards asked (4391): "Although not as a class bearing the worst prison character, are they not most likely to relapse into crime when they become free ?" The answer is, " *Quite certain.*"

Similar evidence respecting the class of men sent out to Australia is given by Mr. MEASOR, who was at the time Deputy-Governor at Chatham. He says, in answer to query 5562, and some following, "In the last ship, the *Lord Palmerston*, which sailed from Chatham to Australia, we sent out as bad a set of men as ever I knew. They were men who had been convicted of very serious offences, all of them, and were very bad Convicts, irrespective of their crimes,—they were extremely bad Convicts. An order was given to select the men who were the most unfit for liberation in this country. Those Convicts have been complained of in Australia since; I know that." How the state of these men who are to form part of the population of a new country must be aggravated by the passage out, is forcibly stated by Mr. MEASOR :—

" 5553.—I have a very great objection to the present mode of transporting convicts. I consider that convict ships are a source of pollution to convicts in every possible way, and of the most horrible description, and you can have very little hope of doing them good, permanently, in a new colony, unless the whole system of transportation is altered with regard to their being thrown together in very close association as they are. I have been informed by convicts over and over again that convict ships are nothing but schools of unnatural crime, and I can hardly wonder at it from the close approximation of one individual to another."

The Governor of Western Australia, Captain A. E. KENNEDY, gives an account which will startle many of the class of men who have been sent out to Western Australia. The following facts were elicited in his examination :—

" 2380.—With respect to the description of convicts who are sent out to Western Australia, I observe in the reports that *several lunatics* had been sent out?—Several.

" 2381.—I believe as many as 28 ?—I cannot speak accurately as to the numbers ; but certainly there was a considerable number.

" 2382.—I am afraid also that men who were still more objectionable, and who had been convicted of unnatural offences, were sent out?—On one occasion, according to the report for 1858, presented to Parliament in 1860, p. 34, it will be found that there were no fewer than 22 who had been convicted of that offence *at one time in the prison*, namely, on the 31st December, 1858.

"2386.—Is it peculiarly objectionable to send out persons who have been convicted of such offences to a colony like Western Australia?—*I think it is objectionable to send them anywhere among Christian people.*

"2391.—I suppose that those who have been guilty of some of the most atrocious offences for which men used formerly to be hanged, you do not think ought to be sent out?—I think that there were no fewer than 27 or 37 murderers in prison in Western Australia at one time in 1861."

Such, then, were the Convicts sent out to the only Colony that would receive them.

Before we proceed to consider the present very satisfactory condition of the penal settlement of Western Australia, as gathered from the evidence of witnesses examined by the Royal Commission of 1863, it will be right for us to be aware of the actual state of things before the system carried out by Governor KENNEDY and Colonel HENDERSON was commenced. We shall then be in a position more fully to appreciate their success, and to see in it the triumphant demonstration of the truth of the principles on which it is founded, and which are here advocated.

Mr. ELLIOT, when a second time summoned as a witness before the Select Committee on Transportation in 1856, produced a dispatch just received from Governor KENNEDY, who had then been only five months in the Colony. (4031). "He commences thus:—'My attention having been drawn to the considerable number of reconvictions of ticket-of-leave holders and conditional-pardon men in this Colony, I deem it my duty to address you on the subject, with a view of your considering that which will, I believe, if persevered in, result in the failure of the reformatory system hitherto so successfully adopted in the Fremantle Convict establishment. There is a strong public feeling growing up against the system, in consequence of the increase of crime and repeated reconvictions of the Convict class, which is much to be deplored in a community which have hitherto received and treated them on an

equal footing with free men; and I am constrained to stake
my belief that the growing discontent is not unreasonable.'
He then incloses a return of reconvictions of Convicts. 'A
perusal of this catalogue of frightful crime will, I think,
satisfy any reasonable mind that association with such miscreants is incompatible with the reformation of ordinary
criminals. Norfolk Island, or other extra-penal establishments, have been hitherto the destination of this class of
incorrigibles. I do not think that ordinary or average prison
officers can be safely intrusted with the management and
control of such men as those contained in the return before
adverted to.' 'No reasonable hope of reclamation of the ordinary class of Convicts can, in my opinion, be entertained
till such characters are removed, not only from communicating with, but out of sight of their fellows.' What I am
about to read is important. 'I do not apprehend that, under
present circumstances, Her Majesty's Government would sanction the additional outlay for an ultral-penal establishment
in this Colony, nor would I recommend it; but I can see no
alternative between such outlay and the signal failure of the
present system if this class of criminals be sent here.' 'The
self-interest which induces the employment of Convicts (which
must be preliminary to their becoming self-supporting) is by
no means so strong as it has been found in other penal
Colonies; and the support and good opinion of the public
in reference to the system once forfeited, a failure must
ensue.' That is the opinion of the new Governor."

With this state of things the expense appears to have
been enormous. "In Lord PANMURE's dispatch of October,
1855, it is stated," says Mr. ELLIOT (4068) "that a number
of Convicts little exceeding 2000 has cost this country upwards
of £80,000 per annum," *i. e.*, £40 per annum for each!

" My own opinion is," Mr. ELLIOT adds (4095), "that the system has
failed, for these reasons : the colony has made no progress; the number
of free people has not substantially increased; no new settlers have come.
I think, therefore, that the colony has not thriven as was hoped; it has

gained nothing but the large Government expenditure. The convicts have not prospered as was anticipated, for there is no employment for them; the evidence upon the table of the Committee shows that they are at a loss how to gain a livelihood. But, thirdly, they have not been reformed, as we all so much hoped; for the latest dispatch from the Governor, which I have to-day submitted, gives evidence that the men begin to conduct themselves very badly. I think it quite natural that there should be a change in this respect. While the number of convicts was small, the free people sufficed to employ them, and they behaved well; but we have poured in fresh convicts, who exceed the demand for labour, and they commit crime; therefore, in all three of the advantages which were looked to, I think the experiment has failed—the colony has not gained—the convicts have not prospered—and they have not reformed."

Such was the state of Western Australia at the time of the report of Captain KENNEDY, soon after his arrival at the Colony, as presented by Mr. ELLIOT to the Committee of 1856. We now shall learn what is its present state from the evidence presented to the Commission of 1863.

The following account of the penal settlement of Western Australia is derived from the evidence before the Commission of Captain A. E. KENNEDY, the Governor of that district from 1855 to 1862, of Colonel HENDERSON, who filled the office of Comptroller of Convicts from 1850 to 1863, and Capt. DU CANE, who went out at the commencement of the Convict system in Western Australia, in command of a party of Sappers and Miners in charge of the works. This district has peculiar advantages for receiving Convicts, on account of the difficulty, if not impossibility, of escaping, and from its climate and natural resources. The old Colony does not extend above 100 miles from the coast;—between that and Mr. STUART'S exploration there is a distance of about 1,000 miles, which is as yet wholly unexplored. There are natural obstacles to extending the Colony, both northwards and southwards, though there are indications of the existence of good land in each direction, which would be available when increased facilities are given. A prison was built at Fremantle for the reception of the Convicts on their first arrival; it is constructed on the plan of an English prison, with very good accommodation for the Convicts; separate sleeping cells for 600 or 700 men, and refractory cells; there are, besides, ticket-of-leave depôts, and altogether the various prison buildings are calculated for about 2000 men. The prison at Fremantle has never, however, been above half-full, except immediately on the arrival of a Convict ship. The labour market has been greatly enlarged since the establishment of the Convict depôt. At first there was great difficulty to obtain work for the ticket-of-leave men, but now, though there is plenty of employment for the prisoners in the immediate neighbourhood of Fremantle, there has been so much demand for labour up the country, that very few remain at Fremantle. Colonel HENDERSON thus describes his system with the Convicts:—When a ship arrived, he always kept the prisoners for a short time at Fremantle to acclimatise them. They were told what they had to expect. Colonel H. addressed them once or twice himself, and told them the treatment they would receive, and the difference between the dealing with them there, and what they would receive at home. Being removed, perhaps for ever, from the land of their birth and from their old associations, and having already undergone punishment, they were now to begin anew. Their future liberty would not depend on their simple abstinence from gross misconduct and determined idleness, but would be the result of their own positive effort to do well, to labour to the utmost of their power, and in all respects to act rightly;—all these points would be indicated by their daily marks, which would be an actual register of their conduct; and on these, their obtaining remission of sentence would depend. Every day's work is recorded according to the amount done, with one, two, or three marks, and for misconduct, a part of the marks is forfeited, according to a fixed scale; these marks are tabulated for the men to see; the Convict can count his marks as he would his money, and knows exactly how near he is to the period of obtaining a ticket - of - leave. Both Captain KENNEDY and

Colonel HENDERSON consider this a great improvement on the former system, which was similar to that now pursued in the English prisons; that was more complicated, less understood by the men, and a constant source of irritation between the men and the overseers. This mark system has been very successful in stimulating the Convicts to industry in their work. This clear and simple system, founded on justice, and administered in the same spirit, proved an excellent means of bringing the men into a right relation with their superior. "As long as they would show me," said Colonel HENDERSON, "that they were really anxious to do well, and were likely to become good settlers in the Colony, I always held out to them every possible inducement to do so. On the other hand, if they showed that they were not likely to do well, they received far more severe treatment, I believe, than they ever got in other Colonies. By that means I acquired, I think, a great influence over their minds and over their conduct." As soon as possible, the Convicts are removed from the prison, and distributed in parties to make roads in different parts of the district. This is a most important preparation for their greater liberty as holders of tickets-of-leave. "I think it must be obvious to any person," says Captain KENNEDY, "that if you send a man out of an English prison, where, according to the opinions of some, he is over-fed and under-worked, and set him loose at once in a new country, where he is really obliged to earn his bread by the sweat of his brow, he will be completely unfit for it, without undergoing some probation. * * * Sending a man from England, unaccustomed to the country, and to the habits of the country, and letting him loose at once, he is sure to fall into crime, or at the very least to be discouraged" (2362, 2358). This road-making confers an immense benefit on the Colony, and is a necessary preparation for all future development of its resources; at the same time it is a peculiarly valuable training for the Convict;—he thus becomes connected with settlers in the neighbourhood, who know his merits, and, if he is a good labouring man, when he acquires his liberty he is immediately taken into service; he becomes accustomed to the rough life of the bush, he gets to know the country better, and loses any exaggerated expectations that he had, as to obtaining high wages. The road parties consist of from 20 to 50 men, and there is usually one warder only with them, never more than two to each party. To assist the warders, some of the best Convicts are selected as constables, and as these obtain five marks a day, and the position is considered one of honour, the post is much coveted, and the attaining it is an incentive to good conduct. For these road parties no buildings are necessary, as the men construct huts themselves, at no expense but their labour; when they have finished their work in one place they make new huts in another. Their provisions are usually contracted for in the immediate neighbourhood, thus bringing them into friendly relation with the neighbouring inhabitants; there is altogether no extra expense connected with these parties. Working on the road parties is regarded as a great privilege by the Convicts,—they like the mode of life, which is much more free than at Fremantle, and such employment is also a step towards obtaining a ticket-of-leave. When this last stage is gained, the Convicts are in a very different position from what they are in England. "The ticket-of-leave system," says Colonel HENDERSON, "has always been, I may say, a reality in Western Australia;--the men were confined to certain districts, and we knew all about them, and could put our hand upon them if we thought it necessary, and if they were guilty of any irregularity, they were immediately returned to the Convict establishment" (6130, 6131). All the conditions are strictly enforced, and the Convicts are at all times required to produce their ticket when desired; they are required not to be out of their houses after ten o'Clock at night. Surveillance is exercised by a vigilant police, but this is no hindrance to the men obtaining work; the ticket-of-leave men are sought after by em-

ployers of labour. A strong hold is obtained over these
men by the power possessed by the Magistrate of summary
jurisdiction; by special legislation he is enabled to sentence
them, without trial, to three years' imprisonment; and the
Governor has the power of revoking their ticket-of-leave, and,
of his own will and pleasure, sending them back to their original
sentence. When men are thus sent back, they are kept under
strict supervision in the establishment without any indulgence,
and only after a time, when their conduct permits, are they again
sent on probationary road parties. Col. HENDERSON states that
the number so sent back is very small, considering that almost
every offence is found out. When ticket-of-leave men serve out
their whole time and are expirees, they are on a perfectly equal
position with ordinary settlers. Many have married respectably,
and have acquired considerable wealth. They are absolutely
free to go wherever they like, and many return to England.
At times, however, a conditional pardon is granted to a license-
holder who has done well before the expiration of his license.
He is then absolutely free, except that he must not return
to England. The Government has then no further responsibility with him. A ticket-of-leave man, on the other
hand, if ill or unable to obtain work, may return to the
Government depôt, to labour on the public works. At first
an allowance of 6d. per diem was made in addition to his
food, and then the men were continually hanging about the
depôt; but this was discontinued, and there is now no undue
desire to throw themselves on the care of the Government;
in fact, they greatly dislike going back to these depôts.

Such are the general features of the system of Convict
management in Western Australia. It will occur to every
one who compares this with that adopted in the Irish Convict
Prisons, that it is founded on the same principles which have
proved so successful in Ireland. In both the results are similar,
that the public feel a confidence in the system adopted with
the Convicts, and are willing to employ them; and that the

relapses are very few. Those who were formerly burdens to the country now most frequently become honest and useful members of society without stigma resting on them; they are themselves the employers of labour, and valuable settlers.

There can be no doubt as to the enormous advantage to society at large of the reformation of these persons, yet we should not be at liberty to sacrifice for it the welfare of the community in which they are placed. It is very satisfactory to learn that this has been actually promoted under the system adopted. Of the physical and worldly advantage derived by this young Colony from the introduction of so much capital and so large a body of labourers, under such judicious guidance, there can be no doubt. Captain KENNEDY tells us that during his government there were 192 bridges built and 219 culverts, and 1030 miles of road cleared, in addition to making and repairing those that were previously in existence. Colonel HENDERSON says (6337) that when the penal establishment was first formed there was really no capital in the country, and almost every one was in debt; the Government Works appeared the only way of disposing of the men. Now the state of things is very much more prosperous, and private enterprise is able to absorb most of the Convict labour under ticket-of-leave. This increase of material prosperity has not been purchased at the expense of morality. Col. HENDERSON says (6128): "The peace and the quiet which prevail in the Colony is something which nobody would believe who did not go there. I may mention to the Commission that Mr. HARGREAVES came at our request to see whether there was gold in the Colony, as it was desirable to set that question at rest; and he expressed himself at the public dinner which was given to me previously to my departure, as being perfectly surprised at the state of quiet and good order which he found to prevail throughout the whole Colony." Captain KENNEDY says (2316) that he believes that the security of life or property has not been diminished, nor any injurious moral effect produced on the free inhabitants by Transportation; in fact, he thinks that there is no part of Her Majesty's dominions where life and property are more secure. A convincing proof in corroboration of this is afforded by the following number of criminal cases tried in the Colony at the only criminal court, the Court of Quarter Sessions, from 1855 to 1860 inclusive. In 1855 there were 56 con- victions; in 1856 they were reduced to 29; in 1857 to 15; in 1858 there were only 11; in 1859, with an increased num- ber of Convicts, they were 17; and in 1860, 23. If we compare these numbers with those in any large town in Eng- land, or in any district of a quarter the extent, we shall perceive the enormous advantage which this new penal settle- ment has over the mother country. It has been apprehended, however, that a large number of ticket-of-leave men make their escape into other Colonies of this new continent, and there spread contamination. That this cannot be the case is definitely proved by the following positive statement of facts by Captain KENNEDY (2319): "The total number of ticket-of-leave men who are not accounted for, or who, in other words, may have escaped, are 42 in 12 years; and of these 42, we know of a certainty that 21 were taken off in American whalers that touch on the coast. When they lose a man, they are of course anxious to get another to take his place. They took away 21; of the others, my belief is that the greater part of them died in the bush in attempting to escape to other Colonies. 42 is the total number, out of nearly 6000 Convicts in round numbers." Every precaution is taken to prevent the escape of Convicts into the other Colonies. The Peninsular and Oriental steamers are the only ones which run between Western Australia and the other Colonies (6245), and they positively refuse to take any conditional-pardon men on board; the few ships which go from the other ports are also afraid to take them, the penalties being so heavy. A police-officer searches every ship before leaving Fremantle for ticket-of-leave men, and, should he find any conditional-pardon man, would at once inform the captain. A migration by land to the other Colonies is, Colonel HENDERSON assures us, physically impossible. The interval between Western Australia and the nearest Colony, South Australia, is 1200 miles—a journey which no white man ever made, except Governor EYRE, who went along the sea beach, and almost died in the attempt. On the east the Colony is hemmed in by a large belt of land, consisting of soft lagoon and sand plains, with a belt of acacia thickets, and scattered gum trees, very difficult to get through; though there is some good pasture land in particular spots, the difficulty has been want of water, and for a long time to come it must remain practically unavailable land. This Colony is, therefore, a peculiarly isolated one, and in that respect well situated for the proper development of the Convict system, and their establishment as free settlers.

The resources of the country for the continued reception of Convicts, was the subject of much inquiry from these experienced gentlemen, by the Commissioners. They state that great difficulties have arisen since 1853, from the uncertainty attending the plans of Government with respect to Convict labour, and the consequent hesitation in investing capital in the Colony. But should these be definitely arranged, they do not doubt but that at least 1000 Convicts might, very profitably to the Colony, be sent over annually; an equal number being thus, on an average, sent into the labour market from those who had obtained their ticket-of-leave. Towards the north, within reasonable limits, there appear to be hardly any bounds to the possible extension of the Colony. The introduction of a regular supply of Convict labour would be a great inducement to the colonization and gradual settlement of this district, because the colonists would thus be always sure of obtaining a supply of workers. The natural resources of the country, if judiciously drawn out, appear to be very great. A mine there has been lately sold in the English market for £80,000, and that part of the country seems to be literally one mass of copper and lead; there are several other mines being worked, but they are not as yet successful, from want of capital and good management. The country to the southward has turned out far better than was expected (6195); there is ample grazing ground for all the cattle which are likely to be required for consumption, a very fair amount for sheep, and a very excellent quantity of land for breeding horses, which, says Colonel HENDERSON, "I think is a far better speculation for Western Australia than breeding either sheep or cattle. * * * * I think that the horse breeding is one of the great stand-by's of the Colony" (6201). Horses are not indigenous to Australia, but some of the best stock in England have been taken out there. The plan adopted is to fence in paddocks, and then to let the horses run at large into the bush, after branding them to mark them, and then hunting them up occasionally to see what are there. They are left in this state until they are old enough to break in, and then they export them to India, where they obtain an excellent market; horses which in Western Australia would have fetched about £28 or £30, there selling at prices varying from £60 to £110 or £115. Colonel HENDERSON states that in the vessel in which he took his passage to Madras on his return home there were 100 horses on board; the voyage was only 28 days in length, and the horses arrived in good condition, while horses which arrived at the same time from other Colonies were in a dreadful state, owing to the length of the voyage. The shortness of the passage to India, in comparison with all other places, will give a permanent superiority to this Colony for traffic in horses, if the market is supplied. Various kinds have been successfully introduced and bred in the Colony, light and well-bred horses, and the heavier kinds, both carriage horses and cart horses; the horses which are sent to India from Australia are very well suited for artillery purposes. "Sir WILLIAM DENNISON has been trying," says Colonel HENDERSON (6283), "to induce the Governor-General to allow him to make a contract to receive so many hundred horses every year from Western Australia at a certain fixed price, and he told me when I was at Madras the other day that he hoped the arrangement would be carried out. That would at once give a first-rate market to Western Australia."

There is a prospect of other trade with India beside horses. The vine flourishes well in Western Australia (6328, 6331), and the olive is equally adapted to the soil and climate. Major SANFORD says in his evidence that on a farm near Perth 1400 gallons of wine were produced from two acres of land. It was a very good red wine, between Burgundy and Port, and appeared likely to become a valuable wine, fit for exportation if kept, but hitherto it has been consumed in the Colony. A number of Spaniards were brought out by a Roman Catholic Bishop to teach the people how to cultivate the vine, and they are carrying out large vineyards and olive groves; the olives are remarkably fine, and oil has been made from them. A peculiar kind of timber, locally called Jarrah, promises to be of very great importance. Major SANFORD says (2808): "That timber belongs only to one district in the Colony,—it is restricted to one corner. I have seen some that has been under water twenty-nine years, and I could see where the sea-worm could not penetrate it; and I saw the sill of the door of a house which had been something like twenty years made, showing where the white ant had tried, but could not penetrate it." There are large forests of this wood in Western Australia. This wood has been found to contain a poisonous quality which affects animals even as large as mice; and it is, therefore, free from attacks by insects; it is hard, rather stronger than fir, and equally good for ships with teak. There is a demand for it in India for railway sleepers, which is likely to be very large.

Such, then, are some of the capabilities of the Colony which is still willing to receive Convicts from us,—because it is practically found that under proper management these persons may become valuable members of society. *Mutual confidence is established*. The regulations made and actively carried out protect the free settlers, and provide for the gradual re-admission of the erring into society. It is a strong proof of this that Captain KENNEDY, on being asked what military force he has at command, in case of an outbreak, replies (2427): "I may commence by saying that there never has been an outbreak, there has never been the slightest trouble, with the exception of one case, and that was merely a religious squabble in the establishment between the Protestants and the Roman Catholics, owing to ill-feeling and bad judgment, I believe, on the part of the clerical gentlemen on both sides. The whole of the military establishment, up to the period of my leaving the Colony, consisted of one weak company of ten troops, and a company of Sappers and Miners, who were not employed in a military capacity at all." 2442. "And you feel no apprehension of an outbreak?—None in the least, and never had any; there is no tendency to it on the part of the Convicts, who are generally dispersed in the way I have described; it is only when they are heaped together that they will become turbulent, but I think they never are so in small numbers." The ordinary number of Convicts that are kept in prison at Fremantle were reduced when he left, he tells us, to 300 and odd. "I might add," Captain KENNEDY continues, "upon the question of Convicts, and the crime that is very rife in other places, *that of offering violence to warders,—that there has been scarcely a case of that in Western Australia.* There was one bad case of a man who was executed for his offence, and there was never a second case after that." 2443. "When employed on the road parties, the Convicts have shown a very good feeling towards their officers. I know of one remarkable instance in the case of a warder who, it was supposed, was almost the severest warder on the establishment, and a man who extracted more work out of his party than any other man did;— there was a land-slip, and that man was buried under the earth, and it is a fact that the men of his party immediately dug him out, showing a degree of alacrity that free men probably would not have shown, and they saved the warder's life thereby;— nobody was present except the warder and the Convicts. They exhibited great zeal in doing it, and great good feeling." Captain KENNEDY does not object to the roughest and even violent men being sent out;—" men," he says (2392), "who have committed robberies with violence are comparatively harmless there, for the simple reason that there are very few people to rob, and that there is nothing portable to steal, so that their occupation is gone. The London thief is the worst man that we get, and I would sooner have any man than him; he will not work if he can help it; I mean the habitual thief." He also objects to clerks and persons of that description who have been convicted of forgery and embezzlement. These generally contrive in some way or other to escape hard labour, and live very often on the produce of their labour in former times;— these set a bad example. The men sent out to Australia should be capable of earning their living by physical labour.

The testimony to the state of the Colony is not alone that of the officials immediately connected with Government Prisons.

The DEAN of PERTH, in Western Australia, gives very valuable evidence respecting the moral condition of the population in general. On being asked (6377), "From your experience of the Colony as a clergyman, what is your opinion of the general conduct and character of the Convicts who have been sent to the Colony?" he replies: "I think that it is very superior to anything which could have been expected from such men in England. Of course there has been a great deal which I have regretted to see, but, on the whole, *I think I may speak of the reformation in outward moral conduct as being very general among the men.*" It will be observed that the Dean is here not speaking of men under confinement, but of those who are at liberty under a ticket-of-leave, to whom, mixed with the other population, the

ministries of the chaplain are directed. Also it is observable
that he is not speaking of interest in religious subjects, and
professions of penitence, which are so often a cloak of hypocrisy
assumed for a particular purpose; he distinctly states that
he limits his remark to their outward conduct and character.
He further adds (6370): "I have no reason to suppose that
the penal establishment has had any injurious moral effect
on the free colonists. I had fears that it might be so, but
I think I might safely say that on the whole I have not seen
any reason to think that it has had such an effect. (6380).
I do not think that the tone of society has been at all demoralised by sending Convicts out." He states that the colonists
generally feel perfectly secure, and that there is not the least
apprehension from Convicts. Dean POWNALL himself says
that his house was very insecure, and had nothing but calico
windows. He gives the following remarkable fact as a proof
of the perfect security of property (3687-9):—"I may mention a house door having no lock upon it, when the lady who
kept the house was surrounded with Convicts. When Governor
KENNEDY stayed at her house he thought it necessary to lock
the front door, and found that there was no lock. She had
only Convict labourers on her large estate; she looked after
the estate, with the assistance of the Convict overseer, and
with none but men of the Convict class employed. She had
no person there who had gone out as a free settler; her son
was there, but he was quite a young man, and unable to
exercise any control over them. This lady's farm had been
a very unprofitable one until Convicts were sent to the Colony,
and since that time it has become gradually more profitable;
it would have been quite impossible for her to have cultivated
the land without Convict labour." Dean POWNALL states his
belief that "one of the reasons of the success which has resulted in Western Australia, so far as the moral character of
the men is concerned, is the absence of temptation to them.
We always take peculiar precautions against putting tempta-

tions in their way.   It is generally known amongst them that we never carry money about with us, or have it in our houses.   We make all our payments in cheques.   If you go for an excursion up the country you take your cheque-book with you, and make your payments, even for so small a sum as £1, by a cheque on the Western Australian Bank."   The two great requirements now existing in the Colony he considers to be some limit to the sale of spirituous liquors, and the opening of Savings' Banks in the different districts.   The want of the latter, and the large number of the former, often is the cause of great evil.   "If you will not take charge of this money," men would frequently say to him, bringing him their year's savings, "we must put it in the hands either of the store-keepers or of the public-house keepers.   In the former case, we shall never see a sixpence of it, they will only let us take it out in goods which we do not want at an extravagant price ;— and, in the other case, we shall have to stop at a public-house till we have drunk away our money." (3690).   The Dean felt compelled to decline the charge, and the consequence was that they had a spree at the public-house for a week or two, and a shepherd who came in on Monday morning with £20 or £30 in his pocket, in about ten days had nothing left.   Governor KENNEDY made efforts to put down public-houses.   If his exertions were seconded, and means arranged for the transmission of small savings or large sums of money to a place of security, a great moral benefit would be conferred on the Colony.   Dean POWNALL believes that if Savings' Banks were formed, many of these men would accumulate capital, and establish themselves in a higher position in life ; the doing so would prevent a great source of moral deterioration, and also enable a more rapid accumulation of capital for the improvement of the Colony. The other conditions of the Colony to which the Dean attributes principally the external reformation of these men, are,—first, as to the absence of temptation already mentioned, there being little in the houses or on the persons of the residents worth taking away;—secondly, and this is a matter of great importance, the wide dispersion of the men, which prevents their congregating and corrupting each other; and,—thirdly, the climate itself, which appears to have a tranquilizing effect on the system, "taking the fierceness and pugnacity out of men of savage character. There is a certain mildness of character in the native population, and the same thing gradually shows itself in the Europeans who are there. There is less readiness to attack, or give blow for blow, than there would be in England."

The great difficulty which appears to exist in Western Australia is the selection of suitable officers. It is evident that no system can be devised in which human beings are to be acted upon, in which much of the successful working must not necessarily depend on the persons employed to carry it out. We Reformatory managers are well aware, that the best judgment we can exercise, the most excellent principles we can adopt, the most perfect system we can employ, are of no avail, if we have not suitable officers in the institution's, who will not only faithfully carry out our directions, but who will throw their whole heart and soul into the work. It is evident that, in proportion as moral agency is made an important part of the system, in such proportion must we seek for officials who are not mere routinists and discipline officers, but who will at the same time act in sympathy with the Convicts, while strictly carrying out the requirements of duty. This combination cannot easily be found, especially in the class of persons from whom such officials must be selected.

While Captain KENNEDY speaks highly of the system adopted in the Colony as stimulating the Convicts to work, he distinctly acknowledges that the success is the greater where there are good warders to look after them, and that any system of managing Convicts in this way must wholly depend upon the efficiency of the persons employed as warders. "I do not think," he says (2355), "too much stress can be laid on that point." He strongly feels the difficulty of getting men of that class who will administer the system conscientiously and honestly. He believes also that men of that grade are very liable to deteriorate in their morale, if too long engaged in the service, and that it is very desirable that new blood, so to speak, should be frequently poured into the work. Another difficulty arises from the low rate of wages given to the staff of prison officers. It is one of the evils arising from grafting an old system in a new country, that their salaries are the same as those in England. In Australia the wages of the labourers are, at the same time, double what they are here; consequently the officers are in a lower position, compared with the men under them, than they would be in England. Captain KENNEDY justly feels that if the advantages were increased which are allowed to officers, who are doing such difficult and unpleasant work, a better class of men might be obtained. He thinks, also, that a stimulus should be held out to them to encourage them to steady good conduct. In Western Australia such a system is adopted towards the police. It is, of course, peculiarly important, under the circumstances of the Colony, to have a good set of men who will stay long enough in the service to carry out the system well;—it is therefore arranged in that service, that every man who does his duty well for a certain number of years, shall acquire fifty acres of land for himself. The hope of this is a great stimulus, and Captain K. recommends a similar arrangement for the warders.

Captain KENNEDY makes, in his evidence, various suggestions which he considers important to the future welfare of Western Australia as a penal settlement, founded on his seven years' experience as Governor of the Colony. In the first place, he greatly objects to men being sent out after a long previous imprisonment in England. He says, emphatically (2609): "I think that lengthened imprisonment is the greatest mistake that ever was committed as to Convicts. *I have no doubt that lengthened imprisonment unfits a man for a life of labour afterwards.* I am perfectly satisfied that after a certain period it ceases altogether to have the desired effect, and a man becomes a sort of routine creature, like a soldier, and goes about his daily business as a Convict, without feeling any irksomness whatever. I think, also, that it stands to reason that associating a man for six and seven years with hundreds of others, who are infinitely worse than himself, is not the way to reform him. (2611). I think that road labour fits them for a life of industry afterwards, and I think it is undesirable to keep them for any lengthened period in prison. I think that keeping them for five or six years in England before they are sent to Australia, is not only useless, but mischievous. I think it does the men more harm than good." In the next place, he considers it undesirable for men to be sent out, who have only a short time to serve before they obtain their ticket-of-leave. When this has been done the men have served the greater part of their time in the Public Works' Prisons in England, and this by no means qualifies them for life in the Colony, as well as the probationary road labour. Of this they ought to have a considerable length of time before being eligible for their ticket-of-leave. When they receive it, after such lengthened experience, they are better prepared to do well, having become acquainted with the inhabitants and the nature of the country. "I think," he says (2666), "that those who are sent out to the Colony ought not to be sent out to be liberated there soon. I think they ought to serve a longer time in the Colony before they get their ticket-of-leave." Four years' probation he would prefer. But the great cause of evil to this Colony and to the others on the Continent of Australia appears, both from his evidence and that of all the other witnesses, the granting of "conditional pardons." "I think," he says, at the conclusion of his evidence (2674), "*that the granting of conditional pardons is so great a mistake that it should not be exercised.*" As long as the Convicts are under ticket-of-leave, their personal liberty is not interfered with, as long as they remain within the prescribed district, and do not injure society by their conduct. They can have over their wives and families if they are well-conducted, and have every opportunity of permanently settling and prospering in their adopted country. The surveillance which is exercised over them, simply exposes them to certain and summary punishment if they break the law. But the men who receive a conditional pardon are absolutely free, except that they may not return to England. There is no longer any control over the Convict who has received a conditional pardon; there is nothing even to prevent him from being on a jury;—the extraordinary anomaly is therefore possible of a man adjudicating on the property and liberty of another, while he has not completed the time of a sentence solemnly passed on him. The practice of granting these pardons to Convicts was likewise a cause of extreme injury and annoyance to the other Colonies, until they took vigorous measures to prevent it. The passage to South Australia can be taken for £7 or £8, a sum which can be easily raised by these men, and large numbers in the early periods left the less prosperous and fertile Colony for more inviting lands. Captain KENNEDY think it very possible that three-fifths may have thus emigrated to South Australia. Heavy complaints on this subject were made to the Commission in the evidence of Mr. R. F. NEWLAND, who had been for ten years a police magistrate in South Australia. He stated that in 1855, 269 persons came from Western Australia to Adelaide, while only 24 returned; in 1856, 438 persons entered against 51 who left; in 1857, 629, against 21 who returned to Western Australia. It was believed in South Australia that a very large proportion, probably one-half of these immigrants, were conditional pardon men and expirees; this created a great excitement, and crime so much increased that an Act was passed in 1857, called the Extradition Act, by which they were to be either subject to three years' penal servitude, or sent back to Western Australia (2877-79). This Act had the desired effect. The numbers fell in 1858 from 629 to 184, and it has steadily diminished, while the numbers who returned to Western Australia rose to 61 in 1860. Though an impression existed in the mind of the witness that about one-tenth of the criminals of his Colony were expirees, or ticket-of-leave men, yet he had no returns to prove this, though they have detectives who had been engaged in the Convict service in Western Australia, and who were able to identify them. With such precautions, and with an anxious desire on the part of the Western Australian Government to prevent annoyance to neighbouring Colonies, it certainly does not appear that any serious objection need be made by them to the Convict settlement in Western Australia, administered on the system which has been here described, and with the improvements and alterations suggested by Governor KENNEDY.

The public prints still announce dissatisfaction in the other Colonies; this is not to be wondered at, while some of the evils probably still remain that arose from former mismanagement;—under the present system it does not appear possible that such evil can be renewed.

With respect to the advantage of a continuance of the employment of Western Australia as a Convict settlement, there appears to be an unanimous feeling and opinion on the part of all the witnesses from that district, that this, *if under proper regulations*, would be a very great advantage to the Colony itself. The revenue of the Colony has very greatly increased since 1850, when the depôt was first established. "To show the increase of cultivation," Major SANFORD says (2824), "in 1857 I went through a district called the Greenough Flats, and there were not above three or four farms at the outside of 100 or 200 acres each; and at the beginning of 1861 I rode through twelve miles of corn land, by three to four miles wide." The resources of the Colony are great if properly developed, and there is power of extension, without interfering with other provinces, whenever an increased population renders this desirable. The morality of the Colony is not deteriorated by the system; on the contrary, the presence of the organised police force, of the expense of which the Home Government pays two-thirds, and of the clergy, of whose salaries the mother country pays one-half, is a great protection and benefit to the free population. The wish is universal throughout the Colony that the system should be continued, and there seems every probability that it may contribute to raise Western Australia into a flourishing condition. A serious hindrance to this, which has been before alluded to, has been the want of money to invest in enterprise, on account of the great uncertainty which has attended the system since 1853;—this has prevented persons from investing capital which may be absolutely lost from want of labour to carry on the undertaking. Should there be a security of this, there is every certainty of a sufficient stimulus being given by the resources of the Colony to attract capital. The witnesses are of opinion that 1000 Convicts might be annually disposed of with very great advantage, and that for many years this number would be easily employed and eventually absorbed into the Colony. The only serious difficulty which presents itself is the disparity of sexes. This is necessarily very great. The inconvenience and evil arising from this are not so great as they would be under other circumstances, because a large proportion of the ticket-of-leave men go into the bush or uncultivated regions where it would be almost impossible to convey a wife and family. Still the subject should be kept in view, so as to devise the best means of remedying the evil. Convict women cannot be sent here. The Colony very properly will not receive such women under any circumstances, to corrupt the new population. Workhouse women, unable to provide for themselves in England, and desiring the opening presented by a new country, ought to be the right class;—but they are not. Their dissolute and degraded habits are found to be most injurious, and they will not be received willingly. Ordinary female emigrants of good character are very likely to do well; they are received into a Government depôt till they are hired, and they are visited by ladies of the place who look after them as well as they can, and give them what advice they require.

With respect to our own country, there cannot be a doubt that, were the expense double what it is, a great benefit would be done to Great Britain by removing from our shores so many Convicts who, even if the very best were selected, would not be likely to do well in the scene of their former criminal life. But, excepting the expense of the voyage, the cost of each Convict in Western Australia does not now exceed on an average £25 each per annum, much less than he would cost in England. We must say, then, that we are greatly indebted to that Colony for delivering us of a burden, and should be ready to take every means in our power to make our Convict depôt there as useful to them as we can.

With respect to the selection of the Convicts who are to be sent over, two points are to be seriously considered. First, at whatever inconveniences to ourselves, we must take care to send over such persons, and these under such conditions, as we learn are adapted to the requirements and circumstances of the Colony. The Governor tells us that they are not afraid to take daring criminals if they are able-bodied, and willing to work, for that many of those who would be most audacious in England, do well there. He would not object even to have London thieves, if they were physically capable of work. But he must not have those who are mentally incapable of guiding themselves, who have committed crimes which render them unfit associates for other human beings, or persons, such as clerks, as have been accustomed to a life exempt from bodily toil, and who, possessing a little property, which relieves them from the necessity to labour, give an example of idleness to the other Convicts which is very injurious.

The Convicts who are sent out should not have been passing through a long imprisonment, which incapacitates both body and mind from healthy exertion, and the greater part of his whole sentence, which should never be less than seven years, should be passed in the Colony, the whole period being under surveillance, and the duration of the Convict's compulsory labour, depending as at present on his own exertions. It may be said that the "exigencies of the service" often require deviations from a system of selection which may be in itself good. The success of so important an experiment as the Western Australian Convict system should not be imperilled for any convenience or advantage connected with home administration. Our own arrangements at home should be adapted to meet the real wants of the Colony which gives us such important help.

Western Australia, then, under a system of Convict management, founded on principles which have proved so beneficial, and which may become much more so when freed from the difficulties under which she has hitherto laboured, appears to offer us most important help while receiving benefit herself. While we ought never to send the dregs of our population into the new country, nor let hardened villains there have free scope for their dishonest practices or lawless violence, yet there are many in our Convict Prisons, and will doubtless be many more when an improved system is adopted in them, who would desire to do well if a fair field were opened to them. Their previous career may render them unfit to be at large where there are ample means of living in luxury by dishonest practices, and where bad associates may be certain to drag them back into crime as soon as they become free. Such as these may turn their misused energies to good purpose where there is little to plunder; where they are removed from those whose very look invites to evil, and the tone of whose voice is a summons to crime; and where they must earn their bread by the sweat of their brow, or starve. Those who have been the "worst" prisoners, whose ungovernable dispositions are always bringing them into punishment, who may even have been engaged in a Portland or a Chatham mutiny,—even those, in the wild, rough life of clearing the roads in the new Colony, living in rude huts among the scattered native residents, to whom their presence is a boon, since it affords a market for their produce, and contributing by their labour to the present benefit and the future advancement of the Colony, — even these worst of Convicts are preparing to become good citizens; — they are once more bound to society by the tie of mutual benefit; — they are making for themselves friends against the day when they gain their title to comparative freedom. Thus the fierce, bad nature, at war with society, and especially with those who are the appointed agents to control him, even this man becomes so subdued and softened, that the single unarmed warder may sleep fearlessly in the very midst of his band of Convicts, with no guardianship save that of the one constable, chosen from among them, whose duty it is to keep watch by night. The settlement of such men in a new country is a great blessing to themselves, and at the same time they return the benefit they receive. But the greatest caution should be adopted in the selection of those persons for *deportation*, a term which may replace the hated one of Transportation. Western Australia does not ask for the "best" of our English Convicts. She does not want those quiet, hypocritical men, who have never done any hard work in their lives, and whose muscles, untrained to labour, are now, perhaps, physically unable to perform it;—men who can go through their prison routine without bad report, fed abundantly, with small exertion, if they have succeeded in interesting the officials to obtain for them an easy post of home work, and who thus go on year after year accumulating good marks and large gratuities. The young Colony does not want these "best" of prisoners. Nor does she desire those Convicts of superior rank in society — clerks,

*employés* of various descriptions — such men as REDPATH and
ROUPELL; these, though they may be esteemed better than
low-born criminals, are positively injurious in a new Colony;
they "cannot dig," and the apparently easy headwork for
which alone they are adapted, and on which they are soon
able to live at ease, introduces a bad element into this Convict settlement, and has anything but a penal aspect.  They
are not only useless and unfit for this new life, but positively
injurious by their example and influence.

How, then, are we to select the Convicts who shall go to
people the new province ?

So great a change of life, so excellent a field for beginning
a new and better mode of existence, is, we have seen, an unspeakable boon to persons whose future in their native country
is clouded with disgrace, and is beset with temptations to evil,
since every place brings associations with crime.  Let it be
represented as such to the Convicts, and let them from the
very commencement of their imprisonment be led to look
forward to it as the goal they will strive to attain.  But
let them clearly understand that they must vigorously exert
themselves, and give unequivocal proofs of true repentance,
as evinced by deeds, not words, before they can attain it.  Let
them pay part of the cost of their passage out by their prison
earnings, and not be allowed to go until they have earned
enough to give what may be considered a fair sum from their
gratuities.  Beside this, let a preference be given to such as
have families, and let them contribute something also towards
the passage out of their wives and children.  The hope of thus
repairing in some degree their past neglect of family ties, will
be a great stimulus to exertion in all who are well-disposed,
and the self-denial and exertion practised in doing so will have
a most beneficial effect on their characters.  Provision should,
of course, be made for the arrival of the families on the other
side of the water; they would, doubtless, be welcomed there,
and would help to solve present difficulties.  The present Act,

having provided for the lengthening of sentences, would enable this system easily to be carried out after a short time; a class of men would thus be sent to Western Australia who had shown a positive determination to do better, and a capacity for work. They would arrive with a good character, and a degree of independence, through having paid, from their prison earnings, part of the expenses of their passage. Under no circumstances should any Convicts be sent who are considered too bad for discharge at home. *We must grapple with our own crime.* The greatest hopes might then be reasonably entertained that, as Western Australia has been so successful under very disadvantageous circumstances, the greatest benefits may be anticipated, under a continuance of the same system, if persons better selected are sent over to form a part of her future population. If such should be the case, when she no longer requires our help, other young states will glady receive similar aid from men who will remain under control and surveillance, until they have proved themselves able to be trusted in perfect freedom.

Under such conditions, provided always that a very greatly improved and really reformatory system of discipline is adopted in our Convict Prisons at home, a system of deportation to another part of the world would be highly beneficial, and may become almost similar to free emigration, after the expiration of sentence.

One difficulty will, however, present itself to the minds of all who have read the extracts from evidence contained in these pages, or who have directed their attention to the subject.

The passage out in Convict ships has always been heard of as of a most demoralising nature, and calculated to undo all good effects which may have arisen from previous discipline.

This difficult problem has, however, been solved by the energy, practical experience, and Christian spirit of a Surgeon-Superintendent of some of these ships, who has given a narrative of his proceedings in a volume entitled "The Convict Ship," by

# 284

OUR CONVICTS.

COLIN ARNOTT BROWNING, M.D., Staff-Surgeon, Royal Navy.* As the volume is not extensively known, copious extracts may be acceptable to our readers, with which we will conclude this chapter.

Dr. BROWNING states in the Preface,—

"When, in the year 1831, the duties and responsibilities involved in the care and management of a convict ship were, for the first time, in the ship *Surrey*, imposed upon me, my inexperience of the nature of the service caused me no small degree of anxiety.

"On my second charge, in the ship *Arab*, in 1834, I entered prepared with a system of instruction and government, the result of my experience, and in which some improvements suggested themselves during our progress to the Colonies. As my third voyage, in the *Elphinstone*, advanced, my plan received still further improvements. Its fitness for the management of *female* convicts was ascertained in the year 1840, when I accomplished, in the ship *Margaret*, my fourth voyage.

"The narrative of the Convict Ship depicts the happy results of this system in operation among 264 convicts in my fifth voyage on board the *Earl Grey ;* and a still more abundant blessing attended my *sixth, seventh* and *eighth* voyages in the *Theresa*, the *Pestonjee Bomonjee*, and *Hashemy.* * * *

"It may be worthy of remark that, on review and comparison of my eight voyages, I find the amount of reformation among the prisoners strikingly to correspond with the degree of diligence and zeal with which the Gospel, in its *Divine simplicity*, was brought to bear, from the hour of embarkation, upon their understandings and hearts. During my first voyage, there was less of Christian instruction, and much less of apparent improvement. *As experience grew, and practical Christianity was from the beginning relied upon, coercion in any form became less and less called for ; and, during my last three voyages, not only were no lashes inflicted, but not a fetter was used, nor a prisoner placed in confinement, or under the charge of a sentry.*"

Dr. BROWNING gives the following account of the instruction and management adopted,—p. 167 :—

"Immediately after the embarkation of the prisoners, or as soon after as possible, the whole body being assembled on the quarter-deck, and the guard drawn up on the poop, the following. or some other suitable address, is delivered :—

"*Address to the Prisoners immediately on their embarkation, and before they are permitted to quit the quarter-deck.*

"This day commences a new era in your existence. The moment you set your feet on the decks you now occupy, you came under the *operation*, and I trust will speedily come under the *influence*, of a system which contemplates

* Sixth Edition. JAMES NISBET & Co., London : 1856.

you as intellectual and moral beings; as beings who necessarily exert an incalculable influence, good or bad, upon each other, upon mankind, and upon the moral universe; as beings, moreover, who can never cease to exist, either in a state of perfect happiness or of unutterable wretchedness. The present moment is the link which connects the *past* with the *future*;—a moment calculated to bring the past most vividly to your recollection, to awaken in your bosoms a deep and anxious solicitude respecting your future career and experience; a moment so full of interest to you and to me, so pregnant with result to every individual now before me, that I feel it difficult to determine what points of consideration I ought to select. It is your present and everlasting welfare that I now seek; and perhaps, you cannot, at this instant, be more profitably exercised, than in honestly and solemnly calling up to your recollection the days of your life that are gone.

"Permit me, then, to ask you, in order that you may put the question, every one of you, secretly to himself, What views do you now entertain of your past life?"

Then follows an excellent practical address which he concludes thus,—p. 179—181 :—

"You now withdraw to your berths, and you will do so in deep and solemn thought. Let every man's mind retire within himself. Let there be no talking, but let all be deep consideration. Look back upon your lives; silently meditate upon, and faithfully apply, every man to himself, that which has been now spoken in great kindness to you all. Let every one consider, that to talk to his neighbour on retiring from this place, is to invade his neighbour's rights, and to interrupt that solemn and secret communion he is now required to hold with his own heart, and with Him who is the searcher of all hearts, and from whom no secrets are hid.

"The following day," Dr. BROWNING continues, "is chiefly occupied with the organization of the people. They are formed into three divisions, and placed under the superintendence of three captains, *cautiously selected from amongst their fellow-prisoners*, according to the character given them in the hulks and prisons, and my own observation of their countenances and general demeanour. Besides the appointment of captains of divisions, as many more of the petty officers are nominated as can be fixed upon consistently with prudence.

"Before mustering the people below for the night, they are assembled on the quarter-deck—the guard being on the poop—to receive the *second* address."

In this Dr. BROWNING enters fully into all the points of discipline and conduct, to which he will require strict attention to be paid. He thus concludes,—p. 195 :—

"The youngest among you must now, in some measure, understand that it is in the strictest sense a *moral discipline* which I desire to see in operation on board this transport. In further proof of which I shall give orders that those irons—the badges of your disgrace—with which you are at present fettered, be removed from the whole of you, at as early a period as is consistent with the discharge of other duties ; and I do most ardently hope, that when I have once caused them to be struck off, you will not, by your conduct, *demand* their being again replaced; for what can be more disgraceful to you, and painful to me, than the clanking of these irons as you walk along the decks ?

" The earliest opportunity is taken of again assembling the people, to announce to them the persons appointed as petty officers, and to state the nature of their duties, and what is reciprocally incumbent upon the people, and those in authority over them.

" The petty officers being drawn up in line, and placed before the people assembled on the quarter-deck, the third address is delivered as formerly from the poop."

After this excellent preparation and instruction as to the principles on which he means to act, Dr. B. arranges the Schools, which, it will be observed, are entirely under the management of persons selected from themselves,—p. 203, *  *  211.

"The whole of the people are now to be formed into schools, according to their degrees of knowledge. To each school a teacher is appointed, and over the whole a *General Inspector*. The teachers are chosen with great care from amongst those who appear to combine with the greatest scholarship the best abilities, the most amiable disposition, and the greatest degree of moral integrity. The peculiar tact necessary to communicate instruction with success, has, with few exceptions, to be acquired.

" The people are again assembled on the quarter-deck, to be informed of the appointment of the Schoolmasters and Inspector, and to listen to an outline of their respective duties. * *

" The first opportunity is next seized for assembling the people, to make them acquainted with the *routine* and *regulations*.

" The routine and miscellaneous regulations having been read to the people assembled on the quarter-deck, they receive the following

"ADDRESS.

" With the duties now exhibited to you, it is requisite that not only the petty officers and schoolmasters, but the whole of you, should make yourselves perfectly familiar ; and you will then take care that the demands which every successive hour makes on your united efforts, are cheerfully and punctually complied with. In every state of society, and especially in *our* little community, *punctuality* and *zeal* in the discharge of duty must be ranked amongst the *cardinal virtues*. Their neglect is confusion and wretchedness; their practice is order and comfort. Their observance is not to be limited to those in office; they are to be characteristics of every member of our community. On this the perfection of our social order must mainly depend.

" I therefore expect soon to see the whole of you so intimately conversant with the duties of every hour of every day of the week, so distinguished by punctuality and zeal, and so under the influence of brotherly love (God of His infinite mercy grant that it may be that love which springs from the belief of His love to you), that our entire apparatus shall work with the most perfect ease and regularity, and steadily produce the anticipated result."

We should gladly enter into more detail respecting the system pursued did space permit, and transcribe more of the excellent observations of Dr. BROWNING.  We must not, however, omit the following account of the School, and the system of discipline pursued,—p. 215—219 :—

" A very short time suffices to familiarise the people with the daily *routine*, and the required duties are speedily executed with a regularity and precision which cannot fail to gratify every enlightened and benevolent observer.  No sooner is the machinery put in motion, than it seems to work by an inherent power, as if, indeed, its *primum mobile* were nothing short of a vital principle. Every hour brings with it its own duties, and the only thing required is, that the petty officers should be occasionally reminded of the demands which the approaching hour will make upon them, and that the people should sometimes feel the influence of my voice, in order to secure that punctuality and des-patch so essentially requisite to the 'carrying on,' with efficiency and comfort, ' of the public duty.'

" The working of ' the school system' is, if possible, more delightful and interesting than ' the plan of management.'  Much, however, depends on the character of the schoolmaster.  The difference in the effects produced on the same class of pupils by teachers of different degrees of skill and zeal, is great, and shews the value of *efficient* instructors, and their vast influence on the acquirement of useful knowledge, and therefore on the future character and destinies of men.  The pupils of a dull and indolent teacher betray, in a marvellous degree, the unhappy characteristics of their master; and the spirit and life of the ardent and industrious schoolmaster are as visibly imbibed by the pupils committed to his care.  I am of necessity shut up to the choice of such teachers as the people themselves supply.  All that I can do myself personally, is occasionally to instruct them how to proceed, and to lecture them seriously on the momentous character of their duties. Charged as is the Surgeon-Superintendent with ' the entire management of the prisoners,' and the whole of the medical duties of the transport, *unassisted*, all he can *daily* attempt is an occasional, and often hasty visit to the schools, the influence of which is perhaps increased by its being always *expected* by the people, and liable to be made at any moment.  However brief and rapid these visits are, they help to maintain a constant intercourse between himself and the schools; they afford him an opportunity of making observations both on teachers and pupils, giving them a word of direction, reproof, or encouragement! and of manifesting a proper interest in the people and the work in which they are engaged.

"In order to prevent my time from being occupied with the minute investigations connected with cases of petty delinquency (an evil of no ordinary magnitude, considering the important purposes to which the time so consumed might be applied), I have found it necessary to form a 'Court of Investigation,' whose prerogative it is to hear all the complaints forwarded by the chief captain and inspector of schools. This court consists of *five* members; namely, four of the most intelligent, judicious and trustworthy of the petty officers; and my clerk, who acts as clerk of the court. They are empowered to cite before them the parties accused, and to call and examine witnesses, in order to ascertain the nature and extent of the alleged offences. They are entrusted with the power of administering *exhortation, warning, admonition and reproof*, and of remonstrating closely and solemnly with such as may be brought before them; with a view always to the improvement of the offender, and the prevention of all impropriety of conduct in future. When the offence, upon enquiry, seems to be of a minor character, and attended with palliating circumstances, and the culprit appears penitent, the court are authorised to dispose of the case, by the administration of reproof and advice, as their judgment may direct; *the reprimand constituting the punishment*. When the accused exhibits a state of mind not quite satisfactory to the court, besides being reproved, duly advised, and cautioned, he is given to understand that he must consider himself in a state of *probation*, under close observation; and is dismissed for the present with the assurance that his next offence will subject him to a more serious punishment, and make it necessary to bring him before the Surgeon-Superintendent.

"This is the severest punishment the court are empowered to inflict; a punishment, too, which they are rarely called upon to administer; and when a case does occur, requiring to be brought to the 'quarter-deck,' it has been so well sifted, and the evidence so completely made out, that, in order to dispose of it *at once*, I have only to cause it to be stated in the presence of the offender; to hear the testimony of the witnesses, who are all assembled to the barricade, ready to appear on the quarter-deck the moment they are called; and to listen to anything which the accused may have to say, whether it be matter of confession, contrition, or exculpation. Thus no time is lost, all is prepared, the witnesses are at hand, the case is made to appear as clear as the day; with scarcely an exception the prisoner confesses his offence, and nothing remains to occupy my time, but to place the delinquency in a just and impressive light, with a view to practical improvement, and to write upon a slip of paper the punishment which I may think it expedient to award.

"The people seem to entertain precisely the views of the court which I desire they should. Men of their own class dealing with them, manifestly produces a species of effect different, if not in *kind*, at least in *intensity*, from that which results from my own personal adjudications. The case is determined as it were by themselves, and appears to be seen by a light which the law itself, and reason, and a sense of justice, supply. A perception of truth, and conviction of right and wrong, influence the minds of the prisoners unmixed with any impressions produced by my immediate presence and authority. Another beneficial tendency of the working of this court, is to lead the people to sit in judgment upon themselves, and to form a just estimate of their own character and conduct.

"As the minds of the people become enlightened, the esteem of my approbation, and dread of incurring my displeasure, increase. Instead of the mere apprehension of punishment, both affection and gratitude soon begin to exert a happy influence; they perceive and feel that I am their *friend;* that my sole aim is their improvement and happiness; that nothing pleases and delights me so much as *real* reformation in principle and behaviour; that nothing causes me greater pain and disappointment than their continuance in immoral and irregular habits, except, indeed, *hypocritical pretensions* to a change of character which does not manifest itself in their temper and conduct. After a little while, therefore, it rarely occurs that the court of investigation have a case to forward to the quarter-deck, and a considerable portion of the people begin, ere long, to act upon far higher principles than a mere respect to *my* feelings and regard to *my* approval."

In the School Dr. B. did not confine himself to dry lessons, but gave simple lectures on natural history, natural philosophy, and other subjects calculated to raise and elevate their minds. Most especially, however, did he devote his efforts to make the men under his care fully acquainted with the Bible, and to direct their minds to the teachings and truths it contains. He also gave them much definite instruction on moral subjects, which might be useful to them in after life. He chiefly aimed, however, to lead them to a true change of heart,—p. 241-2 :—

"Not only must both the moral and the vicious experience a saving change, before they can do anything upon *right principles;* but, *even keeping their eternal salvation out of view,* little good is, in my apprehension, to be expected from what is commonly called 'the *crime class* of our population,' until brought under the illuminating and sanctifying power of the Scriptures, and the gracious influences of the Holy Spirit; for they will, with few exceptions, persevere in a course of iniquity, the bane of social order, and totally unworthy of confidence, until they are brought back to God and to godliness, by the faith of the Gospel. Change of heart is the only ground on which I expect satisfactory change of conduct. So accustomed are some of them to vice; so hardened in iniquity; so utterly devoid of all sense of propriety and decorum; so insensible to the excellencies and attractions of virtue; so sunk in their own estimation, and *(as they apprehend)* in the estimation of mankind; that, if we desire to see these unhappy men become worthy of that degree of trust, without which they cannot be safely permitted to mingle in general society, *we shall aim at nothing short of their conversion to God.* It is my sober conviction, that nothing less than a saving change of heart will warrant our placing confidence in the more hardened and depraved of those who suffer Transportation, or furnish a sufficient guarantee that they will prove safe and useful members of the community. The same observations will, I believe, equally apply to thousands of our population, who escape the punishments both of imprisonment and Transportation.

"*Supreme love to God* is not only the principle upon which alone we can perform even a single work acceptable in his sight, but it also secures active and unwearied obedience to the *whole* of his revealed will. Supreme love to God admits of no substitute. But let this holy and heavenly principle be, by the Spirit of God, generated in any man's heart, and, from that moment, he is under the influence of a mighty and transforming power—a power, the tendency of which is to diffuse itself throughout his whole nature, and reduce to its own holy character all that he is, and feels, thinks, and does."

A voyage spent under such influences, and with such earnest and well-directed effort to benefit the Convicts, could not but produce the best possible effect on them. On their arrival at the place of their destination, an officer of the army came on board, who was also a justice of the peace. He was much struck, and highly delighted with the appearance of the people.

It was with deep emotion that the Convicts parted from the friend who had so devoted his heart and soul and strength to their welfare; at their request, the Inspector of Schools, one of their number, presented to him an address, expressing their unanimous feeling of gratitude to him, appreciation of the great benefits he had conferred on them, and hopes that their future conduct would prove the sincerity of their present resolution, to begin a new and better life.

It is satisfactory to have the following official report of the permanent effect produced by a voyage, passed under such auspices :—

"REPORT OF THE PRINCIPAL SUPERINTENDENT OF CONVICTS.

"*New South Wales.*

"I have the honour to report, for the information of his Excellency the Governor, that the ship *Hashemy* arrived in Port Jackson on the 8th instant, having on board two hundred and twelve convicts from the Millbank, Parkhurst, Pentonville, and Wakefield Prisons, under the superintendence of Dr. BROWNING, R.N.

" On the following day I proceeded on board the vessel and inspected the prisoners, their prison, hospital, &c., and was very much pleased with the cleanly and respectable appearance of the men, and the order and regularity presented by every part of the ship allotted to them. They expressed themselves perfectly satisfied with their provisions, and spoke in the most grateful terms of the unwearied attention of Dr. BROWNING to their wants and interests in every respect during the voyage.

" I beg further to report that, on the 14th instant, after the completion of their muster, the men were permitted to make engagements with persons who were allowed to go on board for that purpose, by an order from me; and it seems worthy of remark that, although at the time of the *Hashemy's* arrival there were four emigrant ships in the harbour, containing about one thousand souls, all these men, with the exception of fifty-nine who were removed to Moreton Bay and Clarence River, where labour was urgently required, were hired to respectable landowners and sheep farmers within six days of their being ready to engage, at wages averaging from £12 to £16 a year, and some mechanics at £28 per annum, the boys receiving from £8 to £11 per annum; besides which, there are now applications in my office from private individuals and others in different parts of the country, for a larger number of this class of labourers than can be supplied by the arrival of several convict ships.

" I cannot conclude my report without expressing the great satisfaction I have felt at the high state of moral feeling exhibited in the conduct and bearing of the convicts by the *Hashemy*; one which made itself apparent to all who went on board that vessel to engage servants, and which I believe to have been effected by the judicious management and discipline of the Surgeon-Superintendent, no doubt acting on minds already humbled by their previous imprisonment, but evidently brought about by his assiduous and constant attention to their moral training. Indeed, to so high a standard has he brought the principles and feelings of these men, that punishment on board during the voyage was unknown, beyond the placing of some one or two in Coventry,—a punishment which was so carried out by the other men that the culprit was as completely in solitary confinement, in the midst of his fellow-prisoners, as if he had been confined in a silent cell in the prison from whence he came; a circumstance unprecedented in any convict ship that ever brought prisoners out here, and is certainly most creditable to the exertions of Dr. BROWNING, as well as to the feelings of the men.

(Signed) " J. M'LEAN.
" *Principal Superintendent of Convicts' Office,*
*Sydney, 25th June,* 1849."

Dr. BROWNING says, p. 267 :—

" Sometime after my return to England, I received a gratifying letter from Captain M'LEAN, acquainting me with the continued good behaviour of my men, and enclosing testimonials from two honourable members of the Legislative Council, in favour of a considerable number whom they had engaged and employed at their respective stations up the country.

"From another gentleman connected with the Colonial Government, and who had the best opportunity of making himself well acquainted with the character of my people, both before and after they debarked, I received a communication, from which I make the following extract:—

"'I have pleasure in stating to you that the convicts by the *Hashemy* still continue to maintain a character for honesty and good conduct unequalled by any prisoners who have arrived here. Their masters speak in high terms of the standard of their morals, and appear to be exceeding grateful to you for the mode of treatment which you must have adopted to bring the men to a sense of their position; you have indeed made an impression on the prisoners' minds, which, under the blessing of Divine Providence, I feel little doubt will be the means of restoring them again to rectitude of conduct. They appear to be influenced, not so much by a fear of punishment as by the dictates of a mind thoroughly cleansed, and sifted by the reformatory process they have gone through. This must indeed be a gratifying proof to you of the excellence of your system over that generally pursued.'"

The following are additional testimonies,—p. 267-9:—

"'My son lately met a gentleman just returned from Australia, and it struck me that his *unwilling* testimony to the good effects of Dr. BROWNING's labours was valuable, as coming from *such* a quarter.

"'Speaking of the convicts, he said—"There are some among them who are shrewd, clever fellows, and they are cunning enough to know that good behaviour is more likely to be advantageous to their interests in the colony than bad; so they become the most consummate hypocrites, and, from the time they land, pretend to be penitent, and they manage to act their part so well that *their conduct is irreproachable, and people are glad to employ them,* and in this way they get on. *They are a complete contrast to the abandoned race who act incorrigibly.*" May not we, who have been behind the scenes, and watched the results of the religious impression produced on board "The Convict Ship," hail this irreproachable conduct as a fruit meet for repentance? That men of the world, who are ignorant of the *power* of the Gospel, should call it hypocrisy, is not wonderful, but it may lead those who are endeavouring to reclaim the wanderer, to thank God and take courage.

(Signed)                          "'E. A.'

"EXTRACT FROM A LETTER WRITTEN BY AN OFFICIAL GENTLEMAN RESIDING IN SYDNEY, AFTER THE PRISONERS HAD BEEN SIXTEEN MONTHS IN THE COLONY.

"'*Sydney, New South Wales, Oct.* 3, 1850.

"'I am happy to be able to assure you that, up to this moment, with very few exceptions, your *Hashemy* men still retain their high character; the doctrines so well impressed upon them have enabled them, in the midst of temptation, to pursue their course in honesty and integrity,—a fact that must be most gratifying to you, and one which proves most conclusively the advantage of the discipline, mainly consisting of scriptural instruction and prayer to God, which you always have adopted in regard to such men while under your charge.'

"Your men have been an example of good conduct to all the ticket-of-leave holders who came out. Up to this time we continue to receive from all those who engaged them, assurances of their being most useful and honest servants."

Dr. BROWNING has done a noble work, worthy of a Christian, in thus proving by actual example how such a voyage may be made subservient to the highest purposes, and productive of permanent benefit to those who are to people a new continent. The influences of the voyage would doubtless be rendered more powerful from the circumstances of seclusion from the outer world and the solitude of the ocean around them, under which they were given; they must bring forth fruit in many, and have a life-long effect. We need not suppose that he alone could have such influence or produce such effects. His volume shows that he would be the last to assume any such peculiar power, and encourages the belief that other equally zealous, loving, and religious persons, availing themselves of his judicious regulations and system, might be the means, as he was, of making the passage from the old country to their new home in Western Australia, the commencement of a happier, because a better, life in this world,—and a preparation for the eternal home in Heaven!

END OF VOLUME I.

PUBLICATION NO. 80: PATTERSON SMITH REPRINT SERIES IN
CRIMINOLOGY, LAW ENFORCEMENT, AND SOCIAL PROBLEMS

# OUR CONVICTS

BY

## MARY CARPENTER

TWO VOLUMES IN ONE

*VOLUME TWO*

*Montclair, New Jersey*
**PATTERSON SMITH**
*1969*

# CONTENTS OF VOLUME II.

# OUR CONVICTS.

## CHAPTER I.

### THE IRISH CONVICT SYSTEM.

THE English and the Irish Convict Systems were both founded on the Act of Parliament of 1853. The object of that Act was to make such changes in the system adopted towards Convicts, as would prepare them for discharge in our own country, since our Colonial provinces were virtually closed against them, Western Australia only consenting still to receive a small number annually. We have seen that in England the system has hitherto been a failure, but have traced that failure, not to the principles on which that and the subsequent one of 1857 were founded, but to certain omissions and additions which were incompatible with the successful working of the principles. We now proceed to the examination of the Irish Convict System, which has fully developed the principles of both those Acts. The results of the ten years during which it has been in operation demonstrate, beyond any possibility of doubt to an impartial observer, not only the truth of the principles embodied in the Acts of Parliament, but also of those moral principles which are so embodied in it as to constitute its peculiar features, and of the excellence of the machinery by which these are brought into action. The wonderful combinations of all these by the founder of the system, Sir WALTER CROFTON, demands from us very close investigation of its principles, and examination of its details.

We cannot obtain a more succinct and lucid account of the rise of the Irish Convict System, and the circumstances under which it was established, than from the evidence of Sir WALTER (then Captain) CROFTON, to the Transportation Committee of 1855-6. As on other occasions, the questions and answers will be blended together so as to form one continuous narrative :—

" I was appointed Chairman of the Directors of Convict Prisons in Ireland under the Act of the 17th and 18th Victoria, in 1854. In 1853 I was on a Commission of Convict Inquiry in Ireland, and for some years previous to that, as a County Magistrate in England, I had given great attention and consideration to the subject of the treatment of criminals generally, and the prevention of crime. I mention this to the Committee to show that any opinion which I may give is not alone derived from my official connection with the subject.

" The state of the Irish Convict Prisons, at the time when this Act into which we are now inquiring was passed, was as deplorable as it is possible to conceive ; the prisoners were morally and physically prostrate in every way. There was a want of the element of hope in them, of education, and of everything one would wish to find in prisoners, and which exists in the Convict depôts in England. The prisons were overcrowded to a great degree, and my statement will be corroborated by my reading a despatch from the Governor of Western Australia, who had just received a large number of Irish Convicts.

" The prisoners had left Ireland before our Board was formed. I will read an extract of a few lines from our first Report, which introduces this despatch :—' The deplorable aspect and apparent destitution of the Irish Convicts appeared to us to require immediate attention, and we have endeavoured as far as possible to remedy this state of things, which contrasts strongly with the condition of those in England. Our opinion is corroborated by extracts appended from the Reports of the Governor, Comptroller-General, and Superintendent of Convicts, &c., in Western Australia, dated 11th September, 1854, and forwarded for the information of the Secretary for the Colonies,—extracts from a despatch from Governor FITZGERALD to the Right Hon. Sir GEORGE GREY, Bart. :—" 11th September, 1854. Some of the Irish prisoners, per ships *Phœbe Dunbar*, and *Robert Small*, have proved in many instances, I regret to say, an exception to this very gratifying state of things ; the result of recent experience and close observation of these men, you will perceive, induces the Comptroller-General to hope *that men from the Irish prisons will not be sent to this Colony with tickets-of-leave.* If, therefore, future drafts be sent, I fully concur with the Comptroller-General in thinking that this class of prisoners, more especially than any other, should remain inmates of the prison at Fremantle, under rigid control, for at least twelve months, to give any hope of sending them forth into the community trained to habits of industry and self-reliance, which they appear to be somewhat indisposed to exercise in general." ' Then there is an extract from the Report of the Superintendent, under date of January 10, 1854, which was two or three months afterwards, with reference to the same subject : ' In the instances of the Irish prisoners received per the ships *Robert Small* and *Phœbe Dunbar*, it was held by judicial and medical authority that their prostrate condition, physically and morally, the result, it was conjectured, of *long imprisonment, low diet, and bad training,* rendered it necessary that they should be subjected to a course of preparatory discipline, arbitrary in duration in some cases, but relative and proportionate to the term of sentence in others, prior to their being exposed to the trials of a strange climate and novel society ; and certain compensating allowances in these arbitrary cases were then discussed and decided upon.' It then says, ' But it may be remarked as a noticeable feature in the idiosyncracy of the Irish prisoners, that is to say, those who arrived direct from Ireland, and who had not undergone the present discipline held applicable to Convicts sentenced in England, that there appears *a singular inaptitude to comprehend the nature of moral agencies, or to be affected by them;* neither do they seem to understand the desirableness, we will say, of self-reliance, or the necessity for the exercise of habits of propriety, industry, and prudence, as a means towards extricating themselves from the consequences of former errors.' I am reading this corroboration of what I have stated to lead the subject to the reason why tickets of license were not issued in Ireland until recently. What the Governor of Western Australia thought that he could not do in Western Australia, viz., to give them tickets of license, we felt, for similar reasons, as Directors of Convict Prisons, we could not recommend in Ireland. These reasons have been pretty well explained from his letter and from what I have stated. I will, however, read a few additional lines from our Report: ' The same feeling which prevents our inflicting on a Colony Convicts who have not been subjected to a proper course of prison discipline, also precludes our bringing forward prisoners for discharge in this country on tickets of license, as in England. *We consider such ticket of license to be a sort of guarantee to the community, that in consequence of a prisoner having been subjected to a proper course of prison discipline and reformatory treatment, he is considered a fit subject to be received and employed by those outside the prison.* Such reformatory course not having hitherto been pursued in this country, we have not felt ourselves justified in recommending the issue of tickets of license.' "

Two points here require special attention. First, the peculiarly low condition of Irish prisoners generally,—and especially of those who had been subjected to the discipline, if such it can be called, of the Irish Convict Prisons then existing. Profoundly ignorant, deficient in any self-reliance, in a state of physical and moral prostration, and unable even to comprehend the nature of moral agency, nothing could be apparently more hopeless than the attempt to *raise* such persons by any kind of prison discipline. And it must be observed that this description of the Irish Convicts as they were does not come from the Director who had the work assigned him of endeavouring to improve them, and who might have been supposed likely to wish to heighten his success by exaggeration of the difficulties he had overcome, but from a high official quarter where a desire existed to receive Convicts in greater numbers. The other point to which we should direct attention is the responsibility which the Directors felt resting upon them, not to release any Convicts on license unless they had good ground for believing that they could safely send them forth into society.

Sir WALTER CROFTON thus continues:—" The first steps that we took were to establish a proper system of discipline to enable us ultimately to carry out the Act. The first part of that system was to remedy the overcrowding which existed. There were upwards of 1000 more in the prisons than they could properly hold, and the Lord-Lieutenant (Lord ST. GERMANS) considering that the best course to relieve this overcrowding was to take the Penal Servitude Act as a basis with regard to the punishments, in which a four years' sentence of penal servitude is considered adequate to seven years' transportation, and six as the maximum of ten years, &c.; we were then instructed to prepare a list of prisoners so circumstanced, and recommend the best conducted that we could find of them for discharge from time to time, absolutely. This was done, and at last the prisons were reduced to some sort of order, so that we could arrange them and establish a proper course of discipline, taking care that the system of separate imprisonment was commenced with, and then following out the English system with regard to public works afterwards, establishing gratuities to give Convicts the element of hope, and induce them to conduct themselves properly.

"There were no Acts of Parliament relating to Ireland

similar to those regulating the management of Pentonville, Millbank, and the prisons here. In fact there was no legal authority till August, 1854, for the management of the Irish Convict Prisons.

"I must trace the matter up to that time, in order to show how it has worked gradually to the present. We found that there was no separation for the juveniles; the juveniles and adults were all together in the Convict Prisons. Our first act, therefore, was to recommend the erection of a Penal Reformatory. I call it a Penal Reformatory to make it as distinct as possible from the general character of a Penal Prison. There are now in the Irish Prisons, out of a number of 2600 males, 700 (I am speaking in round numbers) convicted under 17 years of age. I found, on examination of, perhaps, 180 or 200 of these, that, from bad training and ignorance, they required a certain system to be pursued, which should partake a great deal more of the reformatory element than the penal; therefore this prison was recommended to be of a penal reformatory character, in order to introduce that element. This has been approved, and an Act passed for inclosing Lusk Common for that purpose, which is within eleven or twelve miles of Dublin. In the meantime we separated the juveniles from the adults, and pursued a proper system with them, so far as we were enabled to do so. We then found, by examination in the different prisons, that the educational departments were extremely neglected; that, though there was some teaching, there was no training; and that really the ignorance was the most deplorable thing which could be imagined, not the fault, probably, of the prisoners themselves, but of those who were teaching them. We at once selected two schoolmasters, whose antecedents gave us hopes that they would effect good amongst the prisoners. One was a ragged-school teacher, and the other had been a schoolmaster in a large union, where he had had a great deal of experience. We recommended their being appointed head schoolmasters for the prisons, and also being sent, at the expense of the Government, to visit the different penal and reformatory establishments in this country, for the purpose of seeing the sort of principle which we expected them to act upon, and carry out in the prisons. This they did, and, I am happy to say, with the most gratifying results; for, notwithstanding the state of things which existed formerly, we have been able within this short time to report very differently, and the alteration with regard to the prisons is obvious to any one who visits them. We have been enabled to report now, that 'In our last Report we complained of the inefficient state of the educational departments of the Convict depôts, and stated the importance we conceived should be attached to them in this country, recommending at the same time that they ·should be placed under the inspection of the National Board of Education. Experience has proved that we were correct in our opinion; the report of Mr. M'GAURAN, the head schoolmaster at Mountjoy Prison, showing that, after a very careful examination of the prisoners at that establishment, he found that 96·2 per cent. were almost without any education at all; a fact, we submit, calling for every exertion to render the educational machinery as perfect as possible, in order to open the minds of the prisoners by a system of training as well as teaching. Sensible of the very great importance of establishing a proper system of education in the prisons through which, unfortunately, thousands of human beings must pass, who are in turn subjected to its influence, we are gratified at being enabled to state that, although much of the past year has been taken up in arranging school-rooms, classifying prisoners according to their attainments, appointment of schoolmasters, &c., a great desire has already been evinced by the prisoners to receive instruction; and this is more remarkable, as proceeding from some advanced in age who, at the commencement of the year, attended school with the greatest reluctance,' and that is quite true; it was with

the greatest reluctance we could get them at first to come to
school, but afterwards they came willingly, and the progress
which the prisoners have made within the last twelvemonth
is perfectly marvellous. But then, *the schoolmasters have had
their hearts in the work*, and have led these men's minds, such
as they were, to the utility of education; and certainly the
fruits have been much more than could have been expected.

"One master, I am sorry to say, left us for Australia a few
months ago ; the other is at the Model Prison of Mountjoy.
We trained several other schoolmasters under these two persons,
so that a uniformity of system might prevail throughout the
prisons, and which therefore told, not only with regard to those
prisons which these two masters were in, but throughout the
establishments.

"The course which we adopted with regard to female
Convicts was somewhat similar. We were fortunate in getting
two schoolmistresses, and certainly have attained the greatest
possible results from their appointment. The state of the
female prisoners was really deplorable, and we have large
numbers of them, for in the Convict establishments we now
must have nearly 700 female prisoners.

"The results there have been quite extraordinary. Women
who seemed so lost, that when you entered the prisons, you
felt there was a character about them which was in every
way to be deplored, are now totally different, and persons
who now visited them would see what these schoolmistresses
have achieved, for I look upon the improvement as principally
due to education. The great desire now with the women is
to come to school and be educated and enlightened; formerly
it was their endeavour to keep away from it. The value of
a certain kind of education, not a high education, but a moral
training, is felt throughout the whole establishments, both by
males and females.

"We first thought ourselves justified in adopting the issue

of tickets-of-leave about November last, when we felt that we had some grounds to suppose that they might be issued carefully, and under proper safeguards.

"The plan is by the institution of intermediate establishments between the prisons and the world. We found that men discharged out of the prisons in the ordinary way were perfect children; they did not know what to do; they had not been thinking for themselves for years, and were dependent upon every person they came near; and whatever might have been their intentions to reform, the moment they were outside the prison they fell into their old evil associations again, and were quite astray as to what they should do. This was partly what induced us to recommend a system of intermediate establishments. We thought also that we should be enabled to place them in a position in which the community would be rather more satisfied with the test of their reformation; for unless the community would employ the discharged criminal we felt that whatever we might do in prison, the difficulty was not solved. It is quite clear from what has occurred in England, and what has been going on for some time, that that has been the great difficulty. The people are not satisfied without a test of a man's character, however exemplary you might term him and consider him in the prison, where he is watched by prison officers and every one around him, still it is not considered by the world as satisfactory as if he was placed in a position where he would be exposed to temptation: we therefore recommend the institution of these establishments; where the men would have greater freedom of action."

We omit here the details given to the Committee, and proceed with the general principles and the history of the Intermediate Prisons :—

"In recommending these establishments, we found that there was no new principle to be tested as to the treatment of criminals. We were merely adopting what had been found successful by philanthropic institutions in this country and on

the Continent. All that was novel was its application to the
Convict establishments; and as the success of the philanthropic
institutions which had been tested in this country and on the
Continent was dependent upon individualising and acting on
men in small numbers, through moral agency, our experiment,
if I may so term it, was how we could adopt prison machinery,
that is, the officers of prison establishments to become moral
agents. In consequence of the vacancy of a schoolmaster, we
were enabled to make a fresh appointment, which we termed
that of a lecturer, to the institution in Dublin. He was a person
fortunately with a speciality for the calling, and was practically
conversant with the different reformatory institutions here and
on the Continent. There was therefore no difficulty in that
respect; but we had to adopt the existing prison officers as our
trades' instructors, and, as we hoped, our moral agents; and
there was apparently our difficulty. A shoemaker instructor
was put over his class of shoemakers, and told that he was
to be responsible not only for the industry of the men under
him, but also for their characters; that he was to make himself
conversant with all concerning them. The same was told to
every man in charge of a class; the tailor of his class, the
carpenter, and so on. They were informed that during the
time of instruction at the trades they were to converse with
the prisoners, allude to the subject of the lecture of the
preceding evening which they all attended, and in every way
to act as moral agents throughout the number of hours that
they were with them; in addition to which, they were to aid
in procuring employment, where they could do so, outside the
prison, for the men on discharge. We find this work extremely
well; we have now discharged 51 males on tickets of license,
and 18 females; 49 males have been absolutely discharged,
making a total of 100 males who have passed already through
these intermediate establishments, one at Smithfield, in Dublin,
and the other at Fort Camden, at the mouth of Cork Harbour.
I have had a return, and a very accurate one, collected, of those

who have been discharged on tickets of license upwards of six weeks, and which would afford some test, because the men when first they go out are apt to get into trouble. I have a return of the 23 who were discharged, and who have been out six weeks and upwards; 21 out of 23, I am prepared to prove, from the employers and from themselves, are doing well, and there is every satisfactory idea that they are reformed men. We have 10 or 12 now in Dublin, in employment, who constantly attend the lectures, though discharged from prison, and in many cases their employers come with them, which I think bears testimony to what the lectures have done for the prisoners. Our lecturer has lately, within the last fortnight or three weeks, thought of a plan (and to me it appears a very good plan), of collecting those men who are on licenses in Dublin at fortnightly meetings in the evening, for the purpose of letting them put their savings in the Savings' Bank; and one meeting has already been held, attended by every man in Dublin who has had a ticket of license issued to him, and a deposit of 1s. from his wages has been made by each man to commence with.

"That meeting was about a fortnight ago, and was the first meeting, the only meeting that has yet been held; and they all attended, to put down their shilling each out of their wages. Although I have only made a calculation with regard to those men on tickets of license who have been out that time, yet there are many others who have been absolutely discharged, and have had the benefit, if I may so term it, of these intermediate establishments, who we know are doing well, whom I have seen personally many times; and I am quite sure they are giving satisfaction to their employers, and are going on in an honest course. I have made it my business to have enquiries made respecting them, and I have recently seen the employers of the men myself.

" The results, so far as I have ascertained, are most satisfactory. So far as regards the freedom of agency, which these men have, to do wrong in the establishment, we have on several occasions tried them in this way: I have employed them when public works have required it. A carpenter having been required at the Model Prison for some time, I have tried the experiment, if I may so term it, of sending one of these men every morning to this work, through the city, nearly two miles off, and back again, to return to the lecture in the evening; and he has done this for nearly two months, every day, by himself, no warder with him; and, passing by the public-houses, he returns regularly, and performs the day's work both to the good of the public service and to the satisfaction of the Governor of the prison where he is working. I have sent down other prisoners with messages from one prison to another, and they have returned; many men, a week or a fortnight before the time of their discharge, I have allowed to go out and purchase their tools, so that they may not be out of work for any want of that kind, also their clothes; they have returned punctually. I have found no appearance of anything like drink on them, or of any irregularity whatever. Each man is allowed to spend a certain portion of his earnings; his earnings, perhaps, would average 1s. a week, and he is allowed to spend 6d. of it if he should so desire. There are many who have not drawn a farthing; they prefer keeping the money for the purpose of emigrating, in many cases. Others, again, have bought little matters for their breakfast, such as a herring, and their clothes, and their tools as they have required them, and so on. They dine together in a large hall, which acts as a Mechanics' Institute, and their exercise is taken free from supervision; they are not watched in any way, and we have found no irregularity whatever; it is impossible to find a more orderly establishment in every way with regard either to language or conduct. There were three cases at the first opening of men who were sent from the prisons, with respect to whom, after a fortnight's test, I found, although they came with exemplary characters from the prisons, they were not persons that would do to be trusted; they wanted that sort of watching which we could not give them, and were returned to the prisons. There is always, as will be seen, a sort of nucleus preserved in this establishment; and though large draughts come occasionally of 30 or 35 from the prisons, in the course of three or four days they all settle to their places in consequence of this nucleus which is left, and the establishment goes on orderly enough. We have had 80 in at a time; there are at present only 60. It is important that there should be small numbers, because it gives greater facilities for individualising. With regard to the work performed, there is no doubt that considerably more is done than was ever performed in the prisons. There is an amount of willing industry that we do not find in the prisons generally; and as the trades' instructors in this establishment were the prison officers, they are very good judges with regard to the willing nature of the industry. In addition to this establishment at Smithfield, there are two others; one has been recently opened; the other has been open the same time as Smithfield; it is at the mouth of Cork Harbour. It does not present the same advantages as Smithfield for getting employment for the men, one being in Dublin, and the other isolated; but still I am satisfied that the working of it is good, that the same principle pervades it, and that we have reason to be satisfied with the officers who are there; of course they have been selected for the purpose from the different prisons, but we approve of its internal working.

"It has been in operation the same time as Smithfield; it commenced in January last; and Lord CARLISLE, who has looked thoroughly through the establishments, and is as practically conversant with the Smithfield one as I am, from visiting it three or four times a week, and looking over every book and register connected with it, is so satisfied with its working that he has allowed us to establish others, and I have just opened another at the mouth of Cork Harbour, opposite to Fort Camden, Fort Carlisle, with the same number of prisoners, namely, 85. In a fortnight's time we shall open another industrial establishment in Dublin to hold 70.

"There are 230 prisoners at the present moment on this system; there will in a fortnight's time be 70 more, making 300 in four establishments. We are then going to erect (and they are in the course of erection) eight moveable iron buildings, the same as there were at the Curragh Camp, or at Aldershot, for the troops, to hold 50 in each, so that the same system can be pursued; that is, individualising in each prison or tent, if I may so call it, the 50 prisoners, and keep each sound in itself, with the power of moving these prisons as we wish, or as the public service requires.

"These buildings are just like the soldiers' tents; we have, in fact, taken as a model what they had in the Crimea, at Aldershot, and on the Curragh. They are soldiers' iron rooms, lined, with beds in them to hold 50, and an officer's room on each side; they are inexpensive. The great objection to Convict labour has been that you must find a large public work sufficient to warrant the erection of an expensive prison; and if you combine well-conducted prisoners and indifferently-conducted prisoners, and apply them to that sort of labour, it is necessary to have a kind of security which does cause expense. But if we make a good selection for small works, as we are doing, we need not be particular about the sort of security or the number of prison officers placed over them, and therefore it will be inexpensive labour to the public service. The first two buildings, which will be erected in about six weeks, will be on Lusk Common, about twelve miles from Dublin, and the men will be filtered out of these two prisons of fifties into the community. They will be employed there in erecting our juvenile prison, or rather in commencing it. Men will be brought up from the forts I have spoken of, where they have not the advantages which Smithfield affords, being isolated;

they will be brought up from those establishments to this one at Lusk Common, and as contractors will be doing work close to them, they would be in a place to offer these people employment if they deserve it; their state will be just the same as that of the free labourers, so far as having opportunities of committing themselves. The expense of each of these moveable and lined huts, to hold 50 men and three officers, will be £330.

"I contemplate other advantages as likely to result from the system besides those already mentioned; and in considering that system, it was with a far wider view than merely as regarded tickets of license.

"We believe that it would be a substitute, and a very favourable substitute, for any general system of shortening sentences; it has been some time generally felt that an uncertainty with regard to sentences is a great evil. However convenient (and I quite acknowledge the convenience) it may be for prison authorities to hold out, as an inducement to good prison conduct, that the prisoners should lose 25 per cent. of their punishment, or be released at the end of the third year instead of at the end of the fourth, I cannot think that such a course will tend to genuine reformation. I should be unbelieving in the reformation of any man who would require so strong a stimulus as to be let off one-fourth of his punishment to induce his reformation; I should infinitely prefer to see that man, with a well-modified system of imprisonment, at the termination of his sentence (such as that which I mention) in a situation where he can be tested before he goes out. I should hope that that would be a sufficient stimulus for any good prison conduct; if it was not, I should be very doubtful of the reformation of the man."

Sir WALTER thus expresses his views of the necessity of dealing in our own country with the crime that belongs to us:—

"I believe it to be the best plan to retain them in our own

country, because we have the means of watching them and rendering them powerless with a proper system of police. I believe that there is no country like our own for dealing with such men; I think any spot allocated for that purpose would end in a sort of Norfolk Island again; it would be of no possible advantage. I believe that if we cannot manage those characters with our good police system throughout the country, they cannot be managed elsewhere; but I do not anticipate that they would be any trouble to us."

When men are discharged from the Convict Prisons, information is sent to the police of the district to which he returns.

"If a man has been discharged to his locality, with every professed intention on his part to go on in the same course of crime again, the police have been informed that he intends so doing. There could be no possible compunction in notifying that to the police. A confidential letter is sent to the head of the constabulary of the locality to which I know he is gone, because I pay his fare to that place, and it is notified to the head of the constabulary that such a man has gone there with the professed intention of carrying on his career of crime. In the case of such a man, I have no compunction in marking him; but I should have the greatest in the case of a man who I believed was a reformed character."

We shall not here enter into the details of the working of the system, or of the subsequent adoption of the ticket-of-leave system, and the success which attended it when carried out with strict attention to the conditions of the license. These will be reserved for the next chapter. It is our present object to present a vivid idea of the operation of the system, as derived from the testimonies borne by independent witnesses who have given the subject their personal examination.

The first is from Mr. Recorder HILL, as given in a paper read at the first meeting of the Social Science Association at Birmingham, in October, 1857 :—

" Having learnt from the official reports, and also from private information, that criminals in the Irish Convict Prisons, have been treated from the year 1853 on sound reformatory principles, rapidly developing themselves into an excellent system, I repaired to Ireland, in the month of August last, to investigate for myself the results, so far as the limited period during which it has been in operation permits trustworthy conclusions to be drawn.

" Facilities for the most rigid scrutiny were afforded me in abundance. Of these I availed myself to the best of my ability, and I am under the impression that the facts which I am about to lay before the Section, merit its entire confidence."

Mr. HILL then proceeds to give a full detail of the system, which we must omit, to pass on to his personal observation of the Public Works Prisons, and of the Intermediate Prisons:—

" On the Convict's arrival at Spike Island, he acquires the privilege of earning, by diligence and conduct, certain small gratuities, which are placed to his credit in the accounts of the establishment, and he is furnished with a memorandum-book, in which the increase of this fund is recorded monthly. On admittance to the intermediate stage, he is entitled, in addition to these gratuities, to a small portion of his earnings, which, by unremitting industry during the hours of labour, he may raise to half-a-crown per week. And further, he enjoys, for the first time since his imprisonment, the privilege of drawing out of these earnings, for expenditure, sixpence per week; his choice of articles for purchase being uncontrolled, except as to intoxicating drinks, which are wholly prohibited. These little books are often called for by a director or superior officer, and a friendly consultation ensues as to the state of the prisoner's funds. When it is found that the sixpence has been regularly added to the savings, an occurrence so frequent as to form the rule (spending being the exception), the man is congratulated, not only on his growing store, but on his power of self-command. When the allowance has been accumulated for a time, and is then spent on some article of dress to be worn on his discharge, there is still ground for satisfaction, unless a love of finery has been exhibited. Sometimes, however, the superior shews signs of disappointment, as when, on one occasion, Captain CROFTON found that a prisoner's weekly sixpences had for some months been wasted upon tobacco. No expression of disapproval, however, is suffered to escape, as it would lead the individual to the conclusion that, although he had a nominal right to dispose of his money at his own discretion (or indiscretion), he was in truth under such restraint in its exercise as to paralyze his free agency. The Captain began by asking the man what had originally brought him into trouble. 'Drink,' was his reply. 'Are you not afraid of again being decoyed into the habit of drinking, when you leave this place.' 'Not at all,' was the confident assurance. 'I have now had no drink for years, and I do very well without it.' 'But you were for years without tobacco, and although you suffered much at first, you discovered after a time that tobacco is not essential to your comfort. Yet the moment you are allowed to purchase tobacco you exercise the permission. How can you be sure that as you have not been able to resist tobacco, you shall be able to resist drink when you have the power of obtaining it?' The poor fellow reflected on this conversation, and a subsequent inspection of his book shewed that he had gradually diminished his outlay on the narcotic until he had abandoned it altogether; adding the saving thus produced to his permanent fund.

"When the prison authorities observe that an intermediate man has acquired some capacity for self-control, he is sent out on messages. It is found in practice that he does not abuse this privilege, but having transacted his business with promptitude, he straightway returns. A number of such men will then be entrusted to leave the establishment, for the purpose of performing some work procured for them at a distance from their home, returning every night immediately on the conclusion of the day's labour. Here, again, instances of abuse, such, for instance, as entering a public-house, are rare, if not altogether unknown. The intermediate man, having now established a character, is entrusted with money to make purchases, or to pay bills on behalf of the prison; and what may, perhaps, be justly considered as a surer criterion that his character is known to be deserving, is that such of his comrades as remain at home are in the habit of employing him on commissions to buy for them, and they place in his hands moneys for that purpose. A few months ago a messenger so employed, when he returned, reported that he had lost sixpence belonging to one of his fellows. He was in great distress, but was reassured by the unanimous voice of the whole body, declaring that no thought of malversation had entered their minds. Subsequently, one of the men found the piece of money in an apartment, where it must have been accidentally dropped.

"Meanwhile, the studies begun in Mountjoy and continued in Spike Island are far from being neglected, either by teachers or pupils; and having reference to the habits formed by the training in the lower stages, my hearers will not be surprised to find the individual prepared for the task of self-education, and strongly urged by his approaching change of life to make the best of his opportunities. From the circumstance of Smithfield being situated in Dublin, I had more frequent opportunities of becoming acquainted with the men there placed, than with those at the Forts or at Lusk. The hundred inmates of Smithfield have for their schoolmaster and lecturer, Mr. ORGAN, an able, well-informed, and most devoted public servant, whose appointment reflects great credit on the gentlemen who discovered his value, as he then occupied an obscure position in life. Mr. ORGAN possesses the gift of captivating the hearts while he cultivates the minds of his pupils; and well he deserves his ascendancy over them. He does not limit his exertions to the appointed duties of a teacher. He has been indefatigable in seeking out situations for intermediate men, as they became entitled to their discharge. With regard to those who quit on license, they, as I have already stated, are retained until an approved master admits them into his service.

"Nor does Mr. ORGAN's kind tutelage come to an end on their enlargement. So far as it is possible he watches over them, even when they are far away. He keeps up a frequent and laborious correspondence with all who desire to avail themselves of his services. His successful labours have attracted the attention of the Lord Lieutenant, who not seldom joins the audience at the evening lectures, and takes part in questioning the men on what they have heard. The subjects are multifarious. Outlines of history, sacred and profane ; in particular the history of discovery, illustrated by maps. The study (for so it may be called) of emigration, begun at Spike Island, is continued and pursued into its details. The various forms of government prevailing in the world are canvassed, and the necessity for laws protecting life and property are made evident, even to the understandings and consciences of those by whom they have been violated. Matters of elementary science are explained and illustrated, with a view, among other purposes, to extend the men's knowledge of common things. Principles of political economy are not neglected, especially those which must ever govern the relations between the employer and employed. The students are thus led to see the folly of strikes, how destructive they are to the permanent welfare of working men, promoting only the interests of cunning leaders, who are supported often luxuriously on the sacrifices made by their deluded followers. Saturday afternoon brings a kind of festival, to which the pupils look forward with great interest. The school lessons and the lectures of the prior days form the subject of what is there called competitive examination. The men are divided into two sections, sitting opposite to each other, each division contending for the victory, which is won by the greatest number of successful answers to questions devised by the opponent party. Preparations for this conflict are in progress every night, the inmates of the same dormitory exercising themselves by rehearsals for the coming event; these dormitories being lighted by gas up to a certain hour.

"I was invited to propound questions, and I availed myself of the excellent opportunity thus afforded to test the genuineness of the knowledge acquired by the Smithfield men. Nothing could be more satisfactory. The stock question and the set answer have no place here. It was evident that the students reflected on what they heard; so that humble as their learning is, it performs, perhaps, the most important function of knowlege, it feeds the mind with wholesome nutriment, and occupies it with thoughts supplanting, and, in time, it is to be hoped, utterly excluding, all tendencies to vicious and debasing reveries and conversations.

"At Lusk (fifteen miles from Dublin), I found a body of intermediate men engaged in forming a garden on open heath land, a large tract of which is to be brought under cultivation by Convict labour. Their dwelling, to be supplied with vegetables from the garden, is constructed of corrugated sheet iron, with an interior lining of boards for warmth. It comprehends two distinct erections, each consisting of a single spacious room, which, by the slinging of hammocks, becomes at night a dormitory. One of these rooms is by day their kitchen and houseplace; the other their chapel, school, lecture-room, and library. Each of these two apartments is calculated to give sleeping room to 50 men. They are capable of removal at a slight cost, being light, readily taken to pieces, and as easily reconstructed; consequently they are well adapted for temporary stations like this, which is to be the residence of Convict artificers engaged in building a juvenile prison about to be erected in the immediate neighbourhood. Iron edifices like these have been some time in use at the Forts, and experience has proved them to be very comfortable habitations. The portability of these rooms will overcome the difficulties which have been experienced in employing bodies of men at tasks which are completed within short periods of time. Not being prisons, however, they are only suitable for Convicts who can be held to the spot by moral restraints. But intermediate men are striving to acquire such a character as will recommend them to employers, and thus accelerate their discharge; consequently desertion rarely, if ever, occurs. I heard of no instance in which it had been attempted. Bodies of men so trained may surely be turned to the best account. Thousands of hands might be usefully employed on public works of pressing necessity (like harbours of refuge and coast defences), in which neither private capital, nor that of joint-stock companies, will ever be invested, for the obvious reason that, although indispensable to the community, they cannot be made to yield a revenue. War, emigration, and the rapid expansion of our agriculture, our manufactures, and our commerce, all point to an approaching scarcity of labour. Beyond a doubt, then, the new application of the labour of our criminals, hitherto so little profitable, which the Board has thus admirably devised, challenges immediate and most earnest attention; and we have a right to expect that every improvement which can be suggested in the law controlling the treatment of criminals, so as to bring them at the earliest possible moment to the requisite degree of trustworthiness, will be forthwith made. And no amelioration, believe me, will be so efficacious to that end, as enhancing encouragement to work out their own freedom—a motive which ought not to be confined to the cases of heinous offenders like the Convicts whose discipline forms the subject of this paper, but which should carry its stimulating force into every cell of every prison, purging the administration of justice of the lamentable, nay, revolting absurdity, of withholding a priceless boon from the lesser criminal to confer it on the greater."

Mr. HILL thus concludes his paper:—

"Thus, then, in my humble judgment, the Board of Directors of Irish Convict Prisons have practically solved the problem which has so long perplexed our Government and our Legislature—*What shall we do with our Convicts?* The results of their

great experiment answer thus :—KEEP YOUR PRISONERS UNDER
SOUND AND ENLIGHTENED DISCIPLINE UNTIL THEY ARE REFORMED—
KEEP THEM FOR YOUR OWN SAKE AND FOR THEIRS. THE VAST
MAJORITY OF ALL WHO ENTER YOUR PRISONS AS CRIMINALS CAN
BE SENT BACK INTO THE WORLD, AFTER NO UNREASONABLE TERM
OF PROBATION, HONEST MEN AND USEFUL CITIZENS. LET THE
SMALL MINORITY REMAIN, AND IF DEATH ARRIVE BEFORE REFOR-
MATION, LET THEM REMAIN FOR LIFE."

At the next meeting of the Social Science Association, held
at Liverpool, in 1858, the President of the Section on Punishment and Reformation was the Earl of CARLISLE, the Viceroy
of Ireland. In his opening address he thus speaks:—

" The opening of my recent term of administration in Ireland
was nearly contemporary with the first experiments in the
system of Convict discipline, which has excited so much attention in that country. Whatever may be the merits of that
system in the main features of its conception, and whatever
the success obtained in its practical working, the credit, as
the responsibility, must principally rest with the Chairman of
the Board of Directors, Captain CROFTON. He has been largely
aided by the practised experience and intelligent zeal successively of Captain KNIGHT and Captain WHITTY, and throughout by the benevolent ardour of Mr. LENTAIGNE; he has been
perseveringly seconded, as I know he will be most ready to
admit, by the different members of the Irish Executive, and by
the singular exertions and adaptability of some of his officers
and agents. No one, however, who has watched the progress
of the proceedings, will fail to acknowledge the pervading
influence and inspiration which have been derived and caught
from the perseverance, the enthusiasm, the determination to
succeed, the disbelief in the possibility of failure, which have
distinguished the administrator in chief; and looking back,
as I now can do, to the series of our conferences and expeditions in connexion with this object, as among the most gratifying
recollections of my official career, I feel most happy in having

this opportunity of publicly recording my admiration, my regard, and my gratitude. * * *

"Feeling, then, a right to be thus encouraged and corroborated by actual results and by dry figures, I may the more safely seek to convey the impressions derived from occular observation. I never made a visit to Smithfield during the hours allotted to the evening schooling and lecture without being most pleasantly impressed by the propriety and alertness of demeanour, and by the general absence of all sulkiness or sullenness of either countenance or manner, which distinguished the prisoners. I may here, perhaps, mention that, although I stood among them on these occasions with the full power of giving immediate pardon and freedom to any or all of them, and although occasionally anything particularly striking in the bearing or expressions of some among them might have tempted me to an exercise of partiality in their behalf, I never once allowed myself to interfere with any sentence except in the regular routine, upon the recommendation of the responsible authorities. I almost feel compunction at having proceeded so far without having made mention of the lecturer at the Smithfield and Lusk Reformatories, Mr. ORGAN. I am quite confident that he is one of that privileged number who will have left a mark on their age, not, perhaps, in the ordinary records of fame or precedence, but in the extent and amount of the quiet, unnoticed good he has accomplished, and the wholesome and healing influences he has wrought upon the dispositions and destinies of his fellow-creatures. Accustomed from his first youth to pursue the occupation of a teacher among the humblest and the poorest, he has now given his whole heart to the work of instructing and reclaiming the criminal; and, in addition to the higher qualifications of benevolence and zeal for such an office, he possesses, I believe I should say beyond any person I have ever met with, the faculty of interesting the attention and of making the subject clear to the most obtuse apprehensions. I am quite willing to believe that the system now adopted in Ireland rests upon principles so sound and so true to human experience as to make it in a great degree independent of individual qualities, provided that it be steadily upheld; but I think it would be singularly ungrateful not to admit that for its early and rapid success it was largely indebted to the capacity of Mr. ORGAN to make powerful impressions upon the minds, sometimes sluggish and sullen, sometimes quick and impulsive, with which he was brought into contact, as well as the wholly voluntary and disinterested tenacity with which he clung to the discharged prisoner in his subsequent career, diminishing its risks and shielding him from its temptations. With respect to the general conduct of the prisoners, it is pleasing to find this testimony given by the Superintendent of Smithfield, Mr. GOOD, who had been master of works in the same prison for ten years under the old system, and whom I know to be a very deserving public servant. He says: 'With reference to the conduct of the prisoners, it is gratifying to find that the best feeling exists among them; and, since the introduction of the license system, only five slight breaches of discipline occurred. Most remarkable is the contrast between the men now placed in this establishment and those who were confined here when this was an ordinary Convict Prison. Now they evince a kind, obliging disposition, and a docile spirit; they take advice in good part; they go to work with alacrity; are ready to volunteer their assistance wherever they think it may be required; they seem to have got a new spring of mind, and constantly talk over and ask advice with respect to their future prospects and destinations. Nearly three times the amount of work is obtained as heretofore from the same number of prisoners.' I have referred to the hold which Mr. ORGAN endeavours to establish upon the after career of discharged prisoners. The law provided a map of the county of Dublin, upon which are marked the various stations where they are employed, or

where there is a likelihood of employment being procured
for them. He visits these stations frequently, either for
the purpose of inquiring into the conduct and position of the
men, or of securing fresh employment. Of sixty discharged
prisoners now in the city of Dublin, not one has been out of
employment for more than a few days except from failure of
health. In many cases, as might have been anticipated, the
labour has been of a description not much sought after by
those whose previous lives entitle them justly to greater latitude of choice, such as vitriol-works and the like. This,
however, speaks volumes for those who prefer even such labour
to dishonesty and a recurrence of crime; it speaks surely
not a little for the system which has thus trained and reclaimed them. As a mark of the influence Mr. ORGAN has
been enabled to obtain over the men, even after the period
of confinement is over, he has generally induced them to place
£1 or £2 in the hands of their employers as a security, not
so much for their honesty, as for their regularity and continuance at work; and in case of the man having no earnings
or next to none to his credit, then to consent to a corresponding stoppage for a certain time from his wages. With the
men who are further removed, Mr. ORGAN endeavours to keep
up frequent correspondence. I may very briefly mention one
or two of their statements. One man tells him: 'I must let
you know that I am what you will like to hear, and that is
a non-commissioned officer. I am full corporal, and very soon
to be platoon-sergeant. I hope you will tell all the men in
Smithfield to do as Mr. ORGAN will tell them.' Another tells
him: 'I am earning from 14s. to 16s. a week.' Another
whom he mentions 'is also doing well, and turns out very
well dressed, and earns plenty of money in the coal-pit: he
is earning from 3s. 6d. to 4s. a day, and wishes you long
life and good health.' Another asks for some of his gratuity
money that he may get a kit. Another is going out to Corfu.
The parish priest writes of one: 'I am glad to be able to

make a favourable report of him. He is well-conducted and industrious, and has even purchased a boat, in which he works himself at present.' A housebreaker writes: 'Words cannot express the gratitude I felt when I received your kind letter with the favourable lines contained in it. I sincerely hope I shall never belie the character you were pleased to entertain of me. I have been working at hay this short time back.' The hay reminds me that I perceived on one occasion a discharged prisoner forming one of a gang of hay-makers on my own grounds in the Phœnix Park. He was pointed out to me by the contractor for the job, who gave a good account of him, but I distinctly saw, on my approaching him, that he did not wish for much conversation; he felt very anxious that his antecedents should not be known to his fellow - workmen, and for my own part I felt quite resigned, all Viceroy as I was at the moment, to be cut by a Convict. I will only cite one more comment which, among other things, shows that the supervision of the police is not necessarily considered irksome by the discharged prisoners themselves. This is from a man convicted of larceny, it being his seventh conviction: 'I am living with my father ever since, and I am going on very well. The constabulary are doing everything in their power for my welfare. Your lectures and advice are as fresh in my mind as when I sat there listening to your fatherly expressions, and I will always think of the advice you gave before we left you. No matter who returns you ingratitude after all your trouble, you will always find me grateful, because you acted a father to every one as well as to me. I conclude for the present, thanking God and you for my deliverance from bondage; and may the Almighty reward you and every benevolent man who in the course of time will be an aid in the work of mercy.' "

The next testimony is derived from an article on the "Irish Convict System," in the "Cornhill Magazine," April, 1861.

From this we are tempted to make copious extracts, they present so vivid a picture of the reality :—

"A few weeks since, I found myself, with two friends, traversing a newly-reclaimed common in an agricultural district some fifteen miles from Dublin. A very short time ago the place was all but uninhabited, the heath being in possession of a few squatters, on sufferance, who had been tempted to it by the immunity granted to their class, the absence of rent, and the quality of the soil. More recently, however, the ground had been required for a particular purpose: a body of men, under an energetic leader, were brought to subdue it with the plough, and the old occupants were dispossessed, not entirely without remonstrances or threats of resistance. But the dread authority of the law was against them; and their own leader, a bold and clever man, was disarmed by being appointed to a subordinate office. Under the newly-arrived improvers, the squatters disappeared from the scene, the undulating surface of the common was converted into cultivated fields, 'and laughing Ceres reassumed the plain.' The spot has not quite lost its desolate aspect; although there is a public road through it, and a few buildings are in sight, there is still a broad expanse so devoid of any marked feature that guide-posts are necessary to point the way of the wandering labourer who desires to return home. The work is advancing under the vigorous industry of some fifty men who are employed on the estate, and who may be seen on any working day of the week at their labours. And who are they that are thus, in our own time, colonizing the ancient soil of Ireland, and annexing it to the conquests of modern agriculture? They are Convicts under sentence of penal servitude. Yes, that band of fifty men, clothed in the ordinary garb of rustic labourers, peacefully obeying the orders of two foremen, clothed not very unlike themselves and working with them, are men whose crimes have subjected them to prison and to the discipline of a transient slavery. There are, indeed, no chains ; there are no military guards—not even gaolers—to restrain them ; no fences which they are not in the hourly habit of passing break the broad expanse of the common, with its widely-separated guide-posts pointing the way to the huts which are the prisons of these men. But there is something else far more potent.

" It was while I was engaged in surveying the system of discipline of which the colony at Lusk forms only a portion, that I learned the revolt in Chatham Prison. The details of that violent outbreak amongst the luxuriously-fed Chathamites, who were in open mutiny and refusing to work, were told me on the very day when I was surrounded by Convicts wholly without chains, and hard at work in cold and rain ; and with the Chatham reports fresh in my mind, I heard the civil officers of this open prison at Lusk telling me how the labourers under them, living as I shall show you, upon hard fare, are steady workmen, regular in their duty, and so zealous that, while they are actually purchasing bread as a luxury, they will pursue their toil after the regular hour, in order to help in securing the harvest. This is the result of a system which, with the erring man in the iron grip of the law, has subjected him to something stronger than manacles or lash, and yet, substituting a truly correctional for a merely penal handling, has made sweet the uses even of the bitterest adversity, the adversity of the criminal gaol.

" If we look abroad, beyond the horizon of that strange, unwalled prison, to the general effects of the two systems, English and Irish, we find the same contrast in the broadest results. For instance, in the session before last, a return was obtained by the House of Lords, which shows that of the Convicts out on ticket-of-leave in England nine-tenths relapse into crime, and are actually recommitted to prison for fresh offences ; while, of course, we cannot assume the merely unaccused tenth to be virtuous and pure. In Ireland, even including the criminals released under the old law, the men recommitted are *not* one-fifth of the whole number released, and with all the figures before me, I find great reason to doubt whether they amount to one-tenth.  The Chaplain of Millbank has calculated that considerably more than half—nearly two-thirds—of the men brought to that prison are 'habitual or professional thieves,' 'possessing,' he says, 'great intelligence, but affording little hope of amendment by means of prison discipline.'  A Convict of this class said to him, 'It's not likely I'll work for fifteen shillings a week, when I can get as many pounds.'  The remark of the Convict confirmed the opinion with which the founders of the English system started—that you cannot reform prisoners, but can only export them.  We shall see by and by how far the assumption is justified by facts.

"Statistical figures, however, never suffice to show us the true substance and nature of any two things compared; they do not indicate the actual distinction, they only meet it; and in order to appreciate the striking contrast afforded to the English system, let us see what the Irish system is.  A very brief recapitulation will bring us into the midst of it.  In 1837, Sir WILLIAM MOLESWORTH, the accomplished and patriotic pupil of EDWARD GIBBON WAKEFIELD, demanded that Select Committee on Transportation which reported in 1838, with such force that it became impossible for the Home Government to continue the practice, and, against the will of Australia, transportation was abandoned in 1840.  Attempts were made partially to continue the use of the Colonies as a receptacle for our refuse population; but the Cape of Good Hope actually rebelled against such an experiment; and by 1853 Western Australia was the one Colony willing to receive our Convicts, in small numbers.  The establishments of Bermuda and Gibraltar remain as State Prisons, to which a limited number of prisoners can be consigned.  But since 1853 it has been necessary to provide for the custody of our Convicts at home.  After a laborious investigation in 1850, a Select Committee of the House of Commons had stated the opinion, corroborated by facts and figures, that the majority of convicted criminals can be reformed. In 1855, Captain WALTER CROFTON, who had been appointed to inquire into the state of the Convict Prisons in Ireland, addressed to the Government a communication, citing that opinion, and particularly suggesting two conditions to any complete attempt at a redeeming discipline. The first was, intermediate prisons, in which the Convict could be subjected to trial before his discharge; the reformed, as it were, being filtered away from the unreformed; and the second condition was, such treatment of the whole class as would subject them to the principle of individualization, each man's case being separately handled with reference to his antecedents, his character, and his actual state of mind. Captain CROFTON was placed at the head of the gentlemen appointed as Directors of the Irish Convict Prisons, to carry out the system which he had indicated, and which I have so lately seen at work.

"The system can be best comprehended, as it is administered, upon the principle of individualizing. We will suppose that the criminal—let us call him JOHN CARROL—has already been 'living in crime,' has been before convicted and punished— imprisoned, say, three months for larceny, twelve months for robbery—and is now sentenced for robbery, not to the shortest term of penal servitude, three years, nor to the longest, fifteen, but to the medium term of seven years. Of that period, he must spend at least five years in prison before his release under ticket-of-license. On the 1st of January, 1858, he is admitted to the ordinary prison of Mountjoy, and is at once lodged in a separate cell. As soon as he has entered, it is distinctly explained to him that the period of his detention in that separate cell will depend upon his own conduct. If he is perfectly quiet and orderly, he will be completely isolated even from prison society only for eight months. Should he be less well behaved the period will be the full nine months. Should the criminal fever be upon him in a chronic form, stimulating him to indulge in the excitements of violence—in brawling, striving to communicate with his neighbours, or even in attacking the gaolers—he is soon made to feel how utterly powerless he is, not only by the walls that box him in, but by the reducing of his food to bread and water, and even by flogging.

"Usually, by the end of nine months, or very often in eight months, the Convict is sent to the next prison. If he is a labourer, he is sent to Spike Island, near Queenstown; if he is a mechanic, to the prison of Philipstown. In either case, he is placed in what is called the third class, and is employed upon some branch of useful industry. If he is wholly unacquainted with work he is set to some very simple form of handicraft, such as the making of buckle-straps, or other process equally easy. On his entrance into this class, however, he is again told that his condition while he is in it, and his ultimate promotion to a higher class, will depend exclusively upon his own conduct. No power of 'indulgence' is reposed in the officers of the prison; the system itself is humane, considerate, careful to secure the utmost amount of hope and improvement for the prisoner; and his best reliance consists in the most faithful and strict execution of the system. Any departure from it by the officers would be to embezzle for the benefit of an individual the moral fund available for the whole class. This is all explained to the man in language adapted to his state of education and intelligence; he is made to *feel* that he is himself the true regulator of his own condition in the class and of the period of his leaving it.

"As soon as he is admitted into the third class his conduct is marked down in an account kept for the purpose. The highest number of marks which he can attain during the month for 'discipline,' is three; he is put to school, and the highest number of marks which he can attain for 'school' is likewise three; his 'industry' is also marked with the highest number, three—nine in all; and should he keep up to the highest

standard, as he well may with common diligence and tract-
ability, he can secure his promotion at the end of two months,
having earned eighteen marks.   But he may have lived in
a false pride; he may be intoxicated with the vanity of vindictiveness; he may think it 'manly' to contemn the opportunity
offered to him, and so defy the authority of the officers; and he
may fail to earn his promotion from the third class to the second
in less than six months.   While he is in the third class he is
allowed one penny a week out of his earnings; but for misconduct, according to its degree, his marks may be taken from
him, his money allowance may be stopped, or he may even
be sent back to separate confinement, with the sterner punishments suited to that condition.

"From the third, the Convict, JOHN CARROL, passes into the
second class, where he is allowed twopence a week out of
his earnings; and here he may remain, according to his conduct and the character which he has acquired, as short a
time as six months, or as long a time as seven months, or
even longer.   In the first class, where he is allowed four-
pence a week, his stay may be twelve months, or fifteen;
and in the advanced class, where the allowance is ninepence, it
would in either case be twenty months.   The better conducted
prisoner has passed through the ordinary prison in four years
and three months; the worst conducted, in four years and
nine months.

"In the ordinary prison all these allowances go towards the
money which he is allowed to lay by as a fund on his discharge.   Each prisoner keeps his own account to check that
of the officers; and the men in all classes and of all characters are found to be extremely keen in watching the correctness
of the accounts kept against their name.   They haggle earnestly
over a single mark which is to be allowed or withheld; contest
the accuracy of the record, question the justice of the official
calculation, and, if their own judgment is not satisfied with
the decision of the officers over them, they appeal to the

Governor, or even, in certain cases, to the Chief Director of Convict Prisons. In the cell of a young man who had been confined for robbery, I was told that he had shown his understanding of the prison rules and of the opportunity which they afforded him, by almost unexceptionable good conduct, having misbehaved himself 'only once.'

" 'Not at all, sir!' he exclaimed, earnestly but respectfully, by way of correction to the official statement.

" ' You were reported,' said my informant to him.

" ' Yes, but I was not *punished ;* I was sent to Hospital.'

"The man had been charged, probably, with some neglect of duty, and proved that he was more sick than sinning. Thus, even in the ordinary prison, the men themselves become conscious and active coadjutors in carrying out the system under which they are disciplined, and we shall see, as we advance, how thoroughly they become imbued with its spirit. In proportion as it is rigorously administered it has been found possible to dispense with some of the merely mechanical restraints. In the chapel, for instance, it was in the old time thought necessary to divide the prisoners by partitions; a plan which facilitated various tricks and irreverent idlings during divine service. The partitions have been removed. The place of worship is in itself a room simple enough, but not devoid of a certain tastefulness in its arrangements. The sanctity of the occasion and the collective example operate in a wholesome, though undoubtedly in a cheerful, manner, upon every individual who attends ; and thus by degrees the prisoner is removed from mere separate detention within the four narrow walls that form a kind of live tomb, to live and breathe in the company of his fellow-creatures; he does this with a newly acquired sense of moral necessity, and with the evidences on every side that others as well as himself appreciate the promotion and comfort derivable from good conduct.

" Every circumstance by which he is surrounded, contributes to enlarge and strengthen this influence. As he makes his progress, while yet within the walls of the ordinary prison, the stamp on his own sleeve indicating his class and the number of marks he has earned, and the numbers on the badge of those with whom he is daily associated, are a memento that he has made only so much progress, but still so much. He knows that his opportunities are widening as he goes. He is aware that as he attains promotion the fund lodged to his account is growing in a higher ratio, and will grow yet more largely and rapidly. At every step in his advance it is explained to him that he is gradually marching towards the comparative unrestraint of the Intermediate Prison, whose increased comfort and freedom he is able to appreciate from the progressive experience which he has already had in the ordinary prison. Even the countenances of the companions around him will speak in the same eloquent spirit.

" For there is no greater evidence of the change worked in the race by this hard, matter-of-fact discipline, than the altered expression of the general physiognomy. As soon as the man enters the first prison, the most unmistakeable record of his identity is at once registered in the prison books in the shape of a photographic portrait. ' No, no !' exclaimed an eminent thief, when he was placed before the machine, stretching forth his hands so as to hide his face—' No, no ; you are taking away my bread !' The man was actuated by a prudential regard for his professional interests, when he should once more be released from gaol. As it turned out, however, that very man obtained better employment than thieving, and he need have been under no fear to leave his likeness with the prison authorities. Yet, on proper occasion, the use he apprehended is made of these photographic portraits. If a Convict or ticket-of-leave should go out of bounds, or if a man previously convicted should be arrested, his portrait can be sent to the place where he is captured, and he can be identified. There is, however, a still broader interest in this strange portrait gallery of murderers housebreakers, thieves, and malefactors in general. You see, upon the face of the class, every variety of depraved expression. Some few are scowling villains, fit to tread the most melo-dramatic stage; some cunning enough to satisfy the precon-ceptions of the most self-satisfied scientific physiognomist; not a few, simple-minded, but somewhat blank in aspect, as though they were entirely swayed by the circumstances of the moment. Not a few, also, wear the gay triumphant expression of extreme vanity, as if they would rather be eminent as thieves than not be noticed at all, and were delighted to stand for their portraits, even though it were to the prison photographer. But the largest number of all have a very peculiar expression. If you will allow the eyelids and lips to drop as they will with weari-ness and indifference—if you will let the chest collapse, and the shoulders round themselves with the same listless lack of stamina—and if, while the head is thrown forward, you will slightly lift the face, giving an additional drag as it were to the cheeks, the eyelids, and the lips, you will bring over your countenance exactly the same arrangement which is the common veil assumed by the majority of malefactors pictured in this strange gallery. It is cunning, covered by an affectation of *insouciance*. Your thief *comme il faut* finds it most *distingué*, as well as most diplomatic, to conceal his true qualities under a show of being *blasé*; and his face indicates—all partly put on, but still more natural than he thinks—a want of interest, a want of feeling, and a want of understanding. You see these truly 'low' expressions in almost all the earliest classes of the ordinary prisoners; but as you advance in the series, the expression improves, the scowl is rapidly displaced. The old villain, at his school-books, acquires almost the ingenuous expression of childhood. The half-idiotical simper of vanity is sobered. The melancholy *blasé* affectation passes off, and the general countenance becomes at once more simple, more steady, and more cheerful; until, in the upper classes, you

may find many countenances even above the average out of
doors, in placid self-possession, awakened intelligence, and
amiable content.

"In the first prison the Convict has acquired habits of
industry, either in the prosecution of his own trade, or in
some simple occupation afforded to him.  He has gone through
a certain amount of schooling, tested under able teachers by
periodical examinations, which serve to call forth his own
faculties, and the consciousness of them.  He is associated
with his fellows, under discipline, in the workroom, the school-
room, in the class, and in the chapel; and he has thus been
gradually accustomed to regularity of life, and to a regulated
state of thought.  He has been made to feel how completely
his condition and prospects depend upon his own conduct; and
at every stage, if he has encountered any difficulties of comprehension, they have been cleared away for him by the
explanations of the prison authorities.  But thus far he has
felt under coercion.  The force at first brought to bear upon
him was, in its character, purely penal.  In the earlier stages,
after his release from constant confinement in a separate cell,
the penal element has been largely commingled with tuition and
industry; and, throughout, there has been ceaseless restraint
and coercion; the latter, perhaps, of a moral kind, but not the
less distinctly exercised.  According to the old system, even
of improved prisons, the Convict was thrown upon society fresh
from these coercions and restraints, without character; he
confronted something worse than suspicion—often hopeless
repulsion; the newly-restored liberty was accompanied by
fearful temptations to relapse into crime, the promptings that
way being almost justified by common sense, through the utter
despair of finding honest employment.  Was it not possible
to meet these difficulties—to soften the transition from perfect
restraint to perfect freedom—to show that the prisoner could
continue his better habits even with diminished compulsion,
and thus to provide him with 'a character from his last place,'

though that place should actually be a prison? Captain
WALTER CROFTON saw that these questions could be answered
in the affirmative. In a communication to the Government,
written in November, 1855, he again challenged attention to
the opinion expressed by the Committee of the House of
Commons, that 'the generality of criminals' are 'reformable.'
Already the reformatory element had been mingled with the
penal, but Captain CROFTON proposed to test the efficacy of
the reform, by arrangements which should at once supply the
prisoner with employment, and guarantee his character in prison
as 'exemplary.' The thing wanted was a probationary stage,
to act as a filter in distinguishing the reformed from the unreformed. It was calculated that while this trial stage would
exercise upon the probationer a most direct and important influence of its own, it would show the employer outside that the
quondam criminal had really habits of industry and self-control.
And Captain CROFTON pointed out the influence which such
a system must exercise over the criminal population generally.
These suggestions were at once adopted by the Government
for Ireland in 1855."

We pass over the description given by this writer of the
Intermediate Prisons, and his account of the official arrangements, and the working of the system, as similar information
will be given in the next chapter; we must not, however,
omit some anecdotes, which are valuable as illustrations of
the working of the system, nor a statement of the writer's
own personal observation.

"The occupant of the Intermediate Prison is engaged in
useful labour; the product of his industry has a value of which
some portion goes towards the expenses of the establishment;
and he is thus really repaying a debt to the community. But
some portion is also granted to him as a gratuity, of which
again a fraction is allowed for immediate expenditure. The
utmost amount which he can earn in a week is 2s. 6d. If he
be slack in his industry, of which there are few examples,

or maladroit, he may be unable to earn so much. The greater portion of this remains in charge of the authorities. Sometimes it has been spent on articles absolutely necessary for the prisoner's use; at other times it has been used as an instruction fee to tradesmen; very frequently it has been employed in paying for the passage of the discharged Convict to another country, either where he already had connections, or where he saw an opportunity for employing himself at a distance from the scene of his former troubles. Of his earnings he is allowed sixpence a week to spend, within certain limits, as he likes. He must not, for instance, use it to buy intoxicating drinks; but he may spend it in books, clothing, food, and some other articles.

"I think I noticed a variety in the neck-kerchiefs, which I ascribed to that source; and it is evident that a healthy pleasure would be taken in the variety for the variety's sake, since it contributed to mark the distinction between the homely garb and the old prison uniform. To the library the men contribute a halfpenny a week. The payment is optional, but there is not a single instance of refusal. Nay, on obtaining their discharge, *Convicts not unfrequently leave one shilling, two shillings, or half-a-crown for the library, as a mark of respect to that institution, and of goodwill towards the companions they leave behind. Sometimes, indeed, the departing Convict will leave a contribution, even as much as ten shillings, towards the fund of some fellow-workman, with whom he has formed a friendship.* These little acts, which must be purely spontaneous, go far to indicate the spirit that has been awakened in the tribe.

"I have already mentioned one thing in which the residents of the Intermediate Prison not unfrequently spend a part of their sixpence a week—bread. The fact is quite sufficient to show that the dietary is not excessive, either in quantity or quality; yet the men at Lusk do not grumble, they do not revolt to extort a more luxurious fare, they do not refuse to work. On the contrary, if an extraordinary amount of work is needed—as, for instance, to complete a piece of drainage promptly, or to save the harvest—they throw themselves into the labour with zeal. On such occasions they take evident pleasure in promoting the interests of the establishment, and in evincing their zealous fidelity towards the head of their department; and it is at times like these that they are observed to spend a portion of their little weekly *honorarium* in bread!

"Once a week the inmates of the Intermediate Prison are allowed to send one of their own class out of bounds to purchase the articles on which the sixpence a week is to be spent. In all the time since the beginning of the plan, there have been but three cases of default. In one instance the man so employed was a person of weak mind, who ought, perhaps, not to have been selected; in the other two instances the defaulters had met with old friends, and had been tempted 'just to have a drink.' But in each of these three cases the man was found waiting outside the gates of the Intermediate Prison, looking very foolish. He had been tempted, he had yielded; but he retained his conscience, his hope in the system, and his preference of it over the wild chances and the remorse of flight.

"Another little incident related to me strikingly illustrates this manly and healthy spirit, and especially shows the insight which the men acquire into the laws that so inevitably govern their conduct. When the Chief Director of Convict Prisons was visiting an Intermediate establishment, one of the men approached him, and respectfully challenged inquiry into his request that he might be liberated a fortnight sooner than the period set down for him. He said that his time *would* have expired a fortnight sooner if a certain mark had not been withheld from him in the former prison. I have already said that the men keep their own accounts as a check upon the officers, and that any difference of statement is promptly adjudicated. The petitioner for an earlier release was reminded of this fact, and he admitted that the mark had been withdrawn in strict conformity with rules; but, he said, the offence for which the penalty was enforced was a mere trifle, and 'every-thing depended on his getting out a fortnight sooner.' What 'everything' meant he did not state; but probably it was that he had an opportunity of going abroad with a friend, or of otherwise establishing himself hopefully out of prison. The Chief Director promised to inquire into the case. He did so, and summoned the man before him again. It turned out to be true that the penalty had been inflicted for something that was in itself a trifling nature; but it was a breach of the rules, and when he broke those rules the Convict knew what he was doing. Still he urged it was only a trifle, and that fortnight was 'everything' to him. He was asked to suppose the very common case of a Convict whose behaviour had been absolutely unimpeachable, and to say how such a man, asking to be released a fortnight sooner, as a matter of mere favour, could be refused, if another who had broken the rules, however trivially, could claim the indulgence? The man paused for a moment, and then answered: 'No, sir, I see it would not work.' And he walked away with the air of a man who was satisfied in his own judgment. * * *

"I made a tour of Dublin, à la HAROUN ALRASCHID, for the express purpose of seeing the discharged Convicts actually busy at their daily work. I found them in a great variety of occupa-tions. Some were busy in the most public thoroughfares of Dublin, as labourers. They recognised my companions at a glance, but no notice was taken of them openly, and they went on working without any stop or recognition. There was nothing to distinguish them from the ordinary labourer, except, un-doubtedly, in most instances, a more thoughtful aspect, and a countenance that might be described as more awakened. Other workmen we found busy as labourers in some of the less finished parts of Dublin; and at certain spots they were stationed in no inconsiderable numbers. Others were working within doors, at the manufactory of a busy tradesman, in one of the busiest streets of Dublin—a highway not unlike Newgate Street or

Bishopsgate Street—the tradesman dealing in an article of very general consumption. Others were in a sort of manufactory, homely in appearance, but on an extensive scale, and situated in one of the lowest neighbourhoods of old Dublin. In all the report was the same : the discharged Convicts prove to be steady labourers and good workmen; their employers were quite satisfied, and were ready to employ similar labour again. This evidence was general; its character will come out more distinctly in a few particular instances.

"In one of the humbler streets, an industrious woman has opened a small shop, and her business is prospering. With tears in her eyes, she bore testimony to the regular conduct of her husband, and to the peaceful state of her home : that husband was a discharged Convict, who had been an habitual thief; and, as a drunkard, he had gone to such extremes, that he still bore signs of the delirium tremens with which he was threatened. He now earns twelve shillings a week as a builder's labourer, and assists his wife in paying for their child whom they have put to school.

"Among the very first persons who ventured upon employing a man with a prison character, is an extensive builder. Some of the men whom he thus consented to take have formerly borne the worst of characters. Their conduct with him, however, had been in every respect satisfactory. He has at present four in his employment; one joined his works in 1856, and that man's wages have risen from ten shillings a week to twenty-four shillings; the others have been in the place for about two years.

"The tradesman in the street which I have likened to Newgate Street has in his employment four men, and he made his report on their conduct with the utmost directness and unreserve. He had no complaint to make; in some respects the labourers obtained through Mr. ORGAN are more tractable than the ordinary class of Dublin workmen—less inclined to cavil, less ready to take advantage of their employer in periods

of pressure, more eager to persevere in winning his approval.
One of the men who had been with this gentleman had led a
life of crime for many years; another had been known to the
Dublin police for the last ten years, and, though still young,
had been convicted seven times. These men are surrounded
by property, which malice or negligence might injure, to the
amount of even a hundred pounds. Two of them, including
the man who was convicted seven times, are entrusted with
the collection of bills to the amount of forty or fifty pounds
at a time, and there is not a single instance of inaccuracy.
It is to be remarked that, in this instance as well as in others,
the employer had had several men in his service at different
times, so that he spoke from a varied and lengthened experience.

"The owner of the other manufactory, which I might liken
to a leather-dresser's in the midst of St. Giles's, is himself a
very intelligent man, business-like, and straightforward. His
transactions are extensive, and he evidently has a keen eye
to the main chance. Yet he naturally and properly expressed
strong satisfaction at the consciousness that, while serving
his own interests, he was engaged in a work really beneficial. One of the men employed at this place had been for
nine years 'in crime' before conviction. He has been four
years in his present place, and every day of these four years
he has been steadily earning a good character. The case of
the other man has been still more remarkable. He may be
said to have had extensive connexions in the criminal professions, and he was himself distinguished in his calling as a
desperate burglar. With a fine figure, a manly aspect, and an
agreeable countenance, he has about him much that is considered to distinguish the gentleman. He had for some time
been a 'flash man,' and his ambition as a Don Juan in that
sphere had been gratified by the most remarkable 'success.' A
policeman said of this eminent burglar, that he 'should know
his chisel in any window in Dublin.' The hero was so active and
reckless that it was impossible to capture him, even with the

powerful force brought to bear against him, until two of his ribs had been fractured. Another policeman, a devoted servant of the Irish system, with full confidence in its efficacy, declared that the case of this man, so hardened in crime and so reckless, must be regarded as an exception, in which the ticket-of-license would be inapplicable and unsafe. The fact is, that the man had employed certain qualities which are not bad in themselves, amid adverse circumstances, and probably from childhood, under the influence of a perverse ambition. The thorough discipline of the Intermediate Prison, however, had bent these faculties back into the right direction, and had drawn forth his better faculties. When allusion was made, in his presence, to a brother who had also been convicted, he instantly defended the other's character; remarked that that other had been convicted for the only time in which he had gone astray, and that since his discharge the brother's character had stood higher than his own. In some sense this is true: there was no evidence against the brother except with regard to the offence for which he was convicted; and under his ticket-of-license he got on so well that he is now engaged in trade as an employer, with a rising business. But the man with whom I conversed had also behaved unexceptionably during the three years and more in which he has been with his present employer; so much so that his position has been steadily improved, and he is now selected to sleep in his employer's house. Here he is surrounded by property ready for the market, and quite portable; he is also placed in the midst of a neighbourhood thickly inhabited by men of the very worst character, who would but too gladly take part in any burglary. Yet this accomplished burglar, this man whom the policeman assumed to be incorrigible, whose chisel was known in any window of Dublin, sleeps on the inside of the window, and is trusted by the master without a moment's uneasiness.

"As the counterpart and addition to these cases of men employed, I may give specimens of the applications made by employers. At first, of course, the initiative was taken by the earnest and energetic officers of the system, who were glad to discover men in trade with sufficient understanding and trustfulness to accept the services of the Convicts; but even in this short time the employers have learned to take the initiative. Sometimes they make their application by simply walking up to Smithfield, and asking for the men they want; sometimes they make their application by letter to Mr. ORGAN, asking for workpeople in simple, business-like terms, such as they would use to any well-known agent. I have such letters before me. One writer, a prosperous tradesman, who is altering his house, says, 'Could you send me a decent bricklayer, to build up a wall and do a few other jobs.' Another, a manufacturer, says, 'I can now make room for two of your men, provided they are sober and well able to work. Wages, 10s. a week.' A third, in a large way of business, can employ two or three 'able and willing men.' And so on.

"I have already mentioned the report by the chaplain of Millbank, who says that the larger half of the men at his prison are habitual and professional thieves, and that he has little hope of their amendment; quoting the remark of a Convict: 'It's not likely I'll work for fifteen shillings a week when I can get as many pounds.' Many a Dublin Convict, formerly 'an habitual and professional thief,' could tell this Englishman — and there are some Englishmen in the Irish prisons—that, although he might get fifteen pounds in a lucky week, he cannot possibly pursue that game for any time in Ireland. And the accomplished burglar to whom I have just now referred, could tell the Millbank chaplain that the most ardent and successful in the profession of thieving can be redeemed when proper influences are brought to bear upon them."

In August, 1861, the Social Science Association met at Dublin, and many references to what took place will be found in the volume of the transactions of that year. The

author may be here permitted to give her own personal
observations, as made at the time in three successive papers
in "Once a Week."

"The meeting of the Social Science Association at Dublin,
in August last, afforded to many an opportunity of seeing
and examining for themselves what has lately engaged considerable public attention — the Irish Convict System — as
developed and carried on by the Board of Directors, of
which Captain WALTER CROFTON is the Chairman.

"Even those who have not been called on to pay any special
attention to the management of Convicts, and to the principle
and plan of Convict Prisons, must be aware that some very
radical and important difference must exist between the Irish
and the English Convict Prisons. On our side of the channel it
would require a very great stretch of philanthropy even to
make the trial of taking men into emyloyment, who were
known to be just discharged from Portland or other Convict
Prisons; — those who have come under our knowledge have
been complete failures; — the newspaper police reports continually record offences committed by prisoners discharged
under license or ticket-of-leave; and we know that some of
the most atrocious crimes have been perpetrated by those who
*ought* to have been reformed characters, if long years of training and instruction in Government Prisons could make them
so. The English public does not believe in the reformation of
prisoners by the system adopted in this country.

"The contrary is the case on the other side of the channel.
There is a belief in Ireland that the system adopted in the
Convict Prisons *does* reform those who are the subjects of it;
and the consequence of this belief is, that masters are ready
to receive discharged prisoners into their employment; those
who at first, doubtingly, tried some, now confidently apply

for more. The knowledge that trustworthy, hard-working men are to be obtained by application at the prison for those whose time is completed, is becoming so general, that the grand problem is solved—' What are we to do with our Convicts?' The bulk of them are absorbed into the population as honest labourers, and those whose home connexions make it undesirable for them to remain in their own country, emigrate to others, well prepared to become useful and respectable members of society elsewhere.

"What is the real secret of this marvellous difference?

"And why is it that, while elsewhere we hear of increase of crime, and of reconvictions of those who have already put the country to great expense by years of public maintenance in prison, in Ireland the number of Convicts has actually diminished from 4278, on January 1, 1854, to 1631, on January 1, 1860.

"We desired, then, to avail ourselves of this visit to Dublin to satisfy ourselves fully on these points, and to verify, by personal observation, what we had heard of the Irish Convict System.

"The Reformatory Section of the Association had received an admirable and lucid statement of the system and its results, from a paper on the subject, read by Captain CROFTON himself, which was listened to with the deepest interest, not only by an attentive audience, but by the venerable President, Lord BROUGHAM, who strongly expressed his approbation of it. But we desired also an impartial statement of the whole system, and this was given by the Attorney - General for Ireland in his presidential address. After briefly reviewing the history of Reformatory Schools for juveniles, which are now established in Ireland as in England, he referred to the touching story of the ' Vicar of Wakefield,' in which, a hundred years ago, OLIVER GOLDSMITH developed the true principles which should combine punishment and reformation. ' Throughout the whole prison life of the Convict' (in Ireland), he

continues, 'these guiding principles regulate his treatment.
He enters Mountjoy Prison, and he has there to undergo
the hard discipline of cellular incarceration. He works alone,
not often visited by any one, and with ample opportunity for
meditation and repentance during his nine months of that
probationary state. But he is allowed to have hope of the
future, — a hope to be realised by himself. The shortening
of this period of his separation depends on his good conduct,
and he knows that when it shall have ended he will have
still further opportunity of improving his condition by his
own endeavours. This expectation produces its natural result
in his quiet and orderly demeanour, and his obedience to
authority; in most instances the period of his cellular confinement is accordingly abridged. Then he passes to Spike
Island, or Philipstown, where he labours in association with
others, under the strictest surveillance; there continued good
behaviour enables him to rise from class to class, gaining
all the while something for himself from the fruits of his
toil, until he becomes fit for an Intermediate Prison, where he
has more of freedom and a larger share of his own earnings,
and where the same stimulating and sustaining influence of
hope still operates upon him. By his own efforts he can
lay up a little store for the day of liberation, and by his
own efforts he can hasten the coming of that happy day. If
he will so act as to obtain good marks it is hastened; if he
fails to obtain them it is postponed. Then, during the period
of his detention in the Intermediate Prison, he has, in a
higher degree, the benefit of intellectual and moral culture
which has been offered to him continually, with the higher
blessing of the religious care of a zealous and instructed
chaplain, from the commencement of his incarceration. A lecturer, a gentleman very competent and very devoted to his
duty, addresses to him plain speeches on subjects calculated
to arouse his interest and awaken his faculties. * * * In
very many cases, as part of his penal probation, he is em-

ployed at large in this city and its neighbourhood on such service as the Convict Directors deem suitable for him, or at Lusk, where you will find him discharging the ordinary duties of an agricultural labourer, without enclosure or confinement of any kind; and it is found that he can be so trusted safely, and that neither the city messenger nor the Lusk workman ever dreams of escaping from a control which has no apparatus of bolts and bars to make it effectual. And so the man passes from the prison to his place in society—not his old place, but a higher and better place. He does not make the passage abruptly or without reasonable preparation. Generally he is liberated as the recompense of meritorious conduct before the expiration of his sentence; and the liberation is conditional, subject to be ended if he falls again. And for a time he is under the eye of authority, and finds confirmation of his good purposes in the checks which its supervision puts upon him, and the apprehension of the evil consequences of a return to crime. But, more than this, the continuing guardianship is not at all strongly repressive. To the liberated Convict it is a protection against the influence of those who would turn him back to wickedness, and it gives him a shield against many mischiefs and many misconceptions, which would be entailed by his tainted character, if he had not the opportunity of appeal to the officers of justice, as to his changed life and renewed trustworthiness.'

"Such is a brief sketch, by so high an authority as the Attorney-General, of the system, the working of which we were anxious, personally, to inspect.

"Our first visit was to Lusk Common, one of the Intermediate Prisons, the last stage which the Convict undergoes before receiving liberty. A large party assembled, among them many magistrates, and other influential persons from various parts of England, and an hour's ride brought us from Dublin to Lusk. Had we been merely strangers on a pleasure excursion, we should probably have passed by without especial notice what is,

morally considered, one of the most wonderful spots in the
island. There was nothing to attract any attention. Before
us was a large common, part of which had been reclaimed,
and gave evidence of much skilled labour having been bestowed
on it. Other parts were perfectly wild, and we saw a number
of men working very steadily at the drainage of it. No one
would have noticed that they were not ordinary labourers;
they wore no prison uniform, but the ordinary peasant dress;
they appeared under the control of no gaol official, and no
turnkey was watching them; they were not handling the
pickaxe and spade with the unwilling air of men who were
under compulsion to perform a certain amount of Government
work, but like free labourers who would gladly do as hard
a day's work as they could. It seemed incredible that those
men were prisoners, and even more, men convicted of no
ordinary offences, but who were under long sentences of penal
servitude; such men as those who had burst forth into violent
rebellion at Portland, and who had been, more recently, at
Chatham, controlled only by extraordinary severity, after the
most ferocious outbreaks and outrageous attacks on the officers.
Looking at these men, we could hardly, as an English magistrate remarked, believe what we saw with our own eyes. We
might have waited to converse with some of the prisoners, for
so they really were, and we were quite at liberty to do so,
but delicacy restrained us. Indeed, once observing a group
assembled round one young man, we approached to listen, but
we saw that he was hanging down his head with evident shame,
and found that some one was most injudiciously questioning
him respecting his former life, and his feelings while engaged
in a career of crime;—so we passed on, and gave a courteous
greeting to another, who responded with a manly, respectful air,
not as one who had for ever lost his position in life. The
directors, Captain CROFTON and Captain WHITTY, pointed out
and explained the few and simple buildings. The only dwellings
provided for from fifty to one hundred Convicts, consisted of two

large huts of corrugated iron, each of which would contain accommodation for fifty men and one officer, the beds being so arranged that they could be put out of the way, and the room converted into a dining and sitting room. There were a few simple tenements for the residence of the Superintendent, and for the cooking and bathing of the men; but everything was as informal, plain, and inexpensive as possible. Captain CROFTON pointed out some small houses on the outskirts of the common. Those, he told us, after withdrawing us from the hearing of the men, had been intended for policemen, as it had been considered quite unsafe for a body of criminals to be left with no police near. The houses had never been used; there had never been occasion for any police agency. One Superintendent only has charge of each hut. The few labourers employed with the men at work live in separate houses near.

"After inspecting all parts of the premises, and satisfying ourselves that everything was as open and free as a common farm, and that the men were controlled only by the strong moral influence, which, combined with strict discipline and steady adherence to well-devised laws, constitutes the essence of the system, we felt desirous of learning how far these men were, or rather had been, the same daring criminals who fill our Government prisons in England. Various questions on this subject were put to Captain CROFTON by the gentlemen present, who showed us a table of the offences which had been committed by the very men among whom we had been walking without fear or suspicion. We were astounded to find that they had been guilty of almost every conceivable offence. There were highway robbers, burglars, &c.; murderers only are not admitted here, but must finish their term of imprisonment under the closer confinement of the prisons. We were particularly anxious to ascertain the previous characters of the prisoners, having heard it asserted that the inmates of the Irish Convict Prisons were of a lower grade of crime than those in the sister country. This is not the case, and the following table which he presented to us is a satisfactory proof of this.

SMITHFIELD AND LUSK INTERMEDIATE PRISONS.

Summary of Convictions of Prisoners now in Custody, Aug. 22, 1861.

| Smithfield. | | Lusk. | |
|---|---|---|---|
| 1st Conviction ... ... ... ... | 12 | 1st Conviction ... ... ... ... | 12 |
| 2nd ditto ... ... ... ... | 10 | 2nd ditto ... ... ... ... | 19 |
| 3rd ditto ... ... ... ... | 12 | 3rd ditto ... ... ... ... | 12 |
| 4th ditto ... ... ... ... | 5 | 4th ditto ... ... ... ... | 4 |
| 5th ditto ... ... ... ... | 2 | 5th ditto ... ... ... ... | 7 |
| 6th ditto ... ... ... ... | 1 | 6th ditto ... ... ... ... | 1 |
| 8th ditto ... ... ... ... | 2 | 7th ditto ... ... ... ... | 1 |
| 9th ditto ... ... ... ... | 1 | 8th ditto ... ... ... ... | 2 |
| 10th ditto ... ... ... ... | 2 | 9th ditto ... ... ... ... | 2 |
| 11th ditto ... ... ... ... | 1 | 10th ditto ... ... ... ... | 1 |
| 14th ditto ... ... ... ... | 2 | 12th ditto ... ... ... ... | 2 |
| 15th ditto ... ... ... ... | 1 | 14th ditto ... ... ... ... | 1 |
| 41st ditto ... ... ... ... | 1 | 17th ditto ... ... ... ... | 1 |
| 45th ditto ... ... ... ... | 1 | | |
| Total ... ... ... | 53 | Total ... ... ... | 65 |

Therefore 94 out of the 118 are known " old offenders," some of the remainder being known to the police as bad characters, although not known to have been before convicted in the same county.

"It is said, also, that the English are more unmanageable than the Irish. Our own experience of the criminals of both nations would be directly the reverse of this. There are, besides, many English in the Irish Convict Prisons, and many Irish Convicts in the English Prisons, but their peculiar nationality does not render any different treatment necessary. The objection is futile. The principles and the system which have happily been the means of bringing these outcasts of society into the orderly, respectful, self-controlled men whom we saw, are founded on universal conditions of human nature, and if proved true in one place may be readily adapted to another, by men who, like Captain CROFTON, comprehend them, and possess the personal qualities which are requisite to carry them out. What those qualities are, and what are the pecu-

liarities of the plans, we more fully ascertained on our visits
to the other prisons, which form part of the whole system.
On this occasion we were anxious to learn the actual truth,
and of that we were fully satisfied. The testimony of the
labour-master was no more than we were prepared to expect.

" ' I have been engaged on various public works,' he said,
' for thirty years, yet never before have I had under me a set of
men so well-conducted, so free from bad language, so attentive
to their duty.'

" Dec. 7, 1861."

### No. II.

"Our next visit was to the Intermediate Prison for those Convicts
who had learned trades, the last stage before being discharged,
either on ticket-of-leave, or on completion of sentence. Though
the principles and object of this establishment are exactly the
same as those on which Lusk is founded, yet the development of
these is necessarily modified, to meet the change of circumstances.
Lusk is at a distance from Dublin, and the grand difficulties to
be contended with there are the natural tendency to abscond,
and the danger of association with each other under comparatively little surveillance; here there is an additional peril from
the prisoners being at comparative freedom in the very midst of
the city which had probably been the scene of their crimes, and
which is filled with every allurement to vice. These added
difficulties have been sucessfully surmounted.

" Smithfield is an old prison of the ordinary kind, which,
being at liberty, has been adapted to its present purpose, while
still retaining the cellular arrangement for sleeping. With this
exception there is scarcely anything to remind one of a prison.
The workshops, the large simple dining-room, used also for
evening lectures and other instruction; the cheerful open yard
for exercise, enlivened by small garden plots—all would give one
rather the idea of a model lodging-house with associated workshops, than anything of a penal character. The men were at

dinner when we arrived, and we requested permission to see them at their meal. As we approached the dining-room, we heard the sound of cheerful orderly conversation ; and, on entering, found to our surpise, that there was no superintendent present, but that the prisoners were conducting themselves with as much propriety as ordinary workmen. They have not even separate rations weighed out to them, but the whole fixed quantity of food being placed on the table, they help themselves with due regard to each other's rights. Those who know what care is usually necessary in prisons, workhouses, and even schools, to give to each inmate the exact portion of food appointed, in order to prevent dissatisfaction, will appreciate the admirable tone of feeling which the possibility of such latitude indicates. The men appeared somewhat embarrassed by our presence, and perplexed at what could be the motive of such a visit; we therefore requested to see their library, and one of their number, the librarian, showed us with much pleasure a good collection of useful and interesting books, to which they have free access, purchased partly by the contributions of the prisoners themselves.

"It was Sunday; and after a little friendly intercourse among themselves in the court, the Catholics and Protestants separated into different rooms, where their respective chaplains gave them an afternoon's religious lecture. We meanwhile gained much information from the Superintendent respecting the system adopted : he objects to being designated Governor, desiring that the prison tone should be as much lost sight of as possible. Captain CROFTON was not with us on this occasion, which was on the whole better, as we saw everything in its ordinary condition, without the controlling influence of his presence. Yet his absence only made us more completely perceive how much his spirit pervades the whole. The Superintendent seemed thoroughly imbued with the Captain's principles of management, and spoke in warm terms of their effect on the men. Though all regulations are very strictly carried out, yet, as the prisoners feel that everything is ordered with a regard to their real welfare, and administered with perfect justice, they work with their superiors, instead of against them, as is so commonly the case in prisons; their wills are enlisted, and there is very seldom any cause of complaint. On several occasions some of the men have been employed at work at the prisons in the city at some distance : no difficulty has ever been experienced in marching them to and fro through the crowded city, with a single officer. Some of the men who are the nearest to their final discharge are even permitted to go alone into the city, to carry messages, or to execute commissions. The prisoners are allowed, if they choose, to spend sixpence a week of their earnings in any innocent indulgence ; they entrust with the purchase these privileged messengers, who have never been known to be unfaithful to their trust. A man who had been thus sent out on the preceding day was summoned, and gave us an account of three several expeditions of the kind. The time is of course exactly noted when they go out and return, and the messenger knows that any neglect of duty would be certainly discovered, and would entail on him serious consequences. Still the moral control appeared to us astonishing, which should be more powerful than bolts and bars on one so low and degraded as a Convict! They *had been* Convicts,—they were treated as *men ;* they had been made to feel that they were men not for ever degraded, but who might resume their place in society, or even take one, if they had never yet been regarded as other than outcasts. They comprehended the position in which they were here placed, as men who might be trusted ; and they proved themselves worthy of it.

" The lecture ended, we were invited to be present at a 'competitive examination,' which usually takes place on Saturday evening, but which had been deferred for our benefit. Mr. ORGAN, the lecturer to the prison, gives the men evening lectures on subjects calculated to communicate such knowledge as may be advantageous to them in their future life, besides storing their minds with useful information, and drawing them off

from improper subjects of thought.  He is much more than a
lecturer; he is a friend in the highest and best sense, to those
who, perhaps, never before had a friend worthy of the name;
he sympathises with their difficulties and trials; and when they
are about again to enter into the world, he arranges for their
emigration if they wish to leave the country; does not fear to
advance them for the purpose, from his private purse, the money
which will be afterwards paid to them for their earnings, and
in every way in his power promotes their true interests, and
literally gives himself, his time, his strength, his heart, to the
objects of his anxious care.  In doing so he has had the warm
sympathy, not only of Captain CROFTON and the other prison
directors, but of the Lord-Lieutenant, Lord CARLISLE, who has
even honoured with his presence some of these evening lectures,
and has bestowed on him in his difficult and trying work that
friendly encouragement which is more precious and supporting
than any other human help.  The subjects of the lectures during
the preceding week were as follows:—

SMITHFIELD INTERMEDIATE PRISON.

Lectures for Week commencing Monday, 12th August, 1861.
Monday.—The Sun.  What it Is, and What it Does.
Tuesday.—Labour.  Its Dignity and Rewards.
Wednesday.—Emigration.  Its Advantages and Disadvantages.
Thursday.—Crime.  Its Profit and Loss.
Friday.—Irish Intermediate Prisons.  Their Rise, Progress, and Results.
Saturday.—Competitive Examination.

"Mr. ORGAN gave the men on the present occasion one of
his forcible familiar addresses, and their countenances clearly
indicated how completely he touched their experiences.  We
had now a good opportunity of studying the characters before
us.  Some were grey-headed men, evidently ignorant and stupid,
if not hardened in crime; some quite young, perhaps only
eighteen; the countenances of some were not unpleasant, and
had evidently been greatly softened and refined by the discipline
they had undergone, while the bulk of them were certainly
unprepossessing, though not bad, and were responsive to good

sentiments or advice. One would not have imagined oneself in such an assemblage—all Convicts of a deep dye. Those of us were particularly struck with this, who had elsewhere seen so very different an aspect in a number of Convicts in other prisons, where the hard, dogged, lowering look gives unmistakeable proof of a bad nature checked and repressed, not changed. After the address, the men arranged themselves in two parties, and a man on one side was selected to propose a question to the other. This being satisfactorily answered, the challenge was returned, and each side seemed stimulated by a friendly rivalry to surpass the other, to elicit as much information and call out as much real thought and opinion as possible. Sometimes a discussion arose, in which Mr. ORGAN was called on take a part, which he did, not dictatorially, but with only the superiority arising from his own greater knowledge and better spirit and judgment. The following are the questions which we heard actually discussed on that occasion, and satisfactorily answered:—

1.—Name the remarkable Mountains mentioned in Scripture?
2.—Repeat WOLFE's Lines on the Burial of Sir JOHN MOORE?
3.—Point out the Disadvantages of Strikes?
4.—What Battle confirmed Canada to the British?
5.—With what People did the English Sign the First Treaty of Commerce?
6.—A Captain is obliged to limit the Supply of Provisions to his Crew, owing to a protracted Sea Voyage; can you show the Wisdom of the Step, and How and When can Merchants act upon the same Principle?
7.—In the Reign of what English Monarch was Ireland annexed to the English Crown?
8.—Repeat the Lines on the Spread of the Gospel?
9.—The Qualifications essential to a successful Emigrant?
10.—To what Portion of her Mineral Wealth does Great Britain owe her Greatness?
11.—Who gave Australia to Great Britain, and repeat the Words he expressed on the occasion.
12.—Where, and on what occasion, did our Lord Work the First Miracle?
13.—Name the Great Naval Battles at which Lord NELSON commanded?
14.—Box the Mariner's Compass?
15.—Do the Employers of Discharged Prisoners expect more Fidelity from them than they do from ordinary Workmen?
16.—St. AUGUSTINE on Bad Company?

17.—Who established the Law of Industry, and what were the Words used by him when doing so ?

18.—How is a Shilling made ?

19.—What are Taxes, and how is every Pound sterling collected in Taxes applied ?

20.—The Lay of the Labourer, by HOOD ?

21.—The Maritime Counties of England and Ireland ?

22.—The Great Source of all Crime ?

23.—The Last Words of NELSON ?

24.—How much Money did it cost Great Britain to aboilsh Slavery in her Dominions, and name the Men who distinguished themselves in advocating the Emancipation of Slaves ?

25.—On what occasion did CHRIST teach a Lesson of Frugality ?

26.—MOORE's Lines on WELLINGTON ?

27.—The Epitaph on General WOLFE's Monument ?

28.—When and by whom was Property first Divided ?

" These questions are, of course, founded on the instructions that have been given, and the reading which the men have selected for themselves; the variety of them, and the fitness of the answers in the men's own words, often corrected by each other, sufficiently proved how completely they have made the various topics their own. The subject of strikes especially elicited a long discussion, some taking part for, some against. One young man, who advocated them, seemed quite excited when describing all the circumstances that might lead to a strike ; and as he vividly portrayed the feelings and views of the workmen, the means they adopted to obtain their end, and the progress of the affair, we felt thankful that a youth of so much power for good or ill had been brought under such wise and good influences. The manner in which several noble pieces of poetry were repeated by heart, sufficiently proved what fine powers would have been wasted and perverted, if they had not here been well directed. We had noticed on the walls at Lusk and elsewhere a passage from St. AUGUSTINE on bad company, as follows :—

" ' Bad company is like a nail driven into a post, which, after the first and second blow, may be drawn out with little difficulty, but being once driven up to the head, the pincers cannot take hold to draw it out, but this can only be done by the destruction of the wood.'—ST. AUGUSTINE,

"A gentleman of our party at Lusk had expressed his doubt whether it was not above the comprehension of the prisoners. We therefore requested Mr. ORGAN to ask for an explanation of it; he had never made it, he said, the subject of conversation, but the passage was at once explained by the youth who had advocated strikes, in a way which showed how completely it had been the subject of thought and self-application. Leaving the prisoners with a few words of encouragement and exhortation, we were taken to an outside waiting-room, where were a number of men who, having been set at conditional liberty, came to report themselves as steadily at work, and others who had been for many years free, but who kept up this occasional connection with those who had laboured for their good. These results of the labour and care bestowed were most satisfactory; and still more so were the visits made by some of the association to employers who had many of the late Convicts at work under them, and who spoke highly of their reformed condition.

"We paid another visit to Smithfield with Captain CROFTON, and saw the men at work at their several trades. A certain proportion of the profits is allowed them, so that a good work-man may earn his 2s. 6d. a week, which is laid by for his discharge, except the few pence which he is allowed weekly to spend. Captain C. explained to us the very strict regulations which are adopted, and the system of marks, by which each prisoner can be certain that on his conduct, whatever it is, will depend his future as well as his present position. So exactly are all marks and accounts kept, that a complete check is pre-served both over officers and men, and the Captain can prove or disprove the truth of any charge of unjust treatment. So important an element of the system is this regarded by the directors, that on one occasion the Captain occupied full two hours in investigating the complaint of a Convict, and proving the real state of the case; nor would he rest with the man's admission that 'the Captain was doubtless right,' and that he supposed he had made a mistake. He did not let the matter drop, until he had obtained from him the full admission that he was himself perfectly satisfied. He told us the histories of many whom we saw now perfectly amenable to order, and obedient to duty. It had been no easy task to bring many turbulent and bad spirits to this condition, but the combined powers of personal influence and strict discipline had at length prevailed.

"Another visit was paid to Smithfield before we left the city, and of a most unexpected nature. The Queen and Royal Family spent one Sunday in Dublin, and her august Consort and eldest son spent a portion of the Sabbath in visiting the prisons! It must have been a sight calculated to awaken the deepest emotions, and one worthy of the reign of our beloved Sovereign, who has shown a heart to feel for the lowest of her subjects, to witness the scene that afternoon in the Smithfield Convict Prison; to see the Lord-Lieutenant of the island visit the lecture-room, with Prince Albert and the Heir Apparent of the Crown, and sit down among those men, who, from being a danger and cost to the country, were preparing to become useful and honest citizens of it. We will not intrude on the scene, but will rejoice that our future sovereign has already learnt to consider the welfare of the lowest as much an object of interest as the highest, and that he desires to learn himself, by personal investigation, the real condition even of Convict Prisons.

"Dec. 13, 1861."

## No. III.

"Our last visit to the Irish Convict Prisons for male Convicts was to the first stage in them at Mountjoy. On the Sunday preceding, that also had been visited by his Royal Highness the Prince Consort and the Prince of WALES. Little did the writer of this imagine, while penning the record of their visit to Smith-field Prison, that the illustrious subject of it was on the bed of sickness, which was in a few short hours to be the bed of death! Thus the nation which for more than twenty years had rejoiced not only in the unbroken domestic happiness of their beloved

Sovereign, but in the support and help she received from his wise counsels, has been plunged into deep grief,—a grief which is more than an outward show of ceremonial condolence, the true-heart feeling of a personal loss, and of warm and even affectionate sympathy with our beloved Queen. Such visitations forcibly remind us of the shortness and uncertainty of life, and warn us all to work while it is day, discharging in our several stations the duties to which we have been called by the Supreme Ruler of the Universe, our Heavenly Father. The following tribute to the memory of Her Majesty's august father, the Duke of KENT, extracted from a sermon delivered on the day of the funeral of His Majesty GEORGE III., February 18, 1820, by the writer's father, the late Rev. Dr. LANT CARPENTER, is so strikingly characteristic of her illustrious Consort whom we now so truely mourn, that we may be permitted to insert it here, as harmonising with our feelings at our recent bereavement :—

"'Suddenly, in the vigour of health, and in the enjoyment of the purest sources of temporal happiness, was he removed from the scenes of time. He regarded them in the aspect of responsibility; cherished the charities of domestic life; employed the influence of his rank to effect those purposes which the benevolent Sovereign (his father) would have contemplated with peculiar satisfaction, engaging in the labours necessary to accomplish them with men whose names were not adorned with earthly titles; pursuing them with enlightened zeal and persevering industry, and bearing up under disappointments and discouragements, with a firmness which we may regard as a decisive proof that he had nobler objects in view than the praise of men; that he was influenced by a sense of religious duty, and that he had the strengthening supports of religious principle.'

"Such was the tribute, then, paid to the father of our Sovereign, and such words may be applied to the noble and esteemed Prince whom we lament.*

* *Extract from a Sermon preached in the Chapel of Smithfield Prison, Dublin, by the* Rev. GEORGE B. WHEELER, A.M., Chaplain, *on the day after the Prince Consort's death.*
"Many of you remember that three short months since the PRINCE CONSORT of England stood amongst you. He devoted some hours of his short sojourn in this country to visit the prisoners in this place. He brought with him the

"While at Lusk the prison character of the establishment has been carefully avoided, and at Smithfield very few traces of it exist, at Mountjoy we saw the same general arrangement and system which characterised Pentonville, and gaols built on that model. The ordinary visitor is struck with the extraordinary cleanliness of every part, the brightness of the brass fittings, and the polish of the metal staircases, so fine as to be dangerous to the incautious step. There is a certain beauty in the symmetry and regularity of the whole which, at first sight, removes from the inexperienced observer the anticipated awe and terror. The long galleries, tier above tier, give one the feeling of perfection of adaptation to some special object, which is not unpleasing. The arrangements to save the labour of the officials, and to secure to the inmates of the place a supply of their wants, and a certainty of proper attention in case of sickness, are admirable. We heard no sound. Nothing would have informed us that those small doors on each side of the long galleries were entrances to solitary cells, in each of which was a wretched criminal, to whom for nine long months those four walls shut out the world, and all society save his own gloomy thoughts,—who would there have no retrospect but of his own misspent time and neglected opportunities,

---

heir to the greatest monarchy in all the earth, and the heir, we confidently trust, to the virtues of both his parents. He brought that younger prince, who clung to him so lovingly, and whose sparkling eyes were yet undimmed by tears in life's early day; and thus he taught his children to be considerate and examining. You, my men, can never forget those hours of that Sabbath afternoon. You were witnesses of the deep interest the PRINCE felt in all that concerns humanity. You heard his acute questions. You marked the closeness of his observation, the patience with which he examined all the details of the system instituted here. At that time you were unconscious of his exalted rank. Only two or three knew that our visitor was the nearest to the throne, and had left loyalty to visit us, shut out from the world and by almost all the world forgotten. Let it be remembered here—angels have recorded it elsewhere—that the last public act of the PRINCE CONSORT in Ireland was to set apart some hours of a rare and precious holiday to a thorough and searching examination into the condition of our prisoners here."

or, it may be, grievous wrongs done to his fellow-creatures, a life wasted, a family ruined. We heard no groans of agony, no wail of despair; but the deep unbroken silence in this abode of vice and sorrow was even more oppressive, more suggestive of a misery too great for words, a concentrated mass of human suffering. No door was opened to us—we asked not to see the prisoners. Some years ago we had visited a gaol constructed on the old principle, and the Governor politely ordered that the cell-doors should be thrown open as we passed, that we might see everything. And so, after mounting the narrow stone staircase, we walked through that gallery, and as we passed, a prisoner presented himself at the entrance of every cell. Such mournful specimens of humanity! Such dogged despair! Such unblushing villany! Such hopeless grief! We longed to strive to solace it, to have the satisfaction of doing something to help to save the lost; but we were powerless, and walked on as unheedingly as we could, shrinking from insulting their misery by gazing on it. One drop of comfort and sympathy and advice we did bestow on a young man near his discharge, and that helped him on, and made him feel that when at liberty his help was at hand. But his was a solitary case, and the sight of the prisoners in that gaol almost certain,—the officials told us,—to return to it again, and to continue a life of crime, left on us an impression of horror which has never been removed. We avoided at Mountjoy asking to see the prisoners, not from a fear of the renewal of such an impression, but because we felt that criminals undergoing a penal separation from all around, ought not to be subjected to curious inspection, and that they also should not have any rising shame checked, or even their feelings wounded, by being made the subjects of common observation. But we desired to be assured that the men whom we had seen at Lusk and Smithfield were really criminals of as deep a dye as we had been told, and to learn whether the crimes of which they had been guilty were accidental, or the result of a continued career of vice. Our minds were sufficiently satisfied on this point by an inspection of a book in which is inserted a photograph of each prisoner on his arrival. We could hardly have imagined a collection of heads so low in type, and faces indicating such varied criminality, but uniformly a display of such bad and daring passions. We could scarcely have believed that many of these were the very men whom we had seen under so different an aspect, and with countenances so altered. Only one of all of them did we recognise as the clever young man whom we had noticed taking an active part in the competitive examination; his countenance was then wonderfully changed from the dogged, lowering, vicious look which we saw here. The prisoners, when they arrive in this wicked state, are full of antagonism and hatred to all around, and look with astonishment and often defiance at the strange scene which the interior of this prison presents. Each soon finds that the power over him is more than he can possibly contend against, and he is immured in the cell which must be his abode for nine months. At first this seclusion is absolute and complete, except during exercise, religious worship, evening instruction; and then—though not conducted in separate stalls as at Pentonville—any communication with other prisoners is strictly prevented. It is by degrees felt a great privilege to be allowed to work with the cell-door open during part of the day, then during the whole day; this slight approach to the society of others is esteemed an extreme privilege, and is forfeited for any misconduct. But, in the midst of this strict and severe discipline, a ray of hope is always lighted on the prisoner, for he feels that justice is tempered with mercy. From the very first day of his entering the prison he is made aware that his future condition will entirely depend on his conduct day by day, of which careful records are kept. The treatment of those who have the charge of him, though actuated by strict regard to duty, still manifests that a concern is felt for the welfare of each one individual, and none but those who have had the care of persons, either old or young, who are under sentence of the law, can tell how marvellous is the effect of this feeling alone. The medical officer notices not merely the physical, but the moral state and conduct, and if he hears of peculiar irritability and misbehaviour, he examines whether there is not some physical cause which may be removed. In this he and the Governor act in co-operation, for all are animated by the same spirit. As the Gaol Physician remarked to one of us, ' It seemed as if an electric current had pervaded all the officers.' This will appear to many visionary; but we who were in Dublin at a time when Captain CROFTON had felt it necessary to tender his resignation, became fully assured, from our own personal observation, and from conversation with the various officers, that his spirit did animate the whole establishment of Convict Prisons from beginning to end; so we rejoiced with them when it was arranged that he would remain at his very important post.

" The time of separate confinement being ended, the Convicts are transferred to prisons where they execute Government works. If they are artisans, they are sent to Philipstown, where indoor trades are carried on; if otherwise, they are transferred to Spike Island, near Cork, to carry on Government works on the fortifications. Here their boundary is the limit of the Island, and they are shut in separate cells at nights. This is an immense change to them; from their solitude to be placed in association with their fellow Convicts presents great temptations to insubordination, which, of course, requires the strictest watchfulness. But here, too, the system pursued completely produces its effect. Careful records are made of each Convict's daily conduct and work, by marks which he himself can check, and which he knows will be the means of his rising to higher classes in the Island, and eventually of his being placed in the greater liberty of Lusk. He has here, also, the advantage of the ministrations of the chaplain and the schoolmaster, the latter of whom gives instructive lectures, as at Smithfield and Lusk, calculated to prepare the men for their entrance anew into life. The prisoners do not, when they first come, show themselves by any means reformed, and often give great trouble for some time. Occasionally parties of Convicts from the Colonial Prisons are sent here in a very disorderly condition after their voyage; but all are soon brought into order without any violent outbreak.

"Why is it that under this system there never occur the fearful outrages with which the public have been shocked these last few years? First, we hear of a tremendous rebellion at Portland Prison, which was with difficulty subdued. Then early last year we read of first one and then a second most fearful insurrection, as we must call them, at Chatham, quelled only by an overpowering physical force, and followed by dreadful punishments. Quite recently the public journals give an account of a similar state of things at Dartmoor:—

"'OUTRAGEOUS CONDUCT OF CONVICTS IN DARTMOOR PRISON.

"'Very serious disturbances have for some weeks past [November 2, 1861], we understand, taken place in Dartmoor Prison, where the convicts have been displaying serious symptoms of insubordination and opposition to the regulations of the prison, coupled, as opportunity offered, with most outrageous assaults on the officers more immediately in attendance upon them. To such an extent has their violence been carried, that the prison authorities have for some time been obliged to place extra night officers on duty in the association wards, in which from 80 to 120 of the worst criminals are congregated, without, so far as we hear, any regard to classification or morals. In Dartmoor Prison there are five such wards, where murderers, garotters, robbers, forgers, burglars, and highway robbers, criminals guilty of unnatural offences, and, more deplorable still, youthful thieves and pickpockets, are permitted indiscriminately to herd together in open wards, in which they take their meals and sleep, without any separation or respect for common decency; inasmuch as the convicts in the wards referred to sleep in hammocks placed so close together that one man cannot get in or out without crossing the hammock on his right or left. The moral disorganisation and villany engendered under such circumstances may be easily imagined, and the results have recently been manifested in a shape which calls loudly for remedial measures on the part of the authorities.

"'On a recent occasion the convicts in the association wards concerted a plan for putting out the gas at night, and making a simultaneous assault on the night officers; but, happily, one or two in the plot divulged the secret to the authorities, and precautions were taken by which the fiendish design was frustrated. Notwithstanding this failure, the officers who have in any manner rendered themselves obnoxious have been, for several weeks past, subjected to murderous attacks from these irreclaimable villains, by whom any official who endeavours strictly and impartially to carry out the prison rules, or who, in the exercise of his duty, may bring under the notice of the Governor acts of misconduct, is specially marked out for vengeance. Indeed, things have arrived at such a pitch, that those officers, whose conscience will not allow these hardened ruffians to act as they think proper, are certain, at some time or other, to be attacked and maltreated—the time chosen for such assaults being when they get the obnoxious warder or other warder by himself, or at some distance from his brother officers. As an illustration of the working of the convict system at Dartmoor, we may state that two most respectable and inoffensive officers, named RUNDLE and MASON, were very recently assaulted in the most savage and cowardly manner, the former being attacked by a number of convicts, who came behind him and dealt several violent blows on his head, knocking him down, and while in that position ferociously kicking him with their hobnail boots about the head and stomach, at the same time closing in a circle round the unfortunate man, so that it was some time before RUNDLE's brother officers could render him any assistance, and then not before the severe injuries on his head and different parts of his body had been inflicted. In the case of MASON, who was attacked in the same cowardly manner, he being an unusually strong man, his ruffianly assailants failed to knock him down, and he was enabled to keep them at bay until aid arrived, but not before he had received several severe kicks on the legs and contusions about the eyes, which prevented him for several days from performing his ordinary duty. The principal warder, SHEPHERD, was, not long ago, assaulted and hit on the head and face; an officer named BARNES was also attacked by a prisoner, who struck him on the head with a broom-handle; and, within the last few days, we learn that a most murderous assault was made on an officer named MULES, in one of the association wards, where there were 80 convicts, two of whom struck him from behind several heavy blows on the head with stones, which they had tied up in their handkerchiefs, and with which they beat him most unmercifully about the head and face, inflicting several fractures on the cranium, from the effects of which he now lies dangerously ill, but little hope being entertained of his recovery. Several other officers, whose duties bring them into immediate contact with the prisoners, have likewise been the subject of ferocious attacks, and have received serious injuries.

" ' Such is the " reign of terror" at present existing in Dartmoor Prison ; and unless the most stringent measures are promptly carried out, its condition bids fair to rival, or even eclipse, that of Chatham, during the worst phases of the late mutinous outbreak.'

" Such fearful outbreaks of an evil spirit raging within the establishment are, of course, followed by the consequences described in the conclusion of the same article :—

" ' Some steps in the right direction, however have, we hear, been already taken. Last week, Captain GAMBIER, one of the visiting directors, arrived at the prison, and, with a view of checking the prevailing spirit of insubordination, ordered five or six of the ringleaders to be flogged—a sentence which was immediately carried into effect, three dozen lashes being administered to each of the culprits, who, it may be mentioned, did not evince the smallest signs of contrition for their outrageous misconduct, but, on the contrary, we are told, uttered expressions of savage exultation and defiance. Several convicts, moreover, were ordered to be sent back to the prison at Millbank, where they will be placed in the penal class, and have to undergo very severe discipline. Reduced diet has also been resorted to by Captain GAMBIER with respect to other convicts guilty of mutinous conduct, who, in some cases, are compelled to wear chains or cross-irons, which will, for some time at least, prevent them from using their nailed boots on the heads of the warders of the establishment at Dartmoor, with the abuses of which the public are in general very imperfectly acquainted.'

" Would it be possible that men from prisons like these could be sent to such places as Lusk or Smithfield.

" Only one of our party was able to visit Spike Island, and he was most fully satisfied with that, as we all had been with every part of the system. His testimony was fully in accordance with that of Mr. RECORDER HILL, as given to the Social Science Association at its first meeting at Birmingham, after a recent visit to Spike Island and the other prisons :—

" ' The contrast of expression in the faces of the inmates of Mountjoy and of those of the body advanced to the intermediate stage affords the most striking evidence in favour of the treatment of which they have had the inestimable benefit. This proof of amendment I had ample opportunity of studying, as in my repeated visits I saw the men in every variety of occupation—at their labour, at their meals, during their studies, and in their moments of relaxation. Their countenances, though on the whole inferior in intelligence to the average of free men of their own degree, bore no marks of an evil mind; and while I was being rowed by more than one boat's crew, from island to island, and altogether in their power, it was impossible for me not to feel as secure of their fidelity, as if they had been Thames watermen. In the manners and general demeanour of the intermediate class the desire to improve themselves and to be of service to others was also very apparent.'

" Feb. 8, 1862."

A fourth visit to the Female Convict Prisons is reserved for a future chapter.

Though so many extracts have been already given from the valuable work of the Four Justices, yet we must copy a short passage from their work, embodying some of the observations they made after their visit in October, 1861 :—

"Lusk is a village about twelve miles from Dublin. Powers were obtained by Act of Parliament to enclose an open common there, previously occupied only by 'squatters.' Two huts of corrugated iron, each capable of holding fifty men, were erected at a cost of £320 a piece. A portion of each hut is partitioned off for a warder to sleep in, and the rest serves both as day-room and dormitory for the convicts. A cook-house and offices of the simplest possible character, stand, with the huts, in an enclosure bounded by a mud wall a yard high. A few cottages for warders scattered about the common, complete the whole *matériel* of the 'prison.' All the usual features of a prison may be said—with something of the idiom of the country, though not without high English authority for the phrase—to be 'conspicuous by their absence.'

"As to the *personnel*, we found at the time of our visit about sixty convicts in charge of five warders. The truncheons we saw at Mountjoy, have no place here, and other weapon or chain there is none.

"The obvious question to ask first is—Do not the prisoners often escape? Of more than a thousand men, we are told, who have passed through the prison, only two have attempted it.

"There is a military guard? No. There are police? The answer is instructive. When the establishment at Lusk was first proposed, the residents in the neighbourhood were, not unnaturally, somewhat alarmed at the idea of having a number of thieves and burglars encamped in open quarters near them. To calm these apprehensions, it was proposed that the constabulary should have a station on the common. An iron hut which had been erected elsewhere was brought and set up for the purpose. But no police ever came, for there has never been found the slightest need for them. We were assured by Mr.

COBBE, a magistrate having large property, and himself resident within a few miles, that so unexceptionable has been the conduct of the prisoners, that he has never heard any complaint whatever of misconduct on the part of the prisoners, either within the establishment, or outside.

"Is, then, the non-escape of the prisoners owing to the place being made so comfortable to them that they have no wish to leave it? We certainly failed to find any evidence of such comfort. The men sleep in hammocks in the hut, and all that one can say is, that while they are inside it, they have shelter; but the moment they leave it, they are exposed to every wind of heaven, and to all the rain of that humid climate. In point of mere physical comfort, the advantage is altogether on the side of an ordinary prison, to say nothing of a well-warmed cell at Wakefield or Pentonville. We found most of the men, at the time of our visit, working up to the middle in drains, than which few employments conduce less to comfort. The diet is stated to be not more than the medical officers consider to be necessary for the maintenance of health, and fitness for the hard labour and exposure to which the men are subjected.

"The gratuity is half-a-crown a week, which is rather more than in any one stage at Portland. But it is so much lower in all the previous stages, that a Convict, under a four years' sentence, in Ireland, can only earn half the amount which he could earn, under a similar sentence, in England.

"The men at Lusk are allowed to spend sixpence a week of their gratuity; and we were told that many of them buy bread with it,—an indication that the diet allowed to them is not excessive.

"On the whole we saw no appearance of any indulgence to induce men to remain, as they do, without physical restraint, and submit to strict discipline.

"We have mentioned one independent source, from which we heard of their general good conduct. Another was the rector of the parish, who informed us that the Protestant prisoners attend service at the village church, and conduct themselves with as much propriety as any others of the congregation.

"The aspect of the men whom we saw confirmed the information we received. Neither in dress nor appearance were they distinguishable from ordinary labourers, except, perhaps, as having a somewhat more subdued and staid demeanour. The bailiff, who was superintending their work, told us that having had charge of gangs of labourers in many parts of Ireland, he had never found men more tractable or willing to work than these prisoners; adding, what would rarely be the case with free labourers, that an oath or indecent expression was unheard among them. This statement was confirmed by the other officers. It was difficult to conceive that these were men of the same class as those whose scowling or knavish visages we had seen in photograph or in flesh, in the first stage at Mountjoy; yet undoubtedly they had passed through that prison. [pp. 22, 24.]

"A doubt having been suggested, by what we heard and saw of prisoners in the later stages of their imprisonment, and after discharge, as to whether they really were of the same criminal class as our English Convicts, we examined such specimens of the *raw material*, so to speak, on which the Irish system has to work, as this prison presented. Photographs have been taken of the prisoners on their admission; and certainly, making every allowance for the well-known fact that the photograph does not flatter, a series of physiognomies expressing more unmitigated ruffianism than the volume of portraits which we saw presents, it were difficult to conceive. The living specimens, whom we visited in their cells, had no less the aspect of knavish cunning or sullen brutality, with which our experience at Wakefield has made us familiar. We saw men with whom a tête-à-tête interview produced a sensation decidedly disagreeable, and whose look afforded some excuse for the precaution, objectionable as it seemed to us, by which the warders are armed with truncheons, 'in case,' as was said, 'of an attack by a wicked prisoner.'

"The records of the offences for which the prisoners were convicted, also show that they are persons of much the same class as those with whom we have to deal in the English Convict prisons, thieves and burglars forming a large majority.

"Our experience as regards the Irish prisoner in English prisons, has not led us to believe that he is of more amiable character, or easier to manage and reform, than his 'erring brother,' born on this side the Channel.

"The character of the Irish Convicts previous to the introduction of the improved discipline, was so exceedingly bad, that a special request was sent from Western Australia, September, 1854, that no more of them might be sent to that colony, though it was willing to receive English Convicts.

"After such testimony as to the past, and our own observations as to the present, when we find the remarkable extent to which it has been found practicable to carry the abandonment of 'coercion,' and the substitution of 'moral agencies,' in the later stages of the Irish Convict discipline, and the satisfactory results which have followed, we feel bound to attribute those results to *good management*, and the excellence of the system, rather than to any antecedent superiority in the character of the Irish Convict.

"No doubt, in England, the towns are larger and more numerous, and crime is more highly organised, than in Ireland. But human nature is the same, and criminal perversion needs to be dealt with on the same principles, in both. It is remarkable that, when it was first proposed to established the present Convict System in Ireland, it was said, 'This might do very well in England, but it is wholly inapplicable to the 'peculiar character and circumstances of the people here;' which, *mutato nomine*, is just what we sometimes hear said in England now." [pp. 14, 15.]

It is not only in our own country that the Irish Convict System has elicited the highest admiration and the strongest testimonies to the success of its working. On the Continent, in Australia, in Canada, it is well known and appreciated. As in this chapter, however, we limit ourselvs to testimonies from personal observations, we select only that of Baron VON HOLTZENDORFF, Professor of Law in the University of Berlin. The following extracts are from a translation of parts of a work of his, made by Mrs. LENTAIGNE, of Dublin :—

"In consequence of an invitation to join the meeting of the Social Science Congress, which was about to assemble in Dublin, I proceeded to Ireland in the beginning of August, in the year 1861. As was to be expected, the Convict System of that country held a prominent place amongst the subjects discussed, and by means of that Congress, what *had previously been deemed incredible, was made evident to all who chose by personal investigation to become acquainted with the Irish institutions for the repression of crime.*

"There being much scepticism and jealousy amongst those who had earnestly studied the Irish blue books, a comprehensive critique on the Irish Convict Prisons, and a careful comparison between them and the corresponding institutions in England were necessarily looked forward to, when the discussions of the Congress commenced in Dublin, on the 11th of August, 1861. Besides, every one knew that on this side of St. George's Channel, the Irish System had met with adversaries who had employed their special talents in arguments against the general adoption of that system. But the field of discussion was left open even to them, and every opportunity for the acquirement of information and the discovery of deficiencies was placed at their command.

"The expression of every opinion was allowed in Dublin, and, on that account, the meeting of the Congress there was considered an event, which, in its effects, would not remain without influence on public opinion in England, relative to the existing prison system of that country. For a foreigner, there certainly could be no better opportunity than that presented by the Social Science Congress, of inquiring into the actual condition of the Irish Convict Prisons, and of comparing his own ideas as well as the animadversions of others, with the experienced opinions of competent judges, thus enabling him by the criticism of different individuals to arrive at a correct and definite conclusion on the subject.

"In order that my opinions might not be altogether influenced by the observations of others, and that I might see and inquire in person, I arranged my arrival in Dublin so as to have some days of leisure, before the commencement of the business of the Congress. Sir WALTER CROFTON was prevented by illness from conducting Baron VON DER GÖLTZ and me, through the penal institutions of Dublin; and though I had much reason to regret the circumstance, I could not conceal from myself that his absence contributed to insure the independence of my observations, and an unrestrained freedom of inquiry; for there is a great difference between an object being *shown off* by a friend, and carefully searched into and examined by an impartial inquirer. On the first day of my presence in Dublin, I visited the cellular prisons of Mountjoy, under the guidance of Captain WHITTY, who is at present a member of the Board of Directors, having previously rendered important service at the Prison of Portland. I also repeatedly visited the Intermediate Prison at Smithfield, and saw the agricultural establishment on the commons at Lusk. I inspected at Golden-bridge one of those refuges, which, for Female Convicts, take the place of Intermediate Prisons (this one is managed by Sisters of Mercy), and, finally, before my return to England, I went to Cork and Queenstown, where I had an opportunity of observing the external arrangements of the Convict Depôt at Spike Island."

The Professor's details of the system we omit, and proceed to the concluding observations :—

"I conclude my report with a settled conviction in favour of the Irish system, formed after careful examination, and without prejudice. The facts which I have detailed are incontestable, while the interest I felt in the cause did not permit me to neglect any opportunity for calling attention to defects, if I had observed any, or giving utterance to objections, if I had felt any doubt. I have no object in secrecy; and the Irish Convict Directors are men who, far from shunning criticism, have on all occasions been anxious that public opinion should express itself without reserve. In Ireland there is no mystery, there are no secret proceedings; nor is there any bureaucratic arrogance or red-tapism, which meets the opinions of others with the over-bearing contradiction—'we understand that better.' How little Sir WALTER CROFTON and his colleagues were influenced by blind dogmatism, is shown by the fact that superior to the pride of office, and careless of the praise that was awarded them in the course of their administration, they, when they saw it necessary, effected several alterations in their own work. * *

"All the objections to the Irish System may lead to one question, namely: Are the results which have been undeniably obtained in Ireland to be considered only as phenomena forming exceptions to general rules, but suited to the special circumstances of Ireland, or does the Irish System contain a general truth, as applicable to Anglo-Saxons, Scandinavians, Italians, and Germans, as to Celts? If the general value of the principle followed in Ireland be acknowledged, it would be acting unreasonably not to imitate what has been there proved to be so excellent, for in great social reforms there is just as little principle of nationality as in natural philosophy.

"In England it is asserted that the Irish System is only suitable for Ireland, because the Irish police are better than the English, because the Irish people sympathise with the criminal, and because English Convicts are of such a nature, that in case of deficient supervision, finding a cessation of the strictness with which they had hitherto been watched, they would run away from the Intermediate Prisons, the very day after being placed in them.

"I do not feel myself called upon to decide with regard to the first of the reasons cited, as my knowledge in that respect is not sufficient; but as to the inference to be drawn, I cannot be mistaken. If the English police, whose united numbers are estimated at 20,000 men, are inferior to those of Ireland, it must only follow that they should be improved. That the Irish pattern cannot be equalled, is an assertion that can scarcely be proved, and against such an assumption learned and experienced Englishmen have repeatedly entered their energetic protest. It even seems to me that in some respect Ireland is more unfavourably circumstanced than England, for in consequence of the opposition of parties in Ireland, and the struggle of political passions, the Irish police are not confined, like those in England, to the limited sphere of operation, which, regardless of politics, simply includes the maintenance of public order; and I believe that where the repression of crime is in question, the English police might justly reckon on the approbation and support of the public, at least as securely as those of Ireland.

"With regard to the pretended sympathy of the Irish people with discharged criminals, I must consider such a reproach as more offensive than true. I have already shown the opinion held in Australia with regard to Irish Convicts, but for my own part I have found a deep religious feeling, and a lively sense of morality, amongst the very poorest of the lower classes in Ireland; and during the famine time, thousands preferred to starve, rather than avail themselves of the opportunity to steal.

"Finally, the differences of national character between English and Irish criminals have been referred to, and in order to give a sentimental coloring to the objection arising from this point, it has been alleged that if an English Convict were placed in an Intermediate Prison, his attachment to his family would overcome his resolution, and that he would make use of the favorable opportunity to escape to the society of his relations. Recorder HILL expressed himself most decidedly in contradiction to this opinion, at the meeting of the Social Science Congress, in Dublin, and observed that not only in theory the argument was unsatisfactory, but that experience had proved it was contrary to fact; because, in all the wretchedness of Ireland, family ties were held more sacred than they are in England. The strong attachment of the Irish to their families and relations was, as Mr. HILL explained, shown by the great amount of small sums sent home from America by Irish emigrants, in order to enable their families to follow them, or to relieve them in their distress; and although poor and destitute people went in numbers, the sums sent back, according to Mr. HILL's uncontradicted assertion, far exceeded the amount of money similarly remitted by English emigrants. * * *

" Men have ceased to consider the Irish System as an experiment which requires any longer trial. The plans of Captain MACONOCHIE, who, by his mark system, obtained such brilliant success in Norfolk Island, were wrecked by the indifference of public opinion, and the cold opposition of an administration that believed itself too wise to think that any reform could be necessary. At that time an opinion prevailed that criminals must be got rid of by transportation; but at present the Convict question is one, with regard to which every educated person in England will form a judgment for himself, and every citizen is considered by the Government entitled to an opinion. When an article in favour of the Irish Convict System appeared in the *Cornhill Magazine*, Sir JOSHUA JEBB took advantage of the opportunity to have a similar popular account drawn up in praise of the English system, for the readers of that periodical.* I cannot now foresee whether a settlement of this question will be brought about by a voluntary decision of the English Prison authorities, by fresh outbreaks in the Convict Depôts, or by the matter being brought before Parliament; but I feel convinced that a decision must be eventually come to, and I am warranted in this opinion not only by the moral force of public opinion in England, but also by that consideration of economy, which sees in the repression of crime a saving to every household.

* *Cornhill Magazine*, June, 1861.

"In a few words, the Irish System unites in itself all the correct principles of previous systems of prison discipline, forming a thoroughly re-modelled general organisation, by means of which the Convict, after a series of gradations, is led to liberty, but still kept in check by the deterrent principle of supervision. By this means are reconciled the punishment of crime for the infraction of the laws, and the requirements of society, with the theories of benevolent and compassionate individuals, and the associations which have been formed for the assistance of the discharged offender. Only thus can be obtained the true consciousness in the Convict's mind, of the great injustice which he has entailed on society by his guilt. There still exists much ignorance as to the requirements of justice, and its relations with the object of reformatory discipline in carrying out punishment. Originating in, and founded on justice, the nature of punishment consists in discipline, and should never be otherwise used, than so as to serve the further development of the better qualities of humanity. The cause of punishment can alone be considered as an evil, and its effects should never produce any but good results. A system of punishment which produces torpor and inaction in the mental faculties, is just as unreasonable as the old exploded coercive treatment of the insane. The accomplishment of justice consequently requires the reformation of the offender, by such a system as enables the criminal to perceive the necessity for his punishment, and the amount of his guilt; and it is only by penal discipline that the influencing motives of the judicial sentence can be reproduced in the minds of the Convicts. The reformatory treatment of criminals is indeed not always required, for there are some cases of formal breaches of law, not otherwise criminal, in which it would be unnecessary to require a reformatory treatment. In such cases it is only necessary that the punishment should be a manifestation of deterrent justice, but it ought to be such as would neither prevent moral progress, nor entail the danger of corruption by association. Any punishment producing by its forms of discipline, despair, revengeful and angry feelings, or which blunts the moral perceptions, or produces listlessness, is the greatest crime which a government can commit, and is an outrage against religion, morality and law.

"It is not my object to set forth here how the means of reformation must always vary in their extent and application for different individuals, according to the nature of the criminal's perceptions.

"The Irish system, resting on deep psychological truth, exhibits, in my opinion, those forms of punishment which in affording the greatest number of reformatory means, alone seems efficacious to bring about a transformation of the moral feelings that have become depraved by serious and habitual crime, so as to become rightly disposed to will or wish for what is good and just, and this change must be effected through the free agency of the criminal, who voluntarily submits to the punishment which justice requires, and so gives up the power over his will which no prison bars can control, accepting willingly the restraint in which he is kept, as an atonement for his guilt, and feeling it a duty to submit to the punishment he has deserved.

"It can be of no consequence whether the external arrangements of the Irish institutions be copied, and that associated penal labour for the second stage, precisely as in Ireland, be adopted. It is probable that in a continually modified and graduated system, originating in separation, other forms would, after a time, be arrived at; but the principles embodied in the progressive and graduated mark system, in intermediate prisons, in discharge on license and police surveillance, seem to me quite indispensable; and even when we examine what was effected by the Italian physician, GIROLAMI, as related by MITTERMAIER, there appears nothing more than the same principles on which the Irish System is based.

"There is one circumstance which I must not forget in taking leave of my subject. Forms of government, and prison systems in their effects, and in their execution, are alike dependent on human weakness and human power; and on this account I must acknowledge that the results obtained in Ireland bear witness to an amount of zeal and activity beyond all praise on the part of the Irish officials, from the Viceroy to those whose duty it was to carry out the system. I have seen how Sir WALTER CROFTON almost every day took anxious trouble about the condition and complaints of individual Convicts, how nothing seemed too insignificant for his attention, and how perfectly impressed he was with the sublimity of his task. On one occasion he spent an hour in trying to convince a Convict that he had no right to complain. To him the Irish system is principally indebted for that spirit of humanity, and truly Christian charity which, behind bolts and bars, respects the rights of even the most fallen human natures. When Sir WALTER CROFTON, in the summer before last, announced in Dublin his intention, on account of impaired health, to withdraw from his position, the Social Science Congress gave loud expression to their regret, and Lord BROUGHAM declared his belief that the continuance of the convict system would be endangered by the carrying out of this resolution; but as I am deeply impressed with the truth of the principles on which those institutions are founded, I am of a different opinion.

"That event, which many saw approach, with pain and sincere regret, has since taken place. Sir WALTER CROFTON has retired from the management of the Convict Prisons; but before doing so, the honour of knighthood was conferred on him, in consideration of his services, by the Lord Lieutenant. He is fondly remembered by many who have been raised from the dark paths of depravity to the light of knowledge; and I believe that the monument he has founded will survive him, while his fame will be as great, as the modesty with which he estimates his own merits."

# CHAPTER II.

## THE IRISH CONVICT SYSTEM:
## ITS WORKING.

The testimonies which have been presented to the reader in
the former chapter, given at different times during the last
seven years by persons totally unconnected with each other,
will, probably, leave no doubt in the mind of any unprejudiced
person that a great social problem has been solved in the
Irish Convict System, — that important principles have been
demonstrated to be capable of satisfactory application to one
of the most perplexing and difficult parts of the government
of our country,--that the great and merciful law of the moral
government of the world, revealed to us by the Saviour, that
suffering must follow sin, but that the repentant and returning
prodigal should be received and forgiven, can be and ought
to be the law and guiding spirit of every Christian country;—
this has been proved to have been actually accomplished.
Among our witnesses are persons whose high judicial position
and acquaintance with the Convict class render their testimony most valuable. Many more, who would gladly vouch
for the marvellous success of the system, might be brought from
the country itself;—gentlemen whose knowledge of the criminal
part of the community rendered them hopeless of any true
reformation in them, but who have now great satisfaction in
acknowledging themselves mistaken, as they see facts before
them;—employers of labour, who formerly shrank from the

very idea of giving a Convict work on their premises, but who now even go to the prison doors to solicit their labour, because they cannot be more faithfully served than by those very men who were once the destroyers of the peace and property of society;—and last, not least, the Convicts themselves, who having undergone the just penalty of their evil-doing, which was inflicted with justice tempered by mercy, and having learnt within the prison walls to desire to tread the straight and narrow way, leave them with strong resolve to go and sin no more.

It was probably fortunate that this great experiment, for so it was at the commencement, was tried in an island of no great extent, and under circumstances which permitted the free execution of the plans devised for its accomplishment. But the difficulties to be surmounted in Ireland were probably much greater than would exist in our own island, or elsewhere. These arose not only from the previous mismanagement and bad condition of the Convict Prisons there in existence, as evidenced by the fact of the Commission of investigation sent over by our government, as well as from the extremely low degraded state of the criminal population, testified by the Governor of Western Australia;—but also from the very divided state of society in Ireland, arising from violent religious differences, and from the suspicion and jealousy of the proceedings of the government among a large portion of the inhabitants. If such difficulties as these could be surmounted, in addition to those inseparable from the work itself, the same system and principles would have a still more complete success, when carried out with the experience already gained, and without the serious and peculiar obstacles which were to be encountered in Ireland. They have been completely and triumphantly surmounted there, and the success of the system in that part of the empire, inspires a certainty that the adoption of the same principles, developed in a manner equally adapted to the circumstances of the country, and carried out with the same zeal and devotion, will always produce similar results.

The present admirable condition of the Irish Convict Prisons described in the last chapter, was not produced without long and patient efforts on the part of all concerned in the work, nor without the most unwearied and zealous labour in the Directors, warmly coöperating as they did with their chairman, Sir WALTER, then Captain CROFTON; but it is doubtless to him that the very existence of the system is due. He it was who applied to it the principles which have proved so beneficial; and though he was somewhat shackled by the machinery already existing, he modified and extended it so as to carry out the intentions of the Government, as expressed in the Act of 1853, and gave a unity of action to all the Convict Prisons in Ireland. But the fact of his having planned and developed the system, by no means renders it impossible that other persons should carry out a similar one, if only they act on the same principles and adopt the same means. It is true that he effected much by his own personal influence, both in the development of the system and in the reformation of the prisoners. Yet, greatly as he stimulated the officials by his own strong faith, and inspired them with confidence; much as he excited the Convicts to exertion, and awakened in them hope for themselves by the perception of his hope for them, and by the personal interest which he took in each individual among them; he himself had always greater confidence in the principles on which he worked, than on his own personal share in the execution of the work, and always expressed a certainty that others might produce the same results by the same means. Hence, when in 1862 he was compelled to abandon the work to which he had dedicated his strength and talents, because his health broke down under the increase of labour which fell upon him through the removal by the Government of one of his fellow directors,—he felt sure that the Irish Convict System, being now firmly established, would remain on the same basis as before his withdrawal from the practical development of it. He was right, for it is now conducted as formerly, receiving still the full confidence of the public.

We shall, then, now proceed to a close examination of the actual working of the system, deriving our account of it from pamphlets published at different times by Sir W. CROFTON, and from his evidence before the Royal Commission, with that of Captain WHITTY, at that time sole director.*

The general principles which govern the Irish Convict System, are thus very briefly stated by Sir W. CROFTON :—

"1st. That convicts are better and more reliably trained in small numbers, and by their being made to feel throughout their detention, that their advancement depends on themselves, through the active exercise of qualities opposed to those which have led to their imprisonment.

"2nd. That the exhibition of the labour and training of the convicts in a more natural form, before their liberation, than is practicable in ordinary prisons, is a course obviously calculated to induce the public to assist in their absorption, and thereby to materially diminish the difficulties of the convict question.

"3rd. That the institution of appliances to render the criminal calling more hazardous will assuredly tend to the diminution of crime; and, therefore, that 'Police supervision,' photography, and a systematic communication with the Governors of county gaols, with a view to bring, in all possible cases, former convictions against offenders, and entail lengthened sentences upon them, are matters of the gravest importance, and deserving of the most minute attention."

To illustrate the actual process which each Convict passes through, we may take the case of one, J. B., who may be regarded as a type of the class :—

"J. B. has lived in antagonism to the law, and to all who carry out its biddings. He arrives at his prison chained and scowling at all who approach him—he is angry with himself for not having again been able to elude detection, and for no other cause whatever.

"J. B. is stated to be twenty-eight years of age; his life of crime has given him the appearance of thirty-five. He is now convicted of burglary, and has four former convictions recorded against him. He has received what is termed a certain amount of penal infliction for his different crimes, and has

---

* "A few remarks on the Convict System," 1857; "The Immunity of Habitual Criminals," 1861; "Convict Systems and Transportation : a Lecture delivered at the Philosophical Institution, Bristol," 1862; "A Brief Description of the Irish Convict System," 1862; "Convict Systems and Transportation," 1863; all by Sir WALTER CROFTON.

been on the treadwheel more than once; solitude and darkness also, he has experienced from time to time. He has been violently insubordinate in prison, and has been flogged. He is known to be one of a notorious gang of robbers infesting one of our populous cities. You scan his countenance and there is not one hopeful lineament apparent. You elicit from him that his parents died in a workhouse, from which he absconded. He never had a home."

What do law, humanity, the welfare of society, and of this individual himself, who still has a claim on a Christian community notwithstanding his past misdeeds,—what do all these require from us in our treatment of him?

"1st. We have to punish him for the sake of deterring him and deterring others; but this will make him more hostile than ever. He has suffered mere penal infliction repeatedly, and has returned to prison more hardened than before. Punishment alone has failed to deter him.

"2nd. We have to amend him; but how can this be effected with his mind in a state of hostility to us?

"3rd. We have to train him naturally before we liberate him, or the public will not value the voucher for his conduct; but how is this to be accomplished without the withdrawal of physical force? The last desideratum appears to be utterly hopeless, as the mind again reverts to the figure of the hardened desperado standing in heavy chains before us."

The first and second of these conditions are to be fulfilled in the first and second stages of J. B.'s detention in the Convict Prisons. From the time of his entrance into them, it will be perceived that everything tends to diminish his hostility, and to lead him to cöoperation with the efforts of those who are set over him in preparing him for advancement in his present abode, and final restoration to society. The last condition will be fulfilled in the Intermediate Prisons, which are the peculiar feature of the Irish System. Those who are acquainted with the English Convict Prisons, may not perceive any great difference in external arrangements between those and the first two stages of the Irish Prisons; it is, therefore, important to observe in these the *progressive* nature of all the arrangements, and the efforts made from the very first to treat the prisoner as a rational being, to make him understand

his real position, and to stimulate him to self action.   The
following is a general outline of the different stages :—

### "First Stage.

"Separate imprisonment in a cellular prison at Mountjoy, Dublin, for the
first eight or nine months of the sentence.   Whether the period is eight or
nine months, or even longer, depends upon the conduct of the convict.   If
his conduct is quite unexceptionable, he would be entitled to be removed to
an associated prison (the second stage) in eight months.

"In Ireland it is the practice to make this stage very penal, both by a very
reduced dietary during the first half of the period—viz., four months—and by
the absence of interesting employment during the first three months.   By
the time the convict is required for hard work in the second stage, the
improved dietary in the latter portion of the period in separation, will have
rendered him physically equal to perform it ; and by the end of three months
of the first stage the idler will generally have learned to associate industry
with pleasure.

"The convict learns something very material to his future well-being in the
first stage—he has the advantage of much time devoted to his religious and
secular instruction.

"He learns the whole bearing of the 'Irish Convict System' by means
of scholastic instruction—that he can only reach the Intermediate Prisons
(a special feature and a third stage in the system) through his own exertions,
measured by marks in the second stage of the system.   As the liberation
of the convict within the period of his sentence depends upon the date of his
admission to the intermediate or third stage of the system, it is manifestly to
his own interest, as it is the interest of those placed over him, that he should
be well informed upon this point.   There is a strong mental impression made
consequent on this information.

"As the convict attains knowledge of the system, he feels that, within
certain limits, he is made the arbiter of his own fate.   Antagonism to the
authorities placed over him gradually disappears, and in its stead arises
a conviction that there is a cöoperation where he had formerly anticipated
oppression.

"The first stage will have done good work if it has succeeded in planting
in the mind of the convict that there is an active cöoperation existing
between himself and those placed over him.

"At the end of eight or nine months, as the case may be, the convict
is moved, if a labourer, to Spike Island Prison, to be employed on the fortifications, and if a tradesman, to Philipstown, to be employed at his trade.

### "The Second Stage.

"The peculiar feature of the Irish Convict System in the second stage
is the institution of marks to govern the classification.   The 'Mark System'

is a minute and intelligible monthly record of the power of the convict to govern himself, and very clearly realises to his mind that his progress to liberty, within the period of his sentence, can only be furthered by the cultivation and application of qualities opposed to those which led to his conviction.

" There are different classes to be attained in the second stage, and a certain number of marks are required to be obtained by the convict before he can be promoted from one class to another.

" The maximum number of marks each convict can attain monthly is nine, which are distributed under three different headings—viz., three for discipline, *i. e.*, general regularity and orderly demeanour; three for school, *i. e.*, the attention and desire evinced for improvement, or industry in school; and three for industry, *i. e.*, industry at work, and not skill which may have been previously acquired.

" There are four classes in the second stage—viz., the third (in which the convict is placed on his arrival from the first stage), the second, first, and advanced, or A class.

" It will be possible for a convict to raise himself from the third to the second class in two months, by the acquisition of eighteen marks; from the second to the first in six months, if he has attained fifty-four marks in the second class; and from the first to the A or advanced class in twelve months, provided he has acquired 108 marks in the first class. When the convict has reached the A class his progress is noted monthly as A 1, A 2, &c. Misconduct causes reduction, suspension, or the loss of marks.

" When the convict attains the A class, he is employed (although still in the second stage of his detention) on special works, and kept apart from the other convicts. His school instruction and lectures take place in the evening.

" It will be intelligible that the most successful in combating self, and in climbing the ladder of self-control and industry, will the soonest obtain the required number of marks, and the goal to which they lead—viz., ' The Intermediate Prisons,'—and thence the liberty, for which the convict is supposed to have been made fit, by the lessons of those good schoolmasters, industry, self-control, and self-reliance, succeeded by a very special and natural training.

" It will be seen by the following scale and regulations for carrying out sentences of penal servitude under the Act of 1857 (20 and 21 Vict., c. 3) how much each convict becomes the arbiter of his own fate. The earliest possible periods of removal to Intermediate Prisons apply only to those of the most unexceptionable character, and no remission of the full sentence will take place, unless the prisoner has qualified himself by carefully measured good conduct for passing the periods in the Intermediate Prisons prescribed by the rules; and any delay in this qualification will have the effect of postponing his admission into the Intermediate Prisons, and thereby deferring to the same extent the remission of a portion of his sentence.

| Class and No. of Marks to be gained for Admission to the Intermediate Prisons for different Sentences. | Sentences of Penal Servitude. | Shortest Periods of Imprisonment. | | Periods of Remission on License. |
|---|---|---|---|---|
| | | In Ordinary Prisons. | Shortest Period of detention in Intermediate Prisons. | |
| | | Yrs.   Mths. | Yrs.   Mths. | |
| Class 1st $\frac{108}{90}$ ............ | 3 years | 2   2 | 0   4 | |
| | | 2—\|—6 | | |
| "   6 A, or {6 months in A class} | 4 " | 2   10 | 0   5 | |
| | | 3—\|—3 | | |
| "   14 A, or 14 " | 5 " | 3   6 | 0   6 | |
| | | 4—\|—0 | | |
| "   17 A, or 17 " | 6 " | 3   9 | 0   9 | |
| | | 4—\|—6 | | |
| "   20 A, or 20 " | 7 " | 4   0 | 1   3 | |
| | | 5—\|—3 | | |
| "   28 A, or 28 " | 8 " | 4   8 | 1   4 | |
| | | 6—\|—0 | | |
| "   44 A, or 44 " | 10 " | 6   0 | 1   6 | |
| | | 7—\|—6 | | |
| "   59 A, or 59 " | 12 " | 7   3 | 1   9 | |
| | | 9—\|—0 | | |
| "   68 A, or 68 " | 15 " | 8   0 | 2   0 | |
| | | 10—\|—0 | | |

The periods remitted on License will be proportionate to the length of sentences, and will depend upon the fitness of each convict for release, after a careful consideration has been given to his case by the Government.

"The class and number of marks to be attained by each convict (according to his sentence) before he can be removed to the Intermediate Prisons is shown in the first column. It is evident, therefore, that the time of detention of the convict in the ordinary prison, within the minimum term named in the scale in the third column and the limit of his sentence, depends upon himself; and as he must pass a certain period (named in the fourth column) in the Intermediate Prisons before he can obtain his conditional liberty, the stimulus which he has to overcome self becomes very intelligible.

"Now, however trifling this "Mark System" may appear to those not conversant with its operation, it will be found in practice to realise to the mind of each individual very clearly and fully his progress in self-government and in other desirable qualities. There is not an intelligent officer in the Irish Convict Department who will not bear witness to the intense interest taken by each Convict in the attainment of his marks, and the jealous care with which he notes them.

## "THE THIRD OR INTERMEDIATE STAGE.

" In this stage there are no marks. The result of the self-discipline effected by their attainment is here to be tested before the liberation of the convict·

" 'Individualization' is the ruling principle in these establishments; the number of inmates should, therefore, be small, and not exceed 100.

" The training is special, and the position of the convict made as natural as is possible; no more restraint is exercised over him than would be necessary to maintain order in any well-regulated establishment. At 'Lusk Common,' within fifteen miles of Dublin, there has been for the last five years and a-half an Intermediate Establishment for employing convicts in the reclamation of the land, and for carrying out principles which have proved so beneficial to themselves and to the public.

" The officers in the Intermediate Establishments work with the convicts.

" At 'Lusk' there are only six, and they are unarmed. Physical restraint is therefore impossible, and if possible, it would be out of place, and inconsistent with the principles which the establishments were instituted to enunciate.

" 1st. You have to show to the convict that you really trust him, and give him credit for the amendment he has illustrated by his marks.

" 2nd. You have to show to the public, that the convict, who will soon be restored to liberty for weal or for woe, may upon reasonable grounds be considered as capable of being safely employed.

" How does this become possible ?

" The reply is, that the convict is cöoperating in his own amendment. He cannot ignore the conviction, sooner or later, that the system, however penal in its development, is intended for his benefit; and that, moreover, it has by its stringent regulations and arrangements after the liberation of the Convict, and this is most important to note, made the vocation of crime very unprofitable and hazardous to follow.

" He hears lectures of an interesting and profitable description, which not only point out the wickedness and the danger of criminal pursuits, but show him the course which he should take in order to amend his life, where his labour is required, and his antecedents not likely to entwine him to his ruin. The mind of the convict is in alliance with the minds of those placed over him, and what at first sight might have appeared to be impracticable has become for many years a recorded and gratifying fact.

" It is not averred that the mind of every convict is, in these establishments, bent upon well doing, but that the tone of general feeling is that of desiring to amend, and is in the closest alliance with the system.

" It is evident that this result is the attainment of an enormous power, which it would be impossible to secure by mere routine or mechanical appliances.

" The Convict has felt the intention of the system, the scope of which has been made clear to his mind—that he is an individual whose special case and progress is noted, and very carefully watched in its development."

Having gone through these stages, Sir W. CROFTON says,—

" It is now time to inquire how stands the case of the repeatedly convicted robber J. B., who stood before us scowling and in his chains when last we pictured him. His sentence was fortunately long and in proportion to his criminal career. His prison conduct was for some time reckless and ungovernable; he defied the authorities, and repudiated the marks which chronicled what he could not, or would not obtain.

" Time, however, coupled with reflection and example, had worked a change in his case, as in that of many others; and although his misconduct caused his detention many years longer in the second stage than it need otherwise have been, before he could attain the requirement fixed for the Intermediate Establishments, he at last reached that goal.

" It was difficult to recognise J. B., scowling and defiant at all around him, in J. B. in the Intermediate Establishment, cheerfully and willingly giving his labour, after the ordinary hours, to save the harvest for the State which had not only imprisoned him, but, in its strict requirement, had detained him for years after his better conducted fellow convicts.

" Reader, why was this? The reason is plain. J. B. was at last cöoperating with those who were desirous of amending him. He had realised that the system which governed him, and under which he had for some time struggled and suffered, was innately just, although necessarily severe.

" J. B. has been employed since his liberation at honest industry.

" There are many cases similar to that of J. B., although some greater and some less in degree."

Such is a brief sketch of the Irish Convict System.

The third or Intermediate Stage has been so fully described by the various witnesses whom we have already quoted, that it will be unnecessary to enter into more detail respecting them; but it will be useful to have before us some details of the first and second stages, given by Sir W. CROFTON to the Royal Commissioners; as in previous extracts, the questions and answers are blended, and extraneous matter omitted, so as to form one continued narrative :—

" In Ireland this first stage is made very penal by the omission of meat from the dietary for the first four months. This was at first tried as an experiment. It was my own opinion that the convicts had a larger dietary, when in separation, than was necessary for them. There might be some reason for giving them a better dietary when they were in association on the public works; but in separation it did not appear to me to be necessary. I called upon the medical officer to try an experiment for two months with an absence of meat from the dietary; he tried that experiment; and then I had another experiment tried for three months; and at last we attained four months; when I left Ireland, four months without a meat diet had been in use for some years. I am not at all persuaded in my own mind that four months need be the maximum for the absence of meat. My own opinion is, that if the convicts were given meat one month before they go to the associated labour prisons, it would be quite sufficient for them.

" The absence of interesting employment during the first three months is a feature which is peculiar to the Irish system. I will give the reasons as clearly as I can, and explain why the absence of interesting employment was necessary. What I mean by interesting employment is, the teaching of men trades when they come into the prisons. My observation was, that I found them all at work in their cells, learning shoemaking and all kinds of trades— and requiring, because very few of them in proportion were tradesmen, the attendance of the trades' warders to have constant intercourse with them, in order to obtain instruction. Now we have erected these prisons at an enormous cost for the purpose of creating, as I hope, depressing influences upon the minds of these men, before you work upon them in other ways. I felt that if they could converse, as they must converse in order to receive instruction, with the warders, during nearly the whole of the day, the warders coming backwards and forwards whenever they were required, the effect of the punishment of isolation would be very materially sacrificed. A change was made, and they were given, for the first three months, oakum to pick, and nothing else. To the public there could be no gain in trying to teach these employments, for what is done with these men afterwards? They were sent, nearly all of them, to the public works prisons—and these men were immediately to be made stonecutters and labourers, whom we had endeavoured to make cobblers at a sacrifice of material, and, still worse, of the depressing influences for which the prisons had been built.

" That in most cases a decidedly depressing effect was worked upon the prisoners by this treatment, in the first three months, at Mountjoy prison, I have no doubt; and not only from my own observation, and from the observations of the governors and officers of prisons, but from information obtained from the convicts after their liberation; a natural consequence I think of less diet and the absence of what I have called interesting employment, which had the effect of keeping the separation more distinct for a period of time. After three months, those who had been tradesmen, that is shoemakers and tailors, who did not require any special instruction, were set to work at their trades ; others, who had no trade, were employed in mending the sheets of the prison establishments—in mending clothes, and in boot-closing, employments that do not require any supervision on the part of the officers; but they were not taught any trade.

"A prisoner during his stay at Mountjoy prison is one hour every day at school; but there is a great deal more taught him at Mountjoy than ordinary school instruction; he learns the whole scope of the convict system in Ireland; and when I say that he learns the whole scope of that system, it is an important matter that he should know everything that will be done with him with reference to his marks,—how his progress is recorded,—and how much depends upon his own exertions in every stage, to improve his position.

"This is made the subject of school lectures. The convicts are called up, and on a black board are required to illustrate the mark system, and to explain what will be done with them after they are out. They are made perfectly aware of the police arrangements of the country, and I am satisfied that these arrangements being impressed upon their minds at the commencement of their sentences, induces on their parts a feeling of coöperation with the system; they feel that they cannot pursue crime to the extent which they did formerly with impunity; and I am sure that this knowledge makes a very great impression on the general body of prisoners.

"The system of marks was introduced by Captain KNIGHT, who was at one time governor of Portland Prison, and who afterwards established Portsmouth Prison, and had had considerable experience in organising military prisons.

"The principle of marks was introduced, I believe, in the first instance, by the Archbishop of Dublin or by Captain MACONOCHIE; I am far from thinking that the Irish system of marks is perfect, but it answers the purpose. I know that Captain KNIGHT, who had had the experience I have mentioned, was the person who found a want of record in the English Prisons, and instituted this system in Ireland; and also that Captain WHITTY, who was a director of prisons in this country, after being governor of Portland Prison, a gentleman of great experience, believes it to be a very satisfactory system. I believe that he had thought of a similar scheme before he came to Ireland. Now these marks appear very trifling things in themselves, but they are of the greatest importance to the convicts, and they feel it so. Their position is better realised, and is made more intelligible to them.

"The maximum number of marks that each convict can obtain monthly is nine, but they are distributed under three different headings, namely, three for discipline, that is, for general regularity and orderly demeanour; three for school, that is, for attention and a desire for improvement or industry in the school. I should mention that it is not for a degree of attainment, but for industry in school. It is quite possible for an ignorant man, if learning his letters, to learn his letters industriously, and in that case he would get his maximum number of marks, while another man who could read very well perhaps would not get them; the marks are divided into three, two, and one, three being the highest under each head; three for industry, that is industry at work, not skill, which may have been previously acquired.

"The three heads are discipline, school and work. Now a convict must attain a maximum of marks during his detention to justify his obtaining a full remission of the term authorised by the regulations for the ticket-of-leave.

" This is the notice that is given to the convicts when they enter the prison *(handing in the same)*, and if a man does not accumulate enough marks in the time it is his own fault, and he is kept back till he does. Take the case of a man who is sentenced to three years' penal servitude, he must produce his document, and show that he is in the first class, with 90 marks made, before he can pass into the Intermediate Prison ; if he has been longer than the usual time in attaining them, he would not come into the Intermediate Prison until later, but that would be his own fault and not ours; he must then remain a certain time in the Intermediate Prison in proportion to his sentence, and therefore it not only delays his coming into the Intermediate Prison, but it postpones his obtaining his ticket-of-leave. A proportion is laid down for each sentence, and when you examine the sentences you will find the number who have been sent out on tickets-of-leave, and the periods of remission will show how this system has worked. I should also explain the classes in the stages; there are four classes in the stage at Spike Island, the third, the second and the first, and the advanced or A class. This class was called ' exemplary ' for two or three years, but we thought that the term exemplary was not very applicable to convicts, and it is now called the advanced class. It is possible for a convict to raise himself from the third class to the second class in two months. When they leave the separate prison they go into the third class; they begin low down in that class, on the ground that in separation there is little opportunity of doing much amiss, it does not afford the same test as the other prisons. It would be the highest number of marks attainable (18) by a convict that would get him from the third to the second class in two months. He could get from the second to the first class in six months, provided he attains 54 marks in that period; nine is the maximum for a month, if not attained, the convict gets delayed in each class before he is moved, in consequence of this want of marks telling against him ; then he can get from the first to A or the advanced class in 12 months, provided he has attained 108, that is nine marks a month, 12 times nine making 108. When a convict has reached the A class his progress is noted, as A 1, A 2, and so on ; any misconduct causes a reduction and suspension or a loss of marks.

" A convict has no gratuity in separation, but he has 1*d.* a week in the third class, 2*d.* a week in the second class, and 3*d.* and 4*d.* in the first class, which is divided. That is reserved for the convict to receive when he goes out of prison. It is from 7*d.* to 9*d.* in the advanced or A class. Now I will call the attention of the Commission to the lowness of the gratuities in this system, because it is considered that the convicts should have a long up-hill career for some time as a test. The Directors believe them to be thus better tried before they give them a higher gratuity, which I shall explain when I come to the Intermediate Prisons. In the 3rd class it is 1*d.*, in the second class 2*d.*, and in the first class 3*d.* and 4*d.*, and in the advanced class it is from 7*d.* to 9*d.* Taking the whole of the gratuities in the Intermediate Prisons, and all other prisons, the average amount of the gratuities in Ireland is about one-half of what it is in England.

"When men attain the A class or the advanced class in that stage, they are moved by the system to another part of the establishment, and are employed on special works; the men who are idlers are kept by themselves in a class. The men who are dangerous are kept by themselves also, and withdrawn altogether from the general labourers of the prison. They are subject to very strict treatment; for instance, the idlers, who do not do their work and interfere with the general class, are put by themselves and employed, with very little food; the dietaries are altered specially for them.

"There is another class of men who assault the officers—violent men—who are kept in what is called the dangerous class. They are kept in chains to prevent them doing further mischief, and also only upon such dietary as the medical officer thinks is absolutely necessary for them; but it is very low.

"There is a class of dietary for the idlers, and a class for the dangerous men, and they are kept perfectly separate; their dietary is reduced until they show, by their future conduct, that they deserve to be put into the ordinary labour classes. Now, I attribute to this minute classification of these men, the being able for the last three and a half years to do without flogging, although I may add that I have no objection to find flogging retained as a punishment. *We have not resorted to it during the last three and a half years*, proving, I think, that this kind of classification, under stringent rules, is very advantageous; it is satisfactory to know that although at the commencement there were several in these classes, very few are in them now.

"I can record from actual experience that the marks are of the utmost value; that they are the means of acting upon a man as an individual, and of realising to him his own position and his own means of progress; I know of no other way in which you can equally produce that effect upon him. I am quite satisfied that wherever the system of marks is tried it will succeed.

"There are four persons who are connected with the appointment of the marks; viz., the officer of the gang, the schoolmaster, the principal warders, and the governor; and with regard to the convict, he has the means of seeing the director as to anything which he believes to have been unjustly noted against him.

"I have already called attention to the advanced class; the moment that a man attains a position in that class he is put into a detached portion of the prison, and kept there under a different system. That class have their meals and work together, they are employed on special works at Haulbowline, and have more work, because they have school in the evening; they are dealt with specially in every way; the 1st, 2nd, and 3rd are worked together. They are in a distinct building."

The prisoners are thus prepared for their increased liberty in the intermediate stages in Lusk and Smithfield; there they are fitted for their absolute discharge from the Convict Prisons, or for their conditional freedom under license, or ticket-of-leave. This is the most critical period, and that which is the final and absolute test of the effect of the treatment they have received in the Convict Prisons on these persons who had been living a predatory and lawless life. We have seen that in England all real supervision of the Convict ceases after he has left his place of confinement; while, theoretically, his release is conditional, practically he is nearly in the same position as if he had completed his sentence of punishment. In some respects he is even more at liberty to commit crime, since, in the metropolis, the police have special orders not to exercise the same supervision over him as over suspicious characters in general. We know what the consequences of this procedure have been in England. In Ireland the same Act of Parliament is in operation as in England. Every Convict liberated receives a license endorsed with the same conditions which have been already stated, vol. I, p. 187. These are in Ireland very stringently enforced; a course which has proved to be most beneficial, both to the public and to the Convicts. Attached to the license is appended, in Ireland, the following instructions to the Convict:—

"1. Each convict will report himself to the Constabulary Station of his locality on his arrival in the district, and subsequently on the 1st of each month.

"2. A convict must not change his locality without notifying to his Constabulary Station, in order that his registration may be changed to the locality to which he is about to proceed.

"3. An infringement of these rules, by the convict, will cause it to be assumed that he is leading an idle and irregular life, and thereby entail a revocation of his license.

---

"*Chairman of Board of Directors, Government Prisons' Office,*
*Dublin Castle.*

---

"Constabulary Station at which
to report himself."

The system of photography, and the careful registration of every offence, make it almost impossible for any Convict at large to commit an offence, without his being at once detected as an

old offender, and receiving a sentence proportionally longer.
Since the absolute certainty of detection and punishment is the
most reliable deterrent, the knowledge that crime is thus made
a hazardous calling, proves a very strong stimulant to the
Convicts to abandon it, and to lead a very different life.

The supervision of Convicts at large on ticket-of-leave, is
carried on in the country by the police.  In Dublin there is
a fortnightly visitation of the Convicts by Mr. ORGAN, and a
return made of their employment, conduct, &c.   There are about
150 so visited, many of them having been liberated from prison
upwards of five years.   Inquirers from England, Scotland and
the Continent, have repeatedly tested this fact; and have afterwards satisfied themselves that the antecedents of those visited
by them have been " Habitually Criminal."

The nature of this supervision is so unique, as well as successful, and has not only been the subject of so much discussion,
but has excited so much cavil and scepticism, that it will be well
to take Sir W. CROFTON's own account of it, as given to the
Royal Commissioners, in reply to their very close examination:—

" The Dublin supervision commenced in the year before the supervision of
the constabulary, viz., in January, 1856; the supervision in the country began
in January, 1857.    The plan of the Dublin supervision was that the lecturer
should visit every man who was out on ticket-of-leave officially, and bring in a
fortnightly return to my office, and go into each case with me, and show in the
return the employer's name, the standard of wages, and the conduct of the
men; this fortnightly return was filed in the office afterwards.   I always had
this information checked, when necessary, by a detective inspector of police.
I used to call him in in every case that presented difficulty.   If Mr. ORGAN
found in his visits that there was any obstruction to his obtaining from the
convict full information, he was at once handed over to the observation of the
police, in order that they might see very closely whether there was any chance
of his infringing his license.

" Mr. ORGAN saw these men individually every fortnight, and reported on
them to me, with the names of their employers.   This detective inspector
attended at my office two or three times a week, and when he had any notice
of failures, as he had sometimes, he used to tell me of them; he consulted
with me, and then made a return immediately of the exact state of the case.
We had thus a direct police check upon Mr. ORGAN's reports.   Finding in 1856
that some of the men might go out into the country from Dublin and defeat us

altogether, we were led at once to the necessity of having police supervision in the country.    We were in a very false position as to the public in general, from not being able to account for the ticket-of-leave convicts.    We felt that we must be able to say where these men were, or it would produce such a panic that the men would never get employment at all.    With regard to the supervision in Dublin, nothing can be more strict, for when anything bad is heard about a man his license is revoked immediately, and there is this fortnightly official list kept as a check.    This is merely a portion or extract from the list (*the same being handed in*); extracts from Mr. ORGAN's usual fortnightly reports; he has not confined himself simply to the prisoners discharged on ticket-of-leave, but he has habitually visited, also, other men who have been discharged under the Penal Servitude Act of 1853, whose sentences had expired, but who still resided in Dublin, over whom we have no legal check, but obtain this information.    He has visited them and placed them on our reports as well as the others; it is of course clear that any of these men unconditionally discharged could have closed their doors against him if they had wished, but this visitation has extended over some 400 or 500 people of this class in Dublin.    It is of importance because it brings a certain knowledge of these people to us that could not be attained in any other way, both as to the result of our system and the lives they were leading.    This report refers to what are called the old Act men—that means men who had been under sentence of transportation, and this document is with reference to men who were under sentence of transportation.    The first case that I come to is that of a man whose crime was burglary, there were former convictions, he had been bad in crime for eight years; there is his name, his residence, his employer's name, and his employment, and his wages.    The date of his conviction was in 1852, and he was discharged from the Convict Prisons the 9th September, 1857, he is still reported upon; he commenced to work at 8s. a week, but now his wages are much higher.    He had been sentenced to ten years' transportation; he was convicted in 1852 and his term expired in 1862, he is still on this list.    In the next case the crime was burglary, former convictions, and for years in crime; he was employed under a public body, his name is given, his residence, and wages; he has been out since the 5th July, 1857.    That was a case of ten years' transportation.    It also gives the general conduct of those men; there are observations to every one of them. I think that there are something like 140 men under the supervision of Mr. ORGAN, in Dublin, at this moment.

"I had, when in office, constant communication with the detective officers in the Dublin police, who were assisting Mr. ORGAN in the supervision of these men.    They were a very material assistance to me in carrying out the supervision.    They took a considerable amount of trouble when a case required it.

"Mr. ORGAN always went to the house of the employer and saw the man and the employer.    The man was sent for and Mr. ORGAN then spoke to him.

"I never heard that the circumstance of his going to visit these men so frequently was a means of discovering to their fellow workmen who they were.

The employers themselves, so far from objecting to his visits, encouraged them, and considered them to a very great extent a protection to themselves.

" The slightest infringement of the conditions of the license leads to a revocation of it. *I do not believe—and I have often put this forth when I was in the department—that any case could be proved of a man breaking the conditions of his license in Ireland, and remaining at large; he was sure to be put back to separation, and his license revoked.*

" If we found that a man was within a fortnight of the expiration of his sentence, and had infringed some of the conditions of the ticket-of-leave, we sent that man back to prison, for the sake of the principle. I do not know that it has ever occurred in a case so close as a fortnight, but it has done so close as a month or three weeks. The circumstance of his sentence being so nearly expired did not interfere with that in the slightest degree.

" They were generally easily caught. They were put in the 'Hue and Cry,' a warrant was issued, and there were very few cases in which they baffled us. At first there were a great many shifts and trials to evade, but ultimately and before long, when they found that many had their licenses revoked, and were brought back, they did not even try to baffle us as they did at first.

" In the county prisons, when prisoners are suspected or known to have been convicts, they send up a form containing particulars, with a description of the person suspected or known to be a discharged convict. That comes to the convict prison office, in order that the man may be identified; and very often when it is necessary, if a man at all demurs to his identification, a prison officer is sent down to identify him, and if found guilty of any crime, a letter is in all cases placed on the table of the judical officer, which has been written to the governor of the gaol, the letter being in these terms:—' Government Prisons' Office.—Sir,—The enclosed particulars of —— —— have been compared with the books of this office, and are correct. In the event of his being found guilty of the present charge the directors of convict prisons request that the notice of the judge may be particularly called to the circumstance of his being an 'habitual offender,' with the view of his receiving a sentence proportionate to his perseverance in pursuing a course of crime. Please to notify the result of the trial to this office, and return the enclosure at the same time.' This is a case which actually occurred. A man was convicted for picking pockets. He was a convict, and this course was pursued with him. It entailed upon him a sentence of ten years' penal servitude. His character as an habitual criminal was taken into consideration by the judge. I am able to speak confidently on two most important points— information with regard to habitual offenders being sent in each case to the county prisons; and in the case of ticket-of-leave men that their licenses have been always revoked for an infringement of the conditions.

" It is not very difficult for an officer in Dublin to recognise a man of whom a description is sent from a provincial town. He has had this man perhaps within the last four or five years in his custody, and besides the general description, and the aid of photography, there is a margin left for observations; practically it is found that very few come into the Convict Prisons who have not been known in some way, and whose identification has not been made. The result is that the practice succeeds in a very great majority of cases, and operates very beneficially upon the minds of the convicts.

" The supervision of convicts in the country is thus carried on through the constabulary. There is a notification made to the inspector-general of the constabulary the moment a man is liberated, stating to what district he is going; the man then registers himself with the head of the police, states what he is going to do, where he is going to be employed, and reports himself to him once a month. If he removes from that district, his registration is transferred from the district he is in at that time, to the one to which he goes, so that he is traced from one place to another. If he does anything to infringe the terms of his license, the constabulary report him, and his license is revoked at once.

" He must come himself once a month, and report himself to the police, but it is evident that the police do not confine themselves to that, for, knowing where he is, they would look after him a little oftener, without interfering with him. I can state from my own experience that there is no undue espionage or oppression practised by the police.

" In the first instance I had a very large number of complaints from the convicts generally; they came almost in a body, stating that they would rather be kept to the end of their sentences than go out with such a stigma; but as it was quite evident that they would have had to remain to the end of their sentences, as they could not get out on any other terms, that feeling very shortly vanished, and they preferred being placed under police supervision. I have seen some hundreds of these people after being subjected to supervision, and with the exception of two cases, in which I recollect complaints being made of interference, nothing detrimental occurred. I state distinctly that in my opinion there has been no undue interference on the part of the police. It is quite probable that some man, when doing wrong, would state that he had been interfered with; but I know in general practice it is not true.

" I am quite sure that if police supervision were withdrawn to-morrow from the licensed convicts in Ireland, you would find but little employment for them, and you would have very serious trouble. I have no doubt that it is a very great protection to the public in Ireland."

Sir WALTER CROFTON's mature opinion respecting this system, is expressed in the following statement to the Commissioners. After speaking of the Intermediate Prisons, he says (3151) :—

"Another great point of difference between the English and the Irish Systems was the institution of supervision after liberation, and here I at once acknowledge what has been adduced against us, ' that there must have been very weak faith on the part of the directors in their own system, when they thought it necessary to supplement it by supervision after liberation.' I acknowledge, and I am sure that my colleagues would do the same, that I have a weak faith in any mere prison system, and I think it is far better, both for the public and the convict himself, to check his prison conduct and the prison system by the infallible test of observation when he is at liberty. During the process of classification I had taken the pains to go through somewhere between 2,000 and 3,000 convict cases, and I satisfied myself from their antecedents, and from other points brought to my notice during this examina- tion, that a very great majority belonged to the criminal class, and would in ordinary course return to thieving. It therefore made it imperative, according to my mind, that we should not treat persons as casual offenders, who are in the convict prisons, but expressly as criminals living in crime by habit and repute. It was therefore necessary to surround, by every possible means, the commission of crime by obstructions. It was quite clear that if you could impress upon the minds of this class that if they pursued a course of crime after liberation, they would be brought back to prison again and have length- ened sentences entailed upon them; if you could tell them confidently that the conditions of the licenses would be enforced, it would serve in a great measure to indoctrinate them with the idea that crime would be unprofitable. I am quite sure that the success of the Irish System has been indebted mainly to a feeling on the part of the convicts from the commencement of their sentences, that they could not follow crime as a vocation with impunity. I believe firmly that the great evils which have occurred in England, and the very great expenditure consequent on crime, has arisen from our believing that the majority of the convicts in the government prisons were casual offenders. I am satisfied that there never was a greater delusion. If the police were taken into consultation, as I have always made a point of taking them into consultation in Ireland, the antecedents of these people would be reliably ascertained, and speaking of England I feel sure that the Commission- ers would find that from 70 to 75 per cent. at least live by crime. It is with them a vocation—a business; and I assert that we have no reason to assume that they are only waiting for employment in order to live honestly; on the contrary, we are bound to assume, from their former lives, that they will not do so, and therefore should take such precautions as shall protect society against them; and in the process of protecting society against them, we shall also protect them against themselves, and that I am, from practical experience, prepared to prove. These are the main features of the difference between the two systems, which start from different bases; but it will observed that the Irish Convict System in its procedure makes cases against itself, and therefore its statistical results cannot be fairly compared with any other system."

These extracts from the evidence of the Chairman of the Board of Directors of the Irish Convict Prisons will have given some idea of the principles on which they are conducted,

and of their general management.  The most minute details in
the system having been the subject of deep thought, and the
result of long experience, the evidence of Captain WHITTY,
at that time (March, 1863) sole Director, respecting the dietary,
gratuities, &c., will be valuable.  It will be remembered that
Captain WHITTY had been formerly Governor of Portland
Convict Prison.  Of his management of that prison the Rev. J.
W. MORAN, who was Chaplain there for five years from its commencement in 1848, speaks in high terms.  He says, in his
evidence before the Commission (4745):—" The discipline at
Portland during the years I was there, was in every way
satisfactory.  The discipline was such that it was most remarkable and pleasing.  Captain WHITTY and I laboured together
there.  He was the Governor, as also was Captain KNIGHT,
both of whom are very superior men, and everything was in
the most satisfactory state when I left the prison.  There was
not the same number of prisoners then as there is now—viz.,
about 1,500—but between 900 and 1,000."  Captain WHITTY
was therefore in a position to perceive and point out the
differences of discipline between the English and the Irish
Convict Prisons.  Of this he says, generally,—" I think that
the earlier stages, up to the time that the men come to the
Intermediate Prisons, are certainly more rigid than in England.
That the whole period of confinement in Ireland, up to the
time when they go into the Intermediate Prisons, is a severer
system of punishment than in England."

The following are extracts from his evidence :—

"I think the points in which the Irish System is mainly distinguished
from the English System are, first, the greater stringency in the first period
of the sentence ; that is, in the stage of separate confinement, in which the
prisoners in Ireland receive no meat diet for the first four months, and
have no occupation during the first three months but the distasteful labour of
oakum-picking ; they receive no gratuity during the period of separate confinement, and that generally extends to eight or nine months.  The second
distinction is, a more minute plan of classification on the public works as the
second stage.  It consists in the use of a greater number of successive classes
through which the prisoners have to climb, and can thus be more effectually

sifted in their progress, for the purpose of dealing with them individually. Thirdly, there is a lower scale of gratuity in the earlier stages in the Irish Prisons, the higher rates being reserved for the later and superior classes, which makes this an important object of attainment to the prisoners, inducing in them the habit of looking forward, and of exerting and controlling themselves for a future benefit. Fourthly, the Intermediate Prisons, which are a special means of mental improvement, and of preparing the prisoner for the transition from confinement to liberty, and also of testing this preparation. Fifthly, there is a more rigid enforcement of the conditions on which the prisoners are set at large on license; there is a regular supervision, during the period of such licenses, either by the police or by an officer specially employed for the purpose. Sixthly and lastly, there is a process of tracing back, and placing before the judges, &c., the cases of habitual offenders. These appear to me to be the principal points on which the two systems differ." (3087.)

He thus states the system of gratuities in the Irish Prisons :—

"I am afraid I cannot correctly give you the English gratuities; as to the Irish gratuities, I have prepared a memorandum, but one distinction between the English and the Irish classification I should mention. In England, if a man's conduct is good in separate confinement, on being removed to the public works, he goes immediately into the first class; we require our men who go from separate confinement to commence in the third class, but we make this distinction, if they come with a good character they remain for only two months in that third class, whereas, if they come with a bad character they may be nine months in that class; but they all begin in the third class. I will now state what is the largest amount of gratuity which is attainable by a convict under a sentence of four years' penal servitude. I will take a man of the best character; he would be two months in the third class on public works; and eight weeks at a penny per week would amount to 8d. Then he would be for six months in the second class, or 26 weeks, and for those weeks he would get 2d. a week, making 4s. 4d. Then he would be in the first class twelve months, which are divided into two parts; for the first six months, or 26 weeks, he would receive 3d. a week, and during the second six months in the first class, or 26 weeks, he would receive 4d. a week; the first six months at 3d. yielding 6s. 6d., and the second six months at 4d. yielding 8s. 8d., and the two together for the year making 15s. 2d. Then this man would get into the advanced class, and a four years' man without any prison offences, his conduct being satisfactory, would be in that class 26 weeks; he would here receive 9d. a week, which in 26 weeks would amount to 19s. 6d. By that time he ought to have reached the Intermediate Prison. A four years' man is supposed to remain therein for five months before his discharge, these five months, or about 21 weeks at 2s. 6d. a week in the Intermediate Prison, giving £2 12s. 6d.; the total for a four years' man having a claim to a license would be £4 12s. 2d. (3695.)

"The total amount of gratuities that a man can receive in Ireland with a four years' sentence is about half the amount that he could receive under the same sentence in England, supposing that in both cases he earns the maximum." (3698.)

The dietary is a striking contrast to that in the English Convict Prisons :—

"I have an account here of the dietary for one convict at the Mountjoy Male Prison. On reception, for four months, he gets no meat; he gets in a week 3½ lbs. of oatmeal, 10¼ lbs. of bread, 12½ pints of milk, 2 ounces of rice, and 4 ounces of vegetables; they also get soup which is made of ox heads, but they get no actual meat given to them at all. They get no potatoes. The solid food in this case is only the oatmeal and the bread, and they would be together 14 lbs., 3½ lbs. of oatmeal and 10¼ lbs. of bread in a week. The oatmeal is made into porridge."

"In the next stage at Mountjoy the ordinary diet for the second four months in separation is oatmeal 3½ lbs., bread 10 lbs., milk 12½ pints, beef 1½ lbs. (weighed before cooking), rice 2 ounces, and vegetables 4 ounces, that is merely for the soup. The meat is boiled and made into soup; they get the meat only on two days in the week, Thursdays and Sundays, and that is at the rate of three-quarters of a pound each day, two days in the week. This dietary has been in force since 1860; it began experimentally; for some time it was tried for one month, and then the medical officer approved of its being tried for two months, and then for three months, and now it is the practice for four months. There were no ill effects produced by that diet. In the case of the small number of prisoners who are confined beyond eight months at Mountjoy, they get 12¼ ounces of oatmeal, 12½ ounces of rice, 11 pints of milk, and they also get coffee for breakfast, and some molasses for sweetening it, 11¼ lbs. of bread, 2 lbs. of beef (weighed before cooking), 4 ounces of vegetables, and 8 ounces of potatoes, that is after the eight months, but those men are put into association, and they work out of doors until they are removed; it is a small number only. There is no other diet given at Mounjoy, except to prisoners under prison discipline, who have bread and water."

"I will now give the dietary at Spike Island. The ordinary diet at Spike Island is 24½ ounces of oatmeal, 24½ ounces of rice, 12¼ pints of milk, 13 lbs. of bread, 2 lbs. of beef (weighed before cooking), and two ounces of vegetables. They get meat four times in the week, Tuesdays, Thursdays, Saturdays and Sundays, half-a-pound each day. On the other three days they only get stirabout, bread and milk, on Mondays, Wednesdays and Fridays. In the penal class at Spike Island they get no meat at all. We have two classes there, one called the penal class, and the probation labour class. These last are men who are exceedingly idle, and do nothing but pick oakum. They have a diet without any meat in it at all. They mind their deprivation so much that at present out of 700 men we have only four in that class. A reduction in the diet is very effectual in keeping up the discipline of the prison. I think that the diet at Spike Island is sufficient for the labour that the men perform, to keep them in health and strength. The medical officer never suggests any addition to be made to it. I believe that we have at this time eight in the penal class, four in the probation class, 96 in the third class, and 186 in the second class, 213 in the first class, 115 in advanced class, and 88 in a special class preparing for Intermediate Prisons.

"At Lusk and Smithfield the dietaries are quite different from the others· The Smithfield dietary is 12¼ lbs. of bread, ⅞ of an ounce of tea, 5¼ ounces of sugar, 3⁵⁄₁₆ pints of milk, 34 ounces of beef (weighed before cooking; they have 5 ounces of oatmeal, 5 ounces of vegetables, 10½ lbs. of potatoes, 1¹⁄₁₆ ounce of coffee, a proportion of chicory, and 8⅛ ounces of molasses. That is the Smithfield dietary, and these quantities have all been fixed by the medical officer. The dietary for Lusk is ⅛ of an ounce of tea, ¾ of an ounce of sugar, 21¼ ounces of oatmeal, 21¼ ounces of rice, 11¼ lbs. of bread, 7⁴⁄₁₆ pints of milk, 2¼ lbs. of beef (weighed before cooking), they get that divided in in three days in the week), 14 lbs. of potatoes, five ounces of vegetables, 1⅛ ounce of coffee, a proportion of chicory, and 9⅛ ounces of molasses. I think a higher dietary is not given in any prison in England, but I cannot exactly compare the two. We tried to get it lowered, but the medical officer interfered and said that the men were out all day upon an exposed common, and got very wet, and therefore we had to raise it to that. The medical officer said that the health of the men was failing in consequence of their previous diet, and he said that the men required this to keep up their strength."

### With respect to the labour, Captain WHITTY says :—

"We have very little labour done that is capable of measurement; it is principally different kinds of quarrying work, filling up holes, and paring down the surface of the rock to the sea, to shape the fortification, and there is very little of that kind of work that is capable of being measured. We keep the men steadily at work, and we know what the cost of hired labour would be on the spot; we think that we are fairly justified in going near to that sum. Some of the work can be measured, and that is done by the Royal Engineers' department. We have no clerk of the works, as they have in English prisons, and we depend upon the Royal Engineers' department and their clerk of the works, under whom our men are employed, for the measurements. They report to us if the work is not satisfactory. I think that the men work very fairly there, quite as well as the free labourers. We keep a little under the amount given to the free labourers. We value the labour of each man about 1s. 6d. a day. A trifle under the wages of an ordinary labourer for that sort of work. We find out what labourers are employed for at Spike Island, when a contractor hires them. An able-bodied labourer would earn 1s. 8d. a day at Spike Island.

Captain WHITTY is able to state from his personal official knowledge the very important fact, that since he has been

Director of Convict Prisons in Ireland, there has never been anything in the shape of a mutiny or outbreak in them. He also says:—"I have not noticed any mutinous spirit general among them; we have had once or twice a little symptom of dissatisfaction; there have been violent acts done by individuals or by a few, but no combinations or outbreaks. There have been threats made by the men of one county against the men of another, of a sort of faction fight, but we have always managed to put those things down."

It is unnecessary to quote Captain WHITTY's description of the supervision of the licensed Convicts, as that is in every respect similar to what has been already stated by Sir WALTER CROFTON in his evidence. But our account of the working of the Irish Convict System would be incomplete without the personal testimony of Mr. ORGAN, to whom reference has been so often made in connection with the Intermediate Prisons. The coöperation of a person of zeal, Christian spirit, and sympathising heart, was indispensable in the new and difficult work of supervision over Convicts on license; and at the same time it was essential that such a person should be an official who would strictly conform to the prison regulations, and who, in his labours, which might in a certain sense be termed voluntary, would be still guided by the superior wisdom and judgment of the Directors. Such an individual they were fortunate in finding in Mr. ORGAN, and they have always shown themselves ready to acknowledge his merits. But it would be very erroneous to suppose that he possesses unique qualifications, to which are due the success with which his efforts have been followed, and that it were in vain to hope for the same results if the system were adopted by any other person. Such objection was made, such difficulty started, when Reformatory Schools were first proposed. "Where," it was asked, "shall we find persons who will undertake so unpleasant and difficult a work, or who will have qualifications fitted for it? We know that there are individuals who possess special gifts, and who have had wonderful success in reforming young persons. But where will be found a DEMETZ, a WICHERN? How can we multiply the very few in our own country who have shown equal zeal, and who have had similar success? The Reformatory Schools will be a failure, for we know none who will be able and willing to give themselves to the work." It was answered then, that the work itself would raise up labourers, and prepare them, if faithful and zealous, to be equally successful with those who had first shown them the way. We had confidence in the existence in our country of a sufficient number of able and Christian men and women to afford such help, and our expectations have been realised. The work itself has trained the labourers in it, who humbly desire to be always learners as well as teachers, and who have applied themselves to it with loving hearts and devoted spirits. We cannot then doubt that whenever the Government of our country shall be ready to adopt the system which has been so successful in Ireland, persons will be found to work it with equal zeal and ability, who will encounter fewer difficulties than those which had to be surmounted at the commencement of the new work, because they have the advantage of the experience already acquired. Mr. ORGAN's exertions have obtained for him the esteem of all who are acquainted with them, and we trust that many will be found in our own country to emulate him. We will now, then, turn to his evidence before the Royal Commission. He tells them that he is known in his official position as lecturer to the Irish Intermediate Establishments, an appointment which he has held for more than seven years. His previous occupation was that of Superintendent of the adult evening schools in Dublin. "From early boyhood," he says, "I have been accustomed to appear as a teacher of adult labourers, who, after the close of their daily toil, repaired to the night schools over which I presided, and I have seen those men anxiously embracing the opportunity they had in an evening, but I have never seen greater anxiety or eagerness displayed to improve themselves by men of the non-criminal class than amongst the men from Smithfield and Lusk. Although they do hard work during the day, I have found no difficulty in inducing them to receive instruction for a certain limited time in the evening. They look forward to my going in amongst them with a kind of delight. My duties are to bring before the Convicts of Smithfield and Lusk subjects that are calculated to make them thinking beings. I speak to them upon social questions, such as taxes, strikes, combinations, illegal societies, industry, and honesty; what they have to gain by the commission of crime, and what they have to lose, that is, in a temporal point of view, because I do not allow myself for a moment to infringe upon the duties of any of the respective chaplains. I have before me a copy of a little work of mine, containing the lectures which I deliver to the men, both at Smithfield and at Lusk. The subjects in this little book are— Air; Water; Plants; Canada and her resources; the Ocean; Temperance and Self-control; Australia, past and present; Life, its battles, and how to fight them. My duties are not confined merely to giving lectures, but I exercise a supervision over the discharged Convicts. In addition to that I endeavour to procure employment for these men."

To understand the nature of Mr. ORGAN's work, and his mode of executing it, we must follow him in his details of it:—

"At the outset it was a labour of great difficulty to procure employment for those men on their discharge. I commenced my duties in February, 1856. I drew out a map of the county of Dublin, dividing it into baronies, laying down upon this map the different post towns, also the mills, and factories, and farms, showing the names of the proprietors, the nature of those works, and so on. Having done this, I set out to see such and such employer. Sometimes I was scoffed at, and on more than one occasion the hall door was closed in my face. Still I persevered, and I was very well satisfied, if, after going a distance of 40 or 50 miles, I should meet with one employer who would give one of my Smithfield men a chance to work out his character once more.

When I secured one, I visited both the employer and the employed, and I continue to do so down to the present time. The employer would ask me what control I had, or the government had, over the men. I, of course, explained, but I will give a case in point. Some five years ago I went to a gentleman who was a very large employer, and I saw him. I explained to him my mission. I was a long time in inducing him to give me a chance, but after many repeated visits I did succeed. He took one man. I visited that man once a fortnight, although he had removed from Dublin a distance of ten miles, and I visited the employer. That man succeeded in giving the employer satisfaction, and the employer afterwards applied for another, afterwards for another, and previous to my leaving Dublin this employer wrote the following letter, dated 21st February, 1863 :—'Dear Sir,—In reply to your letter, I beg leave to state that it was at your earnest solicitation that I was induced to take convicts into my employment, in the first instance. I have now had fully five years' experience of them, during which time they have given me universal satisfaction. I have one at present in my employment, in whose honesty I have such confidence that I have made him a sort of watchman, and he has for the last few days detected parties robbing me. Another saved enough to enable him to emigrate to Australia. A third, in shovelling up some manure, found a silver spoon, which he at once gave me. In conclusion I can only say that whenever you have an able-bodied man whom you can recommend, it will afford me much pleasure to give him employment.' This employer was one whom I secured, I assure you, after a great deal of trouble, through the character and conduct of the first man he had employed. I found great difficulty at first in procuring employment for them, but that difficulty has diminished since the employers have had experience of the men. Since such employers as these have been found, the difficulty, of course, does not exist now to so great an extent; but I think that, if I were to go over the same task again with other employers, I should have the same difficulty to encounter.

" My bi-monthly visits are valued very much by employers, who frequently say to me, ' I do not like to speak to the man for doing so and so. You had better do so; he will attend more to what you say than what I say.' I have frequently, in a country place, got 9 or 10 of these men behind a hayrick, and advise them what to do; in many cases they take a greater interest in their employment than ordinary workmen do, because they know that the employers have taken them out of prison, and thrown, as it were, a cloak of protection over them.

" I do not find that there is any sympathy with the criminals amongst the honest classes in Ireland, that would induce them the more readily to take these convicts into employment.

" In my supervision of the convicts who are placed under my charge, I communicate with the detective police on some occasions. I will explain the nature of my supervision, showing how the detective police and I work hand in hand. This letter which I am about to read explains the matter fully :—

'13, Richmond Fair View, Co. Dublin,
'January 10, 1863.

' Sir,—In reply to your inquiry as to my opinion of the working of the ticket-of-leave system in Ireland, I beg leave to submit the following statement of my practical experience day and night of the Smithfield men discharged on license and otherwise, and working and residing in the city and county of Dublin. It is perhaps necessary that I should state that I have been a detective police officer for eleven years, and therefore had an opportunity of making myself acquainted with the working of the new and old system of convict management in Ireland. My experience of the old system was of a most painful character, for the criminals came out of prison worse in fact than they entered, whereas on the other hand I have known very bad characters when discharged from your Intermediate Prisons to engage in steady labour, earning their bread, and absorbed amongst the honest members of the working community. It must have been only by perseverance that any Irish employer of respectable position could be induced to take into his work men who had been habitual thieves and burglars, for the aversion of all men of respectability in Ireland to employ convicts is very great. By this constant intercourse with the directors and yourself, I have on very many occasions been enabled to prevent the commission of additional crime, by visiting the abodes of the persons we had reason to believe intended doing wrong. I have never known a man discharged, and under your supervision, to be convicted of any act bordering upon violence on the person. I think the fact of a numerous and influential class of employers who have many of your discharged convicts in their establishments, is a proof of the great good which has resulted from the working of the Irish Convict System. I am prepared and willing at any time to give information in detail whenever circumstances may require me to do so.

'I remain, &c.,
' TIMOTHY MURPHY,
'To James P. Organ, Esq.,        'Late Acting Inspector, Detective Depart-
5, Mespil, Co., Dublin.'          ment, Dublin Metropolitan Police.

" I divide my visitation reports into three parts, one showing the number under the old Transportation Act; the next showing the number unconditionally discharged, over whom the Government have no control; and the next relates to the Penal Servitude Act of 1857, that gave those short sentences. I will now explain the nature of my supervision. In the visitation form of report there are columns showing, first, the date of a man's conviction, the length of his sentence, the date of his discharge from Smithfield or Lusk, the nature of his last crime, the number of former convictions recorded against him, his name, his residence, the name of his employer, the nature of his employment, the wages which he receives per week, the date if on ticket-of-leave, the date of his time being fully up, and in the margin is a remark upon each man which is made by me. Here is a case, for instance, of a man who was sentenced for ten years for receiving stolen goods, and having under his pillow a blunderbuss; his former character is this,—'A terror to the neighbourhood in which he resides'; his residence is about four miles from Dublin; his employer is Mr. So-and-so; he has remained with that employer since the 9th of April, 1856; he has been from that hour under my supervision; and my last remark was this,—'A man of sober and settled habits, with Mr. So-and-so for the last seven years, wife sober and industrious, has a pig and fowl.' With that kind of connection that exists between me and the discharged convicts, we are not ashamed to know one another, provided no one sees us. I provide employment for all who cannot secure it for themselves.

"Now I will refer to the men under the Act of 1857. The first man on my list was discharged on the 6th of February, 1861; felony was his last crime ; he had been 13 times convicted before, and had been known as a thief since 1845; his name and residence are here put down, and his employment, as before; he was last sentenced to four years; the observation is 'Keeping from crime, contrary to the opinion of many who knew him before.' He has been discharged two years and more now. He is in employment. I know his antecedents, that he was an habitual thief, but in the eleventh hour he gave it up.

"Referring to the connexion between the police and myself, when I find that a man is not going on according to my liking, and he has something suspicious about him, I go to the director, and I either bring the man up if within reach, or tell him about it. I say, 'I do not like the way in which this man is going on;' he may have too smooth an appearance for a hard-working man, or he may be lounging about, or I might find him in his home when he should be out working, or out when he should be in ; then the director takes a note of that; at the same time, if it happens that my suspicions are aroused at night, or when the director is not in the office, and the case is an urgent one, I do not wait for the director to come the following morning, but I go straight to the detective office at the castle-yard ; I there tell the officiating inspector my doubts, and he, as a matter of course, has a close eye upon that man. Then in cases of suspicion I inform the detective authorities; they know that it is their interest and my interest to work hand-in-hand ; and I point out to them sometimes, when I have my documents convenient, the last observation I have made upon the man."

It is very important to observe the manner in which voluntary benevolent effort may thus coöperate with police agency. Mr. O. gives also a valuable testimony to the value of the control thus exercised over the Convicts to the men themselves, by enabling them more easily to get employment. He says :—

"The employers invariably prefer the ticket-of-leave men to convicts who are unconditionally discharged, because they are under more control. The question generally put by employers who have wealth and loose property lying about is, ' How long have the Government control over these men ?' They are always led in a very great degree by the number of years yet to run. Among the list of persons who have employed men who had been discharged from the Intermediate Prisons there are English employers in my district, and they are more generous, in fact, than the Irish. I have found no difficulty in getting English employers to give employment to these men, much less than with the Irish. With regard to any Englishman that I came across, I must say, although I may seem to speak against my own country, that he deals with me more generously. Among those men for whom I have obtained employment there were habitual criminals who had been committing crime for years. I have a case here in which there are 15 reconvictions against a man, and many cases in which there had been varying numbers of previous convictions. Now these men to whom I have referred are not all robbing; I see them every day at hard work. I keep up a regular visitation, and in point of fact I have never done. Those who are released on license are bound to report themselves to me in the same manner as those who are in the country are bound to report themselves to the constabulary. But I do not confine myself to the reports which are made to me by these men. I prefer visiting them at their own homes, and speaking to their employers. I always wish to obtain the opinion of the employer of a man from the employer himself. The police do not exercise any supervison over the convicts in Dublin, except what I have mentioned in the suspicious cases.

" I explain to the persons who employ these men, the control which the Government has over them whilst they are holders of a ticket-of-leave. I always lay the facts clearly before the employers, because if I were not straightforward with them, and I was once detected, I should never be able to show my face again. So that the employers are aware that these men whom they take into their service have been previously in the Convict Prisons. But the men with whom they work are not always aware of that fact. It is the interest of the employers to keep the other workmen in ignorance of the fact; and there is another thing, that if the honest workmen were to know this, I am sure they would take objection to it, and make the place too hot for a discharged prisoner. No difficulty has been found in keeping the matter concealed from the other workmen. The employer always does so. He communicates with me privately, and the other workmen are not acquainted with the characters of the men or their previous mode of life.

" I do not find any indisposition on their part to continue this intercourse with me, which they were obliged to keep up while under their tickets-of-leave; on the contrary, they appear to be grateful for what I have done for them. The success of the system very greatly depends upon its being possible to prevent the men who have been discharged from being recognised as former convicts, but in every case to let the employer know all about them. Also it proves that the Irish are not more tender in their feelings towards criminals than the English.

"The subject of industry very frequently engages our attention, and it is my duty, at least I think so, to explain the state of the home labour market and the foreign market. We never induce, compel, or urge any men to emigrate, and no man emigrates except through a matter of choice; but how does he emigrate? In Smithfield, across the rafters, I have the model of a ship and sails, and I get my young fellows more or less up in the practical working of a ship, and give them a knowledge of the technical terms of the rigging, and so on, and this cultivates in them a taste for the sea; and if they emigrate, they emigrate in this way, that some of them pay part of their passage, and work out the remainder. Some work their passage out. They do not emigrate except as a matter of choice. I do certainly point out to them, as far as I am able, the great advantages of breaking with their former companions, of concealing their shame, and of going where their antecedents are not known. I have a letter here in which one of them writes home for the purpose of bringing his brother and sister out; his brother is a convict at the present time; he himself worked out his passage to some part of America, and he has been writing home now for the purpose of bringing out his brother, and offering money to help the brother out.

"Those who go into the country and have their own friends or their own relations procure employment, I suppose, through them. We have the means of knowing what they are at because they write for their gratuities, and when they do that, or for the balance, they state with whom they are working, and they get no part of their gratuities unless the police authorities, or the head constable to whom each convict reports himself, certifies on the back of the letter that the man wants the money for a useful purpose, that his conduct is good, and that he is being employed by so-and-so. I have nothing to do with the payment of the gratuities except to recommend. For example, suppose I knew that a man wanted to purchase a pig, or to buy a bed or a suit of clothes, I write and say, 'I beg respectfully to recommend that this man may get so-and-so,' knowing that he intends to apply it to a useful purpose. This would apply to the men under my supervision; the police do that with regard to those men who are under their supervision. To those who go abroad the gratuities are paid at once, when it is fully understood that they are going.

"I have known cases in which the old associates of convicts have endeavoured to use their power over them, and from a fear of being betrayed to extort money from them. I have seen their former companions waiting in knots on the morning of their discharge, and endeavouring to induce them to go with them. I have known their former associates to come up 100 miles from different parts of Ireland in order to meet them on the morning of their discharge, and induce them to follow them. When men are on the point of leaving me, I impress upon them to the greatest possible degree the danger that will arise to them, and which they will have to meet amongst their old companions ; because, if a well-disposed convict on being discharged is anxious to earn his bread honestly, and goes in amongst his former companions he is sneered at and he is tormented, in fact he has not any power to resist. I have known also in my tours amongst these people, where there has been a badly-disposed convict, much harm to be done. Whatever improvement might be made in the system of prison discipline, it would still remain very desirable that convicts, after their discharge, should go to some new place where it would be more easy for them to pursue an honest course of life, for I think that the advantages to a man in a new place would be more numerous; at the same time I would not have convicts after their discharge when they were free in the world link themselves with one another, or associate together. I would prefer to separate them and scatter them as much as possible.

" In case a license holder changes his place of residence without reporting himself, I consider that that is a breach of the conditions of the license; he may be robbing. In such a case, Captain WHITTY would notify the case to the police. I believe that he gives a certain time for a man to turn up, say a fortnight or so, and if he does not turn up he is then put in the ' Hue and Cry,' and his license is revoked, for leaving his place of residence without notifying it in the proper manner. The license is always revoked in the case of a man who leaves his place of residence without notifying it to the proper authorities. If they go away from their residences without giving notice, so that we cannot find them out, their names are handed over to the police, and they are put into the ' Hue and Cry;' their license certainly is revoked. Suppose a man remains in his residence in Dublin, but we are aware he is associating with bad characters and frequenting public-houses, that man's license would be revoked."

Mr. ORGAN illustrates, by the following anecdote, the great strictness exercised in revoking licenses, when the terms of them are violated in the smallest degree :—

" An employer, in the county of Dublin, asked me for a trustworthy man. I sent him a man who I thought was a trustworthy man. Driving through a village some ten miles distant from Dublin, on a Sunday evening, I heard some singing in a kind of public-house. I may mention that I am not ashamed, at any hour of the night or day, to go in anywhere. I went into this house to see if there were any of my men there—not that I should have recognised them, if I had seen them. My man was not there. I had a gentleman with me who went to see the working of the system, who was outside, and we saw three men, rather jolly, they were singing a song, and I saw that the centre man was my man. My friend said, ' These fellows seem to be in very good spirits.' 'Yes,' said I. I would not recognise the man; but I drove into town, and on the following Monday morning I went down to Sir WALTER CROFTON's office, and told him the circumstance, and said, 'Remember, sir, that our character is at stake.' And I wrote to the employer asking him to send him the man, which he did. I then brought down the man before Sir WALTER CROFTON, and if it had not been that the employer of the man and his brother came to intercede for him, that man certainly would have been taken up for a violation of his license. This man went back, and what has been the result? An article that was used in the trade of his employer was sent in by a contractor, it was not equal to the sample submitted before the contract was closed; this man told the porter that it would not do, and that the next time he brought in anything of the same kind he would send him back. About a month afterwards another supply of the same article was brought just of the same inferior class, and 5s. were handed to the man as a kind of induce- ment to him to let it pass, and at the same time a promise was made to him of a Christmas-box. My man then went in deliberately to his employer and said, 'Here are 5s.' The employer gave the man the 5s., and told me that as long as he had employment to give, he should never want it. The man got married, and the employer gave the man and his wife work."

Mr. ORGAN truly calls the prison a kind of moral hospital; he shows how completely those established on the Irish Convict System have answered their purpose, by the following testimony :—

"The men at Lusk are lodged all together in one apartment. We have never had a case of complaint from the time the Lusk Prison was opened. There is supervision over them; one man can see the whole. There is a partition, and in it is a window, which, when pushed back, enables you to bring all the men under your eye at once. Of course the men are taught a certain morality, and a very moral tone pervades among them. We trust more to the influence of the men over each other. The officer governs; but I really think the public feeling amongst the men, for they have a public feeling, and a strong one, is equally powerful. In fact, in these convict prisons there is a kind of morality that is understood amongst the convicts, so that one would be likely to bring another to justice if he violated the privileges of the place."

The valuable effects of this moral tone can be fully developed after leaving the prison walls, only by such a system as that adopted in Ireland. When asked by the Commissioners (4699), "Whether, to work the system effectually in Ireland, it would not require some person like himself to be always cognizant of each particular case, and to be watching it when a man came out on ticket-of-leave?" Mr. ORGAN answers—"By bringing them in small numbers previous to their discharge you can individualise. You can convert a prison into a kind of moral hospital; you know each man's disease; you know his antecedents, his connexions, and his inclinations; and so you know more or less of him with respect to recommending his discharge; and after discharge it certainly would be desirable, *for I cannot overrate the importance of supervision.*"

Such is the working of the Irish Convict System. If its results are asked for, reference need only be made to the grand fact that in Ireland there is such general belief in the reformation of Convicts, that they are received back into society, and able to gain an honest livelihood; that employers are not afraid to give them work, and even place them after suitable probation in situations of trust. Tangible proofs of its success can also be given in the very remarkable reduction of crime in the Island, and the very small proportion of relapses.

The statistics of the English Convict Prisons were not brought forward, nor the official reports of reconvictions and revocations of license quoted, because, in the first place, however correct these may be according to the data in possession of the Directors, abundant proof was given, that according to the present mode of working the system, it is impossible that all cases of reconviction should be recognised, and the actual number of relapses known; and next, because the licenses have not in England been revoked whenever the conditions on which they were granted have been violated.

But the statistics of the Irish Convict Prisons are reliable, because adequate means are steadily adopted to identify Convicts who again fall into crime, and very strictly to enforce the conditions of the licenses. We may, then, regard with confidence the statistics of the Irish Convict System, and view with satisfaction the following table given in the Report of the Directors in March of the present year: —

| Year. | In custody in Government Prisons January 1st. | Convicted. | Discharged. |
| --- | --- | --- | --- |
| 1854 | *3933 | 710 | 658 |
| 1855 | 3427 | 518 | 820 |
| 1856 | 3209 | 389 | 1107 |
| 1857 | 2614 | 426 | 910 |
| 1858 | 2277 | 358 | 946 |
| 1859 | 1773 | 322 | 595 |
| 1860 | 1631 | 331 | 524 |
| 1861 | 1492 | 368 | 561 |
| 1862 | 1314 | 592 | 317 |
| 1863 | 1575 | +511 | 326 |
| 1864 | 1768 | — | — |

This table does not contain the number of reconvictions and revocations of license, which alone should be required as an indication of the success of the system. Even if the number of *first* convictions increased, uninfluenced by the Convict Prisons, this could not necessarily be attributed to any defect in the system. Yet we perceive in the table that a very striking decrease of such crime as would entail a sentence of penal servitude, has actually taken place in Ireland since the commencement of the system, and this steadily for seven consecutive years, until the year 1862, when there was a remarkable rise in the number of convictions. But this increase, the Report for that year justly states, " may fairly be attributed to the prevalence of distress in many parts of the country; in corroboration of which it can be stated, from information obtained from official sources, that the numbers confined in the County and City Prisons also increased in that year, and that there was a considerable increase in the number of paupers receiving relief throughout Ireland. The figures in the following table exemplify this statement:—

---

* In addition to this number there were 345 convicts under detention in the county prisons, and several hundred in Bermuda and Gibraltar, who were subsequently discharged in Ireland.

† Four of these are military convicts.

| Years. | Prisoners in County Gaols. | Paupers receiving In-door or Out-door Relief. | In Convict Prisons. |
|---|---|---|---|
| January. | | | |
| 1859 | 2844 | 44,866 | 1773 |
| 1860 | 2535 | 44,929 | 1631 |
| 1861 | 2488 | 50,683 | 1492 |
| 1862 | 2916 | 59,584 | 1314 |
| 1863 | 3055 | 65,847 | 1575 |

"As might be expected," says Capt. WHITTY, then sole Director, "under the circumstances above referred to, the number of reconvictions within the past year shows a considerable increase over the previous years, when the country was in a different state. If the pressure of want leads into the commission of serious crime some who have not been known to have previously thus offended, it is not to be supposed that others who have already been known as criminals would be proof against such an incentive. The practice, moreover, in this country (as described in previous Reports), of systematically bringing to the notice of the Judges and Assistant Barristers full particulars of the antecedents of habitual criminals convicted before them who have previously been in the Convict Prisons, leads directly to such cases being returned to those prisons, instead of being only sentenced to imprisonment in the County Gaols. As this part of the system becomes more developed, and all discharged Convicts come to be subjected to supervision for some period after discharge, it may reasonably be anticipated that but few of them who may return to a course of crime will escape identification and consequent increased severity of sentence upon reconviction."

Hence, the increased number of convictions in the year 1862 cannot in any degree show a failure in the system. It is also very satisfactory to perceive that while the number of paupers and of prisoners in County Gaols increased during the next year, 1863, that of serious offences, involving penal servitude, decreased. The numbers actually within the prisons of course depends on the numbers discharged, as well as on those admitted; and as the number of discharges greatly depends on the length of the sentences awarded by the judge, the numbers actually in confinement must fluctuate accordingly.

During the six years previous to 1862, which was a very exceptional one, the per centage of relapses was only 9·9, not one-tenth of the number discharged. When we know what confirmed criminals, and persons guilty of daring crimes, were in those prisons, this per centage is remarkably small, and of itself an absolute proof of the success of the system.

Including 1862, the statistics stand as given in the following table, which we copy from the Ninth Report:—

"The following are the total numbers of convicts discharged from the beginning of 1856 to the end of 1862:—

|  | On License. | Absolutely. | Totals. |
|---|---|---|---|
| "Total discharged, { Males ... ... | 1,388 | 2,369 | 3,757 } |
| { Females ... | 510 | 693 | 1,203 } 4,960 |

"The numbers returned of the above to Convict Prisons were as follows:—

Re-sentenced ...  ...  ...  ...  ...  ...  ...  510
Licenses revoked  ...  ...  ...  ...  ...  ...  *107

Total ...  ...  ...  ...  ...  617—out of 4,960
                                         or 12.44 per cent."

We may conclude this account of the working of the Irish Convict System with the testimony of the Directors to their continued confidence in it, as given in their Tenth Report, that of the present year:—

"The number of reconvictions has not increased within the year, nor has there been any matter connected with these reconvictions to call for remark, except that the practice of registration and supervision of discharged convicts, the continual communication between the authorities of the city and county gaols and the Directors, concerning prisoners suspected to be convicts with a view to their identification, and the notification to the Judges and Chairman of Quarter Sessions, after conviction, of prisoners thus identified, all continue to work advantageously for the protection of the public, by helping to bring these offenders, as known habitual criminals, under lengthened sentences of penal servitude, instead of being dealt with in many cases by sentences of ordinary imprisonment.

* Viz., 81 males and 26 females. Of these the licenses of 34 males and 21 females were revoked for irregularities—not criminal offences.

" The successful working of the Intermediate Prisons, and of the registration and supervision of convicts after discharge, appears indeed to have been so generally admitted in Ireland, that it would under any circumstances have been almost unnecessary to have now enlarged upon it, or reiterated what has already been presented on the subject in the Directors' Annual Reports.

" They have satisfaction in stating with regard to the registration and supervision by the constabulary of the discharged convicts in the country districts of Ireland, that during the many years that this portion of the Irish Convict System has been in operation, no instance has come to the knowledge of the Directors of persons subjected to this control having had cause of complaint against the constables who had to perform the duties connected with it.

" Of eight male convicts whose licenses were revoked during the year, *two only were thus dealt with* as the consequence of their commission of criminal offences; the remaining six had the privilege of being at large on license withdrawn, in consequence of their breaking the conditions on which they had thus been liberated for a portion of their sentences.

" The conduct of the prisoners generally, both male and female, in all the Convict Prisons, has been good throughout the year, the most unfavourable exceptions being chiefly in the cases of individual prisoners of known evil temper and habits; and there has been no instance of any attempt at combined misconduct in any of the prisons. In large prisons one practically beneficial effect of a consistent and plain system of denoting progress towards known advantages, by means of the attainment of marks for good conduct and industry, is that it operates directly to prevent tendency to combination among the prisoners, even when in continued association; individual interests being clearly defined, as well as the certainty of danger to those interests from any intermeddling or combination, on the part of those who have the desire to maintain them, with other prisoners of an unsteady or actually evil disposition."

We have hitherto given the testimony of eye witnesses only, to the excellence and success of the Irish Convict System. It may be sufficient to convince any impartial person to refer them to the volume of evidence before the Commissioners, a portion of which has been given in this chapter, and to ask them to contrast the effects of the English Convict System, which are patent to every one who gives attention to the subject, with those of the Irish System, which are so universally appreciated in that Island. The Royal Commissioners express in their Report decided approval of the plans adopted in Ireland, after the closest scrutiny. Such approval, followed as it has been already by important changes in the English System, cannot but have great weight. It is valuable also to have the testimony of Lord BROUGHAM, in his inaugural address as President of the Social Science Association at Edinburgh, in 1863; it expresses, as he always has done when alluding to the subject, high appreciation of the Irish Convict System :—

"The attention of our body at the last Congress was, and indeed ever since has been, mainly occupied with the great subject of convict treatment; and we have found fully confirmed by all the inquiries to which it has given rise, the opinion formed at the Dublin Congress, 1861, from a close examination of Sir W. CROFTON's whole proceedings. The regret universally felt at his retirement, owing to ill-health, has been materially lessened by the choice, as his successor, of his friend Captain WHITTY, who had been under him for years, and who has amply justified the selection. The great opposition which the introduction of the system into Great Britain encountered, and the manifest leaning against it of persons high in office, filled all the friends of Social Science with alarm. This has happily been dispelled by the inquiry —first, of the Commission under Lord GREY, and again of the Committee under Lord CARNARVON, in the House of Lords. Unfortunately, some of the most important witnesses were not examined—as Mr. BALME, of Leeds, in neither inquiry, and Mr. SHEPHERD only in the Lords', and our distinguished colleague, the Recorder of Birmingham in neither; but both Reports, and especially that of the Lords' Committee, gave the most signal triumph to the principles, which, for years, both on the Bench and in the National Association, he had been zealously, though temperately, inculcating. We are not therefore surpised that he should have heartily joined the Bristol Association (formed for obtaining an amendment of convict discipline) in petitioning the Sovereign to promote such measures, both executive and legislative, as may carry into effect, without delay, the great improvements so fully sanctioned by seven years' experience in Ireland. The principles are shortly these—every mitigation of a convict's sentence, whether in treatment, diet included, or in duration of the punishment, must be earned by himself, not only in abstaining from offences, but more especially in pursuing a course of industry. On obtaining a ticket-of-leave he must be placed under constant superintendence, and the ticket revoked, not only on his misconduct, but on his leading a vagrant life, and not supporting himself by his industry. Convicts whose sentence has expired are photographed, so as to be recognised in case of new offences; and this, which had been originally suggested by Mr. HILL, and adopted by Sir W. CROFTON, has been favourably mentioned in the Lords' Report, and confirmed by the Governors of the Bristol, Wakefield, and Leeds jails, as well as by the experience of the Irish prisons. The convict is deterred from relapse into crime by the certainty of his being recognised wherever he is committed, the photographs being circulated to all jails."

The Hon. Lord NEAVES, President of the Department of Punishment and Reformation, made, in his opening address at the same Meeting of the Association, the following excellent remarks :—

" The next question that may be considered is : whether the term of penal servitude contained in the criminal's sentence shall be subject to remission during its currency, and if so, on what grounds ?

" A very important difference of opinion here exists, and it cannot be denied that the Memorandum of the Lord Chief Justice of the Queen's Bench, dissenting in this respect from the majority of the Commissioners, is entitled to the greatest weight as an individual authority, and is rested upon grounds deserving of the most serious consideration. I think, however, that the public in general will go along with the views of the majority of the Commissioners, who recommend that prisoners should be allowed to earn a remission of their sentences, by industry recorded by marks, as specially explained in their Report. It will probably be the general opinion that by no other influence could prisoners be induced to commence and persevere in those habits of industry which afford the only hope of their reformation. I regard it as a secondary, or rather as quite an irrelevant matter, that the hope of this remission may make the prisoners more tractable in confinement, and thus lighten the task of governors and warders, or diminish the expense of proper custody, or the necessity of prison punishments. But if *reformation* is an object at all, and if remission of the sentence is the *only* or the *best* means of promoting that end, this seems a legitimate and sufficient reason for adopting it.

" But then this remission, in order to do good and not to do harm, must be *bonâ fide* earned by the prisoner by those very habits of regular labour which it is the object to create.

" To give any remission as a matter of course, which is done in the English and Scottish Systems, appears to me to be wholly at variance with the essential spirit and principle of the plan, even although this remission be liable to be afterwards forfeited by misconduct. In Ireland the remission is not given until it is positively worked for, a most material difference in the operation, or rather in the principle, of the two systems, and I cannot help thinking that much of the failure of the English plan is ascribable to that difference. On this point the Commissioners have arrived at what seems to me a just conclusion.

" Two other great questions are here raised as constituting the main difference between the English and Irish Systems. First, whether there shall be what is called an Intermediate Prison ; and second, whether after the license or remission is granted, it shall be made subject to the supervision of the police, till the expiration of the period of the original sentence. These points have been the subject of much discussion, and I ought to mention that I have recently received the last statement of his views prepared by Sir JOSHUA JEBB, and edited by Lord CHICHESTER. This pamphlet I have no doubt will receive every attention, but it does not appear to have materially altered the state of the controversy; and I shall only here express my belief that, looking to the success of the Irish System where the arrangements referred to exist, and to the failure of the English System where they have never been attempted, the public mind will not be satisfied without a trial of the experiment, as it has been made in Ireland. The Royal Commissioners have recommended their adoption.

" It cannot now, I think, be denied that the Irish System is a great and almost unexpected success. There may at one time have been reason to suspect that its results were mainly owing to the personal energy and character of Sir WALTER CROFTON, by whom it was organised and worked. But I am sure that gentleman will not grudge that the compliment which would thus be due to him individually, should rather be transferred to the system itself, which under the superintendence of his successor, Captain WHITTY, has shown no diminution of its beneficial effects. I am quite aware at the same time, and prepared to expect, that a similar system may not be equally available in England as in Ireland. There may be specialties in the character of Irish crime and Irish criminals, and in the state of public feeling on that subject, as well as in the organisation of the Irish police, that may make a difference in the operation of the plan in that country, as compared with England and Scotland; but we are not as yet entitled to say that these distinctions are so great and vital as that we shall not attempt to assimilate the two systems. After we have done so, we shall be able to judge by experience, and perhaps find adaptations and modifications which may suit the different elements with which we have to deal. It seems impossible to suppose that the English System can be made worse than it is by any alterations that can be borrowed from the Irish.

" The Intermediate Prison seems to afford the fairest prospect that can be suggested for helping the prisoner by these leading strings to stand and go alone, and for giving him a fair chance of his share of employment in the labour market.

" The subsequent supervision of the police is naturally not relished by prisoners, but some questions may here be put with regard to it. Why is it made a condition of the ticket-of-leave, if it is not put in practice? What good can come of convicts who obtain employment only by concealment or false pretences, and who, according to an idea contained in a popular drama, may be kept in terror by their old associates, and thus concussed into conduct to which there would otherwise be no temptation?

" It is impossible to suppose that in the ordinary labour market the liberated convict can ever compete on equal terms with the man of good character. It is not desirable that such should be the case, or that a well-behaved man should have to say that he was refused a situation because his character was good. But the best chance for a convict seems to be the safeguard and test of the Intermediate Prison, and the fair and open recognition of his true character, with a proper supervision as a check and security against relapse."

It is not in our own country only that the Irish Convict System has long been known and appreciated. In the Second Annual Report of the Board of Inspectors of Asylums, Prisons, &c., in Canada, for 1861, Mr. MEREDITH thus speaks, after detailing changes which he recommends to be made in the Provincial Penitentiary or Prison :—"I wish it to be understood that the suggestions which are submitted in this memorandum, for the improvement of the Penitentiary System, are not original. They are taken (modified somewhat to suit the circumstances of the country) from the admirable system which has, for the last eight years, been enforced with such signal success in the Irish Convict Prisons. As an Irishman, I feel proud to think that Ireland should have given birth to a system of discipline which has already done so much towards reforming her criminal population, and which seems likely, with God's blessing, to do so much for the criminals of other countries. Some years ago the Belgian Government adopted the Irish Convict System in their prisons, and the same system has more recently been established in the new kindgom of Italy, under the auspices of the late Count CAVOUR. It would be a source of sincere and lasting gratification to me, if the Board of which I am a member, should prove instrumental in introducing into Canada a system pregnant with such important blessings to the criminal population, as well as to society at large."

We have already seen that the system adopted in Western Australia, is founded on the same principles as those established in Ireland, and that the Mark System, an Intermediate Stage and Supervision after discharge, are there employed with the greatest success.

On the European Continent the Irish System has received warm approbation. In France, M. de MARSANGY, whose work has been already quoted, thus speaks of the Irish Convict System, p. 126 :—

"Tandis que, dans son incompréhensible aveuglement, l'administration anglaise semblait prendre à tâche de discréditer une des plus précieuses institutions du droit pénitentaire moderne, l'Irlande heureusement lui ménageait une éclatante réhabilitation.   Comment y était-elle parvenue? En exécutant religieusement les prescriptions du bill de 1853 et 1857, et en y appliquant cet esprit de prudence, de sagesse et de sollicitude, sans lequel les meilleures lois sont stériles, si même elles ne deviennent funestes.

"En Irlande, disait récemment la *Revue de Dublin*, la mise en pratique du système des *tickets of leave* peut être appelée un *chef-d'œuvre de sagesse;* en Angleterre, c'est *une pure folie.—(Edinburgh Review*, 1863, p. 240).

"En Angleterre, dit la *Revue trimestrielle*, nous n'avons eu à montrer que des erreurs et des fautes.   En Irlande nous n'avons à mentionner que des succès brillants, obtenus dans des circonstances qui étaient de nature à décourager les plus confiants.—(*Quarterly Review*, p. 161; *Westminster Review*, p. 19; *North British Review.* p. 12).

"Quelles étaient ces circonstances si décourageantes et si défavorables? Tout le monde les connaît.   Tandis que l'Angleterre jouit d'une prospérité inouïe, grâce à ses immenses richesses agricoles, commerciales et industrielles, l'Irlande végète, accablée sous la plaie dévorante du paupérisme.   L'ignorance et la misère y poussent incessamment sa population pauvre, tantôt à l'expatriation, plus souvent au crime; et sans l'appui consolateur des idées catholiques, on ne sait ce que serait devenue cette malheureuse contrée.

"Ses malfaiteurs étaient les plus dangereux du Royaume-Uni.   Avant 1853, on en transportait dans les colonies 1000 à 1500 par année.   Leur réputation était telle que, lors du refus par les colonies de recevoir les convicts de la Grande-Bretagne, l'Australie occidentale ne consentit à en recevoir encore '*qu'à la condition qu'ils ne fussent point Irlandais.*' (*Quarterly Review*, p. 16; *Edinburgh Review*, p. 246).

"Dans cet état des choses, on comprend que l'application du système des *tickets of leave* en Irlande ait dû exciter, en 1853, une vive terreur, et que M. M^ACARTNEY ait pu, avec une apparence de raison, déclarer au sein du Parlement que, ' par suite des penchants vicieux des masses dans ce pays les effets de ce système seraient pires en Irlande que partout ailleurs.' (*Quarterly Review*, p. 162).

"Or, ce système de libération préparatoire, dont nous sommes fiers d'avoir été les promoteurs, a, par lui-même, une telle force réformatrice, que, bien qu'introduit en Irlande dans les conditions les plus défavorables, son application dans ce pays n'a cessé depuis dix années, de donner des résultats vraiment merveilleux.   Aussi sommes-nous en droit de conclure que cette expérience est la plus éloquente confirmation de l'efficacité de ce système!"

M. de MARSANGY devotes several chapters of his work to a very close examination of the whole of the Irish System, particularly of the "Libèration Preparatoire," as it is there termed; he strongly contrasts the defects of the English System and the lax administration of existing regulations, with the supervision and strict fulfilment of the conditions of the license in Ireland.

In Germany, Prussia and Belgium, and even Italy, the Irish Convict System has long attracted attention, and won admiration among those who have made the principles of prison discipline and of punishment their study. The lamented Count CAVOUR had entered fully into the system, and was about to have it adopted in his country, when death frustrated this, as well as many other noble intentions. The celebrated Professor MITTERMAIER, of Heidelberg, gave it his warm approbation, and his writings extended the knowledge of the system, as well as excited others to the study of it. The late much esteemed M. L. DAVESIES de PONTES prepared an article for the Revue des Deux Mondes, of September, 1858, which entered very fully into the Irish Convict System, then newly established, and his clear explanations and warm approbation of it excited considerable attention. Above all, the Baron VON HOLTZENDORFF, whose personal narrative has been already cited, did much to draw attention to the important principles which were being developed in our Sister Island. His position as Professor of Criminal Law in the University of Berlin, as well as his extensive knowledge and European celebrity, gave great weight to his exposition of the Irish System in various countries. Among others, his works attracted the attention of M. Van der BRUGGHEN, Ancien Ministre de la Justice des Pays-Bas. In 1856 this gentleman became Minister of Justice in Holland, and after having given in that high position close attention to the effect of various systems of prison discipline, he devoted his time, on retiring from public life, to the preparation of a work on "Punishment as a Means of Moral Reform." On becoming acquainted with the Irish System, through M. de PONTES' article in the Revue des Deux Mondes, he saw the solution of many difficulties. He states in the Introduction to his work :—

" Quoique peu favorablement disposé envers tout esprit et tout nom de système dans une matière, qui, comme j'en avais acquis la conviction, se prête si
peu à des règles générales, à des principes absolus vrais partout et pour tous,
me défiant même d'avance des résultats que chaque novateur en ce genre sait
faire valoir en groupant les chiffres et les données statisques en faveur de sa
théorie, j'avoue que mon premier mouvement fut de m'écrier qu'ici la solution
était donnée du problème de la combinaison de l'emprisonnement solitaire et
collectif, pour les faire concourir au but de la répression pénale, et de la
réforme morale de ceux qu'elle doit atteindre. Je me sentais tout joyeux de
reconnaître dans les idées de Mr. CROFTON des principes aussi simples que
vrais, parcequ'ils sont fondés sur la connaissance du coeur humain tel qu'il est
en réalité partout le même. J'applaudissais surtout à l'idée dominante de tout
ce régime pénitentiaire Irlandais, tel que les pages éloquentes de Mr. DAVESIES
DE PONTES me le faisaient connaître, l'idée qui en est l'âme, pour ainsi dire,
d'où il tire toute sa force, et que Lord STANLEY a exprimée si bien dans ces
belles paroles : ' *The reformation of men can never become a mechanical process*' ; et que le Baron de HOLTZENDORFF, dont j'aurai à parler bientôt et
beaucoup, n'a pas moins bien formulée dans ces termes: ' Il est tout aussi
impossible de. conduire les individus que les peuples par l'oppression à la
liberté.' L'estimable auteur de l'article de la Revue des deux Mondes, que je
viens de citer me semblait également avoir fait ressortir très bien cette impor-
tante vérité, en s'exprimant ainsi : ' *Il paraît rationnel de chercher la réforme
des coupables dans des procédés semblables à ceux qui guérissent les fous, c'est-a-
dire, dans une continuelle gymnastique des facultés morales, dans des épreuves
sans cesse renouvellées, qui leur rendent la force initiale qu'ils ont perdue, ou qui
leur donnent celle qui n'a jamais été en eux.'* "

He did not live to give to the world his enlightened views,
but his manuscript was placed for publication in the hands of
Baron VON HOLTZENDORFF, from whom he had largely quoted in
developing the Irish System, or, we should more justly say, that
of Sir WALTER CROFTON. M. Van der BRUGGHEN thus briefly
but comprehensively states the principle on which that system
is founded, and which the author of this work fully endorses :—

" Nous allons voir comment cette idée, éminemment simple
et éminemment pratique, que la réforme morale consiste avant
tout dans l'affermissement de l'homme intérieur, et que cet affermissement dépend de l'exaltation du sentiment de responsabilité
morale, qui lui-même est inséparable de la liberté de détermina-
tion morale, a été conçue et mise en pratique dans le régime des
prisons d'Irlande par l'Honorable Sir WALTER CROFTON, avec un
succès qui a dépassé toutes les prévisions."

The greater part of the volume is occupied with a description and close analysis of the Irish Convict System; it concludes with this admirable statement by the Baron Von HOLTZENDORFF :—

" Mais le système Irlandais a ce trait particulier, qu'il cherche à développer progressivement et au plus haut degré les facultés intellectuelles et morales du condamné, pour lui faire envisager les dangers de l'avenir, tout en lui montrant dans l'émigration volontaire le chemin le plus court vers le bien.

" Le problème, dont il s'agit pour les sciences sociales, consistera toujours à rechercher pour la répression pénale, le moyen le plus propre de combiner avec le maximum d'énergie dans les forces morales des condamnés le minimum des chances, que la position sociale des libérés pourrait offrir à la récidive. Ce problème, a-t-il été conduit plus près de sa solution par l'auteur du système Irlandais ? C'est ce que nous croyons ! "

We do indeed share the belief of the Baron that this great problem has been solved in the Irish Convict System, and trust that no long period will elapse before it will be adopted by the whole United Kingdom !

# CHAPTER III.

## THE IRISH CONVICT SYSTEM:
### ITS HISTORY.

IN the two preceding chapters some account has been given of the actual condition and working of the Irish Convict Prisons, and of the system upon which they are founded. This system has already attracted so much attention, not only in many countries of Europe, but also in other quarters of the world, and the full comprehension of it is so important to all who desire to adopt it, that we shall now proceed to trace its history from the commencement, and observe the gradual development of it.

The history of the rise and progress of the Irish Convict System as it now exists, is contained in the Reports of the Directors, which are from the commencement peculiarly full and luminous. The early Reports are now out of print, and a series of them is consequently inaccessible to the public; —no apology will therefore be needed for presenting in this chapter full extracts from them.

We have already learnt from Sir W. CROFTON's evidence, the peculiarly low and degraded condition of the Irish Convicts, their condition, both intellectually, morally, and physically, being very far inferior, as testified by the Governor of Western Australia, to those sent out from the English Convict Prisons. The Directors perceived the reasonableness of the refusal of Western Australia to receive such Convicts, and accepted the refusal with a determination on their part to endeavour to raise the subjects of their care to such a condition as to make them good colonists, if not transported felons. They say in their First Annual Report, dated April 26th, 1855 :—"We are quite aware of the great interruption which must arise to the prosecution of the course of treatment the prison authorities in Western Australia are so laudably desirous of carrying out, by the arrival of Irish Convicts in the state described. We cannot for the present, therefore (however desirable it would be on account of our limited accommodation for prisoners), consistently advise the deportation of Convicts from this country to any colony. Those we hope to be enabled to send early in 1856, will, we trust, have given such evidence of reformation, as to induce us to recommend them specially as colonists, when their penal term shall have expired. We shall endeavour to make such deportation a reward for good conduct, and feel assured it will operate as a powerful auxiliary in the cause of reformation."

In every department of the Convict Prisons the Directors had to encounter great difficulties, owing, not only to the inefficient arrangements of the buildings, but from the inefficiency of the officers. "We have found it necessary," they say, "to call for special reports on the character and capabilities of the different officers of the prisons, with a view to remove those who are not qualified for so important a position; and regret to add that we have been compelled to recommend the dismissal of several warders for drunkenness, a crime that cannot be tolerated for an instant in a prison where a good moral example should operate as one of the principal elements of reformation.

"We have endeavoured to assimilate the treatment of the Irish Convicts as far as possible to those of England—*i. e.*, immediately after conviction the male adults will be subjected to separate imprisonment at Mountjoy, Dublin, for a maximum period of nine months, though we hope to be enabled to recommend that an average shorter period should be recognised.

Before undergoing this stage of imprisonment, they are medically inspected, and owing to the diseased state of the Convicts of this country, we regret to say the rejections are very large. We are in hopes, however, and are disposed to believe, from the assurance of one of our Board, well conversant with medical subjects, that we may in most cases be able to carry out some portion of the term by judicious treatment on the part of the Medical Officer at Mountjoy. * *

"We have altered the arrangements that existed in this prison before our Board was formed, and, as we believe, with beneficial effects. * *

"Having adverted to the first part of the system and treatment of the Convicts, which is passed in separate confinement, and devoted almost exclusively to their moral and religious instruction, it remains for us now to describe the manner in which effect will be given to the latter portion of their sentences, while they are employed in labour on the public works, or in the prosecution of trade, when it will be necessary that the utmost care and attention should be paid to strengthen and confirm any improvement that may have been effected during the first period of their confinement; and at the same time to make every exertion to establish habits of industry, and inculcate that *degree of moral feeling and self-reliance which will enable them successfully to struggle against the temptations and difficulties they must encounter in their future connexion with the world.*

"The condition of Spike Island Convict Prison having been detailed in the several Reports of the Commissioners of Convict Inquiry, previous to the appointment of the present Board of Directors, it is unnecessary again to enter very fully into that subject. It is desirable to say that a further and more intimate acquaintance with the discipline and management of that prison does not give us any ground for altering the opinions already submitted to the Government thereon, viz., that under such a system as that hitherto in force, it *would be hopeless to look for any improvement or moral reformation of the prisoners.*

" One of the principal defects has been the inefficiency and unfitness of many of the officers for the performance of the duties required, which in a Public Works' Prison are of a very arduous and responsible nature, and demand (in order to be satisfactorily carried out) men possessing a high moral standard combined with an amount of energy and physical strength found only in persons in the prime of life.

" Heretofore, officers who had been guilty of drunkenness, or who had otherwise misconducted themselves at other prisons, were frequently punished by being sent to do duty at Spike Island, a practice calculated to degrade the character of the officers generally, to lower them in the estimation of the Convicts, and lessen their authority and control. Many of the warders were men much advanced in years, and infirm, therefore totally incapable of efficiently performing any duties requiring either much exertion of body or energy of mind.

" Further, the nature and disposition of the buildings appropriated for prison accommodation at Spike Island, together with the general association of the prisoners, necessitated thereby, must, under any circumstances, prove highly unfavourable to the attainment of the same moral improvement and discipline which have been arrived at in the prisons of late established for the execution of public works in England, and demand a larger staff than has heretofore been employed in this prison, or than would be necessary in suitably constructed buildings. * *

" The numerical insufficiency of the staff heretofore employed has been such, that it has been found impracticable to have the same officers daily in charge of the same prisoners on the works, the evils arising therefrom must be apparent to all : the officers being, of course, comparatively but little acquainted with the character of the prisoners under their charge ; the difficulty of fixing the responsibility for the proper execution of any works in progress on any individual officer, and the impossibility of keeping an efficient record of the conduct and industry of the prisoners, causing a total absence of all stimulus to industry or good conduct on their part.

"The moral and religious improvement of the Convicts have not certainly been made matters of great or sufficient importance, nor has their school instruction received much attention. The chapel, used also as the schoolroom, has heretofore been very little better than a temporary shed; only two schoolmasters have been employed for the instruction of the entire body of the Convicts, which in number has even exceeded 2,000; consequently a large proportion of the prisoners have not attended school at all."

The Board having been in office only since 29th November in the previous year (1854), could not of course be in a position to state that they had rendered the organization of the prison sound and effective in so short a time; but, dating their Report in April, 1855, they are able already to state — "that some considerable and marked improvement has been effected, even to a greater extent than we could have ventured to anticipate from the necessarily partial and very imperfect arrangements which it has as yet been found practicable to make."

The efficiency of the staff being essential to the improvement of the prisoners, the Board at once directed their special attention to this. It will be evident in the following extract that while in the first place they adopted the machinery then employed in the English Prisons, and made the same Act of Parliament the basis of their operations, yet from the very first they were guided by the same principles, which were eventually developed so successfully.

"Proper means are at present taken to ascertain whether candidates for employment in the Convict service are duly qualified, previous to their selection, which is now made on probation for the first six months, during which period the Governor is required to observe carefully and report to the Directors at least every month on their qualifications, abilities, general character, habits, temper, and disposition.    Should these reports not prove satisfactory, and should the Directors be convinced that such persons will not eventually prove fitting and desirable to be intrusted with the charge of prisoners, their services will be dispensed with, and their appointments not confirmed.

" We are establishing a stricter system of discipline among the officers, while at the same time we are endeavouring gradually, as far as circumstances will admit, to remove many discomforts and minor evils under which they have heretofore laboured.   We have taken measures to ensure a careful supervision of their conduct, character, zeal and ability, and to cause such records thereof to be kept, as will enable the Directors at all times to form a correct and sound opinion of their respective merits.   We hope, further, by making the rewards and promotion of the officers contingent solely on their own good conduct, ability and faithful service, to raise their character and elevate their position generally, and thus to render the situations of warders in the Government Prisons more generally sought for by a superior class of the community.

" We have prepared rules for the government of this as well as the other prisons, which have been submitted for approval; they have been framed on and are in accordance with those which have for some time past been advantageously in operation in England, altered and extended in some respects as required by local circumstances, and by the recent alterations in the law substituting 'penal servitude' in lieu of 'transportation.'

" These rules provide for a careful classification of the prisoners, according to their general conduct and character; and their removal from one grade to another is made contingent on their conduct, general demeanour, industry, and the desire evinced by them to profit by the instruction offered, and to derive advantage from the efforts made for their moral and religious improvement.

" A system of gratuities analogous to that which has long

been established in the Convict Prisons in England, has been adopted here as an encouragement and reward for good conduct, and also as a stimulus to industry, which we apprehend to be one of the most important elements in the reformation of criminals, *for if steady and determined habits of industry have not been formed by them, no reasonable hope can be entertained that after they have been discharged from prison, they will be able to gain an honest living, or ever obtain a respectable position in the world, or that any reformation and improvement effected in prison would prove of a permanent nature.*

" We have taken some pains to devise a plain and effective method of concisely recording all the particulars connected with the conduct, character, and industry of the Convicts, and to show the nature and degree of any offences which may be committed by them; and further, in order that they should be made aware of their position and progress in the prison, and of the records which are made concerning them, and also with a view to impress on their minds the importance attached to their good conduct, we have directed that a badge calculated to effect these objects shall be awarded to each Convict every month. The system of classification, gratuities, badges, and the records of conduct and industry, are fully detailed in the rules of the prison, and therefore need not be further dwelt on here.

" The Convicts have been partially classified by the Governor, a work which has been attended with some difficulty, owing to the absence or imperfect nature of any documents from which an opinion could be formed of their respective characters. A stricter system of discipline is now enforced, a careful record of the conduct of the prisoners is kept, and their industry on the works is duly supervised; attention is paid to convince them that by good conduct and industry on their parts, they can alone look for favour or reward. The physical condition and appearance of the Convicts is already ameliorated, and some amount of industry and energy is now displayed by them. On the whole, a marked improvement, apparent even to a casual observer, has taken place."

At the same time that great attention was paid to discipline, much consideration was given by the Directors to the physical condition of the Convicts. Considerable alterations were made in the prisons which were unhealthy. They say :—

"We subjoin a table showing the mortality in the Irish Convict Prisons during the past year, by which it will be seen to how low a state the physical condition of this class of prisoners has been reduced. We therefore felt it to be our duty to provide a higher scale of dietary where necessary, which will give the Convict sufficient strength of constitution to enable him to resist disease; that when his time of penal servitude shall have expired, he will be restored to society with an unimpaired constitution, and with sufficient health and energies to enable him to take a respectable place in the community, and engage in such industrial pursuits as his moral and religious training while under our charge will, we trust, prompt him to follow; while at the same time we have been careful to deprive the Convict of every article which could be considered a luxury, not absolutely necessary for health."

The grand object to be obtained, the restoration to society, is strongly before them in this first Report.

"These objects being, as we hope, obtained by the reformatory system adopted towards the Convict during his detention, it remains to offer him facilities for securing a respectable social position, by affording him the opportunity to exercise the habits of industry which he has acquired, and confirm the reformation effected in his character.

"That it is necessary to afford such facilities to the Convicts on their release arises from the fact, now being proved by daily experience, *that persons are generally most unwilling to employ them*. The Convict having been for a lengthened period withdrawn from all intercourse with the world, finds himself, on his release, unless he returns to his former bad companions (too often the only persons *willing* to receive him), in an isolated position, without friends, thrown on his own resources, and deprived of all means of exercising that industry by which alone he can obtain an honest livelihood. It cannot therefore be a matter of much surprise if an individual under such circumstances should be drawn back to his old haunts, and thus, falling again among his former associates, by degrees resume his original habits and career of crime.

" We deem it to be the duty of all who desire the reformation of the criminal classes to obviate this result—one much to be regretted, and which, we are compelled to admit, tends in a great measure to defeat the efforts made, and the ends proposed by the present Convict System.

"It cannot be denied that difficulties may offer to the adoption of such addition to the system already pursued; at the same time the advantages, both in the diminution of crime and the saving of expense to the country ultimately, which would accrue therefrom must be kept in view.

" In conclusion, we state it as our conviction that a large proportion of the Convicts, when thus tested, will prove themselves steady and industrious workmen, men of good and honest character, and respectable members of the community. We are satisfied it only requires their reformed condition to be generally known and understood, to overcome the prejudice at present existing against employing them among other labourers, and thus enabling them honestly to earn their livelihood, and obtain a respectable social position."

In the First Report of the Directors, the want is strongly expressed of some means of providing employment for the Convicts on their discharge from gaol. But the grand solution of that difficulty, as afforded by the Intermediate Prisons and the subsequent supervision of the Convicts when at liberty, does not appear yet to have occurred to them. It is very interesting and instructive to observe this, because we thus perceive the gradual development of the system in their minds, and we learn how a thorough devotion, heart and mind and powers, to any work, prepares for the discovery of the best means of accomplishing it. Such devoted zeal evidently existed in the Directors, and they communicated it to those who were working under them. When speaking thus of the Directors, we cannot of course forget that it was their Chairman, Sir WALTER CROFTON, who was the main spring of the whole, and that the system in its completed state must be considered his work. But he was most fortunate in having as his fellow Directors such gentlemen as Captain KNIGHT and Mr. LENTAIGNE, who fully entered into the spirit of the undertaking, and brought their own special qualifications and experience to bear on it. Nor was it a less fortunate circumstance that Captain WHITTY, whose evidence has been already quoted, succeeded Captain KNIGHT; and after working zealously with Sir WALTER, then Captain CROFTON, when left sole Director, devoted himself to sustain the system, as he has done, in full efficiency. It is a matter of great satisfaction to all who regard the working out of this admirable system with the deepest interest, to know that Captain WHITTY has now a coadjutor, Mr. P. J. MURRAY, whose intimate acquaintance with the system, and warm sympathy with it, give confidence that he will form an efficient Director. After this explanation, we continue our history.

A year's experience brings the Directors nearer to the solution of their grand difficulty. They say in the Second Report, p. 23, "We are of opinion that the employment of Convicts, selected on account of their general good conduct, &c., in small bodies on public works in various localities, under circumstances of exposure to the ordinary temptations and trials of the world, when the reality and sincerity of their reformation may be fairly and publicly tested, will present the most favourable chances for their gradual absorbtion into the body of the community." This is of course the grand object which, if attained, may be considered the crowning success of all prison discipline. As we proceed, year by year, we shall find that this idea is steadily kept in view by the Directors, until at last society has become so willing to readmit to the labour market the former culprit, who has given reliable proof of repentance, and of a desire and an ability to lead a new life. It is extraordinary that this very willingness has been misunderstood by some persons, and instead of being regarded as a proof of the success of the system, as it should be, is explained by a supposed disregard on the part of the Irish people of the sigma attached to guilt, and to a judicial sentence. How little foundation there is for such an explanation, is proved by the very next sentence in the same Report :—" The public feeling is too general that all Convicts are alike, and they are judged by the standard of the lowest and most degraded. Such being the case, it is not to be wondered at that *all respectable classes shrink from contact with them on their release from prison*, as indeed they may well do, so long as they have a 'prison character' only to refer to, earned under a strict discipline, surveillance and restraint. It is doubtless an established fact, that many of the worst and most hopeless criminals will behave well under such circumstances, and will consequently obtain on discharge a good 'prison character;' therefore, what guarantee can any one have, that in giving employment to a released Convict, he is not harbouring a depraved and unreclaimable criminal, if he has no means beyond this prison character of learning anything about him. It is well known to all who are acquainted with the class to be found in our Convict Prisons, that they present every description and shade of character, and very various degrees of guilt, crime and depravity; that many of the inmates have fallen from weakness, distress and force of circumstances, rather than from absolute and innate natural vice; some are more hardened by a longer career in vice and crime, though still not destitute of all proper feelings, nor without some good ground for hope of their ultimate sincere repentance and permanent reformation; while others, it must be admitted, are, humanly speaking, altogether vicious, almost

dead to any good impressions, and hopelessly irreclaimable ;
but this last class is comparatively small." The task, then,
which was undertaken by the Directors of the Irish Convict
Prisons in 1855, was not easier than that which is still to be
accomplished in England.   There was in that Island, as there is
in our own now, a general dislike in society of contact with any
person bearing the Convict brand, and a profound distrust which
we all feel now of any so called "prison characters." That
distrust was founded, as ours is at present, on a disbelief in the
reformatory nature of the system adopted with Convicts, and
on a perception of the impossibility of any "prison character"
being a real one, because it is formed under a condition in
which the will of the prisoner is absolutely restrained, and in
which artificial appliances enable, and even stimulate him, to
present an appearance of reformation which does not really
exist.  This description of the different classes of prisoners, and
the varied grades of criminality, probably corresponds exactly to
what has been the previous history of the prisoners in all Convict
Prisons in every part of the empire.  Some have endeavoured
to make it believed that Irish Convicts are a less hardened race
than English ones.   We have never heard those who have
practical experience of the management of Convicts, or even of
juvenile delinquents, single out the Irish from the English, as
more amenable to discipline, or less hardened in character, but
rather the reverse.   One very essential difference certainly may
be pointed out between these Irish Convicts of '55, and those
in our English Convict Prisons of '63 ; the former had never
undergone any steady, well-arranged discipline in the ill-managed
prisons which the Commissioners found there ; the latter have
been for years subjected to a system calculated to strengthen
their vicious nature, and to send them forth into society a band
of hardened ruffians, as they have proved themselves.  "We
hope," continue the Directors, "by means of a careful selection
of Convicts, according to their general, as well as 'prison character,' by their employment in small bodies in various localities,

comparatively as freemen (though under surveillance), that the public will gradually become convinced of the difference to which we have alluded, that many of these men are not utterly irreclaimable, and that by degrees they will become willing to extend a helping hand to such as may really prove themselves deserving of their aid and encouragement. We believe that a general desire is felt by the community at large to aid in the restoration of these fallen members of society, though all, or nearly all, shrink from personal contact with them."

The Directors entered on their work with a full knowledge of the difficulties they would have to encounter. "We anticipated," they say, p. 4, "that on the commencement of the new system, whilst in a transition state, both as regards officers and prisoners, many subjects of jarring disappointment and discontent would be likely to arise and cause troubles in the prisons; this was the case to some extent, and called for the exercise of great discrimination and firmness on the part of the local prison authorities. We regret to state that many violent and turbulent offences having occurred in the early part of the year, it became necessary to resort to severe punishments, which, however, were carefully watched by the medical officers; these occurred principally during the disorganization of Philipstown Prison. We are happy to state, however, that the system is now thoroughly understood and appreciated by officers and prisoners, who are aware that although the evil disposed will assuredly receive the treatment their conduct merits, those who have chosen a different course will meet with every encouragement."

It has been sometimes said that the Mark System is good in theory, but that practically it is bad, involving constant disputes between officers and men. The Tenth Report of the Directors confirms this, their Second, that when once well established, it is practically excellent.

The Directors perceived that it was essential to the success of their work to raise the Convicts from their very low and degraded intellectual condition; they knew that this was no easy task, and that it was not sufficient to establish schoolmasters in the gaols, unless they took other measures both to stimulate the teachers, and to rouse to exertion their very ignorant scholars. They thus speak in the same Report of the steps they took, p. 3 :—"In our last Report we complained of the inefficient state of the Educational Departments of the Convict Depôts, and stated the importance we conceived should be attached to them in this country, recommending at the same time that they should be placed under the Inspectors of the National Board of Education. Experience has proved that we were correct in our opinion ; the report of Mr. M'GAURAN, the head schoolmaster at Mountjoy Prison, shows, that after a very careful examination of the prisoners at that establishment, he found that 96·2 per cent. were almost without any education at all; a fact, we submit, calling for every exertion to render the educational machinery as perfect as possible, in order to open the minds of the prisoners, by a system of training as well as teaching."

The distinction here made is a very important one. The mere teacher is generally satisfied that the work is done, if the learner is enabled to master the rudiments of reading, writing and arithmetic, and if a large amount of knowledge is communicated to them; results of this kind may indeed be more easily tested than any other, and therefore are usually deemed sufficiently satisfactory ; but they are comparatively useless to persons in the condition of these prisoners; experience has also proved that they are very inefficient as a reformatory agency, and are indeed often soon lost after the teaching is discontinued. They no more satisfy their real wants, than would large quantities of rich and stimulating food nourish anyone, when a diseased state has deprived his digestive organs of their power of assimilation and nutrition. It is the opening and training of the mental powers, which is the great need of those whose whole intellectual and moral nature has been uncultivated and perverted. Throughout the history and the working of the Irish Convict System, it will be observed that

the great object of awakening, training and directing aright the
intellectual powers of the Convict, has been steadily kept in
view as an important means of reforming him, and preparing
him for society;—to steady perseverance in this object must
much of the success be attributed.

"Sensible of the very great importance," the Directors continue, "of establishing a proper system of education in the prisons,
through which, unfortunately, thousands of human beings must
pass, who are in turn subjected to its influence, we are gratified at
being enabled to state that, although much of the past year has
been taken up with arranging schoolrooms, classifying prisoners
according to their attainments, appointment of schoolmasters,
&c., *a great desire has been evinced by the prisoners to receive instruction;* and this is more remarkable, as proceeding from some
advanced in age, who, at the commencement of the year, attended
school with the greatest reluctance. This applies both to males
and females, and we believe so desirable result has been achieved
through great exertion on the part of the teachers. Lectures
have been established, and attended with visible success; the
great stumbling block to improvement has been the low and
depressing opinion that prisoners in general hold of their own
qualification, believing it to be impossible that they are susceptible of improvement. The exertion required from the instructor
to remove an impression so detrimental of progress, can be of
no ordinary kind, as his constant labour should be that of
illustrating and picturing out to the minds of the instructed;
but this is no light task, and few there are, however gifted they
may be in knowledge, who can really give effect to this desideratum of *all* education, but more especially that of the pauper
and the criminal. Mr. COYLE (an Inspector of the National
Board of Education), has recently visited the Dublin Convict
Prisons' Schools, and made many valuable suggestions, which
we feel confident will advance the cause of education. It is by
the constant visits of the Inspectors, and adopting their suggestions from time to time, that we may hope to render the Prison

Schools what they should be, one of the primary elements of reformation."

Here, as elsewhere, we observe a frank avowal on the part of the Directors of their own shortcomings, and of their willingness and even desire to avail themselves of help and suggestions. Thus, in the same Report, which, issued in the third year of their office, represents the state of the prisons in only the second, they frankly acknowledge that they cannot yet venture to adopt the ticket-of-leave system, which had already been established in England. They state (p. 26):—" The *ticket-of-leave* system has not as yet been brought into actual operation in this country; so large a number of Convicts having remained in the various prisons, who, according to the present state of the law might be considered entitled to their *free* discharge, on the ground of having served, with good conduct the full period under a state of penal servitude, established in lieu of their respective sentences of transportation, that it has not heretofore been deemed safe or expedient to add to this number by discharging still more on tickets of license. This class of Convicts had accumulated in this country to an extent quite unknown in England, owing partly to the want of system which existed formerly in the selection of Convicts for deportation, and partly from their physical *unfitness* for transportation, which, until lately, existed among so large a portion of the Irish Convicts. Subsequent to the appointment of the Commission of Convict Inquiry in 1853 (that is, since April 20th, 1854, when prisoners who had more than completed the proper equivalents of their sentences of transportation were first discharged), there have been 960 released. The class of prisoners who have served over the period of penal servitude established by law, as the equivalent for their sentences of transportation, has been disposed of, and it has become necessary that the system of release on license should now be brought into operation, which, we believe, with due care, may be commenced without giving rise to any serious evils to society.  We foresee that a great difficulty will arise in the disposal of Convicts sent home from Bermuda from time to time in large numbers, with a view to being discharged on tickets of license; we cannot feel justified in pursuing any different course, with regard to recommending them for this indulgence, than what we follow in our own prisons, under the sanction of the Lord Lieutenant.  The conduct of several of the prisoners on their passage home, and since their arrival in this country, appears to render them fitter subjects for a course of separate imprisonment, than discharge on license.  We trust that in future only those whose conduct throughout their imprisonment warrants such an indulgence, will be sent home with that view."

During the next year two Forts had been employed as an Intermediate Stage previous to discharge, and in other respects great progress had been made.  The Directors say in their Third Report:—"Generally speaking, the industry of the Convicts has been very satisfactory, especially of those in the Intermediate Stages at Smithfield, and at Forts Camden and Carlisle.  *The record of industry being known to affect their progress in the advantages of classification* has been a constant stimulus, which we hope will become still more powerful with the men now under sentence of penal servitude, when we are entitled to place before them some more tangible reward than is afforded by the mere increase of earnings, consequent on their attaining higher classification."

It will usually be found that steady industry is a fair indication of good conduct.  Idleness and self-indulgence are the ordinary characteristics of Convicts.  It is therefore satisfactory to learn from the Directors that after so short a trial of their system they can thus report.

They thus continue:—"The conduct of the prisoners generally is shewn by the diminished number of offences committed by prisoners on the public works to have considerably improved, as compared with previous years. *It is satisfactory to know that this diminution has not arisen from any practice on the part of the subordinate officers of overlooking or not reporting offences.* The rules require that no officer or servant, on any pretence whatsoever, through favour or mistaken notions of kindness, shall fail to make an immediate report to the Governor of any misconduct or wilful disobedience of the prison regulations, and it is only by a strict enforcement of this regulation that any steady system of combined rewards and punishments can be thoroughly carried out."

It is evident here that no bribes are held out to the prisoners to induce good behaviour. Reliance is placed by the Directors on sound principles, and a steady undeviating system of discipline. When we remember the state in which the prisoners were found at the commencement of the new system, and that during the year a number of Convicts had been brought back from Bermuda, who were full of dissatisfaction at a supposed breach of faith by the Government respecting the term of their sentence, and who endeavoured to excite the same feeling in others, it is a grand triumph of the system, that an improvement rather than the contrary was observable in the prisons. With great candour the Directors mention, however, some painful exceptions, which show the difficulties they had to contend with at the commencement of their administration :—" There have been, unhappily, some isolated instances of violent and revengeful assaults by Convicts on prison officers and fellow prisoners during the past twelve months, one of which, at Spike Island, in the month of September, terminated fatally for the officer assaulted. In this case several prisoners were ascertained to be implicated with the Convict accused of striking the fatal blow, and have been committed for trial at the next Assizes for the murder, which appears to have been deliberate and prompted by revenge. In this case the Lords of the Treasury have sanctioned the grant of an annuity to the widow of the deceased prison officer. Few of the other cases of assault appear to have originated in any combination of even a small number of prisoners, while in many of them effective assistance has been rendered by other Convicts to the officer attacked."

" The progressive classification and consequent attainment of higher rates of gratuity and other advantages, according to conduct and industry, recorded and denoted by the established badges, continue in general to have excellent effect, and we hope to be authorised to bring the system into more direct application to the cases of penal servitude prisoners during the present year. Hitherto, the fixed period of duration of sentences of this class of prisoners has placed them in a different position from their fellow prisoners under sentence of transportation, and the actual reward attainable by them has been limited to the prospect of acquiring a large amount of gratuity or earnings at the termination of their sentence. When, from misconduct, this hope is lost to them, the badge becomes of little value in their eyes, and the fear of present punishment their only remaining motive of conduct."

It was under the same feeling of disappointment that rebellions and mutinies occurred in the English Convict Prisons;— none occurred in these.

" The more strict enforcement of discipline has led to the collection at Mountjoy Prison of a number of badly conducted prisoners, returned to separate confinement as having proved themselves unfit for association at Spike Island and Philipstown; and this class of Convicts (denominated the penal class in the former prisons) has been the cause of some trouble to the authorities, from their recklessness and unsubmissiveness to discipline. It is actually necessary to have recourse to this means of preventing the evil example of such characters from producing serious bad effects among the Convicts associated on public works, while at the same time the delinquent is visited with a severe punishment, it gives him the opportunity of reflection on the consequences brought on himself by his misconduct; on the whole, however, there has been reason for satisfaction at the number of prisoners of this troublesome description not being greater than it has proved to be."

The following remarks on the kind of officers adapted to such service, will be valuable to all who are concerned in the management of prisons :—

" It has been necessary during the year to discharge several officers from the Convict service, as having proved themselves unfitted for the arduous and responsible duties of prison officers. This is to be expected in a service in which the qualifications are to a certain extent peculiar, and in which, therefore, it is difficult, if not impossible, to decide, without actual experience (whatever may have been a man's antecedents), whether he will eventually become fit for the duties. An extraordinary degree of intelligence is not absolutely necessary in a discipline officer of a Convict Prison; but good temper and a fair degree of discretion, combined with strict moral habits and quiet firmness of character, are qualifications without which he cannot succeed in the discharge of his duties ;—and as the want of them is sure, sooner or later, to bring discredit on any person entrusted with the charge of Convicts, as well as injury to the service itself, it becomes absolutely necessary not to overlook such deficiencies, whatever good qualities may otherwise be possessed by a person whose fitness for such duties is under consideration.

" It gives us great satisfaction to report that the general body of officers in the different prisons have steadily persevered in a zealous and efficient discharge of their duties, and supported our efforts to establish a just and fair course of discipline, and a conviction in the mind of the prisoners that their own advantagement and improvement is cared for, as well as the infliction of the punishment awarded by their sentence."

Having given these extracts from the Third Report of the Directors, which contain only general statements, we now turn to those of the officers for the same year, which strikingly show the results of the adoption of a good system, even at its commencement.

All who are familiar with the effect of the mental state on the physical condition of prisoners under separate confinement, the extreme care required to exclude from this severe trial of the constitution persons of infirm health, and to watch the symptoms which may arise, lest the health of the prisoners should be permanently injured by the ordeal, or, still worse, lest insanity or even suicide should be the termination of this punishment,—will perceive in the facts stated by the officers a striking proof of the wisdom of the system adopted by the Directors, and the truth of the principles on which it is founded.

"It gives me pleasure to report," says the medical officer of Mountjoy separate prison (Report iii., pp. 68, 69), "that the state of the prison during the past year has been comparatively healthy; this is mainly to be attributed to the continuance of the system adopted in the previous year.  *  *  It will be in your recollection that under the former arrangements of this prison, and previous to the alterations adopted by you, it was found necessary to subject the prisoners to a rigid examination, to test their mental and physical fitness for the severe and protracted trials they were in course of being exposed to, which led to very large rejections. But a worse consequence than this ensued; for although every precaution was taken in the original selection, many became enfeebled, and their health gave way eventually under the effects of the prison discipline. *I am happy to report that these evils have been completely removed;* every adult prisoner brought here during the past year, sentenced to transportation or penal servitude, has been received without a single exception, and subjected to the reformatory and separate treatment; and what is still more satisfactory, this important extension of the operations of the system has been unattended by any deterioration of health. From the statistical results stated in the annexed table the sanitary condition of the prison is shown rather to have improved.  *  *  Two cases of insanity appear in the hospital returns; in neither case was the disease induced by the discipline of Mountjoy. One prisoner was insane when committed, and had been sent home from Bermuda in an insane condition; the other had been a patient in the Richmond Lunatic Asylum previous to conviction, after his committal here he got fever and the derangement reappeared. They have been removed to the District Lunatic Asylum. During the period Mountjoy has been open for the reception of prisoners, there has not been a case of insanity attributable to the discipline of the prison."

The following extracts from the Report of the Medical Officer of Smithfield Government Prison point out the bearings of the system on the physical condition of the prisoners. It will be borne in mind that these results are the more remarkable because

they occur in cases where the preceding injurious condition may
have left, and probably did leave, very injurious effects on the
constitution :—

"Any one conversant with the medical statistics of Convict Prisons in
Ireland will see from the preceding Hospital Returns alone that the sanitary
state of the prison during these eleven months was very satisfactory, and
indeed exceptional. This becomes more manifest, however, when we consider
that all the prisoners in confinement here, 251, had previously undergone
long periods of confinement, varying from three and a quarter to six years,
and hence belonged to the class of convicts enfeebled by long confinement,
among whom the serious illness and mortality of former years chiefly occurred.
It is true they were a select class of such prisoners, but very few of them were
strong, many were delicate, and all bore the traces of long confinement, and
moreover they were constantly employed at such trades as shoemaking, tailor-
ing, mat making, &c., and worked more steadily and assiduously than the
convicts here at any former time.

"But the sanitary state of the prison was in reality more favorable than
could be inferred from any mere numerical results, and was most remarkably
manifested in the character of the sickness that prevailed. I would not attach
undue importance to the *total absence of mortality*, which was probably an
accidental circumstance ; but what was really remarkable and significant, all
the diseases of the period occurred so much modified and mitigated in character and form, as clearly indicated that the health of the prisoners was sustained by some peculiar sanitary influence. Thus the cases of fever (six only)
were of a mild and simple type, and they were the only cases of acute disease
that occurred. The bronchitic and catarrhal cases, forming nearly half of all
the cases treated, were merely common colds of more or less severity, and
requiring only a few days residence in hospital for their cure. It was however
in the cases of consumption and scrofula that this modification of morbid
action was most strikingly manifested. These kindred maladies have at all
times been the peculiar scourge of the Convict Prisons in this country, and
probably will long continue to occupy a prominent place in their hospital
records, even under the most enlightened and humane management. Even
these intractable complaints, which, when occurring in prisoners whose health
has been gradually deteriorated by confinement, almost invariably run a continuous and rapid course, were during this period so remarkably modified in
form and character, that except in two or three cases of long existing disease,
they made but little progress, were more amenable to treatment, and in several
instances were completely arrested in their course. Ophthalmia, in all its
forms, is also generally an unmanageable affection in prisons ; the cases in
hospital, chiefly of a strumous character, were, like the other forms of scrofula,
unusually mild. The other chronic ailments, with the exception of one case
of epilepsy, were slight and unimportant.

" To what cause can we attribute this modification of disease and immunity from serious sickness in a class of convicts whose constitutions had been more or less impaired by long confinement? Many causes might be suggested to account for this result.

" Thus, it may be said, the city generally was unusually healthy during the past year; no epidemic disease prevailed; the prison was not over crowded as in former years. These and similar circumstances may have had some influence, but they are inadequate to account for the facts observed in hospital, or for the improvement which was remarkable in the health of the prisoners who worked so steadily and laboriously.

" *This improved sanitary state of the prison dates from the introduction of the reformatory system; and, in my opinion, is attributable to the agency of several concurring salutary influences which this system brings to bear upon the criminal, and which produce as remarkable an improvement in the mental and moral condition, the temper, feelings, character and conduct of the prisoner, as in his general health.* In whatever circumstances the prisoners here are observed, this improved state of feeling is very apparent. In the workshops it is manifested in the cheerfulness, alacrity and assiduity, with which they apply themselves to their laborious occupations, and furnishes a striking contrast to the listlessness, sullenness and gloom, so commonly exhibited by the ordinary convict in similar circumstances. In the school, the earnestness and vivacity with which they engage in their studies, after the fatigue of the day, and the anxiety they evince to acquire information and excel one another, afford still more satisfactory evidence of mental and moral improvement; though at the same time it must be acknowledged that much of this was attributable to the agreeable and skilful manner in which instruction is imparted to them in this prison, by lecturing, diagrams, maps, &c., and to the judicious selection of subjects suited to their capacity, and supplying the kind of information which is attractive and interesting to persons in their condition. In the hospital, also, an improved state of feeling has been equally manifest. It is a common practice among the convicts to endeavour to get into hospital, or to remain there after they are perfectly recovered, in order to avoid the prison duties; *very few cases of this kind have occurred under the new system.* Another, and by no means unfrequent occurrence observed in the Convict Prisons, and more especially among the prisoners whose health has suffered from long confinement, and who have been anticipating their approaching release from prison, is that when the prisoner is attacked with any serious disease, he is at once prostrated in body and mind; comes into the hospital with the gloomy foreboding that he will never leave the prison alive; and lies down, as it were, to die, hopeless and desponding, thus rendering all the resources of art unavailing. A very different spirit prevailed among the prisoners here since the change of management took place. In fact, they appeared to me, in most cases, rather disposed to underrate the seriousness of their sickness, and to rely too much on their improved health, and were only anxious and eager to return to those duties which have ceased to be distasteful to them.

"Those who have had opportunities of observing the powerful influence, for good or evil, that mental feelings and emotions, hope and joy, grief and despondency, exercise upon the human body in sickness and in health, as well as in the world outside as within the walls of a prison, will have no difficulty in comprehending that this buoyant state of mind and hopeful spirit of the prisoners must have largely contributed to produce the improved sanitary condition of the prison during the past year.

"It is almost unnecessary for me to observe that with prisoners in this state of mind, remunerative labour, and the acquisition of interesting and useful knowledge in the school, are, in themselves, sanitary influences of no slight importance.

"Indeed this system of treatment may be regarded as not only reformatory but sanitary to the prisoner, and is brought to bear on him at the period of his imprisonment when he most needs it; so that he is, as it were, prepared, as the period of his liberation from prison approaches, to return to society in such a state of health as will enable him to make good use of the skill and information he has acquired in confinement.

"The observations I have offered are applicable to a great majority of the convicts that were in prison during the past eleven months; there were, however, several who, from obtuseness of mind, or natural depravity, appeared to be little affected by the salutary influences with which they were surrounded. There were also some few committed here in such a weak state of health, that they were unable to avail themselves of the advantages the reformatory system affords to the prisoner.

"I have the honour to be, Gentlemen,

"Your obedient servant,

"The Directors of Convict Prisons."                           "THOMAS BRADY.

The opinion of the influence of the mind over the body here spoken of by the medical officer, as the result of one year's experience of the Irish Convict System, was confirmed by lengthened experience. This is expressed in the following letter, written after an interval of more than six years from the Report just quoted :—

"9, TEMPLE STREET, DUBLIN, 4th May, 1863.

"MADAM,—I have great pleasure in being able to assure you that the remarkable improvement which took place in the sanitary state of the convicts in the Intermediate Prisons, on the establishment of the reformatory system, has been fully sustained ever since.

"The diseases that have occurred, without almost an exception, have been of a simple character and mild form, such as might occur in any family, and requiring merely a few days' residence in hospital for their cure.

"I have observed that the prisoner begins to improve in health from the

moment he passes the threshold of the Intermediate Prison, even though he
be weakly and shattered by previous confinement, and in most instances his
improvement in health is so rapid as to excite the astonishment of those who
have seen him at the time of his admission.  I may observe that the facts
stated here have been repeatedly put forward in my Annual Reports.

" I have the honour to be, Madam,

"Your obedient servant,

" THOMAS BRADY.

" Miss CARPENTER."

The physical improvement of the Convicts, after only two
years working of the newly adopted system, was not greater
than their intellectual and moral progress.   How completely
the system which had been adopted, approved itself by its
results to the various officers, and how much their cöoperation
aided in the working of it, we may learn from extracts from
their Reports to the Directors.   The head Schoolmaster of
Fort Camden thus writes:—

" Of the wisdom and prudence of classifying the convicts, and separating
the well disposed from the viciously inclined, I think our prison here affords
convincing evidence—if evidence were wanting to convince any who have led
the Apostle's admonitions, ' Brethren, be not deceived, evil communications
corrupt good manners.'  For a month or two after the exemplary men were
sent here, a casual observer would say that they ill deserved the character,
were he to perceive all their foibles and murmurings ; but the man who studies
human nature is well aware that these faults occur, and may be found among
society in general, and yet, on the whole, we do not, nor should not pronounce
the community wicked in consequence.   About the 7th of February last (1856)
some exemplary men came here from Spike Island, who had been sent home
from Bermuda, under the impression that they were to obtain immediate
liberty, but being detained they murmured and complained that faith had been
broken with them ; these murmurings seem to have arisen more from miscon-
ception and defective training than from any wilful perversity.  The elements
of dissatisfaction thus generated were beginning to insinuate themselves into
the minds and acts of the other prisoners (whose conduct in general contrasted
forcibly and favourably with those from Bermuda) ; but the religious instruction and admonitions of their chaplains, the good sense and forbearance of the
principal warder, and the other warders in charge of them, together with
the moral and literary instructions imparted in the school, *soon convinced them that all connected with their management had their welfare at
heart;* the feelings of discontent abated, a better spirit was evoked, and they
became more susceptible of moral and religious impressions, so that they are
now governed by the finer feelings and by the affections more than by

restraint or official controul;—they labour well and cheerfully, they pay attention to their school duties, and are punctual in attending morning and evening prayers and other religious obligations. I have frequently stolen unobserved under their windows in the mornings and evenings when they were not under the restraint of an officer, and was edified at their attention to their prayers and books. I might hear a coarse or vulgar expression, but nothing culpable; in this respect their conduct is far more reserved than very many among society even of a better grade."—Third Report, p. 45.

To those who know the extreme difficulty of the teacher in awakening the intellectual powers of those in whom they have been deadened and perverted from childhood, and the irksome and even painful effort required in the adult to master the rudiments of knowledge, the following statement from the report of the same Schoolmaster will be most satisfactory. It will prove that the great end had been already attained,—that of inducing the prisoner to work with his instructor for his own improvement; of enlisting his will, and bringing it into harmony with that of his superiors:—

" Were they," (the prisoners) the Schoolmaster continues, " subjected to a rigorous examination in literary subjects, their progress might appear slow, for many of them were aged men of blunted intellect, and speaking only the Irish language; but this would be an unfair test, for most of them have acquired much useful information, though incapable of answering correctly for want of expression. Those who cannot read or write, so as to gain information from books, have been taught orally and by lecture something of life in general, and are partially educated. It is both amusing and edifying to hear these old men teaching each other geography by pointing out on the maps the several countries, under the Irish names for the different colours that mark them. Those who have learned to read, and who also speak Irish, very generally translate the subjects and substance of their lessons into Irish for those who have failed to learn to read. There was a remarkable instance of the effects of application and perseverance in the case of S. C., an old stolid man, scarcely able to utter a word of English, and not knowing the letters of the alphabet; yet such a desire had he to learn to read, that he applied himself day and night to the task, and though extremely dull and slow, in the course of a few months he could read a first and second book, and was reading the sequel when he was discharged; not only did he improve himself, but he became the medium of improvement to a man named A—, and other aged men, who baffled all attempts to teach them in English, for he translated to them at night what he had learned during the day."—Third Report pp. 47, 48.

As much difficulty is generally experienced in making prison instruction interesting and really beneficial to the prisoner, it will be useful to observe the method pursued, as described by the Schoolmaster in the same report.

" The development of the intellects, and the turning of aged and almost inflexible minds from their natural bias, must be a task of some magnitude, yet I have succeeded in rendering my instructions efficient in that way by consulting the several tastes, by analysing and explaining the simplest and most familiar subjects, and by selecting that kind of instruction most likely to be practicable and useful through life ; but above all, showing by conclusions and morals drawn from the simplest lessons in our national school books, how perverse and grossly mistaken they have been in most of their preconceived opinions, never omitting, when expedient, to place before them the beneficence of Providence, the admirable mechanism and just arrangement of all the works of the Creator, the necessity of regular government, the evils resulting from its want in savage countries, and the iniquity of violating the laws of society, thereby thwarting Providence and paining and injuring our fellow-beings.  These principles I do not very often inculcate by a formal lecture, as I find, by experience, it would be attributed to interested motives, being an officer in the pay of the government, and would not have the desired effect, but I do it rather incidentally ; for in reading the lessons contained in the national school books (which we use) the explanations warrant and admit of such conclusions ; they are not therefore questioned, but very generally received and treasured up in the mind.  The mode of teaching or conveying instructions which I generally pursue is that approved of by Dr. WHATELY in the preface to his 'Lessons on Reasoning,' viz., first preparing questions and ascertaining what the prisoners knew of the given subject ; secondly, giving instructions and explanations; thirdly, examinations; and lastly, recapitulation of the instructions in a very concise form, summing up the essential principles necessary to be impressed on and retained by the mind.  The time allowed for school during the day is employed in teaching the several classes spelling, reading, explanations of lessons, arithmetic, grammar, geography, &c.; and the hour every evening is applied to simultaneous instructions, or lecturing and writing alternately.  The subjects for which they have most taste are reading, writing and arithmetic; and as these are the most likely to be beneficial to them through life, I have encouraged that taste, and paid much attention to those branches.  The maps of the world, and of its several countries are not used for the mere purpose of teaching geography, but serve as great books of history, chronology and morality; because, by their means, I bring vividly and practically before the mind the rise and fall of empires, nations and individuals; the manners, customs, failings, virtues, resources, industrial pursuits, &c., of the different nations exhibited on them ; the advantages arising from international intercourse and commerce; the mutual dependence of nations and individuals, and the folly of national and personal antipathies."

Thus the Schoolmaster does not confine himself to mere educational routine, or to simple culture of the intellectual faculties; he connects them by a natural and easy process with topics bearing on their moral character, and he makes them interesting to themselves personally, because he has a true interest in the welfare of each one of them, and he desires to employ his own superior knowledge and culture for their benefit. He does even more than this,—

" I frequently stimulate the men here," continues the Schoolmaster, Mr. HAROLD, in the same report, " to the future practice of provident and industrial habits, by bringing under their notice the great things accomplished by such persons as WILLIAM HUTTON, and others; by pointing out the necessity of self reliance, as all other expectations of aid from friends or dishonest courses become failures in the end; by recommending *each* to apply himself to some pursuit for which he evinces a taste; by explaining the necessity of husbanding our time properly; by making the changes from one occupation to another serve as so many recreations; and by various other instructions which every day's experience suggests. In teaching agriculture, I adopt a method which is rather the converse of that usually followed, as I introduce first to them the unskilful mode of farming pursued in the neighbourhood of the prison, and the improvements that could be effected by levelling ditches, draining, deep digging, rotation of crops, house feeding, drilling, and a careful preservation of manures. I next proceed to the principles of the science of agriculture, explaining by illustrations and instances the simple compound organic and inorganic substances, the volatile and fixed ingredients in vegetables; the substances that the atmosphere and rains supply, and those which must be added to the land in consequence of the exhaustion caused by cropping. It may not be amiss to state here, that if it were expedient to employ the convicts in general at trades and agriculture, I am convinced it would contribute to humanize, improve and prepare them, for the sort of labour they will have to perform when liberated."

The views here expressed are so different from those entertained by ordinary school teachers, and indicate a scope of attainments and knowledge so varied and superior, that the reader will probably imagine that Mr. HAROLD is a very unique and peculiar master, whose services the Directors were fortunate in securing, but who should not be considered a type of what should be expected in Convict establishments. But throughout the prisons the same principle and spirit pervade those engaged in the different departments. Long extracts of an interesting and instructive character might be made from the Reports of the other teachers, but space forbids, yet we must not omit the following remark in the Report of Mr. BOURKE, the Assistant-Schoolmaster of Spike Island Convict Prison Schools, because it indicates a condition of the Convict mind, very important for the consideration of those who desire to reform it :—

"In the course of my instructions to these men during the past year," he says, 3rd Report, pp. 57 and 58, "I could not help being frequently struck with the vast amount of indifference as to purely scientific or abstract knowledge which existed among them. This I attributed, in the great majority of instances, to two causes : *first, their total ignorance of the pratical bearing of even the commonest and most useful branches of science ; and, secondly, a certain absence of moral energy or elasticity of character*, which would have led them to look beyond their present degraded position to one of future usefulness and respectability, in which knowledge might be applied to beneficial purposes. The removal, therefore, of these causes, and with them of their necessary and immediate effect—the indifference above mentioned,—was a duty to the performance of which I felt the necessity of directing my best and most earnest efforts. Accordingly I have omitted no opportunity of pointing out to these persons the advantages of a good elementary education, the various ways in which it may be and has been useful, and the folly as well as wickedness of despairing to do good because of mere temporary reverses or privations. By these means, as well as by popularizing the subject of instructions so far as to bring it within the easy comprehension of those for whom it is intended, I have succeeded· to a great extent in not only removing the obstacles to, but even creating a taste for, useful knowledge. Of this result, the extensive and increasing demand for books, for the purpose of self improvement in the wards during the evenings, leaves little room to doubt."

If the teachers in the intermediate and advanced classes found the minds of the prisoners in the dull intellectual condition which has been described, we may imagine what was their state of dense ignorance when first received in Mountjoy Prison. This Third Report of the Irish Convict Prisons contains full statements of the methods adopted there by the Schoolmaster, Mr. M'GAURAN, and enforced by him on the assistant teachers ; we will extract a passage showing the spirit and motive which influenced even ordinary and routine teaching, planned as it was with scientific skill, and with admirable adaptation to the wants of the subjects of it :—

"The education which should be imparted," he says, 3rd Report, pp. 74-5, "*in order to be reformatory in its tendency*, must have for its object the implanting right principles in the breasts of the convicts who come within its sphere of action. Its aim must be to engender self-respect, so as to induce shame; to teach the arts of reading, writing and arithmetic,— a knowledge of which is necessary to fill even the humblest situations in life; to infuse a love of honest industry, to cultivate and exercise the reflective and reasoning powers, to foster kind feelings, to instil sound principles, to uproot perverted notions of ' right' and ' wrong,' and to promote good habits. * * * Reading, writing and arithmetic, are taught according to the 'National School system,' with this difference, that the prisoners are treated with all the respect due to mature years, and at the same time all the pains and trouble necessary for infants are taken with them. The prisoners are, in fact, overgrown infants, possessing all their foibles and little whims, without that innocence and simplicity peculiar to childhood, but perfectly childish as regards the desire to be praised in order to gain courage to persevere. * * * I have constantly impressed on each teacher that to be efficient it was essential for him to be at all times cheerful with the prisoners, painstaking and yielding,—yielding without losing his position or compromising his principles; that he should be always on the alert when a prisoner is exerting himself at his lesson, however ludicrous his efforts should appear; to suppress with a resolute disapprobation any attempt on the part of the others to laugh at, or turn into ridicule the prisoner so engaged; and above all, to be particularly cautious himself not to set such an example."

The Chaplains of the Convict Prisons bear a testimony equally strong with that of the Schoolmasters to the effects on the Convicts of the system now adopted; and they also in their Reports indicate the spirit in which the various instructions and ministrations are given,—a spirit of respect for the fellow man and sympathy with his human nature, while they have no fellow-ship with evil doing, or tolerance of misconduct. We shall, therefore, present an extract from the Report of a Chaplain of each of the three denominations, commencing with that of the Protestant Chaplain of Smithfield Prison, dated January 7th, 1857. Its importance will excuse its length.

" Early in the year 1856 a change was made in the class of prisoners sent to this depôt, and since the first of February last we have had only those who, having reached the 'Exemplary Class' in other prisons, were considered deserving of being placed here, in a state of probation, previous to their being deemed eligible for tickets-of-leave. The number of my congregation was, by this change, considerably reduced; but my duties, though rendered of a more pleasing nature, were not at all diminished, either in the time they occupied or the anxiety they involved. The great advantage to be expected from a reformatory institution, which this may now be termed, depends on the individualizing of the men; the acquiring a knowledge of the history, state of mind, past and present, of each, and of his hopes and prospects for the future, as well as the grounds on which he calculates for their realization. Possessed of such intimate knowledge of each case, the chaplain finds the data upon which to work, in a way impossible where a number must be instructed in classes; and the permission granted to men in this establishment of writing frequently to their friends, affords, by the inspection of the letters, an excellent clue to the state of their minds, and also gives some index as to the circumstances and characters of those friends with whom, on their liberation, they will be placed in association.

"Feeling deeply the importance of this, I have always placed myself in communication with the clergyman in whose parish the prisoner's friends live, and under whose ministry he will be placed on his discharge; and I feel thankful that, in every instance, my application has met with a kind and cordial reception. In some cases it was recommended that employment should be sought for the man in some place other than that in which his character had been lost, and to which special circumstances rendered his return imprudent. In others, it appeared that all his family had left the neighbourhood, or were undesirable companions for a reformed man; while, in the majority of instances, kind hearts were ready to receive the returning prodigal, whose sincerity had been tested, not by the ordinary discipline of a prison, but by the peculiar system which can be carried out only in such an establishment as now happily exists here.

"Since the change of this prison to a reformatory institution, in February last, fifteen of my congregation have been liberated therefrom, most of them on tickets-of-leave; several of these have been now at large for six months or upwards. I have kept up frequent correspondence with them and the neighbouring clergy; and *in no instance has any one of them been reported for any misconduct.* Of those fifteen, there is one from whom I have not heard since his liberation; but his antecedents forbid me to be in the least doubt of his good conduct. Of one other I have had rather discouraging private information; but I still hope well of him. With the remaining thirteen I have frequent communication; and truly thankful do I feel to hear how happily most of them are circumstanced.

"I have been for 29 years engaged in ministerial work in parishes in Dublin where the population were chiefly of the lower classes. For 24 years I have been chaplain to prisons in Dublin; and, with that experience, I unhesitatingly say that the men who have been discharged from this prison, under the present system of reformatory training, are, on an average, far superior to most of the same class in life, in cultivated intelligence, moral feelings, and respect for, if not a deep sense of religion.

" I see in the public papers great complaints of the result of the system of ticket-of-leave in England. I do not know whether the system of testing each one through varied stages is the same there as in Ireland, nor do I feel it to be within my province to offer an opinion on the general question ; but I state only the results of facts within my own knowledge when I say that, placed as I am in contact with the convicts in the last stage of the process of restoring them to the society of their fellow-men, my experience is, that the results in Ireland are such as the most sanguine hopes of the supporters of this system could have scarcely anticipated. It is easy for one in my position to trace the effects of the system under which such happy results have been attained. A man, on conviction, is sent first to solitary confinement for six or nine months; there he learns to reflect. He then passes to a course of hard labour in a prison where he mixes with his fellows for two or more years; there he learns order, discipline and industry, and his progress is recorded in monthly judgments, on the quality of which depends his ultimate promotion to the 'Exemplary Class.' Thus hope is awakened and becomes a stimulating principle to his mind. Should he, under the operation of those agencies, prove worthy of being promoted to Smithfield Depôt, his hope dawns into reality; he feels himself on the threshold of liberty, and his best energies and feelings are called into action. Then, in this establishment, those energies are stimulated, and those feelings cultivated, by the most ample provision for religious and secular instruction, combined with constant industrial employment; and the convict, who felt himself an outcast, begins to feel himself a man again.

" It appears to me to be a very important feature in this system that, as each man advances a stage in his course towards reformation, he is at each stage removed to another prison. The very fact of his being thus transferred to a new abode gives to him the idea of *reality* in *progress*, which no nominal promotion would make him feel while he remained in *the same prison*. Every such removal he feels to be a *real sensible step* towards liberty; and the results are obvious. I would add one fact; you have for some time past caused Camden Fort to be appropriated to a special class, selected from Spike Island Prison, and those have been placed under a reformatory system of instruction nearly similar to that established here. Very lately a detachment of prisoners was brought up here from Camden Fort, and it required little experience or observation to see how far superior in mental cultivation, discipline and moral training, they were to even the best men we have hitherto received from the ordinary Government Prisons.

" Such has been my experience during the past year—the first in which this system has been tried in Ireland. I suppose it will receive the consideration of those more fitted to judge of it than I am. One improvement would certainly be most desirable—a facility for the emigration to some other land of those who have no homes, or friends willing to receive them here. Such men, however reformed, are obviously placed in circumstances of great disadvantage in seeking employment at home. Wanting employment, they are exposed to great temptation; and I am sure that, if they could reach another country, most of them would there take that place in the scale of society which adverse circumstances, rather than any moral incapacity, renders it difficult for them to attain in this country.

"I have the honour to be, Gentlemen,

"Your obedient servant,

"THOMAS H. SHORE."

MR. SHORE's opinion has remained unaltered by lengthened experience. After six years he thus writes, May 4, 1863 :— "In every annual Report I have endeavoured to give my views, based on progressive experience, of the working of the Convict system here; so that those Reports, read consecutively, give a full exposition of all my experience. * * * To the 8th Report I would especially refer you, which explains and illustrates, as far as I could do it, the happy effects of this system, with every phase of which I have been so intimately conversant since its first establishment." After referring to particular Reports, he continues :—

"To those views I still adhere, as well as to those quoted in ' Observations on the Treatment of Convicts in Ireland,' by Mr. WHEATLEY BALME, and three other Visiting Justices, who did me the honour to consult me on several points; so that I most unqualifiedly endorse all the views put forth in that book."

We next have the Roman Catholic Chaplain's Report, and then that of the Presbyterian Chaplain :—

"GENTLEMEN,—With your request to state my opinion concerning the Smithfield Prison during the last year I willingly comply.

"Though it is not my custom to praise, I must in justice say that the men committed to my care during the year 1856, called 'exemplary,' were so in reality. For the short period they remained with me, in confinement, their conduct was marked by strict regularity, they attended their religious duties, and exhibited towards each other kindness and charity worthy of imitation. Nearly all, as soon as they obtain liberty, knowing the sad effects of intemperance, spontaneously take the pledge against all intoxicating liquors, and I am delighted to learn from various sources have observed it faithfully, and have proved themselves industrious and good members of society.

"In conclusion, I beg to state that the Superintendent, Mr. Good, and the other officers of the prison, deserve my thanks for their kindness to me, and the anxiety they have manifested to procure anything required for the spiritual wants of the prisoners.

"I remain, Gentlemen, your obedient servant,

"Thomas Nolan, Roman Catholic Chaplain."

"Gentlemen,—My duties as Presbyterian Chaplain to the Smithfield Government Prison, during the year 1856, have been similar to those of the previous one; the usual Sabbath services have been conducted in the prison chapel every Lord's Day; regular weekly visits have been paid to the prisoners; and in my public ministrations, as well as in my private interviews with the men under my care, I have endeavoured to impress upon their minds those instructions which appeared to me most conducive to their temporal and spiritual well-being.    As a matter of duty, I take this opportunity of publicly acknowledging my personal obligation to the Governor, to Mr. Bradfield, and to every subordinate officer in the prison; having been received by them, on all occasions, in a manner both gentlemanly and courteous.    I also consider it my duty further to state that the prison officers of every rank have cheerfully endeavoured to facilitate my efforts in seeking to promote the moral improvement of the men for whose reformation I am chiefly interested.

"It is exceedingly gratifying to me to be able to report the decided change for the better which the arrangements recently made in this establishment have produced upon the prisoners generally.    The air of heartless apathy and careless indifference, which, generally speaking, was manifested by the men in my public and private interviews with them on former occasions, and which were often to me a source of regret and discouragement, are now, I am happy to say, exchanged for feelings of cheerfulness and hope, and an air of self-dependence and self-respect, the all but certain guarantees of a promising future.

"The employing of the prisoners in acquiring some useful trade appears to be an arrangement exceedingly beneficial; as by this means, not only is the expenditure of the service materially liquidated, but I am able to testify that, under the faithful training of the different superintendents, many of the men have acquired, or are acquiring, industrious habits and useful avocations, which, if persevered in, will, it is to be hoped, prevent temptation to crime, and afford them the means of earning an honest and a competent livelihood in after life.

"Of those under my care whose exemplary conduct justified the Government in mitigating their term of punishment under the ticket-of-leave system, I am not aware of a single instance in which good faith has been violated.    On the contrary, I am gratified to learn occasionally, by letters from the north of Ireland, whither some of them have gone, that such parties continue to manifest the same excellent deportment which marked their conduct while in prison, and which justified the authorities in the act of clemency referred to.

" In conclusion I have only to add that the present arrangements in Smith-field Government Prison appear eminently calculated, under the Divine bless-ing, to secure the object intended; and did the public at large, instead of looking with suspicion upon the liberated prisoner, endeavour to second the efforts of Government in promoting his reformation, I am convinced there would be few cases indeed in which it could be said that labour and strength had been spent in vain and for nought.

"I am, Gentlemen, yours very respectfully,

"JAMES EDGAR, Presbyterian Chaplain."

The following are a few among the many letters which have been received respecting discharged Convicts by the superin-tendents and other officers of Smithfield Depôt. They show, not only the satisfactory condition of the Convicts who are now maintaining themselves honestly, but the warm interest still taken in them by those who had before the custody of them.

"T——, *February 22nd*, 1857.

" SIR,—I am glad to inform you that Mr. B—— and his family are doing well. He is in the employment of Mr. S——. He is living soberly, quietly and honestly, and treating his family affectionately. I have seen him at K—— on the 3rd ult., and have heard directly from him on the 19th inst.

" Yours faithfully,

" M. K."

"N——, *Jan. 27th*, 1857.

" SIR,—From your laudable anxiety about B. Q., you will be glad to hear that he is going on well. He is in the employment of a respectable farmer near B——, where he attends his religious duties with punctuality; indeed even before his conviction I never discovered more than the one crime in him, and I believe hunger was the cause; for he applied to his old, bad father for the means of taking him to America, but was refused, though he could give it.

" Faithfully yours,

" J. B."

" L——, *23rd January*, 1857.

" DEAR SIR,—I received your letter and hasten to reply. The young man mentioned in your letter is at present living with his father, and he purposes commencing the coopering trade towards spring; and as regards his character it is unimpeachable, and is strictly honest in the smallest matter.

" Yours very truly,

" E. K."

"C——, *14th November*, 1856.

" SIR,—W. McE., who is still in my service, has requested me to write to you. His brother J. left this for Canada early in May last; and in a few days after he arrived at Montreal, where my sister has been residing for some years, he was employed by a gentleman in the immediate vicinity of the town, and he has continued in his service since that time.  He has written two letters to his brothers, giving a favourable account of the country, and stating that he is quite well and happy.  From the time that he arrived here from Dublin till he left Ireland, he was in my employment, and he conducted himself with the strictest propriety.

" Yours faithfully,

" J. H."

" MY DEAR SIR,—The five men you sent me from the Smithfield Reformatory some months ago, are most willing and industrious poor fellows.  You said you would send a few more hard-working fellows; if they are such you describe, the sooner you send them the better.

" On no account send me any man who is not well-conducted and willing.

" I am, my dear Sir, yours faithfully,

" J. M'D."

In the Fourth Report the Directors speak with satisfaction of the continuance of improvement in the prisons, notwithstanding the difficulties which have been occasioned by the extremely violent and ungovernable spirit of many of the Convicts, which made the work they desired to accomplish one of peculiar difficulty.  In the former Report, Forts Camden and Carlisle, at Cork, and Smithfield, in Dublin, were spoken of as Intermediate Prisons.  In the present one we first hear of Lusk:—

" We have the satisfaction," they say, p. 11, " of reporting, that during the past year we have found the results of the special treatment of Convicts in Intermediate Prisons, on a system explained in our two former Reports, to have quite equalled our expectations.  The conduct of the prisoners, both under detention and after liberation, confirms this statement. We believe that it would be difficult to find any body of men who would behave themselves more submissively to the rules, or give their labour more freely to the public service, than we have found to be the case with the Convicts, who, since the commencement of this system, have been placed in the Intermediate Prisons.

" In April last we located as many Convicts as were at our disposal for the purpose (60), in two iron huts, on Lusk

Common. They were at first employed in levelling the portion of the common on which the huts stand, and forming it into a parade ground and vegetable garden. When this was finished, they were employed in draining the commons, and at spade labour in the fields; the former work, about which they will yet be occupied some time, is excessively heavy, and the Superintendent of Drainage reports most favourably of the willing labour of the prisoners."

Of the disposal of the Convicts after discharge, they thus speak:—

"When the will to emigrate, and, in most cases, to join their friends, is accompanied by the power afforded through their extra industry, it is not surprising to find that a large and an increasing number have left and are leaving the country, the limited amount of their means alone being the impediment.

"*Although we cannot too highly prize, as an important element of reformation, the voluntary emigration of the well-disposed criminals when free, to lands where labour is scarce,* or advocate too strongly its beneficial effects, we are aware that a large number will still remain in their own country, with equal intention of well doing. The experience afforded by two years of many prisoners on license in this city, and of the whole number at present under supervision, induce the most satisfactory conclusions. The fact of employers of high respectability, after long experience, retaining those men in their situations, and still offering work to others of the same class, is the strongest, and perhaps the most satisfactory testimony we can adduce in favour of the system. Many prisoners, sentenced to penal servitude, and discharged from Smithfield, have, by means of their gratuity, bound themselves to tradesmen to be made more perfect in their calling. Although these men are free, a system of visitation, voluntarily submitted to by them, has been kept up, which has been found to be productive of good."

The conclusions to which the Directors have now arrived, are thus stated at the end of their Report:—

"In conclusion, we believe the prison system now pursued in the Convict Department in this country to be as opposed to any encouragement of the evil-doer, as it is favourable to the assistance of the criminal who has suffered a sufficient penalty for his offence, and who desires henceforward to live on the proceeds of his own industry, instead of on that of the community. He needs but the means so to do, and these are acquired through the extra industry, and by the sweat of the brow, of the offender.

"The objection to the system of its offering a premium to crime, if ever made, *can have no place here*. The early stages of discipline are sufficient to convince an inquirer that the objection would be quite invalid. The dietary, from the commencement to the termination of the sentence, is the lowest the Medical Officers will permit. The enforced order, cleanliness and regularity, however impressive of an air of comfort to the casual observer, is, be it remembered, *most repugnant to the previous habits of the criminal, and most thoroughly opposed to his ideas of enjoyment*. We have stated that about seventy-five per cent. pass through the Intermediate Prisons; twenty-five per cent. are at present discharged directly from the ordinary prisons—misconduct and offences having precluded their removal. It is satisfactory, however, to us to be able to observe that this per centage of prisoners cannot be deemed incorrigible. We have many reasons for knowing that after their discharge, when too late, many of these have seen their error, and have endeavoured, though often in vain, to regain the path of honest livelihood. They have left the prison under the ban of misconduct; they have neglected their opportunities, and have joined the world without means to exist, or to obtain employment.

"These may be called an unimpressible class, which will decrease in number as light advances into the prisons, and as the prisoner's future career becomes an object of anxiety to him.

"A portion, however, of the twenty-five per cent. may fairly be called incorrigible. Whether in prison, or at large, their object is the same ; they pursue an unmistakable line of conduct, which must be dealt with strictly and vigorously. The public mind is shocked, from time to time, by the commission of some outrageous crime. If a capital sentence is not carried out, the offenders are, for the most part, to be found in the Convict Prisons, and it will require but little argument to prove, that as with the impressible, so *with the incorrigible, special treatment must be used*. We are of opinion that they should, whilst in prison, be employed, as far as possible, at such labour as will not give them the means of injuring their fellow-prisoners and officers. They should be placed under the special and continual watching of their Chaplain. It may be that the supposed incorrigible may become, and prove himself to be, corrigible. If not, he should be retained to the last hour of his sentence, and when discharged should be placed under such observation as will protect the public from his outrages."

Appended to this Report are memoranda by the chairman respecting the Intermediate Convict Prisons. These enter into very minute details respecting their management and results ; space forbids our inserting here more than an extract from a communication to the Government, dated November, 1855, which shows what a unity of design and what a steadiness of principle characterised the Irish Convict Prisons, from their very commencement.

" The reformability of the generality of criminals has been admitted, after a laborious investigation by a Select Committee of the House of Commons in 1850, and their opinion has been corroborated by facts and figures in abundance. The acknowledged object of all prison treatment being so to direct its deterrent and reformatory course as shall best conduce to the required results, viz., the diminution of crime, it is considered that this result is obtained by a judicious combination of penal and of reformatory treatment. The present system commencing with the deterrent, is followed by a course of penal, and of reformatory discipline. The success of this system it is proposed to test, previous to the release of any prisoner, by the institution of a third stage, in which the reformatory element shall preponderate, as does the deterrent element in the first stage. This course, it is maintained, will protect the community. It will also tend to the present as well as to the future improvement of its guilty members.

"The great difficulty with which discharged prisoners have to contend, is 'the want of employment;' and so long as this difficulty exists, so long will the criminal population, reformed and unreformed, remain a distinct portion of the community; and so long will their absorption be a matter of impossibility. It is obviously, therefore, a primary object to endeavour to remove this obstruction, by considering its cause, and by proposing its remedy. We have been asking the community to receive, and to employ the reformed portion of our discharged criminals; the guarantee for such reformation being, that their character in prison has been exemplary. But the community do not consider that a character obtained under an absence from the temptations to which prisoners would be exposed in the world, a fair test of reformation. They therefore decline accepting this evidence; and refusing to employ such criminals, thus reject the really reformed, who are included in the category as untested.

"The proposed stage of reformatory treatment places a prisoner where he can be assailed by temptations, and where the public will have an opportunity of judging of his reformation, of his industrious habits, and of his general fitness for employment. I firmly believe that it needs but satisfactory evidence of this fact to bring together the employer and those meriting and seeking employment. I firmly believe that this probationary stage, acting as a filterer between the prisons and the public, may be made the means of distinguishing the reformed convicts from the unreformed, before and after leaving their several places of confinement; and I believe the separation, operating as an important channel for amendment and prevention, will exercise an influence over the criminal population, the value of which cannot be too highly appreciated."

The following memorandum will not be without value:—

" MEMORANDUM.                                " DUBLIN CASTLE, 1st January, 1857.
" REGISTRATION AND SUPERVISION OF CONVICTS ON TICKET OF LICENSE.

"His Excellency the Lord Lieutenant being desirous of accurately testing the practical working of the Ticket of License System, by a well-organized system of registration of licensed convicts, whereby they may be brought under special supervision, and a check be laid upon the evil disposed, has been pleased to sanction the following regulations, which are, therefore, circulated for the information and guidance of the constabulary.

" 1. When an offer of employment for a prisoner is accepted, a notification thereof will be made by the Directors of Government Prisons to the Inspector-General of Constabulary, by whom it will be transmitted to the constabulary of the locality in which the employment is to be given, with all necessary particulars for the purpose of being entered in a register at the Constabulary Station.

" 2. Each convict so to be employed will report himself at the appointed

Constabulary Station (the name of which will be given to him) on his arrival in the district, and, subsequently, on the 1st of each month.

"3. A special report is to be made to Head Quarters by the constabulary whenever they shall observe a convict on license guilty of misconduct or leading an irregular life.

"4. A convict is not to change his locality without notifying the circumstances at the Constabulary Station, in order that his registration may be transferred to the place to which he is about to proceed. On his arrival he must report himself to the nearest Constabulary Station (of the name of which he is to be informed), and such transfer is to be reported to Head Quarters for the information of the Directors of Government Prisons.

"5. An infringement of these rules by the convict will cause it to be assumed that he is leading an idle irregular life, and therefore entail the revocation of his license.

"6. Further regulations may hereafter be added to the foregoing should they become necessary.

"It will be obvious that as the employer is in every case made acquainted with the antecedents of the prisoner he wishes to engage, any inquiries that may afterwards be discreetly made, as to character, conduct, &c., cannot in any way affect the prospects of the convict. The managers of the refuges for female prisoners favourably account for ninety-six out of ninety-seven female convicts up to the 31st of August, 1857 (the license of one has been revoked). It appears that on the whole number of 559 convicts on license up to the 30th September, 1857, seventeen licenses have been revoked. It will be observed also that in addition to the stringent observation exercised over forty-two men who are, many of them, exposed to the temptations of the city of Dublin, there is also the very efficient and general supervision of the constabulary. Yet the results, though slight irregularities are always noted, and the terms of the license most strictly enforced,* prove the revocation of rather more than three per cent."

In the Fifth Report of the Directors,—that for 1858,—they are able to speak from the experience of two years of the system they had adopted of Intermediate Prisons and supervision after discharge. They thus speak, p. 10:—

"The 'ticket of license' is not now considered to be a mere indiscriminate discharge after short periods of imprisonment, with a character earned in an artificial state; but a system which protects the public, in employing a convict who is obliged to

---

* As corroboration of the practice pursued, I may add that two of these revocations of license have been on account of irregularity in reporting themselves; three for keeping bad company; one for losing his employment through drink; one for fighting and brawling in the streets; one for defrauding the railway company by travelling without taking a ticket.

register, and one under which, as carried out in this country, it
is scarcely possible that a holder of a 'ticket of license' can persist in a course of crime, and remain at large.  The public are
acquainted with this, appreciate it, and hence their confidence.
We stated that we had a further view than the mere amelioration
of the system of issuing 'tickets of license;' we considered that
the training of Convicts in intermediate establishments would
equally work for good towards the termination of penal servitude
sentences, under the Act of 1853.  We had good grounds for this
statement, because the principles on which the system was based
tended in the first place to improve the criminal, and then to test
his improvement, and thus generate the confidence of the public.
We have had nearly two years' experience of Convicts so sentenced, and who had not the prospects of early liberty to induce
an artificial or hypocritical course of conduct.  We are glad to
have had experience to test in different phases the real worth of
the system.  It has proved of inestimable value to this class of
prisoners, and no greater or better proof can be given than the
fact that for upwards of two years they have been employed
without guards in detached localities on public works, the few
warders with them directing their operations, and themselves
working and contributing to their support.  We state, without
the slightest reservation, that the conduct of these Convicts has
been most unexceptionable, and quite equal to that of any body
of labourers employed for similar purposes.  Many of these
prisoners have been upwards of a year in the intermediate stage.
It would be very difficult to exceed the amount of voluntary
industry given by the Convicts: much has been expected from
them, and much has been accorded by them.  These establishments are not places either of indolence or of indulgence.  The
dietary has been fixed with the concurrence of the medical officer,
as only sufficient for the proper performance of the work required to be done; that it is not excessive, is evinced by the fact
of many prisoners expending their gratuity to purchase bread to
add to their allowance.  Throughout the whole of their prison

treatment, the circumstance of their being criminals has not for one moment been lost sight of; no better testimony can be produced than the fact that so *few return to the prisons.*  \*  \*  \* We are enabled to state, that we have no cause of complaint whatever, and that the conduct of the prisoners in association has been of the most orderly and quiet description, and of such a nature as both to recommend them for employment, and to do the highest credit to their prison discipline, as well as to their special training.  It is not to be supposed that the Convicts so located have been merely casual offenders, or so selected as to give little room to anticipate anything but amenability to the rules.  The exceptions are the casual offenders; nearly the whole of the Convicts have been of the class called ' habitual offenders;' they have been trained to crime, and have followed it as their vocation.  Many have passed through these establishments whose early prison conduct has been of the most reckless and desperate description, but who have subsequently changed their course, and by the attainment of a certain number of marks, representing the value of their industry and conduct, have become entitled to enter the Intermediate Prisons."

In this Report the Directors also enter fully into the subject of the treatment of female Convicts, " to whose reformation," they say, " we attribute more importance even than to the males."  The consideration of this subject is reserved for a special chapter.

The reports of all the officers show so much comprehension of the principles of the system, intelligence, zeal, and hearty coöperation, that it is difficult to make a selection from them. The following passages indicate not only the great difficulties with which they had at first to contend, but the manner in which these were surmounted.

Mr. McGAURAN, the head Schoolmaster of Mountjoy Prison, thus speaks :—

" Two years ago no prisoner, as a general rule, to which there was scarcely an exception, would venture to report another, no matter how much he detested his actions; it would be as much as his life was worth to do so. Since then the custom has become more and more general, the feeling gradually diffusing itself amongst the juvenile prisoners. The adults are not detained sufficiently long *in this prison* to profit so much by our system of teaching and training.

"I found at that time the workshops no better than demoralizing schools; every sort of moral filth and corruption thriving apace; slips of paper, written upon, which I found here and there, proved conclusively that their authors were steeped in the lowest depths of pollution; it utterly beggars description. The hoarse hollow laugh, so frequently elicited, told me but too true, that the conversation indulged in was quite in keeping with the horrible expressions written upon the slips of paper which I had met with. To my mortification I had to endure this state of things for some time, because I could not discover an effective remedy. Never did I feel myself in so great a dilemma. I was fully alive to the danger of using one unguarded word to the juveniles about the heap of moral nuisance I saw daily accumulating. A general could not use more diligence and assiduity, though he might use a higher order of intellect in organizing his plans, or use more of his caution in the carrying out of his operations, than I did in mine. It would take up too much of my report to go into the particulars of this moral siege. * * * To produce the results it is my pleasure now to report, cost me many a sleepless night, and anxious day of toil, but I have been well repaid in witnessing the good effects of my labours, which, had they not the hearty coöperation I was afforded by the local authorities, would have proved utterly inadequate. * * *

"In a schoolmaster's yearly report it is expected that the prisoners' progress should be shown by means of facts and figures. I have given some of the leading facts, but, before I introduce any figures, I beg to make an observation which may not be quite unnecessary to some readers. Figures cannot be used to measure the progress of prisoners in their inward change of character. In an institution of this nature, where all are corrupt, and where reformation is the chief aim, and where everything is made subservient to this great end, the schoolmaster's attention is taken up with more than the teaching of the mere arts, which, taken together, form but the groundwork of education—I mean reading, writing and arithmetic, &c. These important branches are far from being neglected; they are taught upon the most improved principles, and in the most skilful manner, as is admitted by able visitors to the school; but the great object is to reform; these are merely part of the means employed; these are the only ones in my department that can be measured by figures. Conversational lectures of an argumentative nature are frequently employed, at which discussion is freely allowed, when the prisoner is upon an equal footing with the teacher, as far as open discussion goes, and only under restraint when a forgetfulness of the bounds of proper order and decorum is exhibited by him. All our lectures are not argumentative, but any lecture or lesson may become so, when an objection is raised, or when a fact is questioned by a prisoner; a privilege which is never suspended beyond the time which good taste and good sense requires—that is, until the teacher is in readiness to answer it.   I need scarcely remark that such lectures or lessons, whichever people fancy to term them, afford considerable scope for the teacher's skill and tact, besides furnishing admirable exercises for the mental culture of the prisoners.

" An energy of manner in teaching is just as essential as a vigour of expression, to produce a deep lasting impression upon the minds of prisoners; the vigour of expression brings a truth home with convincing force, while the energy of manner, being reflected back, through sympathy, by the hearers, absorbs their attention, sharpens their perceptive powers, and invigorates their judgment.   People of intelligence and education are able, without much effort, to bear up against the drowsy influence of an unenergetic but instructive discourse, because the desire to get knowledge, with which they are possessed, creates an effect opposed in its tendency to that exercised, through sympathy, by the unenergy of manner in the speaker.   Besides, such minds, from being often actively employed, have acquired a degree of buoyancy which renders them less likely to sink under the pressure of external influences, and, from being used to exercise, are less likely to be jaded by a tiresome disquisition.   An audience of respectable people anxious to be instructed, and an audience of prisoners panting for liberty, and not caring for any thing else, is not a distinction without a difference; means found sufficiently effective in one case, will prove utterly impotent in the other. Hence, I lay great stress upon an energetic manner of delivery, as well as the employment of vigorous, sledging expressions in an instructor of prisoners.

" This sort of instruction may be termed our under-ground operations.   Our sapping and mining work cannot be seen on examination by a school inspector. Reformation is the ultimate object of all teaching, training and discipline. Education would have no place in a prison, were it not that it is considered a means of attaining that great end ; and that particular part of education which is calculated to further this object I aim at, and labour to diffuse. Hence, instead of being the mere schoolmaster, I endeavour to be a reformatory agent.   If my object were to show great progress in reading, writing and arithmetic, &c., I could easily do it, by aiming at nothing else, but then I should neglect the principal part of the siege—the sapping and mining operations."

The head Schoolmaster at Spike Island, and Forts Carlisle and Camden, Mr. HAROLD, appears to have had at first still greater difficulties in these associated prisons.   He thus commences his Report :—

" FORT CARLISLE, *January 1st*, 1859.

" GENTLEMEN,—I will preface this Report by a short narrative, for the purpose of exhibiting the striking contrast between Spike Island Prison now, and on the 31st of December, 1855.

" On the 10th of August, 1855, I first came to Spike Island Prison, and having presented to the Governor my letter of appointment, I was conducted by a warder to the school, and placed in charge of it. About a dozen juveniles were in attendance, under the tuition and keeping of two schoolmasters and a warder. The schoolmasters and warder were pacing the floor, the boys were seated at desks, with a spelling book in the hand of each, evidently indifferent about learning, and prepared to give the most unqualified impudence to any one who would dare to urge them to their lessons. I was bewildered by this little scene, for, though comprised in a very limited space, it called into my mind reflections that were not the happiest. After the lapse of a few hours the Local Inspector and Governor informed me that the school was to be remodelled, and that all ages and classes should attend and receive instructions in the school for four hours weekly at least; they also explained to me that arrangements were in progress for dividing all the prisoners into eleven school parties, two of which were intended to be sent alternately to school (one in the forenoon and the other in the afternoon) on each of five working days, and the remaining, or eleventh party, was to attend on the forenoon of Saturday. Each section numbered over one hundred. Captain R. KNIGHT, then a distinguished member of your Board, visited the prison, and pending the general school arrangements, he ordered me to Mountjoy Prison, in order that, previous to entering on active duty, I might obtain some information on convict management, and the mode adopted *there* of imparting instruction to adults. After having spent a week in Mountjoy, and paid special attention to the system established, I returned in very depressed spirits; having there witnessed the vitiated dispositions of the juveniles—exhibited on one or two occasions—which confirmed the opinion I had previously formed, that my life would be miserable in endeavouring to educate men of such a caste. On the 3rd of September subsequently, preparations being made, over one hundred of all ages and classes were ordered to the school, the efficient chief warden, Mr. SPORLE, and I addressed the prisoners assembled in the 'square' on the advantages they would derive from attending to instructions, but to 'all this' they were morbidly insensible. An incident in the first day's proceedings is not unworthy of notice. An assistant schoolmaster distributed books to the several classes, and, by my order, kept an account of the number delivered, but when the tolling of the bell announced a call for dinner, a first book of lessons was missing. I reported the circumstance to the chief warder; every prisoner was stripped to his shirt and searched, and yet the book was not found; this scene of stripping and searching a large number of men, and the apprehension that such would be of frequent occurrence, so disheartened and disgusted me, that I feared my gloomy forebodings would be more than realised. After this occurrence, I had an interview with the chief warder, and we resolved never again to have recourse to a similar search, unless we were satisfied beyond doubt that no mistake could be made in the reckoning of the books. This instance of strict discipline was not without its telling effects, as it showed that nothing could be abstracted from the school without subjecting the whole party present to a trying ordeal, which contributed to preserve the school property in the after times.   During my first five months in the convict service, I was so overworked in arranging, classifying, teaching, prying into character, keeping books of accounts, and withal so anxious for the success of my undertaking, that little more would have carried me off the stage of existence.   In the Spike, Carlisle and Camden Prisons, there were then 1,435 of all ages, and with this great number the work of education and reformation was a serious undertaking.   In my former reports I detailed the system established, the rules laid down, the exertions made, the difficulties encountered for the promotion of the slow but steady progress of these mis-guided people.   I also drew some real pictures of them in the different stages of their servitude, and showed clearly the salutary effects of Carlisle and Camden as Intermediate Prisons.

"On the 31st of December, 1855, there were 1,435 convicts in Spike and the two Forts, whose conduct, appearance and bearing, were more forbidding than I have described; but the number in these prisons on the 31st of December, 1858, is only 565, and their conduct, with few exceptions, improved beyond the most sanguine expectations; so that notwithstanding my original misgivings, I am now proud of being the very humblest of the instruments employed in this great moral reformation.   Let it be granted, by way of argument, that the discharged convicts have not been reformed, as a con-sequence they must have come back to Spike, then our prisons would still be as full as they were in 1855; but they are less by 870, therefore they have not come back, and we may justly and safely infer that they have been amal-gamated with, and have become good members of society.   Should this reformation continue successful, both in prison and out of it, Ireland will soon be as free from crime as history represents her to be in the days of BRYAN BOROIMHE—

> A single gaol,
> In Bryan's reign,
> Did all the criminals contain.

"The moral reformation that has been effected in these prisons during the last three years is decidedly attributable to your system of management, and particularly to your strictness in the following cases:—

"The attention you have paid to the selection, training, and improvement of your officers, who are, with few exceptions, a superior class of men, most of them well-educated, all of them fairly so; most of them believing in the 'moral force' principle—for, if not, and therefore acting contrary to their convictions, their zeal would be only apparent, and consequently unsuccessful most of them sensible of the importance of their charge, conversant with the exact nature of their duties, impressed with the necessity of showing good example, patient and persevering in their efforts to lead those intrusted to their care to the path which turns away from evil and leads to good. When wilful and perverse violations of the laws and rules of the prison deserve and require punishment, it is inflicted calmly, dispassionately and judiciously, by your order, or by the order of the Local Inspector or Governor, and not by the warders at their own discretion, as was the case formerly, in too many instances. There is something peculiar in the Irish character, capable of being changed from evil to good by kindness, which could never be accomplished by harshness. There is something also in the very mode of uttering or conveying a rebuke or command that touches the heart and begets feelings for or against authority. During my long experience in public institutions, I have observed that kindness and clemency invariably succeed in bettering the conduct and condition of the inmates of those institutions. Severity may, through fear, curb for a time the fierce passions of the irritated, and thereby spare the authorities trouble ; but those suppressed passions ultimately explode like an ignited powder-mine, the eruption being the greater in the ratio of the pressure. *The total absence of religious bias in the administration of the prison laws and rules, both as regards officers and prisoners, and their promotions, has not failed to secure that respect and obedience which seldom attends partiality, especially in Ireland, where the people are very sensitive in religious matters.* An instance of this came under my notice in the beginning of the year 1856, on interrogating a number of convicts who had returned from Bermuda. Though they attended school there, they made no improvement; this they regretted, and appeared sensible of their folly, but urged as a cause that the schoolmaster was a proselyte, and that they feared to learn anything from him ; which is a proof that unless the prisoner entertains some respect for the officer placed over him, his teachings will be ineffectual. I do not hear any objections raised by any of the parties that have since arrived; and those who have lately returned are much improved since the new arrangements there became properly developed. The punishment of dismissal invariably inflicted on any of your officers who were so unfortunate as to indulge in spirituous liquors is an admirable corrective; for if the rule in this case were less exemplary, and if in the wards or schools, or on the works, any officer, be he schoolmaster, warder, or other functionary, should so far forget his duty as to have even the scent of liquor upon his person, he thereby contributes to undermine the foundation laid for progressive improvement, and renders null and void all exhortations and lectures against intoxication, that fruitful source of crime.

" The utility of requiring the men in the Intermediate Prisons to keep and make up weekly accounts of the respective amounts of their gratuities, cannot be overrated, and the good effect it produces on their minds, shows at once the wisdom of the conceptions of him who originated the idea; without due consideration, this may appear insignificant, but by a little reflection and observation, one is convinced of its importance and influence in exciting in the prisoners a desire for the possession of more money. That it stimulates to provident and economical habits I feel assured, from the many instances that have come under my own observation of men who had previously laid out their three pence weekly on tobacco, now leaving it in reserve to increase the small sums that will be coming to them on discharge, when they may be able to convert it to some good use for their future support. They are making calculations daily; the young to know if they would have as much as would take them to America or the Colonies; the more aged speculating on some industrial pursuit in which to invest their slender reserves when they get home. Here let me observe that some of those formerly set no value on their gratuities; but now, if through mistake any of the warders are short one penny in his calculations, the prisoner at once reminds him of it and has it rectified. Thus, by telling them frequently the amounts of their gratuities, they are reminded that they have so much money, and it naturally begets a desire to have more, which is evident from their eagerness to add to whatever they have to their credit already.

" In Fort Camden I have frequently stood with each of the warders for the space of an hour watching the men at their work, and I never heard him speak to any of them to urge them to work better; nor was there the slightest necessity, for they worked with a uniform steadiness and diligence worthy of approbation, more like men of the world working for their employers than prisoners influenced by the fear of punishment. The furtive glance which the prisoner in the earlier stages of his confinement casts at his officer, to know if he is watching him, is abandoned here, and he is led to believe that a certain amount of confidence is reposed in him, which stimulates him to industry. This training gradually leads to trustworthiness and integrity, which will be of the utmost importance to the prisoners when they are cast upon the world again.

" An intimate acquaintance with the habits, feelings, failings, and even the virtues of a large number of congregated convicts, enabled me to make some suggestions in my former reports on subjects to which I need not now advert, as they have been all ably discussed by your chairman in his ' Memoranda,' and other papers; neither will I enumerate the lectures and instructions each and every day delivered and imparted by myself and my assistants through the year, as such a course would be ostentatious; they are all recorded in the ' Daily Report Book,' which, with the Register and other books, may be consulted by those who are interested in the reformatory movement; they form part of the annals of the prison, will remain in its archives, and a succeeding generation may not think them unworthy of a glance. It is now an aphorism that systems of improvement look well on paper, whilst practical results are not commensurate with the display. *But the progress of reformation in the Convict Prisons has exceeded all and every one of the written and published anticipations.*

" More than three-fourths of the Camden prisoners have been transferred to Smithfield and Lusk during the year; with every party a school classification sheet was forwarded, together with their copy-books. Amongst them there were many educated men, but the following—W. H., J. M'G., and J. B.— I mention with pride and pleasure, on account of their extensive acquirements, good sense, and unexceptionable conduct. The following extract from a letter to me of the last-mentioned will show his high sense of propriety and the purity of his intentions:—

"'DUBLIN CITY, *December* 26, 1858.

"'DEAR SIR,—I was discharged on yesterday morning with five pounds, and am now waiting for to-morrow, when, with God's blessing, I shall start for Liverpool; when I get there I shall wait for the first opportunity of sailing for New Orleans, of which I have heard a very good account, and where, I have no doubt, with the assistance of God, and the help of these testimonials, I shall get good employment. I am extremely thankful, sir, for your very generous solicitude for my welfare, as also to those reverend gentlemen who have been so kind as to give me a starting point again to work by ; and I now solemnly promise, in the face of Heaven, that sooner than betray the great confidence which you placed in me, I shall die from whatever cause it may please God to send me.

"' M. HAROLD, &c.'                                                    "J. B.

"I have closely observed the attention paid to their religious duties by the men in Carlisle and Camden, and I have only to say that the fervency of many of them often caused me to blush for my own remissness. I will close this part of the subject by repeating an extract from my last report. If a Christian element is not infused into, and mixed up with education, feeble indeed will be the good influences of other teachings; this is the province of the several chaplains who have all laboured incessantly to promote it; consequently those who are truly influenced by religious motives are not few, and their examples and advices to their fellow-prisoners are most salutary. As the Christian Sabbath is specially dedicated to God, any lectures or instructions I could impart to *all*, would not be well adapted to the sacred solemnity of the day; I therefore assembled the Roman Catholics, who are 90 per cent. of the whole, and read for them some chapters in pious books with which we are supplied, and which explain in the simplest and most effective manner their duties to God, to themselves, and to their neighbours, with the awful consequences of neglecting them."

After speaking of the zeal and diligence of the officers, warders, and Schoolmasters, Mr. HAROLD thus concludes :—

"To you, gentlemen, I feel grateful for your kind indulgence and other favours; I also thank the Local Inspector, Governor, Chief Warder, and Chaplains of every persuasion, for their kind attention.

"I am, gentlemen, your most obedient humble servant,

"MICHAEL HAROLD, Head Schoolmaster.

"To the Chairman and Directors of
Government Prisons, Dublin Castle."

Mr. RYAN, one of the Assistant Schoolmasters, makes in his Report the following judicious remarks :—

"Having before made a passing allusion to the conduct of the men, I shall not dwell longer on the subject here, except to state briefly my views of the influences which are here brought to bear with a view to reforming them. In the first place, then, the number of prisoners being so small, each working party is small in proportion; the officer over same has thus an opportunity of making himself thoroughly acquainted with their dispositions and habits. Their failings are as well, if not better known to him than to themselves; he observes every deviation from the path of duty, reasons the delinquent into a formal compliance, and thus the prisoner is compelled to suppress, for a time at least, those irregularities which are too often the results of an ill-regulated and unsettled mind.  This surveillance continues; the prisoner is watchful to guard against those failings to which he is most prone, and the habitual absti- nence from such faults produces a certain power of self-controul, which acquires strength with time, causes a desire for an indulgence in such out- bursts of passion to die away, becomes instrumental in the formation of habits of industry and perseverance, and secretly impels him to a continuance in the practice of an upright line of conduct when the restraint has been removed. The warders, too, are not quite so formal as they need to be in Spike Island, nor yet so familiar as to weaken in any way that obedience which it is their duty to secure.  Their conversation and example have a humanizing influence over the prisoners, and effect, to a certain extent, a refinement of minds and morals which in a prison conducted under more strict regulations would be utterly impracticable; thus we see that every officer, and every employment, become instrumental in promoting the good work.

"In the school we find another and very potent auxiliary: here all restraint is set aside, obedience and order are secured more by appeals to their good sense than by rigid discipline.  All are under the teacher's eye; he knows each and every one, calls them by their names, and for the time carefully avoids numbers, badges, and everything calculated to awaken in their minds a sense of their unhappy situations, unless in cases where it is necessary to refer to such as a reminder of the misfortunes they have brought upon themselves by their thoughtless indiscretions.  Teacher and pupils recognise each other, have a mutual dependence on one another, and by a little forbearance and encourage- ment on the part of the former, a reciprocity of action is established, which in many instances is attended with the most happy results.  The lessons which they read have all a moral tendency, and serve the double purpose of per- fecting them in their reading, and of fostering within their breasts a love of the great Author of our existence, by giving them more extended notions of his power, wisdom, and goodness, of his concern for his creatures, and of the ingratitude of sinful man in defying his holy law.  They also point out their duties towards themselvs and their fellow-beings, inculcate a love of industry and labour, the necessity for patience and fortitude under trials and sufferings, a deference and submission to the laws of the country; in fact, they lay before them, as in a map, all their duties, social and moral, and with the expositions, repetitions, and interrogations of the teacher, they can hardly fail to make some impression even on the most obdurate heart; and if to these agencies you add the sacred ministrations of the Chaplains, the efficacy of which in an undertaking of this kind is so obvious as to need no comment from me, you cannot avoid the conclusion, that a prisoner subjected to such discipline for a period of five or six months, must be very callous and bereft of every feeling of Christianity, who is not somewhat reformed on discharge from Carlisle."

Full extracts have already been given from Mr. ORGAN's evidence to the Commission, still it may be useful to gather from his Report to the Directors some of his early experience. The importance of supervision to the men themselves, he illustrates by the case of one of the license-holders who was accused of murder, and thrown into Naas Gaol. Mr. ORGAN knew where the man was lodging, and believed that he was steadily at work. He at once made the necessary inquiries, wrote particulars proving an *alibi*, and arrived at the gaol almost simultaneously with his letter, in order to recognise the prisoner, and ascertain if he held a ticket of license. The suspected man was discharged soon after his visit, there being the clearest and most perfect *alibi*. This could probably not have been obtained by the man, at any rate without much difficulty and lengthened detention, had not the supervision, regularly exercised, enabled Mr. ORGAN thus to prove it. The Lecturer continues in his Report, p. 119,—

" This circumstance suggested to me the propriety of calling a meeting of all discharged prisoners in my district, with a view to point out to them the necessity and importance of making known to me at all times their intentions to change their residence, whether within or without my district, and to caution them against the selection of low lodging-houses.

" Accordingly the meeting was convened; and if there existed no other proof of the results of the training of these men previous to their discharge, that which manifested itself in each and every one of the men assembled was, in in my mind, sufficient to remove the doubts and prejudices of those having no confidence or belief in the reformation of the adult criminal.

" The men cheerfully attended, and wore the appearance of hard work and contentment. No gaudy dress or outward show, bordering upon the ridiculous, was visible amongst them. Their wages rated from 5s. with, to 24s. per per week without food. The meeting included scavengers, paviers'-attendants, bacon-curers, factory, agricultural and building labourers, shoemakers, tailors, masons, carpenters, and stone-cutters. Their ages varied from seventeen to forty-five years. Amongst them were many who heretofore were trainers of burglars and pickpockets. The former highwayman, once the terror of the locality in which he resided, was to be seen there now content and happy on weekly wages merely sufficient to keep the wolf from the door,—a sum he thought it beneath him to steal, much less to work for, in days gone by.

" I had, previous to the meeting, prepared a paper entitled ' Crime, its causes and results,' which I then and there read ; and, having exhorted them to persevere in honest industry, pointed out to them the manliness and comforts of their present position, and dwelt upon and contrasted the miseries of their past lives with the comparative happy independence of their present station. The meeting was adjourned until such time as I may deem prudent or advisable to convene a similar one."

Mr. ORGAN next speaks of his efforts to procure employment for the men,—

" Let it never be supposed that finding employment for discharged prisoners can ever be accomplished without great exertion, quick observation, and a regular organized plan of action, together with a fair knowledge of the sources of employment in the surrounding districts.

" Some years must elapse before employers can generally be induced to apply at a reformatory prison (although many have done so) for men to till their farms, build their houses, or work their mills. But they can and have been induced to give employment to prisoners upon the recommendation of responsible and respectable persons. What then to be desired is a helping hand from this class; but, as I have just observed, *in no country is it more difficult to enlist the sympathy for a convict, or to obtain the means to assist him when discharged, than in Ireland.* This may appear startling, but it is true ; and it will be admitted by the reader that there are few more practically qualified to offer an opinion upon the matter than the writer of this report, whose experience in the reformatory world is entirely practical.

" Let those who suppose that the providing of employment for discharged prisoners is an easier task in Ireland than elsewhere, know, perhaps for the first time, that I have frequently ridden, and on a Sunday too, twenty miles and upwards to provide employment for a single man previous to his discharge ;. and, perhaps, in endeavouring to obtain the employment, I had to meet disappointment, contumely, or downright insult. And again I have known men frequently to walk from fourteen to twenty-six miles in search of honest employment,—men who heretofore were the curse of the community in which they resided. I do not mention this with a view to enlist praise for my exertions in training or providing employment for the Smithfield men. I have never yet made known the difficulties with which I had to contend, and which I had to overcome; nor do I intend to do so; but I mention these facts for the sole purpose of removing the erroneous impressions which have been published in an official report in England, and which I regret you have prohibited me from noticing in detail. * * *

" During the past year the circle of employers increased considerably. In order to procure the assistance of these good-hearted men, much was to be done to remove their prejudices and allay their fears. I have frequently sat hours with some of them whose assistance I valued most, explaining the principles of our convict management and the training of our prisoners.

" I may here mention a case where force of truthful argument, and represen-
tation of authenticated facts secured for me the assistance of one of the best
employers it has ever been my good fortune to number amongst the friends of
our cause.

" Returning one morning last October from Naas gaol, where my official
duties led me, I happened to meet a gentleman of business-like appearance,
whom I had never before encountered. I thought I could do no harm by
introducing myself to him. He turned out to be what his benevolent countenance indicated—a good and generous-hearted man—and what was more, a
very liberal employer. I opened the discourse as prudently and as cautiously
as I could, and endeavoured to elicit from him his opinions upon the state of
the country with regard to crime. As usual, the ticket-of-leave question
turned up, and he told me what a horrible class of beings ticket-of-leave men
were, and of the appalling crimes committed by them, and that one of them
was at that time imprisoned in Naas gaol charged with the crime of murder.
This was coming to the point which I desired most, and to which I eagerly
looked forward. It was my turn to reply; so I did. What I said is unnecessary to repeat here; but whether I succeeded in bringing the gentleman over
to my views may be judged from the fact, that five of my men were in his
employment in about a fortnight afterwards. A copy of his letter to me
relating to these men I have already inserted.

" It is in this way, and by availing myself of every opportunity which offers
that the demand by times for our prisoners exceeds the supply.

" I could record several similar cases did space admit, or circumstances
require it.

" Employers, such as the gentleman just mentioned, when made aware of
the conditional liberty of our license men, and what is expected from them,
together with the supervision which I exercise over them, feel comparatively
secure from acts of dishonesty or bad conduct on the part of our men, though
their fears and misgivings have hitherto led them to suspect, and frequently
to prematurely and unjustly condemn."

The Sixth Report of the Directors, for the year 1859, contains
the following very important statement :—

" We do not, in this Report, consider it to be necessary to
recapitulate the merits and the details of the 'Intermediate
System.' We have stated them very fully in our Reports for
1856, 1857, and 1858. To the latter Report we particularly
invite attention, as a comparison is there drawn between the
anticipations expected in our earlier reports, and the results
which had been attained at the end of 1858. We now, after
another year's experience of these results, extending over

2,300 prisoners, are able completely to confirm the strong opinions we have always expressed of their value. We would not for one moment withhold the credit due to those in our department who have laboured unremittingly in promoting the reformation of the criminal and his well-doing on liberation; but we feel bound to repeat our opinion that the system pursued would be incomplete in its action if unaccompanied by the powerful adjuncts of 'conditional liberation' and registration until the expiration of sentences. We have found them to operate as wholesome checks on the criminal, to protect the public, and to be the means—the only means of which we are aware—of effectually scattering 'the criminal class.'

"By their use crime may, for the first time, be rendered a hazardous and an unprofitable calling.

"All authorities agree in the importance of making punishment more certain. Without registration this is scarcely possible; and it is of daily occurrence that 'hardened offenders,' not identified by the police-officers, escape with very trifling punishment. This immunity from the consequences of crime enters very fully into the calculation of the criminal classes, and tends more than any other cause to recruit their ranks. So long as this immunity is suffered to exist so long shall we fail to reap full benefit from our very heavy expenditure, incurred for the purpose of arresting the progress of crime.

"On the one hand, the State pays £55,000 per annum for the maintenance of juveniles in Reformatory Schools, and it is an expenditure which is well and zealously administered by the managers of these establishments; but, on the other hand, it suffers the adult and hardened offender to train the young to his own calling, the immunity with which he is enabled to do so forming no slight element in the recommendation to his pupil of the advantages of a criminal course.

"Without some measures of a more aggressive nature are taken against persons known to belong to the 'criminal class,' in vain may we hope to reduce the vast Convict expenditure with which the United Kingdom is now burdened, amounting to £370,154 per annum for Home Service, and £209,399 per annum for Colonial Service (Civil Service Estimates for 1859), in addition to a sum of £530,285 for county and borough prisons (Judicial Statistics, 1858, page 34); in vain may we hope for results proportionate to our police expenditure, amounting in England alone to £1,447,000.* In the second volume of Judicial Statistics, published in June, 1859, it is estimated that crime costs England ten millions annually, and it is stated that there are many heavy items omitted such as Judge's salaries, cost of Convicts in the Colonies, &c., which show this sum to be an under-estimate. It is, at all events, sufficiently alarming to call for the adoption of the most stringent measures to repress crime, and to prevent the very dangerous aggression upon our social state, which will otherwise be infallibly caused by the liberation in the United Kingdom of thousands of criminals formerly sent out of the country. We have now had some years' experience of the registration of criminals in Ireland, and of their habits and conduct both within and without the walls of the prisons. We feel that we should not be performing our duty if we failed to record as our opinion, that by having recourse to conditional liberation and registration, and by thus giving effect to the twelfth, fifteenth, and sixteenth Resolutions of the Committee of the House of Commons, which sat in 1856, on those points, crime and its cost might be very materially reduced throughout the United Kingdom.

"We have stated that Intermediate Prisons would, without the assistance of conditional liberation and registration, be of themselves incomplete; so, on the other hand, without the preliminary treatment of Intermediate Prisons, conditional liberation would be incomplete and unsatisfactory in its results. The system must be taken as a whole to be of full value. It should be felt that each criminal, previous to

* Judicial Statistics for 1858, page 34.

his liberation, has been invited to cöoperate in his own improvement, and that he has been made aware of the stringent course which will be pursued towards him after his liberation.

"If he then fails and again follows crime as a vocation, no possible sympathy can be felt for him. It would be unjust to the public that such a criminal should receive any sentence but that of a very long term of servitude.

"The results of closing the opportunities of committing crime, by the early re-incarceration of the offender who still intends following it as a vocation, will very frequently be to cause the pursuance on his part of a very outrageous line of conduct when again placed in prison. Disappointment at his career of crime being suddenly checked, and anger at having been detected, have combined to conduce to such a result. We have several instances of the kind, and are glad to find that instead of preying upon society the offenders are within the walls of the prisons.

"The greater part of our prison offences are committed by this class of prisoners, and it is well that it should be so.

"This appears to be the proper time to disabuse the minds of many persons with regard to the type of criminality in this country for several years past. Out of Ireland all that is heard or heeded of her crime is connected with agrarian outrages, and it is therefore assumed that the crime of the country for the greater part takes that form.

"Nothing can be further from the truth than this assumption. For many years past, the criminals whom we have discharged, and of whom we write, have been for the greater portion members of the criminal class, burglars, felons, pickpockets, &c., known to the police as following crime as a vocation. It is necessary that this statement should be distinctly made, and as clearly understood, or a full appreciation cannot otherwise be felt of the success of the Convict System pursued in this country."

The following testimony to the improved health of the Con-

victs at Philipstown, where Convicts are sent whose state of
health renders it undesirable to expose them to the bracing
climate of Spike Island, is given by Dr. CARR, the medical
officer of that prison :—

"The mortality per-centage of $1\frac{70}{1000}$ in the year's amount of prisoners—the
numbers and ordinary nature of the cases (as compared with former years),
treated in the hospital, which contained *only* 13 *patients on* 31*st December*—
the diminished applications of trivial descriptions at the dispensary—the
evident decrease of invalid admissions into this prison, my disbelief of such
class being retained in other prisons—all point out that the leavens of
phthisis, scrofula, and other deadly afflictions, that carried such former
disastrous sway, have almost entirely disappeared—that the convict community at large has attained a healthy position, *superior to that of the general
population of Ireland* (provable by the difference of mortality in those two
classes)—while the *remarkable diminution of crime*, together with the improved condition and circumstances of the people who heretofore supplied
the pabula of Convict Prison mortality, portend *the great improbability* of
future recurrent consequences of revolting disease so painfully developed
on former occasions."

The Seventh Report, for 1860, contains no new features, but
satisfactory statements respecting results. While the numbers
for whom there was accommodation in the Government Prisons
amounted to 3000, the Convicts actually in them on the 1st of
January, 1861, were only 1076 males, and 416 females,—total,
1492, or not half the number for whom accommodation was provided. Would that such a statement could be made respecting
the English Convict Prisons! Why should we be content to
continue a system, productive of so much evil to the Convicts
themselves, and to the country, when a way so much better is
opened to us? Why should the country be content to see in
England one Government Prison added to another, and even the
County Gaols called into requisition to contain the thousands
annually added to our Convict population?

After giving the number of annual discharges up to that time,
which is contained in the table copied in the last chapter, p. 116,
the Directors refer to the fact, that all the Convicts have been
disposed of in Ireland, or by free emigration. Not to speak of
the moral triumph thus achieved, the pecuniary saving to the

country was enormous, considering the expense of transporting every Convict. The Directors say,—

"We also append a return of the number of Convicts sent from Ireland to penal colonies from 1849 to 1853, and state at the same time the fact that since the latter year no deportation has taken place. We believe, that by giving this return, and making this statement, an opinion will be better formed of the success of the Irish Convict System.

TRANSPORTED FROM IRELAND.

| In 1849 | ... ... ... ... ... ... ... ... | 1543 |
|---|---|---|
| " 1850 | ... ... ... ... ... ... ... ... | 775 |
| " 1851 | ... ... ... ... ... ... ... ... | 1082 |
| " 1852 | ... ... ... ... ... ... ... ... | 1296 |
| " 1853 | ... ... ... ... ... ... ... ... | 604 |

"In giving these figures, and in stating that the Irish Convict System has been enabled to dispose of its own Convicts without deportation, we are far from wishing to convey that we are opposed to a well-regulated system for the removal of Convicts to Western Australia. On the contrary, we believe that such a course would tend to amend the criminal, and be advantageous both to the mother country and the colony. * * *

"We have reason to be satisfied with the state of the prisons, and consider that the Reports made by the Governors of the desire on the part of the Convicts to attain high classification, and the confirmation afforded of this opinion by our own constant communication with them, evinces that it answers the purpose for which it was intended, and is the means of promoting industry, self-reliance and self-restraint, on the part of the Convicts. The marks which govern the classification, and are the rewards of certain desirable qualifications in the Convicts, are obviously the best means of realizing to the mind of the individual his actual progress, and the cause of that progress. We have many years' experience of the system, and are, therefore, qualified to give an opinion. We observe, by the latest reports from the penal establishments of Western Australia, that marks have been recently introduced into the Convict System carried on in that Colony, and with the best results."

The following passages in their Report are also important :—

" We have reported a diminution in the number of criminals in the Convict establishments for some years past. We do not think it probable that a further decrease can take place for some time to come, until the results of the Reformatory Schools, and other means of arresting crime in the germ, can be felt in the community. The appliances in force in this country for bringing old offenders to justice, the rigid enforcement of good conduct on the part of those liberated on license, the very great difficulty with which an old inmate of the Convict Prisons would be surrounded in carrying on crime without detection ; the systematized manner of proving former convictions, in order to again bring an old offender under a sentence of penal servitude, are all reasons which very obviously conduce to fill the Convict Prisons.

" We stated in our last Report that—

" ' Under any successful prison system the inevitable result of a diminution in the total number of prisoners will be, that as that total number decreases, the proportion of incorrigibles included in it must become greater. It may be compared to a sifting process, by which the refuse would only be left at last.'

" In dealing with this class, therefore, which will be mainly composed of old offenders, we feel it to be absolutely necessary to record that ' time' can alone enable us to present reliable hopes of their amendment, and to earnestly plead that for this purpose, as well as for the protection of the public, longer sentences may be given to them than has heretofore been the practice. * * *

" Although 5,560 Convicts were discharged from the Government Prisons between January, 1854, and January, 1861, there remained only 1,492 in them on the 1st January, 1861 ; 1,462 out of the 5,560 were discharged on license, and only 89 have been revoked, which does not amount to 7 per cent. Included in this number are the cases of 30 Convicts whose licenses were revoked for irregularities not criminal. We give additional value to these statistics by stating, that we do not believe a case can be proved of a Convict having been reported for infringing the conditions of his license, and still remaining at large in this country. * * *

" Concurrently with the appliances for the detection of old offenders, we are enabled to point to the very small number of Convicts in our establishments; and when we further state that we are enabled to employ our Convicts before liberation, for the public service, in a state almost analogous to that of freedom, and thus to illustrate the system which has led to this final stage of training, we submit that we shall have done more to evince success, than conveying it by a very lengthened report. What the Intermediate Prisons have been to the male Convicts, the Refuges have proved to be to the females; and we cannot be too thankful that, some years since, ladies were found willing to undertake this very grave and responsible charge. Success has attended their labours in even a greater degree than could have been expected."

The Reports of the Officers are as satisfactory as in former years. They all indicate earnestness, interest in their work, and satisfaction with the system. A great cordiality appears to prevail among all the officers, as indicated by the frequent thanks expressed by the Chaplains and Schoolmasters to the other officers for their kindness and cöoperation. Catholics and Protestants are here on a perfect equality, and all share the feelings expressed by the Protestant Chaplain, Mr. SHORE, at the conclusion of his Report :—

" I desire to express my grateful acknowledgments of the unremitting kindness, attention, and assistance I have received from the Governor, the Deputy-Governor, the Chief Warder, and, without exception, from every officer of the establishment; and if Providence has vouchsafed a blessing on my labours here, I am sensible how much I am indebted for it to their cöoperation.

" To yourselves, gentlemen, I have so frequently had occasion to express my grateful sense of the courtesy and kind assistance I have experienced from you ever since the Government Prisons have been placed under your direction, that I need now only say, that during the past year, I have found that courtesy and kindness just the same as ever."

The following vivid picture derived from the Report for the next year, 1861, of Mr. HAROLD, the head Schoolmaster of Spike Island, shows the degree in which the officers enter into the system pursued :—

"Let me suppose that any gentleman of intelligence and discrimination had visited Spike Island previous to the introduction of the present system. What would he behold? By day, a number of men dressed in the uniform garb of degradation, sullenly and reluctantly tugging at the ropes by which they were harnessed to a truck, laden with stones or other materials; others sinking the shaft of a mine, or levelling the hills and filling the hollows; all obeying through fear, unmindful of any other but the basest of motives. Should this visitor be permitted to take a night view of the prison,—peeping through the circular apertures in the doors, what would he behold? A solitary lurid lamp in each apartment, a number of men stretched upon their straitened beds, like a dead mass, devoid of animation, the monotony only relieved by an occasional murmur or morose complaint, and a corresponding reply of 'silence' from the vigilant turnkey. I now leave this gentleman to draw his own conclusions, and to record them in his memory.

"The month of December, '61, arrives; the same gentleman incidentally arrives at Queenstown, recollects his former visit to the island, has heard of the great reform in convict management, and crosses the lee channel in order to ascertain whether report speaks truly or not. He sees a strong party of men at the pier, embarking for Haulbowline, dressed in a garb uniform in appearance, but bright and cheerful-looking also. They are superintended by warders, only needing the weapon of 'moral force' to secure obedience. Proceeding through the island, he meets several parties employed as formerly in the various Government works, but indicating by two distinct garbs, and by blue and red facings on one of these garbs, that the different degrees of merit are recorded, and exhibited, and rewarded. Visiting the several workshops, he will find some articles well executed by convict artizans. Entering the day-school he will behold three teachers, with all the essential appliances, earnestly and actively communicating instructions to a large number of attentive prisoners. Night approaches—the bell tolls—the sections are gathered— and those with the gray, the blue, and the red collars, are conducted individually to separate apartments, clean, well ventilated, and supplied with a few rude necessary articles of furniture. Conspicuous in every little dormitory may be seen a small library, consisting of about a score of the most approved and useful books, published by the Commissioners of Education, with religious and other approved works. After a spare but wholesome supper, each prisoner —being supplied with a light—sits down to his library, in which he finds something to interest and instruct him until eight o'clock, when, after prayer, he retires to rest. Let our visitor be now conducted by the Sergeant of the Guard to the D and B associated prisons, he will see them well but cheaply lighted, with 100 men in one and 80 in the other, either sitting in an attentive

attitude, hearing short moral lectures from their respective teachers, or carefully applying themselves to reading, writing and arithmetic, and other useful
educational studies.  The two hours evening school time terminates, all
retire to their dormitories, where those who desire to read may assemble
around the tables and prosecute their studies under the presidency of an educated and judicious warder; those who wish to go to rest may do so, study or
reading not being compulsory further than the school-hours.  Our visitor may
now be reminded to 'look on this picture and on that;' but, as before, we
leave him to form his own opinions; yet, in reply to his inquiries, we must
inform him of the nature of the *changes*, and of the objects contemplated and
effected by them."

After explaining the system, he adds :—

" I now leave it to this visitor to say whether this course of discipline and
moral training will be likely to render them better members of society hereafter than they were previous to conviction."

It is clear that the Schoolmaster's hopes were realised, from
the following letters written by employers who had given work
to the Convicts.  They are all addressed to Mr. ORGAN :—

" *March 3rd*, 1861.

" DEAR SIR,—You have asked me to state my opinion of the men you sent
me from Smithfield in the course of the last five years; I have no objection to
do so.

" I have found them to be industrious men, and anxious to give satisfaction.
I have four of them at present in my employment, and one of them has been
acting as foreman for the last two years.

" Yours very truly, &c.

"  ———

" J. P. ORGAN, Esq.

" P.S.—I can give employment to a few more good men just now."

" *8th Feb.*, 1861.

" SIR,—I can now make room for four good willing labourers, a*t* 10*s.* per
week, if you know of any honest inclined men.

" Yours truly,

" J. R."

" *Feb.* 25, 1861.

" DEAR SIR,—I believe I have about 100 of your men at present employed,
and as far as I can see they are all sober, hard-working fellows.  They are
very attentive to their work, and appear very sober men.  Some of them have
been employed by me upwards of two years ago.

" Yours truly,

" JNO. D.

" J. P, ORGAN,"

"My Dear Sir,—Please send me two or three of your best men in the morning.  See that you send none but sober industrious men.

"Yours faithfully,

"A. L.

"J. Organ, Esq."

"City Hall, Dublin, Feb. 25th, 1861.

"Dear Sir,—I believe I have about 10 of your men at present employed, and so far as I can see they are all sober, hard-working fellows.  They are very attentive to their work, and appear very sober men.  Some of them have been employed by me upwards of two years ago.

"Very truly yours, &c.

"———.

"To J. P. Organ, Esq."

"Tobacco and Snuff Manufactory,
"2, Francis Street, Dublin, Feb. 26th, 1861.

"Dear Sir,—I have at present in my establishment four of your men, some of whom have been with me for two years; they continue to give me satisfaction, in consequence of which I have recently raised their wages. I consider them trustworthy and sober men.  I must say they have it in their power to rob me, at any time, but I have never known them to do so.

"I remain, dear Sir, yours respectfully, &c.,

"———.

"Mr. Organ."

"12, Bull Alley, Feb. 26th, 1861.

"Mr. Organ—Dear Sir,—The two men you recommended, one about four years ago, are doing well.  I feel no hesitation in pronouncing them honest, as I have tested their sincerity on many occasions, both of them being in the habit of delivering my goods through town and receiving payment for them often to the amount of forty to fifty pounds.  I have raised their wages from time to time, as I considered them deserving of any kindness I could conscientiously show them.

"I remain, your most obedient servant, &c.,

"———.

2, Bath Avenue, 27th February, 1861.

"Dear Sir,—The men you sent me are still working for me.  I have four of them employed close by myself, and I must say their conduct is satisfactory. D., who came to me four years ago, has 24s. a week now; he had only 12s. when he first came.  I have kept them all through the year, though I discharged some very good workmen.  The two labourers have 11s. a week each, and the last bricklayer you sent me has been raised from 18s. to 26s. per week.

"Yours truly, &c.,

"———.

"To J. P. Organ, Esq."

In the Eighth Report we learn that already two prisons had
been closed, Forts Carlisle and Camden, which had been employed for the intermediate stage.  The Directors say:—

"It will be observed by the Reports of the Local Inspector of
Spike Island, and the Governors and Superintendents of the
different Convict Establishments, that they are in a very satisfactory state; that the prisoners continue to appreciate the 'Mark
System,' and evince a great desire to attain high classification.
'Marks' are obviously very simple and intelligible means of
realizing to the mind of each Convict his progress in industry
and self-control.  In the separate or first stage of imprisonment
at Mountjoy, in Dublin, the marks, classification, and entire
Convict System, are made the subject of explanatory lectures on
the part of the Schoolmasters; the Convict thus becomes perfectly aware both of the importance of endeavouring to amend
himself, and of the little chance with which, when liberated, he
can prosecute a criminal calling without incurring very great
hazard.  After seven years' experience of the 'Mark System,'
we are entirely of opinion that it has been most successful in its
results.

"In our Annual Reports for the last six years we have so
constantly stated the importance we attach to the institution of
'Intermediate Prisons' for male, and 'Refuges' for female Convicts, and the good results which have attended their adoption in
this country, that we need scarcely now do more than confirm
these statements, and reiterate our opinion of the intimate knowledge of each Convict, which is afforded by training him under
a more natural course before his liberation.      *     *     *

"Since January, 1854, 6,121 Convicts have been liberated in
Ireland; and since the establishment of Intermediate Prisons,
upwards of six years since, *only ten per cent. of all classes of
Convicts liberated from the Government Prisons since that time have
returned to them.*  To give value to this statement, it is especially
necessary to note the appliances in Ireland for bringing old
offenders to justice, and that, in addition to these appliances, the

period named is not sufficiently long to make recognition impossible in small establishments.* With regard to licensed Convicts, who are included in the above number, we can state that all cases of proved infringement of the stringent conditions attached to such licenses have been followed by their revocation.†   *   *

"Our prison expenditure is very low. According to our present estimate, the Convicts in our different establishments do not cost more than £24 10s. each,‡ without deducting the value of their labour, which it will be seen by the Reports of the Governors, &c., is very considerable and satisfactory. It must be borne in mind that the reduced number of Convicts in the establishments causes the charge per head to be greater than if the number was larger ; because the salaries of the superior officers remain the same, and are spread over a smaller area. When our establishments were more filled the cost per head of each Convict was not so much as it is now."

A reference is here made to the proceeds of the work of the Convicts. In Mountjoy Prison, containing men in the early stages, work is not performed which can be reported as profitable, though a large number of articles are made for prison use.

At Spike Island, the second stage, the Governor states the daily average of men at work during the year, to be 475 ; the estimated value of their work is £12,540.

At Philipstown there are 104 effective and light-labour prisoners, employed on trades and other skilled labour. The profit on these is £1,684, being about £16 a head on every prisoner.

At Smithfield and Lusk Intermediate Prisons, where the average number of prisoners for the year was 90, the profit on

---

"* The altered appearance and different age of these men renders personal recognition in large prisons after a lapse of time almost impossible, and statistics formed on such data most unreliable. The Irish regulations are therefore of the greatest importance."

"† Not 7 per cent. have been revoked, and these are included in the 10 per cent. given above."

"‡ Inclusive of buildings this charge would be raised to £25 13s."

labour amounts to £1,971 14s. 10d., making the average earnings of each effective prisoner £21 18s. 2d.

It is worthy of remark that in proportion as there is greater
liberty, the profit on the labour of the prisoner increases, until,
in the Intermediate Prisons, each man nearly pays the expense to
which he puts the country by his incarceration.

The number of Convicts discharged during the operation of
the new system was stated to be above 6,000; of these many
had left the country, but those who remained required constant
supervision; the system of registration of crime, the revocation
of sentences, and the other means which had proved so successful in reducing the number of convictions, required constant and
vigilant personal attention on the part of the Directors. Even
those who emigrated were a source of anxiety and care. Hence
the diminution of the number of Convicts within the prisons did
not materially lighten the amount of personal labour of the
Directors, as the development of the system beyond the prison
walls was proportionally increased. It was thus a matter of
great surprise and grief to all interested in the system, that the
Board which was carrying out so admirable a work was about to
be disturbed, by the removal from it, by the Government, of one
of its number.

"In May last," we read near the close of the Eighth Report,
"our late colleague, Mr. LENTAIGNE, was appointed to the office
of ' Inspector-General of Prisons.' It was with great regret that
we received the notification of his transfer. We felt not only
that the department would suffer through the loss of a Director,
but that it would especially do so through the loss of a gentleman who had devoted himself unceasingly to the improvements
connected with the ' Irish Convict System.'

"Since that period this department has been conducted,
therefore, with materially reduced power of direction and supervision. The Irish Convict System has been much indebted for
its success to the very minute attention paid to its details.
Unless concerned in its practical working, it would be difficult

to realise the importance and value of this attention being given, and of the occupation of time thereby entailed upon the Directors.*

"It has not been possible to attend to these details as well as heretofore, and it is therefore to be expected that the system will suffer in its results."

It was doubtless the anxiety expressed in the last sentence, together with the over-strain of work caused by the removal of one of his coadjutors, which finally compelled Sir W. CROFTON to resign his charge, owing to the serious injury his health was sustaining. In doing so he had the satisfaction of having proved, as stated in the last paragraph of the same Report, "that the Irish Convict System, after many years of trial, has resulted both in efficiency and economy. 'Efficiency,' proved by the orderly conduct of the Convicts, and by the empty state of the prisons, notwithstanding the strict appliances in force for bringing old offenders to justice. 'Economy,' by the very low cost of the Irish Convict Establishments, although it is obvious that the supervision of a small number of prisoners is always proportionably more expensive."

Captain WHITTY was then left the sole Director of the Irish Prisons, and thus speaks, in the Ninth Report, of the change which had been made, and its probable effect on the working of the system :—

"In referring to the important change that has taken place within the year in the arrangements of superintending the Convict Prisons Department in Ireland, it would be unnecessary for me to enlarge on the great loss that the public service has sustained by the retirement, on account of ill-health (in May last), of Sir WALTER CROFTON, C.B., the late Chairman of the Board of Directors, who with his first colleagues, Capt. KNIGHT and Mr. LENTAIGNE, founded and developed the Convict System,

---

"* The refuges for female convicts, the arrangements of the farm at 'Lusk Intermediate Establishment,' and the proceedings with regard to liberated Convicts, fall under the supervision of the Directors."

which is allowed to have worked so satisfactorily in Ireland, and has attracted so much public attention and favourable notice in other countries.

"The change referred to consisted in the present abolition of the Board of Directors, and in leaving the superintendence to the charge of myself, the only remaining Director, with the aid of two Inspectors, Captain BARLOW, previously Local Inspector of Spike Island Prison, and Mr. NETTERVILLE, previously Governor of Mountjoy Male Prison. The closing of Philipstown Prison had reduced to a certain extent the duties of general superintendence, and the change above described caused a saving in the expense of superintendence of over £500 a year; but the nature of the Irish Convict System required such constant and minute attention on the part of the Directors themselves, to the individual cases of the prisoners in the progress of classification, and in otherwise adjusting the process of marks for the right use of the Intermediate Prisons, that it may be considered as still experimental whether only one officer, with the power of a Director, can carry out those objects and perform the general duties as efficiently as was practicable under the former plan of superintendence.

"Alterations have been proposed in the rules, for the purpose of giving increased powers to the Inspectors; but in the possible continued absence of the Director from illness or other cause, inconvenience to the service might still arise; and I feel also called upon to state that I have already experienced the result of the change in the heavy increase of labour and responsibility that must fall upon the person entrusted with the duties of sole Director, however zealously the Inspectors may perform the visiting and other duties that properly belong to their office."

But there was no relaxation of effort on the part of the officials, because the Director who had stimulated and helped them on had been obliged to leave them. Mr. ORGAN thus writes respecting the Lusk and Smithfield Intermediate Prisons in his Report, dated January, 1863 : —

"Simplicity of life and cheerfulness of disposition, even when engaged in the most severe and menial labour, characterize the reformatory system of prison management, as carried out upon the Lusk Farm. The food of the men is coarse but wholesome, yet sometimes insufficient. Their work is most laborious and irksome at some periods of the year, so much so, that I have frequently heard them say that they toiled harder upon the commons of Lusk than in any prison through which they had previously passed. I have often paused to admire the once vicious, destitute town-thief plying his spade and pickaxe as he stood in drain or ditch, cold and wet, reclaiming the barren common. At the most unpleasant and laborious work, cheerfulness shows itself in the man; and though, perhaps, heretofore sulky, repulsive, and sullen, yet here we find the same man amenable to every rule, obliging and obedient to every officer, hopeful and willing under every circumstance, and hypocritical under none. The vice and wretchedness of their former lives they only remember to avoid ; for, imbued with the spirit of self-dependence, animated with hopeful confidence in the future, and cheered and stimulated by the happy success of their former prison comrades in the honest labour market at home and abroad, they appear unmindful of everything save the two great and guiding motives, the hope of liberty and hope of honest employment, when discharged.

"The course of instruction pursued with the men of this prison is similar to that carried out in Smithfield. The anxiety of all to improve is highly edifying and encouraging. Few men have had greater experience in the field of adult education than myself, for I have devoted my whole lifetime to the instruction of the labouring poor. I therefore may venture to offer an opinion upon the subject. Now, I have always considered it, as natural for a *man* to attend school in the evening as it is for a *child* to attend school during the day. The mind of the adult is most composed after the day's toil, and useful and interesting instruction in the evening is prized by him as a great boon.

"During a practical experience of twenty-three years, I feel myself justified in stating, that I have never known men to have embraced the opportunites afforded for their mental culture more earnestly than the prisoners of Lusk and Smithfield.

"I know they appreciate my lectures, and I also know they have a kind regard for myself; hence it is they repose in me their confidence, and, to a great extent, permit me to shape their destinies. I cannot well express the relationship, if I may be allowed to use the expression, which exists between the men of the Intermediate Prison and myself. It may suffice to say, that their after well-being is, and ever has been, to me, since my connexion with them, an absorbing thought. I have laboured to raise their minds and hearts from the vicious, warped, and prejudiced condition in which I found them ; and, after a long practical experience, I can only say, that I have, in many instances succeeded, and in other cases failed. My own especial position in the service is a very wracking, wearying one, ever chequered with hope and fear, joy and sorrow, perpetual solicitude, occasional despondency, but unbroken confidence in the ultimate success of that arduous but good and useful cause in which it is my pride to be engaged.

" Lusk is a grand preparatory stage for prisoners to fit them for their after occupation in life, whether they return to the country districts from which they came, or enter upon the adventurous career of an emigrant—as many of them do. There is something very hopeful in the way the prisoners at Lusk take to their labour, and the great interest they evince in having everything go right about the farm. Should an animal be ill, or the weather be unfavourable to their work, they manifest as great an anxiety as if they themselves were personally concerned. This is a very admirable trait in their character, and one, too, which has won for many of them the respect of their employers, when they exchanged the restraint of the prison code for the independent freedom of honest occupation."

The following letters show, also, that the confidence of the public in the system remained unshaken :—

"2, BATH AVENUE, 24th January, 1863.

" DEAR SIR,—After repeated solicitations, I took into my employment one of the men you recommended. Finding him to be steady and correct, I took another of them, and being satisfied with his conduct, I took in as many as I had an opportunity of employing—sometimes five or six, *and found every one of them to give great satisfaction, being attentive to their work, and acting soberly and honestly.*

"I have but one of them employed at present. But I hope soon to be able to take in more hands, and *could not desire better than those men you recommend.*

Your obedient servant, &c.,
" To J. P. ORGAN, Esq."                                        " ———.

" THE NATIONAL MANURE COMPANY OFFICE,
"15, LOWER ORMOND QUAY, DUBLIN, 28th January, 1863.
"—— ORGAN, Esq., Smithfield Prisons.

" SIR,—In answer to your inquiries respecting the various men I have had from you during the past five years, it affords me very great satisfaction to be able to state that in all cases I have found the men most attentive to their work, and most tractable to manage ; ever willing and ready to do whatever is required of them, and most anxious to make themselves useful; the training they have received previous to being sent to those willing to employ them seems thus roughly to have broken them into discipline, such as you do not find amongst the ordinary labourers of the country, and you know I have had some considerable experience in the management and direction of large numbers of workpeople of all kinds both in this country and in England. I may add that having occasion to go a good deal in the neighbourhood of the huts at Lusk, I have been astonished to see from 30 to 40 men at work over the Company's farm, with so few warders to look after them.

"I remain, yours obediently, &c.,

"———."

"BLACKROCK, *Jan.* 30*th*, 1863.

"—— ORGAN, Esq.,

"DEAR SIR,—I feel great pleasure in speaking most favourably of the discharged prisoners who have been in my employment from time to time.

"Of course I took them solely upon your recommendation, and, indeed, for upwards of twelve months one of your men had charge of my building materials—lead, paints, tools, &c., &c. I found him strictly honest and faithful. I have no objection at any time to lend you my assistance in your good work, for I am convinced of the great necessity of assisting the convict after his discharge, and above all keeping a friendly eye over him. A long license over a man seems to me a great protection to honesty to his employers.

"I am, dear Sir, yours very truly, &c.,

"———."

It is fortunate for the stability of the Irish Convict System that another Director now shares with Captain WHITTY his great labours, which, as we have seen, are not of a mere routine kind, but involve a degree of personal influence and responsibility which cannot be supplied by any subordinate officer. The Tenth Report states (p. 8) : "With reference to the observations made in the last Annual Report by the then sole Director respecting the difficulty of providing for the due performance of the duties that formerly devolved on a Board of Directors, further experience having shown the necessity for the appointment of an additional Director, and Mr. MURRAY, the Inspector of Juvenile Reformatories, having in November last been appointed to that office (still retaining charge of the duties of his former appointment), we are enabled by the experience of some months to report that, with the aid of Captain BARLOW and Mr. NETTERVILLE, as Inspectors, the duties of supervision and management of the present Convict Prisons can be effectively conducted." The present satisfactory state of the various establishments has already been quoted from the same Report, pp. 118, 119, in the last chapter.

The foregoing simple narrative of the actual progress of the work will, we trust, give a feeling of absolute reality to those who, after reading the various accounts of the Intermediate Prisons, which have, from time to time, come before the public, may have been disposed to believe them an illusion, a pleasing fiction, something too wonderful to be entitled to belief. It could not be imagined that the solution of one of our chief social difficulties had been effected in that Island which, in other respects, has been so great a source of anxiety to our rulers. Yet it is actually the case. Eminent continental jurists who had arrived at philosophical conclusions based on deep principles of government, and on the laws of human nature, found to their surprise and pleasure that these principles had actually been developed in Ireland, and acted on for a sufficient number of years to prove their soundness. It is not probable that the Directors of the Irish Prisons had any philosophical system before them when they began their work. They came to it with a full appreciation of what had been already done in England. They had the same Act, that of 1853, as the basis of their operations, and they determined to work out the principles of that Act to the utmost of their power. They found peculiar and unexpected difficulties in their way, which they had to surmount. The disposal of the Convicts by trans-portation was suddenly cut off from them, and henceforth they must discharge their prisoners at home. An especial aversion existed in the Irish mind to contact with those who had endured a penal sentence. The unfortunate men themselves were in a very low state of degradation, physical, intellectual and moral; hence they were not in a condition to enter the labour market, even if it had been ready to receive them. The Government Prisons were in a most unsatisfactory state, both as regarded arrangement, accommodation, and even sanitary condition. The officers also were very ill adapted to their work, and it was necessary to train almost a new staff of subordinates. This was not so easy a matter; for though it has been asserted that it was more easy to adapt the new system to Irish than to English prisoners, experience proves that peculiar qualifications are required in controlling the Irish. Many officers, many schoolmasters, may be very efficient with the English, who would be totally incapable of acting satisfactorily with the Irish of the lower classes. The Irish are excessively sensitive to wrong and injustice, whether real or imaginary; yet they are equally susceptible of kindness and sympathy, and extremely grateful for them, especially when received from persons in a higher rank, and where there can be no possible suspicion of a sinister motive. It is not, however, always easy to meet with officials who possess such moral qualities as will thus obtain their confidence, and secure their willing obedience. The Directors indeed state in the First Report that they apprehend greater difficulties than have existed in England, with regard to the character of the prisoners, especially as a large number of those who were at that time in the prisons were brought into their criminal position by want of work and extreme distress. We have yet to learn that the Saxon is less amenable to reason and to moral influence than the Celt, and if the means adopted to surmount the difficulties which were adopted with the Irish Convicts were permanently successful, there can be no doubt that they would be so with the Convicts of Great Britain.

The means employed were not mere outward appliances, When the Irish Convict System is spoken of, mere mechanical arrangements are not intended; these might be adopted elsewhere and fail, if the spirit were not infused into them which animated all concerned in working it in Ireland. There, from the first day of his entrance, the Convict was taught and gradually led to feel, that though he had, through his own misdoing, lost his personal liberty, yet that it was for himself to controul his own will and bring it into conformity with law and duty; and though he had apparently lost the power of shaping his own

destiny, yet that in reality he still possessed it, and that his
future, whether for good or for evil, would depend absolutely
on himself.   The Convict, by degrees, felt hopes of himself
and remembered he was a man, a member of society, one
who might fill an honourable place in it, because he perceived that those put in authority over him remembered
it too, and had hopes of him, and confidence in him.   How
could those Convicts fail to comprehend that there was a true
human sympathy with them, when the Chief Director devoted
his time and labour to converse individually with each one
of the four thousand thus incarcerated, learn his difficulties,
trials and temptations, study his character, and thus be prepared to give him the friendly advice he needed when again
in the world ?   Combined with this sympathy was strict justice ; to every one the inevitable consequences of his own actions were certain to follow, whether good or bad.   Here was
a law established founded on right and equity and truth, and
every one was bound to obey it, whether officer or prisoner.
There was no favour, no partiality, no bribery, no indulgence for
any one, whether high or low.   How could the Convicts do
otherwise than respect this justice, and feel willing to obey a
righteous law, when they knew that any one of them might
appeal to the Director if he thought himself aggrieved, and that
his case would certainly receive an impartial investigation !

A perfect freedom from religious differences constitutes another
important feature in the Irish Convict System.   This is at all
times difficult to attain, wherever persons of different religious
denominations are working together in the same establishment ;
it would be particularly so in Ireland, where, unhappily,
glaring instances of hostility, arising from religious differences,
are continually occurring.   The true spirit of Christ should display itself in mutual forbearance, and in that respect for the
religious opinions of others which we desire for ourselves.   Such
has been found in the Irish Convict Prisons, where judicious regu-

lations, strict justice, and mutual courtesy have enabled Catholic and Protestant officers to work in their respective spheres, without interference in their duty, and with mutual courtesy. This is evident in the Reports of the officers;—we have personally witnessed it. The effect of such genuine religious toleration cannot be too highly estimated.

May these be ever the features of the Irish Convict System, and may it continue, as it has done, thus to blend justice with mercy, and to bring back the erring and wandering into the fold of Christian society !

# CHAPTER IV.

## FEMALE CONVICTS.

THE treatment of Female Convicts is a subject of great importance and of peculiar difficulty; yet it has not hitherto received that full consideration which it requires, if any hope is to be entertained of arriving at a solution of it.

It is frequently imagined, even publicly asserted, that Convict women are so hopelessly bad that it is useless to attempt any reformation of them. Such an opinion is founded on the knowledge of such cases as those which have been presented at the commencement of this work, and which are frequently occurring in the public prints; on the very painful exhibition of female vice in police-courts among the unhappy women who are lost to all sense of shame; and, not least, from the descriptions of the scenes that occur in the Convict Prisons, which have been given to the public by the Prison Matron. We acknowledge that the reformation of such women is a very difficult work, but at the same time believe that the difficulties are not insurmountable, if a right system is adopted; we believe, too, that the strong impression which prevails as to the impossibility of reforming women who have once entered on a career of crime, arises more from the exhibition to the public of the extraordinary excess of female Convicts who have been forced into an unnatural state of excitement by injudicious treatment, than from the real conviction of experienced persons who have judiciously and perseveringly endeavoured to reform them.

It is unnecessary in this place to dilate on the influence which every woman exercises, for good or for evil; in the sphere in which she is placed; it is too generally acknowledged to need proof.

The incalculable benefit conferred by the early influence on her children of a good mother can be attested not only by those who have risen up to call her blessed, but by society generally.

And, on the other hand, no one can estimate the evil which is caused to society, both directly and indirectly, by a wicked one.

The importance of the work of female reformation cannot indeed be doubted, for no one can calculate the amount of crime which may be saved to the country by the rescue of a single woman from a vicious life.

The actual cost to the public of a bad mother, in the punishment and reformation of her children, is shown by the following cases, which came under the writer's personal knowledge a few years since :—

" We will cite two instances which prove the enormous cost to society of a bad woman who is a mother. Mrs. L—— was left a widow with three sons and three daughters. We saw the latter in gaol together, some ten years ago;—the eldest brother was then under a ten years' sentence in Parkhurst Juvenile Prison ; the second boy was in prison ; the youngest was in the Workhouse ; the mother was living as she chose. This was the eighth conviction of her three girls, the youngest of whom was only fifteen ! They had lived together in London by picking pockets, at which they were adepts; once it was attempted to get them into a Refuge, but the mother soon removed them. The eldest daughter was then under sentence of penal servitude. She completed her time at Brixton, but was soon in gaol under another name, and is now again in Brixton Convict Prison. A conditional pardon was obtained for the two others in different voluntary institutions. After many disappointments, and much perseverance with them, they emigrated—one to Canada, one to the United States, as female servants, and reports were heard from each as doing well. The youngest boy was maintained for some years in a Workhouse Industrial School, then ran away, and was lost sight of; the second, after five or six imprisonments, was placed as a voluntary in a Reformatory, from which he emigrated with a fair character to Australia, and has been heard of as doing well. The eldest was discharged with a ticket-of-leave from Parkhurst, his conduct having been good there, his fare was paid to emigrate with the gratuity he received on his discharge; but he left the ship, returned to the scene of his former life, and after living at large on the fruits of crime for some weeks, he was taken up for burglary, convicted, and sentenced to fourteen years' penal servitude. How much has that one woman cost to the Government and to society through her children !

"Again.—About seven years ago, two young girls were brought from gaol, to be, if possible, saved in a Refuge under the care of benevolent ladies, from an abandoned mother who came to claim them. They were useful to her, and she considered that she had a right to their services, for she had paid a high price to have them trained in the most approved modes of picking pockets, by a professional London thief. Her husband was in a respectable way of business, but she had driven him from her by her dissolute practices, and he was in America. The younger daughter, a bright, clever girl, was sent as a voluntary to a distant Reformatory, but the mother speedily followed and removed her. This girl and her brother, pursuing, with their mother, their unlawful calling, were soon arrested, and sent, under sentence, for five years to Reformatories. Even there the mother's evil influence pursued them. Constantly did she defeat all the efforts that were made to reclaim the poor girl, insinuating drops of fatal poison into her soul ; and when at last her time of detention was expired, she carried her off to plunge her again into crime, from which she has been only stopped by a sentence of six years' penal servitude. The elder daughter, in the meantime, first corrupted all the girls in the Refuge where she was received, teaching them the various modes of picking pockets she had learnt, and then went out to practise them again. After two years' imprisonment, which only served to teach her caution, she pursued her unlawful trade so successfully, that, being a good daughter, she *six* times, as she once told a lady, set up her mother in business ! This wicked woman, the mother, has not only been bringing up her own children in crime, but, as she herself informed a lady, had trained at least fifty young girls to thieving, travelling with them in first-class carriages and living at inns. She was just then professing penitence for these sins, and got admittance into a London refuge to spend the winter comfortably. What did she teach the inmates there ?"

These two women had probably never been in prison. They were too artful to run the risk of detection themselves. The police of various towns were frequently endeavouring to discover the track of the last mentioned woman, hoping to obtain a sentence of transportation for her, but unavailingly. There was no possibility of making any effort to reform these wretched beings, because they were free, they had no desire to alter their course of life, and would not submit willingly to the restrictions which would be requisite, if any hope of improvement could be entertained. Hence the peculiar importance, not only of using every effort to elevate the female sex generally, especially those of a low and degraded condition, but of availing ourselves of the opportunity of reformation which is presented by a long term of detention being awarded to a woman who has broken the laws of her country. Such an opportunity is opened to the Government in the Female Convict Prisons. There appears hitherto to have been a complete failure in them, as to any such result as might have been hoped,—the reformation of the women committed to them.

We shall in this chapter consider the English Female Convict System and its results; we shall then endeavour to point out the cause of these, and show the effect of different principles of treatment in the Irish Female Convict Prisons.

Let us first inquire what is the work which is to be done in the Female Convict Prisons?

The system and arrangements in them must necessarily differ from those for male Convicts, for there is a very great difference between the inmates. Female Convicts are, as a class, even more morally degraded than men. As a general rule, it will be found that women are not brought before a public tribunal except for very aggravated crimes, or for a long course of vice. We may attribute this partly to a degree of forbearance which usually exists in the stronger towards the weaker sex; and partly to the fact that they are, when engaging in crime, most commonly the accomplices of their male connections, or shielded by them. From these causes, we learn that in the United States it is rare ever to see women in prison; in our country the proportion of female Convicts to males is usually not one-third of the whole number. But for these very reasons they are especially bad, more deeply hardened than those of the other sex in the same position. They generally, perhaps always, spring from a portion of society more completely cut off from the honest and respectable portion of society, and therefore more lost to shame. At the present day we find in our Convict establishments men who have moved in the higher walks of life, as well as among the lower, middle, and the mechanic class. They have known how, by a plausible hypocrisy, not incorrectly called a "homage to virtue," to keep up a character, and to associate with the rspectable portion of society; such persons appreciate to some extent, if not the true value of reputation, at least its uses. They know the feelings and principles acknowledged as good in the world; and if they have not the spirit of religion in their hearts, they are at least acquainted with its teachings, which may at a future time come with power into their souls. But Convict women usually spring from a portion of society quite cut off from intercourse with that in which exists any self-respect, and they are entirely lost to shame or reputation. During an acquaintance for more than a quarter of a century with two or three hundred families of the labouring class, some of them very low in character, and living in the worst parts of a crowded city, a case has never come before us of a woman being even brought before the magistrates, still less sent to prison. Since, during the last sixteen years, that acquaintance has been extended to the very lowest families that could be brought under the notice of the City Missionary or the master of a Ragged School, only one case of a woman being in prison has ever been heard of among them. A much shorter acquaintance with girls in a Reformatory has disclosed various cases of wretched mothers being in prison, whose progeny had sprung up as much cut off from all Christian or civilized influences, as if they had been born in a heathen country. These poor women, these female Convicts, will then, we believe, usually provo to belong to a pariah class, which exists in our state as a something fearfully rotten and polluted, and which diffuses its upas poison around, undermining the very foundations of society.

The women of this degraded portion of society will be generally found to differ in many respects from those belonging to a higher sphere. Their intellectual powers are low, and from having been left uncultivated, are in a state of torpidity from which it is very difficult to rouse them. Without discussing the comparative intellectual powers of adults of the two sexes in

general, experience of the education of the youth of each in
various ranks of society enables us to state confidently, that while
in the upper classes, with equal opportunities, the intellects of
girls develop more rapidly than those of boys, in good schools for
the labouring classes there is an equality between the two sexes;
but in the lowest class, that below the boundary line which the
decent labouring poor never willingly pass, the girls do not in
general display the slightest interest in learning, and it is indeed
extremely difficult to incite them to any degree of mental applica-
cation, while boys of the same class, and even of the same family,
readily receive it, and show positive pleasure in the culture of their
minds. This peculiarly low intellectual condition in females of the
lowest social grade is accompanied by a very strong development
of the passions and of the lower nature. Extreme excitability,
violent and even frantic outbursts of passion, a duplicity and disregard of truth hardly conceivable in the better classes of society,
render all attempts to improve them peculiarly difficult. And if,
added to all this, what is holiest and best in woman has been perverted and diseased by unlawful intercourse with the other sex,
as is very frequently the case, there is engendered in her a hardness of heart, a corruption of the whole nature, which would seem
to make absolute reformation almost impossible. We have
heard one who had had large experience in the temperance cause
declare that he never yet had known a reformed female drunkard,
though he could point to multitudes of men who had been
rescued from the sway of intoxicating liquors. Most seldom is
any real change observable in a woman who has arrived at
maturity in so degraded a condition. We need not say how
strongly such experience points to the necessity of rescuing young
girls who are growing up under such contaminating influences
before it is too late, and placing them, with legal controul,
under circumstances where they may become useful members of
society.

In order to have any prospect of success in the reformation of
women in this very degraded and, we may say, abnormal condi-

tion, for their characteristics differ essentially from those of the labouring, middle and upper classes, there must exist, in the first place, firm steady controul, against which it is evidently hopeless to rebel, combined with a strict and vigilant discipline, administered with the most impartial justice. This is a primary condition of reformatory work in general, but absolutely essential in this. We well remember the violent outbursts of passion, the rebellious spirit, the deception, the suspicion, the constant annoyance with which we had to contend in the early days of our Girls' Reformatories ; these have given way to willing obedience, perfect confidence in their superiors, and a general openness, since a thorough steady discipline was established in our Schools ; until this was accomplished, little permanent improvement could be anticipated. In the next place, to provide abundance of active useful work is absolutely necessary. The restless excitable nature of these women requires a vent in something ; they should have full employment, of a kind which will exercise their muscles and fully occupy their minds, so as to calm their spirits and satisfy them with the feeling of having accomplished something. The importance of this also we have fully proved in our Reformatories for girls ;—it is even more essential in establishments for women. These two primary conditions having been arranged satisfactorily, considerable attention must at the same time be paid to the culture of the intellectual powers. These, we have already stated, are more deadened, or perverted to a bad use in women than in men. There is far greater difficulty in stimulating girls who have passed their childhood in neglect, than boys. The effort of learning to read is to such often positively painful, and without the greatest skill, kindness, and firmness combined on the part of the teacher, the young person would succumb to the difficulty. The effort once made and a triumph achieved, an important step in reformation is attained, for stores of interesting information are now open which will fill the mind, instead of the pernicious thoughts which formerly harboured there.  Intellectual effort, which would be very easy and pleasant to a child of six years old, is extremely difficult and unpleasant to a girl of sixteen, still more so to a woman of thirty or upwards ;—a mastery over it once gained, not only an intellectual but a moral power is acquired, both of which facilitate the work of reformation.  Another essential part of the work of reforming such women as have been described, is the healthy development of their affections.  These are peculiarly strong in the female sex, and may be made the means of calling out the highest virtues, the most genuine self-devotion ; when perverted, as we saw them in JANE CAMERON, they may be and are frequently made an instrument of much evil; but in a woman they can never be utterly lost. It will then be essential to the success of any system which has as its object the reformation of women, that scope should be given to the affectional part of the woman's nature, and that this should be enlisted on the side of virtue.

That all these conditions should be fulfilled in a Convict Prison does certainly appear very difficult ; yet, if they are essential to success, no labour, no expense, should be deemed too great to develop a system which should embody them all, and do the work required,—reform female Convicts.  The expense which a bad woman is to the public who comes forth from a lengthened confinement in a Government Gaol unreformed, is far greater than any possible cost which might have been incurred in reforming her; the evil she has done within the prison to those around her is very great, and extends the poisonous influence to a widely-extending circle, when the women she has corrupted go out into the world; on her own discharge she emerges from her seclusion only to plunge into greater excesses than before, and to perpetuate and intensify the pollution of the moral atmosphere from which she had been temporarily withdrawn.

We shall now proceed to describe the system adopted in England for female Convicts, as derived from official sources.

The treatment of female Convicts is thus stated by Sir J. JEBB in his evidence to the Royal Commission (662): "All female Convicts are first sent to Millbank, where they go through two stages of discipline; then they go to Brixton, where they go through three more stages of discipline, and then a proportion of them come to Fulham, and go through two stages." (661). "I should not like to have them there for more than a year if I could help it, but the exigencies of the service required them sometimes to be there for 16 or 18 months; it depends upon the number coming in under sentence of penal servitude and the number of those who are going out by the expiration of their time. We must relieve Brixton; all however go to Millbank first." It appears, then, that there is no system on which female Convicts can absolutely rely, and which will afford a steady stimulus to them in their prison progress. Their removal from Brixton to Fulham depends rather on convenience and circumstances, called the "exigencies of the service," than on a settled principle, and on their conduct and diligence. In reply to a question (665) whether there is any absolute rule as to the time for which a female Convict is sentenced? the answer is "No. We have adhered as nearly as we can to 12 months. It depends upon the vacancies which occur. The three prisons, Millbank, Brixton and Fulham, all work together." It will be observed, that though Fulham is generally called a Refuge, it is absolutely, as here designated, a *prison*. The principle of it is a slight improvement in the condition of the Convicts, and a variety of employments, with a nearer prospect of release. They receive also rather larger gratuities, and somewhat better diet. It is, however, strictly under prison management, and the prisoners there are not under license, but absolutely under sentence.

The Fulham Refuge was opened in May, 1856, and is thus described by Sir J. JEBB (657): "The number of women accommodated there is 180. The discipline is somewhat relaxed from what it is under penal servitude at Brixton, and they are engaged in every kind of industrial employment, such as washing and needlework, but especially in washing. There are upwards of 100 women employed daily in the laundry, and they thus acquire the knowledge of a very valuable occupation by which to obtain their living on being released, and they realize a considerable amount for the Government."—659 \* \* \* "Some of these women have earned as much as £20 a year, paid into the Exchequer. This is the return for 1862 :—

*Fulham Refuge Washing Account for the year ended Dec. 31st, 1862.*

|  | £ | s. | d. |
|---|---|---|---|
| For private families, 41,004 doz. and 7 @ 1/- ... | 2050 | 4 | 7 |
| For the establishment, 15,050 doz. and 8 @ 1/- ... | 752 | 10 | 8 |
|  | 2802 | 15 | 3 |
| Cost of materials ... ... ... ... £601 18 11 |  |  |  |
| Paid for carriage of linen ... ... ... 109 16 6— | 711 | 15 | 5 |
| Balance in favour of the establishment ... | £2090 | 19 | 10 |

Ninety women being employed in the laundry, the average earnings of each, calculated from balance £2,090 19s. 10d., is about £23 4s. 7¾d." It is explained by the Lady Superintendent, in her Report, that more than 90 are employed, but as the routine of the day does not allow them a full day's work, the computation is made for the work as done by 90 full-time women.

This computation does not of course include rent of premises, the wages of skilled instructors, the use of apparatus, &c., and therefore cannot be regarded as clear profit. Still it is very satisfactory that the women work so well as to have cleared so large an amount towards their maintenance.

The Chief Director having thus stated the system adopted with regard to the female Convicts, says that upon the whole there is more trouble with them than with the males. " I think so," he says (765), " because they are not so amenable to punishment, and their offences are of a different character, and depend very much upon impulse. If they quarrel one with another, they will set to work and break the windows in their cells, and tear up their clothes, all without any assignable reason, and then they will sit down and burst out crying. They are difficult people to manage." Such a condition as is here described by the Chief Director, surely is an unmistakable sign of extraordinary mismanagement. That such violent bursts of wilful violence and passion should be frequent among the inmates of any establishment, indicates a bad tone pervading it, and a want of due controul; but that it should occur in a Government gaol, where all needful appliances are accessible, is surprising. Still more so is it to hear the Director conclude his statement by simply remarking, "They are difficult people to manage, *but on the whole we have been successful*, for which we are mainly indebted to the admirable character of the officers." Such a state of things would usually be considered a glaring failure, rather than a success; nor can we imagine any reformatory influence pervading an establishment where scenes of wild excitement have any frequency.

The number of prisoners at Brixton is about 600, the number of officers is about 40, or one officer to every 15 prisoners. In our Reformatories we consider one to every ten inmates a fair staff: as the adult criminals are necessarily far more difficult to manage than our Reformatory boys and girls, and require far stricter surveillance and discipline, we may easily imagine what hard and difficult work these officials must have to undergo, and how it must tell upon their health and strength, as well as power of exertion.

The Chief Director believes that the female officers perform their duties admirably; he acknowledges that they have "hard work, but not more than they can get through if in good health. The hours," he says (766), "are necessarily long. The officers are forced to get up at half-past five, or a quarter to six o'clock. The Convicts are not locked up until five or later. Some of the Matrons are kept on till eight o'clock, but some of them are relieved from duty about six." Captain O'BRIEN, the Director who has especial charge of the Female Prisons, states (2223):

" The female officers and warders are on duty at Millbank on
alternate days 12 hours, and 15 hours including their breakfast,
tea, and dinner time.   They are not allowed to go out during
the day, unless on special duty."   On being asked (2230) :
"Does it not strike you that it is too great a strain both upon
the body and the mind of the female warders to keep them so
constantly on such severe duty ?"—he replies,  " I do; the
number of officers that there are both in Millbank and Brixton
Prisons is small; and in Millbank, both for the males as well
as the females, the hours are very long, and they cannot get out
so often as I think they ought to get out, the consequence is
that towards the close of the day I am told that some of the
officers get irritable and extremely cross with the prisoners, and
that other officers get so tired out, they really do not much care
whether the prisoners about them conduct themselves well or
ill : that is what I am told."   The same witness also says
(2232): " I have no hesitation in saying that the prison is
rather under-officered than otherwise; the fact is that the rule
which has been pursued has been to keep the number of officers
as low as possible.   I have occasionally asked for a greater
number of officers, and I have been answered, 'No, they cost
too much, we must look to the expenses;' upon the whole we
should do better if the number of the officers was increased."

We learn from the evidence that Brixton Prison is very
healthy, that there are very few deaths; the Convicts in the
infirmary are many of them invalids who came from Millbank
in that state.   The frequent indisposition of the female officers
is therefore owing to overwork, of which the Chaplain thus
speaks (4809): " I think that they are decidedly overworked ;
the hours are too long for an efficient staff, because, if illness
happens to overtake three or four of the Matrons, the duty
thus becomes excessive ; and, of course, as to leave, a Matron
may be looking forward every other night to leave from six
o'clock, but she cannot have that indulgence if some one else
is ill,—she must take her place."   (4810).   " *They are, a*

*great many of them, laid up with illness, and they look very much worn out at times.* If the staff was larger, perhaps the Superintendent might be able to give an earlier leave of absence once or twice a week, and in that way give them a little time to recruit."

After hearing the account of the work imposed on the female warders, and that of a most wearing kind, it is not surprising that they are frequently ill. The inquiry was made of Dr. GUY, the medical attendant of Millbank (3123) : " Whether the strain on the minds and bodies of the female warders, from the amount of work expected from them, is greater than it ought to be?" His reply is important. "I think it is greater than it ought to be. *I know that their work is extremely difficult and sometimes dangerous,* it is very wearying work that they have to perform, and I think I am bound to say that I think they are not always sufficiently considered; I have oftentimes thought it right to make recommendations for an improvement in their quarters; and I do not think that these recommendations have been so promptly considered as I think they would have been if they had been prisoners and not warders. I consider it right to say this, though I know there are difficulties in the way."

We have seen elsewhere that the cells of the female warders are in some cases near to those of the prisoners, and exposed to the disturbing noises maliciously made by those wretched women. Under female officers so overworked by continual strain, and constant contact with Convicts so depraved, it will easily be perceived that strong daring women feel that they have the power in their own hands of exercising annoyance to their superiors, and disturbing the order of the prison. Captain O'BRIEN says that these are a minority among the whole, and that many of the women go through the prisons without any report at all; but he candidly acknowledges that he does not think that there are many cases in which anything like reformation take place during their confinement at Brixton. Yet he says that he thinks that the system of treatment there is judicious and well regulated !

The general regulations are the same in the female as in the male Convict Prisons, with a slight alteration as regards remission of sentences.

The punishments inflicted appear to be quite inefficacious in even preserving discipline, and to be defied by the women. Captain O'BRIEN says (2112): "When the women who are thoroughly bad misconduct themselves over and over again, it is impossible to punish them any more, for their health will not bear it, and it does them no good. I think it sometimes renders them worse than they were before, and they become so utterly depraved, and so detestable in every way, that really I can scarcely speak of them with common magnanimity." The following occurs in the same evidence :—

"2164. You have stated, I think, that in your opinion the women defeat you in the matter of punishment, that is, that no punishment that you can inflict has any effect upon them?—Yes, to a great extent.

"2165. And no punishment has been tried, so far as I have understood you, of a different kind from that which is applied to the men, excepting in degree?—No.

"2166. You have stated that confinement in a dark cell, upon bread and water diet, is the only kind of punishment that has been applied to the women, and that that has totally failed?—Yes.

"2167. And the only suggestion that it has occurred to you to make is the village stocks?—Yes."

Captain O'BRIEN has had the supervision of the female Convicts since 1849. He further says:—

"2173. I was aware that the mode of punishment was ineffectual; I was always aware of that, but it has only been lately that it has occurred to me that the use of the stocks might be a good addition to the present rules.

"2174. That was the special mode in which you thought of changing the punishment?—Yes.

"2175. But at what period, since you first commenced the supervision of the female prisoners, did you come to the conclusion that the existing mode of punishing the females was altogether inefficient?—Very soon after I came to have anything to do with them.

"2176. But no formal notice of the opinion you entertained has been given either to Sir JOSHUA JEBB or to the Home Office?—It has appeared in the reports made to Parliament, although I cannot at this moment lay my hands upon them, and to this effect, that punishments when carried to a great extent with the very bad women become absolutely useless and cannot be carried out,

218 OUR CONVICTS.

for with women who deserve punishment over and over again, the punishment
we give them does not stop them from committing the prison offences for
which we order the punishment."

Surely, then, if the present system has totally failed, there
must be something radically wrong in it, and it ought to be
changed. Fuller particulars respecting the punishment of the
women are given by Dr. GUY, the Medical Attendant at
Millbank Prison, in his evidence,—

"3107. Some injury to health arises from the repeated punishments which
the worst class bring upon themselves, both of the men and of the women. It
is impossible to shut up men or women in dark cells on bread and water over
and over again without producing some effect upon their health. I may state
to the Commission that I am a strong advocate for flogging, on medical grounds,
and because I consider it the most merciful punishment of which I have any
knowledge. Unfortunately it applies only to the men. As to the women who
are given to tearing their clothes and smashing their windows, if they are put
into a dark cell, they shout and sing and make merry. They know that there are
prisoners not very far off them, who can hear their noise, and they like to go
on in that strange way; and I think that if it were possible to inflict upon
them some short bodily pain, it would be much more merciful. In the case of
the man, I think that flogging is particularly advantageous.

"3108. What do you think of the stocks?— Captain O'BRIEN told me in
conversation that he thought it would be well to introduce the stocks, and
I think it essential that something of the kind should be adopted. Our difficulty now in the case of a woman is this, that the worst punishment we can
inflict upon her is to put her into a dark cell for three days with bread and
water, and she comes out at the end of that time, and very soon goes back
again. But she is always conscious that there are people in her neighbourhood who will be worried by her noise, and you cannot unfortunately put her
anywhere where she will not be heard. She knows that the prisoners near
her are rather interested in hearing her shouting and singing, and what is
wanted is to keep her in a cell where she will not be heard, or place her in the
stocks. And yet another thing is wanted. If you put a woman into the stocks,
so as to prevent her from following her *favourite amusement of lying on the
floor and drumming* with her feet against the door, she still retains the use of
her tongue, and will make a great disturbance, *especially if she knows that the
officers are sleeping near her, or that there are sick prisoners at hand.* I think,
therefore, that the Governor should have the power of ordering such a prisoner
to be carried bodily away, and put where she could disturb no one.

"3109. I thought you had at Millbank Prison cells which were out of
hearing?—No, we have no such cells; they are out of hearing of the neighbourhood, but they are not out of hearing of the prisoners. I have often wished
that there could be such separate cells, but I have always been met by the

statement that the expense would be too great. I mean cells that would be so isolated that a woman might know she was alone and disturbing no one.

"3120. It has been stated that a very common offence on the part of the female convicts is to tear up their blankets, and that invariably when they have done that, new blankets are given them?—It was so at Millbank until lately.

"3121. Is it not desirable that they should feel the bad effects of tearing their blankets?—I think it desirable that a prisoner should always feel the effects of his own misconduct, wilfully brought upon himself, *but this he does not do at present,* for the theory is that we medical men are bound to do all we can to prevent a prisoner from hurting himself; more than that, we have before us the fear of a jury, if anything should happen, which jury would probably consist of the petty tradesmen of Westminster, and would be apt to contain at least some friends of the criminal class."

In the morbid and unnatural state in which the Convict women evidently are in the Government Prisons, we are not surprised that deception is carried to a remarkable height among them, that being one of the very prominent features of women of a degraded condition. Dr. GUY gives us the following illustration of it in the conduct of female Convicts:—

"It may be important," he says (3142), "that the Commissioners should know, and that the public should know, the extraordinary cases that we have to deal with. A short time ago, at one of my monthly inspections, I observed a woman who was looking ill, and putting on an expression of great depression. She seemed to be low spirited, and asked to see me. Those who wish to see me are always able to do so, and to speak to me. I saw this woman; she was looking low spirited, and she had rather a weak expression of countenance. She was taken into the Infirmary, and immediately pretended to be imbecile. She put on a look of imbecility, and never spoke except in monosyllables, or in very few words at a time. If she was washed in cold water, she would ask for more, and in a very idiotic, foolish way. All our tests failed to show whether she was of sound or unsound mind, although we were convinced that she was not; but we could not say that she might not be of unsound mind. In five months that woman voided her own excreta on her own person, having another prisoner to wash her; and at the end of five months she got tired of it, and confessed that she had deceived us; that she had been putting this on all the time, and she hoped she should not be punished. These are the cases that we have to deal with."

A counterpart of this is found in the pages of the "Prison Matron:"—

"One woman in Millbank Infirmary took a fancied neglect of the doctor so much to heart, that on his next appearance she sprang from her bed and seized the poker with the intention of splitting his head open. 'I'll learn you to say I don't want any arrowroot, you beggar,' she screeched forth. The same woman, in the days of her convalescence, and probably to prolong her stay in the Infirmary, feigned a trance with such excellent effect as for a time even to puzzle the surgeon in attendance. It was more a state of coma than of trance, and necessitated the administration of beef-tea with a tea-spoon. After the surgeon was perfectly convinced of the trick, and had read her a lecture on her wickedness as she lay on her bed, in as rigid and death-like a position as she could assume, she maintained her inflexible position for two days, and was only brought to reason by the mixture of a little assafœtida with her beef-tea, at which fresh insult she sprang up in bed and assailed the attendant with a torrent of invective, only to be heard in its true strength and richness in the wards of our Government Prisons."

The frequent effort to escape from work by shamming sickness is a feature of the Male Convict Prisons, where the inmates do not take an interest in their occupation, or feel a moral stimulus to try to do their duty, whether they like it or not. Yet, generally, there appears to be no complaint in the Female Prisons of unwillingness to work, but rather of a want of occupation for them. Mr. MORAN says that there are 600 prisoners there; about 100 are occupied in baking for the different Convict Prisons, some are employed in the kitchen and in baking, and the others in needlework when they can get employment from the great houses, but this is very uncertain. Thus a large proportion of all the female prisoners in Millbank and Brixton have no active occupation; nothing whereby they may learn habits of diligence, and acquire the means of obtaining an honest livelihood when their term of imprisonment expires. This want of active exertion is a serious hindrance to any beneficial effect which might otherwise arise from the training and instruction intended to be given to the Convicts. It appears strange that the means of remedying this very serious defect did not engage the attention of the Commissioners.

The state of education among the female Convicts is very low; far inferior to what it is among male prisoners. This will not be a matter of surprise to those who are acquainted with the con-

dition of the lowest grade of women in our country, and of the
ordinary educational state of the convicted girls who are admitted
into our Reformatories, three-fourths of whom are usually destitute of the simple elements of education.    Mr. MORAN tells us—
(4771): "Out of 1,706 female prisoners who entered Brixton
Prison from 1853 to 1858, 851 of them were entirely uneducated,
615 could read and write; but they had learnt that in other
prisons before they came into our prison; 50 of them could read
a little, and 10 might be said to be tolerably educated out of that
number.    Their religious knowledge was very limited indeed;
they were hardly acquainted with anything; at all events nothing
to serve as a principle to guide them."    We find, then, that all
the female Convicts, except a few isolated and exceptional cases,
were without any education but what they had received in the
gaols to which they had been previously committed.    This
reveals a fearful state of things, and is suggestive of the most
serious reflection.    The deficiency in reading and writing may
not, it will be thought, indicate absolute dense ignorance and
degradation; various circumstances may have operated to prevent these women from having had, when young, the opportunity
of receiving instruction; their parents may have been too poor to
pay for their schooling; or they may have been compelled by the
size of a rapidly increasing family to retain at home their older
girls to help in family cares.    The painful fact is that they have
been so isolated from all Christian sympathy, that it was in the
gaol that they had to learn the simplest rudiments of religion.
Four schoolmistresses are employed in teaching the Convicts at
Brixton, and there are two lady Scripture-readers, whose visits
are much valued by the prisoners.

The record of punishments for 1861 in Millbank Prison presents some very remarkable results.    It will be remembered that
this prison is intended for the reception of Convicts, both male
and female, in the first stage of punishment, and in separation.
The following is an abstract of the return :—

MALES.

|  | Adults. | Juveniles. | Total. |
|---|---|---|---|
| Handcuffs ... ... ... ... ... ... ... ... | 58 | — | 58 |
| Dark & Refractory Cells and minor punishments | 399 | 4 | 403 |
| Whipped with a Cat or Birch ... ... ... ... | 9 | 3 | 12 |
| Total of punishments ... ... ... ... ... ... | 466 | 7 | 473 |
| Admonished, and not punished ... ... ... ... | 416 | 2 | 418 |
| Total ... | 882 | 9 | 891 |

FEMALES.

|  | Adults. | Juveniles. | Total. |
|---|---|---|---|
| Handcuffs ... ... ... ... ... ... ... ... | 41 | 11 | 52 |
| Straight Waistcoats ... ... ... ... ... ... | 287 | 116 | 403 |
| Dark & Refractory Cells and minor punishments | 569 | 45 | 614 |
| Total of punishments ... ... ... ... ... ... | 897 | 172 | 1069 |
| Admonished, and not punished ... ... ... ... | 574 | 73 | 647 |
| Total ... | 1471 | 245 | 1716 |

The number of male prisoners, Dec. 31st, was 560. Daily average, 515
"        "    female    "        "       422.    "        "      469

It thus appears that while the number of punishments of the male Convicts during the year, 473, did not amount to an average of one each, the punishments of the females, 1,069, amounted to more than two for each individual. Again, there are only nine cases of corporal punishment among the males, while the severe and very degrading punishment of a straight waistcoat has been inflicted on the females 403 times, or, on an average, more than daily! These numbers do not call forth any special comment in the Report of the Directors, nor do any peculiar exciting causes appear to exist on the part of the women. On the contrary, very serious offences were committed on the male side of the prison during the year;—two murderous assaults on officers occurred; three Convicts escaped by the exercise of much and long ingenious effort; four suicidal attempts were made by two Convicts; ten men were removed to lunatic asylums, and only two women; there were seven deaths of men, and only two of women; the admissions of men to the Infirmary were 515, while those of women were only 226. This remarkable disparity in the punishments inflicted on the two sexes, and the peculiarly severe character of the punishments of the women, leads to the conclusion that such punishments are in themselves quite ineffi- cacious, and that some different system ought to be adopted. Very possibly a large proportion of the punishments may have been inflicted on a comparatively small number of persons. When these are passed on to the Associated Prison at Brixton, the mischief they do among the other Convicts is incalculable. The Superintendent at Brixton Prison states, in her Report,—"We have, as usual, had a great many reports among the apparently incorrigible, who were comparatively a small number, yet too many for the discipline which without them would prevail in this prison. * * * It is much to be regretted that, reformation being so important an element in this prison, with the further object also of preparing many for the Refuge at Fulham, there should still exist the necessity for our receiving and retaining some incorrigible prisoners, whose influence and example decide many for evil who appear just on the verge of becoming improved."

Another important point in this return of punishments is the large number of punishments of *girls* in the Convict Prisons. Since young persons up to the age of 16 can now be received under sentence in Reformatories, it certainly is a very remarkable fact, that while only seven punishments of male juveniles are recorded, there are as many as 172 for young female delinquents, 127 of these punishments being of handcuffs and strait waistcoats. Such punishments have no place in Reformatories. If they are needed in establish- ments where there are the means of controul which do not exist in Schools, the inference may surely be drawn, that a system which requires so much punishment is not likely to produce any permanent moral effect, either within the prison walls or beyond them in the world.

In the year 1862 the Superintendent's Report states that the punishments have been fewer—796. Out of 921 prisoners who had been in the prison during the year, 565 had not been reported for any offence, more than half the reports (1305) having been incurred by 59 prisoners only.

Very few observations are usually made respecting the women in the general Reports; Mr. DE RENZI makes this remark respecting their intellectual culture, in his Report of Millbank Prison for 1862 :—" In the case of the women who are taught individually in their cells, not like the men, collectively in school, not only is there the absence of any powerfully stimulating motive to quicken their perceptions, and awaken their interest and attention, but there is a strong counter motive in the weekly gratuity allowed for work, which varies in amount according to the quantity of work done." The desire for work and interest in it does not seem to arise solely from the stimulus given by the gratuities. The Convicts appear to have an absolute pleasure in occupation, thus differing from the male prisoners. The Superintendent of Brixton Prison writes in her Report for 1861 :—

" The prisoners are always very anxious for employment; it is only the very bad who are disposed to be idle, and even some of these have asked and been supplied with work while in punishment cells. The invalids have been industrious; some have persevered in endeavouring to do needle-work, when hardly equal to the exertion; but of the invalid prisoners we receive from Millbank, many are wholly incapacitated from working at all; and as our Infirmary is always full, our work return is thereby lessened; still a great deal of work has been done, and as a body the prisoners are very industrious."

This feature in the women is a valuable one, which might be turned to very great advantage if an effective system were adopted.

Great difficulties arise in this prison from the presence of the refractory Convicts, when thus placed in association with the better disposed. Complaint is made on this head in several of the Reports, as well as in that of the Lady Superintendent of Brixton Prison already quoted. The Chaplain of that Prison thus speaks on the subject :—

" Those who have passed through the discipline at Millbank determined to set at defiance all who were disposed to help them, and all means used for their improvement, cannot be spoken of hopefully. Great difficulty is experienced in dealing with such refractory women in an associated prison.

" It is much to be regretted that they are ever removed from Millbank until they have exhibited some signs of amendment, and gained such a standing in the prison as good conduct can alone secure. This, obviously, is the design of the established regulations, the departures from which I apprehend have been occasioned by the state of health of the prisoners, either mental or physical, or both.

" If I may venture to repeat what I have more than once expressed, it does seem most important that women of this class should be treated in a *special manner* and in a *special place*, and that they should be placed under medical treatment, as their presence among other prisoners operates most injuriously upon those around them, and constitutes one of the chief difficulties in carrying out the discipline of this prison. I trust, however, that the evil may soon be remedied, when the new establishment at Broadmoor is completed.

" The difficulty of dealing with such refractory women can be understood by those only who have experience in such matters. And few can conceive the lengths to which they will go, and the stratagems to which they will resort, in order to try and have their own way. Nevertheless, even among this class, kind, patient, firm and Christian effort has not been unattended with success, and several can be pointed out taking their places among the orderly and well-conducted, in the first and second classes, who were once as bad as can well be conceived."

Very great uneasiness is expressed by the Superintendents of this and of Fulham Refuge, or Prison, respecting the fate of the women under their charge when again in the world. The Superintendent of Fulham Refuge says, in her Report for the same year :—

" In my general remarks under this head I trust that I may be permitted to digress a little.

" The most desirable way of disposing of our women on discharge has for some time past occupied my anxious and serious attention, and more so since the ' Discharged Prisoners' Aid Society' has been compelled from want of funds to relinquish its valuable labours on behalf of female prisoners.

" As it is impossible for the Superintendent of a prison, from the very nature of her duties, to be possessed of the facilities for procuring situations or employment for prisoners upon their discharge, that are at the disposal of a Society which for so many years has been what I may term a most important and needful *auxiliary* to this prison, I trust that some means will be devised as a substitute for the loss we have sustained. As an expedient I think that a matron might, with advantage, be engaged whose special duty it would be to procure employment and temporary lodgings for such cases as have hitherto been received by the Discharged Prisoners' Aid Society.

" I think this might be tried with every hope of success, either under the Prisoners' Aid Society, or in more immediate communication with this establishment. Such an agency would necessarily be circumscribed, as it would only meet the cases hitherto provided for in London through other means. I would gladly impose upon myself any additional labour which such a plan would involve.  *  *  *

" The reconviction of some of the most promising women who have ever been in this prison, and of whom we had formed the highest opinion, whilst it proves how little reliance can be placed on characters acquired when under any kind of restraint, has made me think very seriously for some time past of various plans to prevent a relapse into crime. Those I have named appear to me very simple and practicable. There are doubtless some 'missing links' yet to be found before there will be a commensurate amount of good for the means used and exertions made on behalf of prisoners."

The Reports for the next year, 1862, confirm the same experience. The Superintendent of Brixton Prison says :—

" My experience satisfies me that female convicts, as a body, cannot bear to be idle. The present public distress shows it more particularly, as we cannot obtain an adequate supply of needlework. Unless actively employed they become restless and desponding, and brood over the wretchedness their crimes have entailed on husbands and children ; that this is the case with many I am quite sure ; therefore it appears to me that although sedentary, monotonous, and uninteresting employment, with separation, is a right and salutary punishment for a considerable time during the first stage of imprisonment, it would, *if persisted in for a more lengthened period, augment cases of insanity and of suicide.* 159 have been reported for slight offences arising from irritability, such as a hasty word or action, soon repented of, but not to be excused, it being highly necessary to enforce strict discipline ; hence the benefit of badges, and of remission of a portion of their sentences ; they are great accessories to the rigid fulfilment of the end of penal servitude ; take these away, and we should have to deal with two extremes, stubborn, unimpressionable logs, or furies, giving as much trouble and doing as much mischief as can be imagined by spirits actuated by no other motive than sullenness or revenge ; and so unimproved and friendless, that all hope would be at an end of their ever desiring to lead better lives upon their discharge."

Though Fulham Refuge is intended for the most promising of the Convicts, the Report of the Superintendent is not more hopeful than before. She says :—

" I am glad to say that there has been a decrease of reports and punishments this year, whilst the daily average of prisoners has been the same, viz.,
174. Last year there were 115 reports, 75 prisoners reported, and 64
punished. This year there have been 99 reports, 67 prisoners reported,
43 punished, and 55 punishments.

" Having frequently been struck with the low and depraved class of women
which now come under my charge, I am surprised at being able to give so
satisfactory a report of their general conduct. At the same time, *I cannot but
be aware that the duties of the officers are far more trying than in former years,
and that it is only by untiring exertions on their part that such a degree of
order can be maintained.* Often have I to encourage the officers, and myself as
well, with the hope that the worst of our criminal class is being brought under
the power of the law, instead of being at large to exercise their evil influence
over those less depraved and criminal than themselves; and thus we trust
that, although our labours are more arduous, good is being done to the country
at large."

Of the conduct of many of the women who are advanced to
Fulham, and allowed to remain there, we may form some
opinion from the fact, that though the Superintendent states that
the conduct of the prisoners has been generally very satisfactory,
yet there is a record of 57 punishments,—nine having been
punished twice ; two three times ; one four times ; and one even
five times. It might have been imagined that women who were
in this last stage, which is supposed to test their fitness for
freedom, ought not to have required absolute punishment to keep
them under controul, and that if they once so conducted themselves as to require correction, they would be sent back to
Millbank. It is not a matter of surprise that the public should
be unwilling to trust women who require such severity to keep
them from serious misconduct.

Such is the only insight which we can obtain into the general
working of the female Convict Prisons from official sources.
Vague rumours of course, from time to time, give some insight
into the " secrets of the prison house;" the volumes of the Prison
Matron give a vivid picture of their internal working. Respecting
the reliable nature of this work we cannot entertain any doubt, as
it is referred to by the Royal Commissioners in their interrogations of the Chief Director, and no doubt is expressed by them or

by him of the truth of the statements it contains; no suspicion
appears to be entertained in it of serious faults in the system,
and the greatest deference and respect is everywhere shown to
the Directors, to one of whom the book is dedicated.  In doing
so the author says,—"That I have written very earnestly—to
the utmost of my power, very truthfully,—a record of prison life,
I trust may form my excuse for dedicating this work to you.
Much that may appear strange herein, I pray you to believe, is
devoid of all exaggeration.  Much that might have been more
highly coloured and effective, through the agency of fiction, is
related after the simple manner of its occurrence."  As the
work has reached a third edition, without any doubt being
thrown on the accuracy of its statements, a few extracts will
here be given, which serve as an illustration of the various
official statements that have been already quoted.

The Prison Matron gives this painful description of the women
generally :—

"To see some of these women hour by hour, and listen to them in their
mad defiance, rage, and blasphemy, almost constrains one to believe that
they are creatures of another mould and race, born with no idea of God's
truth, and destined to die in their own benighted ignorance.

"As a class, they are desperately wicked—deceitful, crafty, malicious, lewd,
and void of common feeling.  With their various temperaments there are
various ways of humouring them into obedience, and sometimes a chance
of inducing them to act and think judiciously; but it can be readily imagined
that all the vices under the sun are exemplified in these hundreds of women,
with but a sparse sprinkling of those virtues which should naturally adorn
and dignify womanhood.

> For men at most differ as Heaven and earth,
> But women, worst and best, as Heaven and hell,

asserts our greatest living poet; and no two lines, I fear, are more true to
human nature.

"In the penal classes of the male prisons there is not one man to match
the worst inmates of our female prisons.  There are some women so wholly
and entirely bad, that chaplains give them up in despair, prison rules prove
failures, and punishment has no effect, save to bring the prisoners to 'death's
door,' on the threshold of which their guilty tongues still curse and revile,
and one must let them have their way, or see them die.  Some women are
less easy to tame than the creatures of the jungle, and one is almost sceptical
of believing that they have ever known an innocent childhood or a better

life. And yet, strange as it may appear, these women are not always in for the worst crimes: there are few, if any murderesses amongst them; they have been chiefly convicted of theft after theft, accompanied by violence, and they are satanically proud of the offences that have brought them within the jurisdiction of the law. \* \* \*

"The great difference between the male and the female prisoners is this love of display under difficulties. It is a subject almost inexhaustible, and on which a whole volume could be written. Personal appearance is almost wholly disregarded by the men; by the women it seems never forgotten for an instant, inciting them to breach of discipline and defiance of all rule, and making them bold and stratagetic. Checked too roughly, it leads to violent outbursts of temper that will throw a whole ward into confusion.

"To check this vanity, to baffle the many means which prisoners find for their gratification in the indulgence of it, is one of the most trying and incessant tasks of the prison matron. There are times even, when, with a very vicious woman, who has no self-controul, and whom physical restraint transforms into a wild beast rather than a human being, a little harmless variation in the arrangement of the hair or the style of the bonnet is tacitly overlooked.

"There are some women at Millbank and Brixton Prisons who have undergone every method of punishment, who have defied, fought against, and worn out those that inflicted it, and who, with health impaired by constant severity, are still as reckless and dangerous as in the days when prison rules were new to them. Kindness, severity, moral reproof, have all been tried and failed, and disciplinarians of the strictest school can do no more with them. Such women are at last humoured by thoughtful prison matrons; there remains no other way to keep them quiet. This may be subversive—is to a certain extent subversive—of true discipline, but a strict observance of the rules would inevitably kill the woman, whose indomitable spirit would last till her dying day."

The same author has shown us in "JANE CAMERON," that even such women as these may be softened and subdued by the influence of one of her own sex of a higher and better nature, which throws itself into sympathy with her own. It is evident that to work effectively with women such as here described, however, requires, in officials, no little firmness, experience, tact, and, above all, deep Christian love; but they should be aided in this difficult work by a system wisely planned and firmly supported.

The Prison Matron thus speaks of her fellow-workers, in "JANE CAMERON," vol. ii., p. 58 :—

"In our female prisons it may be easily imagined there is a sprinkling of these hard, unsympathetic officers,—good officers, in the main, so far as discipline is concerned, but possessed of no tact with the women ; unable, after years of service, to understand them, constantly exciting the prisoners by those little exhibitions of authority, which are according to rule, but which have been quietly 'dropped' by the majority of their fellow workers. Such matrons do more harm than good, gain but a sulky obedience from the well-behaved prisoners, and elicit passionate outbursts from the unruly. They are the Javerts of female prison life, making no effort to study the characters or the temperaments of their women, and keeping up a confusion in the wards that is inexplicable to the authorities. Orderly and precise matrons, but nothing more; they are like the orderly and precise mothers whom we meet with sometimes, who regulate their children's lives on a similar principle, and whose children invariably turn out wrong;—after all their trouble, all their care.

"And if children with harsh mothers, or with mothers of the very opposite character, who have never a will to exert, go wrong, so those children of a larger growth, female convicts—but children in so many things—do not exhibit any great improvement when a strict disciplinarian, or an easy, foolish matron, has the management of them. To hit the happy medium is the good fortune of not a few, however: experience will always teach the right way to a perceptive mind."

Thus we perceive that a system of temporising, or humouring the individual feelings of each woman, is regarded as absolutely necessary under the existing system. It probably is so simply to carry on the existing general order, without continual violent outbursts of passion. But that such is the case proves a great defect in the system adopted. We know by painful experience in the early days of our Girls' Reformatories, that such a course is absolutely subversive, not only of all real discipline, but also of all hope of reformation. A daring and rebellious girl was once overheard to say to her companions, "The more we stands out, the better they treats us." She gave her teachers a lesson which they never forgot. We have known a Schoolmistress, acting on the principle recommended in the foregoing extract, tolerate the impertinence or constant petty disobedience of some bad and wilful girl ;—this produced the most injurious effects ;— the girl felt that she had established for herself the privilege of acting as she chose, provided she kept within due limits, and imagined that she had infused a dread of provoking her into the mind of her instructress;—the other inmates learnt a lesson that they had only to be sufficiently daring and intolerable, to obtain the same privilege for themselves. We are told that the fear of the Lord is the beginning of wisdom; it is true, also, that there is no commencement of reformation until a fear of disobedience, and a principle and practise of duty are thoroughly established. This uncertainty of the course to be pursued with her, leads the woman to still greater lengths, for she finds that she can, by management, carry her point with the Director himself. The Convicts have the privilege of seeing the Director, if they request it, on one day in the week. The following is a specimen of such an interview, as given by the Prison Matron :—

" ' Well, JONES, what have you to say to me ?' possibly inquires the Director.

" ' If you please, sir,' dropping a curtsey, ' I want to stop away from Fulham. I hear, sir, as how I'm to go on to the Refuge, and I'd rather not go, if you please, sir. Oh ! I'd so much rather stop !'

" ' For what reason ?'

" ' Why, sir, I've never had a report here, sir; and I likes my officer, and knows 'em all like, and am very comfor'ble. And you see, sir, I've a bit of a temper, and shall be all strange and worited in a new place, and sure to break out, sir, and be sent to Millbank, sir, again. And if you'll only be so kind as to let me stop, sir.'

" The Director mentions the advantages of Fulham over Brixton ; but the woman expresses her objection more firmly, and perhaps there is a little conversation between the Director and the Lady-Superintendent oʰ the merits of the case.

" In a matter of this description the issue is doubtful ; now and then a woman receives permission to remain ; at times, Brixton is full of women, and Fulham the reverse, and, *nolens volens*, the prisoner must go.

" When permission to stay has been refused, a woman will occasionally break her windows, and thus, by the laws of the prison, prevent her transfer to the Refuge. This act is invariably punished by the removal of the prisoner to Millbank, to the silent system and coir-picking again. * * *

" Occasionally a woman, bursting with her imaginary wrongs, enters into a full detail of the ill treatment she has received from Miss R., or Miss W., or the principal, who may be standing at her side. Such a report on her conduct is unjust or exaggerated, or wholly false ; she has been always set upon, whilst others just as bad—' fifty times wuss, sir,—have been let off, or winked at.  Then there's lot of favourites!—and because she don't care to follow suit and curry favour, she's served so, and reported on, and trodden under foot.  And all she's got to say is, that it had better be altered, that's all—she's stood enough of it!'

" One woman who pleaded for an investigation into her report, and was refused, went back to her cell and hanged herself."

The outbreaks are now well known as a peculiar feature of these Convict Prisons.  They are a natural consequence of the excitability and bad feeling of the women under the system prevailing there.

" In prison," our author says, " the example of breaking out is displayed so often, and the monotony becomes, to a wild spirit, so wearisome and heart-breaking, that to disturb the stillness of their dreary abode and to give some animation to the unvarying round of their enforced duties, the offence is committed, and the glass is shivered by the pewter pints!

" One break out is almost sure to be followed by another; for the pulse beats high in these caged natures, and their blood is soon warmed by tumult and excitement.

" One matron, of a somewhat impulsive disposition—who has since left the service—once told me in confidence, and with a comical expression of horror on her countenance, that she was afraid she should break out herself, the temptation appeared so irresistible.

" 'I have been used to so different a life—father, mother, brothers, and sisters, all round me, light-hearted and happy—that it's like becoming a prisoner oneself to follow this tedious and incessant occupation.  I assure you, Miss ——, that when I hear the glass shattering, and the women screaming, my temples throb, my ears tingle, and I want to break something, dreadfully!'

" I believe I have already remarked that some of these 'breakings out' are parts of a cool, deliberate attempt to obtain removal to a dark or refractory cell, adjacent to a favourite companion who has recently committed a similar offence.  At both prisons madness is very often feigned, and windows and tables are broken for the sake of fellowship both night and day; and occa-sionally there are suspicions of unfair treatment, slights and jealousies, to render the woman's actions somewhat consistent with her feelings.  With the malicious, it is a morbid satisfaction to destroy prison property.  'I'll serve 'em out for putting me in here!' is often the remark with which an act of wholesale damage is accompanied.

" In one year at Millbank Prison, one hundred and fifty-four cases of destruction of prison property occurred; that there are some women so des-perately wicked—so resolved to resist all efforts to make them less abandoned or intemperate than they have always been—that it is often necessary to lay four or five reports in the course of the week, for two months in succession, before the Superintendent, in order to keep up anything like a semblance of discipline in the wards to which these women belong.

"In former days women were contented with tearing their blankets into a few strips; but as these fragments were available for 'prison flannels' it became a general rule to devote a little more time to the work of demolition, so as to make quite certain that the infinitesimal portions should render no further service to the State."

Though the official testimony already given, fully proves in general terms the violence of the outbreaks, yet as it is well to realise the kind of evil involved in them, and the difficulties the officials have to contend with, we copy the following scene from " JANE CAMERON." It is evidently sketched from life.

"She had become naturally enough, perhaps, a more thoughtful woman, and even then she hesitated. When the cell door was closed, prayers had been said, and the gas put out, she arose and softly paced the limits of her cell in the darkness, until reflection vanished and a wild determination set in. She had been imposed upon, and was thought an easy woman that would stand all manner of nonsense. She—JANE CAMERON, who had been one of the worst of Glasgow girls! She gave up trying to be good; she could not stand remaining any longer quiet and passive; life was horrible; any thing was preferable, for variety's sake. She laughed once or twice at the sensation there would be created in the wards presently, when the officer was on night duty, and all was hushed and at rest.

"She thought herself into a mad state;—it is easy for a solitary woman to do this—and she regretted the absence of her broom, which had been given out according to rule when she had received her gruel supper in her 'pint.' When all was still, CAMERON proceeded to tear her blankets and bedding; after the first rip or two it became an easy and gratifying task; she began to sing over it after a while. Then she leaped on her table, and sprang up at the window, 'pint' in hand, and hesitated. It was her first grave offence; should she do it, or should she not? She stood there and trembled for a while, then thought of her wrongs again, and of her fellow-convicts, who would laugh at her if she halted half way, and finally with a whirl of her hand she battered at the glass with her 'pint,' and screamed.

"The death-like stillness of the ward was over; the spell was broken; the matron came hurrying to the scene; the outer bell was rung for assistance; the prisoners turned out of their beds and began hammering against the doors for information; one woman cried forth, 'Bravo, CAMERON! Give it 'em, my gal and another swore that the next time she got a chance CAMERON had better look out, for waking her from her first sleep in that fool's way. 'If you wanted to break out, why did'nt you come it in the day-time?' she grumbled.

"The excitement of entrenching on the stillness of her life, the quiescence of her daily existence, was now in full force; she was proud of the noise she had created, and of the attention she had drawn upon herself; she regretted the absence of more windows, and tried hard in the few minutes that intervened to break up her table for defensive purposes. And when the door was flung back by the male officers, she made a rush at them like a tigress, and fought them, scratched their faces, and tried to bite them, till, overpowered, she was borne away to the 'dark.'

" In the dark cell she proceeded to stamp with her feet, beat the door with her hands, and scream after the approved convict fashion, until startled almost out of her life by a hoarse voice at her side.

" ' Give it 'em. I have schreech'd myself hoarse, and now its your turn.'

" ' Wha be ye'? cried CAMERON.

" ' HUTCHINSON. I smashed yesterday; we're half on the smash, and they'll be obliged to fill it now. I thought some one had been here before. You're CAMERON ? '

" ' Ay.'

" ' Thought you were a quiet un,' was the observation ; ' no good being quiet in Millbank. I like a row; and I've *rowed* till I've lost my voice. I can kick still, though. Hoo! Hark here!'

" And away went the heels of HUTCHINSON on the slanting wooden boards which formed, and still form, the place of rest for the ' dark' inmates.

" When the blankets and rug were passed in to CAMERON, she tore them up after the usual fashion, and received hearty plaudits from her companion, who had torn up hers at an earlier hour of the night.

" ' Keep it up, CAMERON !' said the woman. ' We'll do a song now. I'll sing; I've a beautiful voice. The screw sleeps above—*your* screw— and we'll keep her frisky.'

" The news was satisfactory to CAMERON, who sang and kicked her heels during the rest of the night, or the early morning, in the hope that the uproar would reach from the cell to the ears of the matron above her. In the morning came bread and water, which HUTCHINSON accepted, being hungry and which CAMERON flung back at the matron through the trap. In the morning came news of the sentence; three days in the ' dark,' with bread and water. But the ' dark' was a change; there was no work for her, but she had found a companion, and they could talk together of the ' bonnie days' when they were free. They compared experiences, took notes, told each other much of their respective lives, promised to consider themselves ' pals ' from that time forth, and to write to each other, passing the epistle on from hand to hand in the airing ground or the chapel. When there was a chance they would break out together again, and perhaps be shut up together just as they were then."

These fits of uncontrolled and desperate passion sometimes end in insanity; attempts, either real or feigned, at self-de-struction are not uncommon. One dreadful instance occurred, in which a woman, in a fit of wild jealousy and desperation, threw herself over a parapet and was dashed to pieces on the pavement below. Sometimes their excited feelings, and the vain attempts made by the officials to controul them, bring on a fit of illness. But even this has little effect in subduing their evil spirit, which remains with them until death closes the mournful scene. The Prison Matron says :—

"The same ingratitude, and selfishness and callousness are evinced towards each other; and to the prison officers, the same duplicity, craft, and vindictive feeling. There are women whom nothing will soften, whom no kindness will affect.

"'Breaks out' occur even in the infirmary; the passion of jealousy, to which all prisoners are prone, leading them to imagine that too much attention has been shown to one invalid, and too much neglect to their own selfish requirements. A woman will break out at a supposed slight, and struggle from her bed to wreak her vengeance on the crockery near her. One prisoner in Millbank Infirmary took a fancied neglect of the doctor so much to heart, that on his next appearance, she sprang from her bed, and seized the poker with the intention of splitting his head open. 'I'll learn you to say I don't want any arrowroot, you beggar!' she screeched forth."

We will not copy any more of these revolting scenes, nor describe the deliberate attempt of a woman to murder a Matron, or other wild outbreaks, the dangers to which the officials are exposed in the discharge of their duty. In the Report of the Superintendent of Brixton Prison for 1863, two assaults on Matrons are spoken of in one year, which sufficiently indicates the risk of health, if not of life, which they incur. Yet there are interspersed in these volumes many tender and beautiful traits, which show how much might have been done to soften even these women had the right means been adopted, had it been made a part of the system to call out the better parts of the nature. One of these Convicts made literally a bosom friend of a mouse she had succeeded in taming, and her grief at its death was inconsolable. Another lured a sparrow to her cell, and almost broke her heart when the little creature came to an untimely end. One is reminded by these incidents of the prisoner in the Bastille and his spiders. Sometimes a woman will run the risk of a report, and even punishment, to possess herself of a flower.

"I have a remembrance," the Prison Matron says, "of looking through the 'inspection' of a cell some years ago, and perceiving a prisoner, with her elbows on the table, staring at a common daisy, which she had plucked from the central patch of grass during her rounds—one of those rude, repulsive, but not wholly bad prisoners, from whom no display of sentiment was anticipated. Yet the wistful look of that woman at her stolen prize was a gleam of as true sentiment as ever breathed in a poet's lines. A painter might have made much of her position, and a philosopher might have moralized concerning it—for the woman wept at last, dropped her head down on the table between her linked hands, and shed bitter tears silently and noiselessly. The prison daisy must have spoken of the old, innocent times—of the fields she crossed once with old friends—perhaps of daisies like unto that before her, which were growing on a mother's grave.

"Six months afterwards I saw that flower pressed between the leaves of her Bible—a little treasure I should not have had the heart to take away, had there been any laws of confiscation concerning daisies in 'the books.'"

The romantic and devoted attachment of the Convicts to their "pals," individuals for whom they have conceived a prison friendship, is generally very injurious; but the same power of affection, if rightly directed, might be the means of great good. A Convict has been kept from a violation of the rules, or even from an outbreak, by regard to some particular Matron who had given her a kind look or word. JANE CAMERON was saved from moral destruction by such influence. Humouring and indulgence are very injurious to these women,—but Christian charity is never without its power over them.

To one more point we must allude, the Prison Schools. It has been already stated that the instruction of such women is a very difficult task, and that the intellectual nature of females, both young and old, in this degraded condition, is far more obtuse and difficult of culture than that of males. But this very fact renders it doubly important that every effort should be made to awaken their deadened powers, and to supply them with mental food which may take the place of the garbage which had hitherto been their nurture. But it has not been so in these prisons, as we have gathered from the official evidence; we have also the following account from the Prison Matron :—

" In justice to my subject, I must say, that the schooling system is far from a perfect one—does not work well, even irritates the women. Perhaps it would be hard for most of us to sit down late in life to learn school lessons; to these woman who have known no lessons in their childhood, whose minds are set to ignorance, and on whom a ray of light is torture, the prison school is almost unendurable.

" I cannot think that so much attention has been given to the schools as the subject is deserving of. The machinery to do good is existent, but it appears to me that it is not fairly worked. *There is no incentive to learn,* and the women sit down to their lessons with more doggedness and moroseness than they exhibit when they turn to their daily labour.

" 'What's the good of learning at this time of life ?' one woman will say. And I have often heard another exclaim, 'I'd rather have six months—nine months—longer sentence, than this sort of work. It's awful hard !'

" They sit at their desks, a posse of unruly children, more ignorant and unteachable than any child can possibly be, growling discontent over their lessons, and seeking to evade them. Over such a grisly array of pupils the two schoolmistresses in attendance possess little, if any power. * * * *

" The women are taught once a-week in classes of fifty at a time ; the wing women generally of a morning, from ten till half-past twelve; the old prison women, and consequently the worst behaved, of an afternoon, and for a period of time somewhat less than woman of the second or first class. The slight alteration of teaching the women in smaller classes has been recently tried with satisfactory results."

The length of time here allowed for schooling is evidently insufficient to produce any sufficient effect, or even to enable the Schoolmistresses to acquire any influence over their inapt scholars. To secure tolerable order, a Matron is obliged to watch the classes while the lessons are being given by the two Schoolmistresses. The following is the result :—

" The schoolmistress appeals to the matron on duty if there be too much talking, and the matron calls to order and reproves the unruly. Bible reading in classes is adopted by those who have a fair knowledge of their letters, and a strange gabble of sounds it is proceeding from these women. There is, however, an objection to reading aloud amongst them, and it is only by the matron's continual remonstrance that the majority of the women can be induced to read·at all. Those who have yet their letters to learn have special lessons given them, and great is the difficulty to surmount the first barriers in the way of education. Women more ignorant and stupid than

these prisoners it is impossible to conceive; teaching them becomes a hopeless task—the little progress made one week is entirely forgotten the next,
and has to be re-learned, with the same stolidity of manners and vacuity of
countenance.   Teaching for two hours, or two hours and a half, once a-week,
with no lessons to learn in the interim, is a burlesque of teaching with such
indocile pupils.

" Reading in Bible-class and a writing lesson constitute almost all the
school duties required of the women.   Originally copy books were given to
them, until the leaves began to disappear, and to be used for furtive correspondence; latterly a single sheet of paper is laid before each woman, and
collected at the end of school hours, the performance thereon being duly
criticized.

" At one period an attempt was made to teach the elementary rules of arithmetic, a variation which unfortunately proved a signal failure.   It was the
last feather on the camel's back, and the women would have nothing to do
with such arduous mental exertion.   To do them justice, they made the
attempt; but the extraordinary answers that were returned to questions the
most simple, and the shouts of laughter from the women at the desks at the
blunders of those who had found courage to respond, were subversive of good
order, often of good temper."

It is evident that schooling so conducted is worse than useless,
and cannot have the effect of elevating the condition of these
women.

After such pictures of prison life, we cannot wonder at the
unwillingness displayed by the public to take into their houses
women from the Convict Prisons, however well they may have
submitted themselves to the discipline required.   No one would
wish to admit into a well-ordered household any one who had
been even cognizant of such proceedings, though she had taken
no active share in them.   Besides, coming as most of the female
Convicts do from very degraded homes, they are totally unfit for
ordinary civilized life, for which the mechanical routine of a
prison does not afford the slightest preparation.   In fact, even if
placed in domestic service through the special interest and effort
of some kind lady visitor, they find themselves wholly unprepared for it.   The Prison Matron gives us instances of their
suddenly leaving comfortable places of service, through a yearn-
ing after their old life.

The present state of the Female Convict Prisons does not,

then, afford us the slightest hope of any improvement in the
Female Convicts. Indeed, the Rev. GEO. DE RENZI, Chaplain
of Millbank Convict Prison, states in his Report for 1861,
(p. 74): "The most discouraging feature in our criminal returns
of late years has been the sad, but too certain, evidence which
they contained *of an extensive and extending demoralization of the
female portion of the community*." Though he expresses a hope
that this is somewhat decreasing, yet there does not appear
any ground for such expectation while the penal establishments
which were intended to diminish crime are so completely failing
in their object.

We now proceed to bring forward some distinct proofs that
the Female Convict Prisons are not reforming women and
decreasing the crime of the country, but the reverse. The
Report of the Directors for 1863 contain some important statements. We learn from them (p. 6) that "316 Convicts were
discharged on license during the year 1863, and 39 on expiration
of sentence, two received pardons, six were removed to lunatic
asylums, and 20 died, making a total disposed of in the year
of 383." The number of cases of death and insanity appear
remarkably large, considering the attention paid to dietary and
medical treatment. Such results would lead to attribute much
of the evil to the mental condition of the Convicts which might
be remedied by a change of system. Those who are accustomed
to the care of morally diseased females are well aware how much
the health is affected by restlessness, excitement of the bad
passions, and that dreadful void in the nature which is produced
by the want of interesting occupation, and of a natural scope for
the affections. 437 Convicts were received, the Report tells us,
into the Goverment Prisons during the year 1863. "Of these
127, or 29 per cent., were reconvicted; 39 of them were reconvicted during the currency of their former sentences, and 88
subsequent thereto, and, in addition to these, 15 licenses were
revoked, making a total of 142 reconvictions or revocations of
licenses." The greater number of these 142 offences of women

who had already undergone penal servitude were such as did not involve any very serious legal offence, 119 being cases of larceny. But though the crimes for which these women have received a fresh sentence of penal servitude do not themselves imply any deep depravity in them, yet they do incontestably prove that these discharged Convicts have resumed their former criminal mode of life, and that they are again the centre of the most baneful influences. So the Directors evidently perceive, for they continue :—"But though the return of crimes for which women are sent to prison under sentences of penal servitude would seem to show that, so far as they are personally concerned, they do not belong to what may be called the dangerous classes of society, there can be no doubt that their male associates do, and experience goes far to show that it is female influence exerted in some way or another, and not, as is often supposed, intoxication, which is the source of so much crime."

We cannot accept, as the real origin of the evil, the following reasons which are assigned:—"The large increase in the number of reconvictions arises partly from the rapid discharge of the women under the effect of the comparatively short sentences of recent years, the want of means for assisting and supervising them on discharge, and in some degree, perhaps, from defective prison arrangements."

The adoption of an entirely wrong system of treatment appears to be the true cause of the bulk of those reconvictions; a longer detention in the Convict Prisons would probably not have reduced them eventually, but only postponed the evil. The large proportion (29 per cent.) of reconvictions which have been *recognised* cannot, of course, be regarded as the actual per-centage of relapses into crime of those who have passed through the Convict Prisons. We have already seen how many escape recognition, and this would be particularly easy as regards women. The police state that they find it more difficult to fix in their minds the lineaments of women than of men; indeed, the attempt is sometimes almost ineffectual to discover a female Convict who has endeavoured to conceal her identity. It will, besides, be observed that the committals to County Prisons are not included in this return. The actual per-centage of female relapses probably more nearly approaches that given by the four Wakefield Magistrates, viz., 50 per cent. of the women who were sent into penal servitude from Wakefield Gaol.

This is no new condition of female Convicts after their treatment in the Government Gaols; Captain O'BRIEN states in his evidence to the Committe of 1856, "I am sorry to say that the conduct of the women released on license is very bad. I believe that a great many of these women, especially the older ones, will sooner or later find their way back to imprisonment" (749). Mr. BRENNAN, Police Inspector in the Metropolis, states to the same Committee that he does not know one woman who has been released on ticket-of-leave, and is doing well (3302).

How little it is possible to form a judgment of the actual results of the Convict treatment of females, from the statistics of those gaols, is shown by the following statements made in the evidence of the Chaplain of Brixton Prison. He tells the Commissioners (4832), that since the establishment of that prison, 2320 female Convicts have been discharged, and only 227 recommitted; this would be not quite 12 per cent., a very moderate number, considering the bad character of these women. He states that this number fairly represents the number who have been reconvicted, because these prisons receive all the prisoners who are reconvicted. When asked (4838) : "A much larger proportion than those have probably fallen into crime?" he replies : "I daresay it would be so, but, at the same time, as most of the prisoners return to their homes, and as they would be known in the neighbourhood if they had committed offences before, they would probably receive sentences of penal servitude." From such statements we should naturally infer that this number of relapses of nearly 12 per cent. nearly represents the truth. What is our astonishment to learn from

a pamphlet in the hands of the Commissioners, the last Report
from the Liverpool Gaol, — " it there appears," reads the
O'CONNOR DON (4840), " that out of 207 female Convicts released
between the years 1856 and 1859, 73 have been recommitted,
or about 35 per cent !"

The Report of the Governor of the Borough Gaol, presented
to the Mayor, Recorder, and Magistrates of Liverpool on
November 3, 1862, gives us the following appalling facts respecting the state of female crime, as indicated by the gaol
statistics. The total number of commitments of *female* prisoners
during the year ending September 30, 1862, was 4440 adults
and 78 juveniles. " The number of persons committed last
year," he adds, " are more than have been committed during
any year since we have occupied this prison, except the year
1857." * * * " Up to the 18th of August last, the numbers of cells on both sides of the prison were sufficient for
the separate confinement of all prisoners in custody here, and
for all the past year the cells on the male side of the prison
have continued sufficient for the male prisoners ; but on the
before-mentioned day, and for several days afterwards, the
number of female prisoners became greater than the number
of cells on that side of the prison ; so that I have been
occasionally compelled to place two women together in such a
number of cells as the excess of numbers required." The
excess of adult females committed over the preceding year, he
tells us, is no less than 712, while there is a decrease in the
juveniles of five, indicating the continued good effect of reformatories, without which, as in former times, the juvenile convictions
would probably have shown even a more rapid increase than the
adults. " The number of adult females, who were committed
here last year," he adds, " exceeded the number of adult males
by 21, viz., 4440 adult females against 4419 adult males." Such
facts deserve careful consideration, and especially as the proportion of female commitments to male throughout the kingdom,
does not generally exceed one-third of that of males, certainly

not one-half, while here in Liverpool there is not only a great
increase over former years, but the actual number of women
in gaol exceeds that of men, instead of being one-third or
one-half. All large towns present numberless temptations to
vice, and in Liverpool dens of iniquity of the most dangerous
character abound; and seaport towns, especially one so situated
as Liverpool, are much exposed to be the residence of large
numbers of dissolute characters. Besides, the very elaborate
Police, as well as Gaol Reports, which are prepared in Liverpool,
do not often in other places come before the public eye, to startle
it with an enormous amount of female depravity. Liverpool
must not therefore be held up as peculiarly entitled to unen-
viable notoriety, and we must endeavour to ascertain some
special reason for this immense *increase* of female crime there.
We are enabled by the Report of the Chaplain of the Gaol,
Rev. T. CARTER, to form some idea of the share of this which
may be given to our Female Convict Prisons.

" The large number," he says, " of recommitments of adults of both sexes
cannot but have attracted your notice : and those gentlemen who have been
more immediately connected with the administration of justice, in your police
and sessions courts, will no doubt have had their attention drawn from time
to time to the great number of offences committed by returned penal servitude
prisoners and holders of tickets-of-leave. The full extent of this evil, however, does not lie upon the surface. Some little investigation is needful to
discover its proportions. I have not gone very minutely into the question,
nor am I able to state in precise figures the number of returned convicts who
have been committed to this gaol during the last year. Some idea, though,
may be formed, when I say that of the sessions cases *alone* 71 (40 males and
31 females) were returned convicts, in many instances holders of tickets-of-
leave even at the time of their further conviction ; and on the last day of the
official year there were under conviction in this gaol 55 who were recognized
as belonging to that category.

"Further, I have inquired into the present doings and mode of life of all
the females who have been sentenced to penal servitude between the 1st of
June, 1856, and the 31st May, 1859, and I beg to submit the following as the
result:—241 were sentenced to various periods of penal servitude during
those three years, of whom 34 are still under detention in convict prisons,
leaving 207 who are supposed to have undergone their sentences ; of these
207, 97 cannot be traced, because many have only just received their liberty ;
others may in all probability have emigrated or passed to other localities

beyond the reach of my inquiry;* 73 have been recommitted, several sub-jected to second like sentences; 17 are known to be living disorderly lives and maintaining themselves by crime; 7 have been pardoned on medical grounds, dead, or lunatics; 4 are known to have migrated to other localities, and all trace is lost; 1 is in a refuge in London; whilst only 8 are known to be so far doing well.

"Now, these figures exhibit a fearful state of things. I give them as plain facts, and leave others to draw their own deductions from them. One con-clusion, however, 'cannot be evaded, namely, that the *present mode of treat-ment adopted in our convict prisons is a complete failure.* Nearly the whole of those women—certainly a large proportion of them—have been returned to Liverpool to mix again with our population, and to spread *the leaven of their pernicious influence* with this condition in their hands endorsed on their license—'To produce a forfeiture of the license it is by no means necessary that the holder should be convicted of any new offence. If she associates with notoriously bad characters, leads an idle or dissolute life, or has no visible means of obtaining an honest livelihood, &c., it will be assumed that she is about to relapse into crime, and she will be at once apprehended and recom-mitted to prison under her original sentence.' But this intimation is a dead letter—a mere idle threat. I do not know of a single instance wherein it has ever been enforced; indeed, how is it possible that it should be carried into effect where there not only exists no machinery, no organized arrangements for enforcing the condition, but whilst the heads of the convict department, with singular inconsistency, discountenance all interference."

Here, then, we have one most important cause of the great increase of female crime in Liverpool. In the figures given us by Mr. CARTER there can be no mistake, because they are founded, not on vague report or supposition, but on positive information obtained through a well-organised police and other official aids. The conviction he expresses of the "complete failure" of the present system adopted in our Female Convict Prisons is not one founded alone on the conclusive statistics just quoted, which show that only eight women are known to be doing well out of 241 sent to the Convict Gaols; they are based on very long and close personal observation of the results, as well as the causes of female crime, and all who have been working at the reformatory cause know well how important and valuable have been the contributions he has made to it from the very first. Mr. CARTER's statements are

---

"* Of those ' not known' others were committed shortly after this Report was written."

always based on the experience he has gained from his daily work in the Liverpool Borough Gaol for a long course of years. This testimony, and the conclusions he has arrived at, are founded on actual *results*. Such extraordinary failures cannot arise from any inefficiency in the officials of the Convict Prisons, respecting whom high testimony is borne by the Directors in their Reports; it is the system adopted which must be *completely wrong*, and can *never* do what is intended, *i.e., reform female Convicts.*

The statistics of other prisons where the same careful investigation has been made would support this conclusion. Numberless cases might be cited from Police Reports, where peculiarly accomplished thieves and female pickpockets prove to be ticket-of-leave women, or some that have received a long training in a Convict Prison; they are, indeed, of such frequent occurrence as to attract little attention. Two instances will suffice :—

" SHOP-LIFTING IN BROADMEAD.

" ANN BARNES, *alias* MURPHY, a respectably dressed and modest-looking young woman, but an old offender, was charged with stealing two pieces of riband, collars, and other articles, value £1 10s. 5d., the property of Miss HUTCHINGS. The complainant, in partnership with her sister, keeps a haber-dasher's shop in Broadmead, and from her statement it appeared that on Monday the prisoner, in company with a man and another female, came into her shop at about five o'clock in the afternoon. The man asked to be allowed to look at a necktie, which he pointed out in the window. This was handed to him, and he ultimately purchased it. While he was examining the necktie the prisoner and the other female inquired respecting some riband, and the complainant's sister showed them several descriptions, which they turned over a great many times before they said how much they required, and at length, being pressed as to the quantity they would have, the prisoner said that she only wanted three quarters of a yard with which to trim her child's hat. The sister of the complainant observed that it was a small order, and at length cut off the quantity named from a piece of riband worth 1s. a yard. The pair of females next asked to look at some collars, and accordingly a box containing them was produced. Each of the women took up the collars, threw them down, and turned them about for a considerable time; and, after much consultation, they selected a collar at 7½d., and that concluded their purchases. Whilst they were standing close to the counter before leaving, the complainant's sister perceived the end of a piece of riband hanging from beneath the prisoner's jacket, and she charged her with having the riband concealed, which the other indignantly denied. The sister of the complainant upon this caught hold of the end of the riband and pulled out a quantity, which had been secreted beneath the prisoner's jacket. In addition to the riband two new pocket-handkerchiefs were exposed, which appeared likewise to have been hidden. The complainant, who was in the shop, perceiving the turn which affairs had taken, ran round the counter and caught hold of the accused by the shoulder, and whilst she had her thus, she noticed some collars hanging out of the prisoner's pocket, and she charged her with stealing them. To this accusation the prisoner said that she did not know they were there, and that some one else must have put them in her pocket. The complainant drew out the collars, and in doing so saw that the accused had another piece of riband in her pocket. She then became exceedingly abusive, and whilst the complainant caught firm hold of her in order to detain her, she (the prisoner) pulled her head and hurt it very much. The complainant keeps a young man to assist her in the business, but he happened to be out at the time, and she therefore ran into the shop of Mr. COOPER, shoemaker, next door, to ask him if he would help her in securing the accused. The prisoner seized the opportunity to run away, but in leaving the shop she dropped three silk handkerchiefs. The other two persons who accompanied her to the complainant's shop had already taken themselves off. P.C. 46 stated that he was on duty in the Horsefair, on Monday evening, when he perceived a crowd, and in the midst of the people was the prisoner, who was then without the hat and jacket which she had worn when she robbed the complainant. She darted away from the mob, and ran up a court near; but was at last apprehended, and her hat and jacket found in a water-closet. Mr. WILLIAMS remarked that *the accused had only been home on a ticket-of-leave for a fortnight. She retorted that she had served her full time* for the offence of which she had been convicted. Mr. WILLIAMS stated that she was apprehended some time since for a robbery, and whilst in gaol was confined of a fine child, which, through the kind exertions of Mr. Alderman FORD, had been received into a Roman Catholic establishment, the mother being of that persuasion. The prisoner protested that she was innocent of the present charge; but the Magistrates said a jury would require to be convinced of that. For the present they remanded her, that if possible her companions might be apprehended."—*Bristol Daily Post, May* 20, 1863.

If we mentally follow this wretched woman to her home, and see around her the companions and accomplices of her crimes, we may form some small conception of the baneful influence she must shed around her, and shudder at the life to which her infant must be destined, if not removed from her keeping. All this daring crime, it will be observed, is shortly after the training she has received in a Convict Prison.

Here is another instance extracted from the same paper, of June 17, 1864:—

"ATTEMPTING TO PICK POCKETS AT THE AGRICULTURAL SHOW.

"JOHN and SARAH WILLIAMS, two well-dressed individuals, were charged with being concerned with others in attempting to pick the pockets of several persons in the Agricultural Show, Durdham-down. A detective officer of the metropolitan police force, named COATHUPE, stated that he was on duty at the Agricultural Show, on Durdham-down, on the previous day. At four o'clock he saw the two prisoners there, and, suspecting them, he followed them. He saw the female prisoner place herself beside another female, and put her hand into her pocket. The male prisoner was close to her. He inquired of the lady if she had anything in her pocket, and she said she had not. Afterwards he saw the female prisoner put her hand into another lady's pocket. On inquiring of the latter she said she had only a pocket-handkerchief in her pocket, and that had not been taken. Saw the accused make several other attempts, and the male prisoner was with her the whole of the time. They walked arm in arm. A detective from Liverpool proved *that he had known the female prisoner for the last fourteen years. She was a thief and had been twice sentenced to penal servitude.* Prisoner: It's false. Mr. ALMAN, who appeared for the accused, contended that there was no charge proved against the prisoners, inasmuch as it had not been shown that there was any property on the persons alluded to. The Magistrate considered it a clear case, and sentenced the prisoners to six weeks' hard labour."

It does, indeed, seem useless to sentence this woman again to penal servitude on the existing system, but is it just to society that she should be at large to prey upon it after an imprisonment of only six weeks?

The evil done by these women who have passed some years in the Convict Prison is not limited to their injury to society when at large. They carry their contaminating influence into the County Gaols to which they are committed, and there attempt to incite insubordination, by a repetition of the daring insolence to which they have been accustomed. "I will show you how they carry on at Brixton," said a woman who had been committed to a County Gaol, after being in penal servitude, and she suited the action to the words, endeavouring to create disturbance where there had always been good order and discipline. From numerous official quarters have we heard that the scenes never do occur in well-ordered gaols which the evidence before the Commission proves to be frequent at Brixton. The very same women who have been well-conducted prisoners, and have gained the favourable opinion of their warders, while in County Gaols, have returned to them, after being at Brixton, violent and coarse in the extreme, attempting to enact scenes such as they had witnessed there.

The following is an instance of this from the Chaplain of the Bristol City Gaol, dated July 20, 1864 :—

"In answer to your inquiry, I am very happy to be able to assure you that I have never seen but one specimen of a planned insubordination on the part of female prisoners in this gaol, during the five years that I have been Chaplain. The circumstances were these,—

"Three women—ELLEN S—, EMMA M—, and MARY ANN B—, were tried at the last October Sessions for extensive shoplifting. They had all only just arrived in Bristol, having previously been convicted together for a similar offence in London, and having undergone together a sentence of four years penal servitude, passed upon them in June, 1860. They were thus all three on *ticket-of-leave* when they came to Bristol, 'travelling,' as they termed it. ELLEN S— was 24 years old, and had already had *two* sentences of four years' penal servitude. EMMA M— was also 24 years of age. MARY ANN B— was 44 years old, having been several times convicted, as far as I could ascertain. At the October Sessions in Bristol they were convicted and sentenced, M— to seven years; S— to six years; and B— to five years' penal servitude.

"At the same Sessions, ELIZABETH F—, aged 18, was also sentenced to four years' penal servitude, after two previous convictions.

"These four prisoners were placed near together in our gaol, awaiting the time of their removal to Millbank. After locking-up time, viz., between eight and nine o'clock on the night of the 17th of December, the three prisoners, S—, M—, and F—, began to sing and shout, and call out to one another as loudly as they could. Upon being remonstrated with they were very violent, and threatened to injure the female warders if they endeavoured to restrain them 'from having their fun out.' They proceeded to tear up their bedding, and threw a great portion of it into the yard below through their cell windows. This disturbance amongst them continued all night, and so threatening was their manner that it was considered desirable to send for one of the male officers to put their hands together in handcuffs.

"When I saw them early on the following morning they were still very noisy and irritable, but they received my remonstrances with tolerable civility; and F— and M— promised to desist from their ill-behaviour. S— was still defiant, and declared that nothing should stop her. However, in the afternoon all three were perfectly quiet, and on the following day they seemed really sorry for their outbreak, and thanked me for what I had said to them. They gave no further trouble during the remainder of their stay in Bristol Gaol. "I remain, dear MISS CARPENTER,

"Yours very faithfully,

"CHARLES BRITTAN, Chaplain.

"P.S.—The motive these prisoners assigned for their misconduct was rage at the length of their sentences. S—, it appeared afterwards, had further planned a disturbance in chapel, intending to scramble out of her own pew, and then to let the other women loose, merely for mischief sake.

"At the time F— was convicted, her mother and her sister were also in the gaol."

It is possible that many of the evils which have been enumerated may be referred by those connected with the Convict Prisons to the difficulty experienced by these women in getting employment; — but how can it be expected that the public should be willing to take them into employment, when they know so many instances of their again plunging into crime very soon after the discipline they had gone through; not only so, but when they hear of the "smashings" and numerous punishments even in Fulham Refuge, which is appropriated to the best women. In the last Report of the Convict Prisons the Chaplain states that, "In the month of August, 1863, several of the *first-class women* who had been transferred from Brixton (to Parkhurst Prison) manifested a very insubordinate spirit; they become very riotous." It is true that the Chaplain adds that in a few days they all settled down again, but, nevertheless, the disorder was of so serious a character that he makes it a subject of praise in the male prisoners in the neighbouring premises, that they showed no symptoms of sympathy "during the *great disturbance in August last*, among the female prisoners who had been transferred from Brixton."

None will now probably hesitate to acknowledge that the system adopted in the Female Convict Prisons fails in any reformatory effect. Let us now endeavour to point out the causes of this.

First.—In the penal stage, there should be such firm and steady discipline as would soon remove from the prisoners the temptation to these violent outbreaks; their savage wildness ought to be subdued, and must be so before there can be any reformation. As long as a woman in so wicked a state finds that she can create an excitement in the prison among the officers, gratify her malignant spirit by the destruction of prison property, and enjoy the society of some one as wicked as herself in the dark cells, the outbreaks described to the Commissioners will continually occur. *At whatever cost*, cells should be made separate from each other, where two prisoners should never be together under any circumstances, and where they should not have the power of annoying the officers. An occasional isolated fit of passion easily subdued will then take the place of planned outbreaks. When these have somewhat subsided, which they will do when the prisoners know that they cannot effect by them their wicked intentions, the work of the Matrons and Warders will be much lighter and less wearing to their health and spirits, and they will be more able to throw the necessary spirit and power into their labours. But, to keep up a steady discipline, it is necessary that there should be a sufficient staff of able officials. It must always be remembered that the nature of women being much more susceptible than that of men, female officers are much more easily prostrated, both physically and mentally, than males;—consequently it is of the greatest importance that they should have no more laid on them than they can bear without injury. The staff should be sufficiently large to allow this; the hours of duty should be shortened, with intervals of relaxation beyond the prison walls, and arrangements made for regular and frequent holidays, by which they may retain the tone and vigour of their minds. Experience has proved to the writer that it is only by such means that officials can be retained in a condition adequate to their arduous work. Justice to faithful officers requires this; the public service will receive what is of more value than pecuniary outlay, by granting it to them.

Secondly.—The women should, from the very first, be made clearly to understand that their future prospects depend on themselves alone;—such arrangements should be made as will secure this, and impress on their minds a feeling of strict justice. The Mark System, described as adopted with so much success in the Irish Male Convict Prisons, has an equally valuable effect in those for female Convicts, and would doubtless be equally valuable here. The regret expressed by the Chaplain that the women had less interest in their schooling, because it occupied the time in which they might have earned marks for work, clearly indicates this; if marks were awarded for lessons also, the same stimulus would apply to both. Experience has shown that this Mark System is the most certain and effective means of stimulating to self-exertion, and inspiring a sense of justice. But under no circumstances should women be removed from their separation in the first prison, until they are really prepared for association with others. When the change is made to Brixton, they should always be sent back into separation, if their conduct proves that they are unfit for society. The Brixton Prison might then become as well ordered as the Superintendent desires. The women would thus have no excuse for complaints of favouritism, nor would they endeavour to make their own will, as is now so often the case, decide in what prison they shall be.

Thirdly.—There ought to be full and active employment provided for the women when they have passed through the first and solitary stage; in this, coir-picking and shirt-making may be sufficient occupation, but afterwards, something very different should be arranged. In this respect the female Convicts labour under a great disadvantage, as compared with the inmates of the Public Works Prisons. The men have varied labour in the open air, calculated to exercise their muscles, to occupy their minds, to give them the healthful influences of nature, and to prepare them to gain an honest livelihood. Nothing is wanting for them in this respect. But the women have no suitable occupation thus to occupy them, and prepare them for future life, to give a natural and healthful character to their actual prison existence, which is one dreadful, monotonous routine. Even the very Matron felt it at times difficult to controul the painful irritability which was engendered by the dreary sameness; what, then, must these women experience who have been accustomed to an exciting and unrestrained life. Many sink under it, we have already seen; others, if not absolutely insane, become idiotic in their deportment, or perfectly childish. All efforts to vary their life by the exercise of their ingenuity in making various little articles, are repressed by the prison regulations; their only change is the monotonous walk in the prison yard, where the sight of a flower is hardly ever enjoyed, and the possession of one an irregularity connived at. The eagerness of the women to have the privilege of yielding domestic services to the Matrons, and generally to do any active work, shows what they might become were suitable arrangements made. But without such provision, who can wonder at the amount of ill-feeling displayed by women thrown back for years on their own vicious thoughts.

Fourthly.—The numbers should never be so large in an Associated Prison as to prevent the possibility of a personal influence being exerted by the officers over the Convicts. Until such is the case, no moral tone can pervade the establishment, and until this does exist no improvement can be anticipated. If a right principle is infused at the commencement, and the Convicts have learnt that they are treated with justice and with kindness also, when they find that those set over them are actuated by a desire to benefit them instead of to punish them, they will be ready to receive the good influences which may be exerted over them by the Matron. But while the numbers are so large, without any absolute separation, it is quite impossible that any real influence should be exerted. We have seen in the

Irish Convict Prisons how strong a feeling of individual interest exists between the male officers and the Convicts; women would be still more easily influenced by this. The Prison Matron has shown us how sensitive these poor women are to kindness, and how strong are their yearnings for personal affection; these characteristics of female nature might be made subservient to the highest, purposes if due advantage were taken of them.

Fifthly.—Considerable attention should be paid to the intellectual culture of the women, as a means of raising them from their present degraded condition. That this can be done, if right measures are taken, experience elsewhere has proved; and that it will be an important element in their reformation, no doubt can be entertained. In the existing state of the Female Convict Prisons, it is inevitable that the women should be totally careless of intellectual improvement, but if the alterations here proposed were made, they would gladly welcome the opportunities presented to them.

Sixthly.—The assistance of male warders should be called in as little as possible. The mere fact of the employment of such in controlling females has a most injurious effect. The women become excited and maddened almost to frenzy, and put forth a strength perfectly incredible to those who have not witnessed it. From the Prison Matron's narrative it appears certain, that to produce a scene with the male warders, is the direct object of many of the worst women. Though it may be necessary to retain the possibility of employing the greater strength of men under peculiar and rare circumstances, yet generally, with judicious management, it would be far easier to controul violent women by female than by male officers. The Chaplain of a well-ordered County Gaol for women has stated that there never has been need of employing male officers in the prison, and he believes that it would be most injurious to do so. Yet extremely bad women are brought there; on one occasion one was dragged with difficulty to the gaol by three policemen ; — they were not admitted within the walls, and the woman soon yielded to the firm discipline, and to the moral influence of which she was at once·made sensible.   Cases are very rare in well - managed gaols in which such agency is employed.

We have not here entered into details, because those can best be planned by those who are actually developing the principles.   But in all, there should be that careful study of the effects of treatment which alone can guide to improvement.   No preconceived theories, or mechanical arrangements, or desire of economy, should interfere in the execution of a work, which, in its indirect, as well as its direct results on society, yields in importance to few others.

The grand object to be aimed at, however, is not to make good prisoners, but to send out into the world reformed women.   Even if, by the changes here suggested, these prisons were made models of good conduct, and were pervaded by an excellent influence, no confidence could be felt respecting the future of the Convict women, when withdrawn from the artificial condition and the supporting influences under which they have been living.   The Superintendent of Fulham Refuge laments that some of the most promising prisoners turned out failures.   This must always be expected under any purely prison system ;—no one can be trained for freedom in bondage.   The best prisoners, — those who can completely yield to the discipline enforced, and who can keep quite clear of reports,—such even may be thoroughly bad women.   Some degree of freedom of action alone can test the true character of the individual.   What, then, is to be done for the female Convicts ?

The Intermediate Prisons, which we have so strongly advocated for male Convicts, and which have been so successful in Ireland, cannot, it is evident, be employed for women.   Nor indeed, if it were possible, would they answer the end intended, as they cannot prepare for domestic life, which will be the destination of most of the women. This difficulty was very strongly felt by the Directors of the Irish Convict Prisons at the commencement of their work. We shall do well to follow them in the progress of the experiment they tried, and having learnt how they succeeded, we may perceive the way to similar success in our treatment of English female Convicts.

The condition of the Female Convict Prisons in Ireland was even worse than that of those for males, when the Directors first undertook the charge. The female Convicts who had been transported to Western Australia had been so bad that the Colony absolutely refused to receive any others. The Directors say in their First Report :—

"Our proportion of female criminals is very large, and it is much to be deplored that such is the case, considering the influence for good or evil that women must exercise on the rising generation. This large proportion may, in a great measure, be ascribed to the circumstances of the country, and want of industrial employment. A prison is now erecting at Mountjoy for the reception of 600 female Convicts; which will, we trust, enable us, from its construction, to carry out such penal and reformatory treatment as will induce habits of reflection and amendment, and will also relieve the County Gaols from the great inconvenience to which they are subjected through the reception of Government prisoners. Pending its erection, however, we are endeavouring to ameliorate, if possible, the condition of those confined in Grangegorman and Cork Prisons, which, unfortunately, can only hold a portion of our Convicts. Towards attaining this object, education adapted to the wants of that class, and engendering habits of industry, are the great adjuncts to the religious influence inculcated by their chaplains. With regard to education, the Female Prison Schools, in common with the others, will be placed under the inspection of the National Board of Education. Heretofore instruction has been limited to those under twenty-seven or twenty-eight years : we have given directions that there should be no limit as to age provided there is a disposition to acquire information.

" Respecting industrial training, we have desired that all the Convicts should, in turn, receive instruction in cooking, laundry, sewing, knitting, cleaning, &c., instead of confining a certain number to a particular occupation; although this plan tends to the work not being so well performed, we prefer it on account of the advantages gained by the individuals receiving general instruction.

" It has been a custom to admit Convicts into the prison with their children sometimes at the age of five or six years; we cannot consider such places, with their necessary associations, advantageous for education of the young, and recommend its discontinuance, excepting in cases of children under two years of age."

In their Second Report they show that immediate good results have followed the adoption of their plans. They say :—

" With regard to female Convicts, we have devoted much attention to carry out the plans proposed in our last year's Report concerning them, and have observed a manifest improvement in their general demeanour and conduct. This we attribute in some measure to the efforts made by our teachers to open their minds by education, and to engender habits of self-controul. Many, instead of sullenly brooding over their past life, now look forward with hope to the future. Even women advanced in life, who have spent most of their career in prison, and who at first would not attend school, and seemed incapable of understanding the advantages of education, are now amongst the most assiduous in their classes. A difference in their conduct is already apparent; they are more orderly and obedient to the rules, and make efforts to exercise that self-command, the want of which has so often led them into crime. We trust that under the new arrangements in the prisons, and a system of Refuges and patronage on discharge, which we are now advocating, many Convicts formerly considered irreclaimable, will finish their career as good members of society.

"On the subject of education, Mrs. LIDWELL, the Superintendent of the Cork Depôt, expresses herself as follows,—'I find that the effect of school instruction has been, in most instances, to awaken, as it were, the minds of the prisoners, and improve their natural comprehensions, to make them more docile, more easily brought to see the value of cleanliness and order, and to inspire them with a considerable feeling of self-respect; many of them seem by education to have become better able to understand the folly and wickedness of their previous lives, and experience a strong feeling of repentance. I have observed, too, that as they make progress in school education, their conduct in the prison proportionally improves; and that some who have come from the County Gaols with very turbulent characters, and apparently of very violent dispositions, become, under the influence of education, conformable to discipline.

"Mr. SYNNOTT, the Governor, and Mrs. RAWLINS, the Superintendent of Grangegorman, both dwell on the importance of this training. Prisoners are subjected on conviction to four months separate confinement, as far as the accommodation at our disposal will admit, after which they are removed to the industrial classes, and employed in work suitable to their sex. The system of badges and gratuities work particularly well as applied to the female Convicts, and calls forth good qualities which would otherwise have lain dormant. Mr. SYNNOTT says,—' Classification and the badges have already proved to be of great moment, and are well calculated as auxiliaries in producing happy results, and a further and more healthful development of individual merit.' Mrs. RAWLINS states,— ' The prisoners in the higher classes have exhibited much anxiety to keep their position, while those in the lower endeavour, in many instances, to raise themselves, and have tried to overcome dispositions which bring them into blame.' "

The minds of the Directors were even then awakened to the

importance of devising some plan for the gradual introduction
to liberty of the female Convicts, while at the same time
they should be brought into personal contact of ladies unconnected with the prisons, who would devote to them their
voluntary benevolent effort.    They continue :—

"Great difficulties present themselves in the final disposal of
female Convicts.   A man can obtain employment in various
ways in out-door service, not requiring, in all cases, special
reference to character, and at work which is not open to females
in this country.   A woman, immediately on discharge from
prison, is totally deprived of any honest means of obtaining a
livelihood.   Persons of her own class will object to associate in
labour with her, even if employers were willing to give her
work; and the well-conducted portion of the community object
to receive with their families, or domestic servants, persons so
circumstanced, without a stronger guarantee and proof of their
real and permanent reformation, than would be afforded by a
prison character."

How to effect this was the grand problem to be solved.   The
difficulty is thus concisely set forth by the Directors.   "A
Government Institution would answer for a mere Refuge, *but not
as a medium through which the individual will be established in society;*
for under any rules it will be looked upon as a prison, and on
the discharge of the inmates the same difficulties will be felt as
at present in our Convict Depôts."

To give such confidence to the public in the reformation
of these unhappy women, as to make families willing to
receive them into their domestic circle, it was necessary
that the female Convicts should not only have gone through
some such intermediate stage as the men, but that they
should have had some kind of trial of the sincerity of their
reformation without the restraint of the prison walls, or the
guardianship of government officials.   The plan proposed by the
Directors admirably combined these objects.   "For this reason,"
they continue, "instead of increasing the existing Government

Prison Establishments—a plan attended with much expense, delay, and difficulty—we proposed, in December last, to the Irish Government, that Convicts whose conduct had been exemplary should be drafted into existing private charitable institutions willing to receive them, where the disposition of each inmate would be studied, and the certificate of character founded on that study, together with recommendations, which would then be considered sufficiently satisfactory to obtain her employment; the prisoners, in all such institutions, should be under the general supervision and inspection of the Convict Directors. In order to carry out this plan, a certain number of exemplary Convicts should be selected from the Government Prisons, at periods varying according to circumstances, previous to the time when in the usual course they would become eligible for discharge, and be sent to such private establishments, and not released therefrom under at least three months; and not then unless immediate and proper employment should offer, excepting, however, cases where prisoners become regularly entitled to their discharges, from having completed their sentence, and special cases to be determined on by the Directors and sanctioned by the Executive. Should, however, a prisoner misconduct herself, she would be liable to recommittal to the Convict Depôt, to undergo her original sentence. It is obviously most desirable to enlist public sympathy and interest in any scheme for the employment of discharged female prisoners; this object we consider will be best attained in the manner proposed."

Here we have the first sketch of a plan which has succeeded admirably.

Mrs. LIDWELL, the Lady-Superintendent of the Cork Female Prison, thus alludes to the same need in her Report:—

"A great difficulty under which I labour in the management of the prison, is the want of suitable employment with which to keep the prisoners in constant and useful occupation. The store is now crowded with shirts and socks made by the prisoners, of which I have no means of disposal. The shirts have the convict stripe on them, and therefore could not be sold to any but a Government Prison. Forty women are constantly employed in the laundry, who, in addition to the ordinary work of the prison, also do the washing of the Spike Island Depôt. Then in cooking, cleaning, and assisting in the stores, there is employment for about fifty more; and the rest, then, when not engaged in school, I am forced to employ in sewing and knitting, in which branches, as I have said, there is already a large accumulation of work done.

"I have to state to the Directors that I am greatly impressed with the advantage to the prisoners of transmission to the refuges, previous to being finally discharged. Those who are well-conducted fear to leave the prison directly, as they feel conscious they cannot obtain honest employment, with the disgrace of conviction attaching immediately to them; and it would be very desirable that the same advantage should be granted to the prisoners sentenced to penal servitude. I have now in the prison some of that class, who are extremely well-conducted, and would, I make no doubt, prove excellent members of society.

"I have the honour to be, gentlemen, your obedient servant,

"DELIA J. LIDWELL, *Superintendent.*

"The Directors of Convict Prisons, Castle, Dublin."

On the 20th of September, 1858, the new Female Prison at Mountjoy was entered by Mrs. LIDWELL with 20 Convicts, the remainder followed in drafts in charge of the constabulary, always attended by some of the female officers. The prison was in a very unfinished state, yet Mrs. LIDWELL is able to state in her Report:—

"I am happy to be able to say that, notwithstanding the drawbacks incidental to an unfinished prison, the conduct of the prisoners has been, on the whole, good, and I estimate their progress as decidedly satisfactory. The system of classification, by marks earned through good conduct, industry at work, and attention to school, has produced most excellent results upon, not only the habits, but it is not too much to say, upon the very characters of the prisoners. It is the most powerful incentive to good that in my experience has yet been tried.

"Great benefit, too, has been effected by the change from association to cells, inasmuch as it prevents the communication amongst the prisoners that was not merely idle but most injurious, as the chief burthen of their conversations frequently consisted of allusions to their past ill-spent lives, and these not always of a repentant character. Many of the prisoners themselves acknowledge, and I believe sincerely feel, the benefit they have derived from this change. I have heard them thank God for it, as it weaned them from sin and evil companions. This may, of course, be affected in some cases, but I have reason to believe that it is in general a genuine expression of feeling.

"A great deal has been effected for the moral improvement of the prisoners by the attendance of the Chaplains, and by their exhortations ; much is also due to the religious instruction imparted by the Sisters of Mercy to Roman Catholic , prisoners, and by Protestant lady visitors to those of their own persuasion. My experience, however, leads me to disapprove of visits by the ladies of either creed, paid individually to the prisoners in their cells for the purpose of affording religious instruction. It has a tendency to impress the prisoners with an idea of their own consequence, and incline them to become presuming. They look upon it rather as an opportunity of talking than one of learning, and after a little time there is a decided tendency on the part of the prisoner to seek to become too familiar with her instructress. In time they begin to regard the attendance of their kind teachers rather in the light of visits of condolence than as admonitions to prevent them from a recurrence to their evil ways ; while, therefore, I am most anxious to have the religious instructions continued in the different rooms set apart for the purpose, I am of opinion that it has been for the advantage of the prisoners that the cellular visits have ceased.

"The school has wrought immense benefit : it has given healthy occupation to the prisoners' minds ; and while it has developed an amazing amount of intelligence amongst them, seems to have given a better tone to their mode of thinking. Those who are remarkable for attention at school are seldom to be found amongst the ill-conducted or disorderly. The alteration in the school routine, devised by Captain CROFTON, has effected most important results for the better. By the former system the prisoners went but twice a-week to school, remaining there from three to four hours ; now they are at school every day, though but for one hour. This new arrangement has the effect of keeping the attention of the prisoners more alive ; they learn with a great deal more rapidity, and have got rid of the disposition to waste, in talking, any portion of the time allowed for school. I think it right to state that these arrangements have been zealously and efficiently carried out by the School Matrons.

"I should be glad to have all children over the age of four years (even though the mother's period of imprisonment be not expired) removed to some juvenile reformatory institution. Their presence is injurious to discipline, while they are themselves liable to be contaminated by the bad example and possibly bad teaching of their mothers."

These Refuges were established. It required some moral courage, or rather a strong faith and a devoted love in these ladies, to undertake the custody and care, unaided by means of punishment, of physical restraint, of women who had sprung from "a class so depraved, and hitherto deemed so incorrigible," continues the Report, "as to be absolutely rejected by the colonists of Western Australia, a Colony whose vitality at the present moment depends on an increase of the female sex." But they did undertake the charge, and here are the results up to the close of 1858. *Vide* Fifth Report, p. 18 :—

| | |
|---|---:|
| Entered Refuges from the Convict Prison ... ... ... ... | 232 |
| Still remaining ... ... ... ... ... ... ... ... ... | 88 |
| To be accounted for ... ... ... ... ... ... ... ... | 144 |
| Emigrated ... ... ... ... ... ... ... ... ... ... | 40 |
| Sent to situations, or returned to husbands and families... | 60 |
| Returned to parents and friends (six of these are likely to relapse) ... ... ... ... ... ... ... ... ... ... | 24 |
| Married ... ... ... ... ... ... ... ... ... ... ... | 3 |
| Sent to Magdalen Asylum ... ... ... ... ... ... ... | 5 |
| Sent back to prison to complete their sentences ... ... | 11 |
| Escaped (the only one up to the present time) ... ... ... | 1 |
| | 144 |

Those who were sent back to the Convict Prison from being unprepared for the Refuge cannot be considered as relapses. "Only two," the Directors say, "have been reconvicted and sent to the Convict Prison, and the information with regard to these cases may be considered positive, and therefore satisfactory ;"—positive, on account of the complete system of supervision of the police and registration of offences established by the Irish Government.

"It is a subject of sincere gratification to us to be enabled to report results far exceeding what we ever anticipated. By means of 'individualization,' a large number of women far advanced in criminal courses have been thus returned to the community to lead honest and industrious lives. When at liberty a protecting hand has still been with them; the weak have been protected, the over-confident cautioned."

The success of these Refuges has steadily increased. It is not confined to the individuals enjoying the benefit of them; for the indirect effect of them on the inmates of the prisons is very great. The Convicts not only look forward with hope to obtaining the privilege of entering the Refuges through their own steady efforts, but a feeling is imparted to them all that benevolent interest in their welfare is felt, not only by those whom duty places near them, but beyond the walls, among those who have no connexion with them, save that which the Samaritan had with the wounded and perishing traveller.

These Refuges form also a valuable link to society, for they are accessible to the public, whose cöoperation is so important. Many from England who, in 1861, attended the Social Science Association in Dublin, closely inspected them, and received every desired information as to their working. All were struck with the changed look and manner of the women from what had been noticed in the earlier stages. There was nothing to remind one that they had even been in prison; and they were ready to converse with visitors with full assurance of sympathy respecting their future prospects. In the autumn of the same year, the four Yorkshire Magistrates who went over, closely scrutinized this important part of the Irish Convict System. In their published "Observations," they say :—

"We visited two Refuges in Dublin—a larger one for Roman Catholic women, who are the most numerous, at Golden Bridge; and a smaller one for Protestants in Heytesbury-street. The former is conducted by Sisters of Mercy, some of whom were ladies of high social position. * * * The women are generally found exhibiting the most willing obedience to discipline, and among them misconduct of any kind is extremely rare. Considering that many of them are women who have been convicted over and over again, the fact speaks volumes for the salutary effect of the training they have previously undergone in prison. No difficulty was said to be found in procuring situations for them, which shows how well the Refuge answers the purpose for which it was intended. The Protestant Refuge is under the charge of a Matron, superintended by a committee of lady visitors. We were much struck by the apparent industry displayed in the washhouse and laundry. * * * That, under these circumstances, women—and those women convicts—should be found to work as hard for the benefit of the institution where they are detained, as they would for themselves out of doors, appears to us a result of very high import, in a moral as well as in a financial point of view. It shows that an influence *yet unknown on this side the channel* has been brought to bear on the correction of that fault which is the special characteristic of the criminal class, viz., dislike of hard work."

To this may be added the personal testimony of the writer, as given in "Once a Week," June 7, 1862.

"IRISH CONVICT SYSTEM.

FEMALE PRISONS.

No. IV.

"It is always a painful sight to see degraded women; but, on our recent visit to Dublin, we determined at once to encounter it, and our first visit in the capital of our Sister Isle was to the Mountjoy Female Convict Prison.

"It was the Sabbath, and it was an appropriate employment of the day consecrated to Him who came to seek and to save the lost, to worship with the prisoners. There are three distinct places of worship in Mountjoy Prison. The largest is for the Roman Catholics, adapted to the performance of the rites of their religion. A very plain, simple apartment is occupied by those attending the ministry of the Presbyterians, and a large chapel is simply arranged for worship, conducted according to the custom of the Church of England.

"In many prisons the Convicts are arranged at public worship each in a separate cell or partition, so as to see and be seen by the minister only,—as if even in the presence of our Heavenly Father, and engaged in His worship, the prison idea must still pervade the service, and everything social be banished. In other gaols, where there is not this separation, but all worship God together, as an absolute separation between the two sexes is necessary, the women are out of sight in a gallery. Thus have we worshipped under the ministry of the late lamented Rev. JOHN CLAY, whose services in the Preston Gaol were most impressive, and who carried with him to the Throne of Grace the hearts of all his hearers. Here, however, the women were alone in the chapel with the clergyman and female officers, without any apparent formality or restraint. A painful history might be read on many of the countenances before us;—vice dreadfully disfigures the features of a woman, and no one could have been here without having gone through a long course of crime. But all were joining with apparent devotion and interest, every one who could do so following the service in the prayer-books; the earnest practical exhortations, which were addressed to them in the sermon, were received apparently with self-application and intelligent interest.

"The service concluded, the Lady-Superintendent of the whole prison (who had not been present, being a Roman Catholic), showed us the general arrangements of the establishment, though of course we were obliged to defer our observation of the ordinary working of it to a week day. One feature of it struck us particularly. In England the difficulties seem insuperable to the admission into gaols, workhouses, and even infirmaries, of benevolent lady visitors of different religious denominations. In Ireland, where parties run high, we anticipated still greater difficulties; yet here—in this Convict Prison—the grand problem is solved, for not only are the female officers of different religious denominations all working harmoniously together—but Catholic, Church of England, and Presbyterian ladies all visit the prisoners, with excellent effect, and no interference with each other interrupts the harmony of the establishment. All there are engaged in one great work, and sympathise with each other in it; judicious regulations being laid down, which no one attempts to interfere with. Each prisoner on entrance states her religious profession, and is expected to keep to it; and the ladies of each denomination visit only those of the same religion: they meet them in class, and, as occasion presents itself, gain such knowledge of them as enables the visitors to lend a helping hand to the women when discharged. A good influence is thus obtained: there is no proselytism; the motives of the ladies cannot be questioned by the prisoners— they come only to fulfil Christian duty; and these wretched women, who are cut off from society through their own crimes, here can feel that there are those who care for their souls, and who are desirous of giving them Christian sympathy. None but those who personally know it, can comprehend the deep import of the words, 'I was in prison and ye visited me.'

"We had been told to be sure to see the Infant School in

the gaol! We were startled and shocked at the bare idea. Are there even infants round whom the prison walls are closed? Had not our Reformatory and Industrial Schools been successful in preserving young children from such an unnatural condition? And then we remembered a dreadful sight which we had once witnessed. In an Associated Gaol, we had been taken to a large room appropriated to nursing mothers with their infants! The room was full, and the spectacle awful! The faces of those mothers can never be forgotten, for they exhibited every species of hideous vice and degradation. And these were to give the first impressions to the young immortal beings who were unhappily their children, and who were imbibing from them the tainted streams of life. And not only from its own mother would each child derive its early impressions,—her face might perchance be softened by a smile of maternal love,—but all around there were other wicked mothers, whose looks and voices would be bad and even fiendlike at times: and the poor little child would catch its first notions of life from the worst specimens of humanity. A convict mother must entail misery on her offspring, and we found that in Mountjoy Prison an attempt was being made to mitigate the evil. All women are by law allowed to have with them very young children in the prison; if the sentence is long, the poor child may have dreary years to spend in this abode;—for what mercy would it be to it to send it forth into the world uncared for, unprovided for? Hence this Infant School, to which we were now conducted. It was not indeed as cheerful and happy a looking place as we should like to see young children in;—we could not but notice strong thick walls outside the school-room, which spoke clearly to us the dreadful word 'prison.' But the officials told us that these poor little things were not conscious of their peculiar position, and did not consider that they were in gaol, but in 'Mrs. LIDWELL's workhouse,' as they called it. They looked cheerful, happy, healthy, and clean, in their Sunday pinafores; and their teacher seemed fond of them, and so did the worthy

Superintendent, Mrs. LIDWELL; and they certainly looked better and more cared for than did the poor children we afterwards saw in one of the Dublin workhouses. We were told, and readily believed it, that it produced an excellent effect on the mothers, who were unhappily there as Convicts, to know that their children were within reach, and that if their conduct was good they would be allowed the Sabbath privilege of having their young ones under their own care for a time;—perhaps there they first began to think of their solemn responsibilities as mothers. Under existing circumstances, this Infant School in a Convict Prison is good and beneficial,—the best thing that can be done for the child : but surely it ought not to be so. Surely no young child should enter on life's training under such a stigma as having been bred in a gaol!—surely society should take care that its young members should be properly educated somewhere, when the parent is removed by the arm of the law;—surely a workhouse school should be a more appropriate and happy home than one in a gaol. It is not so at present! May it be so ere long!

"We next visited Mountjoy on a week day. This prison contains both the first and second stages of the female Convicts. In consideration of the greater susceptibility of women, the time of entire separation is four months instead of eight, conditional of course on good conduct and industry; if these are not satisfactory, the time is extended. The general arrangements and system are similar to those of the men, and through all is there the same individual watchfulness and care, combined with strict regulations; a sense of justice blending with all in the mind of the prisoners. We visited the second stage, the associated work-room, where a large number of women were engaged in needlework, under superintendence. It was well for them to have this occupation to draw off their thoughts from themselves. One hour in every day they receive a lesson in the schoolroom. There we found intelligent schoolmistresses engaged closely, each with a class

which she received in rotation.  It was a strange sight to
see elderly women in spectacles standing in class, spelling
out the Irish lesson books, which are so familiar to our
children.  But we were much astonished at the proficiency
which some, even of these, had made.  We know the extreme
difficulty which is experienced by young persons, who have
been early neglected, in overcoming the mysterious combinations of letters into syllables, and the connection between these
forms and the corresponding sounds.  It was, therefore, a
remarkable and significant fact, that only one hour a-day,
well and actively employed with real goodwill to learn, should
have produced such results.  The women greatly appreciate
this hour's instruction; faculties before dormant are excited
and exercised; and thoughts are opened to them which excite
new ideas and aspirations.  Some of the classes had attained
considerable proficiency, and their teachers were evidently proud
of them.  More advanced stages of the women were engaged
in various kinds of house-work and cooking, and a number
in washing and ironing.  These occupations seemed more
calculated than the needlework to rouse their energies in a
right direction, and to draw off their thoughts from themselves;
consequently their countenances look better, and indeed as the
stages advanced it was easy to trace an improvement in expression.  Hard work is a most important element of training,
and a great aid in subduing bad passions.  One woman, of
stalwart appearance, was working with great zeal at a washing-
machine: she had been guilty of manslaughter!  One shuddered
to think of what she must have been capable when her passions
were wild and unregulated.  But though the faces of many
were bad, yet we could perceive, as we advanced, a great
softening of expression, and in none did we observe that sullen,
dogged, and rebellious look, which indicates that the governed
and the governing party are not working harmoniously.  The
most advanced at Mountjoy are placed in a 'preparatory class.'

  "Now the establishment of an 'intermediate stage' for women,

corresponding to the Lusk and Smithfield for men, was long
a difficult and perplexing problem. Yet it was necessary to
solve it. Why are the public unwilling to take into their
employment persons who have come straight from prison,
however good those prisons may be? Simply because they
do not believe in the reformation of the prisoners, and with
justice; for, where the will is absolutely enthralled, it is impossible to tell how an individual will act when the restraint
is removed. It is one of the grand secrets of the success of
the Irish Convict Prisons, which is acknowledged by all who
personally study the subject, that this principle is understoood
and acted on. But the women could not with safety be allowed
the same liberty as the men. Not only would the difference in
character to which we have alluded prevent this, but the
dangers of the streets to females, especially of this class, would
render such liberty most unsuitable. Under these perplexities,
the Directors availed themselves of the voluntary zeal and
devotion which offered to take charge of the women who should
be considered worthy of the privilege of an intermediate stage.
The nuns of Golden Bridge, who had already considerable experience in the care of a Penitentiary, undertook the charge of
such Catholic Convict women as should be sent to them. They
are there still under their sentence of detention, and subject,
as at Lusk and Smithfield, to be sent back to Mountjoy should
their conduct prove unsatisfactory, and they are under the constant inspection of the Directors; but, in other respects, they are
under the management of the nuns. There we saw them, and
remarked a most favourable change in their appearance and
deportment; indeed had we not been aware that they were
Convicts, we should not have imagined it from anything we
observed. The women were chiefly engaged in laundry-work,
cheerfully and actively. We conversed with several of them,
and found them all anxious to lead a new life, and preparing for
it. Golden Bridge has large grounds connected with it, which

afford to the women the salutary influences of out-door occupation; there are the garden and potato-ground to be cultivated, and the pigs and poultry to be attended to; the care of animals is generally beneficial, and intercourse with nature always is so. These, combined with the religious and moral influences exercised by the nuns, and their Christian interest in them, afford an excellent preparation for future life. There is also a Protestant institution of a similar kind in Heytesbury-street, superintended by ladies; the number here is small, but the same object is in view; and here, as at Golden Bridge, the ladies who undertake the charge keep a friendly watchfulness over the women when they go out into the world. The plan has answered admirably. The women fully appreciate the kindness which is shown them, and the efforts which are made for their good, and they go forth again to the world in a very different position from what they could have done from any prison. The public, too, place confidence in the characters which they receive from the ladies who have the management of these institutions, and know to what influences they have been subjected. Hence they are not unwilling to receive these women into domestic service; and many are satisfactorily placed out, while others emigrate. This plan has not been in operation as long as the Intermediate Prison for men, but hitherto it has answered admirably and gives good promise. The same principle is in operation here as at Lusk, and produces the same results.

"'Individualisation,' says Captain CROFTON,* 'is the ruling principle in these establishments. The result of the self-discipline effected by the attainment of marks is here to be tested before the liberation of the Convict. The training is special, and the position of the Convict made as natural as possible; no more restraint being exercised than would be necessary to maintain order in any well regulated establishment. *The Convict*

* *Vide* "A Brief Description of the Irish Convict System." By Captain W. CROFTON. Printed and published by E. FAITHFUL & Co., Victoria Press.

*is cöoperating in his own amendment.'* Most satisfactory is it that Captain CROFTON has been able to add (p. 21): 'After nearly six years' experience, it has been found that the public are satisfied with the tests afforded by the modification of prison life evinced in these Refuges, and are well disposed to cöoperate with the managers and sisterhoods in their kind and charitable work.'"

Of the effect of these Refuges, and of the conduct of the women in them, a sufficient proof is given in the following table, contained in the Appendix to the Report of the Commissioners, p. 204 :—

SUPPLEMENTAL RETURN of the NUMBER of FEMALE CONVICTS released under ORDERS of LICENSE from the Year 1856 to the Year 1862 inclusive, showing the Number returned to the Convict Prisons, either by having had their License revoked for trifling Offences, or being sentenced to Penal Servitude or Transportation.

| Years. | Number Licensed. | Total Number of Female Convicts who have been re-convicted or Licenses revoked from 1856 to 1861 inclusive, detailed in previous Return, 2, furnished on 2nd January, 1863. | | Number of Female Convicts who have been re-convicted or Licenses revoked in 1862. | | Total revoked to 31st Dec., 1862. | Total re-convicted to 31st December, 1862. | Grand Total. | Per-centage. | |
|---|---|---|---|---|---|---|---|---|---|---|
| | | Revoked. | Re-convicted. | Revoked. | Re-convicted. | | | | Revoked. | Re-convicted.† |
| 1856 | 51 | 1 | — | — | — | 1 | — | 1 | 2 | |
| 1857 | 46 | 2 | 3 | — | — | 2 | 3 | 5 | 4.3 | 6.5 |
| 1858 | 113 | 8 | — | — | — | 8 | — | 8 | 7 | — |
| 1859 | 100 | 2 | 1 | — | — | 2 | 1 | 3 | 2 | 1 |
| 1860 | 75 | 4 | — | — | — | 4 | — | 4 | 5.3 | — |
| 1861 | 68 | 2 | — | 6 | — | 8 | — | 8 | 11.7 | — |
| 1862 | 57 | — | — | 1 | — | 1 | — | 1 | 1.7 | — |
| | 510 | 19 | 4 | 7 | — | 26* | 4 | 30 | 5 | ·8 |

\* Of this number 21 have had their licenses revoked for misconduct in the Refuges.

† Cases in which the Convict has been re-convicted, and the license also revoked, are included under the former head.

(Signed)     J. S. WHITTY,

February 11, 1863.           Director of Convict Prisons.

We must also copy from the same source (Report of Commissioners, p. 240) the following important letter:—

"LETTER FROM MISS KIRWAN AS TO THE REFUGES FOR FEMALE CONVICTS IN IRELAND.

"ST. VINCENT'S REFORMATORY,
"GOLDEN BRIDGE, DUBLIN, *April* 2, 1863.

"SIR,—Having heard that evidence has been received by the Royal Commission to the effect that I was of opinion that we laboured under a great disadvantage in the management of female convicts in Ireland, in consequence of their having to look forward to detention in a refuge instead of absolute liberty, and having been asked to give my opinion on this point, as well as to explain our general management, I beg to offer the following remarks. I have never found the convicts discontented either here or at Mountjoy Prison (which we visit three times a week) in consequence of not being discharged at the same period of their sentence as the men are sent on license; nor have I ever heard the authorities at the prison complain of disorder arising there because the women have to look forward to the refuges, as they have been made to understand the object for which the refuge was established, and they are fully aware that their future position in life depends on the habits and character they acquire here. Those we receive under long sentences are discharged by an extension of license at the same period of their sentences as the men (under the same sentence) are discharged from the Intermediate Prisons; but those who have been sentenced to three or four years penal servitude have to be retained longer in the refuge than the men in an Intermediate Prison, for the following reasons:—

"1st. It is generally admitted that it is more difficult to reform a woman than a man, who has the additional check of supervision when liberated.

"2ndly. The public would have no confidence in their reformation unless they spent a considerable time under our care in comparative liberty and in offices of trust. Men are more frequently employed at outdoor work, whereas women are generally engaged in household duties, often with valuable property under their charge, therefore they require more time for training and testing them.

"3rdly. The females of the criminal class are essentially idle and ignorant to helplessness, consequently it takes time to enable them to conquer their former habits, and to acquire new ones; heart, head, and hands have to be taught, or rather first untaught, and then retaught. It is not enough to let them see the evils of a life of crime, but we must teach them how to earn their bread honestly in future, and put them in the way of doing so.

"The women are sent here from the Government Prison at the same period of their sentences as the male prisoners become eligible to be transferred to an Intermediate Prison, and they are selected in the same manner, with a few exceptions, since the short sentences came into use.

"For instance, women advanced in life, who have been convicted, in some cases a hundred or a hundred and fifty times, and who only become eligible by marks for the refuge near the close of a three years' sentence,—these we do not take, as humanly speaking we could not expect to find, after long habits of crime, a permanent improvement to take place in a few months, and feeling doubtful of their reformation we could not recommend them to the employment of our honest neighbours; therefore no good could be effected.

"This will bring before you the great disadvantage we have been labouring under since the long sentences of transportation were changed for the present short sentences of penal servitude. As well as I can observe, the prospect of a short sentence does not deter an habitual offender from a life of crime; but, on the contrary, the regular life in prison, rest, and good medical care are sometimes an advantage to her. She does not devote herself to self-improvement and exert herself to gain her marks, as she knows she must soon be discharged, when she returns to her old habits with renewed vigour; whereas when a woman is sentenced to seven years' penal servitude, no matter what her antecedents may have been, she gets subdued, and begins to 'Lay down her mind to be good' (as they usually say) being fully aware that the term of her imprisonment, within certain limits, entirely depends on her conduct, and she sees it is her interest to earn her marks. She is removed to the refuge at the appointed time, where she is taught all the duties of a domestic and farm servant, and when she acquires habits of industry, self-controul, and self-respect, she is provided with suitable employment and perseveres in a good life for the future.

"I am, &c.,

"(Signed)   Sister Mary Magdalen Kirwan.

"To the Secretary to the
  "Penal Servitude Acts Commission."

In Ireland, the public has fully coöperated in the work undertaken by the managers of the Refuges, in restoring these women to society. Increased experience only confirms the truth of the principle on which they are founded. The ladies who take an interest in these Refuges have full opportunity of judging of the competency of the women, and the sincerity of their reformation; they are therefore in a position to recommend them, and the public place confidence in their recommendation. The women also find themselves still, on their actual discharge, under the friendly surveillance of those who have already proved their true interest in them, by their earnest efforts for their reformation.

A similar system would surely be very beneficial in our own country. It is true that in Ireland peculiar facilities existed for commencing the work for the Convict women, through the instrumentality of ladies in monastic institutions who rejoice to devote themselves to it, and who were aided and encouraged by their own religious organizations throughout the country. But Protestant ladies were also soon found equally zealous in the work, and who carried it on equally well. There are in England many benevolent institutions supported by the benevolent zeal of ladies; surely a sufficient number would be found to engage in the work, and enter into a generous rivalry with the Sister Isle, in seeking to save these lost ones. The Christian women of England are those who must exert themselves to save their fellow women, the female Convicts.

It is no easy or amateur work which we call on them to undertake; but it is one which is worth much toil,—much personal sacrifice,—much devotion of heart and soul and strength; and those who do so devote themselves to it will feel that they have not laboured in vain, if they are made the blessed instruments of saving only a few women, and enabling them to lead those around them in the ways of virtue, instead of luring them on to vice.

What then do we propose?

We must endeavour to awaken those who have the controul of the Female Convict Prisons to the evils which are now existing in them, and urge their being placed on an entirely different system, so that each woman may feel that she is working onward in coöperation with her officers towards her own amendment. It is essential that this should be done before any hope can be entertained that voluntary effort will be effectual, whether made through the instrumentality of Prisoners' Aid Societies, Patronage Societies, as on the Continent, or Refuges, as in Ireland. To attempt to work with women such as we know that many of the inmates of the Convict Prisons are at present, would be followed by almost certain failure, discourage future attempts, and infuse disbelief of the principles of voluntary benevolent effort in Intermediate Establishments. It is unnecessary here to recapitulate what changes ought to be made in our Female Convict Prisons, to insure for them any reformatory influence. We have but to work our existing prisons on the principles which have been proved true in Ireland. They are founded on the grand and universal laws of human nature, which must therefore be adapted to England as well as to our sister isle.

The Convict Prisons having been placed on a right basis, authority must be obtained from the Secretary of State for the transmission of prisoners from the Convict Prisons to the voluntary Refuges, under license, with an allowance for their maintenance, as in the Irish Refuges. Such authority from the Government is absolutely necessary. Without it any persons are, of course, competent to establish Refuges for the reception of discharged prisoners, when quite at liberty, but there would then be no hold over them; and it is certain, from past experience, that such efforts would be of little avail to help in the reformation of female Convicts; the bad would not wish to submit to such further restraint, and it is probable that only a few, even of the well-disposed, would be willing to stay so long as to prepare them to do well at liberty. The detention under license, which would be strictly revoked for misconduct, is essential to the success of such a plan. How complete that may be, will, of course, depend on the previous training of the women in the Convict Prisons, and on the manner in which the Refuges themselves are conducted. But with an earnest desire to do good to those unhappy women, and with the adoption of judicious means, there need be no serious doubt that such Refuges will prove an inestimable boon conferred on the female Convicts of our country, and, through them, on society.

It is unnecessary here to enter into any details respecting the management of Refuges. These can best be ascertained by those who propose to establish them, from direct communication with ladies who have already gained experience in conducting similar institutions. The work itself will also instruct those who are humbly anxious to learn how to do it, that they may be the instruments of saving their fellow-creatures.

We trust that the time is not far distant when the needful preparatory steps having been taken by the Government, the women of England and Scotland will come forward to put their hands to this great work, and never turn back, until, with God's blessing, it is accomplished.

# CHAPTER V.

## IMPROVEMENTS.

THE position at present occupied by the criminal portion of our community must arouse the anxiety and excite the serious consideration of all who direct their attention to it,—while it inspires a painful feeling of insecurity in society, and exposes the unwary and unprotected to frequent injury of property, and even of life.

It is impossible, in our country, to defend ourselves against the attacks of those who make crime their profession. If we live in regions infested by brigands, and where the Government is unsettled, we anticipate exposure to danger and act accordingly; we dare not go out unarmed and undefended against the ruffians whose very garb indicates their calling, whose demeanour at once points them out as disturbers of the public peace. But here, in civilised England, in the central part of that Empire, which assumes the position of the most free, the most enlightened, and the best governed in the world, peaceable citizens are not able to pursue their honest callings, or go about their lawful avocations in peace and safety,—they are perplexed by the extraordinary inconsistencies which the most dull must perceive, in the laws of their country or in the administration of them,—they find by painful experience that instead of living under a powerful government, capable of protecting them against enemies both external and internal, their rulers even stand aghast in utter perplexity when assailed

by the foes of their own household,—the Convicts whom they
had so luxuriously fed, carefully nurtured, magnificently lodged,
and from whom they thought they might reasonably expect, at
least, a grateful return in good conduct and quiet demeanour.

These enemies who are the plague and disgrace of our land
are not those against whom we can easily defend ourselves,
because they do not appear among us with any outward indications by which we can at once discriminate them. The ordinary
inmates of our provincial gaols come from our midst, and return
again to their place in society, whatever it may be, not further
contaminated by their abode there, unless it be their ill fortune
to be incarcerated in a prison where separate confinement has
not yet been adopted. They usually spring from a class of
persons with whom respectable labouring persons cautiously
avoid any contact, their external appearance clearly indicates
them, and their low dissolute lives at once point them out as
persons not to be trusted. Those who are accidental offenders,
who have been " overtaken in a fault," usually return to their
own connections, and are absorbed again into society in the same
position from whence they left their homes, or, at any rate,
provision is made for their re-establishing themselves elsewhere.
But the case is very different with those who are discharged
from the Government Convict Prisons. They cannot be easily
distinguished from the general mass of the people. The experienced and penetrating may indeed occasionally detect them,
by observing the strange contrast of their good clothing, and
excellent physical condition, with a bearing evidently not that
of a hard-working man, and may feel suspicious of a peculiar
cut of the hair, and a kind of prison gait. But these indications soon wear off;—and when we see besides us in a shop
a respectable-looking young woman, we little suspect that she
is one of a gang of accomplished thieves who have learnt
their art in the Government establishments, and that she will
shortly hand the contents of our pockets to her friends in
the street. The auditor at an instructive lecture, at a club

for working-men, his mind absorbed in scientific details, little anticipates leaving the lecture-hall without his purse, which has been abstracted by one whom he supposed to be a fellow listener, but who was really a professional pickpocket. Nor should the congregation, retiring from their worship, have to learn, as they do, that they cannot safely lay upon the plate of offerings a portion of the gold and silver they carry with them, without the remainder being artfully abstracted by some one who had seemed to be a fellow worshipper! It is impossible to defend oneself against such insidious marauders, except by living in a state of perpetual suspicion and most inconvenient caution. No ordinary care can protect respectable houses, supposed to contain property, from the attacks of burglars, and from the destruction of legal documents more valuable than gold. And when, in all these cases, the culprit is brought to justice, then we hear, to our surprise, of "a genteel-looking young man," of "a young woman of respectable appearance and pleasing demeanour," but eventually discover either that they have been long pursuing a course of undetected vice, or that they have not long returned from a Convict Prison.

Such is the insecurity of our country,—such the immunity of crime,—such the result of our present treatment of it.

No one can have thoughtfully read the facts brought forward in the first volume of this work, or studied the bearing of the extracts from the evidence laid before the Royal Commission, without feeling painfully impressed with the nature of the crime existing in our country, and with the worse than uselessness of the method adopted of dealing with it. It is also very alarming to know that we cannot by any possible means gain a knowledge of the numbers or strength of our enemy, or even make an approximation to the real amount of crime in the country. The published statistics give only the numbers of apprehensions, of commitments, and of convictions. They may show the numbers of imprisonments which have taken place during the year, but do not give the very slightest knowledge of the number of *persons* who have been summarily convicted of crime. In these, and the returns of convictions, some persons may have been counted several times over, having incurred several punishments. It is perfectly impossible to ascertain this by the existing machinery; because, even if the number of reconvictions in a year of one individual can be ascertained in one county or district, it is impossible to prove that the same person may not have been convicted in several other counties or districts during the year. This will be easily understood by referring to the histories given by the pickpockets under sentence of transportation in Preston Gaol; those persons took care to move from one locality to another, where their previous criminal history would not be known. Less possible is it to form the slightest conception from the statistics how many of the offenders have been convicted year after year, and how many are newly enlisted in the ranks of crime during the year. Again, the number of apprehensions during the year throughout the country are even less reliable as indications of the actual number of offenders against the law, but they do very clearly indicate some approximation to the actual amount of deeds committed which are injurious to the well-being of society. In a large number of the instances in which persons are brought before the magistrates, the individual is acquitted from insufficient evidence, or the complainant does not appear, or the offender is "cautioned and discharged." Yet it is probable that in no cases, except those simply involving breach of police or municipal regulations, is any one brought before the magistrates without being a suspicious character, or without having been guilty of some serious offence, if not of this identical one. The number of commitments cannot give any clue to the number of ill-disposed persons or habitual offenders in any place, but they certainly indicate whether or not there is a large amount of crime there. It is of great importance that we should know both this, the peculiar nature of crime in each district, and the real number of offenders in the country, with the number of their reconvictions, if we may hope for any effectual repression of crime.

The improvements we would suggest in this chapter are, first those directly connected with our Convict Prisons, and next those which appear desirable, with a view to the general repression and diminution of crime in the country, and the consequent protection of society.

The evidence brought before the Royal Commission led them to pass various very important resolutions relative to the actual state of Convict treatment. After analyzing the criminal statistics, they say (par. 30, 31) :—

* * "But, allowing for the influence of other causes, from the evidence we have received there seems reason to believe that the recent increase of offences is at least partly attributable to defects in the system of punishment now in force, and to the fact that there has been an accumulation of discharged convicts at home, owing to the comparatively small number sent to a penal colony since 1853.

"Penal servitude, under the present system, appears not to be sufficiently dreaded, either by those who have undergone it, or by the criminal classes in general. That many of the former are not effectually deterred from pursuing a course of crime by the fear of incurring this punishment again, is shown by the fact that a large per centage of those discharged from convict prisons are known to be reconvicted, while many more probably are so, but escape detection from the absence of any effectual means of ascertaining the previous history of those convicted of offences : and the accounts given of penal servitude by discharged convicts, and the fact that they generally come back so soon to their former haunts, tend to prevent it from being regarded with fear by their associates. It appears, indeed, that in some (though doubtless very exceptional) cases, crimes have even been committed for the sole purpose of obtaining the advantages which the offenders have supposed a sentence of penal servitude to confer."

It appears surprising that they should report in the next paragraph that this "want of sufficient efficacy in the present system of punishment, does not arise from any error in its principles, or from its general arrangements being injudicious ;" still, other parts of their Report fully endorse the system adopted in Ireland, in the particular points on which it differs from the English Convict System. Thus, the general principle is adopted by the Commissioners that Convicts should *earn* the remission of part of their sentences by their own industry and efforts, which are to be registered by marks. They say (par. 38):—

* * "The experience, both of this and of other countries, has demonstrated that it is impossible to compel convicts to work hard by mere coercion, the attempt to do so having invariably failed, while it has produced a brutalizing effect on their minds, and increased their previous aversion to labour. On this ground the late Captain MACONOCHIE, many years ago, recommended that the punishment to be inflicted upon criminals should be measured not by time, but by the amount of labour they should be compelled to perform before regaining their freedom, and he devised an ingenious mode of recording their daily industry by marks, for the purpose of determining when they should have a right to their discharge. This proposal met with so much approval from the Government of the day, that Captain MACONOCHIE was sent to Norfolk Island for the purpose of trying the system he had recommended in the management of the convicts detained there. The experiment did not succeed, for reasons which were sufficiently obvious, but into which we need not now enter. The failure, however, did not afford any reason for condemning the principle on which the scheme was founded, and, in fact, that principle has been adopted, to a greater or less extent, in all the various schemes of penal discipline which have been tried in the last twenty-five years. The result has been to establish the conclusion, that the hope of earning some remission of their punishment is the most powerful incentive to good conduct and industry, which can be brought to act upon the minds of prisoners."

The difference between this principle and that in practice in the English prisons is clearly stated in the next paragraph :—

* * "Referring to the account we have already given of the regulations in question, we have to observe, that those now in force in England seem to us to be needlessly complicated, and to have the fault, *that they do not hold out to convicts a partial remission of their punishment as a reward to be earned by good conduct and industry, but assume that this remission will be granted unless more or less of the proffered advantage should be forfeited as a penalty, in consequence of the convicts having failed to deserve it.* The distinction between this system, and that of making whatever remission of punishment is allowed to a convict something which he must earn, we consider to be one of great importance. We also think it an objection to these regulations, that they allow a part of the time which a convict has been ordered to lose for misconduct to be afterwards restored to him. The Irish rules requiring convicts to gain a certain number of marks in order to establish a claim to a remission of punishment, make a nearer approach to what we think would be the best system."

Closely connected with this principle is the Mark System, and the importance of letting the remission of time be *earned* by the Convict's own exertions.    On this subject they thus speak in par.   38 :—

" Such is the opinion unanimously expressed by all who have had the opportunity of observing its effect, while employed in the mangement of convicts, whether at home or in the colonies.   Their opinion is confirmed by the experience gained in carrying into effect the Act of 1853, under which convicts were made to serve the full time for which they were sentenced. Under this system the convicts were found to be more sulky, more difficult to manage, and much less industrious, than under the opposite one.   Attempts were made to provide a substitute for the hope of obtaining an earlier release, by granting various other advantages to prisoners as a reward for good conduct, but none of the indulgences which were granted to them with this view, proved to have nearly so powerful an effect upon their minds as the prospect of obtaining an abridgment of their punishment."*

The Commissioners highly approved the more penal character

---

* " In the Report on Convict Prisons, by Sir JOSHUA JEBB, lately presented to Parliament, the effect of the refusal of all remission of punishment to convicts under the Act of 1853 is thus described (p. 18):—

" ' The consequence was, that as hope diminished a dogged and discontented submission to discipline arose among the convicts, very different from the cheerful and ready obedience of former times, and the example of those who were suffering under disappointment spreading to others who had no such grievance to complain of, created great difficulties.

" ' Successive stages of discipline, each having some amelioration, were substituted for the remission of sentence ; but these were insufficient to re-establish the good feeling which had prevailed ; and until every man sentenced between 1853 and 1857 (altogether about 10,000) were disposed of, the state of the Convict Prisons was much less satisfactory than previously, or than it is at present.'

" And the following passage is quoted from a memorandum by Captain WHITTY, dated 13th July, 1853 :—

" ' The question of dealing on public work with the convicts under sentence of penal servitude is becoming a very serious one, and presses for immediate consideration and settlement.

" ' If their sentence of penal servitude is to be considered as one of actual imprisonment for the whole period awarded, their position becomes entirely different from that of men under sentence of transportation with whom they are associated ; the main inducement to good conduct and industry, which has hitherto operated so beneficially in the management of the latter, will be wanting, and it is to be apprehended that the penal servitude men will become generally reckless and indifferent, and that the incorrigible class, which has been almost extinguished under the system of the last few years, will comprise a very large proportion of the whole number.

" ' Hitherto the moral influence of the system in force, by which reward for good conduct and improvement has been combined with due punishment for the reverse, has enabled the prison authorities to employ the convicts on the public works with confidence and good effect ; but if the fear of punishment alone is to be the motive to obedience and exertion in the mind of the convicts so employed, an entirely new system of guarding and coercing the prisoners will become necessary, and it is much to be apprehended that any such system, though necessarily expensive in its machinery, would be unprofitable in all its results.'"

given to the first stage of penal servitude. They find that the period of separate confinement has been so much diminished from want of suitable premises, as to make the average time of this, which is the real period of punishment, on an average only seven months and twenty days. With respect to this they say (par. 48) :—

\* \* " Arrangements ought at once to be made for remedying this. We are of opinion that convicts ought to be kept in separate confinement for the full period of nine months, except in the case of prisoners who are found unable to undergo it so long without serious injury to their bodily or mental health. No considerations of expense, whether connected with the necessity for additional buildings, or with the loss of the labour of the convicts, ought to be allowed to prevent this stage of punishment from being continued for the time prescribed by the regulations. We think, too, that though separate confinement, even under the present system, is, as has been said, extremely distasteful to convicts, this wholesome effect on their minds might be increased. It has been already mentioned that in Ireland the diet is lower during the first four months; and that no work is given to the prisoners for the first three months, except such as is of a simple and monotonous character, in which they require little or no instruction. This practice has been adopted because it has been found that by far the greater number of convicts have no knowledge of any trade, and when first taught one, must necessarily be constantly visited by their instructor, whose visits tend to mitigate the irksomeness of separate confinement. There appears to us to be much force in the reasons which induced the Directors of the Irish Convict Prisons to adopt these means of rendering separate imprisonment more formidable, and we therefore recommend that attempts should be made, with due caution, to give a more deterrent character to separate imprisonment in the English Prisons."

The mode of classification in the Irish Associated Prisons they much prefer, thus avoiding the danger of parading together a whole army of Convicts, whose great united physical force must be a strong temptation to rebellion. They also recommend the system of schooling adopted in the Irish Prisons. They thus speak (par. 54) :—

" There is no reason why the convicts in Public Works Prisons should not have their schooling after working hours, as is the case in Ireland. Two hours' schooling on alternate evenings might, without difficulty, be given to each convict, and an endeavour ought to be made to improve the quality of the instruction. For the purpose of having school in the evening it would be necessary to build additional class rooms, and an increase in the staff of officers would also be required. Such an increase is, however, wanted at all events, as we shall have occasion to mention later."

These are all very valuable improvements recommended by the Commissioners.

The evidence brought before the Commissioners respecting the working in England of the Ticket-of-Leave System is most important. They do not, however, abandon the principle on which it is founded, because the working of it has hitherto been so unsatisfactory and, indeed, so dangerous to the public in this country, for they perceive that the evils have arisen from the neglect of the conditions on which the licenses have been granted. On this subject they make the following statement, in the 42nd and 43rd paragraphs:—

"We see nothing in the result of the experiment of discharging convicts under license, as it has been hitherto tried, to lead us to anticipate that such a system would fail if carried into effect in a different manner. We believe, on the contrary, that this system, coupled with a general prolongation of sentences of penal servitude, and arrangements for placing convicts when so discharged under effective controul and supervision, would afford the best prospect of giving to society a real protection against criminals, without subjecting them to undue severity. No doubt there would be much difficulty in securing an effective supervision of convicts discharged at home under license, but the object is one of such extreme importance that it ought to be attempted. With this view, we are of opinion that license holders ought to be placed under the supervision of an officer of the convict department, who, with proper assistants, should discharge with respect to them the duties performed in Dublin by Mr. ORGAN. As in Dublin, the support of the police ought to be given, when required, to the officers entrusted with this task, but in other cases the police should abstain from any interference with the license holders, in order not to increase the difficulty of their obtaining employment. Some changes in the law would be necessary, in order to enable the Government to exercise a proper authority over this class of convicts. In the first place, in order that a license holder may be compelled to preserve his license, it ought to be made an offence for him not to produce it when duly required; and there ought to be a power given to apprehend license holders believed to have been guilty of misconduct before the actual revocation of their licenses. Provision should also be made for enabling magistrates to hear evidence upon oath, as to any breach of the conditions indorsed upon the license, imputed to a license holder, and to adjudicate upon the fact, with a view to the revocation, or, in trivial cases, the suspension for a longer or shorter time of the convict's license. Above all, it ought to be provided, that if a license holder

is convicted of any serious offence, this shall be considered such a breach
of the conditions of his license as to cancel it, making him liable to be
remanded to a convict prison for the whole portion of his original sentence
that remained unexpired when he was discharged, *to which should be added
the term of any new sentence he might have incurred.* This last provision
would remove one of the causes which has most tended to render nugatory
the conditions indorsed upon licenses. * * * We are of opinion, that by
the arrangements we have now suggested, the discharge of convicts at home,
under license, might be so guarded as to render them less dangerous to
society than heretofore, since those among them who attempted to resume
their habits of crime would speedily be sent back to punishment."

The Commissioners continue, however, to express their fears
that men under these conditions will not find it easy to obtain
an honest livelihood.    It is quite certain that in the present
condition of the English Convict Prisons, such would be the
case.    The public have no confidence in the training given in
them.    The Chief Director himself considered that it would be
unsafe to attempt any Intermediate Prisons, similar to Lusk
and Smithfield in Ireland, for the English Convicts; he well
knew that they were not fitted for such an approach to liberty;
how, then, can the public trust them in the labour market ?    It
was this very difficulty that led the Irish Directors to try the
experiment of the Intermediate Prisons, which at first appeared
a very daring one, but which was justified by its entire success,
for they are an essential link between absolute imprisonment
and conditional freedom.    Without this link, the system falls
to pieces, and no subsequent appliances of police supervision
or voluntary benevolent effort can supply the want of the
missing link, can obtain public confidence, and make a prison
character a reliable one.    The Intermediate Prison System
was approved by some of the Commissioners, and the following
paragraph was adopted to follow paragraph 64 (pp. 113, 114);
at a subsequent sitting, however, on the motion of the Recorder,
it was omitted.

" A system of labour in association, accompanied with as small an amount
of restraint as is necessary to secure discipline and industry, has been tried
in the later periods of detention in Ireland with considerable success.  Its
chief recommendations are, that the semi-liberty which it offers is a test

of improvement, and fits the convict (who has undergone a severe and depressing course of punishment) for re-entry into life, while it affords an additional inducement to good conduct and industry in the earlier stages of imprisonment. In its nature this intermediate system somewhat resembles the mode of treatment adopted towards the road parties in Western Australia. At Lusk, fifty men work at every description of agricultural labour in open fields, under the care of five warders. At Smithfield, in Dublin, they work at trades, and one of their number is employed daily in carrying messages through the city. Insubordination in these prisons is unknown, and though they have been established for some years there have only been three attempts at escape. Seventy-five per cent. of convicts released in Ireland have passed through these prisons. We see no reason why a system which appears to have had considerable success in Ireland, should not at least be tried in England, for those convicts who cannot be removed to Western Australia."

The Commissioners saw the great evil of the present system of gratuities, by which the worst prisoners, having the longest sentences, may obtain the largest sums of money on their discharge, and recommend, in this also, an approach to the Irish System. On various other points they recommend improvements.

On the subject of transportation the Commisioners state strongly their opinion that no new penal settlements ought to be formed, and that the proposals which have been made to establish one on some wild inclement climate is perfectly untenable. The evidence respecting Western Australia, from which copious extracts have been made in a preceding chapter, leads them strongly to recommend a continuance of the transfer of a large number of our Convicts to that country.

With respect to the improvement of the Female Convict Prisons, the Commissioners find themselves unable to offer any suggestions, hence there appears, at present, no prospect of any attempt at change in those abodes of vice.

Many of the suggestions of the Commissioners can be carried out without any change in the law of the land; but as it was conceived that those respecting the licenses, or tickets-of-leave, required fresh legislation, to confer on the Government sufficient powers, an Act of Parliament was passed (July 25, 1864) to amend the previous Penal Servitude Acts, containing the following important clauses :—

"A license granted under the said Penal Servitude Acts, or any of them, may be in the form set forth in Schedule (A.) to this Act annexed, and may be written, printed, or lithographed.  If any holder of a license granted in the form set forth in the said Schedule (A.) is convicted, either by the verdict of a jury, or upon his own confession, of any offence for which he is indicted, his license shall be forthwith forfeited by virtue of such conviction; or if any holder of a license granted under the said Penal Servitude Acts, or any of them, who shall be at large in the United Kingdom, shall, unless prevented by illness or other unavoidable cause, fail to *report himself personally*, if in *Great Britain* to the Chief Police Station of the Borough or Police Division, and if in *Ireland* to the Constabulary Station of the locality, to which he may *go, within three days after his arrival therein*, and being a male subsequently once in each month, at such time and place, in such manner, and to such person as the Chief Officer of the Constabulary Force to which such station belongs shall appoint, or shall change his residence from one police district to another without having previously notified the same to the Police or Constabulary Station to which he last reported himself, he shall be deemed guilty of a misdemeanour, and may be summarily convicted thereof, and his license shall be forthwith forfeited by virtue of such conviction, but he shall not be liable to any other punishment by virtue of such conviction.

" If any holder of a license granted in the form set forth in the said Schedule (A.),—

" 1. Fails to produce his license when required to do so by any Judge, Justice of the Peace, Sheriff, Sheriff Substitute, Police or other Magistrate before whom he may be brought charged with any offence, or by any constable or officer of the police in whose custody he may be, and also fails to make any reasonable excuse why he does not produce the same; or

" 2. Breaks any of the other conditions of his license by an act that is not of itself punishable either upon indictment or upon summary conviction ;

He shall be deemed guilty of an offence punishable summarily by imprisonment for any period not exceeding three months, with or without hard labour.

" Any constable or police officer may, without warrant, take into custody any holder of such a license whom he may reasonably suspect of having committed any offence, or having broken any of the conditions of his license, and may detain him in custody until he can be taken before a Justice of the Peace or other competent Magistrate, and dealt with according to law."

In this Act are embodied other important changes in the administration of our criminal law.  These are so set forth by the Secretary of State in a Circular addressed to the Judges and Recorders.  The substance of these alterations and their bearing on the administration of the law are so luminously stated by Mr. Recorder HILL, in his recent Charge to the Grand Jury at Birmingham, that we cannot do better than present extracts from it. Speaking of the Circular, Mr. HILL says :—

"'The principal change,' writes Sir GEORGE GREY, 'in the law which is effected by this statute is the abolition of sentences of penal servitude of four and three years, leaving the sentence of five years as the shortest that can be passed in any case, and authorizing it in those cases where only sentences of four or three years could have been passed before. This will have the effect of increasing the severity of the penal law, which, owing to the very frequent use of the short sentences referred to, had, in the opinion of the Royal Commissioners, who lately investigated this subject, become too much relaxed. With the same object, another very important provision is added; that a person convicted of a crime, punishable with penal servitude, after having been previously convicted of felony, if the judge in his discretion thinks that the punishment of penal servitude should be inflicted, shall not be so sentenced for a shorter period than seven years. It will be observed that in all these cases the alternative sentence of imprisonment is not interfered with. In that respect the law continues as it stood before the passing of the late statute. The remainder, and by far the larger portion of the Act, refers to the granting to convicts under this sentence licenses to be at large before its expiration, and introduces various regulations for the purpose of preventing the misconduct of such persons between the time of their release and that at which they would have been by law entitled to their liberty. I do not think it necessary to occupy your time with any observations on this part of the subject, except to remark that, among other safeguards of the public, it is enacted that the conviction of a license-holder upon indictment for any offence involves not merely a revocation of his license, but it remits him to his original sentence as it stood when his license was granted, and this in addition to any punishment to which he may be sentenced upon such indictment. In accordance with the strong recommendation of the Royal Commissioners, an important modification is about to be introduced into the Convict System, in reference to the granting of remissions. Instead of these being granted as a reward of general good conduct, as heretofore, they are now to be earned by industry alone. General good conduct—such as implicit obedience to all prison rules—will be as indispensable as before, but will of itself count as nothing towards the obtaining the remission of a portion of the sentence. That can only be gained by steady and laborious industry, the degree of which will be measured and recorded every day by the assignment to each convict of a certain number of marks. A maximum amount of remission is fixed

as hereinafter stated, as the utmost which can be attained by perfect
industry, and the number of marks is so regulated that a convict must
obtain the maximum number of marks every day, without any deduction
for misconduct, in order to get the maximum remission.  The sentence
therefore is absolutely certain up to a certain point, but may possibly
extend beyond that point and will inevitably do so unless the convict
persistently and strenuously exerts himself.'

" The principle adopted in the scale of remissions for industry and good
conduct, gives a maximum reduction of somewhat less than one-fourth part
of the sentences upon men, and one-third part of the sentences upon women.
Wholesome restrictions have been introduced, it appears, in the quantity of
food allowed, and also in the amount of gratuities given on their discharge to
convicts adjudged to penal servitude.  Thus, gentlemen, you will perceive
that the new provisions are characterised by augmented severity, and when
you learn that they are made in conformity with the views not only of the
Legislature and the Executive Government, but that they echo, as it were,
the opinions of public bodies charged by authority, or who had charged themselves with the duty of careful investigation into the working of our criminal
law, I think you will agree with me that our new Penal Servitude Act forms
an epoch in our legislation."

Mr. HILL then adverts to the extreme severity of the criminal
law in past times, and the reversion to excessive consideration
of the personal feelings of the criminal which have recently
characterised its administration.   He thus continues :—

" The impulse which wrought the mitigation of our criminal code was one
rather of sentiment than of reflection.  We revolted from the pain inflicted
on ourselves through the sufferings of the criminal, and our own feelings once
relieved, we forgot to ask ourselves whether we were treating the object of our
sympathy so as to promote his permanent advantage.  We forgot that to
discharge him from prison while under the influence of false principles and
the coercion of evil habits was to leave him in a state of slavery more
surely incompatible with his welfare here and hereafter, than any state
which could result from the harshest visitations of human jurisprudence.
If, then, the changes which have been lately made are such as to promote
his reformation, and ensure his persistence in the right path after it has
been recovered, true and genuine mercy will be far from receiving any shock
by what has been done.   And this, I humbly believe, will be the consequence should the new spirit breathed into the treatment of criminals permanently actuate all who take part in giving effect to our laws.  You must
have been struck, gentlemen, with the complete change of principle on
which remission is henceforth to be granted.  Passive obedience to prison
rules, however indispensable it may be to good order, has little tendency
to reform the character, and will therefore do little to ensure an honest

course of life after discharge. Industry is the ground on which we must build, and in order that industry practised in the gaol may continue after the prisoner is at large, it must be willing industry, and hence the value of the remission which is held up to him as its reward; whereas industry produced by fear of punishment, even in the comparatively few instances where it is so produced, will, by the painful associations with which all memory of it must be accompanied, relax itself and fall into desuetude, when, by regaining his liberty, the convict has left his fears behind him. The extended duration of his sentence will afford him a sufficient time to make his industry habitual, and it is to confirmed habits we must mainly look to protect him against relapse. Thus the interests of the criminal have been, we see, as carefully considered as the interests of society; both moving onwards hand in hand. But the benefits to each do not rest here. The hour of discharge arrives, and the well-disposed prisoner, having now to meet his greatest peril, is not abandoned. He takes his gratuity, which preserves him for a time at least from the overwhelming temptation produced by want. He has to report himself to the head of the police in the district to which he resorts, and he thereby establishes a relation between himself and a public officer, who, both by duty, and, speaking from experience, I will say also by inclination, will befriend him, so long as his conduct deserves it, and who will exercise over his actions the powerful influences of hope and fear. It is often assumed that the vigilance, which it is the duty of the police to exercise over discharged offenders, is necessarily of a hostile character; but that is not so. A ticket-of-leave man, when his ticket becomes what it always ought to have been, a testimonial that the holder is a person who has given evidence of his earnest desire to do well, and of his possessing the requisite qualifications for pursuing an honest course of life, will find the head of the police in his district a protector against ill-founded suspicion, to which an ex-convict is naturally ever obnoxious. And when, in addition to the testimonial which the ticket-of-leave man brings from his prison, he can safely refer to the police for a certificate that he has continued to deserve the remission which has been granted to him, surely he must thus obtain facilities for procuring employment which will constitute a new and invaluable privilege; while, on the other hand, his consciousness that any breach of the conditions on which he holds his license to be at large, will, the moment it becomes known, ensure his being forthwith deprived of his liberty, must give additional force to his good resolutions. The interval, then, between his discharge on ticket-of-leave, and the expiration of the sentence pronounced upon him by the Judge, is made a season of regulated responsibility. It is an additional stage of probation, furnishing motives to good conduct which will only cease to act, when, such probation being fully accomplished, he regains the footing of his neighbours, who have never fallen into that miserable adversity which is the offspring of crime."—*Birmingham Daily Post*, Oct. 25, 1864.

We rejoice, then, that a decided step has been taken towards improvement in our criminal legislature. Our machinery is improved in some important particulars. We begin to perceive our errors, and to desire that they shall be corrected. This is doubtless a matter of congratulation. But our rulers do not yet appear to see the radical cause of the great injury wrought by the vast number of discharged criminals in our midst. The Commissioners lament the difficulty which these men find in obtaining employment, and yet do not appear to have discovered that the whole system of the Government Prisons is totally unfit to prepare them to do so. They heard from the Western Australian witnesses that the longer men are trained under their system, the more unfit they are to earn their living by hard work, even in another country where they are carefully guarded from temptation, and have every stimulus to exertion. They had the testimony of the Government officers themselves, who, apparently quite unconsciously, have revealed to the public what, indeed, was vaguely known before, the immoral condition of the Convicts, the state of chronic antagonism in which they live with their officers, so that every precaution requires to be constantly adopted to prevent an outbreak or serious injury to the officers,—yet they do not perceive, they state in their Report, that the principles on which the English Convict System is founded is wrong! The very fact that the system adopted in Ireland appears to an ordinary observer to have a general resemblance in its early stages to the English System, while its results are so marvellously different, — clearly points to the conclusion that it is founded on a totally distinct principle. The various alterations in the machinery of the Convict Prisons, and in points of detail, which are proposed by the Commissioners, are in accordance with the Irish System, and are valuable as part of the system ; yet, taken alone they may make the English Government Prisons somewhat safer, but cannot reform the criminals. The reformation of the Convicts ought, however, to be a fundamental object. The good organization of extensive Convict establishments is not an end, but a means, and if it fails to accomplish the great object—the reformation of the offender, after he has suffered the punishment due to his crime—it is useless. The principles on which punishment and reformation should be blended, are so clearly set forth by M. VAN BRUGGHEN in the work already quoted, that we offer a translation of the passage [Chapter I., p. 33]:—

" The State or society being obliged to use compulsory privation of the liberty of natural action as the chief means of penal retribution, repression, and penal intimidation, thereby contracts towards those who are the subjects of it an absolute obligation to provide, not only for their physical existence, but to furnish them the means of supplying the wants of their intellectual and moral nature, which their dependent condition prevents them from procuring for themselves.

"This duty of the State, put in general terms, and without exactly analyzing its source or its nature, will now hardly meet with any opposition in the public opinion of modern society. It is chiefly owing to the generous efforts of a HOWARD and an ELIZABETH FRY that it has acquired this conscience. All that for a century has been effected in Europe and in America under the influence of religious sentiments and Christian philanthropy, to improve in every way the condition of prisons, and to soften the lot of those who must there atone for their outrages against the peace of society,—sufficiently proves that the public conscience has long been awakened on that point, and requires no further proofs. We desire here only to discover the real foundation of this social duty, because it is on the just appreciation of it that the judicious choice depends of the means which the State ought to employ, and which are at its disposal. It is .to the ulterior development of this fundamental principle that the following paragraph relates.

" The obligation of the State, which is here discussed, is not founded on the moral duty of society to exercise collectively through its government the Christian virtue of charity, of brotherly love, or, in other terms, of philanthropy, more or less Christian. For, although every society rests on a moral basis, and every society is more or less impregnated with Christianity, through the fact of its historical development on the religious and moral basis of the Gospel, yet this society, considered as a moral personage, is destitute of that real personality which alone can be the spring and centre of the feelings, and of religious and moral acts.

" Nor does the duty of which we are speaking spring directly from the interest of society in its own preservation, which should lead the State to consider as an advantage the moral reform of individuals dangerous to its peace, with whom it must, in proportion as other more inhuman means of repression fail, always fill its prisons in greater number, to release them, after a fixed time, more corrupt and more furious, to be the terror of the population.

" But this obligation arises, in the first place, as a positive and absolute right, belonging to those towards whom retributive justice is exercised, from the very nature of the right of punishing, which political power is called upon to exercise. For this right, embracing the different motives of penal repression, retribution, as well as the intimidation and protection of society, has its true basis only in that law of moral order, founded by the Supreme Legislator, and impressed in the nature of man created after His own image, *that suffering must always be the necessary and inevitable consequence of evil, in order to change this evil into good.* ' We suffer,' says VINET, ' because God has made punishment the inevitable companion of sin; we suffer, because suffering is the needful road to lead us to Him who cleanseth from sin.' It is only under this aspect that the right of punishing, placed on its true moral basis, loses the odious character of simple vengeance, or of egotistic violence, which is exercised by most only to secure their own protection.

" The distinction here established is very important. It gives

at once a sure foundation to the absolute obligation which rests
on the State, not only to attend to the moral wants of the
prisoners, but to make their very punishment conduce, as it
ought to do, to the amendment of their moral life ;—an obligation from which it cannot withdraw, without abusing the right
of punishment which belongs to it, in order to make it degene-
rate, by losing its moral character of justice, which is at the
same time retributive and restorative, into a simple act of
violence, exercised by the strongest against the weak."

Now it cannot be doubted that it is the intention of those
who have the controul of the English Convict System, to make
it conduce to the ends here so clearly and forcibly stated.
But practically it has not had that effect. The punishment of
the Convicts does not conduce "to the advancement of their
moral life ;" that has been sufficiently proved by the condition
of the prisons, by the aggravated criminality of those who
have experienced their discipline, and by their frequent reconvictions ; the high moral character of justice is thus seriously
lowered in our country. Public opinion has long decided that it
it is not restorative. It is not even retributive ; our highest
secondary punishment cannot be an object of dread, if crimes are
perpetrated for the express object of obtaining admission to
Convict Prisons. Captain CARTWRIGHT, the Governor of Gloucester Gaol, mentions, in a letter to the Commissioners, the
case of ten men who were convicted of arson at the Gloucester
Winter Assizes, and sentenced to six years' penal servitude.
Many of these men made distinct statements that their object
was to get a sentence of penal servitude, as they should thus
" learn a trade, and get plenty of money." "All of these men,"
Captain CARTWRIGHT concludes, after giving particulars of their
cases, "gave themselves up to the police after committing the
offence, and I entertain no doubt whatever that their sole object
was to get a long confinement in the Government Prison. When
I spoke to them, on admission, of the heinousness of their crime,
they assured me they had no malice against the unfortunate

owners of the property they respectively destroyed." Thus the country was put to the expense of at least £2000, in the punishment and maintenance of these men, through the temptation presented by the premium on crime held out by our present penal system. Nor can it be a subject of wonder that men tramping from one place to another, as these were, and sleeping in Workhouses, should listen to the representations of those of their number, who had been in Convict Prisons, as to the superior comforts of a penal establishment. One who had experienced them gave such a description as is contained in the following. A correspondent of the *Times* writes :—

"Soon after my appointment to Fiddington a released convict returned to his home in my parish. As I had known him from my boyhood, and as he had been for some time my father's servant, I was anxious to act the parson's part towards him. Accordingly I lost no time in giving him suitable employment, with good wages. One morning, while thus engaged, he requested me to sign a 'bit of paper' for him, as he wanted to draw some money. 'Draw some money, CHARLES! and what money can you have to draw?' 'Why, you see, sir, we are enabled to earn somewhat in prison, and when we are released we can claim our allowances.' 'Well, CHARLES, I will sign your paper; but, first of all, tell me a little about your prison experiences;' and from his lips I wrote down the following:—

"'March 29, 1859.—I have been convicted of poaching five times, of petty felony once, and of felony once. Upon my last conviction, at Taunton, I was incarcerated eight months at Bath. From there I was removed to Dartmoor Prison, where I remained three years and four months; and during that period I have earned £12 9s. 7d., for steady conduct and work. Our prison life is as follows:—We attend chapel twice a day, and the hours of work are from seven a.m. to half-past four or five p.m. But we are not required to work hard, nor are we allowed to do overwork. Our cells are comfortable, and our fare very good; for we get roast mutton twice a week and roast beef twice a week. We are, too, allowed to mix and converse together during the hours of work, but not within the prison walls. Now, sir, I don't want to get there again, but I may say I am certain of this, that no man in this parish can live as I lived in Dartmoor Prison during the last twelve months—reckoning lodging and clothes—upon 10s. a week.'

"I could not refrain asking him, 'If thirty lashes were inflicted upon the second conviction, do you think men would go on offending as you have done?' 'Well, you see, sir, that would alter the whole thing, uncommonly, and make them keep clear as much as possible, no doubt.' I need scarcely add that CHARLES was soon 'wanted;' for, as prison discipline possessed no terrors for him, he was soon back at his old quarters, 'living as no man in the parish could live on 10s. a week' at the public cost.  I am, sir, your obedient servant, F. S. RAWLINGS, late Rector of Fiddington, Somerset.  Netley, Aug. 19, 1864."

Such evils can never exist in the Irish Convict System, which has been proved to be both "retributive and restorative," and thus to accomplish the highest objects of justice, both to society and to the individual.  The principles of this have been so fully stated, that it is unnecessary here to recapitulate them.  The expressed approbation of the Commissioners of so many points of the system, and the public attention drawn to it, will, we trust, at no distant period, lead to the thorough adoption of its principles in our English Convict Prisons.  These principles are especially adapted to the female prisons, as shown in the former Chapter.  To the treatment of English Convicts, we trust the Irish System will be speedily applied.  The necessity of radical change in our hitherto ineffective penal system is urgent.

The possibility of our any longer throwing the burden of the crime of England upon our Colonists in Australia, appears now to be finally settled.  The strong expostulations and determined opposition on the part of all, except Western Australia, to the reception of Convicts on any part of the shores of that grand new Continent has produced the effect which was to be anticipated.  The following announcement has just appeared in a leader of the *Times* of November 18th:—" We have now the pleasure of stating what is no longer a secret, that no such policy" (of resisting the public opinon of those large communities respecting transportation) " is contemplated by her Majesty's Government, and that, subject to the approval of Parliament, *transportation to the Australian Continent will cease within a limited period*."

Thus we are suffering the punishment we have brought upon ourselves by so long disregarding their remonstrances as to the kind of Convicts who should be sent, and the conditions under which they should be there.  Yet should we be

prevented from ever again sending our Convicts from our own
shores, we shall be only in the same position in which Ireland
was, when she applied the noble remedy of reforming her
criminals, and allowing them to go to another country only
as free men, and at their own expense.

When the right principle is once established in our Convict
Prisons, there will not be the same difficulty in dealing with
those who appear incorrigible, both from their conduct within
the prison and from their frequent reconvictions. From these
the public ought to be protected. Why should such a man
as the following be allowed to draw others into crime, and to
prey upon the public :—

### "AN INCURABLE THIEF.

"At the Middlesex Session last week (August, 1864) an elderly man,
named JOHN WILLIAMS, was sentenced to ten years' penal servitude for
burglary. Inspector POTTER said he had known the prisoner JOHN WILLIAMS,
*alias* THOMAS DORMER, *alias* JOHNSON, for about 15 years, and he was one
of the men concerned in stealing the Queen's plate from a van on its
route from the Great Western Railway at Paddington to Buckingham Palace,
about eight years ago. The driver to whom the van was intrusted was
induced by the prisoner's companions to go into a public-house and take
drink till he became the worse for liquor, and while he was in this state
four men abstracted the chest containing the plate from the van. From
the muddled state the driver was in he was unable to identify either of
the men, but there was no doubt that they were the persons who committed
the robbery. He was also charged with being concerned in several jewel
robberies, and amongst them one on the premises of Mr. MAYWOOD, in
whose house his son was employed. The prisoner was apprehended and
tried for this robbery and acquitted, but two men with him were tried at
the Central Criminal Court in January of the present year, and each sentenced to be kept in penal servitude for ten years. Witness then apprehended him. He was convicted *seven years ago at the Central Criminal
Court* for burglary, when he was indicted for stealing a large quantity
of silk from a warehouse in Covent-garden, and he was sentenced to be kept
in penal servitude *for six years, of which sentence he served five years,
when he was liberated with a ticket-of-leave. Since that time he had been
engaged in burglaries, and was the constant associate of returned convicts.*"

And why should society be injured by one who is justly
designated (like one who was tried at the Somerset Epiphany
Sessions, 1864) "throughout his life a bad fellow :"—

"JOHN BROOK, 44, labourer, pleaded guilty to stealing a small quantity of bread and pork, the property of ANN MIZEN, at Weston, on the 23rd November. It appeared that he had spent most of his life in gaol and in penal servitude, and for this offence he was sentenced to seven years' penal servitude."

The Recorder of Birmingham made important remarks on a number of cases of this kind, which were brought before him at the General Quarter Sessions, April 11th, 1864 :—

" Of our 128 prisoners, 68 have been previously convicted, and all but seven convicted of felony. Of the 61 convicted of felony, 16 have had to endure penal servitude, three of the 16 having twice experienced that punishment. One of the three has received a sentence of six years, and afterwards one of five years. Another, two sentences of six years each, and a third has been visited with a sentence of fifteen years' transportation, and again of six years' penal servitude. The career of the last-mentioned prisoner is melancholy indeed. Eleven convictions stand against his name. In March, 1850, he was sentenced, at the Maidstone Assizes, to fifteen years' transportation for stealing a watch, and yet he was ready for conviction at the Bedford January Sessions of 1857, when six years and three quarters only of his long term had expired, for stealing 15 lbs. of cheese, for which offence he was awarded six years' penal servitude. And he is now to be indicted before you for another felony; that is to say he has been in trouble for two distinct felonies, both committed prior to the expiration of that sentence of 1850. Gentlemen, can this be right? Could such a state of things have existed if the prisoner under the first-mentioned sentences had been kept in salutary and well-conducted training, until he had worked himself out of prison by industry and good conduct. Under such treatment he must either have given satisfactory evidence of reformation or he would have been detained in confinement at home or abroad until the year 1865. If, then, he had been discharged on the ground of his merits, and had enjoyed the privilege of a well-conducted supervision, the probability is that the community would have been spared his two latter detected offences, forming, it is not rash to believe, only a small portion of the undetected crimes committed during the period of his liberation. On the other hand, if he had not manifested improvement sufficiently marked to justify his conditional discharge, in that case these intermediate offences could not have been committed, and the public would have had the benefit of what the celebrated jurist JEREMY BENTHAM calls incapacitation; to which he justly attributes great importance. * * * Nine of our prisoners have recorded against them each five or more convictions! Again I ask if this can be right? Ought we to shrink from the duty of permanently incapacitating by imprisonment malefactors who have given such conclusive evidence that their being at large must be inconsistent with public safety? Not that I would deprive them of all hope of eventual restoration to freedom.

If by a long probation they can yet prove that they may be entrusted with self-guidance, let them go; but, gentlemen, you cannot but feel that their chance of liberation would be, as it ought to be, very remote, and that in the great majority of instances their fate would be sealed for life. Let no parsimonious feeling interpose between us and such a safeguard for our families and our property. Depend upon it, however expensive a prisoner in confinement may be, yet it is better, even in a strictly financial point of view, to dole out to him the necessaries of life by the hand of authority, than to permit him to roam the country and help himself—to say nothing of the cruelly unequal burden which falls on the individuals who happened to be plundered; and not to mention the fear of outrage which we know by experience from time to time spreads abroad alarms, the pain and misery of which are indicated by panics rising to a height but little justified by the facts which have produced them."

Surely, as Mr. HILL remarks, expense ought not to have any consideration when the safety of society is in question; no length of detention can be too great to secure from fresh acts of violence such persons as those referred to in the following leader in the *Times* of December 1, 1862 :—

"The November session of the Central Criminal Court in the year 1862 will long be memorable in the annals of crime. In this month alone twenty-seven persons have been indicted, and twenty-four convicted, of savage outrages in the streets of the metropolis. In almost all of these cases there was evidence of an organized plot in which others besides the prisoners were implicated. In some of them the violence employed was such as to endanger life; in some it was aggravated by the most gratuitous brutality after the robbery had been effected. One at least of these crimes was committed by day-light, several in the most public places, such as Holborn and Cockspur-street. Ruffians as they were, many of the prisoners had ostensible callings or trades, and seem to have banded themselves together for predatory expeditions on a system resembling the Indian 'thuggee.' Most of them exhibited an impudent and defiant demeanour on the trial, and not one, so far as we know, expressed or betrayed the slightest contrition. Like the sanguinary fanatics of the French Revolution, they showed to the last every symptom of a reprobate conscience, and seemed to accept their doom as a fatality incident to an ambitious career. Need we add that the majority of them, however young in years, were veterans in lawless depravity. Of those who were sentenced on Saturday, one had undergone a nominal term of four years' penal servitude, a second of three years, besides *fourteen* other convictions, a third of six years, eighteen months of which had been remitted; a fourth had been convicted three times, and had been known to the police for years as the 'constant associate of the worst of thieves;' a fifth and sixth had been 'for many months hanging about the night-houses in the Haymarket on the look out for drunken persons; a seventh had been 'the constaut associate of thieves, and sum-marily convicted several times;' an eighth had been 'twelve times in custody for felony and assaults;' a ninth, his accomplice, had been four times in the hands of the police; a tenth was believed to be the same person who had been condemned to four years' penal servitude, and had left Portland but a few months; an eleventh was a thief by trade; a twelfth was 'known to have been in the House of Correction;' a thirteenth was a ticket-of-leave man, sentenced to 'seven years' transportation' (we presume, penal servitude) in April, 1857; a fourteenth and fifteenth had previous convictions for felony proved against them, and a sixteenth had been 'sent to a reformatory' for four years."

Such men as these, placed among the ordinary inmates of a gaol in any degree of association, must diffuse around them a most dangerous influence; and, while the safety of society requires that they should be detained in confinement until they have given reliable proof of reformation, the reformatory character of the Convict Prisons demands that they should not be permanent inmates of them, impressing their own character on the inmates, and making absolutely necessary restrictions which otherwise might have become less penal in the advanced stages. Prisoners of such a class were formerly sent to people a new colony; now they must remain at home, and it becomes very important that they should be placed in a separate and more penal Convict Prison, where arrangements should be made to provide more penal restriction, where they should be debarred from many of the advantages which they enjoy in the other Convict Prisons, and yet where the same principles of management which have been advocated in these volumes, should have full force. There should still be the possibility of the amelioration of their condition, and still a stimulus given to self-improvement, even if they should be destined never again to live at large in the world, condemned for their crimes to incarceration for life. Such a separate establishment has been strongly advocated by many persons highly experienced in Convict treatment. Such a prison, conducted on the principles here advocated, and containing within its boundaries a sufficient enclosure of land, might be made to contribute very largely

to its own expenses, as we saw was the case in the later stages
of the Irish Prisons; those persons who are under life sentences might be safely detained there, and the public no longer
witness the anomaly of crimes being actually committed by
those whom they believed from their sentence to be for ever
prevented from injuring the public.  The Commissioners make
some  very important observations on this subject (par. 83) :—

" Sentences for life should, we think, be only passed on men guilty of very
aggravated crimes, but when passed, they ought really to imply that those
who have incurred them, shall never again be allowed to return to society,
either at home, or in a colony, unless the mercy of the Crown should be
extended to them on special grounds.  After a certain time, if they behave
well, the severity of their punishment might properly be relaxed, but they
never ought to regain even the qualified freedom of the holder of a ticket-of-
leave.  *If, however, they are to be kept in perpetual confinement, this punishment may be inflicted more safely and more conveniently at home than in
a colony.*  Should this rule as to the enforcement of sentences for life be
adopted, the courts before which offenders are tried would naturally make
a distinction between the most atrocious criminals, and those whose guilt,
though aggravated, is one degree less, by passing sentences for life on the
former only, and on the latter sentences for a definite, though in some
cases, a very long term of years."

Should such arrangements be made by the Government, we
may hope that a very important step has been taken towards
removing that great blot on our criminal legislature, the
punishment of death.   It is, indeed, a hideous remnant of
our antiquated draconic code, and its continued existence
in our country springs from a servile obedience to the law
of them of old time, " an eye for an eye, a tooth for a
tooth," from which the Saviour came to set us free.  This is
not the place to enter on a discussion of that topic, which
is, indeed, at present the subject of parliamentary inquiry.
The public mind is beginning to revolt against it; juries
dread the responsibility of giving a verdict which may prematurely cut off an innocent person; all the pleas on which
capital punishment has been defended are gradually dropping
away; and the various cases which have occurred, even during
the present year, must have made the Government see, as the

people do, how very difficult it is to draw the line where mercy should be exercised, or remission of the sentence granted. At the present moment, when the young foreigner, against whom popular indignation had been so strongly excited, and whose guilt of a heartless and atrocious murder none doubted, excites great sympathy, now that a legal verdict has been found against him, and his numbered days are fast flying, thousands would gladly unite to obtain his reprieve, were there the very smallest chance of such effort proving successful ;—for though the circumstantial evidence against him seems complete, yet is there not a possibility, the merest possibility, that he has spoken truly, that some of the witnesses have given false evidence,—that he did *not* commit the foul act ? *  Multitudes of such cases have occurred where an innocent man has died the felon's death, and there has been no recal! Many, on the other hand, who were really guilty, and who ought not to have been again in society, have been allowed to go at large on a verdict of not guilty, simply because the jury feared to bring on the culprit an irrevocable sentence, while there was the slightest shadow of a doubt of his guilt; thus justice has been defeated by the severity of its enactments. If, however, there were such a prison as was indicated by the Commissioners, where the criminal under a life sentence should be always confined, unless his innocence should be proved, there would cease to be one of the strongest reasons for continuing the awful punishment at which humanity shudders, and from which the public feeling of our country increasingly shrinks.

We now proceed to consider some of the improvements which appear necessary to put an effective check on the crime of the country.

In the first place, there is a great want existing in the country of any general and uniform system of the registration

---

* Since this was written, the unhappy man has met his fate, and at the last moment confessed his crime.

of criminals.   Careful records may be, indeed, kept of the
number of committals and convictions, but as we have before
remarked, this gives no information respecting the number
of individuals who have been engaged in criminal acts, still
less does it indicate the number of recommittals and reconvictions.   From time to time an experienced eye may detect the
same individual as an old offender, and sagacious efforts may
lead to discovery of the antecedents of the culprit.   But there
is no recognised and established means of ascertaining these.

Mr. WEATHERHEAD, Governor of Holloway Prison, states
to the Commission :—"There is," he says (526), "extreme
difficulty in discovering previous convictions, particularly in
case of the old incorrigible thief, or the clever thief.   He
escapes the former conviction better than a man who has
been seldom in prison, and that class generally travel from
county to county, or from one prison to another, and their
former convictions are never brought to light against them."
Out of the 20 or 30 whom Mr. WEATHERHEAD ascertained to
have been in Convict Prisons only about four were known at
their trial to have been previously under sentence of penal
servitude.

We have seen that in the Irish Convict System photography
was found a most valuable help in this.   Even before it was
employed there, Captain GARDNER, Governor of the Bristol
Gaol, had made important use of it, and stated it in a circular
addressed to the Governors of Gaols in December, 1854 :—

"The advantages which I have myself seen derived from the use of
photography, as an aid to the administration of criminal justice are such, that
I am induced to make an effort to procure its general adoption throughout
the kingdom.

"The importance of being enabled, in the cases of all hardened criminals,
to prove previous convictions must be self-evident to dwell upon, neither does
it require argument to show that the difficulties hitherto in the way of such
proofs have been always numerous and often insurmountable.

"When the convict has been sent back for a second time to the same gaol,
the required evidence has been easily procurable, but it is well known to
all who have been concerned in criminal administration that the most cun-

ning, the most skilled, and the most daring offenders are migratory in their habits; that they do not locate themselves in a particular town or district, but extend their ravages to wherever there is the most open field for crime, or where the chances of plunder most present themselves; that this is the case will be attested by the police of almost every large city, whose experience will have failed to connect the most extensive and best planned robberies with their resident known thieves.

"A knowledge of the foregoing truths induced me, a few years ago, to desiderate some mode by which descriptions of committed prisoners suspected of previous convictions might be circulated among the Governors of leading gaols, but numerous difficulties at first present themselves; periodical visits of inspection might be useful, but they would have two great disadvantages: first, they would withdraw the Governor or confidential officer too frequently from his gaol duties; and secondly, they would entail expenses which the counties could not bear; written descriptions, in very marked cases, might be effective, but as, in the great majority of instances, it would be found impossible to make them sufficiently precise, they would only tend, where parties were sent to identify, to frequent disappointments and useless expense.

"Photography then suggested itself to my mind, and it became at once apparent that if I could devise some means of making the operation sufficiently sudden, I might in scores of cases, even without the knowledge of the prisoner, procure his likeness, a very icon of himself, of which, being capable of multiplication to any extent, I might transmit a copy to wherever it might promise to lead to useful results.

"Twelve months' continuous study of the system has enabled me to perfect it. I have now an apparatus in my gaol which I use daily. I have rendered it most subservient to the object for which it was designed, and through its use have brought to justice several hardened offenders who, being unknown in my neighbourhood, would otherwise have escaped with inadequate punishment.

"J. H. came into the Bristol Gaol upon commitment for trial, a perfect stranger to me and my officers. He was well attired, but very illiterate; the state of his hands convinced me that he had not done any hard work; whilst the superiority of his apparel over his attainments led me to suspect that he was a practised thief. I forwarded his likeness to several places, and soon received information that he had been convicted in London and Dublin. The London officer, who recognised him by his portrait, was subpœnaed as a witness, picked him out from amongst thirty or forty other prisoners, and gave evidence on his trial in October last, which led the Recorder to sentence him to six years' penal servitude.

"J. D. came to the gaol wholly unknown. His person and manners induced me to suspect that it was not his first appearance in a place of confinement, and having made several copies of his portrait, I sent them round to the Governors of different prisons. He was recognised as having been convicted at Wells; the necessary witness was subpœnaed, his former conviction proved, and he was sentenced to four years' penal servitude.

"I could mention several instances in which some most notorious thieves, strangers to this part, have been brought to proper punishment.

"Such having been my own experience, I now appeal to the Governors of other gaols to aid me in carrying out the system upon a broad and national scale. The cost of an apparatus complete will not exceed ten pounds, and it may be worked at an expense of about five pounds per annum.

"I have only to add my wish that you should bring this communication under the notice of your Visiting Justices, and to say, should the authorities of any district consider that I can help them by instructing their officers in the exercise of this most useful art, I shall be happy to do so free of all expense."

This general system has not yet been adopted in our country, but wherever photography has been tried, it has proved very valuable. The Governor of the Bedford County Gaol, in a special report on its employment, says:—"I feel convinced that tramps and vagabonds who wander from town to town, committing petty depredations, will, as far as they can, avoid those prisons in which photography is employed."

Again, the Government Inspector of Prisons for the Southern District, Mr. JOHN G. PERRY, in his return to the Home Secretary, says, speaking of the employment of photography :— "Its application, as might be expected, is distasteful to prisoners, and probably acts in some measure as a check on future misconduct, as the prisoners, being conscious of the use that is made of their portraits, have a great dread of exposure from their agency."

By the general employment of photography in connection with a well-devised and steadily executed system of registration throughout the country, it would be easy to ascertain which are our casual offenders, and which the habitual criminals, who now so often escape detection or incur only a slight punishment, by passing from one county, where they are known, to another, where, under a fresh name, they pass for first-convicted transgressors. It is most important to the country that this system should be adopted if we would repress crime in the land. To the criminal himself it would be an act of mercy, for what can be more mistaken kindness to any one than to allow him to continue in a sinful course? The Christian minister is here at perfect harmony with the administrator of justice.

"Let us now infer from this," says F. ROBERTSON, "a great truth,—*the influence of non-detection*. They who have done wrong congratulate themselves upon not being found out. Boys sin by disobedience; men commit crimes against society and their natural impulse is to hush all up, and if what they have done is undiscovered to consider it a happy escape. Now the worst misfortune that can happen is to sin and to escape detection;—shame and sorrow do God's work as nothing else can do it. We can readily conceive that, if this shame and scandal had been hushed up, then the offender would have thought it a fortunate escape, and sinned again. A sin undetected is the soil out of which fresh sin will grow. Somehow, like a bullet wound, the extraneous evil *must* come out in the face of day, be *found* out, or else be acknowledged by confession." *

It is thus most important, both for the ends of justice and for the reformation of the offender, that every means should be adopted which may make crime a difficult calling, and which may lead to the detection of those who require, for the safety of society and for their own benefit, a long and reformatory treatment. Besides, we have seen, from facts stated in the early part of this work, what erroneous ideas have been formed of the effects of particular systems, from the want of such certainty of ascertaining former convictions, as would test the effect of treatment which was supposed to be reformatory. Surely a complete system of registration of offences would be one of the first great improvements.

Secondly, the great uncertainty of judicial sentences, and the very different punishment awarded to the same offences by different judges, has a most injurious effect on the public mind, and especially on that of the criminal class. Sir RICHARD

---

* F. ROBERTSON'S "Lectures on the Corinthians," p. 457.

MAYNE'S opinion is founded on a long experience as Commissioner of the Metropolitan Police since the foundation of the force in 1829, and is therefore very important. He says (1659): "I believe it is not too strong a word to use to say that the administration of the law with regard to the widely varying degrees of punishment at the present day is a scandal. Some of the judges, I think, pass sentences of eighteen months for an offence that another judge would pass a sentence of five years or more of penal servitude.

"1660.—The law gives them almost unlimited discretion whether they will pass a very long sentence of penal servitude, or a very short sentence of imprisonment?—Yes.

"1661.—You are of opinion that that latitude is universally large?—Yes.

"1662.—Does it not make it perfectly uncertain and a species of lottery?—Yes; *the police consider it so*; they often report to me with regard to a case,—So-and-so will be tried before such a Judge, and he will get a very light punishment."

Illustrations of Sir R. MAYNE'S opinion are common. In the Central Criminal Court of December 4, 1863, as recorded in the *Times* of December 5, we find a man, CHARLES WRIGHT, 26, indicted for a burglary. The Jury found the prisoner guilty, and the RECORDER sentenced him to *nine months'* imprisonment with hard labour.

In the next case we learn that

"The jury having convicted WEST, a police constable was called, and deposed that the prisoner had spent about six years in a gaol within the last twelve years. He was convicted in October, 1859, at Maidstone, of stealing cloth belonging to the London, Chatham, and Dover Railway Company, and sentenced to eighteen months' imprisonment. In July, 1861, he was sentenced to two years' imprisonment for uttering counterfeit coin. While in prison on that conviction, he attempted to commit suicide by cutting his throat. He was then removed to a lunatic asylum, from which he afterwards escaped, taking with him some of the property of the institution. He had been previously under confinement in the gaol of Hertfordshire, and while there he assaulted and garotted a warder, for which he afterwards underwent *eighteen months'* imprisonment with hard labour,

" The RECORDER sentenced the prisoner to be kept to penal servitude for six years."

Thus a long career of crime, indicating a settled habit of vice, with repeated acts of violence, has a sentence of only six years. But we next find that a man who has nearly murdered another is restrained only for eighteen months.

" DANIEL HENRIGHT, 48, a labourer, was indicted for feloniously *wounding* PATRICK RILEY, with intent *to do him some grievous bodily harm.*

" Mr. NICHOLSON was counsel for the prosecution; and Mr. MONTAGUE WILLIAMS for the defence.

" The RECORDER, in summing up the case to the jury, said it was a *serious matter and not be treated lightly.* He would not do Irishmen the injustice to suppose that such barbarity was at all common among them. To strike an unarmed man, sitting quietly at his supper, with a weapon such as had been described, was in the last degree disgraceful. The question for the jury, however, was whether the prisoner intended to do the prosecutor some grievous bodily harm, and they would judge of the intent by the weapon which had been used.

" The Jury, without hesitation, returned a verdict of guilty.

" The RECORDER, after commenting on the cowardice of striking a man on the head with a hammer and disabling him before he could turn round to defend himself, sentenced the prisoner to *eighteen months*' hard labour."

In the same paper we find in the Western Circuit, at Winchester, that a soldier, VALENTINE BAMBRICK, was indicted for violently assaulting and robbing a man. The offence was proved, and the case was aggravated. The law had been recently passed awarding corporal punishment for such an offence.

" The learned Judge having summed up,

" The Jury found the prisoner guilty.

" The Judge said he should defer passing sentence till the morning.

" BAMBRICK : It is of no consequence what you do now. I don't care about losing my pension; but I have lost my position. I don't care what you do with me. You may hang me if you like.

" This morning his Lordship passed sentence. He said, — VALENTINE BAMBRICK, I don't know that I ever had a more painful duty than in considering your case. I have felt great anxiety about it, and have considered everything you urged in your defence; but the evidence which satisfied the jury has satisfied me, and it does appear to me to be *as clear a case as ever was tried.* You say you had a witness, and that witness might have put some other construction on the matter. If you had made an application to have your trial postponed, I should have been the first to listen to your application, and I can't help thinking, from the intelligence you displayed, you must have been aware that you could have made such an application. I am bound to say that I don't think any witness could have altered the facts. You were found in a deadly struggle with another man. He was under you, and the witness said that when he found you RUSSELL was almost choked and suffocated by the pressure of your hand on his throat. It is perfectly clear that he was robbed of his medals, and some of them were found at the house where the woman lodged. How could they have come there? How did they come from the breast of RUSSELL? I have no doubt you have exhibited great gallantry and great courage, and have well entitled yourself to the Victoria Cross. Had it not been for your character, I should have put in force the provisions of a recent statute, and subjected you to personal castigation, but, as it is, I deal with your case with great regret. I should have been delighted if the jury could have seen their way to a doubt. I believe that you must have been under the influence of drink, for there was no adequate motive for your act, for the medals are only of trifling value. *Your punishment must be very severe. It must be penal servitude for three years.*

"BAMBRICK: There won't be a bigger robber in England than I shall be when I come out."

Is three years' penal servitude a very severe sentence for almost murdering a man! Are the lives of the public of so little value?

The following is a still more striking illustration of the uncertainty of punishment, extracted from the *Morning Star*, Feb. 24, 1863:—

### THAMES.

"ANNE STEPHENS, a servant girl, about 17 years of age, was brought before Mr. WOOLRYCH, charged with committing several robberies.

"After these were proved, and it appeared that they were of a very daring kind, other evidence was given, from which it appeared the prisoner was very unmanageable in the Refuge where she was sheltered, and that she had been in the service of a gentleman, who took her out of the Refuge, and in return for the kindness of the gentleman and his wife she robbed them of clothes and other property.

"The prisoner's mother said the prisoner always was a very unmanageable girl.

"The prisoner pleaded guilty.

"Mr. WOOLRYCH said the prisoner was a most hardened offender, an ungrateful and incorrigible thief, who had repaid kindness with ingratitude, and shamefully plundered her benefactors. *All attempts to reclaim the prisoner had been in vain, and he would try what the severe but wholesome discipline of a gaol would effect.* He sentenced the prisoner *to be impri-soned for four months* in the House of Correction and kept to hard labour."

The prisoner's conduct is truly characterised by her judge. But is an imprisonment of four months a punishment at all commensurate with the enormity of her offence. She had committed three distinct and separate crimes. Emboldened by her success in the first serious breach of trust, for which alone she merited a severe punishment, she abuses the confidence of her benefactor and robs her, and thus commits a very serious robbery on her mistress; this alone, we might have supposed, would have sent her to trial and brought upon her a sentence of penal servitude, especially taken in connection with her previous instruction and training in a Refuge. Many young girls are made Convicts for what would appear far less crimes. But this bad and daring young woman, with whom crime was evidently a settled habit, and who had already become an adept in the commission of it, has only four months' imprisonment, which can neither reform nor deter her, and whence she will probably go forth to prey with greater impunity on society. In all these cases the judges were doubtless influenced by excellent motives and wise reasons; —but the public can perceive only the inconsistencies and uncertainty.

A very striking case of this uncertainty of punishment is mentioned by Mr. AVORY, Clerk of Arraigns at the Central Criminal Court, in his evidence to the Royal Commission. He says (1910, 1917):—

"I have been shown an instance, which is fresh upon my memory now, of two judges sitting at the same time in the same assize town, in different courts, and who tried cases of poaching accompanied with violence to game-keepers; in the one case the prisoner was sentenced to ten years' transportation, and in the other to one year's imprisonment. The circumstances were as identical as they could well be. Some judges give them a week in a case of that sort. In the absence of violence, a week is not at all an uncommon thing for night poaching, armed. And other judges pass a severe sentence if there is no violence.

"In the sentences of persons convicted after a previous conviction for felony, when that is charged in the indictment, I have known a prisoner to have a smaller sentence than on the first occasion. That may arise from various circumstances. In the first place, the former conviction may have been many years before, and the accused may have behaved himself well for ten years, and then have fallen into some small crime."

The possibility of such glaring inconsistencies must be highly injurious, and must certainly have a tendency to diminish that reverence for law which is so important.

Mr. SIDNEY GURNEY, Clerk of Assize on the Western Circuit, gives a similar testimony in his evidence (1867, 1871):—

"There is great variety in the sentences passed by the different judges for the same offences, and committed under similar circumstances, without any reason for the difference that I can discover. I believe that rape is an instance in which some judges pass a very severe sentence, and others a moderate one. I have found that that discrepancy applies to all classes of crimes. It has existed to such an extent that while for the same offence one judge would inflict imprisonment, another judge would inflict penal servitude."

It can hardly be doubted after such evidence as this, and much more might be easily adduced, that it would be most important to give some greater certainty to the awards of the law, without interfering with that discretionary power in judges which is so important a feature of our legislature.

The third improvement here suggested is, that sentences should be cumulative;—that is, that a frequent repetition of offences, though not themselves serious, should be followed by long reformatory treatment.

The subject of cumulative sentences is viewed thus by Sir R. MAYNE:—

"1763.—I think that the repetition of very small short sentences is greatly increasing, and is a very great evil. I think that it might be reasonably made an indictable offence, and punishable after a certain number of times when there was a repetition of small offences for which the punishments are now summary convictions. Take that remarkable case to which I have referred many times in which the men were convicted who attacked Mr. PILKINGTON; one of the parties had been convicted nine times, and at last he received a sentence of penal servitude; he had just been released when he committed that offence; the two men were released at the end of May, and I think that in July the offence was committed.

"1766.—What I understand you to suggest is that it would be a good thing that several summary convictions should be made cumulative?—Yes, and make them an indictable offence punished accordingly."

The reason and justice of this seems obvious. If a person is pursuing a course of conduct which is contrary to law and injurious to society, and if repeated punishments fail to produce any effect, or to check the individual in his vicious career, the perseverance in such illegal course and, as it may be regarded, defiance of law, ought itself to be regarded as a crime involving a long course of punishment and reformatory treatment. It is almost impossible to calculate the evil to society caused by the presence of individuals who thus live in a manner regardless of law; the evil to the individual is not less of allowing him to continue such a course, and thus become callous to the disgrace and punishment of the gaol; and the cost to the public of his continual apprehensions, convictions and imprisonments, is far more than his incarceration in a prison, where he would be made to earn a portion, at least, of the cost of his maintenance.

As the law at present stands the same person is sentenced repeatedly, becomes habituated to a month's imprisonment in a gaol where his comforts are attended to, and he returns to his old haunts and associates, nothing daunted, as in this case :—

"ROBERT SCURRY was brought up on remand charged with stealing a cow-heel, value 4*d.*, from the stand of Mr. MARSH, in the High-street Market, on Saturday night. A witness named WILSON deposed to *seeing the prisoner snatch the cow-heel off the stand*, and run away. P.C. MAY found the prisoner a few minutes afterwards surrounded *by four or five companions*. Suspecting that something was wrong, he went up to them, and *found the prisoner in possession of the cow-heel*. He took him to the market, where WILSON pointed out to him the stall from which he had seen the prisoner steal it. He asserted that he did not take the cow-heel. He had been before the magistrates on *three or four previous* occasions, and was sentenced to one month's imprisonment."—*Bristol Post*, April 29, 1864.

It should not be considered an excuse that drunkenness is the cause of crime, or even of disorderly conduct. Many of the most serious crimes are perpetrated by persons under the influence of liquor, and excessive annoyance to the public caused by persons in this degraded condition. If such persons as the following know that they should receive a long incarceration, and compulsory abstinence from drink, they would be more cautious :—

### "ANOTHER INVETERATE TOPER.

"James Kelly, a dirty-looking old man, was charged with being drunk and incapable of taking care of himself. P.C. 152 found him at six o'clock on Sunday evening lying down in Old Market-street. Mr. Castle: He has been here before? Mr. Williams: At least *two hundred times.* You told him when he was last here that you would call upon him to find sureties. Prisoner: Just give me one trial more. If you'll let me off I'll go into Wales. Mr. Williams said he had promised that a score times. Mr. Castle said the magistrates must keep their word with him, and they called upon him to find two sureties in £10 each to keep the peace. He would be committed to gaol till he found them. Prisoner: Can't you let me go to Wales? Mr. Williams: No, you must go to gaol. You were there for eleven months out of twelve before. The prisoner was then removed."

For women such a course would be particularly useful. Such degraded beings as the following might thus be saved :—

"Joanna McGrath for the Sixteenth Time. — *This notorious and incorrigible woman was brought up charged with being drunk and incapable.* Defendant now begged Mr. Alderman Homfray to 'forgive her jist this once, and she wouldn't do it again.' She was committed to prison for one month's hard labour, and said, on leaving the dock, 'Oh! sure, then, Mr. Homfray, isn't that too bad, anyhow.' "—*Bristol Post,* Newport Sessions, December 24, 1863.

### "AN INCORRIGIBLE.

"Martha Channon, an old woman who has been repeatedly before the Bench, was charged with having been found drunk and disorderly in Gloucester-lane. P.C. 180 found her at one o'clock in the morning sitting on a door-step with her clothes half-stripped from her person, and cursing and swearing vehemently. In her defence, she said a friend gave her a share of a few pints, which overcame her. Some persons then followed her, and, knowing that she had money in her pocket, attacked her, and tore her clothes. P.C. 180 said that *there was not a day in the week that she was not drunk,* and the Magistrates fined her five shillings and costs, or seven days' imprisonment."— *Bristol Post,* July, 1863.

### "TWO HUNDRED TIMES IN PRISON.

"A little old woman, answering to the name of Anne Haynes, came curtseying into court and took her place as defendant, as though she did so by force of habit. Mr. BRICE : This is Mrs. HAYNES. The aged defendant acknowledged the introduction by another curtsey, Mr. BRICE : Why you are a good deal more decent than usual. Defendant: Yes, sir. Mr. WILLIAMS : She has not been in prison for some little time. Defendant: No, I have been deputy-nurse at the workhouse, but they stopped my butter and tea, and I came out. Mr. BRICE : Well, you must go back again, for if you don't, and can get any money or credit to-night, you will be here on another charge of drunkenness to-morrow. It is no use to commit her,—she has been two hundred times in prison. The old woman curtseyed to each of the Magistrates, and, taking her dismissal, retired."—*Bristol Post*, July, 1863.

Persons of this class are a constant annoyance and expense in every large town; most Magistrates will recognise the description given of them by Mr. SMITH, the Governor of Edinburgh Gaol, in his evidence to the Commissioners (5075, 5083):—

" The number of short sentences is so great that it is quite possible for a prisoner to undergo twelve sentences in a year; I have known that to be the case for being drunk and disorderly, and offences committed on the street. I do not happen to remember the number of recommitments at this moment, but it is large, and will always be large, because there are such a number of short sentences for offences of that class,—street offences, drunkenness and assaults. I think it exceeds 40 per cent. There is a class of drunken and disorderly people who are continually taken before the magistrates. There are also persons who are very frequently convicted of petty thefts. Those persons, after several convictions, are still only sentenced to imprisonment for short periods."

A large proportion of such as these eventually enter the Convict Prisons after having completed their curriculum of crime, as it has been aptly called. Mr. WEATHERHEAD states (5214) that out of 382 prisoners, he has 60 who have been from two to six times in Holloway Prison. One-sixth of the whole have usually been persons who have been there before, and many others have been before in other prisons, though how many cannot be accurately ascertained from want of any general method of registering offenders. Altogether about one-third of the prisoners who are relapsed Convicts have had from two to ten previous convictions (5210).

This principle of cumulative punishment would be particularly important in its influence on the female sex of the criminal class. When a woman has once undergone imprisonment she has lost her position in society, feels herself degraded, and becomes more and more reckless and hardened until she enters the Convict Prison.

Rev. J. MORAN, Chaplain of Brixton Convict Prison, states in his evidence before the Commission (4778, 4784) that it is generally after repeated convictions and confinement in the County Prisons that women are sent to the Government Prisons. Some have had 14, and some as many as 40 previous convictions. One woman from Liverpool had had 47 convictions, and when she now received a long sentence of penal servitude, it was not in consequence of the previous convictions, but on account of the nature of her crime.

What will be the condition of the wretched woman mentioned below when eventually she arrives at the Convict Prisons?

" CATHERINE O'BRIEN, 20, was indicted for having feloniously wounded EDWARD THOMPSON DOWNES, with intent to do him some grievous bodily harm. * * *

" The jury found the prisoner guilty of unlawfully wounding.

" It was then proved that she had been thirty or forty times in custody for robberies, violence and drunkenness, within the last seven years, and that she was a woman of the worst class.

The COMMON SERJEANT, in passing sentence, said the jury had certainly taken the mildest view of the case, which was one of misdemeanour. This was one of a class of offences deserving the severest punishment, because the treatment sailors received in houses of this description was grievous in the extreme. The unfortunate men were inveigled in, then the door was fastened, and because they insisted on going out the clothes were torn off their backs. It was the act of Providence that the man had escaped from death, and it was fortunate for the prisoner that she had not been found guilty of the felony. She had thought him helpless because he had been drinking, and had evidently thought that she might commit the greatest atrocities upon him. As it was, the sentence was that she be imprisoned and kept at hard labour in the House of Correction for eighteen calendar months."—*Times*, Dec. 5th, 1863.

Surely such an offence as this woman has now committed, after her 30 or 40 offences, might have obtained for her a sufficiently long sentence to give a prospect of reformation.

The subject of cumulative punishment will, it is hoped, receive the attention of the Legislature. Taken in connection with the registration of offences, aided by photography, it would be a most important means of diminishing the numbers of the criminal class, and of the repression of crime in the country. That it may produce that great end, however, it is evident that it will be necessary, not only that our Convict Prisons should have undergone an entire change, but that the County Gaols should all of them be established on sound principles. This subject does not come within the scope of the present work, but it is one especially requiring the attention of the County Magistrates. The revelations made last Session before Lord CARNARVON's Committee in the Lords must have surprised many that such a state of things could have existed in our country. The principles which have been found true in the Irish Convict System might be applied to the common gaols in a manner adapted to their special requirements. They have already been embodied in a Report on Prison Discipline adopted at the Hampshire Quarter Sessions, January, 1864, and have been subsequently carried out with excellent results in Winchester Gaol.*

The same principles have already been tried with great success in the Yorkshire West Riding Prison at Wakefield. Mr. EDWARD SHEPHERD, the Governor, whose long experience in that important post has led to his having been more than once summoned as a witness on prison discipline before Parliamentary Committees, accompanied the four Justices to Dublin in the autumn of 1861, on their important mission of thoroughly investigating the Irish System. On his return, with their sanction, he introduced the system into his prison, and at the following meeting of the Social Science Association, at London, read a paper on the subject, from which we will introduce the following passages, which are valuable, not only as being the result of long experience, but as showing the effect of a tried principle:—

" Although the discipline carried out in our county and local prisons is as various as the prisons themselves,—from unrestrained communication to

---

* The Report is contained in a pamphlet by the Earl of CARNARVON on Prison Discipline. London: MURRAY.

the strictest separate confinement, yet there is *one* principle common to all,—*punishment*.

" What is the raw material to be wrought upon ? It is often a sad mass of coarse and unclean stuff, and must undergo many processes of purification. The antecedents of an old offender are generally marked upon his features. His evil passions have left their trace upon his countenance. His idleness or hatred of labour is visible in every movement.

" Having never acquired self-controul, he has no idea of regulating his own will, or submitting to the will of others. Living in crime, and adding vice to vice, losing all habits of cleanliness and decorum, and recklessly careless of himself, he is brought as a criminal to prison ; degraded in body and mind, deservedly to be punished; but surely, also, to be pitied, and surely likewise, if possible, to be purified and reformed.

" Such a criminal as I have described, then, is brought to prison habitually lazy, bad tempered and insubordinate. He is punished for every manifestation of these vices, and for every infraction of the prison rules ; and, if the ordinary prison punishment fail in controlling him, he is frequently further punished and degraded by flogging. The motive presented to his mind is not hope, but fear. Punishment has gradually less and less influence over him, and he becomes hardened to it. What can be expected of such a man when his imprisonment expires, but that he will commit further crime, and be again sent to prison. Ought such a man, with a character so thoroughly depraved and hardened, to be treated in prison exactly the same as the incidental criminal ? It is, I consider, one great fault of the present discipline that it deals with both alike,—it applies its discipline not only without regard to individuality, but without respect to class—first offenders and habitual criminals—prisoners for long, and those for short sentences. Prison inmates, whose conduct is good, or whose behaviour is bad, are alike under the rule of identical discipline.

" Every Governor of a prison can bring forward instances where a criminal is undoubtedly influenced for good. He learns to controul his temper, to render willing obedience to the prison rules, and to the order of the officers. He becomes industrious, cleanly in person and habits, anxious for instruction, and grateful for kindness. His sullen, defiant look and manners are gone, and are replaced by a cheerful and comparatively happy expression of countenance. This is no ideal portrait, every manager of a reformatory knows its truth, and we noticed this change of countenance in many of the convicts in the Intermediate Prisons in Ireland.   *   *   *

" The superior motive of hope is neglected in our present discipline. There is no privilege or reward to stimulate to healthy action ; there is only punishment to deter from wrong-doing, and whilst penalties are arranged for every possible infraction of prison rules, it must appear hard to the prisoner that there is no indulgence awarded for persevering obedience to them.

" What may naturally be expected, almost invariably ensues. The prisoner so far studies the rules of the prison as to avoid punishment, and in 99 cases out of 100, when even the surface appears fair, and the character good, the man is not really reformed, but only rendered cautious, and on his return to society, he soon becomes an item in our recommittals."

Mr. SHEPHERD then proceeds to examine the statistics of crime connected with his prison, and proves that there has been an actual increase of recommittals during the last 12 years, especially of persons recommitted four times and upwards :—

" This would seem to shew that the maximum of our prison discipline has the minimum of reformatory or even deterring success.

" Then I say, advisedly, there is a necessity for introducing a reformatory system in to our county and local prisons.

" We cannot be told that it is impossible to reform the adult and hardened criminal; we know what has been done in Ireland, and what has been done there can be done elsewhere.

" Limited as we are by the present conditions of the law, the Visiting Justices resolved to try in the West Riding Prison an experiment which should introduce such of the features of the Irish System as under the circumstances could be appropriated.

" This alteration in the discipline was introduced in November last, and I will limit myself to such statements as will simply illustrate the working and the general principle sought to be carried out.

" All convicted prisoners on their reception are placed in the probation class on the lowest diet, and kept as strictly separate as the law will allow.

" After 14 days of continued good conduct some alteration is made in the severity of the discipline, a different employment and out-door exercises are given. These slight relaxations are intended to show the prisoner that he has advanced one step.

" After a further probation of a month's continued good conduct, other indulgences are granted in increased exercise, a greater variety of books, educational instruction, and an improved dietary. This latter seems solely an animal one, but it must be considered that those to whom it is applied are often little better than animal beings, whose appetites have the principal rule over them, and if we can induce these to subserve their moral good we are turning them to a worthy use. This privilege of better dietary is likewise requisite when we recollect that for the lowest class the minimum has been given (or rather, I should say, ought to be given) that is compatible with health, and that the active employment in labour in the next classes requires also an improved diet.

" The machinery by which a prisoner raises himself from a lower to a higher class is the same as we saw in active operation in Ireland, namely, the system of marks. By this system a prisoner is no longer treated in the mass, his individual character comes under observation. A notice is given to him shewing the indulgences he will receive on his advancement to the next higher class, and an explanation of the marks, by what such advance can be obtained.   *   *   *

" A prisoner soon understands and appreciates the value of these marks, and when he finds he has received only one mark for his work, he at once determines to exert himself to gain more, and as my daily experience shews, he takes especial care that no mistake is made against himself.

" It is when I come to speak of results, that I must apologize to the section for introducing an experiment to their notice which has been for so short a time in operation. The first noticeable fact is an increase in the labour of the prisoners, but the most observable effect of the experiment is the improved conduct of the prisoners.

" The average number of misconduct reports of a nature so slight as to require only a caution, was in the year 1860, 140 per month on population of 560, or 25 per cent. In the five months in 1862, that is since the introduction of this new discipline, there have been 106 reports per month of a like nature on a population, averaging 695, or 15 per cent., but it is when the prison offences are repeated, or when they are of a more serious nature, requiring actual prison punishment, that the great difference of conduct shews itself. In the year 1861, 91 prisoners were punished monthly, or 16 per cent. on the population, and since January last 41 per month, or only 6 per cent. have been punished.

" But the good effects of the new discipline are shown more markedly by the progressive decrease in punishments monthly. In January last 84 prisoners were punished, in February 40, in March 43, in April 25, and in May only 14, and this on a population of above 700."

We may hope to see a great change in the Criminal Class if the three improvements which have been suggested are carried into effect, viz.,—1st. Strict registration of criminals, aided by photography; 2. Greater certainty and uniformity of judicial sentences; and 3rd. Cumulative sentences; and if, at the same time, there are the changes in County Gaols desired in the Report of Lord CARNARVON's Committee, and which have been adopted with so much success at Wakefield and Winchester.

The Criminal Class may be divided into—

1st. Casual Offenders.

2nd. Those who are leading an idle and dissolute life, and who are in the frequent commission of petty offences.

3rd. Habitual Offenders, who make crime their calling.

The Casual Offenders will, it may be confidently expected, be more commonly checked than at present by a short but severe imprisonment, when this is duly registered against them, and their identity secured by photographs, so as *certainly* to entail on them a more severe punishment for a future offence.

The Second Class, if awarded, on a second offence, a sentence long enough for reformatory treatment, will be checked in the evil they are doing to society, and will have the opportunity of reformation. If they do not avail themselves of it after at least a year's imprisonment, being now well known and suspicious characters, their next conviction will bring on them a sentence of not less than five years of penal servitude.

The Third Class, under an *effective administration* of the present Act of Parliament, on a fresh conviction, will be recognised as old offenders, and instead of a few months' imprisonment, as so often at present, will receive not less than seven years' penal servitude. The public will thus be protected, and they themselves have an opportunity of reformation. But if they again offend, the time must still be lengthened, and they must never be at large until they have proved it is safe for society that they should be so.

A lengthened or even a life imprisonment in the case of obdurate offenders is in accordance with the principles advocated at the Committee of 1856. Captain MACONOCHIE, in his evidence to that Committee, says (3728): "If he did not become good with one such punishment, he would become better with a second, and better still with a third, and progressively he would be an altered man, I am confident. He would either be an altered man, or (which is another point that I wish very much to impress upon the Committee) *he would be shut up, through his own fault, for life; because in the administration of punishment I would show extreme severity to frequent reconvictions.*"

Mr. Recorder HILL forcibly sets forth this principle to the same Committee :—"You must be content that they *shall be retained until habits of industry are formed,—until moderate skill in some useful occupation is acquired,—until the great lesson of self-controul is mastered,—in short, until the Convict ceases to be a criminal, resolves to fulfil his duty to God and to man, and has surmounted all obstacles against carrying such resolutions into successful action.* But as no training, however enlightened and vigilant, will produce its intended effects on every individual subjected to its discipline, *what are we to do with the incurable?* We must face this question: we must not flinch from answering, that *we propose to detain them in prison until they are released by death.* You keep the maniac in a prison (which you call an asylum) under similar conditions; you guard against his escape until he is taken from you, either because he is restored to sanity, or has departed to another world. If innocent misfortune may and must be so treated, why not thus deal with incorrigible depravity? \* \* \* It is my belief, that if long terms of punishment, even to perpetuity, were placed before the public mind, as indissolubly connected with the privilege to the Convict of working out his own redemption from thraldom by proving himself fit for liberty, it would require no great lapse of time to produce the change in opinion which I contemplate." \*

Many years of painful experience have elapsed since the Recorder uttered these words, and since the Committee of 1856 supported the principles of punishment, which, where they have been adopted, have been proved to be so sound, and so important for the repression of crime, the security of society, and the reformation of the offenders, three ends equal in importance and in unity with each other.

The public has suffered much in that interval, from the increase in their midst of crime of a peculiarly audacious and dangerous description. We have learnt that no laws,

---

\* Appendix to Second Report from the Select Committee on Transportation, 1856, p. 187.

however excellent,—the adoption of no principles, however sound,—are of any avail, unless there is a vigorous administration of them. We have discovered what are the errors and defects which have brought upon us the enormous and incalculable evils which we have endured. Let the public now join in hearty cöoperation with the Government in enforcing the energetic administration of the law in the repression of crime, and in such treatment of OUR CONVICTS as may return a large proportion of them to society REFORMED.

# CHAPTER VI.

## PREVENTION.

THE treatment of our Convicts is entirely in the hands of the Government, and society has no power of changing it, except through the influence of public opinion, which it is the object of this work to awaken.

The prevention of crime rests, to a great extent, with the community;—in this a Government cannot do more than make such enactments as may be necessary to promote the welfare of society, and to second individual effort;—it is the duty of every man and of every woman to do something, either by direct exertion or by example and influence, to weaken the power of evil, and to prevent the enormous criminality which exists in our land.

Those who have carefully studied the evidence adduced in the course of this work, will, it is presumed, fully admit that it is most important, both economically and morally, that every possible means should be adopted to check the supply of Convicts to our prisons, by using preventive measures.

Under the system which has been adopted during the last ten years this has been impossible, because the prisons themselves have increased the enormity of the crime of the country, and because the numbers of unreformed persons thrown into society under the shelter of a ticket-of-leave, have given little hope that any efforts would be availing to stem the torrent of crime which was inundating our nation. But now that a new system is, we hope, being inaugurated, and that habitual offenders will no longer enjoy the immunity which has hitherto been accorded to them, it is for society to do its part in aiding in the great work of the repression of crime throughout the country.

There are already in our land many movements and agencies which have for their direct object the diminution of immorality and the incentives to crime. Some of these we shall briefly indicate, leaving the advocacy of them to those who devote themselves specially to each object.

The Temperance Cause stands first in importance. Every one who has paid any attention to the causes of crime, or even to the ordinary police reports in the public press, must be fully aware how many crimes of violence are committed under the influence of intoxicating liquor. All who notice coroner's inquests well know how many persons annually sacrifice their lives to strong drink. The testimonies of medical men, the declarations of Judges, the evidence of Governors and Chaplains of gaols, all point to the same cause of a large proportion of the crime of our country. It surely, then, is the duty of all who know these things, and desire to benefit their fellow-creatures, to help those who are weak to stand against temptation; it behoves all to give aid and sympathy to those who are endeavouring to promote this great cause. The marvellous change produced in Ireland when Father MATTHEW enlisted his thousands and millions in the ranks of temperance, sufficiently proves what might be done in England were a sufficiently united effort made throughout the country to discountenance drinking usages, and thus to undermine the causes of drunkenness.

The efforts made to check the great Social Evil open another large field for moral effort. It cannot be doubted that with this is connected some of the most degraded immorality of our times, and that the infamous houses which are suffered to exist among us supply many cases of felony to our police courts,

and a large amount of crime to our Convict Prisons; and none
can tell how many murders have been perpetrated in them.
Laws do exist which might be put in operation for their suppression, if there were a sufficiently earnest and determined
spirit in society to enforce them. If the law is not sufficiently
strong, let efforts be made to have it amended. This would be
a more effective check on the crying disgrace to our land, than
any number of institutions to receive the unhappy victims of
this permitted evil. The following extracts from the Report
of the Police Establishment of Liverpool, for the year ending
29th September, 1864, speak volumes on these two causes of
crime:—

"Drunkenness, and *the offences consequent thereon*, are large.
(See table) :—

|  | 1861 | 1862 | 1863 | 1864 |
|---|---|---|---|---|
| Drunkenness ... ... ... ... | 9832 | 12076 | 13914 | 14002 |
| Assaults on Police ... ... | 1165 | 1283 | 1389 | 1398 |
| Common Assaults ... ... ... | 1733 | 1942 | 1707 | 1865 |
| Totals ... ... ... ... | 12730 | 15301 | 17010 | 17265 |

"The figures of the above extract show what the police have
to contend with; and in order to suppress the sale of liquor
within prohibited hours, I have for some time past doubled the
number of men to do duty in plain clothes on Saturday night
and Sunday (p. 7).

"Table No. 6 gives the class of persons apprehended or
proceeded against, either by indictment, as per Table No. 1,
or dealt with summarily, as per Table No. 2. Of the former
class, 299 males and 255 females were known thieves, 258
prostitutes, 1 male was a vagrant on tramp, 24 males and 15
females habitual drunkards, 7 males were of former good
character, and the characters of 821 males and 445 females
unknown to the police. Of the class proceeded against sum-

marily 685 males and 461 females were known thieves, 2580
prostitutes, 76 males and 10 females were tramps, 20 males
and 1 female were suspicious characters, 1603 males and 1346
females habitual drunkards, 29 males and 2 females were of
previous good character, 23,011 males and 6624 females of
character unknown: most of the last numbers would doubtless
be of good character, having been proceeded against by
information.

"Table No. 7 gives the depredators, offenders, and suspected
persons at large, and includes, under the different classes
specified, all those who have habitually frequented the district,
the calculation being based upon the ascertained number in the
month of September. Known thieves and depredators under
16 years of age, 41 males and 21 females; 16 and above, 154
males and 117 females; receivers of stolen goods, all above
16 years, 47 males and 29 females; prostitutes under 16 years
27, above 16 years 2316; suspected persons 16 years and above,
62 males and 54 females; vagrants and tramps under 16, 30
males and 5 females; 16 years and above, 231 males and 35
females.

"Table No. 8 gives the number of houses of bad character;
receivers of stolen goods, 39; public houses, the resort of thieves
and prostitutes, 234; beer-houses, do., 96; coffee-houses, do.,
72; other suspected houses, do., 45; brothels and houses of
ill-fame, 906; and tramps' lodging-houses, 126; making a total
of 1473 houses of bad character within the borough."—p. 9.

While there is no effective repression of these enormous evils
in our large towns, *crime must abound.* How long must the
police proclaim these awful facts, without moving the citizens
to preventive action?

The Diffusion of a Pure Literature, affording both enter-
tainment and instruction at a cheap rate to the labouring
population, is another valuable agency. It may gradually
take the place of the immoral and sensational reading which
has led so many astray, and has directly incited to deeds of

violence, as well as to a life of vice, as we have already proved.

Societies for Improving the Dwellings of the Labouring Classes, and in many ways for promoting their elevation and comfort, are doing a good work for society, but they cannot be relied on for producing any but a very remote and indirect influence on the criminal class. These efforts are most excellent, and it is certainly right that those who are blessed with influence and means should so employ them. But let not the superior attractiveness of these efforts blind any to the great need which exists, even for the sake of the respectable portion of the community, of using active and vigorous efforts to subdue, by moral and Christian means, the criminal class, which has attained such enormous strength in our country.

Much may be done by the means which have been indicated, at least to check the aggressive nature of the criminality which is around us, and to protect from outrage the respectable portion of the community. If the improvements are carried into effect which were indicated in the last chapter, and if such action were taken as would repress the two enormous evils spoken of at the commencement of this, a great change would be apparent. But we cannot anticipate in adults any such radical change as may be hoped for in the young. It is no less the interest than it is the duty of both the Government and of society to take care that *due training and education shall be given to the neglected and destitute children of this generation*, who will become the men and women of the next. It is to the consideration of this branch of the subject that the present chapter will be devoted.

A neglected and ill-trained childhood is usually the commencement of a felon's life. The consideration which has been given in this work to the question,—"How are our Convicts made?" must have proved to the reader that, in a large proportion of cases, the child was led into a life of crime by circumstances over which he had no controul;—that, in others, a want of right parental guidance failed to check the commencement of evil. Children and adults formerly were punished alike. Though the great inconsistency and evil of this treatment of children had forced itself strongly on those whose official duty had brought them into contact with such cases; yet the attention of the Legislature was not called specially to the subject until, in the year 1847, a Select Committee of the House of Lords directed its attention to the "Execution of the Criminal Law, especially respecting juvenile offenders and transportation." The two subjects would not, at first sight, appear to have any close connection with each other, and yet there was a deep significance in their union. The subjects of transportation were found, in a large number of cases, to have begun their career of crime as juvenile offenders. How to deal with these two questions was the subject of long and anxious discussion, and the examination of many witnesses of high judicial experience. As the result of their deliberations they thus speak in their Report :—

"That the contamination of a gaol, as gaols are usually managed, may often prove fatal, and must always be hurtful to boys committed for a first offence, and thus for a very trifling act they may become trained to the worst of crimes, is clear enough. But the evidence gives a frightful picture of the effects which are thus produced. In Liverpool, of fourteen cases, selected at random by the magistrates, there were several of the boys under twelve who in the space of three or four years had been above fifteen times committed ; and the average of the whole fourteen was no less than nine times."

The Committee recommends for such offenders the adoption, by way of trial, of Reformatory Institutions. There was much difference of opinion on other topics, but perfect unanimity on one—the last resolution. The Report says :—

"Upon one subject the whole of the evidence and all the opinions are quite unanimous, *the good that may be hoped from education, meaning thereby a sound moral and religious training*, commencing in infant schools, and followed up in schools for older pupils; to these, where it is practicable, *industrial training should be added*. There seems, in the general opinion, to be no other means that afford even a chance of lessening the number of offenders, and diminishing the atrocity of their crimes."

This Committee was followed by another in the House of Commons, in 1850, on Prison Discipline, before which was brought much important evidence respecting the effect of imprisonment on juveniles, in addition to that which had been tried before the Committee of the Lords. The unanimity of opinion among these as to the necessity of an entirely new course of treatment to be adopted towards criminal and neglected children, led to the assembling of a Conference at Birmingham, interested in the object, in December, 1851.

The following circular, which had been signed by all those who convened the Conference, was the basis of its deliberation, and the substance of it was embodied in resolutions, which were unanimously passed by the Meeting : —

"A CONSIDERATION OF THE CONDITION AND TREATMENT OF THE 'PERISHING AND DANGEROUS CLASSES' OF CHILDREN AND JUVENILE OFFENDERS, WITH A VIEW OF PROCURING SUCH LEGISLATIVE ENACTMENTS AS MAY PRODUCE A BENEFICIAL CHANGE IN THEIR ACTUAL CONDITION AND THEIR PROSPECTS.

"The children whose condition requires the notice of the Conference are,—

" First,—*Those who have not yet subjected themselves to the grasp of the law,* but who, by reason of the vice, neglect or extreme poverty of their parents, are inadmissable to the existing School Establishments, and consequently must grow up without any education; almost inevitably forming part of the 'perishing and dangerous classes,' and ultimately becoming criminal.

" Secondly,—*Those who are already subjecting themselves to police interference,* by vagrancy, mendicancy, or petty infringement of the law.

" Thirdly,—*Those who have been convicted of felony,* or such misdemeanour as involves dishonesty.

"The provisions to be made for these three classes are,—

" For the first, *Free Day Schools.*

" For the second, *Industrial Feeding Schools,* with compulsory attendance.

" For the third, *Penal Reformatory Schools.*

"Legislative enactments needed to bring such schools into operation are,—

" For the Free Day Schools, *such extension of the present Government Grants, from the Committe of Council on Education, as may secure their maintenance in an effective condition,* they being by their nature at present excluded from aid, yet requiring it in a far higher degree than those on whom it is conferred.

" For the Industrial Feeding Schools, *authority to Magistrates to enforce attendance at such Schools, on children of the second class, and to require payment to the supporters of the School for each child from the parish in which the child resides, with a power to the parish officer to obtain the outlay from the parent, except in cases of inability.*

" For the Penal Reformatory Schools, *authority to Magistrates and Judges to commit juvenile offenders to such Schools instead of to prison, with power of detention to the Governor during the appointed period, the charge of maintenance being enforced as above.*

---

" In this statement of the object of the Conference, it is assumed that society has a right to protect itself from the injury and loss which it at present suffers from this class of children ;—that the existing system does not so deter or reform as to protect society ;—and that EDUCATION, including both instruction and training, is the only means of effecting any material diminution of juvenile crime.

" Also, that in *all* the Schools above named, the object in view is, not so much to give a certain amount of secular knowledge, or to enforce a temporary restraint, as to train up useful and self-supporting members of society, acting on a religious principle ; hence, *they will be best conducted by individual bodies, with close and rigid inspection by the State as to their effective working.*

" The parent has a double duty to discharge towards his child ; first, to supply him with the means of subsistence ; secondly, to train him in the way he should go. It is, therefore, further assumed that, by neglecting the second part of his responsibility, he ought not to be permitted to escape the first."

The first result of this Conference was to draw public attention to the enormous expense to the country, and evil to the childen, of the system which had been adopted towards them. The statements of Judges, Recorders, Governors and Chaplains of gaols at that Conference demonstrated, what we briefly indicated in the former part of this work, that a succession of criminals is being provided for the country by the existing system, and that a cruel injustice was being done by it to the children. But no remedy could be applied to this state of things without the authority of Parliament. Two Reformatory Schools, one at Red Hill, the other at Stretton-on-Dunsmore, were then in successful operation ; but they

could not grapple with the evil, as they had no legal detention of the inmates.　Children could not be sent to them by
a magisterial sentence.　Hence, though much good was undoubtedly being done by those schools to the individuals under
their care, and who were willing to remain there, they could
exercise no influence over those who most required such
guidance, but who would *not* be willing to remain under
controul.　Besides, it would be unreasonable to expect that
voluntary contributions would be adequate to the support of
a sufficient number of such schools to meet the wants of the
country; and, indeed, it would not be right to throw on
private benevolence what should be a national work, as it
would be a national benefit.　Again, without legal authority,
it would be impossible to levy contributions on the parents
towards the maintenance of their children, and this was an
important part of the plan, in order to prevent these schools
from becoming a premium on the neglect of ill-disposed
parents.　And yet, while the schools could not be established
without legislative enactments, it was considered essential to
the success of them that they should be under voluntary
management, and that combined with good industrial training,
and a sound moral, intellectual and religious education, there
should be the kindly influence of a home.

As a preliminary measure, those members of Parliament
who had taken an active interest in the Conference, and
promoted the movement, obtained the appointment of a Select
Committee of the House of Commons to inquire into the
condition of criminal and destitute children.　The sittings of
this Committee continued during 1852 and 1853, and it
examined a large number of witnesses; not only those who
had had practical experience of the results of training on
criminal and destitute children, but Governors and Chaplains
of gaols, and other persons whose official position had enabled
them to form a judgment on the subject.　The resolutions

of the Committee respecting criminal children, were as
follows :—

"1. That it is the opinion of this Committee that a great amount of
juvenile destitution, ignorance, vagrancy, and crime, has long existed in
this country, for which no adequate remedy has yet been provided.

"2. That the existence of similar evils in France, Germany, Switzerland,
Belgium, and the United States, has been met by vigorous efforts in those
countries; and, in the opinion of this Committee, sound policy requires
that this country should promptly adopt measures for the same purpose.

"3. That it appears to this Committee to be established by the evidence,
that a large proportion of the present aggregate of crime might be prevented, and thousands of miserable human beings, who have before them
under our present system nothing but a•hopeless career of wickedness and
vice, might be converted into virtuous, honest, and industrious citizens, if
due care were taken to rescue destitute, neglected, and criminal children
from the dangers and temptations incident to their position.

"4. That a great proportion of the criminal children of this country,
especially those convicted of first offences, appear rather to require systematic
education, care, and industrial occupation, than mere punishment.

"5. That the common gaols and houses of correction do not generally
provide suitable means for the educational or corrective treatment of young
children, who ought, when guilty of crime, to be treated in a manner different
from the ordinary punishments of adult criminals.

"6. That various private reformatory establishments for young criminals
have proved successful, but are not sure of permanent support; and are
deficient in legal controul over the inmates.

"7. That penal reformatory establishments ought to be instituted for the
detention and correction of criminal children convicted before magistrates
or courts of justice of serious offences.

"8. That such penal reformatory establishments ought to be founded
and supported entirely at the public cost, and to be under the care and
inspection of the Government.

"9. That reformatory schools should be established for the education
and correction of children convicted of minor offences.

"10. That such reformatory schools should be founded and supported
partially by local rates and partially by contributions from the State, and
that power should be given for raising the necessary amount of local rates.

"11. That power should be given to the Government to contract with
the managers of reformatory schools, founded and supported by voluntary
contributions, for the care and maintenance of criminal children within
such institutions.

"12. That the delinquency of children, in consequence of which they
may become subjects of penal or reformatory discipline, ought not to relieve parents from their liability to maintain them.

" 13. That in any legislation upon this subject, it is essential that power should be given, under such restrictions as may be necessary to prevent hardship or injustice, to recover from parents the whole or a portion of the cost of the maintenance of their children while detained in reformatory institutions.

" 14. That it is also essential that power should be given to detain children placed in such institutions so long as may be necessary for their reformation; provided always that no child be so detained after the age of 16.

" 15. That the summary jurisdiction, with respect to criminal children, given to magistrates by 10 & 11 Vic. c. 82, has had a beneficial tendency, as far as it has been exercised.

" 16. That, in addition to the discretion which is given by that statute to any court before which a child is charged with any minor offence to dismiss such child on sureties being found for its future good behaviour, a power should be given in such cases, in default of such sureties, to send the child to a reformatory school.

" 17. That if during any child's detention in a reformatory school satisfactory sureties should be offered for its future good behaviour, there should be power to release such child from further detention.

" 18. That, irrespectively of the high moral considerations which are involved in this subject, this Committee desire to express their belief, that whatever may be the cost of such schools and establishments, *they would be productive of great pecuniary saving, by the effect which they would have in diminishing the sources from which our criminal population is now constantly recruited, and thereby reducing the great cost of the administration of the criminal law.*"

This Committee was followed by another Reformatory Conference at the close of 1853, and in the following summer, mainly through the persevering efforts of the Right Hon. C. B. ADDERLEY, M.P., the Reformatory School Act (17 and 18 Vict. c. 86) became the law of the land, on the 10th of August, 1854. This Act is permissive and experimental; it gives the power to all Magistrates, Recorders and Judges, to sentence to these Reformatory Schools children who have committed any act punishable with not less than fourteen days of previous imprisonment, but does not require them to do so; it leaves the establishment of these Schools to voluntary benevolence; they are to be inspected by some person appointed by the Secretary of State, and on being certified by him as fit and proper for the purpose, children may be sentenced to them by Magistrates or Judges for a certain number of years. The chief provisions of this and three subsequent Acts* are as follows:—

The School remains under the sole direction of the voluntary managers; but the Secretary of State may inspect it by his inspectors at any time he pleases; if the state of the School is not satisfactory he may withdraw the certificate, and the School then ceases to be a Reformatory School under the meaning of the Act. The Secretary of State thus acts in *loco parentis* to the child, and when placing him in a School satisfies himself that it is fit and proper for his training.

The Secretary of State makes a grant for a fixed sum per head for each child sentenced to the School, as long as he is in it. In addition to this, counties or boroughs may, if they think fit, raise a county rate, and make an agreement with the managers of any School to contribute towards its support.

The Secretary of State has the power of discharging the child at any time; this is frequently done when the managers make application on the score of good conduct. The manager of the School may grant a license to any inmate, half of whose time of detention has expired, to be at large on trial, under the responsibility of the School.

The parents of the children are compelled to pay whatever may be ordered by the Magistrates towards the expense of the child while in the School, and this contribution relieves the treasury.

This is a general outline of the conditions under which children are placed in Reformatory Schools.

Of the working of the Reformatory Schools the Education Commissioners thus speak in their Report. After giving full details of their working from the Report of H.M. Inspector, Rev. S. TURNER, for 1859-60, they say:—

"A considerable diminution of juvenile crime has also taken place since

---

* 18, 19 Vict. c. 87; 19, 20 Vict. c. 109; 20, 21 Vict. c. 55.

the establishment of the system. Mr. TURNER makes the following statement on this subject.*

" 'It may probably be fairly urged, that some portion of the diminution
which has taken place in the number of juvenile delinquents may be
attributed to other and more general agencies than reformatory schools,
or the legislation which they have carried out. Increased employment,
active recruiting, more diffused education, ragged schools, &c., have no
doubt all contributed to absorb into honest life, or to wean and prevent
from criminal courses, many that would else have been inmates of our
prisons. But having now observed for many years the ebb and flow of
our juvenile criminal statistics, and watched their connexion with the
changes of our social circumstances and position, I confess that I do
not find any traces of so marked, so steady, and so increasing an impression on the criminal population as we find during the four years
for which the reformatory system, properly so called, has been at work.

" 'It must be remembered, also, that in those four years the population
at large, and therefore the class from which young offenders are mainly
supplied, have steadily increased, so that we might have expected an
addition to their numbers of 5 per cent. in 1859, as compared with
1855, instead of a decrease of 36; that the police of the country has
been put upon a much more effective footing, and the discovery and
apprehension of offenders made more certain; that the tendency to resort
to summary convictions and short sentences would necessarily multiply
the amount of commitments in each year, by allowing the offender to
appear twice or thrice in the same or different prisons during the twelvemonth; and, most of all, that the number of commitments of criminals
of older age rather increased than decreased in the three years 1856,
1857, 1858, and has only lessened materially in the year 1859.

" 'I am brought, therefore, to the conclusion that the marked decline
which can be traced during the last four years in that youthful delinquency which was spreading so much previously has resulted more especially from the operation of the Acts of 1854 and 1855 (the 17 & 18
Vic. c. 86, and the 18 & 19 Vic. c. 87), and that the principles which
these statutes recognized, and which have since been so steadily carried
out, may be safely relied on as the true instruments for the repression
and prevention of juvenile crime.'

" Upon the whole," the Commissioners conclude, " none of the institutions
connected with education appear to be in a more satisfactory condition than
the Reformatories. We have no recommendations to make respecting them,
as apart from the excellent manner in which they appear to be working, their
establishment is still so recent that the time for such alteration as may be
required has not yet arrived."

It is unnecessary here to enter into the system generally

---

* Report 1859-60, pp. 15, 16.

adopted in Reformatories, as it has frequently been before the public; we may refer any who desire information on the subject to a small work by the present author: "Suggestions on the Management of Reformatories."*

Mr. TURNER's subsequent Reports are by no means less satisfactory than that quoted by the Commissioners, and there is every ground for hope that as the managers of Schools become more experienced the results will improve. Without referring to figures, we can point to the fact that public confidence in the Reformatory System is steadily increasing, and that society is willing to receive children who have been trained in these Schools and to give them employment. They are even sought for in domestic service. The nature of juvenile crime is also greatly modified; instead of our boys and girls coming to the Schools after six or even eight imprisonments, as was frequently the case ten or twelve years ago, they are usually sent to us before they have been so greatly hardened by familiarity with the gaol and frequent crime; thus an offending member of a family is removed, before all the younger branches of it are contaminated. Cases of juveniles who have been convicted several times can now hardly be met with in the country. Formerly it was no unusual thing for two, three, or even four, members of the same family to be in Reformatories, now it is a case of rare occurrence for a second to be received from the same household. The fact of a son or daughter being forcibly removed is now regarded as it ought to be, as a great calamity, especially since the parent is compelled to make a weekly payment; many cases have occurred in which parents have become in consequence more careful of their other children.

There cannot, then, be a doubt that the Reformatory Schools are doing an important work as a preventive measure, and as arresting the progress of the supply of crime to the country; they also confer a great benefit on the young persons themselves, who seemed destined, without such help, to a life of crime. But

* Published by the Reformatory and Refuge Union, Suffolk Street, Pal Mall, London.

the entrance to the Reformatory is through the prison; to be
received in one, the child must have committed a crime, and
must have received the brand of the gaol.   It was the desire
of the promoters of the reformatory movement that children
never should have in early life that stigma attached to them,
and that the school should take the place of the prison.   Under
the existing Act, however, that cannot be the case, and it
therefore appeared increasingly important that the second
object of the Birmingham Conference should be obtained—
the Certified Industrial School, to which young persons may
be sent, under a Magistrate's warrant, without having received
the stigma of a gaol.   Such a measure was at length obtained,
and on August 17, 1857, the Industrial Schools' Act was passed,
20, 21 Vict., c. 48.   The class of children is thus described in
the last amendment of the Act, passed August 6, 1861 (24,
25 Vict., c. 113) :—

> " I.—Any child apparently under the age of fourteen years found begging
> or receiving alms, or being in any street or public place for the pur-
> pose of begging or reciving alms.
>
> " II.—Any child apparently under the age of fourteen years that is found
> wandering, and not having any home or settled place of abode, or any
> visible means of subsistence, or frequents the company of reputed
> thieves.
>
> " III.—Any child apparently under the age of twelve years who, having
> committed an offence punishable by imprisonment or some less punish-
> ment, ought nevertheless, in the opinion of the justices, regard being
> had to his age, and to the circumstances of the case, to be sent to
> an Industrial School.
>
> " IV.—Any child under the age of fourteen years, whose parent represents
> that he is unable to controul him, and that he desires such child to be
> sent to an Industrial School, in pursuance of this Act, and who,
> at the same time, gives such undertaking or other security as may
> be approved of by the justices before whom he is brought, in pursuance
> of this Act, to pay all expenses incurred for the maintenance of such
> child at school."

The tenth section provides that *any* person may bring before
Justices any child that is hereinbefore declared to be liable
to be sent to an Industrial School.

With respect to the maintenance of such children, sec. 17
provides that the Commissioners of Her Majesty's Treasury

may contribute toward it out of the monies provided by Parliament;—and section 18 enacts that Justices committing the child, or Justices having jurisdiction within the district where the School is situate, or where the parent of such child shall reside, upon application of any person appointed by the Secretary of State for that purpose, shall have authority to make an order on the parent of such child for payment towards the expenses of his maintenance.

In this Act, then, as in the Reformatory Schools' Act, parents are compelled to pay towards the maintenance of the child, and there is the power of licensing; here, the Magistrates, instead of the Secretary of State, may discharge the child, provided there is sufficient security of his being able to maintain himself. No children can be sentenced to a Certified Industrial School who have ever been in prison, or who are above fourteen years of age.

The value of these Schools is very great, and, as far as they have become known, they are much appreciated by the public. No stigma is attached to any boy who has been in an Industrial School, and as the inmates are less hardened, greater liberty can be allowed them, and they can more easily find their place in society than from Reformatories. They remove the child who was in danger of becoming criminal, before he has actually joined the ranks of crime, before he knows the interior of a prison, which may now remain an object of awe and dread to him. Unfortunately, however, those Schools have not yet become general; being regarded by the Government as experimental, the Act extended only to January 1, 1867, a circumstance which imposed a natural obstacle to the establishment of institutions which might eventually be abandoned. We trust, however, that of this there is no danger, for as the class of children diminishes who have undergone imprisonment, the Reformatories may be diminished in number, and reserved for the more hardened and the older offenders, as they receive young persons up to the age of sixteen. Many children are now sent to Reformatories who might have been placed in Industrial Schools without a prison brand, simply because no Certified Industrial

School was at hand to receive them. It cannot be doubted, however, that as there has been no difficulty on the part of the public in establishing a sufficient number of Reformatory Schools, the call will be responded to whenever the necessity is felt.

If we compare Reformatory and Certified Industrial Schools, it is evident that the latter should be preferred whenever a child is admissible under the conditions of the Act, supposing, of course, that both are under equally good management; because he does not receive any criminal stigma, and will be more quickly prepared to enter into the world. The expense to the public is also much greater in the case of a Reformatory than of an Industrial School. In the former, the allowance from the Treasury is six shillings per week for each inmate, with an allowance, in many cases, of two shillings per week from county or borough rates; in the latter, the Treasury allowance is only five shillings, without any addition from rates. In each case the expenditure is of course supplemented by voluntary contributions. The actual cost of Reformatories is necessarily greater than Industrial Schools, because the character of the inmates requires a larger and more expensive staff, to conduct the School efficiently, as well as more costly arrangements in various other respects.

Both Reformatory and Industrial Schools having thus been shown to answer the purpose intended, wherever they have been efficiently conducted on sound principles, and the Government having made all the enactments required for their maintenance, it is a matter of surprise and sorrow that so little progress has yet been made in arresting the frequent imprisonments of young children, which were shown in a former chapter to be the sure means of perpetuating a succession of Convicts. Abundant testimony was brought forward, and much more might have been adduced, to prove that, however well regulated a gaol may be, it is not, by its very nature, *a fit place for a child*, a young person of immature age; *that it does not produce the intended effect of deterring from crime;* that committal to one stamps a child for life ; that it is, therefore, an expensive procedure. Surely to affix a stigma which can never be effaced on a young child who has not a legal right to controul his own actions, is an enormous inconsistency, and a cruel injustice. The law of England carefully guards parental rights, and to a certain extent enforces parental responsibility. The child of 14 has no right, however much he may deem it for his future advantage in life, without the consent of his father, to apprentice himself to a trade, whereby he may secure for himself the power of obtaining an honest living. If he may not do what is right, because he is under the responsibility of his father, why is he to be punished because his father has so neglected his duty as to allow him to do what is wrong? In some places, we have heard that parents are punished, if, through their neglect, their children are injurious to society; and so they ought to be. The ordinary treatment of children is never the same as that of adults ; we do not expect from a boy or girl the knowledge of life, the wisdom which can be alone derived from experience, the power of guiding his actions, the development of conscience, or the physical condition of a man or woman. The vagaries of boys are never looked upon in the upper classes with a serious eye ; and if they commit actions which are legally criminal, parental correction is administered. And yet a contrary course is pursued as soon as a young boy of the lowest class of society proves by his conduct that he is ignorant of his duty, deficient in principle, and totally unfit to guide himself. Then the massive prison walls are opened to receive him, ponderous keys are turned on him, an officer waits on him, he has rights which he can assert, he is treated as a man. The late City Solicitor, Mr. CHARLES PEARSON, stated to the Lords' Committee :—

"I think that the law of England is not fairly dealt by in its administration as regards children. By the common law of England, a child *under years of discretion* is not taken to be *capax doli*. By the theory of our law it is necessary that you should prove against a child charged with crime, a precocious capacity for evil, or, as Lord HALE describes it, a mischievous discretion. I press with great submission upon your Lordships, as legislators, the propriety of applying this principle of the common law in this respect to poor, neglected, and destitute children."

But this course is still pursued in our Police Courts; young boys are still so frequently sent to gaol for trifling offences, that it would appear that no impression has been made by all the efforts to awaken public opinion on the subject. For robbing gardens of apples, for breach of police regulations, young boys are constantly sentenced to short imprisonments. The Rev. W. C. OSBORNE, the Chaplain of Bath Gaol, who, for a long series of years, has especially devoted his attention to the condition of juvenile delinquents, has frequently called public attention to the great evil which is caused by the imprisonment of children; he calculates that about 10,000 children are annually sent to prison, and states, in a memorial to both Houses of Parliament in 1860, that "during the last three years the number of juvenile offenders committed to prison has been 31,758 (one-sixth being females), of whom only 2890 have been at the expiration of their prison time removed to Reformatory Schools."

As long as this system continues, no permanent effect will be produced on the juvenile crime of the kingdom. Isolated individuals who are sent to Reformatories may be saved, and may be enabled to lead an honest life, instead of that of a Convict, but the mass of crime remains comparatively untouched, and for ever recruited by new additions. In November, 1862, the Governor of Liverpool Gaol states in his Report, that there were committed to his prison during the last year 537 juvenile offenders—459 males, 78 females. Of these only 108 were sent to Reformatories. In 1863 there were 562 committed, and only 122 sent to Reformatories. As Liverpool has always taken a prominent position in the Reformatory movement, and the excellent Chaplain of the Gaol, Rev. T. CARTER, has borne an active share in it, we may anticipate still more unsatisfactory returns from the whole country.

The Report of the Liverpool Gaol for this year contains important statistics. The Governor presents the following table:—

RETURN OF THE NUMBER OF COMMITTALS TO THE LIVERPOOL BOROUGH GAOL
DURING THE LAST NINE YEARS, ENDING 30TH SEPTEMBER, 1864.

| YEARS | MALES | | FEMALES | | TOTAL | | GRAND TOTAL |
|---|---|---|---|---|---|---|---|
| | Adults | Juveniles | Adults | Juveniles | Adults | Juveniles | |
| 1856 | 4010 | 710 | 4134 | 285 | 8144 | 995 | 9139 |
| 1857 | 4326 | 616 | 4538 | 177 | 8864 | 793 | 9657 |
| 1858 | 4075 | 387 | 3028 | 99 | 7103 | 486 | 7589 |
| 1859 | 3857 | 404 | 3713 | 88 | 7570 | 492 | 8062 |
| 1860 | 3387 | 293 | 3664 | 68 | 7051 | 361 | 7412 |
| 1861 | 3558 | 335 | 3728 | 83 | 7286 | 418 | 7704 |
| 1862 | 4419 | 459 | 4440 | 78 | 8859 | 537 | 9396 |
| 1863 | 5010 | 481 | 4924 | 81 | 9934 | 562 | 10496 |
| 1864 | 4746 | 272 | 4828 | 67 | 9574 | 339 | 9913 |

We here see that while adult crime has increased, juvenile crime has diminished nearly one-third of what it was before the commencement of Reformatories; the girls, indeed, are only one-sixth in number. Yet but a very small proportion, not one-fourth, have been sent to Reformatories, as we learn from the following table from the Report of the Rev. T. CARTER:—

TABLE OF THE NUMBER OF JUVENILES OF BOTH SEXES COMMITTED DURING THE LAST TEN YEARS, SHOWING THE PROPORTION REMANDED FOR INQUIRY, AND THE NUMBER SENT TO REFORMATORIES AFTER SUCH INQUIRY.

| Year | Committed | Of whom Remanded for inquiry | Sent to Reformatories after such inquiry |
|---|---|---|---|
| 1855 | 990 | 27 | 19 |
| 1856 | 995 | 254 | 133 |
| 1857 | 793 | 467 | 233 |
| 1858 | 486 | 287 | 117 |
| 1859 | 492 | 277 | 103 |
| 1860 | 361 | 277 | 112 |
| 1861 | 418 | 388 | 103 |
| 1862 | 537 | 473 | 108 |
| 1863 | 562 | 524 | 122 |
| 1864* | 633 | 547 | 132 |

\* From the 25th January in this year all remanded cases have been detained in Bridewell and not sent, as in former years, to the gaol; hence a large proportion of these numbers will not be found in the gaol returns.

Reformatories cannot check the supply, but reform those sent to them, and it is very satisfactory to learn from Major GREIG, the Chief-Constable of Police, that the committals of juveniles above 16 have been on the decrease; as that is the most dangerous age, it is evident that Reformatories have already had their influence in checking the supply of daring, reckless young persons, notwithstanding the enormous incentives to crime in Liverpool.

What, then, remains for the Government to do, in order to give full effect to present enactments, and to arrest the progress of juvenile crime?

The real effect of Reformatories cannot be proved while these constant imprisonments of children continue, nor is it just to them that they should be so treated in their immature state.

The experience of the last ten years has shown that it cannot be expected from Magistrates, when children are brought before them, to weigh all the varied arguments which may be adduced respecting their disposal. Some Magistrates may be disposed too readily to send children to Reformatory and Industrial Schools; others may not have attended to the subject, and be too unwilling to do so. It is a short and ready way to send a boy to prison, and this is therefore often done without consideration of the future consequences. The next time he appears before the Bench the boy receives another short sentence, and thus the same course is repeated which has so long been deprecated; he may not be remembered, and other Magistrates may be sitting. There can be no uniform system adopted without legal enactments.

The law at present leaves it in the power of Magistrates to deliver over children to their parents for chastisement, or to caution and discharge them. A child may also be remanded for further consideration of his case, and examination of his circumstances. He should, however, under no circumstances be sent to prison if under 14, except as a preliminary to a Reformatory. If the child has been guilty of some misdemeanour which indeed requires correction, but which does not imply serious wickedness, let him be handed over, *as would be the case in the higher classes*, to parental chastisement, the father being warned that a repetition of such misdemeanour, or continued neglect of his child, will be followed with serious consequences. If the child has been previously brought before the Magistrate, or is proved to be habitually in a state of incipient crime or transgression, coming under the provisions of the Industrial Schools' Act, let him be sentenced to one, the parent being compelled to pay the utmost his means will allow towards his maintenance. The child thereby will have no taint of crime affixed to him, and after good training of a few years will probably come out a hard-working boy, easily finding employment. Should the case be still more serious, the Reformatories can receive him; the character obtained there will decide his future prospects in life. The expense of the Reformatory will be far less to the Government than a continued career of crime, terminating in penal servitude.

A system of this kind steadily pursued would throw the responsibility of the child (where it ought to be) upon the parents, and is entirely in accordance with the recommendations of the 15th and 16th resolutions of the Select Committee of 1853.

Let, then, efforts be made to obtain a short Act, rendering it unlawful to send any child to prison under the age of 14, except as a preliminary to a Reformatory. This would not be a "premium on crime," for cases are rare in which parents do not esteem it a great misfortune to be deprived of all right over their children; nor do wild unrestrained boys and girls think it a privilege to be confined in a school, and obliged to conform to regulations.

When the Reformatory System for children has thus had a fair trial, then, and not before, may we expect to find a sensible effect produced on the population in the diminution of juvenile crime.

Another most important preventive measure, if we desire to check the progress of crime, and to diminish the great hereditary pauper class from which springs so large an amount of criminality, is a complete change in what are called Pauper Schools. The present system, both indirectly and directly, leads to crime. In the third chapter of the former volume we saw the miserable boys taken from the workhouse before the Bench of Magistrates because the master was unable to induce them to work. And then they were introduced to the gaol, and perhaps learnt, as this was a second offence in one case, that this was a more desirable abode;—they were enlisted in the criminal class. This is no isolated case.

The subject of the treatment of pauper children is too extensive for more than a passing consideration in this place. Of the direct effect of the present system in fostering crime, abundant testimonies might be cited. The Select Committee of 1853 entered fully on this subject, and passed the two following resolutions :—

"19. That the education given in workhouses, although improved of late, has not been sufficiently directed to industrial training, which the Committee deem to be of especial value, as affording the best means of enabling children to provide for themselves the means of independent support upon leaving the workhouse.

"20. That it is essential for the future welfare of children in workhouses that such arrangements should be made as will prevent the possibility of their intermixing with the adult classes, to the moral detriment of the children."

The late Mr. NASSAU SENIOR, one of the Education Commissioners, speaks thus of the Workhouse at Southampton, which he visited, "The paupers, they (the master and mistress) said, are a tribe, the same names, from the same families and the same streets fill the Workhouse; it sometimes contains three generations!"—Report of Education Commissioners, p. 358.

The Assistant Commissioner, Mr. CUMIN, thus speaks of the Workhouse Schools which came under his observation, "I know nothing more pathetic than a Workhouse School. * *

Doòmed by necessity never to know the meaning of the familiar word home—cut off from the exercise of the ordinary affections—many of them diseased in body and feeble in mind—these poor children exhibit little of the vigour and joyousness of youth. *Listless and subservient in manner, they seem to be broken down by misfortune before they have entered into life.*"—p. 356.

The prison authorities can now testify, as Mr. DAVIS, the Ordinary of Newgate, did some years ago, to the Lords' Committee, that "there is a close connection between the scum of a Workhouse and juvenile offenders." The general voice of the public assigns to the Workhouse boy or girl one of the lowest places in the community; this fact is too notorious to need proof. But ought this to be so? What have these poor children done to incur disgrace? No child can be a pauper *per se.* By the order of Providence, young children, immature beings, are unable to provide their own maintenance, or to take care of themselves. The parent is the natural guardian of the child; if that source fails, society must undertake the charge, but is the child to be a sufferer on this account, or should he incur odium? No one can supply to the child the love and fostering care which a good parent would give, but on that very account should not every effort be made to supply the place of this to the unoffending child? But it is not so in our country!

The pauper condition itself presents difficulties which cannot be removed from Workhouse Schools under the existing Poor Law regulations. The pauper stamp is impressed on young children who ought to be rising freely into life;—they have a sense of bondage; they are cut off from ordinary life, and their ignorance of it makes them enter it unprepared, from Schools which might be otherwise good. They cannot possess property, for paupers have none, and this deprives them of the possibility of learning some of the most important lessons to fit them for society. How can an orphan child brought up in a Workhouse School know what are the rights and duties of

property; the use and value of money; the necessity of providence and economy to maintain an independent position in the
world? And he must, therefore, go forth into it unprepared!
And what can there be in a Workhouse School in any way to
supply the influences the Creator designed to exist in a home?
The recipients of public charity, as such, have nothing to supply
the child's craving for affection, and they feel no gratitude for
what is given grudgingly, and to which they know they have a
right. There are "inherent and ineradicable evils," in Workhouse Schools. Independently of these, the Schools cannot
materially improve while they continue under the management
of a body of persons who are elected for qualifications by no
means indicating fitness for the education of the young, and
whose very duties are often antagonistic to it.

"An intimate experience," says Mr. SYMONS, in his Report for 1854, "of
the views and tendencies of the guardian class satisfies me that it would
be difficult to select men who are less friendly to it or more unqualified
by sympathy or aptitude to take part in the work. Neither is there anything
in the functions or objects of poor-law administration in the slightest degree
germane to education or the moral training of children. The chief office
of the guardian is at once to repress and relieve adult pauperism. The
tendency of his duty is to maximise prevention by minimising relief; to
stimulate self-exertion and deter dependence by the smallness of the succour
and irksome concomitants. He has to apply a discipline sufficiently penal to
probe poverty, test its reality, prevent fraud, and discriminate between the
claims of helpless indigence and wilful idleness.

" No one of these duties or requirements applies to the pauper child. He is
seldom, if ever, a pauper by choice. His dependence is always his misfortune; his pauperism is an hereditary ailment, not an acquired habit; his
condition is not his fault. So far from meriting correction, the penalties
of poverty, which fall properly on the adult, would be causeless cruelties
if inflicted on the child. We have no right even to deter his possible lapse
into the same category by embittering the dependence which he cannot help,
and limiting the alms which he has a right to have. The very principle
which in the one case suggests the economy of relief, requires in the other
liberal benevolence, generous sympathy, and the kindest reformatory appliances. Such a work is not akin to that of awarding labour tests, limiting
dietaries, scrutinising claims, protecting rates, inspecting supplies, and
superintending the current administration of a workhouse. *I do not scruple,
therefore, to say that the placing of pauper children under the local government*

*of a board constituted quite differently is one of the main necessities of the case."—'* Suggestions on Popular Education,' by NASSAU SENIOR, p. 95.

Commissioners, Inspectors, all agree in lamenting in Guardians " a rooted distrust of any plans involving outlay ;" and " a morbid dread of what is termed ' over education,' " (*vide* Educational Report.) Individually they may be estimable and benevolent men, but collectively, with a few honourable exceptions, this is their general character as Boards of Guardians,— a character completely unfitting them for the care of children, and precluding the introduction into the Schools under their management of that voluntary benevolent and Christian influence which is essential to the accomplishment of the object intended. This, we have seen, is strongly the opinion of the late Mr. JELINGER SYMONS, Her Majesty's Inspector of Workhouse Schools.

There are, indeed, some Workhouse Schools where there is as much a home feeling as can possibly be given to the establishment. But these are exceptions. A dreary listlessness, a want of the brightness and energy of youth, is usually obvious among the inmates. These faults are apparently inseparable from the present system. The efforts of the Workhouse Visiting Society have done much, and, where permitted, will do much more to shed a kind influence into the Workhouse. But this is merely palliative, the radical evil remains.

The following suggestions as to an entire separation of the children from Workhouse associations were made in evidence to the Poor Law Committee of 1861, and are in accordance with a plan proposed for the establishment of District Schools. They are offered here for consideration :—

" First.—It should be made unlawful for any children under sixteen years of age to be taken into the Workhouse, or into any establishment connected with the Workhouse within three miles of it.

" Secondly.—The management of all pauper children should be placed in the hands of a School Committee, to be annually chosen by the ratepayers. The School for girls must be under the immediate management of a Committee of ladies.

"Thirdly.—All Schools intended for resident pauper children should be certified as fit and proper for their purpose by the Secretary of State, to whom their condition should be annually reported, and who should have power to withdraw the certificate.

"Fourthly.—Where no School exists in any district fit for the reception and proper training of pauper children, the Guardians should vote a sum for the erection and suitable furnishing of one, under the direction of the School Committee.

"Fifthly.—The Guardians should pay to the School Committee a weekly sum, not more than 5s., for the entire maintenance and instruction of each pauper child.

"Sixthly.—All Pauper Schools must be industrial in their character; should the School Committee think fit, the Pauper Industrial School may be certified by the Secretary of State for the reception of vagrant children, under the regulations of the Industrial Schools' Act. In like manner any School Committee may contract with the Managers of a Certified Industrial School to receive pauper children with the payment from the Guardians of 5s. a week.

"Seventhly.—The Guardians shall be obliged to pay for the schooling of all children receiving out-door relief, under the provisions of DENISON's Act. The parents may select what School they please, provided it is one under the inspection of the Committee of Council on Education. The payment for the schooling of out-door pauper children is to be in addition to the relief, and their regular attendance a condition of receiving relief."

On such a system the enlightened and benevolent effort of the country would be enlisted in the work of raising the children of paupers, and the destitute orphans of England, into a self-supporting and independent position. England has given these children food and clothing, and education and shelter. Where these are afforded in abundance, where there are even handsome edifices erected for the purpose, which seem to mock, by their splendid exterior, and by the refinement and convenience of the interior, the poverty of the inmates, even then there is in these abodes a sensible lack of all that can make opening life joyous ; the faces, the manner, the very bearing of the children show that they want that love which is the essential of their nature,— that they can never be happy there. The call has been responded to on behalf of the criminal children, and will surely be so when the nation summons the benevolent, the Christian-hearted men and women of England to watch over the pauper children, and establish for them schools calculated to give them a good training for future life, with the independence of spirit which should be found in every Briton.

Our preventive measures must not, however, pause here. Much will have been done when we have learnt how to arrest the progress of future pauperism and crime in the young persons who are actually in our hands. But this proceeding will leave our purpose only half effected, if there remains below these a whole pariah class from which others will constantly supply our Reformatories, our Certified Industrial and our Workhouse Schools ;—as well may we expect to infuse a sanitary condition into an unhealthy and badly-drained locality, by erecting hospitals for the cure of those who are in a state of disease imbibed from the polluted miasma. We must endeavour vigorously to bring elevating influences to bear on the portion of the community whence criminals are supplied to our police courts, our gaols, our Convict Prisons.

The very existence of this class may be unknown to the upper and middle portion of society, as they are to be found in parts of the great cities unfrequented by respectable persons ; but they may be seen in large numbers when a great exciting cause arises, whether a mob, or a trial of some of their associates, or an execution (a scene which should inspire a sickening horror into any person of common humanity), when their wild yells and heartless demeanour reveal the worse than heathen barbarism which is in our midst. Let us mentally follow these wretched beings to their homes, if such they can be called, and form some conception what the children must be who are brought up under such influences.

The testimony of the present writer three years ago at the Birmingham Conference is, unhappily, still true :—

"To perceive the existence of this class, it is necessary only to walk, as I have done, through whole districts of Liverpool, endeavouring to discover among those squalid courts and alleys some of the families whence children have been rescued as brands from the burning, and sent to a Reformatory ;—to go into the swarming by-streets of the old town of Warrington, and there find the wretched children so unaccustomed to even the casual notice of one of the civilised class, that they stared with astonishment when I addressed to them words of kindness. It needs but to walk, as I have, at all hours, through the Lewins' Mead district of Bristol, unhappily by no means unique in its character in that ancient city, to perceive the fearful evil, and see year after year pass without any material alteration in it. Decades of years glide by, and it is still the same. Half a century ago its infamous character was such that a respectable labouring man, whose road lay through it to convey a lady home on Sabbath evenings from her place of worship, declared that the language and scenes to which he was exposed made him feel as if he were going 'out of heaven into the bottomless pit.' When, some years ago, I gave a lesson to a Ragged School in this district on the destruction of Sodom, the wickedness and riot described in the Scripture narrative appeared to the children merely a portraiture of familiar scenes ; and they all acknowledged that if Lewins' Mead had been the subject of the patriarch's prayer, to save it from destruction, not ten good men could be found here any more than there. Nine years ago I stated in my evidence before the Commons' Committee the condition of this part of the city, which is such as to render it seldom visited by the police, who dare not singly cope with so vicious a population. Within this very month, as I walked through it, the whole thoroughfare was crowded with combatants, leaving no space for passengers ; and a policeman at hand angrily refused me to interfere, until supported by several others."

Such scenes as these are familiar to persons who are acquainted with the back slums of the metropolis.

Let us realise the consequence to the community of whole districts remaining in this state of isolated barbarism, and reflect how impossible it is for the children to emerge from it unhelped. Not only must they grow up to be no better than their parents, and perpetuate such a condition of things, but there is a constant tendency in them to drag down others from the class above them, whose natural dispositions or circumstances indicate a proclivity to crime. Workhouse Inspectors have long perceived the existence of this untaught and uncivilised class; from observing the condition of the inmates of the Workhouse, they have known that this class was not reached by the educational agencies of the country. This portion of our population is nearly untouched by any institutions of our country,—except the poorhouse, the police-force, and the gaol. They are in a state of semi-barbarism. They are slaves of their lower instincts and passions; they have no care for what does not immediately concern their present needs; nor will they sacrifice their convenience or their money to obtain education for their children, for they no more comprehend its true value than a man blind from birth can understand the nature of sight. They live in a state of ignorance of all that constitutes civilised society, a practical ignorance of man's immortal nature and destiny,—an ignorance which degrades below the brute creation, that *does* fulfil after its kind the end for which the Creator gave existence; which chains the sense and debases by sensual indulgence; which makes men hunger only for the bread which perisheth, and not for that which is the nutriment of true life; which makes them thirst only for that which stimulates to maddenning frenzy, preventing them from receiving the waters of life. Such is, in faint and few words, the meaning which is really hidden under the simple word "*ignorance*," but which is too often lost sight of in our anxiety to convey rudiments of book-learning, which we most falsely suppose will be an antidote to crime. And the effect of such ignorance is not only that the individuals labouring under it are utterly unfit to hold any social position in the State; not only that they are without such *practical* acquaintance with the laws of God and man as will withhold them from the crime into which they are continually led by the desire of sensual gratification; but that they live in a state of entire isolation from the comparatively virtuous and respectable portions of society, and consequently more or less in absolute antagonism to it. The consequence of this necessarily is that our Workhouses are filled with them, as our Inspectors testify, and that our Reformatories are recruited from the same sources, as we ourselves are fully aware,—children in the lowest depths of ignorance, who have never received any Christian sympathy or instruction. The Chaplains of our Convict Prisons bear the same testimony:—

"The religious and moral condition of the prisoners may be shortly but truly and accurately described, in apostolical language, as that of men 'living without God in the world.' * * * In most cases there has been an utter and habitual neglect of all the requirements commonly regarded as essential to even a nominal Christian life."

So speaks the Chaplain of Millbank Prison, in the present year, and in the former one the Chaplain of Dartmoor Prison testified:—

"Many demand our pity as much as our censure, considering their extraction, and the deplorable circumstances which have overshadowed them from their birth. Not a few of them first saw the light in the 'guilt-gardens' which disgrace our great cities. It would have been little short of the miraculous if these unfortunate ones had turned out better than they have. What would have been the career of any of us, had we been born in a community of thieves and depraved beings, breathing an atmosphere of oaths and obscenity, looking upon everything we could grasp as our spoil, and regarding every one whom we could overcome as our prey."

The Police Report of Liverpool for this year shows the following alarming amount of ignorance in that town:—

## " EDUCATION.

" Comparative statement for four years :—

| Years. | Read and Write well. | Read and Write imperfectly. | Read only. | Neither Read nor Write. |
|---|---|---|---|---|
| 1861 | 796 | 9890 | 1873 | 7187 |
| 1862 | 616 | 11563 | 2584 | 9178 |
| 1863 | 477 | 13111 | 2799 | 9842 |
| 1864 | 328 | 12637 | 2604 | 10280 |

"This is the lowest degree of education compared with any preceding year, and quite in keeping with the figures contained in the foregoing tables (p. 8)." These tables give the nature of the crimes committed, the number of persons apprehended, the arrests for drunkenness, the thousands of juvenile offenders, "painfully on the increase," under the age of sixteen. No wonder is this, while ignorance and drunkenness prevent the moral growth of the rising generation!

A great and glaring wrong is being done to the children of our land in being thus suffered to grow up in heathen ignorance. It is no fault of theirs that they are so situated. Each young being that enters this world is a child of the same Heavenly Father with ourselves, and has an immortal spirit. The State protects its body from starvation, but "man liveth not by bread alone." The children who grow up *untaught* and *uncared-for* in our *Christian* and *civilised* country do not owe *restitution* to society when they have infringed its laws, which they have never been taught, or when they become dependent on it for physical support, from never having had a proper training of the powers which the loving Creator has given them. *Society owes restitution to them* for having left them in this condition,—passed by, as it were, on the other side of the world's highway. This the present writer can forcibly state from her own experience, having for eighteen long years been watching the fearful odds with which these poor children are compelled to fight the battle of life, who spring into existence in the midst of the dense ignorance which has been here faintly pourtrayed.

The education of this class of the population was the subject of the resolution already quoted in the Lords' Committee of 1847. No steps were then taken by the Government, or have been taken since, to carry out the intention of the resolution.

The only agency that has ever attempted to grapple with the difficult work described in the Report of the Lords' Committee, and indicated by the foregoing extract, is that commonly called the Ragged School, a movement which began about the year 1846. Its object was to afford the very kind of education described in the resolution already quoted. The founders of Ragged Schools sought out the very lowest and most ne͏ children they could find, endeavoured to give them moral and religious training, to civilise them, to teach them honest industry, and to let them know practically that they were not regarded as the offscourings of the earth, the refuse of society, —that there were those who cared for their souls. The work was a difficult one, but they persevered in it, and eighteen years of long and painful experience have only convinced them more and more forcibly, that this is the very work most wanting in England. They began as a doubtful experiment, regarded with sceptical eyes by those who took an interest in education generally; they were not sympathised with by those devoted to the interests of their peculiar churches, and who desired *especially* to augment their numbers. Hence, there has always been a great difficulty in obtaining funds for the necessary expenses of such Schools, which have often been inefficient from want of proper machinery and teaching powers, and which never have existed in the numbers necessary for the wants of the population.

Such was the position of the question at the first Birmingham

Conference. The Ragged Schools had indeed led the way in the case of many of its promoters to the perception of the necessity of further agencies for those children whom they could not reach, owing to their being too deeply sunk in crime, though still young, to be voluntary attendants at a day school. They had done an important work in penetrating the dark places of our cities; even if they could not remove the darkness, they led the way to more extended and effective efforts. The Committee of Council on Education was at that time encouraging voluntary effort by grants in aid of Schools, under certain conditions; but these, however well adapted to the labouring portion of the population, were totally unfit for such ignorant and semi-barbarous children. Not only so, but a strong disinclination was expressed by the Council to give any portion of the grant to this most neglected and destitute part of the community. A memorial was sent by the Conference to the Committee of Council, setting forth the need of help, and the reasons why the present provisions were unavailable for Ragged Schools,—but in vain.

The Select Committee of the House of Commons in 1852-53 thus spoke in the 23rd and 24th resolutions:—

"23. That the Ragged Schools existing in England and Scotland, and recently introduced into Ireland, especially the ragged industrial feeding schools, at present supported by voluntary subscriptions, or, as in Glasgow, by local rates, have produced beneficial effects on the children of the most destitute classes of society inhabiting large towns.

"24. That voluntary contributions have been found inadequate to supply the number of such schools at present required in the metropolis, and other cities and towns; and therefore they should not be excluded from the aid of the National Grant, under the distribution of the Committee of Council for Education; great care being necessary in framing the minutes applicable to this description of schools, so as not to fetter private exertions, or to exclude men eminently qualified to fill the laborious and difficult position of teachers, by the requirement of too high an educational certificate."

But the Government of our country has never yet acknowledged this responsibility to protect the child from ignorance as well as from starvation; it has never effectually aided, still less stimulated to exertion, the large number of voluntary labourers who have shown themselves willing to give devoted efforts to this work. If only they could obtain sufficient pecuniary means to sustain Schools for this class of children in due efficiency, they were ready to go to the high-ways and bye-ways, search them out, and invite them to come in, holding them there by the bonds of Christian love. Instead of welcoming such help to do for the country what the Lords' Committee could only recommend, and what no government machinery could possibly effect, the educational grants of the country have been most unaccountably directed to help those abundantly who could well help themselves; the Educational Council have not only ignored the very existence of this large portion of the population, but, until the present minutes have been passed, by their regulations have actually cut them off from receiving any direct educational help. The Government has built gigantic prisons, and spent annually enormous sums to maintain and controul those who have been brought to this desperate condition by early neglect;— by spending a pound annually in educating the child for a few years, the expense might have been saved of maintaining him for many years in a Convict Prison, at a rate of more than forty pounds per annum.

Remonstrances and entreaties for suitable help have been frequently addressed, but in vain, to the Committee of Council on Education. Once, and once only, in June, 1856, was a minute issued specially adapted to the real wants of this class of Schools, and calculated at the same time to stimulate to exertion. But, unfortunately, it was burdened with an allowance for food, which was evidently out of place in an educational grant, and which exposed it to great abuses. Hence, conditions were afterwards annexed which nullified its operations, and it was withdrawn before the end of the next year, another minute being substituted which gave no help, except for industrial work.

But the need of help was increasingly felt in the country.

Considerable difficulty existed, however, in obtaining a united effort on the part of the Managers of the Ragged Schools.

Those in London, and others connected with their Society, have generally expressed an unwillingness to receive aid, from a fear of interference with the religious influence which they desired to exercise on their children. Besides, they never aimed at any high scholastic standard, and feared that any attempt to make their Schools conformable to Government requirements might prove injurious to them. But the question was not whether the Managers of certain Schools wished to obtain help, but whether it was an important general principle that help should be given by the Government in the education of that portion of the population which must otherwise remain uneducated. A third Conference was held at Birmingham in January, 1861, founded on the principle, — *" That it is the duty of the State, both as regards society in general and each individual composing it, to provide education for those who cannot obtain it for themselves."* The principles of this Conference were supported by Lord BROUGHAM, by Lord SHAFTESBURY, whose name has ever been foremost in all that concerns the education and elevation of this class of the community, Sir J. S. PAKINGTON, who presided over the Conference, Sir STAFFORD NORTHCOTE, Rev. Dr. GUTHRIE, who had so forcibly and practically supported the claims of this class in Edinburgh, Sheriff WATSON, of Aberdeen, and a number of noblemen and gentlemen whose position or professional duties led them to a deep conviction of the necessity of providing for the education of the perishing and dangerous classes.

Thus a very strong and united testimony was given to the principle that if any class of the population is to be helped to obtain education, *a priori* this class should receive especial help, for the welfare of society, as well as for the individual.

But no change was made by the Council.

The Royal Westminster Education Commission proposed questions on the subject, through the late NASSAU SENIOR, Esq.

The following answer given respecting Ragged Schools by the writer, is a sample of their general results.

"A whole district has been improved. Twelve years ago, Lewin's Mead, Bristol, and the neighbouring courts and alleys, swarmed with juvenile thieves; it was not unusual for two or three in a single family to be known depredators and convicted thieves; it was considered an honour for a boy to be the acknowledged head of a gang; twenty-five were in one year in prison who were occasional attendants at the Ragged School. The neighbouring National, British and Infant Schools, bordering on this district, exercised no influence over it. But now, for more than ten years no child has been in prison in attendance at this Ragged School, and though the district is still very low, being chiefly inhabited by the poor Irish, yet juvenile crime is most rare in it, a convicted thief being almost unknown in it. The shopkeepers have expressed their great satisfaction at the increased security of property. In some districts of Bristol, as well as of London, Gloucester, and other places, the bulk of the scholars have been so far improved as to be drafted into National Schools. The possibility of this depends on the nature of that part of the population. The parents of the children have often been induced to make an effort to improve the condition of their children, by the combined action of the school discipline on the scholars, and the home visitation and influence of the master and managers. Numberless children who were growing up in ignorance and vice, have, through the influence of Ragged Schools, become useful and self-supporting members of society."

In the spring of 1861 a Parliamentary Committee investigated the condition of the neglected and destitute children, and strong evidence was brought before it, showing the necessity for education for this portion of the population.

The complete change introduced by the Revised Educational Code rendered it expedient that we should suspend for a time our efforts to obtain aid for our Schools, until we had given a fair trial to the effect of its provisions.

The present position of the question is this:—

The Government has not yet recognised the necessity of directing the educational grants of the country to the portion of the population which requires aid the most, and which has been proved unable to obtain it, by voluntary effort only.

Nor has the Government practically acknowledged the duty to society, nor the advantage to itself, of arresting the constantly increasing sources of crime, by the preventive measure of education of the class which chiefly supplies the criminal ranks.

The Government has now, in the Revised Code, withdrawn the

regulations which *prevented* the Ragged Schools from the possibility of receiving any portion of the aid given to other Schools· But the regulations which are framed for a higher class of children, are necessarily *quite unfitted for these.* We willingly accept "results" as a fair test of the efficiency of a School, and its claim for aid, but we contend that the results to be justly required from Schools for this class of children are of a different kind from those to be expected from the higher class of the labouring population. If the results required in the latter case are purely intellectual, those in the former should embrace the moral and physical training of the children. There is, however, another circumstance which prevents Ragged Schools from obtaining aid under the existing minutes. While the Revised Code bases its grants upon results, it requires, we must be allowed to say, with great inconsistency, that these results shall be obtained only with a *particular machinery,* which it defines. It is not sufficient that a master shall have raised his scholars to the required standard, and conducted his School in a perfectly satisfactory manner; no grant will be awarded unless he himself has gone through a prescribed course of training, and has undergone a certain examination which does indeed test the knowledge he possesses on certain subjects, but *not* his power of *teaching,* nor his *moral influence.* If this limitation is felt to be injurious in the higher Schools, as is proved by the strong remonstrances on the subject made in Parliament, how much more must it be injurious in these Schools, for which the certificated teachers rarely possess qualifications. The effect has already practically been to exclude excellent Ragged Schools from the small help they before received, and to leave others in their previous unaided condition. The 10,000 in Liverpool and the thousands elsewhere remain uneducated, still to swell the criminal class.

Thus the portion of the population *most* requiring educational aid, both for their own sakes and for that of society in general, is still practically excluded from receiving it from the Government of the country. There must be special provision made for them.

These children are not paupers; they cannot receive education from the Workhouse Schools. Parliament annually grants £30,000 for the education of those who are so; why should there be any hesitation in affording it to those who are thoroughly neglected and falling into crime, or who are struggling to keep themselves from dependence, but unable to pay for education. They cannot be placed in Certified Industrial Schools, as some have suggested, for what have they done that they could come under the provisions of the Act, and be placed under magisterial sentence? They are running wildly in the streets; their training is neglected,—that can be given them at a comparatively small expense to the public, perhaps sixpence per week, in a Ragged School; but they have not committed acts which would bring them under the provisions of the Industrial Schools' Act;—why, indeed, should we wish unnecessarily to remove them from their parents, and charge the Treasury with five shillings a week for each one under magisterial sentence?

It is to be deeply regretted that those who interest themselves in the education of the labouring population of the country, and extend their efforts to the middle classes, which ought to be able to help themselves,—that such persons should entirely overlook the crying wants of these neglected ones, who, unhelped, must continue to remain in dense ignorance. It must be, then, for those who are striving to carry on a Christian warfare against the crime of our land, it is for them to take up the cause of those who are perishing for lack of knowledge, and to endeavour to induce the Government to take this preventive measure, which yields in importance to no other in our country, for on it depends the diminution of crime, and the well-being of the present generation,—the highest welfare of the next.

# CHAPTER VII.

## CÖOPERATION OF SOCIETY.

OUR task is well-nigh completed! It has been a painful one, probably, both to reader and to writer, to follow our Convicts in their lawless career, living in defiance of God and of man; to see them dogged and defiant in incarceration; to behold them, when in partial liberty, only more daring, more hostile to society, gathering strength for new outrages; to find them again in the world, schooled to new modes of wickedness, corrupting all within their sphere, preying on the peaceful part of society, and, as it were, licensed marauders, until they should, by some extraordinary deed of wickedness, again put themselves within the grasp of the law. It was necessary to know the evil, in order to seek for a cure;—to learn the causes of it, that we may discover means of preventing its constant recurrence.

We have not, however, been exclusively occupied with scenes of vice. We have had the happiness of contemplating order, diligence, a spirit of brotherly kindness and Christian obedience, succeeding a life of reckless lawlessness,—and this in a Convict Prison. We have seen the men who formerly were ruffians of various descriptions, skilful house-breakers, men who preferred a life of dishonest idleness to one of honest labour,—we have seen these very men, after their time of penal servitude had been completed, go forth in voluntary subjection to the law of the land, engaging in humble laborious work among their fellows, atoning to society for their past misdeeds by their present virtuous lives.

We trust, then, that faith in human nature, and in the power of the good and the true, has thus been strengthened, not shaken by the foregoing survey, and that many have been incited to put to themselves the question,—"What shall *we*,— shall *I* do?" It is the object of this concluding chapter to point out some of the ways in which society may thus cöoperate with the Government.

Belief in the possibility of the amelioration of every human being as long as he remains in the world, is essential to any efforts that are to be made for the improvement of that portion of our fellow-creatures who are the subject of our consideration. Without this, all our plans for their benefit will be devoid of that spirit and vigour and hopefulness, which are essential to their success. With this confidence, appealing to the better nature of our fellow-being, showing him that we regard him as a child of the same Heavenly Father as ourselves, that we recognise the immortal nature within him, which his sins had caused him to forget; efforts for his good, which might otherwise be poor and insignificant, become fraught with a power which astonishes him who makes them, and inspires the conviction, "Not I, but the grace of God which is in me." With this strong faith, disappointment and failure do not discourage, but only incite to new and better efforts. None could have come in contact with more degraded characters than Captain MACONOCHIE, but we have seen that his confidence in the possibility of elevating them never left him, and that he found gratitude and improvement, where the reverse was anticipated. So with MONTESINOS and OBERMAIER. So with Sir WALTER CROFTON. After having come in contact with so many thousands of Convicts, his faith in their susceptibility of improvement has been unshaken, and he has been heard to say, "I should hesitate to pronounce any Convict incorrigible." He mentioned in illustration the following instance :–

"Some years ago there was a convict in the Irish Government Prisons who had sprung from a criminal family and passed his life in acts of daring. For some time his conduct in the prisons was very audacious, and he resisted all efforts to improve him. At length, however, he began to endeavour to do well, and by slow degrees worked his way through the various stages and classes, until he acquired the privilege of going out on ticket-of-leave. A situation was procured for him. But on mentioning this to the Superintendent of Police, he entreated that so dangerous a step might not be taken, as he considered it impossible that a man with such antecedents and such connections could live in safety in the very scene of his former misdeeds. But the prison authorities felt more confidence, and the man was released, Sir W. CROFTON requesting him to call at his office once a fortnight, and let him know of his well-being; the police being also desired to observe him. For some time all went on smoothly, until one morning the man appeared in great despair, exclaiming that he was undone, and could never show his face any more. Sir WALTER was alarmed, and inquired the cause of his trouble. The poor man explained that as he was working a gentleman rode by, whose house he had broken into when he was convicted of burglary. The gentleman had evidently recognised him, and eyed him closely. He would henceforth be a marked man, and no longer able to continue in his place of work. His friend, the Director, reassured him, and promised to communicate with the gentleman, whom he satisfied, on the authority of the police, that the man was evidently leading an honest life. The man persevered: after a time rescued a younger brother from a bad course, and took him to work with him; he subsequently married respectably, and trained up his children in the way they should go."

This was the man who had been pronounced incorrigible.

A striking example of the susceptibility of even the most apparently hardened and hopeless to the influence of Christian love appealing to their inner nature, is found in the records of Dr. TUCKERMAN, of Boston, U. S., who, in November, 1826, originated the "Ministry at Large" in America, or, as we term it, "Domestic Mission:"—

"Early in the year 1827, as I was one morning on my way to the north part of this city, my attention was arrested by a crowd about the door of the United States Court House; and upon inquiry into the cause of it, I was informed that two pirates were about to receive sentence of death. I immediately entered the Court, and was soon very near and in front of the prisoners. Here a spectacle was brought before me more painful than language can express. Nothing can be more unlike than was the countenance of each of these prisoners to that of the other. That of one expressed all the rage of a demon, and that of the other the strongest possible contempt,

Judge STORY arose, and asked them if they had any cause to assign why the sentence of death should not be pronounced upon them? The first to whom I have referred, at once, and in all the madness of the most murderous rage, poured out a torrent of the most profane and revengeful language upon the District Attorney and the Court. The other with a sardonic grin—for it could hardly be called a smile—replied only, 'the sooner the better.' Judge STORY said that he had witnessed many very affecting scenes in the discharge of his judicial duties, but never one so painful as on that occasion. The sentence having been pronounced upon them, they were remanded to prison. It was quite impossible that I should take the course I had marked out for myself for the morning; and having followed these men to the prison, and obtained admission, I asked the turnkey to beg of one of them permission to enter his cell, with a view only to any services which it might be in my power to render him. The turnkey entered a cell, but very soon returned and said to me, 'he will not allow you to enter.' The door was on a jar; and I entered the cell, saying to the turnkey, 'please to come for me in an hour.' He adjusted the bolts, turned the key in the lock, and left us. I offered my hand to the prisoner, which I think he did not take. I assured him of my great desire to serve him. His reply was: 'I only wish to be in hell, where it is hot, and not in this cold place.' The hour passed, and the turnkey returned. Not the smallest apparent moral progress had been made in that hour, except in the circum-stance that this unhappy man had consented to my request to pass an hour of the next day with him. He had said, in reply to my request to visit him again, 'you may come if you choose. I care nothing about it.' I went the next day, and the next, and the next; and endeavoured by every means in my power to get at his heart, and to make some impression there. I also closed each visit with prayer. It was now, however, quite perceptible that a change of feelings had begun in him. He had a father and mother living, and I had addressed myself in every way to his filial sensibilities. There seemed to be no other chord in his heart from which a moral vibra-tion was to be obtained. I think it was on the fifth or sixth day of my visits to him that he said 'amen' at the conclusion of my prayers. He was now desirous and glad to see me. The remembrance of his parents was the great restorative of his sensibilities. On about the tenth or twelfth day of my visits he fell upon his knees, when we prayed together. He had now a very deep sense of his guilt, and the character of his penitence was most peculiarly filial. God was revealed to him as his Father, and his heart was penetrated and bowed as the heart of a greatly guilty but sincerely repenting child. Every thought and care and interest was absorbed in the single desire of the mercy, the forgiveness of his Heavenly Father. I passed an hour with this man every day during, I think, thirty-four or thirty-five days; and never have I heard such sup-plications, such entreaties for mercy as I heard from his lips. In the midst of one of my prayers he broke out in such impassioned and importunate cries to God that it seemed to me as if the very stones of his cell might have responded to them. My own heart was well nigh broken by his anguish. And he died, apparently the most contrite being I have ever known. Whether other modes of appeal to him might have been as effectual, I know not. It is enough, and I bless God that this to which I have referred was at least a principal means of his moral recovery."

Let such faith and hope and love for the soul of the most obdurate be carried into our Convict Prisons, and the results will be proportionate.

The Select Committee of 1856, after hearing what might have been regarded as very discouraging evidence respecting the result of Convict training in the Government Prisons, were yet so satisfied with the evidence of others who had adopted a different system, that they made the following statement, as the nineteenth resolution of their Report:—

" That the Committee concurs with some of the most experienced witnesses they have examined, in the opinion that a great majority of convicted prisoners are open to the same good motives and good impulses which influence other human beings, and therefore that a system of encouragement to good conduct, and *endeavours to inspire feelings of self-respect, self-reliance, and hopefulness for the future,* which have been tried in some of our largest establishments, ought to be adopted, so far as is practicable, without impairing the penal and deterrent character, essential to any system of imprisonment."

Now this resolution is a recognition by the Committee of the very important principle, that no mechanical means, but the introduction of human sympathies and spritual influences into a prison system, constitutes the real reformatory power. It is through human agency that a renovating influence is to be introduced into our Convict Prisons, and into society at large. "Man cannot be reformed by mechanical means," our statesman has said, and the words found an echo in distant lands; they point to no new truth, and express a very old experience, but they are important as an acknowledgement of a great truth in a higher quarter.

It is, then, essential to enlist voluntary effort in the work of reformation. When we use this term, we wish to indicate a willing heartfelt effort to promote the welfare of our fellow-beings,

We are all perfectly aware that whatever we do of our own
free will, throwing our heart and soul and strength into it,
we accomplish far better and more effectually than what we do
compulsorily.  No slave under the lash, no prisoner fearing the
eye of his jailor, will do the work of a free labourer, stimulated
only by his own spirit; no mere officials, however well paid by
their superiors, will ever toil by night and by day, in season and
out of season, like those who, animated by the love of God and
of man, voluntarily devote their powers to their work, and are
willing, if need be, to sacrifice themselves to it.  Probably in no
country does there exist so large an amount of this voluntary
action as in our own, because in none is there so great a
degree of freedom combined with a reverence for law.  But that
this individual voluntary effort should be successful, it must be
united with knowledge how best to work, power to effect what
is good, and pecuniary means to provide the necesssary
machinery.  If all these are combined in those persons who
desire to accomplish any work, the most valuable results may
be anticipated.  A close relation is established between those
who thus give their time, their labour, and their means, and
those who receive benefits of the most important nature.  The
receipt of alms, or maintenance at the public cost, is degrading
to the nature, and never inspires gratitude, but is received with
insolent dependence, or even with arrogant assumption as a
right.  But unpurchased efforts, and self-sacrifice for the good
of our fellow-creatures, are more calculated than anything else,
if judiciously directed, to awaken and strengthen the better
parts of the nature, and to make it even doubtful which is the
most blessed, to give or to receive.

There is besides a deeper and even more important element
in voluntary and benevolent effort, which, from its very nature,
cannot be absolutely defined, and which, if genuine, shrinks
from observation,—the religious element.  This is not an in-
culcation of creeds, or even the communication of religious
truth; these may, of course, be intrusted to an official paid

to give routine instruction in them. But we mean that awakening of the religious principle within, which is effected through Divine grace, by the spiritual action of one soul upon another; that Divine sympathy which, viewing in every human being, however mean or low to outward view, however young or however old, an immortal soul, and a child of the same Father, will be ready, following in the steps of the Saviour, to feel his weakness and bear his burden, and to draw him towards holiness " with the cords of a man." This is the true voluntary element; this is the water which can be obtained only " without money and without price," and is the best restorative to those who are thirsting for the waters of life.

Now, we would by no means be supposed to say that this voluntary and essentially religious element cannot co-exist with an official position; it can, and frequently does so;—it has, indeed, peculiar power when it is found there. Without it, those who are paid to do certain duties in Gaols, Workhouses, or other institutions, may perform them with scrupulous exactness and zealous fidelity, as regards their instructions and the wishes of their superiors, and yet establish no friendly relations between themselves and the objects of their care. If the duties they have to perform are unpleasant ones, there will exist an hostility and antagonism between them, or at best a sullen acquiescence, to avoid punishment. But if the same duties are performed with the spirit just described, which is full of healing virtue, then the driest routine is fraught with interest, and painful drudgery is even transformed into a labour of love.

The remarkable union in the Irish Convict System of voluntary effort and a wisely directed sympathy, with a judiciously planned system of routine work, constitutes its peculiar feature, and the grand secret of its success. And it was because every one working in it, from the Director to the most subordinate official, was animated more or less by the same spirit, and made the work a personal and voluntary, as well as a paid

and official one, that the admirably planned system has had
the success which has attended it.

Seldom have we met with a more striking instance of daily
and voluntary self-sacrifice in an official position than in the
late Rev. JOHN CLAY, who, as Prison Chaplain, gave to his
work an amount of devoted labour, with warm sympathy and
spiritual help, which eventually exhausted his physical frame,
and the full results of which only the last day can reveal.
Truly, as his son has beautifully said in the dedication of his
father's memoirs to Mr. Recorder HILL, " He spent and lost
his life in the holy war against sin and ignorance."

It is to this element that our Reformatories and Industrial
Schools owe their peculiar excellence, and their influence on
the wayward and misdirected children who are placed in them.
In a well conducted Institution, the officials, whether male or
female, regard not their own personal comfort, nor keep within
the strict terms of "the bond," but go beyond it in time and
labour, and do not find it wearisome, because they love it, feel
a personal interest in it, and desire above all the true welfare
of their young charge.   They are fellow-labourers with those
to whose responsibility the children are intrusted by the Government,- and the children feel that they are under the care of
friends who love them.   These are paid officials, yet they do not
their duty as hirelings, but with the zeal of voluntary workers.

Even among the police of our country, a body of men who
are usually considered so hostile to the class of persons before
us, may be found, and we have ourselves observed it, as genuine
a desire and effort to benefit their fellow-creatures, as can be
met with anywhere.   We have heard a Superintendent of Police
rejoice, with a very excusable pride, in the hope that his town
was better than it would be without him, for that he not only
prevented much crime by a strict attention to duty, but helped
those in difficulty, who sought him as a friend for aid and
council.   The young boys whom he had been the means of
sending to a Reformatory, have come to him on their discharge

as to a father, for advice and encouragement; and when he sees a poor young girl driven into crime by the circumstances of her home, he spares no pains to get her placed in a suitable Reformatory. We have known another exert himself to save from the prison brand young boys and girls who were wandering through his county uncared for, and beg, as a personal favour, for their admission into an Industrial School. Many instances of kindness and earnestness to assist those who have gone astray may be constantly found in the police force, where even ordinary officials have been glad to give a helping hand to persons who had been marked characters, but had shown a desire to begin a new life. Such has already been the result of the supervision of licenseholders, where commenced under the provisions of the new Act.

Let us now consider some of the ways in which the voluntary cöoperation of Society with the Government is needed in the great work of the repression and prevention of crime.

By the recent legislation a way is opened by the Government in which the unofficial and purely voluntary aid of Society is not only required, but even invited to assist in the restoration of our Convicts, helping them on their discharge to obtain work, and giving them encouragement to lead a better life. When the Government has done its part in adopting the best possible means for the reformation of our Convicts, and has proved to the public that they may again be trusted, since they have done well in partial liberty, it is for Society also to do its part in giving them kind and Christian help.

Much has already been attempted in various parts of the country in aid of prisoners discharged from the common gaols. We know how valuable were the labours of the Rev. J. CLAY, of Preston, in this respect. Without any Society or "Refuge for Discharged Prisoners" to assist him, he enlisted in the service many voluntary helpers, and the police also; obtained work for the men on their discharge, and kept a friendly surveillance over them which proved most valuable. At Wakefield, the Governor of the Gaol, Mr. E. SHEPHERD, himself organised an Industrial Home for discharged prisoners. The men lived as in a well-ordered lodging-house, and paid their expenses by their own work, so that the Institution had the rare merit of being self-supporting. Mr. SHEPHERD thus speaks of it in his farewell address to the Magistrates, on his resignation, after thirty-eight years of service:—

"I have also given considerable time and thought to the subject of the reformation of criminals. About seven years ago I established in the vicinity of the prison an 'Industrial Home,' whereat released prisoners might obtain employment, and earn a livelihood until they had an opportunity of meeting with other occupation. This Institution, though entirely independent of the prison, has proved a most useful and beneficial auxiliary to that establishment. I received kind offers of pecuniary assistance from several of the Magistrates, when I first opened the 'Industrial Home;' but I am happy to say that I have not found it necessary to avail myself of their offers, but have managed to render it self-supporting. It has, in short, been successful in every respect. Its value, as a Reformatory Institution, is proved by the fact that 734 released prisoners have been inmates since the opening, and of that number at least 300 are now known to be honestly earning their living by various occupations, the majority of whom are settled in Wakefield or its neighbourhood."

In July, 1862, an important Act was passed (25 & 26 Vic., c. 44) to second the efforts made by individuals in aid of discharged prisoners. This Act enables the Visiting Justices of a prison to make a grant, not exceeding £2 in any one case, to the Treasurer of a properly certified Discharged Prisoners' Aid Society, upon an undertaking being signed by the Secretary that such money shall be expended, in accordance with the requirements of the Act, in behalf of a prisoner discharged from such prison.

The following is the mode of its operation in Birmingham:—

" Upon an application for assistance being received, the amount of gratuity due to the applicant, and his wish as to how it is to be expended, are first ascertained. The agent visits him at the address given, and reports as to whether the general circumstances of the case look promising or otherwise. If the man has no home, the first object is to see him respectably lodged; or if the neighbourhood he has selected for himself appears to be undesirable, an endeavour is made to induce him to change it. If these preliminaries cannot be satisfactorily arranged the case is dismissed. But if the man seems likely to benefit by the assistance rendered, then the gratuity is applied for in his behalf; and, when this has been received, the society becomes responsible for the way in which it is expended. A home having been provided, and suitable clothes obtained, the next object is to see him employed. Work is either sought out for him, or he is encouraged to seek it for himself. If the man is a labourer there is comparatively little difficulty in the matter, but in other cases a considerable delay is frequently experienced, the want of a good character being a great barrier to his getting employment. It is here that the friendly offices of the Society are chiefly called into requisition. His former employers are applied to, places of work are suggested to him, or else he is provided with the means of setting up for himself. From time to time he receives the friendly visits of the agent, whose duty it is to report what the convict is doing, and, under the direction of the Committee, to assist him in every way that lies in his power. These visits are continued even after the convict has drawn the whole of his gratuity from the society; and it is gratifying to report that while the agent has never had cause to complain of rudeness or incivility on the part of any prisoner assisted by the society, he has frequently found them most grateful for the advice and the assistance that they have received. In some instances, especially where the discharged convict is accustomed to, and is capable of, rough manual labour, or where a man's past career, and the companionship of former associates, seem likely to prove an hindrance to him in carrying out his good resolutions in this country, the Committee have recommended emigration.

"When a discharged convict expresses a readiness to emigrate, an outfit is provided for him, and he is sent to Liverpool with as little delay as possible, where he has to report himself to the Society's Emigration Agent. His passage is paid; and on his reaching his destination, the balance of his gratuity is made over to him by the captain of the vessel in which he sails. In almost all other cases the society withholds for some time a portion of the convict's gratuity, as a guarantee for his good behaviour."—Fourth Rep.

The London Prisoners' Aid Society in London state in their Seventh Annual Report that the number of cases annually entertained by the Society has been as follows:—

| | 1857 | 1858 | 1859 | 1860 | 1861 | 1862 | 1863 | Total. |
|---|---|---|---|---|---|---|---|---|
| | 49 | 315 | 440 | 741 | 769 | 689 | 451 | 3454 |
| Of whom there have been assisted to emigrate | 12 | 97 | 95 | 167 | 223 | 254 | 163 | 1011 |
| There have been aided in other ways | 37 | 218 | 345 | 574 | 546 | 435 | 288 | 2443 |

From the 1st January to the 31st May, in the present year, 165 cases have been entertained by the Society, of whom 71 have been assisted to emigrate; making a total of 3619 cases entertained, of whom 1082 have emigrated.

Many other societies are in operation throughout the country to effect the same excellent objects.

Of not less value are the efforts of individuals, of whom the excellent THOMAS WRIGHT, of Manchester, stands foremost in the present day; his exertions on behalf of his suffering and sinning fellow-creatures are too well known to need more than a passing allusion. The name of ELIZABETH FRY will always be foremost among those who have visited the prisoner, and striven most effectively to ameliorate the condition of our gaols. But the humbler one of SARAH MARTIN is no less deserving of record, and her labours were more calculated to stimulate to emulation, because without any advantages of talents, position or wealth, the results of her labours showed what might be effected by a sincere desire to serve her fellow-creatures in the spirit of Christ. She died in 1843, at the age of 52, at Yarmouth, where a memorial window was erected to her by subscription in the Parish Church. The following is extracted from an interesting memoir of her in "Our Exemplars, Poor and Rich:"—*

"Bravery, self-devotion and indomitable perseverance, were needed to carry her through the scenes she witnessed, and to win for her the marvellous influence she acquired over even the most depraved. The confidence she inspired in the sincerity of her purpose,—and here lay the secret of her success,—is shown by her having, during the whole period of her ministrations, met with insult but from one prisoner; though for some years, it is grievous to state, a trunkey, by his bad character and conduct, greatly distressed her.

"She was not long in perceiving the necessity of giving religious instruction to the inmates of the gaol, of separating the juvenile from the old offenders, of providing schooling for all, and what was more important still, regular employment, by which, besides removing the fatal snare of idleness, means could be afforded to the prisoner of earning a small sum for his support when discharged; and the vital importance of not abandoning him at this critical moment of his career also impressed itself early upon her mind. These topics were then gradually attracting attention; but while, year after year, the various methods by which such improvements might be accomplished were under discussion outside our gaols, SARAH MARTIN had applied herself single-handed to the task, and at Yarmouth had actually wrought those ameliorations in prison discipline which public men were baffled in their efforts to achieve.

---

* 12mo., CASSELL, London.

"Reading the Scriptures during a short visit was what she first attempted. Finding that there was no Divine worship or observance of Sunday in the gaol, her next step was to organise services for that day; the duties of both reader and preacher soon devolving upon herself. Of the afternoon service she was relieved in 1831, but she continued it in the morning until her last illness obliged her, in 1843, to give it up. Captain WILLIAMS, the Inspector of Prisons, who speaks of her in terms of the highest appreciation in several reports, writes in the second of these,—'Sunday, November 29th, 1835; attended Divine service in the prison; * * * a female, resident in the town, officiated; her voice was exceedingly melodious, her delivery emphatic, and her enunciation exceedingly distinct. The service was the Liturgy of the Church of England; two psalms were sung by the whole of the prisoners, and extremely well, much better than I have frequently heard in our best appointed churches. A written discourse, of her own composition, was read by her; it was of a purely moral tendency, involving no doctrinal points, and admirably suited to the hearers.'"

Women should always be those to carry Christian sympathy to the helpless and sinning of their own sex. SARAH MARTIN began her ministrations in the Workhouse. The dreary depths of those establishments have now been penetrated by many zealous and devoted women, who have organised themselves into a Workhouse Visiting Society· The result of this voluntary effort has already been excellent. In the Dublin Workhouse the women were formerly in so daring and violent a state that it was not deemed safe for ladies to go into the female wards without protection from the inmates; on one occasion *fourteen* female paupers were tried for setting fire to the Union, and were condemned by the Judge to penal servitude. Yet, after the visiting of the ladies commenced, in a short time a softening effect was produced, and the time of the visits was anticipated by the inmates with the greatest delight. The effect of the cöoperation of ladies in the Refuges in Ireland for female Convicts has already been spoken of. Many Refuges and Homes for those women who require Christian help to restore them to society after their fall from virtue or their imprisonment, are in successful operation in our country under the management of ladies, but as yet no efforts have been made for discharged female Convicts. Probably hopelessness of success has been the cause of this. But we trust that such a change will ere long be effected in our Convict Prisons, and such arrangements made by Government, as will render possible the establishment of such Refuges for our female Convicts as have been carried on so successfully in Ireland. Then we may feel a confidence that the Christian women of England will respond to the call, and will devote themselves to the restoration of their erring sisters.

But our whole work will not be done when we have completed the arduous task of restoring our Convicts, or, rather, when we have made every possible effort to restore such as are willing to return to the path of duty. It is not enough to help those who have already become Convicts, we must give a timely helping hand to those who are in danger of becoming so. We must increasingly use our best exertions to restore those who have taken the first step in the ordinary gaols, and, above all, we must devote our especial efforts to the improvement of the class from which the criminals spring. But to produce the needed effect on the criminal portion of the community there must be not only isolated efforts but a general coöperation of society in the work. The dying words of Judge TALFOURD, coming to us from the seat of judgment as the last testimony of a great and good man, should never be forgotten. But the warning has not yet been attended to. There is not yet sufficient sympathy existing in our country between the different classes of the community; "they that are strong" have not yet learnt to bear with those that are spiritually weak, and lighten them of their burden, or help them to bear it wisely and well. The "respectable" classes have rejoiced that they are not as other men are, thieves, pickpockets, burglars, Convicts; and go down to their homes from the house of prayer, or dwell in intellectual refinement, justified in their contempt and repugnance for them. It has been said that one-half the world knows not what the other half suffers. It is true, and until the upper half does know, from the exercise of genuine sympathy, the sufferings of the lower from sin and ignorance, these will not be materially diminished.

Let, then, every one, whether in a wide or narrow circle, resolve to do something to promote the welfare of others, by *personal effort*. The giving of money is not enough. There are multitudes who will gratify their kindly feelings by pecuniary sacrifice; the enormous sums raised in our country for the support of foreign missions, and of the various benevolent institutions, sufficiently testifies to this; but these are not enough, nor do they purchase for the donor an indemnity for the neglect of the more precious charity of personal kindness. There are multitudes of charitable societies conducted by a few real workers under the patronage of persons of rank, with a long array of names which conceal their small amount of action. Institutions and Societies are valuable instrumentalities in aid of personal effort, but cannot take its place; in reality the true value of these institutions is the amount of true Christian charity and personal influence of which they are made the medium. This personal effort may develop itself in a variety of ways. It is not in the power of all to become visitors of the poor; they may be unfitted for the work, or prevented from engaging in it by higher claims of duty. All cannot teach the young, but they may give encouragement to those who do so, and enhance the value of this by their sympathy which, if truly felt, may find various ways of expressing itself. Every one may avoid placing temptations in the way of their fellow-creatures. When we offer up for ourselves the daily prayer, "Lead us not into temptation," it is our bounden duty not to lead others into them. How many of the frauds which have recently been committed on a gigantic scale, have indirectly been caused by the want of close and regular inspection of accounts by Directors, who have thus helped to fill our Convict Prisons. How large a number of young persons have been first led into crime through their employers placing too great a confidence in them, and thus taxing their honesty beyond its strength to resist. How many domestic servants have been led into theft and lost their character through the culpable neglect of their mistress

respecting money or articles of value. The Recorder of Birmingham has enlarged forcibly in his Charges on the duty
of society in this respect. None, indeed, who see the very
unguarded exposure of goods in shops, can wonder at the
numerous thefts which are caused by the practise. Surely
persons who throw such temptation in the way of the young
or unprincipled, are themselves answerable for the sin. We
knew a youth who, falling before such a temptation, was led,
almost from the door of the School, to the cells of a Convict
Prison. In this way, then, does it behove society not to add to
the burden of crime in the country, but to cöoperate with
the Government in its efforts to repress crime by removing
the causes of temptation.

Another, among many other ways, may be mentioned in which
individuals may do great good, and much strengthen the hands
of Government. There are various important laws which have
been made by the Legislature for the suppression of houses
of ill-fame, receiving-houses of stolen goods, and others of an
immoral character, which remain virtually a dead letter through
want of cöoperation on the part of society in carrying them into
effect. It is evidently the intention of the Legislature that no
direct incitements to be evil should be tolerated. Yet all these
criminal resorts and open allurements to sin flourish among us,
and remain unblushingly in our midst in the face of day. They
must be connived at, or this could not still continue to be the
case. Every one who knows of the existence of such places is
bound as a Christian man and a good citizen to do all in his
power to suppress them, and thus cöoperate with the Government. If existing legislation is not sufficient, let efforts be
made to improve it.

The condition in which the young of our country are growing
up, or as it has been truly expressed, are dragged up, to take
the place of the present generation in the ranks of crime and
pauperism, should especially engage the attention of Society, and
enlist extensive voluntary effort. It is not known to the bulk

of the middle and upper classes of society;—it cannot be known, for no words can give an adequate idea of it to those who have not personally witnessed it. The back slums, the poverty-stricken lanes and alleys, the dens of vice, the hundreds of houses of sin, which the police of Liverpool and other towns know to exist, are hidden from the gaze of those who frequent the better portion of crowded cities; for only a few solitary individuals from them dare occasionally to obtrude their wretchedness on the well-dressed public. This is no new state of things. Nearly thirty years ago Dr. TUCKERMAN wrote:—

"I have seen a boy in our House of Correction for the third time for intemperance, when he was only fifteen years old. I have also seen one at fourteen years of age broken down by infirmities induced by the same cause, And often, even at that age is the deep and strong depravity within most distinctly shown in the eye, the countenance, and the whole air and manner of boys. Such boys are to be seen upon our wharves, and about our markets. But are they observed? Or what interest is excited in respect to them? I remember that when I was once dining in London with a circle of as intelligent men as I knew in that metropolis, some of whom were baristers, I asked them, if in their way to Westminster Hall, or to any of their Courts, they had never particularly regarded the appearance of very great numbers of wild. ragged and filthy boys, almost constantly to be seen in certain streets; or if, when seeing them, they had never thought of the probability that sooner or later these boys would be arraigned as criminals, for or against whom they would plead, and who would be transported or hung for crimes? The reply was, that they had but casually noticed them! Yet utterly neglected as were these many hundreds of children by those who might have been their saviours, and educated as these children were in crime and for crime, their moral responsibility for the condition in which they are, and for the offences for which they will be condemned, seems to me much smaller than is that of those whose disregard of them is a chief cause of their condition."

There are "very great numbers of wild, ragged and filthy boys, almost constantly to be seen in certain streets" of the metropolis now as then. The ignorance of their existence, and of their spiritual wants, is as great now as it was then. If those who do know them entreat for some adequate help for the education and even the civilization of these neglected children, it is refused by the dispensers of the Educational Grants of Parliament, and they are told that the Workhouses and Industrial Schools are for these, not the education which is destined for the labouring classes. How, indeed, can the Work-houses and Industrial Schools contain these myriads? Or how can they be compelled to enter them? Ten thousand make known their ignorance annually in the Liverpool Police Courts, but the Legislature does not attend to their cry;—who shall proclaim the wants of the other tens of thousands who do not make known their ignorance through their crime? It is the upper portion of society, bound to them by Christian sympathy, who should discover their need, comprehend the dreadful ignorance which exists in our land, and never cease from their personal efforts and their appeals for help, until such provision is made for them as was shown by the Lords' Committee so long ago to be needed, if the progress of crime in our country is to be arrested.

Not until then, not until all our children are educated, and the criminal class is brought under Christian influence, will the duty be fulfilled by society, which was so forcibly laid before us by the lamented Prince Consort, at the close of his address at the Educational Conferenee :—

" It is our duty—the duty of those whom Providence has removed from this awful struggle and placed beyond this fearful danger—manfully, unceasingly, and untiringly |to aid by advice, assistance and example, the great bulk of the people, who, without such aid, must almost inevitably succumb to the difficulty of their task. They will not cast from them the aiding hand, and the Almighty will bless the labours of those who work in His cause."

Thus may all labour together, Government and people, for the regeneration of the misguided and neglected in our country, and for the restoration to society of " OUR CONVICTS."

*December* 17, 1864.

PATTERSON SMITH REPRINT SERIES IN
CRIMINOLOGY, LAW ENFORCEMENT, AND SOCIAL PROBLEMS